Volume One

Xlib Programming Manual

for Version 11 of the X Window System

by Adrian Nye

O'Reilly & Associates, Inc.

Revision and Printing History

First Printing, August 1988.
Second Printing, November 1988. Small errors corrected.

Small Print

Table of Contents

Figures

Examples

Tables

Preface

By convention, a preface describes the book itself, while the introduction describes the subject matter. You should read through the preface to get an idea of how the book is organized, the conventions it follows, and so on.

In This Chapter:

Preface

About This Manual

This manual describes the X library, the C Language programming interface to Version 11 of the X Window System. The X library, known as Xlib, is the lowest level of programming interface to X. This library enables a programmer to write applications with an advanced user interface based on windows on the screen, with complete network transparency, that will run without changes on many types of workstations and personal computers.

Xlib is powerful enough to write effective applications without additional programming tools, and is necessary for certain tasks even in applications written with higher-level "toolkits."

There are a number of these toolkits for X programming, the most notable being the DEC/MIT toolkit Xt, the Andrew toolkit developed by IBM and Carnegie-Mellon University, and the InterViews toolkit from Stanford. These toolkits are still evolving, and none of them is currently part of the X standard, although Xt is being considered for inclusion. Toolkits simplify the process of application writing considerably, providing a number of *widgets* that implement menus, command buttons, and other common features of the user interface.

This manual does not describe Xt or any other toolkit. Our intention is to provide complete documentation of the Xt toolkit in a future volume of our X Window System series. Nonetheless, all the material described in this book is essential for understanding and using the toolkits since the toolkits themselves are written using Xlib.

In Release 1 of Xlib, the resource manager (for parsing the command line and merging user preferences) was a separate library, which had been developed as part of the Xt toolkit. As of Release 2, parts of the resource manager have been incorporated into Xlib. This volume documents the Release 2 resource manager. This manual also describes the X11 routines that were provided for compatibility with X Version 10, chiefly in Appendix B, *X10 Compatibility*.

Summary of Contents

This manual is divided into two volumes. This is the first volume, the *Xlib Programming Manual*. It provides a conceptual introduction to Xlib, including tutorial material and numerous programming examples. Arranged by task or topic, each chapter brings together a group of Xlib functions, describes the conceptual foundation they are based on, and illustrates how they are most often used in writing applications (or in the case of the last chapter, window managers). Volume One is structured so as to be useful as a tutorial and also as a task-oriented reference.

The second volume, the *Xlib Reference Manual*, includes reference pages for each of the Xlib functions, organized alphabetically for ease of reference; a permuted index; and numerous appendices and quick reference aids.

Volume One and Volume Two are designed to be used together. To get the most out of the examples in Volume One, you will need the exact calling sequences of each function from Volume Two. To understand fully how to use each of the functions described in Volume Two, all but the most experienced X "hacker" will need the explanation and examples in Volume One.

Both volumes include material from the original Xlib and X11 Protocol documentation provided by MIT, as well as from other documents provided on the MIT release tape. We have done our best to incorporate all of the useful information from the MIT documentation, to correct code references we found to be in error, to reorganize and present it in a more useful form, and to supplement it with conceptual material, tutorials, reference aids, and examples. In other words, this manual is not only a replacement, but is a superset of the MIT documentation.

Those of you familiar with the MIT documentation will recognize that each reference page in Volume Two includes the detailed description of the routine found in Gettys, Newman, and Scheifler's *Xlib–C Language X Interface*, plus in many cases additional text that clarifies ambiguities and describes the context in which the routine would be used. We have also added cross-references to related reference pages and to where additional information can be found in Volume One.

How to Use This Manual

Volume One is intended as an introduction to all the basic concepts of X programming, and also as a useful reference for many of the most common programming techniques. It is divided into fourteen chapters, which describe and demonstrate the use of the X programming library, and numerous appendices.

You will find it necessary to read at least Chapters 1, 2, and 3 before attempting to program with the X library. Chapter 1, *Introduction*, provides a discussion of the context in which X programs operate. Chapter 2, *X Concepts*, describes the conceptual foundations underlying X programming. Chapter 3, *Basic Window Program*, presents a simple program.

Chapters 4 through 9 (*Window Attributes*, *The Graphics Context*, *Drawing Graphics and Text*, *Color*, *Events*, and *The Keyboard and Pointer*) discuss various programming techniques that are used in all X programs. These chapters can be read as a tutorial and consulted for reference later.

Chapter 10, *Interclient Communication*, is a description of communication between applications and between applications and the window manager, including properties and selections. The proposed conventions for interclient communications are presented in Appendix F, Proposed Interclient Communication Conventions.

Chapter 11, *Managing User Preferences*, describes the facilities provided for database management, parsing the command line, and managing user preferences. Xlib calls this the resource manager.

Chapter 12, *A Complete Application*, provides an example of a complete application. This chapter is especially useful in demonstrating managing user preferences with the resource manager.

Chapter 13, *Other Programming Techniques*, describes programming techniques that will be useful to some but not all programs. It should be scanned for applicable techniques and read in detail when needed for a particular project.

Chapter 14, *Window Management*, describes what window managers do and how they work. This information should provide a more complete knowledge of the variety of contexts in which X applications may function. It also describes the Xlib functions that are intended primarily for window management. A simple window manager program is described.

Appendix A, *Glossary*, gives you somewhere to turn should you run across a term that you are unfamiliar with. Some care has been taken to see that all terms are defined where they are first used in the text, but this assumes a sequential reading of the manual.

Appendix B, *X10 Compatibility*, describes the routines supported in X11 for compatibility with X Version 10.

Appendix C, *Writing Extensions to X*, is a guide to writing extensions to X. This is for experienced X programmers only. It is provided so that this manual can serve as a complete replacement for the MIT Xlib documentation.

Appendix D, *The* basecalc *Application*, presents the complete code for *basecalc*, the complete application described in Chapter 12, *A Complete Application*.

Appendix E, *Event Reference*, describes each event type in a reference page format. Included is how to select the events, when they are generated, the contents of the event structures, and notes on how to use them. This information is vital in using the numerous events.

Appendix F, *Proposed Interclient Communication Conventions*, describes the conventions for interclient communication that were proposed in Release 2. Though these conventions are likely to be modified in future releases, future conventions are promised to be backward-compatible. This appendix is based upon David Rosenthal's *Inter-Client Communications Conventions Manual*, which was released in draft form with Release 2.

Appendix G, *Release Notes*, described the changes between Release 1 and Release 2. This manual describes Release 2, but notes any changes necessary to make the code work with Release 1.

Finally, Appendix H, *Sources of Additional Information*, lists where to get the X software, companies that offer training in X programming, and description of additional books on the subject that will be published soon.

Volume Two consists of a permuted index, reference pages to each library function, and appendices that cover macros, structures, function groups, events, fonts, colors, cursors, keysyms, and errors. Finally, Volume Two concludes with at-a-glance charts that help in setting the graphics context (GC) and the window attributes. This volume should be consulted to obtain the specifics of calling each Xlib function.

Example Programs

The example programs described in this manual and other demos are available from O'Reilly and Associates, Inc. on an MS-DOS 1.2 Meg floppy. We have chosen this format because most programmers have access to a PC from which they can upload the software to the system where they run X.

Send us U.S. $10 plus shipping and we'll send you the diskette containing the example programs.

Assumptions

Readers should be proficient in the C programming language, although examples are provided for infrequently used features of the language that are necessary or useful when programming with X. In addition, general familiarity with the principles of raster graphics will be helpful.

Font Conventions Used in This Manual

Italics are used for:

- UNIX pathnames, filenames, program names, user command names, and options for user commands
- New terms where they are defined

`Typewriter Font` is used for:

- Anything that would be typed verbatim into code, such as examples of source code and text on the screen

- The contents of include files, such as structure types, structure members, symbols (defined constants and bit flags), and macros

- Xlib functions

- Names of subroutines of the example programs

Italic Typewriter Font is used for:

- Arguments to Xlib functions, since they could be typed in code as shown but are arbitrary

Helvetica Italics are used for:

- Titles of examples, figures, and tables

Boldface is used for:

- Chapter and section headings

Related Documents

The C Programming Language by B. W. Kernighan and D. M. Ritchie

The following documents are included on the X11 source tape:

Xt Toolkit Intrinsics, by Joel McCormack, Paul Asente and Ralph Swick
Xt Toolkit Widgets, by Ralph Swick and Terry Weissman
Xlib–C Language X Interface, by Jim Gettys, Ron Newman, and Robert Scheifler

Two more books on the X Window System are now being developed at O'Reilly and Associates, Inc., and are expected to be published in the Fall of 1988:

Volume Three — *X Window System User's Guide*
Volume Four — *Programming with the Xt Toolkit*

Requests For Comments

Please write to tell us about any flaws you find in this manual or how you think it could be improved, to help us provide you with the best documentation possible.

Our U.S. mail address, e-mail address, and phone number are as follows:

O'Reilly and Associates, Inc.
981 Chestnut St.
Newton, MA 02164
(617) 527-4210

UUCP: uunet!ora!adrian   ARPA: adrian@ora.UU.NET

Licensing Information

This manual has been designed for licensing and customization by manufacturers or distributors of systems supporting X11. As of this writing, it has been licensed by Masscomp, Motorola, Apollo Computer, Silicon Graphics, and Stellar Computer. For information on licensing, call O'Reilly & Associates, Inc. at 617-527-4210, or send e-mail to tim@ora.UU.NET.

Acknowledgements

The information contained in this manual is based in part on *Xlib–C Language X Interface*, written by Jim Gettys, Ron Newman, and Robert Scheifler, and the *X Window System Protocol, Version 11*, by Robert Scheifler (with many contributors). The X Window System software and these documents were written under the auspices of Project Athena at MIT. In addition, this manual includes material from Oliver Jones' Xlib tutorial presentation, which was given at the MIT X Conference in January 1988, and from David Rosenthal's *Inter-Client Communication Conventions Manual*.

I'd like to thank the people who helped this book come into being. It was Tim O'Reilly who originally sent me out on a contract to write a manual for X Version 10 for a workstation manufacturer, and later to another company to write a manual for X Version 11, from which this book began. I've learned most of what I know about computers and technical writing while working for Tim. For this book he acted as an editor, he helped me reorganize several chapters, he worked on the *Color* and *Managing User Preferences* chapters when time was too short for me to do it, and he kept my spirits up through this long project. While I was concentrating on the details, his eye was on the overall presentation, and his efforts improved the book enormously.

This book would not be as good (and we might still be working on it) had it not been for Daniel Gilly. Daniel was my production assistant for critical periods in the project. He dealt with formatting issues, checked for consistent usage of terms and noticed irregularities in content, and edited files from written corrections by me and by others. His job was to take as much of the work off me as possible, and with his technical skill and knowledge of UNIX he did that very well.

This manual has benefitted from the work and assistance of the entire staff of O'Reilly and Associates, Inc. Susan Willing was responsible for graphics and design, and she proofed many drafts of the book; Linda Mui tailored the troff macros to the design by Sue Willing and myself, and was invaluable in the final production process; John Strang figured out the Release 2 resource manager and wrote the section on that topic; Karen Cakebread edited a draft of the manual and established some conventions for terms and format. Peter Mui executed the "at-a-glance" tables for the inside back cover; Tom Scanlon entered written edits and performed copy fitting; Linda Walsh updated the index of the book; Valerie Quercia, Tom Van Raalte, and Donna Woonteiler all contributed in some small ways; and Cathy Brennan, Suzanne Van Hove, and Jill Berlin fielded many calls from people interested in the X manual, and saved me all the time that would have taken. A special thanks to everyone at

O'Reilly and Associates for putting up with my habits of printer and terminal hogging, lugging X books around, recycling paper, and for generally being good at what they do and good-natured to boot.

I would also like to thank the people from other companies that reviewed the book or otherwise made this project possible: John Posner, Barry Kingsbury, and Jeffrey Vroom of Stellar Computer; Oliver Jones of Apollo Computer; Sam Black, Jeff Graber, and Janet Egan of Masscomp; Al Tabayoyon, Paul Shearer, and many others from Tektronix; Robert Scheifler and Jim Fulton of the X Consortium (who helped with the *Color* and *Managing User Preferences* chapters), and Peter Winston II and Aub Harden of Integrated Computer Solutions. Despite the efforts of the reviewers and everyone else, any errors that remain are my own.

— *Adrian Nye*

1
Introduction

This chapter gives the big picture: what X is all about, and some fundamentals of how it works. Everyone should look at this chapter, though readers who are already familiar with X may only want to skim it.

In This Chapter:

1

Introduction

In March 1988, the Massachusetts Institute of Technology released what may well become one of the most significant software technologies of the 1990s: Version 11 of the X Window System, commonly referred to as X11. X11 may not change the world, but it is likely to change the world of workstations.

The X Window System is being adopted as a standard by nearly every workstation manufacturer, and should eventually replace or be supported under their proprietary windowing systems. Versions will also be available for personal computers.

For the first time, portable applications can be written for an entire class of machines, rather than for a single manufacturer's equipment. Programmers can write in a single graphics language and expect their applications to work without significant modifications on dozens of different computers.

What's more, since X is a network-based windowing system, applications can run in a network of systems from different vendors. Programs can be run on a remote computer and the results displayed on a local workstation. Proprietary networks have been around for a while. However, network cooperation of *different* computers has been held up by the lack of a common applications language. Now there is one.

Vendors hope that X will lead to a software explosion similar to the one that occurred in response to the PC standard on microcomputers.

1.1 Versions of X

X was developed jointly by MIT's Project Athena and Digital Equipment Corporation, with contributions from many other companies. It was masterminded by Robert Scheifler, Jim Gettys, and colleagues at MIT, though it owes some debt to the "W" windowing package developed by Paul Asente at Stanford.

There have been numerous research versions of X. Version 10, Release 4 (popularly known as X10.4), which was released in 1986, became the basis for several commercial products. Development of most X10.4 products was curtailed, however, when it became apparent that Version 11 would not be compatible with it. Version 11, Release 1 became available in September 1987, and Release 2 in March 1988.

Version 11 is a complete window programming package. It offers much more flexibility in the areas of supported display features, window manager styles, and support for multiple screens, and provides better performance than X Version 10. It is fully extensible. But just as important, the X11 subroutine library (Xlib) is expected to be stable for several years, and to be at least a de facto industry standard. That means that programs written with this library will not need major revisions because of software updates. While there may be additions to this library, there won't be incompatible changes to it.

With X11 Release 2, control of X has passed from MIT to the X Consortium, an association of major computer manufacturers who plan to support the X standard. The Consortium was formed in January 1988, and includes virtually all large computer manufacturers. Many software houses and universities are associate members, who don't have a voice in controlling the standard, but receive advance access to newly released software.

1.2 X Window System Concepts

The X Window System is complex, but it is based on a few premises that can be quickly understood.

1.2.1 Displays and Screens

The first and most obvious thing to note about X is that it is a windowing system for bit-mapped graphics displays.* It supports color as well as monochrome and gray-scale displays.

A slightly unusual feature is that a *display* is defined as a workstation consisting of a keyboard, a pointing device such as a mouse, and *one or more* screens. Multiple screens can work together, with mouse movement allowed to cross physical screen boundaries. As long as multiple screens are controlled by a single user with a single keyboard and pointing device, they comprise only a single display (see Figure 1-1).

---

* In bitmapped graphics, each dot on the screen, (called a *pixel*, or picture element), corresponds to one or more bits in memory. Programs modify the display simply by writing to display memory. Bitmapped graphics are also referred to as raster graphics, since most bitmapped displays use television-type scan line technology: the entire screen is continually refreshed by an electron beam scanning across the face of the display tube one scan line, or raster, at a time. The term bitmapped graphics (or memory-mapped graphics) is more general, since it also applies to other dot-oriented displays, such as LCD screens. We assume that you are familiar with the basic principles of bitmapped graphics.

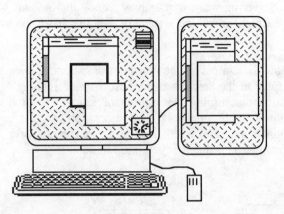

Figure 1-1. A display consisting of more than one screen

1.2.2 The Server–Client Model

The next thing to note is that X is a network-oriented windowing system. An application need not be running on the same system that actually supports the display. While many applications will execute locally, other applications may execute on other machines, sending requests across the network to a particular display, and receiving keyboard and pointer events from the system controlling the display.

At this point, only TCP/IP and DECnet networks are supported, though that will change before long.

The program that controls each display is known as a *server*. At first, this usage of the term server may seem a little odd—when you sit at a workstation, you tend to think of a server as something across the network (such as a file or print server), rather than the local program that controls your own display. The thing to remember is that your display is accessible to other systems across the network, and for those systems the code executing in your system does act as a true display server.

The server acts as an intermediary between user programs (called *clients* or *applications*) running on either the local or remote systems, and the resources of the local system. The server performs the following tasks:

- Allows access to the display by multiple clients.

- Interprets network messages from clients.

- Passes user input to the clients by sending network messages.

- Does two-dimensional drawing—graphics are performed by the display server rather than by the client.

- Maintains complex data structures, including windows, cursors, fonts, and "graphics contexts," as *resources* that can be shared between clients, and referred to simply by resource IDs. Server-maintained resources reduce the amount of data that has to be maintained by each client and the amount of data that has to be transferred over the network.

Since the X Window System makes the network transparent to clients, these programs may connect to any display in the network if the host they are running on has permission from the server that controls that display. Most programs connect to the display from the host on which they were invoked. In a network environment, however, it is common for a user to have programs running on several different hosts in the network, all invoked from and displaying their windows on a single screen (see Figure 1-2).

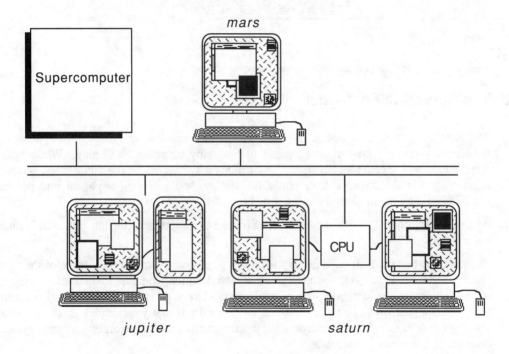

Figure 1-2. Applications can run on any system across the network

Actually, any of the hosts can be used for processing by any of the servers, if the servers have permission. This use of the network is known as *distributed processing*. Distributed processing helps solve the problem of unbalanced system loads. When one host machine is overloaded, the user of that machine can arrange for some of the programs to run on other hosts.

For example, a relatively underpowered PC can run an X server and act like a terminal while all the clients run on more powerful systems across the network, with their results displayed on the PC screen.

1.2.3 Window Management

Another important concept in X programming is that clients don't actually control such things as where a window appears or what size it is. Given multiprocessor, multiclient access to the same workstation, clients must not be dependent on a particular window configuration. Instead, a client gives *hints* about how and where it would like to be displayed. The screen layout or appearance and the style of user interaction with the system are left up to a separate program, called the *window manager*.

The window manager is just another program written with the X library, except that it is given special authority to control the layout of windows on the screen. The window manager typically allows the user to move or resize windows, start new applications, and control the stacking of windows on the screen, but only according to the window manager's window layout policy. A *window layout policy* is a set of rules that specify allowable sizes and positions of windows and icons.

Unlike citizens, the window manager has rights but not responsibilities. Programs must be prepared to cooperate with any type of window manager or with none at all (there are fairly simple ways to prepare programs for these contingencies). The standard window manager *uwm* does not enforce any window layout policy, but clients should still assume that there could be one. For example, the window manager must be informed of the desired size of a new window before the window is displayed on the screen. If the window manager does not accept the desired window size and position, the program must be prepared to accept a different size or position, or be able to display a message such as "Too small!"

If you are having trouble visualizing this situation, imagine a window manager where no windows are allowed to overlap. This is known as a *tiled* window manager. The Siemens RTL tiled window manager lets only transient windows overlap. The window manager *uwm*, on the other hand, is referred to as *real-estate-driven* because keyboard input is automatically assigned to whatever window the pointer currently happens to be in.

There is at least one other window manager variety that you might encounter, called a *listener*. Its distinguishing feature is that it assigns all keyboard input to a single window when that window is selected by clicking on it with the pointer. A listener may or may not allow windows to overlap. Apple Macintosh™ users will recognize this type of interface.

X is somewhat unusual in that it doesn't mandate a particular type of window manager. Its developers have tried to make X itself as free of window management or user interface policy as possible. And while the X11 distribution includes *uwm* as a sample window manager, individual manufacturers are expected to write their own window managers and user interface guidelines.

In the long run, the developers of X may well have made the right choice, in that the lack of clear user interface guidelines will allow a period of experimentation in which the marketplace could come up with better designs than are presently available. Some industry observers, however, decry this move, pointing out that it undercuts X's appeal as a standard user platform—X *programs* may be portable across systems from multiple vendors, but if users have to deal with a different user interface on each system, half the benefit of that portability will be lost. Until a clear user interface standard emerges from the marketplace, developers must be careful to write their programs in such a way that they can run under different window managers and user interface conventions.

1.2.4 Events

As in any mouse-driven window system, an X client must be prepared to respond to any one of many different asynchronous *events*. Events include user input (keypress, mouse click, or mouse movement) as well as interaction with other programs. (For example, if an obscured portion of a window is exposed when another overlapping window is moved, closed, or resized, the client must redraw it.) Events of many different types can occur at any time and in any order. They are placed on a queue in the order they occur, but can be handled by clients in any order. Event-driven programming makes it natural to let the user tell the program what to do instead of vice versa.

The need to handle events is a major difference between programming under a window system and traditional UNIX or PC programming. X programs do not use the standard C functions for getting characters, and they do not poll for input. Instead there are functions for receiving events, and then the program must branch according to the type of event and perform the appropriate response.

1.2.5 Extensions to X

The final thing to know about X is that it is *extensible*. The code includes a defined mechanism for incorporating extensions, so that vendors aren't forced to hack up the existing system in incompatible ways when adding features. These extensions are used just like the core Xlib routines and perform at the same level.

Among the extensions currently being developed are support for 2-D spline curves, for 3-D graphics, and for display PostScript.

1.3 X Window System Software Architecture

By now, we have described enough to draw a simple picture of the X Window System architecture (Figure 1-3).

- **A display server** is a program that runs on each system that supports a graphics display, keyboard, and mouse. The server is as device-independent as possible, but does include some device-dependent code. The X release from MIT includes sample monochrome and color servers for Sun 2, 3, and 4 systems; DEC systems under ULTRIX; Apollo systems under DOMAIN/IX; HP Topcat, Catseye, or Renaissance systems; and IBM RT systems. Commercially developed servers are or will be available from most major workstation vendors. In addition, companies such as Graphics Software Systems, Interactive Systems, and Locus Computing offer server implementations for PCs.

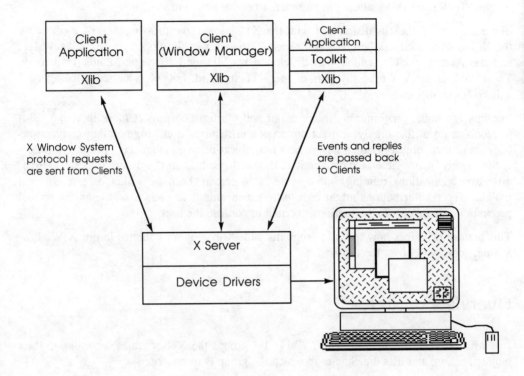

Figure 1-3. Clients communicate with the server via Xlib calls

- **Applications** communicate with the server by means of calls to a low-level library of C-language routines known as *Xlib*. Xlib provides functions for connecting to a particular display server, creating windows, drawing graphics, responding to events, and so on. Xlib calls are translated to protocol requests that are passed either to the local server or to another server across the network. Some of the many sample applications available on the X release include *xterm* (a terminal emulator), *xcalc* (a calculator), *xmh* (a mail handler), *xclock* (a clock), and a teX previewer.

- **The window manager** is just another program written with the X library, except that by convention it is given special authority to control the layout of windows on the screen.

Client is a slightly more general term than *application*, although they are almost synonymous. All clients except the window manager are called applications. When a statement in this book applies only to the window manager or only to the applications managed by the window manager, the appropriate term is used. In other instances, whichever term seems more natural is used.

Applications and window managers can be written solely with Xlib or with a set of higher-level subroutine libraries known as *toolkits*. Toolkits implement a set of user interface features such as menus or command buttons (referred to generically as toolkit *widgets*) and allow applications to manipulate these features using object-oriented programming techniques. Toolkit *intrinsics* allow programmers to create new widgets.

There are several toolkits distributed with the X11 release, the most notable of them being the Xt toolkit (called Xtk before X11 Release 2), which was developed by Digital and MIT, and the Andrew toolkit, which was developed by MIT and Carnegie-Mellon University. These toolkits are not officially part of the X11 standard, but Xt is currently being considered for inclusion.

Toolkits can make programming much easier and the finished project more thorough. But the toolkits do utilize highly abstract concepts and require strict programming conventions because of their object-oriented design in a non-object-oriented language. Another problem is the variety of user interface conventions that will result from the different toolkits. Imagine two applications running side-by-side on a screen, each of which uses a different toolkit. The pointer buttons might have different meanings in each window, unless special precautions are taken. This situation is certain to confuse the user.

This manual describes how to write programs with Xlib. Future volumes in our X Window System series will cover the toolkits.

1.4 Overview of Xlib

Just what does the X library contain? Table 1-1 groups the Xlib routines according to their major function, and lists the chapter in which the group is discussed.

Table 1-1. Xlib Routines by Function

Function Group	Description	Chapter
Color	Routines to change the way colors drawn by an application are interpreted on the screen.	Chapter 7
Cursors	Routines to change the shape and colors of the image that tracks the pointer around the screen.	Chapter 6
Data Management	Several mechanisms to associate data with windows or numbers.	Chapter 13
Display Connection	Routines to connect and disconnect an application with a display, possibly across the network.	Chapter 3
Display and Server Specifications	Macros and equivalent functions are provided that provide information about a particular server implementation and the connected display hardware.	Volume One, throughout; Volume Two, Appendix C
Drawing	Routines to draw dots, lines, rectangles, polygons, and arcs, and an analogous set to fill the last three.	Chapter 6

Table 1-1. Xlib Routines by Function (continued)

Function Group	Description	Chapter
Errors	Routines to set the functions called when errors occur.	Chapter 2
Events	Routines to get input from the user, from other applications, and from the server. In X these are collectively called events.	Chapter 8
Extensions	Routines to find out what extensions are available on a particular server, and get information about how to use one.	Chapter 13
Fonts	Routines to list available fonts, load fonts, and find out their characteristics.	Chapter 6
Geometry	Routines to manipulate and translate geometry specifications.	Chapter 11
Graphics Context	Routines to set the way drawing requests are interpreted.	Chapter 5
Host Access	Routines to control access from other machines connected in a network.	Chapter 13
Images	Routines to get, display, or manipulate screen images.	Chapter 6
Interclient Communication	Routines enabling any client to make available information for any other client to read.	Chapter 10
Keyboard	Functions to modify the way keyboard input is handled, including the keyboard mapping.	Chapter 9
Pointer	Functions to modify the way pointer input is handled.	Chapter 9
Regions	Routines to do perform mathematical operations on polygonal regions.	Chapter 6
Resource Management	Routines to make managing user preferences and command line arguments easier.	Chapter 11, Chapter 12
Screen Saver	Routines to set the operating characteristics of the daemon that blanks the screen when the keyboard and pointer have been idle for a time.	Chapter 13
Text	Routines for drawing text, and for determining the size of a string to be drawn.	Chapter 6
User Preferences	Routines for setting and getting the keyboard click and auto-repeat settings.	Chapter 9

Table 1-1. Xlib Routines by Function (continued)

Function Group	Description	Chapter
Window Attributes	Routines for setting and getting the current characteristics of a window.	Chapter 4
Window Life	Routines to create or destroy a window.	Chapter 3
Window Management	Routines to allow the manipulation of windows around the screen, changing their size, their visibility on the screen, and their apparent position above or below other windows.	Chapter 14

As you can see, Xlib provides a lot of functionality. X was designed to allow any style of user interface, and that requires a very flexible set of routines. But not all the routines are necessary or intended for writing normal applications. Many are intended for window management or for other specialized purposes.

A more detailed listing that provides the name and a brief description of the routines in each group can be found in Volume Two, Appendix A, *Function Group Summary*.

2
X Concepts

This chapter introduces the concepts that underly X programming. You should read this chapter even if you are the type of person who likes to jump right into the code. (If you're desperate, you can skip ahead to Chapter 3, and return to this chapter when you get confused.) "An hour or so spent reading about the system in general can save many hours of programming that leads to a dead end when the approach turns out to be wrong."

In This Chapter:

In This Chapter (continued):

When learning a new programming language, many programmers prefer to look at a few code samples and then begin programming right away, looking up more information as they need it. This book is organized so that most of it is useful both as a tutorial and as a reference. There are lots of code samples and fragments in this manual to help the person who likes to read code more than words. Around the code they will find many of the concepts described that are necessary for understanding that particular example.

The "just look at the examples" approach works up to a point. It allows a sharp individual to get "something" running in a very short time. But eventually programmers find that in order to get the most out of a system—and sometimes even to get it do anything useful—a lot of underlying issues must be understood. In X, there are a lot of interrelated concepts and assumptions that are so basic that the programmer should know them cold. An hour or so spent reading about the system in general can save many hours of programming that leads to a dead end when the approach turns out to be wrong.

This chapter describes those underlying issues and assumptions that are so important to programming with Xlib. It goes into considerably more detail than the brief conceptual overview provided in Chapter 1. After reading this chapter, you will be well prepared to understand the rest of this book and will have a sound idea of what is required to write an X application. This chapter describes how Xlib works, window concepts and characteristics, graphics, and events, and reviews the issues that you will need to think about in order to program.

2.1 How Xlib Works

Let's start by describing the problem that X was designed to solve, and then describe how it goes about solving it.

First of all, X was designed to provide windows on bitmapped terminals. This has been done before, but not in a way designed to be easily portable to many different brands of hardware, from PCs to supercomputers. The code was designed to stress easy portability, even between different operating systems, but still to allow high performance.

Second, X was designed to allow many different types of machines to cooperate within a network. This was one of the major innovations in the X design. There are several standard networking protocols, but there was lacking a widely-adopted standard for a higher level protocol specifying what should be sent over the network to drive a window system. The first thing that was determined about X was the protocol used to communicate across the network.

Third, the developers of X decided that it should not require (or even imply) a particular style of user interface. Practically speaking, X would not have been adopted as a standard by many companies if had implied a user interface incompatible with their proprietary window systems. In addition, the developers of X felt that the issues surrounding the design of a window-based user interface for X were not sufficiently worked out at present. An important design goal was thus to make X "policy free."

To accomplish these goals, the X Window System had to be designed from the bottom up. To work over a network, there had to be programs running at both ends of the connection to send and receive the information and to interpret it. The end that controls the display and input devices was named the server. At the other end are clients—programs written using Xlib to interface with the X protocol (see Figure 2-1).

Actually, although this book describes Xlib, the C-language interface to the X protocol, there is also a Lisp interface and there are likely to be others. Any language binding that can generate and receive X Protocol requests can communicate with a server and be used with the X Window System. But at present, Xlib is the most popular programming interface used with X, because C is so widely available.

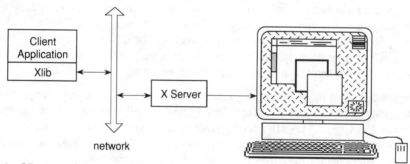

Figure 2-1. Clients and servers

2.1.1 The X Protocol

The X Protocol specifies what makes up each packet of information that gets transferred between the server and Xlib in both directions. Even when the server and Xlib are running on the same machine, the protocol is used for communication, through some internal channel instead of the external network. There are four types of packets that get transferred via the protocol: requests, replies, events, and errors.

A protocol request is generated by Xlib and sent to the server. A protocol request can carry a wide variety of information, such as a specification for drawing a line, or changing the color value in a cell in a colormap, or an inquiry about the current size of a window. Most Xlib routines generate protocol requests. The exceptions are routines that only affect data structures local to Xlib, and don't affect the server (regions and the resource manager are the primary examples).

A protocol reply is sent from the server to Xlib in response to certain requests. Not all requests are answered by replies—only the ones that request information. Requests that specify drawing, for example, don't generate replies. When Xlib receives a reply, it places the requested data into the arguments or returned value of the Xlib routine that generated the request. An Xlib routine that requires a reply is called a *round-trip request*. Round-trip requests have to be minimized in clients because they lower performance when there are network delays.

An event is sent from the server to Xlib, and contains information about a device action, or about a side-effect of a previous request. The data contained in events is quite varied because it is the principal method by which clients get information. Events are kept in a queue in Xlib, and can be read one at a time by the client.

An error is like an event, but it is handled slightly differently within Xlib. Errors cannot be read by the Xlib calls that read events. Instead, errors are sent to one of two error handling routines in Xlib. One handles recoverable errors, and the other handles fatal errors. The default error handlers simply print a message and exit; either or both can be replaced by a client-specific error handling routine.

2.1.2 Buffering

Xlib saves up requests instead of sending them to the server immediately, so that the client program can continue running instead of waiting to gain access to the network after every Xlib call. This is possible because most Xlib calls do not require immediate action by the server. This grouping of requests by the client before sending them over the network also increases the performance of some networks, because it makes the network transactions longer and less numerous, reducing the total overhead involved.

Xlib sends the buffer full of requests to the server under three conditions. The most common is when an application calls a Xlib routine to wait for an event, but no matching event is currently available on Xlib's queue. Since in this case the application must wait for an appropriate event anyway, it makes sense to flush the request buffer.* Secondly, Xlib calls that get information from the server requiring an immediate reply and therefore the request buffer is sent while the information is being returned. Thirdly, the client would like to be able to flush the request buffer manually in situations where no user events and no calls to query the server are expected.

Let's look at how this works in practice. While an application is running, Xlib queues up requests for the server. The server, meanwhile, sends events to Xlib as soon after the user causes them as the network allows—it does not queue them or group them (except under rare conditions involving grabs discussed in Section 9.4). When the client application asks the user for input, it could, for example, draw a string that asks a question. This request sits on the request queue within Xlib. Then the application calls the event reading routine to get the answer. But normally, the answer won't be there yet because the user hasn't seen the question! So, Xlib flushes the request buffer, and the question will appear on the user's screen. Then, the user will type the answer, the event will be sent to Xlib, and the program can continue.

Using Xlib calls, the client can flush the connection in three ways: by calling a routine that requires an immediate reply (a routine with `Query`, `Fetch`, or `Get` in its name); by calling

_____

*We are referring to the operation of Release 2 of Xlib here. In Release 1, the request buffer was flushed whenever a call that waited for an event was issued, regardless of whether the needed events were already available to Xlib. This caused unnecessary flushing that reduced client performance.

certain event-reading routines when no matching event exists on Xlib's queue; or by calling the routines XFlush or XSync.* The first of these actions says to the server, "I need some information; please act on these requests right away and then give me the information. The second says, "I'm waiting for a certain kind of event, so I'll check if you already sent the event over to Xlib. If not, please act on these requests immediately and then I'll be waiting for the event." The last one says, "I don't need any information from you now, but I need you to act on these requests immediately." Normally, the last method is not used because there are enough of the first two types of Xlib calls in the client to make the transactions frequent enough.

You should already know that Xlib maintains a queue of the events for each server that an application is connected to (see Figure 2-2). Whenever events arrive from the server, they are queued until the client reads them.

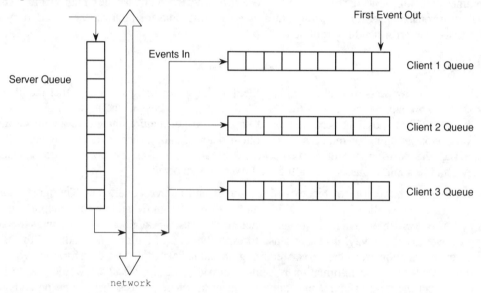

Figure 2-2. The server's event queue and each client's event queue

The fact that Xlib queues both input and output is very important in application programming, and especially in debugging. It means that drawing requests won't appear in a window until the output buffer is flushed. It means that errors are not discovered by the server until the queue of requests arrive and are processed, which happens only after Xlib flushes the request buffer. Once discovered, the error is reported immediately to the client. In other words, several Xlib routines may be called before an error caused by an earlier routine is reported. These are two of the most visible examples of the effects of buffering. See Section 2.6.3 for more details on how buffering affects programming and debugging.

---

* In this manual, whenever you see typewriter font (such as that used for the routine XSync), it means this word would be typed verbatim into C code as a symbol, structure name, structure member, or Xlib routine. Italic typewriter font is used for dummy arguments to Xlib routines, since they could be typed into code as shown but are arbitrary. The argument names used in this volume are the same as the names used on the reference pages in Volume Two, *Xlib Reference Manual*.

2.1.3 Resources

X uses several techniques to reduce network traffic. One major technique is to have the server maintain complex abstractions such as windows or fonts and allocate an integer ID number for each one as a nickname to be used by clients. Each of these abstractions is called a *resource*. A resource can be a window, pixmap, colormap, cursor, font or graphics context (these will be described in a moment).

Whenever an operation is to be performed on a window (or any other resource), the ID of the window is used in one argument to the routine. This means that instead of an entire structure full of data being sent over the network with an Xlib routine call, only a single integer that refers to that structure need be sent. Remember that since the client and the server may be running on different machines, pointers can't be used to refer to structures. The caveat of the resource approach is that the client must query the server when it needs information about resources, which, as mentioned above, leads to network delays. As it turns out, clients normally don't need to query the server very often, and the resource abstraction greatly simplifies programs.

2.1.4 Properties and Atoms

The developers of X needed a way to allow clients to communicate arbitrary data with each other, and they came up with *properties*. A *property* is a packet of information associated with a window, made available to all the clients running under a server. Properties are used by clients to store information that other clients might need or want to know, and to read that information when set by other clients.

An *atom* is an ID that uniquely identifies a particular property. Atoms are used to refer to properties in routine calls so that the server doesn't need to send arbitrary-length property-name strings over the network. Atoms for properties are analogous to the IDs used to refer to resources, except that both an atom and a window are needed to uniquely identify a property. The same atom would be used to identify a property on one window as on another—only the window is different in the calls to set or read this property on two windows. Only the type Atom is ever used in client code; properties are the underlying data managed by the server.

Some atoms are defined when the server initializes. These atoms identify properties whose contents have a certain meaning known by all clients. The properties themselves don't have valid contents until clients or the window manager sets them. The meaning of the data in a property is solely by convention. A group of related clients or an extension may define other properties and atoms that will have a meaning known to all the clients in the group or using the extension.

One of the most important uses of properties is to communicate information from applications to the window manager and vice versa. The application sets the *standard properties* on its top-level window to specify the range of sizes it prefers for its top-level window, and other information. These properties are called "standard" because they are the minimum set that an application should specify. Properties also communicate the other way; for example, the window manager specifies what sizes of icon pixmaps it prefers.

The atoms for window manager communication and for a few other standard uses are defined when the server initializes, but the corresponding properties are not set on particular windows until clients set them.

For more information on properties and atoms, see Section 10.1.

2.1.5 The Window Manager

The window manager is just another client written with Xlib, but by convention it is given special responsibilities. It mediates competing demands for the physical resources of a display including screen space and the colormap. Usually it has a user interface to allow the user to move windows about on the screen, resize them, and start new applications.

While applications must respect the authority of the window manager, they must also be able to operate properly when no window manager is running. This is treading a fine line in a number of areas. For example, one convention says that an application that creates its own colormap should leave the responsibility of installing the colormap to the window manager. But obviously that would preclude the application from operating properly without a window manager. The truth of the matter is that window management under X is not yet well understood. No reliable conventions exist for some aspects of it. For this reason, current window managers and current applications don't always follow even the rules that are well accepted. The lesson to learn from this is to exercise caution when using existing applications as models.

Much of the communication between clients and the window manager and vice versa occurs through properties. Many of the properties are known as *hints* because they may not necessarily be honored by the window manager, even if one is running. An application must be prepared for the window manager to ignore, modify, or honor the preferences it indicates through the window manager hints. The atoms for these properties are defined when the server initializes, but the properties themselves don't have valid contents until applications or the window manager set them.

Quite a few of the features of Xlib and its routines exist only to give the window manager the mechanism to enforce its authority. They should not be used by normal applications, except as allowed in the conventions described in Appendix F, *Proposed Interclient Communication Conventions*. It is important to understand them to write applications that deal properly with the window manager.

One such feature is called *substructure redirection*. *Substructure* refers to the size, position, and overlapping order of the children of a window. *Redirection* refers to the requests by applications to change the configuration of these windows being sent to the window manager for approval instead of actually getting acted upon. Substructure redirection allows a window manager to intercept any request by an application to change the size, position, border width, or stacking order (known collectively as the window configuration) of its top-level windows on the screen. Any application request to change the configuration of its top-level window will be canceled, and instead, an event will be sent to the window manager indicating the arguments used in the reconfiguration request. The window manager can then decide what size, position, and stacking order to grant the application, and the window manager will reconfigure the window to those dimensions. For temporary windows such as pop-up menus and dialog boxes, the substructure redirect feature can be turned off using a window attribute.

Substructure redirection has two significant implications for applications. The first is that the application cannot assume that the configuration it specifies for a window will actually be reflected in the window on the screen. This is true whether the configuration was set by creating the window or by reconfiguring the window. That means that the application must always determine the new configuration of the window before drawing into it. It can do this by selecting a certain event type which contains the window configuration.

The second important implication of substructure redirection concerns the mapping of a top-level window. Because the window manager can intercept the mapping request, and it might take some time before the window manager decides on a window configuration and maps the window itself, an application can't assume that the window is visible immediately. That means it can't draw into the window immediately. The application must wait until it receives an event indicating that the window is visible before drawing into the window.

Communicating with the window manager, and window management in general, is a long story which we'll describe more fully in Chapter 3, *Basic Window Program*, and Chapter 10, *Interclient Communication*. Chapter 14, *Window Management*, gives an example of a simple window manager and describes communication with applications from the window manager's perspective.

Now you should have an idea of how Xlib works. Let's move on to a description of windows.

2.2 What Are Windows?

An X server controls a bitmapped screen. In order to make it easier to view and control many different tasks at the same time, this screen can be divided up into smaller areas called windows. A window is a rectangular area that works in several ways like a miniature screen. Windows on the screen can be arranged so they all are visible or so they cover each other completely or partially. A window may be any size.

Each window (on a screen running X) can be involved in a different activity, and the windows currently in use are placed so they are at least partially visible. The window manager lets you move a different window to the top when necessary, or rearrange the size and position of the windows.

What you may not have realized is that some of these windows, such as the ones created by the mail handler *xmh*, are made up of many layered windows of various sizes. The scroll bars, title bar, command buttons and other features of the user interface are actually separate windows that provide information to the user or allow for input providing convenient control (see Figure 2-3). There is more here than meets the eye.

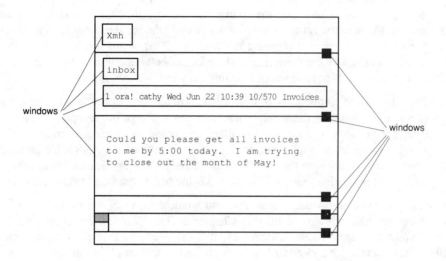

Figure 2-3. The windows used to create an instance of the xmh application

2.2.1 Window Characteristics

What are the characteristics of a window? There are many.*

First of all, a window always has a *parent* window, which is assigned as the window is created. Each window is contained within the limits of its parent. The window cannot display output in areas outside itself, and cannot receive input from the keyboard or the pointer while the pointer is outside itself (unless a *grab* or *keyboard focus* is in effect, as described in Sections 8.3.2.1 and 8.3.2.2). Every window fits in a hierarchy set up by its children, its parent, its parent's parent, and so on. The very first window, the only one that has no parent, is called the root window and fills the entire screen. The root window is created by the X server as it starts up.

Second, a window has a *position*, which locates its upper-left corner relative to its parent's corner, a certain *width* and *height*, and usually a *border*. These characteristics are shown in Figure 2-4. By convention, the window width and height do not include the border. Since several windows may have the same parent, a window must also have a *stacking order* among these windows to determine which will be visible if they overlap. These four characteristics are collectively know as the *window configuration* because they affect the layout of windows on the screen.

---

* Do read this section even if you are already familiar with windowing systems, to make sure you understand X's particular implementation of windowing.

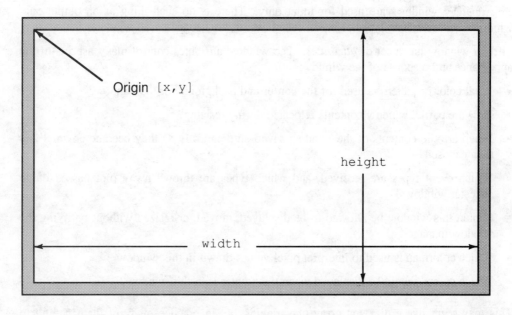

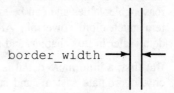

Figure 2-4. Elements of the window configuration

To summarize, the window configuration includes:

- A window's *width* and *height* in pixels, not including the border.

- A window's *border*. It can vary in width; zero makes the border invisible.

- A window's particular position on the screen, specified by *x* and *y* in pixels relative to the upper-left corner of the parent window, not including the border of either window.

- A window's particular *stacking order* among the windows with the same parent.

The width, height and position are collectively called the window *geometry*. Applications often allow users to specify the geometry and border width of the window as a command line argument or through the user defaults mechanism.

Third, a window has characteristics referred to as *depth* and *visual type*, which together determine its color characteristics. The depth is the number of bits available for each pixel to represent color (or gray scales). The visual type represents the way pixel values are translated to produce color or monochrome output on the monitor.

Fourth, a window has a *class* of either InputOutput or InputOnly. As the names imply, InputOutput windows may receive input and may be used to display output, and InputOnly windows are used for input only. There is no such thing as an output-only window because certain types of input, called events, are needed by all windows.

Fifth, a window has a set of *attributes*. The window attributes control many aspects of the appearance and response of the window:

- What color or pattern is used for the border and background of the window?

- How are partial window contents relocated during resizing?

- When are the contents of the window saved automatically as they become covered and then exposed?

- Which event types are received, and which types are thrown away (not passed on to ancestor windows)?

- Should this window be allowed to be displayed, moved, or resized without notifying the window manager?

- Which colormap is used to interpret pixel values drawn in this window?

- Which cursor should be displayed when the pointer is in this window?

This may seem like a dizzying array of variables, but in practice many of them default to reasonable values and can be safely ignored. And the flexibility they provide makes the system much more powerful. All of these window characteristics will be explained in more detail later in this chapter, and most will be covered again later in the book.

But first, a little more detail is necessary on the basic framework of X: the window hierarchy, coordinate system, and stacking order. These are the subjects of the next three sections.

2.2.2 Tree Hierarchy

Windows are arranged in a hierarchy like a family tree, except that only one parent is required to create a child window. There is a separate hierarchy for each screen. At the top is the *root* window, which fills the entire screen and is created when the server initializes. The first windows to be created by each client are children of the root window. In the client's call to XCreateWindow or XCreateSimpleWindow (either of which creates a new window), the root window is the parent.

The children of the root window are special because they are the top-level windows of each application, and they are managed by the window manager. Chapter 3, *Basic Window Program*, describes the special procedures required of clients before displaying, moving, or resizing one of these windows.

Each child may also have its own child windows. These child windows of the top-level windows are used to create application features like command buttons and scroll bars.

Figure 2-5 shows a window hierarchy as it might appear on the screen, and Figure 2-6 shows the same hierarchy in schematic form. Note that the windows *A* through *G* represent subwindows of each application, which may not overlap like this in real applications. Normally the subwindows are used as command buttons or panes which are laid out in non-overlapping fashion. Pop-up menus would overlap the command buttons, but command buttons would not overlap each other. However, this hypothetical hierarchy serves to demonstrate the stacking order and the window hierarchy.

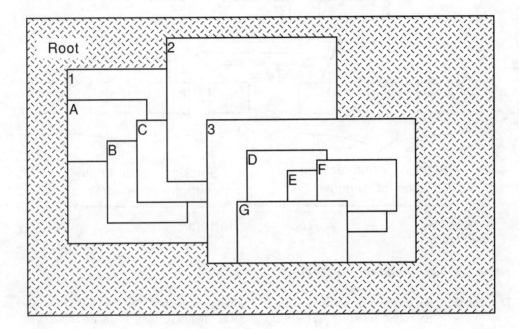

Figure 2-5. A sample window hierarchy on the screen

A child may be positioned partially or completely outside its parent window, but output to the child is displayed and input received only in the area where the child overlaps with the parent. Figure 2-5 shows that the child windows do not extend beyond the borders of the parent even when they are positioned in such a way that they would otherwise overlap the parent's edge. (For example, in Figure 2-5, window *G* will not be drawn beyond the bottom of window *3* even if its height would suggest that it should.) If a window is moved in such a way that it would extend beyond the parent, it is clipped, so that only the part overlapping the parent is displayed.

These are the terms used to describe subsets of the window hierarchy:

Parent   the window used when creating a child window.

Child   a window created with another window as parent.

Subwindow   synonymous with child. Not the same as descendant.

Siblings   windows created with the same parent (brothers and sisters).

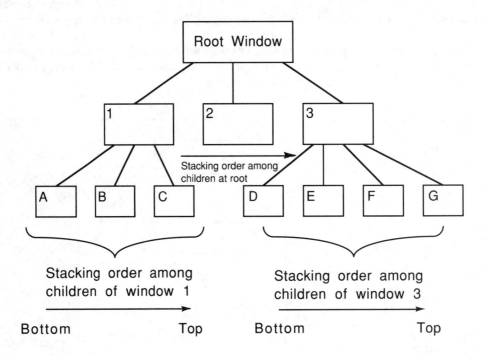

Figure 2-6. Sample window hierarchy in schematic form

Descendants   the children of a window, their children, and so on. Descendants could also be called *inferiors*. This term is more inclusive than *child* or *subwindow*, since it can include several generations in the window hierarchy.

Ancestors   the parent of a window, its parent, and so on, including the root window. Ancestors could also be called *superiors*.

2.2.3 Coordinate System

In the X Window System:

- The horizontal axis is *x* and the vertical axis is *y*.

- *x* and *y* are 0 at the upper-left corner inside the border (if there is one) of the window currently in use. This point is referred to as the window's *origin*. All measurements for placing graphics and for positioning subwindows are made from the origin. When we say that a point is *relative to* a window, this means that the x and y coordinates of the point are measured from the window's origin.

Figure 2-7 demonstrates the coordinate system on a window on the screen.

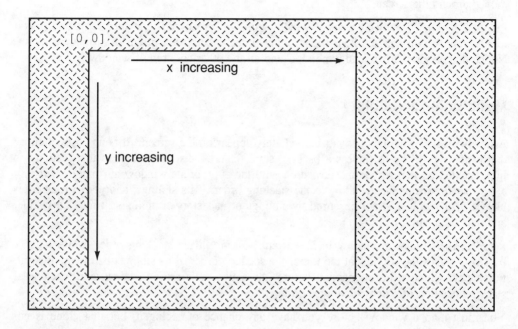

Figure 2-7. The X coordinate system

When you specify the size of an X window, the width and height values are the number of usable pixels inside the window's border in the *x* and *y* directions. Each window is given a unique identifying number (ID) when it is created. All the routines that affect a particular window use a window ID as an argument and act in this window environment, so positions in the window are specified relative to the upper-left corner inside the border. It is not necessary to know the position of a window to correctly locate subwindows or draw graphics within the window.

For example, to create a window using `XCreateWindow` or `XCreateSimpleWindow`, you supply an offset from the upper-left corner of the parent to position the new window. When the parent moves, the new window stays in the same position relative to its parent.

2.2.4 Window Stacking Order

When one window overlaps another, the one on top obscures part of the other window. The stacking order determines which window appears on top. This order can be changed with various routines to raise, lower, or circulate windows relative to their siblings. These routines affect only a group of siblings and their descendants but not their ancestors.

Child windows always stay in front of their parent. When a window with children is moved in the stacking order, all its child windows move with it, just as they do when the parent is moved around the screen.

Figure 2-6 and 2-5 showed a set of windows on the screen and their hierarchy, and if you look carefully you can see how the stacking order affects each group of sibling windows. Notice that window 2 is above window C and all the other children of window 1.

2.2.5 Mapping and Visibility

A newly created window does not immediately appear on the screen. It is an abstract entity that cannot be drawn to (unless a backing store feature—discussed later in this section—is implemented on that server and turned on with the appropriate window attribute). *Mapping* a new window adds that window to the stacking order of its siblings, and marks it as eligible for display. If it is not obscured by siblings or ancestors of siblings, it may be visible, and only then can it be drawn to.

XMapWindow maps a window in its current position in the stacking order, while XMap-Raised places the window at the top of the stacking order of its siblings before mapping it. For a new window, never mapped before, these two calls are equivalent since the initial stacking position of a new window is on top.

You must map a window before you have any chance of seeing it, but that alone is not enough. A number of factors can affect whether any window, newly created or already mapped, is visible:

1. The window must be mapped with XMapWindow or related routines.

2. All of the window's ancestors must be mapped.

3. The window must not be obscured by visible sibling windows or their ancestors. If sibling windows are overlapping, whether or not a window is obscured depends on the stacking order. The stacking order can be manipulated with XConfigureWindow or XRestackWindows.

4. The output buffer must be flushed with a call to XFlush or by a function that requests information from the server. More information on this topic was provided in Section 2.1.2.

5. The initial mapping of a top-level window is a special case, since the window's visibility may be delayed by the window manager. For complicated reasons, a client must wait for the first Expose event before assuming that its window is visible and drawing into it. It is not important to understand why this is true at this point. See Section 2.1.5 if you are curious.

An important consequence of these rules, and one of the reasons for them, is that unmapping a window (with XUnmapWindow) erases the window and all its descendants from the screen. X allows you (or actually, the window manager) to control the placement and visibility of an entire client made up of a hierarchy of windows simply by manipulating the top-level window.

The window configuration and window attributes are maintained when a window is unmapped. But, it is important to remember that the X server does not automatically preserve the visible contents of a window. Graphic operations on a window that is not visible, or that is unmapped, have no effect. Graphics visible in a window will be erased when that window is obscured and then exposed. For these reasons it is important for the client to be prepared to redraw the contents of the window on demand, as described in Section 2.5.

On some high-performance servers, a "backing store" feature is available that maintains the window contents when a window is unmapped or covered by other windows, so that the window is automatically refreshed with the current contents when it becomes visible again. This feature is expensive in terms of computing resources and should be invoked only for windows whose contents are difficult to recreate. On many types of equipment this feature is not supported, so for the sake of portability, programs should be capable of recreating the contents of their windows in other ways. This portability is particularly important in X because network environments often employ various brands of equipment.

Mapping is done with the XMapWindow or XMapSubwindows routines. Unmapping is done with the XUnmapWindow or XUnmapSubwindows routines.

2.3 Introduction to X Graphics

This section provides a brief introduction to the terms and concepts used in graphics under the X Window System. You will see these terms used in Chapters 3 and 4 before we get to a serious treatment of graphics in Chapters 5, 6, and 7.

2.3.1 Pixels and Colors

The X Window System is designed to control bitmapped graphics displays. In the simplest black and white display, there is a single bit per pixel: the state of that bit determines whether the pixel will be black or white. In color systems, or on monochrome systems allowing gray scale displays, there are multiple bits per pixel.

The state of the multiple bits assigned to each pixel does not directly control the color or gray-scale intensity of that pixel. Instead, they are used as an index to a lookup table called a colormap, as shown in Figure 2-8. On a color display, a pixel consists of separate red, green, and blue phosphors, each sensitive to a separate electron beam; the relative intensity of these three colors fools the eye into thinking it sees a single color. Accordingly, the colormap contains an array of red, green, and blue (RGB) triples. In other words, if the value of the bits for a given pixel is 14, the RGB values of the fourteenth member of the colormap will be displayed at that location on the screen.

Each member of a colormap is called a *colorcell*, each of which translates a pixel value into a specified set of red, green, and blue values. All bitmapped displays have at least one hardware colormap, though in the case of a single-plane monochrome screen it may consist of only two colorcells. In most cases, all clients share the single colormap by allocating only the number of colorcells they need and sharing as many as possible. When clients

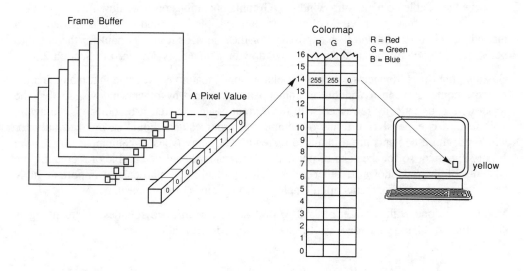

Figure 2-8. Mapping of pixel value into color through colormap

have special requirements, however, X allows them to create virtual colormaps which are then swapped into the hardware colormap (if it is writable) when necessary.

Note that each window can potentially specify a different colormap. This is the significance of the fact that the colormap is a window attribute.

2.3.2 Pixels and Planes

The number of bits per pixel is also referred to as the number of *planes* in the graphics display. Black and white systems have a single plane, color displays have from 4 to 28 planes, and gray-scale displays usually have from 2 to 4 planes. X11 supports up to 32 planes.

As can be inferred from the previous discussion of bits per pixel as an index to the colormap, the number of possible colors or shades of gray that can be *simultaneously* displayed on the screen is 2^n where n is the number of planes in the display. (Of course, additional colors can be made available even on a system with only a few planes, at the cost of existing colors, simply by loading different RGB values into the colormap if it is writable.)

All graphics calculations are performed on the pixel values before they are translated into RGB. The *source* pixel values specified in a drawing request and the *old destination* pixel values are combined according to a plane mask, clip mask, and logical function to arrive at the *final destination* pixel values. The plane mask, clip mask, and logical function are aspects of a structure called the graphics context (GC) and are described in Chapter 5, *The Graphics Context*.

The macros `BlackPixel` and `WhitePixel` return pixel values that map to black and white using the default colormap for that screen. These macros are intended for use in monochrome programs, and sometimes for default borders or backgrounds on color displays. On color hardware, the colors of black and white may sometimes be redefined by the user, depending on whether the colormap is read/write or read-only.

2.3.3 Pixmaps and Drawables

A window is not the only valid destination for drawing. *Pixmaps* are also valid destinations for most graphics requests. Windows and pixmaps are collectively known as *drawables*.

A pixmap is an array of pixel values. It has a depth just like a window. It does not, however, have a position relative to any other window or pixmap, and it does not have window attributes such as a colormap. All of those things affect a pixmap only when it is copied into a window.

Some routines operate only on pixmaps or only on windows. These routines specify either `Pixmap` or `Window` as the argument. If either is allowed, the argument to the Xlib routine will be specified as a `Drawable`. All the drawing routines specify the `Drawable` argument type.

A pixmap is not susceptible to being covered by other windows. Windows, on the other hand, may only be drawn to usefully when they are visible, since their contents are not maintained when they are obscured or unmapped (unless the backing store feature is available and in effect).

Pixmaps are maintained in memory, but they don't appear on the screen until copied to an existing visible window. To be copied directly, the pixmap must have the same depth as the window it is to be copied to. Once copied, the colormap associated with the window is used to translate the pixel values from the pixmap to visible colors. After copying, additional drawing into the pixmap does *not* appear in the window.

In short, windows have the disadvantage that, when they are not visible, drawing to them won't do anything. But a pixmap, which represents an area of the screen, resides in memory and can be drawn to at any time. Unfortunately, pixmaps have disadvantages too as destinations for drawing. They must be copied into a visible window before the user can see them. This copying can have performance penalties. Off-screen memory used for pixmaps should be regarded as a precious resource because it may be limited in quantity.

A pixmap of depth 1 is known as a *bitmap*, though there is no separate type or resource called `Bitmap`. A bitmap is a two-dimensional array of bits used for many purposes including cursor definitions, fonts, and templates for two-color pictures. Each bit represents a single pixel value that is either set (1) or unset (0). Depending on the visual type, these pixel values can be interpreted as two colors, or simply as black and white.

2.3.4 Drawing and the Graphics Context

As in any graphics language, X provides routines for drawing points, lines, rectangles, polygons, arcs, text, and so on. Routines that draw graphics are generically called *graphics primitives*. But in X, a given graphics primitive does not contain all the information needed to draw a particular graphic. A resource called the *graphics context* (GC) specifies the remaining variables, such as the line width, colors, and fill patterns. A GC is specified as an argument to the drawing routine, and modifies the appearance of everything that is drawn into the drawable.

The GC must be created by the client before any drawing is done. The created GC is stored in the server, so that the information it contains does not have to be sent with every graphics primitive. This improves the performance of drawing significantly since it reduces the traffic over the connection between Xlib and the server. All GC settings apply to all graphics drawn using that GC.

More than one GC can be created, and each can be set with different values. This allows a program to switch between GCs and get different effects with the same graphics primitive.

2.3.5 Tiles and Stipples

When pixmaps are used for patterning an area, such as for the background of a window or in a drawing request, they are often referred to as *tiles* or *stipples*.

A *tile* is a pixmap with the same depth as the drawable it is used to pattern. The tile is typically 16-by-16 pixels wide but can be other sizes depending on the hardware (see XQuery-BestTile). It is typically composed of only two different pixel values since this is the easiest type to create, but multiple pixel values are permitted. Areas drawn by any of the drawing routines can be tiled by replicating a tile specified in the GC. The background and border of windows can be tiled with the tile specified in the window attributes; the tile chosen is not affected by the GC.

A *stipple* is a pixmap of depth 1. A stipple is used in conjunction with a foreground pixel value and sometimes a background pixel value to pattern an area in a way similar to a tile. There are two styles of stippling that can be set in the graphics context. In one, set bits in the stipple are drawn in the foreground color, and unset bits are drawn in the background color. In the other, only the set bits in the stipple are drawn in the foreground pixel value, and the pixels in the destination represented by unset bits in the stipple are not changed. Like tiling, stippling affects only those pixels that are selected by the graphics request, such as the pixels drawn for a line or a character. Stipples are only present in the GC, and cannot be used for window backgrounds.

Figure 2-9 shows how a tile is used to pattern the background of a window.

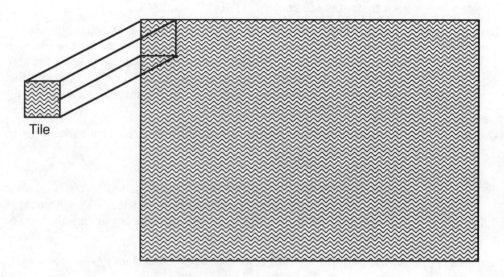

Tile

Figure 2-9. Tiling of a window background

2.4 More on Window Characteristics

This section expands on the overview of window characteristics in Section 2.2.1 and describes in more detail the window attributes, window configuration, class, and depth and visual.

2.4.1 Window Attributes

The *window attributes* consist of information about how a window is to look and act. Each window has a separate set of attributes, which can be set with XSetWindowAttributes, or in some cases with routines that change individual attributes. The attributes control the following window features:

Background   can be a solid color, pattern, or transparent.

Border   can be a solid color or pattern.

Bit Gravity   determines how partial window contents are preserved when a window is resized.

Window Gravity   determines how child windows are relocated when a window is resized.

Backing   provides hints about when a window's contents should be automatically saved, which display planes should be saved, and what pixel value is to be used when restoring unsaved planes. Not all servers are capable of

backing. Check the value returned from the `DoesBackingStore`
macro to determine whether this feature is supported on a particular
screen on your server.

Saving Under   provides hints about whether or not the screen area beneath a window
should be saved while a window such as a pop-up menu is in place, to
save obscured windows from having to redraw themselves when the pop-
up is removed. Not all servers can save under windows. You can find
out whether this feature is supported on a particular screen with the
`DoesSaveUnders` macro.

Events   indicate which events should be received, and which events should not be
sent to ancestor windows.

Substructure Redirect Override
determines whether this window should be allowed to be mapped on the
screen without intervention by the window manager. This override is
usually done for menus and other windows that are frequently mapped
and then almost immediately unmapped again.

Colormap   determines which virtual colormap should be used for this window.

Cursor   determines which cursor should be displayed when the pointer is in this
window.

It may clarify the picture to describe the features that window attributes *do not* affect. Setting the window attributes does not determine the size or position of a window, its parent, or
its border width; these comprise the window configuration. Setting the window attributes
does not affect the depth, class, or visual of a window; these are set when the window is
created. Attributes do not determine how graphics requests are interpreted; this is the job of
the graphics context (GC).

2.4.2 Window Configuration

A window's configuration consists of its position, width and height, border width, and stacking position, as described in Section 2.2.1. These factors are handled differently from the
window attributes (even though they are stored internally in the `XWindowAttributes`
structure) for an important reason: changes in a window's configuration can affect window
layout and therefore must be changed in cooperation with the window manager.

We won't go into detail here about how the application must interact with the window
manager when attempting to map a window or change a window's configuration. Suffice to
say for now that the application must do this so that the window manager can be responsible
for controlling what is on the screen and where. See Chapter 3, *Basic Window Program* for
an introduction to client-window manager interaction, and Chapter 10, *Interclient Communication*, for a complete description.

2.4.3 Class: InputOutput and InputOnly Windows

The X Window System provides two classes of windows: InputOutput and Input-Only. The main difference between the two classes is that an InputOnly window cannot be used as a drawable (a destination for a graphics request). Consequently, InputOnly windows have a more limited set of window attributes, have no border and a transparent background, and cannot have InputOutput windows as children.

InputOnly windows make an invisible area of the screen in which input has a different purpose but the display is not changed. InputOnly windows usually are assigned a different cursor to distinguish them.

The class of a window is assigned at creation and cannot be changed.

2.4.4 Depth and Visual

The depth and visual of a window are assigned at creation and cannot be changed. The *depth* is the number of planes that are to be used to represent gray scales or color within a window; depth is also the number of bits per pixel. The maximum depth allowable for an InputOutput window is the number of planes supported by the screen it is associated with. If a screen has twelve planes, a window may have at most twelve bits per pixel and therefore there are at most 2^{12} possible different shades of gray or color.

The depth of an InputOnly window is always 0. For InputOutput windows, the symbol CopyFromParent, when used as the *depth* argument in XCreateWindow, copies the depth of the parent window.

The *visual* accounts for the differences between various types of display hardware in determining the way pixel values are translated into visible colors within a particular window. A screen may support only one or several types of visuals. An XVisualInfo structure contains all the information about a particular visual. One member of XVisualInfo is the visual class, which has one of the values PseudoColor, StaticColor, Direct-Color, TrueColor, GrayScale, or StaticGray. These values specify the characteristics of the colormaps that can be used with the window; whether the colormap is read-only or read/write, color or monochrome, and whether it is split into three primary colors or composite. Other members of XVisualInfo specify the valid range of pixel values, how many bits of the pixel are allocated to red, green, and blue, and several other variables.

Both the depth and visual are inherited from the parent when a window is created with XCreateSimpleWindow. For more information on the visual class, see Chapter 7, *Color*.

2.4.5 Icons

An *icon* is a small marker window that indicates that a larger "main" window exists and is available but is not currently mapped on the screen.

Most window managers allow the user to *iconify* an application to get it out of the way without destroying it. Deiconifying an application is faster and more convenient than creating a window and running the application from scratch. Also, the iconified application keeps running whatever processes it was at work on when iconified (unless the application is programmed to halt when it is iconified). When input is required, the program may either wait until the window is deiconified, or accept input in the icon.

Figure 2-10 shows an *xterm* window before and after it is iconified. The Release 2 incarnation of *xterm* does not create an icon pixmap, and therefore simply draws its icon name into the icon.

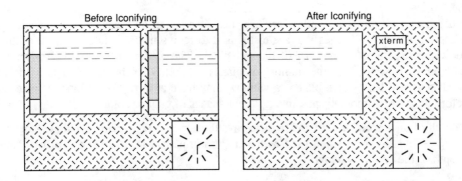

Figure 2-10. An application and its icon

Icon windows are managed by the window manager. Through the window manager hints (which will be detailed in Section 3.2.8 and Chapter 10, *Interclient Communication*), an application passes, as a minimum, its icon's name and pixmap to be displayed in the icon window. If an application needs to perform operations on its own icon window (perhaps to be able to change the background at any time, as the mail handler *xmh* does to indicate that mail has arrived), it can pass the window ID to the window manager. Otherwise, the window manager will create the icon window.

The window manager may specify in a property on the root window what sizes of icon pixmaps it prefers. If this property is set, the application should attempt to provide an icon pixmap of an acceptable size. The window manager may also specify where icons will be placed. These are optional features of the window manager that may not be present. In fact, most versions of the window manager *uwm* do not specify icon sizes or control icon location.

2.4.6 Special Characteristics of the Root Window

The root window is created when the X server program is initialized. The root window's characteristics differ slightly from those of other windows.

The root window is an InputOutput window. It is always mapped. Its size cannot be changed. Its upper-left corner is always at the upper-left corner of the screen, where the global coordinates are (0,0). The root window has a zero-width border. Its size is accessible from macros that will be described in Chapter 3, *Basic Window Program*.

The default attributes of the root window include a background pixmap with diagonal cross-hatchings, the default colormap, and a default cursor that is a large X. Any of these can be changed. The background can be changed to a single pixel value instead of a pixmap, if desired. The event mask attribute can be changed, but by default no events that occur in the root window are sent to any client. None of the other attributes are applicable to the root window. See Chapter 4, *Window Attributes*, for more information on setting window attributes.

The root window is not generally iconified by the window manager because, among other reasons, it can't be unmapped.

2.5 Introduction to Events

This section provides a brief introduction to events. You will need this knowledge to fully understand Chapter 3, *Basic Window Program*, and each window attribute described in Chapter 4, *Window Attributes*. Events are covered completely in Chapter 8, *Events*, and Chapter 9, *The Keyboard and Pointer*.

2.5.1 What Is an Event?

Moving the pointer or pressing a keyboard key causes an input *event* to occur. These are two of the simplest and most common event types, but there are many others. An event is a packet of information that is generated by the server when certain actions occur, and is queued for later use by one or more clients. The queued events can be read at any subsequent time by any client running on the same server.

Here are some other sorts of events:

• Mouse (or other pointer) button pressed or released

• Window mapped or unmapped

• Mouse crossing a window boundary

These event types are usually used for user input and to control a user interface. A second purpose of events is to allow various clients to communicate with each other and with the window manager. The events that report the following actions are usually used for the second purpose.

- A client may request that all keyboard input be sent to a particular window regardless of the pointer position; this is called a *keyboard focus* window. Changing keyboard focus from one window to another causes FocusIn and FocusOut events, indicating to the client whether or not it can expect further keyboard events.

- Changing the mapping between keyboard keys and codes they generate causes a KeymapNotify event to be sent to all clients.

- Reparenting a window is sometimes done by the window manager to add a frame to windows on the screen. This action causes a ReparentNotify event.

- When window gravity (an attribute of each window that controls its positioning relative to its parent when the parent is resized) is in effect, a GravityNotify event is generated.

- A PropertyNotify event is generated when a client changes a property on a window.

- SelectionNotify, SelectionClear, and SelectionRequest events are used to communicate back and forth between a client that is allowing a user to select a section of text (or other information) and a client that is allowing the user to place the information in its window. Some of these events are sent with XSendEvent.

At this point it is only important to understand in general what events are, not precisely what each one is for or how to use them. Chapter 8, *Events*, and Chapter 9, *The Keyboard and Pointer* will provide complete details.

2.5.2 Selection and Propagation of Events

A client must select the event types that are needed for each window. The selection is made by calling XSelectInput, which sets the event_mask window attribute, or by setting that attribute with the more general XChangeWindowAttributes routine.

For example, a scroll bar may require mouse button events but not keyboard events, while the main window of an application may require keyboard but not mouse events. One would select different event types on each of these windows.

Keyboard and pointer events are generated in the smallest window enclosing the pointer (or grabbing the pointer, as discussed in Section 8.3.2.2). Then an event of one of these types propagates upward through the window hierarchy until the event type is found in the event_mask or do_not_propagate_mask attributes of the window. If the event is found in an event_mask first (or in both on the same window) then the event is queued, and if it is found in a do_not_propagate_mask first then it is thrown away. If the event is queued, the ID of the window that finally received the event is put in the window member of the event structure.

The do_not_propagate_mask can only be set with XChangeWindowAttributes. Events other than keyboard and pointer events do not propagate. They occur in the window in which they were selected when the appropriate action occurs.

For most types of events, a copy of an event can be sent to more than one client if each client has selected that event type. Each client has its own event mask for each window, even though there is only one window ID and one set of window attributes. The client that created the window need not do anything to cooperate. The second client that wants to get an event from a window that it didn't create simply needs to select the desired event types with XSelectInput on that window. A duplicate event is sent to each window, and these events propagate independently up through the hierarchy.

2.5.3 The Event Queue

What do we mean when we say that an event is queued? Each client has its own event queue which receives the selected events in the order they are sent by the server, as was shown in Figure 2-2.

The client then can remove the event at any time and process it according to its type and the other information in each event structure. There are several functions that get input, and they differ in how many windows are monitored and what types of events are sought. The client can also read events on the queue without removing them, remove one and then put it back, or clear the queue by throwing away all the events. Events can also be created by a program to send messages to the window manager or other programs.

2.5.4 An Event Structure

XExposeEvent is one of the most important events, and its event structure is shown in Example 2-1. It is generated when an area of a window becomes visible on the screen, and indicates that the client must redraw that area. This happens when a window is moved, resized, iconified, deiconified, or has its border width changed, or when an obscuring window is unmapped. Exposure events are common and can happen at any time since they may be caused by the actions of other clients.

Example 2-1. An event structure

```
typedef struct {
    int type;
    unsigned long serial;   /* # of last request processed by server */
    Bool send_event;   /* true if this came from a SendEvent request */
    Display *display;  /* display the event was read from */
    Window window;
    int x, y;
    int width, height;
    int count;              /* if nonzero, more expose events follow */
} XExposeEvent;
```

The type of event is reported in every event structure. The window to which the event propagated is reported in the *window* member, present in all but five event types (those dealing with selections and graphics exposure). All other information in the event structures is specific to certain event types and is described in detail in Appendix E, *Event Reference*.

2.5.5 The Event Loop

Because events can arrive in any order, the structure of code to handle them is predetermined. Every program contains an event loop in which each event is received and processed. Normally this loop is implemented as an infinite `while` loop, beginning with an event-getting routine, and followed by a C-language `switch` statement that branches according to the event type. Within each branch for an event type there may be additional branches corresponding to the window in which the event occurred.

The loop will almost always include exposure events. X does not normally keep track of the contents of the obscured regions of windows. It is the responsibility of the program to make sure that the window contents can be redrawn when exposure occurs. The program must be prepared to receive and act on an exposure event at any time, meaning at every event-gathering routine. A program may work perfectly as long as there are no other programs running, but that is not good enough in a window environment!

When a window is first mapped, the first function of the program must be to read the exposure event that is generated by mapping the window, and respond to the size, position, and border width allowed by the window manager. Then the program can draw the window's contents. As it turns out, this is also how the program should respond when an exposure event arrives at any later time. The first drawing and later redrawing are done in exactly the same way, using the same code.

2.6 How to Program with Xlib

This section reviews what is important to know about X programming before you write any code. Describing what goes into the design, writing, and debugging of X programs should give you a better start when you begin your own programming.

The basic program described in Chapter 3, *Basic Window Program*, illustrates many of the issues described here.

2.6.1 Designing an X Application

Let's begin by outlining the major tasks any X application must perform.

From the user's standpoint, almost any application under any window system will do the obvious things: create a window on the screen of an appropriate size, determine a position for some text and/or graphics within the window, draw into the window, and accept keyboard and/or pointer input, changing the screen accordingly. Essentially, the top-level window of the application is treated very much like the whole screen would be treated on a PC. These tasks are straightforward and most programmers should find them familiar.

There are, of course, a few complications resulting from the unique features of window systems in general and the X Window System in particular. These complications determine the design requirements for an application that is to run under X.

2.6.1.1 Design Requirements

The following three paragraphs describe the things X applications must do that are not obvious. These are things that must be done for the application to operate properly under X, but that the average user might not notice or know about.

First, X allows workstations to be connected in a network, in which any host or node may run X programs and display them on any other node, given permission. This means that the program must be able to accept the user's specification of which display to use. (Note that each display has its own server, so choosing the display is equivalent to establishing the connection between the client and a particular server.) This requirement turns out to be built in, and it is described in Section 3.2.2.

Second, the application must be responsible in its use of the limited resources of the display, chiefly screen space and colormaps. This is because there may be many applications running concurrently on a single screen, sharing those limited resources. The client in charge of managing these limited resources is the window manager. There are certain requirements for communication between the window manager and each application to ensure that competing needs can be fairly arbitrated, and to help make sure that the user sees a consistent user interface. These requirements are not difficult to meet for simple applications, but they get more complex for serious applications since the conventions for window management are not completely firm. This area is described in Chapter 10, *Interclient Communication*.

Third, other clients may be moved over your client and then moved away, requiring your client to redraw its window or windows. X cannot maintain the contents of an unlimited number of overlapping windows, and it is inefficient for it to try to maintain even a few. Your client will be told when redrawing is necessary and in what areas. This requirement is not hard to meet, but it encourages programming in a way that records the current "state" of each window so that it can be redrawn. The handling of exposure is described in Section 3.2.13.

In a nutshell, these three aspects are all that is required of an X program beyond its basic functionality. Fortunately, for most clients without unique needs such as a custom colormap, these requirements are straightforward to satisfy.

2.6.1.2 The User Interface

The first step in designing an application will be to determine what its features will be. Determining how the user will invoke those features is probably the next step. This means designing a user interface.

X was purposely designed to be "policy-free," and therefore it does not come with a standard user interface like many other window systems do. All parts of the user-interface you will have to write yourself, unless you choose to use one of the toolkits that are available. That means you must write menus, command buttons, dialog boxes, and so forth, and determine how they are to be used. Although there are many ways to write these user-interface features, there is a simple implementation of a menu in the *winman* program shown in Chapter 14, *Window Management*, and an example of a dialog box routine in Chapter 9, *The Keyboard and Pointer*. The writing of a command button routine should be straightforward.

The key elements that interact in the design of a user interface are the hierarchy of windows and the selection and processing of events. The user interface is chiefly made up of the processing of pointer and keyboard events. Since these device events propagate through the hierarchy depending on whether they are selected, both the hierarchy and the selection together determine how events are received. For every user action there must be a path (possibly unique, possibly common for several different user actions) through the event handling code that yields some sort of response to the user, either by a visible change, a message, or a beep. Therefore the job of the event loop is to distinguish all the possible user actions and invoke the proper code. In the main event loop, each case statement for an event type must then have another switch depending on the window which received the event, before calling the function that performs the action the user requested. The event type and the window in which it occurred are only two of the most common event structure members—there may be additional switch statements based on other members too, such as which keys or buttons were being held while a key or button press occurred.

Especially for complex programs, a careful design of the window heirarchy and selection of events can simplify the code and save hours of debugging. I recommend drawing out the hierarchy of windows and the types of events selected by each one, and then drawing in the events that will be propagated to ancestor windows. This helps find problems before any code is written.

2.6.2 Writing an X Application

The best way to start writing an X application is probably to copy the existing application that is most similar to your intended purpose, or to start from a skeleton program such as *basicwin*, described in Chapter 3, *Basic Window Program*. Be aware that many current applications, even in the standard distribution, do not follow the current conventions for interclient communication. One goal for Release 3 of X11 from MIT is to bring the standard applications up to snuff.

The following sections describe some basic facts about the actual process of coding and compiling an application.

2.6.2.1 The User Defaults

An application should not hardcode all the options that are possible under X, such as colors and fonts. It should allow the user to specify the colors of all windows, the font to use, the display and screen to use, the initial size and position of the application, and a large number of other standard and application specific options. The problem is that there are too many of these options to be specified on the command line every time the application is invoked.

The developers of X have designed a better way for the user to specify options. The user places the desired options in a file using a particular format, and runs the X application *xrdb* specifying this file as a command line argument. *xrdb* places a property on the root window whose value is the contents of this file. Applications use a set of Xlib routines collectively called the resource manager to return a setting for each variable required. The routine XGetDefault makes this process quite easy for the application. If the user has not called *xrdb* to set the property on the root window, XGetDefault reads in a file called *.Xdefaults* in the user's home directory. The application itself should contain a default value for each variable in case neither of these sources contains a default for any of them.

The user defaults contains key/value pairs. A key/value pair may apply only to a particular window within a particular application, to an entire application, to a certain class of applications such as editors, or to all applications. The algorithm used to find the value for a particular variable operates quite differently from a normal database manager. Given an incomplete specification of a key, it uses an algorithm to determine which of the keys in the defaults is the best match and returns the indicated value. It always returns only one value. This is much different from a normal database manager which would return many values if the key were too general.

The resource manager and getting user defaults is described in detail in Chapter 11, *Managing User Preferences*.

2.6.2.2 Compiling and Linking X Programs

To use all the functions in the X library, you need to include *<X11/Xlib.h>*, *<X11/Xutil.h>*, *<X11/keysym.h>*, and *<X11/Xresource.h>*. These files define data structures, macros, and symbols and declare the types of functions. To compile and link your program with all the available Xlib libraries, including a symbol table for a symbolic debugger, use:

```
cc -g -o outputfile inputfile.c -lX
```

The *-lX* option specifies linking with the standard X library, Xlib.

A set of routines to make it easier to port programs from X Version 10 to Version 11 is provided in a separate library. To use the X Version 10 compatibility functions, include *<X11/X10.h>* in your source file and link with both the *-lX* and *-loldX* options to your *cc* command.

The library options may have different names on certain systems. For example, Xlib may be loaded with *-lX11* rather than *-lX* to distinguish X11 from X10 when both are supported. In addition, in Release 1 *-lXrm* is used to link with the resource manager routines. This option is no longer needed in Release 2, since the resource manager has been integrated into Xlib.

You will probably want to use *make*(1) when compiling time could be saved by compiling smaller functions separately before linking. (For more information, see the Nutshell Handbook *Managing Projects with Make*.)

2.6.2.3 Naming Conventions

There are a number of conventions for the naming of Xlib functions and constants. You should be familiar with these conventions in order to name your own functions and constants properly. The major conventions are:

* The names of all Xlib functions begin with an X (capital x). Compound words are constructed by capitalizing the first letter of each word. For example, a typical function name is XAllocColor.

- The names of most user-visible data structures and structure types begin with an X. The only exceptions are `Depth`, `Display`, `GC`, `Screen`, `ScreenFormat`, and `Visual`. Pointers to these six structures are quite commonly used in programs, but their members should not be accessed except through pre-existing macros, with the possible exception of `Visual`.

- The names of all members of data structures use lower case. Compound words, where needed, are constructed with underscores (_).

- The names of macros do not begin with an X. To distinguish macros from user symbols (which are all caps), the first letter of each word in the macro is capitalized. The function form of each macro has the same name as the macro but with a leading X. (The macros used for quarks are an exception to this rule, perhaps because they were once part of a separate library. Their names begin with Xrm.)

- The names of symbols defined in X include files (#defined constants) use mixed case, with the first letter of each word capitalized, and do not begin with X. Lower case symbols are reserved for variables and all upper case for user symbols, according to existing convention. The only exception is that predefined atom names use all upper case letters, with underscores separating the words. Atom names begin with *XA_* to distinguish them from user constants.

You should choose constants and routine names that won't be confused with standard Xlib functions, macros, or constants. User function names should not begin with X, and perhaps should not have the first letter of every word capitalized. User constants should be all upper case. Variable names can be lower case as usual, with underscores separating the words if desired, since X structure member references will always be accompanied by the variable declared as the structure.

2.6.2.4 Using Structures, Symbols, and Masks

Xlib programming takes advantage of many structure definitions and defined constants. This style of programming may be unfamiliar to some programmers. We will describe how structures and constants are typically used so that the idea will be familiar when you see the examples.

Pointers to structures are the major way of specifying data to and returning data from Xlib routines. If the routine returns data, the returned value will be a pointer to the data structure, unless the routine returns more than one structure, in which case one or all of the structures will be arguments. In some routines (primarily those concerning color), a pointer-to-structure argument specifies some information and returns some other information.

When setting the characteristics of an X resource such as a set of window attributes, a graphics context, the cells in a colormap, or a hardware characteristic (such as key click), both a structure and a mask are specified as arguments. The *mask* specifies which values in the specified structure should be read when updating the resource values. One bit in the mask is assigned to each member in the structure, and a special constant is defined in the Xlib include files to represent that member when constructing the mask. Each of the mask constants has one bit set. The mask argument is made by combining any number of the mask constants with the bitwise OR operator (|). For example, the CWBackground-

`Pixmap` constant is used to indicate that the `background_pixmap` member of the specified window attributes structure is to be read and the corresponding member in the resource changed.

The other major use of defined constants in Xlib (other than for masks) is as values for structure members themselves. They indicate which of a number of alternatives is true. For example, several of the structure members can have only the values `True` or `False`. As another example, the `type` member of each event structure can have one of 33 different values, each represented by a different defined constant such as `Expose`.

Defined constants are also used to provide convenient names for atoms. As described in Section 2.1.4, an atom is an integer value identifying a property. Atoms are used to avoid passing arbitrary-length property-name strings back and forth between the client and the server. Using defined constants to give names to atoms gives convenience without extra overhead. Defined constants are also used as returned values.

2.6.2.5 Performance Optimizing

While designing, writing, and debugging your application you can look for ways to improve its performance.

Whenever possible, you should use Xlib functions that do not require protocol replies. That is, in functions that are called frequently, avoid Xlib routines with names containing `Get`, `Query`, or `Fetch`. Most of these functions return information from the server, and as such they are subject to network delays and will slow down your application.

In general, keep the feedback loop between the user's action and the program's response as short as possible.

2.6.3 Debugging an X Application

All programmers know that debugging is by far the most difficult and time-consuming aspect of programming. This is where you catch all the problems caused during the writing stage and often also problems in the design stage. One can rarely foresee all the issues when designing a program.

There are some techniques that make debugging X applications easier. One, of course, is to have good tools. The C program checker *lint* helps find problems such as mismatches in the number of arguments to a function, variables declared but not used, or misused pointers. Although it often finds something to complain about that you don't consider an error, it also provides useful information.

Use of a good debugger such as *dbx* avoids the need to continually place `printf` statements in the code and recompile.

The standard application *xwininfo* is good for displaying information about a window, including its window ID and name, parent and children IDs and names, all the window attributes, and the window manager hints set for that window. Use the *-all* option or see the *xwininfo* reference page in Volume Three, *X Window System User's Guide*, for information on printing just the needed information.

The standard application *xprop*, which displays the name, type and value of each property set on a window, is useful in debugging applications that set or read properties. It can also display font properties. These applications are described in Volume Three, *X Window System User's Guide*.

One of the most common places to have difficulty debugging is in event handling. For this reason, I recommend that all programs under development contain `printf` statements at the beginning of each branch of their event handling, so that the programmer can watch the sequence of events in one window and the visible performance of the application in another. This print statement can be placed within a compile-time `#ifdef DEBUG, #endif` pair so that all the print statements can be taken out of the compiled code by simply commenting out the definition of the symbol `DEBUG` and recompiling. Although the event types are coded as numbers and will normally be printed that way by the printf statements, they are easily translated back into event types using the technique described in Section 8.2.5.

X applications are difficult to test thoroughly. Here are some of the miscellaneous tests you should put your application through.

- Be sure to try all combinations of raising and and lowering different windows to test the application's response to exposure. Does it redraw unnecessarily?
- Try all combinations of pressing and releasing different pointer buttons to see if anything breaks.
- Try operating the program in a busy network environment.
- Try the application on a variety of different servers. Does it work on both color and monochrome systems?
- What happens when you type function keys or other unique keys on a particular keyboard?
- Is it possible to crash the application by specifying the wrong set of defaults or command line arguments?

If your application can pass all these tests, you've done a good job.

2.6.3.1 Errors

There are really two levels of error handling in programs using Xlib. The first level you implement yourself by monitoring the return status of the routines that request resources. This allows the client to modify the arguments of the request and try again. The second level is usually caused by a programming error, or a fatal system error. These types are processed later and are handled by two separate error handling functions that can be set by the client but by default simply print a message and exit the client.

As an example of the first level of error handling, a client should always check to see whether it was successfully connected to the display server with `XOpenDisplay` before proceeding. If this connection did not succeed, the client should print a message to *stderr* indicating what happened, and which display it attempted to open. This process will be demonstrated in Chapter 3, *Basic Window Program*.

The reason why this type of error message is not built in becomes clear when you understand that X errors are processed like events. They are generated when something goes wrong, and queued until the client flushes the output buffer. If you wait until the buffer is flushed to allow the standard error handler to catch and report the error, you will have lost the information of what went wrong, and lost the chance to recover from it. If you monitor the returned value, you could conceivably allow the program or the user to keep changing the arguments until the call succeeded.

Fatal errors, such as a broken connection with the server, are unrecoverable conditions and invoke the XIOErrorHandler. User errors occur when routine arguments don't conform to accepted ranges, or when IDs do not match existing resources, etc. These types of errors are sent to XErrorHandler. Both error handlers by default display an intelligible (if not intelligent) message and then exit. The possible error messages and their general causes are listed in Volume Two, Appendix B, *Error Messages and Protocol Requests*. These error messages also specify which protocol request caused the error, which you can also look up in Volume Two, Appendix B, to determine which Xlib routine may have caused the error. This mapping is not unique because several Xlib routines often generate the same protocol request.

User-defined error handling routines will be called from the error handlers if you pass procedure names to XSetIOErrorHandler or XSetErrorHandler. If either is passed a NULL function pointer, the respective default handler will be reinstated.

If you write your own error handling routines, it is recommended that you use XGetError-Text or XGetErrorDatabaseText to get the string describing an error code, so that the codes of extensions can be handled properly. XGetErrorDatabaseText uses the resource manager to provide further error messages from the file *XErrorDB*, located by default in */usr/lib/X11*.

Only the error handling routines receive error events and these events cannot be selected or received by windows.

2.6.3.2 The XErrorEvent Structure

Example 2-2 shows the XErrorEvent structure and its members. The value of each member of this structure is displayed by the default error handlers.

Example 2-2. The XErrorEvent structure

```
typedef struct _XErrorEvent {
        int type;
        Display *display;          /* display the event was read from */
        XID resourceid;            /* resource ID */
        unsigned long serial;      /* serial number of failed request */
        char error_code;           /* error code of failed request */
        char request_code;         /* major opcode of failed request */
        char minor_code;           /* minor opcode of failed request */
} XErrorEvent;
```

- The serial member is the number of requests sent over the network connection since it was opened, starting from 1. The difference between serial and the last request processed as reported in error messages tells you how many requests to count back in order to find the request that caused the error.

- The `request_code` is a protocol representation of the name of the procedure that failed; these are decoded in Volume Two, Appendix B, *Error Messages and Protocol Requests*.

- The `error_code` is one of the items described in Volume Two, Appendix B.

- The `minor_code` is zero unless the request is part of an extension. If it is, the `minor_code` indicates which request in the extension caused the error.

- The `resource_id` indicates one of the resources (window, colormap, etc.) that was associated with the request that caused the error.

2.6.3.3 Synchronizing Errors

Since error events are not displayed precisely when they occur, it is often informative to look up the protocol request as well as the error code to determine which function the error occurred in. You can't rely on the debugger to indicate where the error occurred.

In particularly difficult situations, it is useful to use `XSynchronize` to make sure that errors are displayed as soon as they occur. When `XSynchronize` is invoked, the performance of graphics will be drastically reduced. The same result occurs by setting the global variable `_Xdebug` to any nonzero value when running a program under a debugger (UNIX only).

3
Basic Window Program

Every Xlib program has a similar structure. This chapter shows a simple program that puts up a window and handles events in that window. You can use this simple application as a template for your own, more complex applications.

In This Chapter:

3
Basic Window Program

This chapter presents a simple program that demonstrates the fundamentals of programming with the X library. All clients will use the techniques described and demonstrated here.

The basic program presented in this chapter fulfills all the requirements for a basic application outlined at the end of Chapter 2, *X Concepts*, and illustrates some of the most important X concepts and programming issues. You should have read Chapter 2 before proceeding.

The program performs these operations:

- Connects the client to an X server with XOpenDisplay, and exits gracefully if the connection could not be made.

- Gets information about the physical screen, and uses it to calculate the desired size of the window.

- Creates a window with XCreateSimpleWindow.

- Sets standard properties for the window manager.

- Selects the types of events it needs to receive.

- Loads the font to be used for printing text.

- Creates a graphics context to control the action of drawing requests.

- Displays the window with XMapWindow.

- Loops for events.

- Responds to the Expose event resulting from mapping the window (and any other Expose event that might come along later) by calling routines to place text and graphics. If the window is too small to perform its intended function, it displays an appropriate message.

- Receives ConfigureNotify events, indicating that the window has been resized by the window manager. The new window size is provided in the event structure.

- Keeps handling events until a KeyPress or ButtonPress event arrives, then closes the display connection and exits.

The program does not perform the following operations, which are required of a robust X client:

- Allow the user to specify command line options and read the resource database.

- Handle colors.

For more information on these topics, see Chapter 12, *A Complete Application*.

3.1 Running the Program

If you have the diskette of sample programs (available from O'Reilly and Associates, Inc.—see Preface for ordering information) and a workstation that runs X, you can try out this program by compiling *examples/basicwin.c*. See the description of how to compile X programs in Section 2.6.2.2.

The program just displays a window with some text and graphics drawn into it. Figure 3-1 shows the output of the program. The one useful thing it does is tell you the size and depth of the current screen.

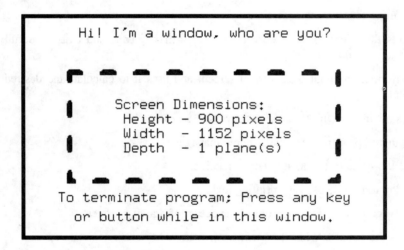

```
          Hi! I'm a window, who are you?


      ┌ ─ ─ ─ ─ ─ ─ ─ ┐

      │     Screen Dimensions:         │
      │        Height - 900 pixels     │
      │        Width  - 1152 pixels    │
      │        Depth  - 1 plane(s)     │

      └ ─ ─ ─ ─ ─ ─ ─ ┘

        To terminate program; Press any key
          or button while in this window.
```

Figure 3-1. Output of the basicwin program

Without further ado, let's begin to look at the code.

3.2 The Main of basicwin

As usual, the code is composed of a main program and several subroutines. The main does everything described at the start of this chapter except create the GC, load the font, and draw the text and graphics. These tasks are done in the get_GC, load_font, draw_text and draw_graphics routines, which are shown with the complete code in Section 3.2.20, but not described fully until Chapter 6, *Drawing Graphics and Text*. You can get the general idea of what they do just by looking at them, though.

In the following sections, the code is shown and described in small pieces. In some cases the relevant declarations of variables are shown again in each segment of the code as well as at the top of the program (where they would normally appear). This has been done to increase clarity when showing the individual pieces of the program.

3.2.1 Include Files and Declarations

Example 3-1 shows the include files and declarations from *basicwin.c*.

Example 3-1. basicwin — include files and declarations

```
/* Xlib include files */
#include <X11/Xlib.h>
#include <X11/Xutil.h>
#include <X11/Xos.h>

/* standard C include file */
#include <stdio.h>

/* bitmap data for icon */
#include "bitmaps/icon_bitmap"

#define BITMAPDEPTH 1

/* Display and screen are used as arguments to nearly every Xlib
 * routine, so it simplifies routine calls to declare them global.
 * If there were additional source files, these variables would be
 * declared 'extern' in them. */
Display *display;
int screen;

void main(argc, argv)
int argc;
char **argv;
{
    Window win;
    unsigned int width, height;     /* window size */
    int x = 0, y = 0;               /* window position */
    unsigned int border_width = 4;  /* border four pixels wide */
    unsigned int display_width, display_height;
    char *window_name = "Basic Window Program";
    char *icon_name = "basicwin";
```

Example 3-1. basicwin — include files and declarations (continued)

```
        Pixmap icon_pixmap;
        XSizeHints size_hints;          /* preferred sizes */
        XEvent report;                  /* structure for event information */
        GC gc;                          /* ID of graphics context */
        XFontStruct *font_info;         /* structure containing font info */
        char *display_name = NULL;      /* server to connect to; NULL means
                                         * connect to server specified in
                                         * environment variable DISPLAY */
```

Let's begin with the include files. The three include files *<X11/Xlib.h>*, *<X11/Xutil.h>*, and *<X11/Xos.h>* are needed in virtually all Xlib programs. The *<X11/Xlib.h>* file contains declarations of structure types used in Xlib functions. *<X11/Xlib.h>* in turn includes *<X11/X.h>*, which sets up many defined constants. *<X11/Xutil.h>* contains more structure definitions and defined constants for certain groups of Xlib functions. Many of the structures and constant definitions from these include files are described in this manual with the functions in which they are used. Structures and constants are also presented on many of the reference pages in Volume Two, *Xlib Reference Manual*, if the routine on that page uses a structure or defined constant as an argument or return value. Volume Two, Appendix F, *Structure Reference*, provides an alphabetical listing of structures; Volume Two, Appendix G, *Symbol Reference*, provides the definitions of constants.

The final include file referenced in the Example 3-1 is *<X11/Xos.h>*, which attempts to make programs as portable as possible by including certain files depending on the version of UNIX for which the program is being compiled. This include file is not absolutely necessary but it is useful.

Now let's move on to all the strange new types that appear in Example 3-1. The Window, Display, Pixmap, XSizeHints, and XEvent types used in this program are all defined in *<X11/Xlib.h>*. A brief description of each is given here, but you will need to see the code that uses each variable to fully understand them.

- Window is a unique integer identifier (ID) that is returned by XCreateWindow or XCreateSimpleWindow and is thereafter used by the program to refer to the created window resource. The ID for a window is assigned by the server and can be used by any application.

- Display is a large structure that contains information about the server and screens. It is filled only after this program connects to a server by calling XOpenDisplay.

- Pixmap is an integer ID like Window, but for a pixmap resource. The pixmap in this case is a picture to display in the icon for the window.

- XSizeHints is a structure that is used to provide the window manager with information about the preferred sizes and size increments for the top-level window of the application.

- XEvent is a union that stores information about an event. It can be interpreted as one of many individual structure types depending on the type of event.

These declarations are repeated in the sections of code below in which they are used to avoid the need to flip back and forth.

3.2.2 Connecting to a Server

XOpenDisplay connects an Xlib program to a server. The code shown in Example 3-2 that calls XOpenDisplay will appear in all Xlib programs.

Example 3-2. basicwin — connecting to the server

```
char *display_name = NULL;
Display *display;
int screen;
    .
    .
    .

/* connect to X server */

if ( (display=XOpenDisplay(display_name)) == NULL )
{
    (void) fprintf( stderr, "basicwin: cannot connect to \
            X server %s\n", XDisplayName(display_name));
    exit ( -1 );
}

screen = DefaultScreen(display);
```

basicwin

The *display_name* argument to XOpenDisplay specifies which server to connect to. This may be any server on the network, and could be specified on the command line in a more complete application than this one. (See Sections 2.6.2.1 and 11.1 for a discussion of how to process command line arguments and user-specified default values in an X program.) When *display_name* is not specified by the user, it should be set to NULL, which causes XOpenDisplay to connect to the server listed in the UNIX environment DISPLAY variable. You can view the current contents of the DISPLAY environment variable by using the UNIX command:

```
echo $DISPLAY
```

It can be changed by typing:

```
setenv DISPLAY display_name                    (C Shell)
```

or

```
DISPLAY=display_name; export DISPLAY           (Bourne Shell)
```

xterm normally sets the DISPLAY variable when you login to a remote machine, to make sure that when you execute X applications from that terminal, your output will be displayed on the screen from which you typed the command.

Both the DISPLAY environment variable and the *display_name* argument to XOpen-Display have the same format. The format is *host:server.screen*, in which *host* refers to the machine name; *server*, the server number on that machine; and *screen*, the screen number on that server.*

The server number can be thought of as the number of the user on a particular host. The *server* number is always zero on a single-user workstation, and may be nonzero only if a single host is supporting more than one user. A single host supporting more than user is uncommon because it requires a separate set of wires for the keyboard, pointer, and display of each user, all running to the central host.

The .*screen* part is optional, and only specifies which screen is returned by the Default-Screen macro (more on macros in a minute). You can still use any or all of the screens controlled by the specified server. For example, Perseus:0.1 instructs the server you are running the program on to connect to server 0 on the host called Perseus, and that the default screen on that server for this program will be screen 1.†

The XOpenDisplay routine returns a pointer to a structure of type Display. If the connection is successful, the structure will be filled with information about the server and each of its screens. If the attempt to create a connection fails, XOpenDisplay returns NULL. The code in Example 3-2 above checks to make sure this returned pointer is not NULL before proceeding. The message printed when the connection fails includes the text returned by the XDisplayName function. This function returns *display_name* or, if that is NULL, the UNIX environment DISPLAY variable. XDisplayName is necessary since without it, there would be no way to tell the user to what server an attempt to connect was made.

The client might not succeed in connecting to a server for a number of reasons. Most likely, the *display_name* variable or DISPLAY environment variable does not specify a valid server that is connected via the network to the machine you are running the program on. Or perhaps the network is out of order. Another possibility is that the server and client use different versions of the X protocol. X Version 11 programs are not compatible with X Version 10 and vice versa, so that if such a connection is attempted, a error message such "protocol mismatch" should be printed, since the connection will partially succeed. All releases of X Version 11, however, *are* compatible since they use the same protocol.

Finally, the host you are running the client on may not be on the *host access list* of the server you are trying to display on. The host access list is a simple permission mechanism. A server reads the list of hosts as it starts up and may be connected only to clients running on these hosts. There are commands to add and remove hosts from the access list, but these can be called only from clients running on the host whose list is being changed. In all these

---

*MIT's manuals describe this format as *host:display.screen*, using *display* instead of *server*. Since most people think of screens and displays as virtually the same thing, their description leads to confusion. The second member in the string really identifies which server on a particular host to connect to. Each of these servers would support a user.

†Note that most servers only control a single screen. However, X does support multiple screens. These may actually be separate physical devices, but they can also be logical devices. For example, the sample server for Sun workstations on the X11 distribution allows a single physical screen to be used as both a color screen and a monochrome screen. Both screens can be active at the same time: moving the pointer off the edge of one screen moves the pointer onto the other, showing the entire contents of the other screen in the process. This is a useful feature because color is by definition somewhat slower than monochrome, so programs can be edited and debugged on the monochrome screen but then tested on the color screen.

cases the code shown in Example 3-2 will simply print the name of the server to which the connection failed, and no further information.

If Example 3-2 executes successfully past opening the display, we can begin to set up variables for use in the rest of the program. The first of these is the global variable `screen`, set to the return value of the `DefaultScreen` macro. `screen` will be used throughout the program to indicate which screen on the server our operations are to affect. It is important to use the `DefaultScreen` macro rather than to hardcode 0 as the screen used by the client, because even without command line parsing in the client, this allows the user to set the default screen by setting the *.screen* element of the DISPLAY environment variable.

The variable `screen` can actually be any integral value between 0 and the value returned by `(ScreenCount(display) - 1)` inclusive. The `ScreenCount` macro returns the number of screens on the connected server. Since we only intend to use one of the screens, we can be satisfied with using the default screen.

3.2.3 Display Macros

We have just described all the macros used in the context of connecting with a display. They all get their information from the `Display` structure returned by `XOpenDisplay`. But this is not the only useful information we can get from the `Display` structure. There are numerous other macros that supply information about the characteristics of the server and its screens. We will describe these macros where they come in handy in this book. The complete set of macros that access the members of the `Display` structure is listed and described in Volume Two, Appendix C, *Macros*. They tell you whether the server supports certain features like backing store and motion history buffers, the protocol version and release and the name of the server vendor, and the byte order used for images on the server. The `Display` structure also provides information about each screen, such as the root window dimensions and the number of planes.

The macros are provided both for convenience and because the `Display` structure is intended to be opaque; clients shouldn't access its members directly. The reason for it being opaque is that Xlib's authors want to retain the option to change the members in the `Display` structure without making existing clients obsolete.

But the fact is that Xlib's authors have not provided enough macros to eliminate the temptation to access the members directly. There are at least two members of the `Display` structure for which no macros are provided that are definitely needed in certain fairly common situations. These cases are noted in Chapter 9, *The Keyboard and Pointer*, and Chapter 11, *Managing User Preferences*. You will not be struck dead if you access these members directly, but you should at least flag the places where you access them so that you know where to look if the clients stops working in a later release.

3.2.4 Getting Window Information

Most clients need to know the size of the screen so that the output can be tailored to look the same—or to look good—on any display. There are two ways to get this information. You can access members of the `Display` structure to get information about the root window, or you can use `XGetGeometry` or `XGetWindowAttributes` to get the root window's dimensions. The first method, using the macros for accessing information from the `Display` structure, works only for the root window. The second and third methods, reading the window geometry or attributes, work for any window.

To get the dimensions of a screen in pixels, you can use the macros `DisplayWidth` and `DisplayHeight`. The macros `DisplayWidthMM` and `DisplayHeightMM` return the screen dimensions in millimeters. These four macros get their information locally from the `Display` structure, so they are fast and efficient. The ratio of width in millimeters to width in pixels gives you a measurement of the spacing between pixels horizontally, and the same process can be used to determine the vertical pixel spacing. This can be important because when you draw a circle, it will look more like an ellipse on screens that don't have the same pixel spacing in both directions (usually inexpensive PC servers). You can tailor your drawing to compensate for this effect.

The second and third ways to get the geometry of a window are to use `XGetGeometry`, or to get all the window attributes using `XGetWindowAttributes`. The difference between these two routines is that `XGetWindowAttributes` gets much more information, and actually calls `XGetGeometry` itself. These methods have the disadvantage that they get information from the server, requiring a round-trip request that is subject to network delays. We show this method here because, for any window other than the root window, this is the only way to get window information.

The following code fragments demonstrate the three ways of getting root window information. *basicwin* uses the macros method because in this case we need information about the root window, and this is the most efficient way to get it.

Example 3-3 shows the macros method; Example 3-4, the `XGetGeometry` method; and Example 3-5, the `XGetWindowAttributes` method.

Example 3-3. Code fragment for getting display dimensions — using macros

```
Display *display;
int screen;
unsigned int display_width, display_height;
    .
    .
/* open display */
    .
    .
/* display size is a member of display structure */
display_width = DisplayWidth(display, screen);
display_height = DisplayHeight(display, screen);
```

Example 3-4. Another way to get window size — using XGetGeometry

```
Display *display;
int screen;
Drawable root;
int x, y;
unsigned int width, height;
unsigned int border_width;
unsigned int depth;
    .
    .
    .
/* open display */
    .
    .
    .
/* get geometry info about root window */
if (XGetGeometry(display, RootWindow(display, screen), &root, &x,
        &y, &width, &height, &border_width, &depth) == False)
    {
    fprintf(stderr, "basicwin: can't get root window geometry\n");
    exit(-1);
    }
display_width = width;
display_height = height;
```

Example 3-5. A third way to get window size — using XGetWindowAttributes

```
Display *display;
int screen;
XWindowAttributes windowattr; /* (this declaration at top) */
    .
    .
    .
/* open display */
    .
    .
    .
/* fill attribute structure with info about root window */
XGetWindowAttributes(display, RootWindow(display, screen),
        &windowattr);
display_width = windowattr.width;
display_height = windowattr.height;
```

3.2.5 Creating Windows

The next steps are to create a window and place it in relation to the root window. Actually, a window's position relative to its parent is usually determined before the window is created, since these coordinates can be specified as arguments to the routine that creates the window. But creating a window that is a child of the root window is a special case, in which the position is not important because a window manager will usually allow the user to position the window as it appears on the screen. Therefore, the coordinates used are specified arbitrarily as (0, 0). Even if a window manager is not running, the window will appear on the screen at the upper-left corner, ready to be moved to a convenient position.

Example 3-6 shows this simple process.

The only new thing in Example 3-6 is the use of several new macros in the call to create a window.

Let's talk about `RootWindow` first. Each screen has its own root window. To create a window on a particular screen, you use the root window on that screen as the parent. That window can then only be used on that screen. The ID of the root window on a particular screen is returned by the `RootWindow` macro. The first generation of windows on a screen (known as the top-level windows) should always use this macro to specify the parent. `XCreateSimpleWindow` makes a new window with a parent, size (`win_width`, `win_height`), position (`win_x`, `win_y`), border width, border pixel value, and background pixel value. All other attributes of the window are taken from the parent, in this case the root window. If we wanted to specify any or all the attributes instead of inheriting them from the parent, we would have to use `XCreateWindow` instead of `XCreateSimpleWindow`.

3.2.6 Color Strategy

Applications do not choose pixel values, they choose colors and are returned pixel values by a routine they call that allocates colors or the display macros `BlackPixel` or `WhitePixel`.*

This example is a monochrome application, but it will work on both monochrome and color screens. We use the `WhitePixel` macro to specify the background pixel value (in the call to create the window), and set the foreground in the GC to be the contrasting value returned

---

* `BlackPixel` and `WhitePixel` are no longer constants as the were in X Version 10. Pixel values must not be hardcoded.

by `BlackPixel`. The border pixel value is also set to `BlackPixel`. The background and border pixel values are set with the last two arguments of the call that creates the window in Example 3-6. The foreground pixel value is set in the `getGC` routine in the manner described in Section 5.1.1.

As you may recall from Chapter 2, pixel values represent colors, but they will be translated by a colormap before being displayed on the screen. These macros return the pixel values corresponding to two distinguishable colors in the default colormap, which might not actually be black and white. The visible color corresponding to a pixel value may change if the colormap is modified, or if the default colormap is uninstalled and a new colormap is installed. Therefore it is possible, though unlikely, that these colors will not be distinguishable.

There is nothing an application can do to avoid this possibility, but using `XQueryColors`, it could find out the RGB values corresponding to the pixel values returned by `Black-Pixel` and `WhitePixel`, and then use an algorithm to determine whether they are sufficiently distinguishable.

Color is described in more detail in Chapter 7, *Color*.

3.2.7 Preparing an Icon Pixmap

An application should create an icon design for itself, so that if a window manager is running and the user iconifies the application, the icon will be recognizable as belonging to the particular application. Exactly how to tell the window manager about this pixmap will be described in the next section, but first let's talk about how to create the pixmap.

The program should take two steps in creating the pixmap: It should find out what sizes of icon are acceptable to the window manager, and then create a pixmap of an appropriate size. Since most current window managers don't specify icon sizes, and it is difficult to know how to respond in a reasonable way, this issue can be ignored for the present. Eventually, when standard window managers specify standard icon sizes, applications would use `XGet-IconSizes` to determine which window manager was in operation and have a icon bitmap for each one.

Example 3-7 shows the simple process of creating a pixmap for the icon.

Example 3-7. basicwin — creating an icon pixmap

```
#include "bitmaps/icon_bitmap"

void main(argc, argv)
int argc;
char **argv;
{
    /* other declarations */
     .
     .
     .
    Pixmap icon_pixmap;
```

Example 3-7. basicwin — creating an icon pixmap (continued)

```
/* open display, create window, etc. */

/* might someday want to use XGetIconSizes to get the icon sizes
 * specified by the window manager, to determine which of several
 * icon bitmap files to use, but only when some standard window
 * managers set these. */

/* Create pixmap of depth 1 (bitmap) for icon */
icon_pixmap = XCreateBitmapFromData(display, win, icon_bitmap_bits,
        icon_bitmap_width, icon_bitmap_height);
    .
    .
    .
```

An icon design can be created using the standard X application *bitmap*. You run *bitmap* with a filename and dimensions as command line arguments like so:

```
% bitmap icon_bitmap 40x40
```

Then you use the pointer to draw your bitmap. For more information on the bitmap editor, see Volume Three, *X Window System User's Guide*. Normally the icon carries some symbolic representation of the application, so use your imagination. *bitmap* creates an ASCII file that looks like Example 3-8. This particular bitmap is a little small for an icon, being only 20 pixels on a side. A more typical size would be about 40 pixels on a side.

Example 3-8. Format of bitmap files

```
#define icon_bitmap_width 20
#define icon_bitmap_height 20
static char icon_bitmap_bits[] = {
   0x60, 0x00, 0x01, 0xb0, 0x00, 0x07, 0x0c, 0x03, 0x00, 0x04, 0x04, 0x00,
   0xc2, 0x18, 0x00, 0x03, 0x30, 0x00, 0x01, 0x60, 0x00, 0xf1, 0xdf, 0x00,
   0xc1, 0xf0, 0x01, 0x82, 0x01, 0x00, 0x02, 0x03, 0x00, 0x02, 0x0c, 0x00,
   0x02, 0x38, 0x00, 0x04, 0x60, 0x00, 0x04, 0xe0, 0x00, 0x04, 0x38, 0x00,
   0x84, 0x06, 0x00, 0x14, 0x14, 0x00, 0x0c, 0x34, 0x00, 0x00, 0x00, 0x00};
```

The bitmap format shown in Example 3-8 is not used only in XCreateBitmapFrom-Data. It is also used by the Xlib functions XWriteBitmapFile and XReadBitmap-File.

3.2.8 Communicating with the Window Manager

Before mapping the window (which displays it on the screen), an application must set the standard properties to tell the window manager at least a few essential things about the application.

You may remember from Chapter 2, *X Concepts*, that a property is a collection of information that is readable and writable by any client, and is usually used to communicate between clients. The standard properties are part of the convention for communication between the window manager and each application.

You may also remember that a property is associated with a particular window. The standard properties are associated with the top-level window of the application. This is how the server keeps track of the standard properties of all the different applications and has them ready for the window manager to read them.

Several routines are provided that allow the application to easily set these properties; analogous routines allow the window manager to read them. The routine that was designed to set all the most important properties for a quick application is XSetStandardProperties. Any real application will also set other properties for the window manager.

The minimum set of properties that an application must set are:

- Window name

- Icon name

- Icon pixmap

- Command name and arguments

- Number of arguments

- Preferred window sizes

We'll say more about each of these after you have seen the code that sets them. Example 3-9 shows the code that sets the standard properties.

Example 3-9. basicwin — setting standard properties

```
void main(argc, argv)
int argc;
char **argv;
{
    .
    .
    .
    /* to be displayed in window manager's title bar of window, if any */
    char *window_name = "Basic Window Program";

    /* to be displayed in icon */
    char *icon_name = "basicwin";
    Pixmap icon_pixmap;

    XSizeHints size_hints; /* structure containing preferred sizes */
```

Example 3-9. basicwin — setting standard properties (continued)

```
/* open display, create window, create icon pixmap */
    .
    .
    .

/* initalize size hint property for window manager */
    size_hints.flags = PSize | PMinSize;
    size_hints.width = width;
    size_hints.height = height;
    size_hints.min_width = 350;
    size_hints.min_height = 250;

/* set properties for window manager (always before mapping) */
    XSetStandardProperties(display, win, window_name, icon_name,
        icon_pixmap, argv, argc, &size_hints);
```

It is important to realize that these properties are only hints. A hint is information that might or might not be used. There may be no window manager running, or the window manager may ignore some or all of the hints. Therefore, an application should not depend on anything having been done with the information provided in the standard properties. For example, take the window name hint. Some window managers will use this information to display a title bar above or beside each top-level window, showing the application's name. The proper and obvious thing for the application to do would be to set the window name to be the application's name. But if the application were an editor, it could try to set its window name to the name of the current file. This plan would fall through if no window manager were running.

The icon name and icon pixmap are both set to allow the window manager to make a good icon. Current window managers often display just the icon pixmap, unless no pixmap is specified, in which case they use the icon name. Other window managers may use both. If the icon name is not set, the convention within window managers is to use the window name as the icon name; if the window name is not specified either, then they will use the last element of the command line. However, a well-written application should set both.

The UNIX shell command name and arguments are passed into *main* in the standard fashion from the command line, as argv and argc. These can be used directly as arguments in the call to set the standard properties. This information might be used by the window manager to restart or duplicate the application when so instructed by the user.

And last but not least, the window size hints property is a structure that specifies the sizes, positions, and aspect ratios preferred by the user or the program for this application. The XSizeHints structure is shown in Example 3-10.

Example 3-10. The XSizeHints structure

```
typedef struct {
        long flags;          /* marks defined fields in this structure */
        int x, y;
        int width, height;
```

Example 3-10. The XSizeHints structure (continued)

```
        int min_width, min_height;
        int max_width, max_height;
        int width_inc, height_inc;
        struct {
                int x;  /* numerator */
                int y;  /* denominator */
        } min_aspect, max_aspect;
} XSizeHints;
```

You might ask, "How would the user be involved in specifying the size hints, when they have to be set even before a window appears?" X provides a mechanism that allows the user to specify the preferred geometry on the command line or in a setup file that contains application defaults. A more complete application would check these values and use them to overrule any conflicting preference of the window manager. On the other hand, if the program itself picked the size or position, then the window manager's choice should take precedence. The flags member of XSizeHints, shown in Example 3-10, indicates which members are specified by the program, which by the user, and which are not set at all. In Example 3-9, the symbols used to set flags are PSize and PMinSize. These indicate that the program is specifying its desired size and its minimum useful size. The symbols used for other members of XSizeHints are shown on the reference page for XSetStandardProperties in Volume Two.

Let's describe the other members of XSizeHints. The x, y, width, and height members are simply the desired position and size for the window. These should be the same values used in creating that top-level window in the first place. If the window manager has no window layout policy then these members will be honored when the window is created.

The rest of the size hints are there for when the window needs to be resized, either because of the window manager's layout policy or because the user has requested the resize. min_height and min_width should be the minimum dimensions (in pixels) in which the application can still function normally. Many window managers will not allow the user to resize the window smaller than min_width and min_height. max_width and max_height are analogous to min_width and min_height but are less critical for most applications. width_inc and height_inc indicate to the window manager that it should resize the window in steps of a convenient size above min_width and min_height and below max_width and max_height, if possible.

Here is an example of size increments. A text editor application would like its window to be resized in increments of the font width and height if it used constant-width fonts. What's more, the application often likes to interpret its dimensions in terms of width_inc and height_inc. Instead of requiring the user to specify dimensions on the command line in pixels, an editor could require dimensions in characters, which would be translated into pixels by multiplying them by width_inc and height_inc respectively. The window manager *uwm* interprets dimensions this way if the application sets width_inc and height_inc.

3.2.9 Selecting Desired Event Types

The next step is to select the event types the application will require. Our simple program must receive events for three reasons: to redraw itself in case of exposure, to recalculate its contents when it is resized, and to receive a button or key press indicating that the user is finished with the application.

The program must select these types of events specifically, since by default it won't receive the kinds of input it needs. Example 3-11 shows the line of code that selects events.

Example 3-11. basicwin — selecting desired event types

```
/* Select event types wanted */
XSelectInput(display, win, ExposureMask | KeyPressMask |
    ButtonPressMask | StructureNotifyMask);
```

The event mask constants are combined with a bitwise OR since they are really setting bits in a single value.

ExposureMask selects Expose events, which occur when the window is first displayed and whenever it becomes visible after being obscured. Expose events signal that the application should redraw itself.

X provides separate events for depressing and releasing both keyboard keys and pointer buttons. KeyPressMask selects only KeyPress and ButtonPressMask selects only ButtonPress events. ButtonRelease and KeyRelease events would be selected by separate masks, ButtonReleaseMask and KeyReleaseMask, but they are not needed in this application.

StructureNotifyMask selects a number of event types, specifically Circulate-Notify, ConfigureNotify, DestroyNotify, GravityNotify, MapNotify, ReparentNotify, and UnmapNotify. The only one of these we need for our application is ConfigureNotify, which informs the application of its window's new size when it has been resized. We could get away without selecting this event type, but any real application would use it because it allows an increase in performance. Without this event type, on every Expose event the application would have to use XGetGeometry to find out its current size. This is a request that requires a reply from the server and therefore is subject to network delays.

The rest of the event types selected by StructureNotifyMask are described in Chapter 8, *Events*.

3.2.10 Creating Resources

The next step in the application is to create any other X resources that are needed. Resources are collections of information managed by the server and referred to in the application by an ID number. Items with the types `Colormap`, `Cursor`, `Font`, `GC`, `Pixmap`, and `Window` are resources. They should be created once and the ID kept, rather than creating and deleting them in frequently-called subroutines. That's why they are normally created in `main` or in a subroutine called only once from `main`.

In this program we have already created two resources: a window and the icon pixmap. We still need to load a font for the text, and to create a graphics context to draw both text and graphics into the window. These operations are done in the routines `load_font` and `get_GC`, called just before mapping the window. We're going to delay describing these routines until Chapters 5 and 6, in order to keep this chapter to manageable proportions. However, the complete code for *basicwin* including these functions is listed at the end of this chapter, in case you want a sneak preview.

3.2.11 Window Mapping

Finally we are ready to display the window. Note that we have done all that preparation before mapping the window for good reason. The window manager hints must be set so that the window manager can handle the mapping properly, and events must be selected so that the first `Expose` will arrive and tell the application to draw into its window.

Example 3-12 shows the code that maps the window:

Example 3-12. basicwin — mapping the window

```
/* Display window */
XMapWindow(display, win);
```

You may remember from Chapter 2, *X Concepts*, that in order for a window to be visible it must meet five conditions:

1. The window must be mapped with `XMapWindow` or related routines.

2. All its ancestors must be mapped. This condition is always satisfied for the children of the root window, the top-level windows of each application.

3. The window must not be obscured by visible sibling windows or their ancestors. If sibling windows do overlap, whether or not a window is obscured depends on the stacking order. When first mapped, a window appears on top of its siblings, which will be on top of all windows if its parent is the root window.

4. The output buffer must be flushed. This topic will be described in the next section.

5. The initial mapping of a top-level window is a special case, since the window's visibility may be delayed by the window manager. For complicated reasons, an application must wait for the first `Expose` event before assuming that its window is visible and drawing into it.

3.2.12 Flushing the Output Buffer

`XMapWindow` causes an output request that instructs the server to display the window on the screen. Like all other output requests, this one is queued until a routine that queries the server (most routines whose names contain `Get`, `Fetch`, or `Query`), an event-reading routine, or a routine such as `XFlush` or `XSync`, is called. The server operates more efficiently over the network this way because output requests and events are sent in groups.

The `XFlush` command instructs the server to process all queued output requests right away. This routine is rarely necessary because of the event loop which we describe next, since the event-getting call also flushes the output buffer quite frequently. Even in programs that don't require user input, exposure events must be handled to keep the window refreshed on the screen. The reading of these events sends the output requests. `XFlush` is necessary only when something drawn must be visible before the next input occurs.

3.2.13 Setting Up an Event Gathering Loop

X programs are event-driven, which means that after setting up all the X resources and window manager hints as described up to this point, the program performs all further actions only in response to events. The event-gathering loop is a way to respond to events, performing the appropriate action depending on the type of event and the information contained in the event structure.

The event loop is normally a closed loop, in which one of the event types with certain contents defined by the application indicates that the user wants to exit. In some existing applications such as *xclock*, the loop is completely closed, and therefore the only way to terminate the program is to find the process ID from the shell and kill it, but this is not exemplary program behavior.

The choice of which events are received by the application is made when the application selects input or sets the `event_mask` attribute. The event loop must make sure to properly handle every event type selected. One of the most common debugging problems is for there to be a difference between the events handled and those selected.

Have a look at the code in Example 3-13, before we describe it in more specific terms.

Example 3-13. basicwin — processing events

```
#define SMALL 1
#define OK 0
        .
        .
        .

/* get events, use first Expose to display text and graphics;
 * ConfigureNotify to indicate a resize; ButtonPress or KeyPress
 * to exit */
while (1)  {
        XNextEvent(display, &report);
        switch  (report.type) {
```

Example 3-13. basicwin — processing events (continued)

```
        case Expose:
                if (window_size == SMALL)
                /* if window was resized too small to use */
                        TooSmall(win, gc, font_info);
                else {
                        /* place text in window */
                        draw_text(win, gc, font_info, width, height);

                        /* place graphics in window, */
                        draw_graphics(win, gc, width, height);
                }
                break;
        case ConfigureNotify:
                /* window has been resized, change width and
                 * height to send to draw_text and draw_graphics
                 * in next Expose */
                width = report.xconfigure.width;
                height = report.xconfigure.height;
                if ((width < size_hints.min_width) ||
                        (height < size_hints.min_height))
                        /* if window was resized too small to use */
                        window_size = SMALL;
                else
                        window_size = OK;
                break;
        case ButtonPress:
                /* trickle down into KeyPress (no break) */
        case KeyPress:
                XUnloadFont(display, font_info->fid);
                XFreeGC(display, gc);
                XCloseDisplay(display);
                exit(1);
        default:
                /* all events selected by StructureNotifyMask
                 * except ConfigureNotify are thrown away here,
                 * since nothing is done with them */
                break;
        } /* end switch */
} /* end while */
```

Example 3-13 is framed by an infinite while loop. Just inside the top of the loop is the
XNextEvent statement which gets an event structure from the queue Xlib maintains for
the application, and puts the pointer to it in the variable report. You might assume that the
event loop could have been written:

```
while (XNextEvent(dpy, &event)) {
        .
        .
        .
}
```

but this is not the case. XNextEvent returns void; it only returns when there is an event to return. Errors are handled through a separate error handling mechanism, not through the returned value. So it is necessary to write the event loop:

```
while (1) {
    XNextEvent(dpy, &event);

}
```

Right after XNextEvent is a switch statement that branches depending on the event type. There is one case for each of the four types of events: Expose, ConfigureNotify, ButtonPress, and KeyPress.

3.2.13.1 Repainting the Window

Expose events occur when a window becomes visible on the screen, after being obscured or unmapped. They occur because the X Window System does not normally save the contents of regions of windows obscured by other windows or not mapped. The contents of windows need to be redrawn when they are exposed.

The code for Expose events draws or redraws the contents of the application's window. This code will be reached when the window is first mapped, and whenever a portion of the window becomes visible.

An application can respond to Expose events by refreshing only the parts of the window exposed, or by refreshing the entire window. The former is possible because the event structure for each Expose event carries the position and dimensions of a single rectangular exposed area, as shown in Example 3-14.

Example 3-14. The XExposeEvent structure

```
typedef struct {
    int type;
    unsigned long serial;/* # of last request processed by server */
    Bool send_event;      /* true if this came from SendEvent request */
    Display *display;      /* display the event was read from */
    Window window;
    int x, y;
    int width, height;
    int count;            /* if nonzero, at least this many more */
} XExposeEvent;
```

Several Expose events can occur because of a single window manager operation, as shown in Figure 3-2. If window E were raised, four Expose events would be sent to it. The height and width members in each event structure would correspond to the dimensions of the area where each of the windows overlapped window E, and the x and y members would specify the upper-left corner of each area relative to the origin of window E. All the Expose events generated by a single action are guaranteed to be contiguous in the event queue.

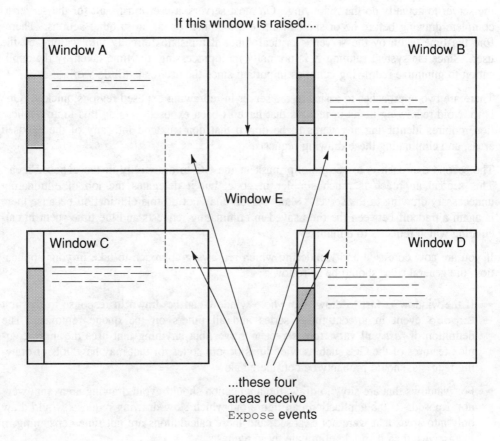

If this window is raised...

Window A

Window B

Window E

Window C

Window D

...these four
areas receive
Expose events

Figure 3-2. Multiple Expose events generated from a single user action

Whether an application should draw the whole window or just the exposed parts depends on the complexity of the drawing in the window. If all of the window contents are simple for both the application and the server to draw, the window contents can be redrawn without a performance problem. This approach works well as long as the window is only redrawn once even if multiple Expose events occur because of a single user action. One trick is to monitor the count member of the Expose event structure, and ignore the Expose events (don't redraw the window) until this member is 0. An even better method is to search the entire queue, removing all Expose events that occurred on the window, before redrawing. This technique is demonstrated a little later in Example 3-15.

On the other hand, if a window has any elements that can be time-consuming for either the application or the server to redraw, then the application should only redraw the time-consuming elements if they are actually within the exposed areas.

The issue here is redrawing time, which has two components under the application's control: the time the application takes to process the redrawing instructions, and the time it takes for the server to actually do the redrawing. On most servers, a user must wait for the server to complete drawing before he or she can move the pointer or go on to other actions. Therefore the time taken by the server is critical, since it translates directly into waiting by the user. Since the system running X is normally multiprocessing, the time taken by the application to minimize redrawing is not as important since the user can still do work.

There are two approaches to assisting the server in redrawing exposed regions quickly. One is to avoid redrawing items in regions that haven't been exposed. Doing this in an application requires identifying any items to be drawn that don't extend into any of the exposed areas, and eliminating these drawing requests.

The second approach is to set the clip mask in the GC to draw only in the exposed areas. This second approach is much simpler in code, but it delegates the job of eliminating unnecessary drawing to the server. Many servers may not do this elimination because there is again a tradeoff between the time saved in eliminating requests and the time spent in calculating which requests to eliminate.

If you are now confused and wondering which redrawing approach to take in your application, the general rules should be as follows:

- If the window is fast to draw, the whole window can be drawn in response to the first Expose event in a contiguous series and all others on the queue removed. The definition of *fast* will vary from server to server, but anything that uses the more complex features of the GC, such as wide lines or join styles, or that may have lots of drawing requests, should probably be considered slow.

- For windows that are slow to draw, the application should avoid drawing areas that were not exposed. If the application can figure out which slow drawing requests would draw only into areas that were not exposed, and these calculations are not time consuming in themselves, then it should eliminate these requests.

- For windows that are slow to draw, the second best approach is to set a clip mask to allow the server to eliminate unnecessary requests. (This will work only if the server has been designed to do so.) The application can combine all the areas in a contiguous series of expose events into a single clip mask, and set this clip mask into the GC. The code for this is only slightly more complex than the approach for the window that is fast to draw.

- Whichever approach is taken, the application should search the whole queue for Expose events and process them before redrawing. Of all the tricks described here this is the simplest, but it can have a significant impact on performance.

Since the image used by the *basicwin* application is simple, the application can redraw the entire window upon receiving the last contiguous Expose event with little performance penalty. But we'll also show you the other approach, as if the window were more complex. Example 3-15 shows the first method from the list above, and Example 3-16 shows the third method. Either of these could be used as a replacement for the code that handles Expose events in Example 3-13 above.

The second method in the list above is not shown here because it is hard to demonstrate in a way that is transferable to other applications. I'll just describe it in a little more detail instead. Let's say that we're writing a spreadsheet application, and designing the exposure event handling. In the spreadsheet it would be easy to determine which cells were affected by the exposure because the cells are arranged along horizontal rows and in columns. Upon getting an Expose event, the application could easily determine which cells overlapped the exposed area and then redraw only those. The same could not be said of a painting program, in which some drawing primitives could be diagonal, or drawn with wierd line styles. It would be very hard to determine whether a particular primitive drawn in the painting program intersects with an exposed region. In general, any application that draws most or all of its graphics horizontally or vertically can benefit from this technique. One example of an application written this way is *xterm*, and you can look at the code for that if you can get it.

Example 3-15. Handling Expose events for simple window contents

```
#define SMALL 1
#define OK 0

int window_size = 0;    /* OK, or too SMALL to display contents */
    .
    .
    .

    switch  (report.type) {
    case Expose:
        /* get rid of all other Expose events on queue */
        while (XCheckTypedEvent(display, Expose, &report));

        /* if window was resized too small to use */
        if (window_size == SMALL)
            TooSmall(win, gc, font_info);
        else {
            /* place text in window */
            draw_text(win, gc, font_info, width, height);

            /* place graphics in window, */
            draw_graphics(win, gc, width, height);
        }
        break;
```

The new technique shown in Example 3-15 is the line of code that calls XCheckTyped-Event. This line searches through the queue and removes all Expose events. Whatever caused each later Expose events must be complete for there to be an Expose event in the first place. Therefore, only one redrawing is necessary to update the screen. Keeping the later Expose events would cause unnecessary redrawing of the window.

Note that if our application had more than one window, we would not be able to indiscriminately throw away all the Expose events without first checking to see which window each event occurred on. In that case we could use similar code substituting XCheckTyped-WindowEvent and adding an argument specifying the window we were planning to redraw.

Example 3-16 shows a technique that could be used for more complicated windows. It creates a single Region composed of the union of all the rectangles in each Expose event. Regions are described fully in Chapter 6, *Drawing Graphics and Text*, but you should be able to understand this example anyway.

Example 3-16. Handling Expose events for complex window contents

```
#define SMALL 1
#define OK 0

int window_size = 0;   /* OK, or too SMALL to display contents */
Region region;         /* coalesces rectangles from all Expose events*/
XRectangle rectangle;  /* places Expose rectangles in here */
    .
    .
    .

/* create region for exposure event processing */
region = XCreateRegion();
    .
    .
    .

    switch (report.type) {
    case Expose:
        /* start with an empty region */
        region = XCreateRegion();

        /* add this event and any Expose events remaining in
            queue to region */
        do {
            /* set rectangle to be exposed area */
            rectangle.x = (short) report.xexpose.x;
            rectangle.y = (short) report.xexpose.y;
            rectangle.width = (unsigned short) report.xexpose.width;
            rectangle.height = (unsigned short) report.xexpose.height;

            /* union this rect into a region */
            XUnionRectWithRegion(&rectangle, region, region);
        } while (XCheckTypedEvent(display, Expose, &report));

        /* set clip_mask of GC to region */
        XSetRegion(display, gc, region);

        if (window_size == SMALL)
            /* if window was resized too small to use */
            TooSmall(win, gc, font_info);
        else {
            /* place text in window */
            draw_text(win, gc, font_info, width, height);

            /* place graphics in window, */
            draw_graphics(win, gc, width, height);
        }
        XDestroyRegion(region);
        break;
```

Being able to redraw the contents of its windows is important for most applications, but for a few applications it might be very difficult or impossible. There is another method that might be used in such a situation. The application could draw into a pixmap and then copy the pixmap to the window each time the window should change. That way the complete window contents would always be available for redrawing the window on `Expose` events. The disadvantage of this approach is that the server might not have sufficient memory to store many pixmaps in memory (especially on color displays), or it might be slow about copying the pixmap into the window. But this would probably be a logical way to handle exposure in an application that performs double-buffering.*

On high-performance graphics workstations a feature known as a backing store might also be available to assist in redrawing windows. When available, this feature can be turned on for any window that really requires it. With the backing store on, the server can maintain the contents of the window when it is obscured and even when it is unmapped, and capture drawing to the window while it is in one of these states. The one situation that the backing store cannot fully take care of is resizing the window. This is because it is assumed that most applications need to recalculate the dimensions of their contents to fit a new window size. The application can set an attribute called bit gravity to retain part of the window during a resize, but part of the window is still going to need redrawing if the window is resized larger.

In case you might be wondering, we have intentionally not described the `draw_text` and `draw_graphics` routines here. They are described in Sections 6.2.6 and 6.1.2. But if you are still curious, they are included in the listing of *basicwin* at the end of this chapter.

3.2.14 When Can I Draw?

There is often confusion about when an application is permitted to draw into its windows. You might think it would work to draw immediately after the `XMapWindow` request that displays a window on the screen. But that won't always work with all styles of window manager. The rule is that no drawing is allowed until the first `Expose` event arrives.

The reason involves a feature of X called substructure redirection, introduced in Section 2.1.5 and described more fully in Section 14.2.

---

* Double-buffering is an animation technique that hides the drawing process from the viewer. In this process a pixmap is drawn into and then copied to a window when the image is complete.

On some hardware it is possible to directly view a pixmap in a window without having to copy it, though this is an extension to X and not a standard feature. In this case there would be an additional pixmap that swaps roles with the first whenever a new image is complete.

3.2.15 When Will My Drawing Appear?

Another characteristic of X that often confuses newcomers is the fact that graphics drawn may not appear on the screen immediately. It is easy to write a program that properly performs a number of drawing calls but that never makes anything appear on the screen. This is a side-effect of the fact that X is designed to operate over a network, as was described in theoretical terms in Section 2.1.2. We'll describe it in more practical terms here.

What happens is that the requests are queued up in Xlib, waiting for something to happen that requires an immediate communication with the server. Xlib will not send requests of any kind to the server until such an occurrence. The requests are saved up as a packet so they can be sent over the network more efficiently.

The queue of requests waiting to be sent to the server is called the *output buffer*. The requests are accumulated in the output buffer until a call to (1) any routine which requests information from the X server (for example, XGetWindowAttributes, XQuery-Pointer, XLoadFont); (2) certain requests for getting events (XPending, XNext-Event, XWindowEvent, XMaskEvent); (3) XFlush; or (4) XSync. Actually, a routine in (2) that gets events triggers a communication with the server only if there is no event on Xlib's event queue that matches what the routine is looking for. Only if the routines are waiting for an event do they trigger the exchange.

Any of these actions is said to flush the output buffer, which means that all requests up to this point will be acted on by the server. Novice programmers who neglect to call one of these routines will notice that their drawing requests haven't been honored. They don't realize that *none* of their X requests that require communication with the server have been honored.

But does it really take a lot of care to make sure that the output buffer gets flushed? Not usually. Since good X programs are event-driven, they often call routines that get events. If an application handles event types that occur frequently, such as pointer or keyboard events, there is nothing to worry about. If the application needs to get information from the server by making a call containing the word Query, Get, or Fetch, no problem is likely. On the other hand, an output-only application that handles only Expose events would certainly need to call XFlush once in a while to make sure that its drawing was honored in a timely fashion.

3.2.16 Handling Resizing of the Window

The ConfigureNotify event tells the application that the window was resized. In this program, we pass this information to the routines that draw text, so that they can position things properly. We also see if the new size is less than the minimum useful size that we set as a size hint for the window manager. If it is smaller in either dimension, then we set the flag window_size so that the next time an Expose event arrives, we display the message "Too Small" instead of the usual text.

Example 3-17 shows the code that handles the ConfigureNotify event.

Example 3-17. basicwin — the ConfigureNotify event

```
#define SMALL 1
#define OK 0

    XEvent report;
        int window_size = 0;   /* OK, or too SMALL to display contents */
        .
        .
        .

        case ConfigureNotify:
                /* window has been resized, change width and
                 * height to send to draw_text and draw_graphics
                 * in next Expose */
                width = report.xconfigure.width;
                height = report.xconfigure.height;
                if ((width < size_hints.min_width) ||
                            (height < size_hints.min_height))
                        window_size = SMALL;
                else
                        window_size = OK;
                break;
```

Note that when the window is first mapped, the ConfigureNotify event appears on the queue *before* the first Expose event. This means that the code works even if the window manager modifies the window's size before allowing it to be displayed. The initial ConfigureNotify updates the application's knowledge of the window size, and the following Expose event allows the application to draw the window's contents.

If we had not selected ConfigureNotify events, the code for Expose would have to be modified to check the dimensions in the first Expose event, so that it knew the correct window size. It would have to query the server for the window size in response to subsequent Expose events, because these events describe only the exposed area, not the entire window.

3.2.17 Exiting the Program

This program uses a key or button press to exit. This is not a very demanding use of KeyPress and ButtonPress events. For a description of how to use keyboard and pointer events for more advanced purposes, see Chapter 9, *The Keyboard and Pointer*.

To cleanly exit, a client should free all the memory it has allocated, particularly X resources, and then close the display connection with XCloseDisplay. Example 3-18 shows the code that performs these functions in *basicwin*.

basicwin

Example 3-18. Closing the display connection and freeing resources

```
case ButtonPress:
        /* trickle down into KeyPress (no break) */
case KeyPress:
        XUnloadFont(display, font_info->fid);
        XFreeGC(display, gc);
        XCloseDisplay(display);
        exit(1);
```

It is good practice to use XCloseDisplay even though the connection to the server is closed automatically when a process exits. Otherwise, pending errors might not be reported.

3.2.18 Error Handling

Although there doesn't appear to be much in the way of error handling code in this example, the question of error handling has been fully considered:

- On the XOpenDisplay call, we check for the error return, tell the user what server the attempt was made to connect to, and exit gracefully.

- For all other errors, we depend on the default error handling mechanism. These errors might be a programming error (all of which we hope to eliminate) or a fatal error such as losing the connection with the server. When a client gets an error event from the server, the library code invokes an error handler. The client is free to override the default handler, which prints an informative message and exits. But for this example, we've simply relied on the default handler.

It is important to note that not all errors cause the error handler to be invoked. This fact does not show itself in this example. Some errors, such as failure to open a font, are indicated by returned values of type Status. The returned values may be True or False. In general, any routine that returns Status will need its return value tested, because it will have bypassed the error handling mechanism.

3.2.19 Summary

The basic steps that were taken in this program are as follows:

- Open connection to server.
- Make sure connection succeeded, print error and exit if not.
- Get display dimensions.
- Calculate desired size of window and create window.
- Create pixmap for icon.
- Initialize XSizeHint structure.
- Set standard properties for window manager.

- Select desired event types.

- Map window.

- Set up event gathering loop.

- If event is of type `Expose`, draw contents of window.

- If event is of type `ConfigureNotify`, recalculate dimensions of window.

- If event is `ButtonPress` or `KeyPress`, close the display and exit.

The order of these steps is important up to the point where the window is mapped. Within the event loop, the order of events cannot be completely predicted.

3.2.20 Complete Code for basicwin

Example 3-19. basicwin — in its entirety

```c
#include <X11/Xlib.h>
#include <X11/Xutil.h>
#include <X11/Xos.h>

#include <stdio.h>

#include "bitmaps/icon_bitmap"
#define BITMAPDEPTH 1

/* Display and screen are used as arguments to nearly every Xlib
 * routine, so it simplifies routine calls to declare them global.
 * If there were additional source files, these variables would be
 * declared 'extern' in them. */
Display *display;
int screen;

/* values for window_size in main, is window big enough to be useful */
#define SMALL 1
#define OK 0

void main(argc, argv)
int argc;
char **argv;
{
    Window win;
    unsigned int width, height;      /* window size */
    int x = 0, y = 0;                /* window position */
    unsigned int border_width = 4;   /* border four pixels wide */
    unsigned int display_width, display_height;
    char *window_name = "Basic Window Program";
    char *icon_name = "basicwin";
    Pixmap icon_pixmap;
    XSizeHints size_hints;
    XEvent report;
    GC gc;
    XFontStruct *font_info;
```

Example 3-19. basicwin — in its entirety (continued)

```
    char *display_name = NULL;
    int window_size = 0;   /* OK, or too SMALL to display contents */

    /* connect to X server */

    if ( (display=XOpenDisplay(display_name)) == NULL )
    {
        (void) fprintf( stderr,
                "basicwin: cannot connect to X server %s\n",
                XDisplayName(display_name));
        exit( -1 );
    }

    /* get screen size from display structure macro */
    screen = DefaultScreen(display);

    display_width = DisplayWidth(display, screen);
    display_height = DisplayHeight(display, screen);

    /* size window with enough room for text */
    width = display_width/3, height = display_height/4;

    /* create opaque window */
    win = XCreateSimpleWindow(display, RootWindow(display,screen),
            x, y, width, height, border_width,
            BlackPixel(display, screen),
            WhitePixel(display,screen));

    /* Create pixmap of depth 1 (bitmap) for icon */
    icon_pixmap = XCreateBitmapFromData(display, win, icon_bitmap_bits,
            icon_bitmap_width, icon_bitmap_height);

    /* initalize size hint property for window manager */
    size_hints.flags = PPosition | PSize | PMinSize;
    size_hints.x = x;
    size_hints.y = y;
    size_hints.width = width;
    size_hints.height = height;
    size_hints.min_width = 350;
    size_hints.min_height = 250;

    /* set properties for window manager (always before mapping) */
    XSetStandardProperties(display, win, window_name, icon_name,
        icon_pixmap, argv, argc, &size_hints);

    /* Select event types wanted */
    XSelectInput(display, win, ExposureMask | KeyPressMask |
            ButtonPressMask | StructureNotifyMask);

    load_font(&font_info);

    /* create GC for text and drawing */
    get_GC(win, &gc, font_info);

    /* Display window */
```

Example 3-19. basicwin — in its entirety (continued)

```
    XMapWindow(display, win);

    /* get events, use first Expose to display text and graphics;
     * ConfigureNotify to indicate a resize; ButtonPress or KeyPress
     * to exit */
    while (1)   {
        XNextEvent(display, &report);
        switch (report.type) {
        case Expose:
            /* get rid of all other Expose events on the queue */
            while (XCheckTypedEvent(display, Expose, &report));
            if (window_size == SMALL)
                /* if window was resized too small to use */
                    TooSmall(win, gc, font_info);
            else {
                /* place text in window */
                    draw_text(win, gc, font_info, width, height);

                /* place graphics in window, */
                    draw_graphics(win, gc, width, height);
            }
            break;
        case ConfigureNotify:
            /* window has been resized, change width and
             * height to send to draw_text and draw_graphics
             * in next Expose */
            width = report.xconfigure.width;
            height = report.xconfigure.height;
            if ((width < size_hints.min_width) ||
                    (height < size_hints.min_height))
                    window_size = SMALL;
            else
                    window_size = OK;
            break;
        case ButtonPress:
            /* trickle down into KeyPress (no break) */
        case KeyPress:
            XUnloadFont(display, font_info->fid);
            XFreeGC(display, gc);
            XCloseDisplay(display);
            exit(1);
        default:
            /* all events selected by StructureNotifyMask
             * except ConfigureNotify are thrown away here,
             * since nothing is done with them */
            break;
        } /* end switch */
    } /* end while */
}

get_GC(win, gc, font_info)
Window win;
GC *gc;
XFontStruct *font_info;
{
```

Example 3-19. basicwin — in its entirety (continued)

```
        unsigned long valuemask = 0; /* ignore XGCvalues and use defaults */
        XGCValues values;
        unsigned int line_width = 6;
        int line_style = LineOnOffDash;
        int cap_style = CapRound;
        int join_style = JoinRound;
        int dash_offset = 0;
        static char dash_list[] = {
            12, 24    };
        int list_length = 2;

        /* Create default graphics context */
        *gc = XCreateGC(display, win, valuemask, &values);

        /* specify font */
        XSetFont(display, *gc, font_info->fid);

        /* specify black foreground since default may be white on white */
        XSetForeground(display, *gc, BlackPixel(display,screen));

        /* set line attributes */
        XSetLineAttributes(display, *gc, line_width, line_style, cap_style,
                join_style);

        /* set dashes to be line_width in length */
        XSetDashes(display, *gc, dash_offset, dash_list, list_length);
}

load_font(font_info)
XFontStruct **font_info;
{
        char *fontname = "9x15";

        /* Access font */
        if ((*font_info = XLoadQueryFont(display,fontname)) == NULL)
        {
            (void) fprintf( stderr, "Basic: Cannot open 9x15 font\n");
            exit( -1 );
        }
}

draw_text(win, gc, font_info, win_width, win_height)
Window win;
GC gc;
XFontStruct *font_info;
unsigned int win_width, win_height;
{
        int y = 20;    /* offset from corner of window*/
        char *string1 = "Hi! I'm a window, who are you?";
        char *string2 = "To terminate program; Press any key";
        char *string3 = "or button while in this window.";
        char *string4 = "Screen Dimensions:";
        int len1, len2, len3, len4;
        int width1, width2, width3;
        char cd_height[50], cd_width[50], cd_depth[50];
```

Example 3-19. basicwin — in its entirety (continued)

```
int font_height;
int initial_y_offset, x_offset;


/* need length for both XTextWidth and XDrawString */
len1 = strlen(string1);
len2 = strlen(string2);
len3 = strlen(string3);

/* get string widths for centering */
width1 = XTextWidth(font_info, string1, len1);
width2 = XTextWidth(font_info, string2, len2);
width3 = XTextWidth(font_info, string3, len3);

/* output text, centered on each line */
XDrawString(display,win,gc,(win_width - width1)/2,y,string1,len1);
XDrawString(display,win,gc,(win_width - width2)/2,
        (int)(win_height - 35),string2,len2);
XDrawString(display,win,gc,(win_width - width3)/2,
        (int)(win_height - 15),string3,len3);

/* copy numbers into string variables */
(void) sprintf(cd_height, " Height - %d pixels",
        DisplayHeight(display,screen));
(void) sprintf(cd_width, " Width  - %d pixels",
        DisplayWidth(display,screen));
(void) sprintf(cd_depth, " Depth  - %d plane(s)",
        DefaultDepth(display, screen));

/* reuse these for same purpose */
len4 = strlen(string4);
len1 = strlen(cd_height);
len2 = strlen(cd_width);
len3 = strlen(cd_depth);

font_height = font_info->max_bounds.ascent +
        font_info->max_bounds.descent;

/* To center strings vertically, we place the first string
 * so that the top of it is two font_heights above the center
 * of the window.  Since the baseline of the string is what we
 * need to locate for XDrawString, and the baseline is one
 * font_info->max_bounds.ascent below the top of the chacter,
 * the final offset of the origin up from the center of the
 * window is one font_height + one descent. */

initial_y_offset = win_height/2 - font_height -
        font_info->max_bounds.descent;
x_offset = (int) win_width/4;
XDrawString(display, win, gc, x_offset, (int) initial_y_offset,
        string4,len4);
```

Example 3-19. basicwin — in its entirety (continued)

```
        XDrawString(display, win, gc, x_offset, (int) initial_y_offset +
                font_height,cd_height,len1);
        XDrawString(display, win, gc, x_offset, (int) initial_y_offset +
                2 * font_height,cd_width,len2);
        XDrawString(display, win, gc, x_offset, (int) initial_y_offset +
                3 * font_height,cd_depth,len3);
}


draw_graphics(win, gc, window_width, window_height)
Window win;
GC gc;
unsigned int window_width, window_height;
{
        int x, y;
        unsigned int width, height;

        height = window_height/2;
        width = 3 * window_width/4;
        x = window_width/2 - width/2;   /* center */
        y = window_height/2 - height/2;
        XDrawRectangle(display, win, gc, x, y, width, height);
}

TooSmall(win, gc, font_info)
Window win;
GC gc;
XFontStruct *font_info;
{
        char *string1 = "Too Small";
        int y_offset, x_offset;

        y_offset = font_info->max_bounds.ascent + 2;
        x_offset = 2;

        /* output text, centered on each line */
        XDrawString(display, win, gc, x_offset, y_offset, string1,
                strlen(string1));
}
```

4
Window Attributes

The window attributes control a window's background and border pattern or color, the events that should be queued for it, and so on. This chapter describes how to set and get window attributes, and provides a detailed description of each attribute. Everyone should read this chapter.

In This Chapter:

Attributes

4
Window Attributes

Now that you know a little about events and X concepts in general, we can go back and describe the window attributes thoroughly. The window attributes were introduced in Section 2.2.1 and described in more detail in Section 2.4.1. You should have read those sections before proceeding. You will continue to find this chapter useful as a reference even when you're an experienced X programmer. A useful quick-reference to the window attributes is also provided inside the back cover of Volume Two.

4.1 Setting Window Attributes

Window attributes can be set while creating a window with XCreateWindow, or afterward with a call to XChangeWindowAttributes. When creating a window with XCreate-SimpleWindow, the attributes are inherited from the parent. There are also several routines for changing the background and border attributes individually.

The procedure is the same for setting the attributes with XCreateWindow or XChange-WindowAttributes. You set the members of an XSetWindowAttributes structure to the desired values, create a mask indicating which members you have set, and call the routine to create the window or change the attributes.

4.2 The Window Attribute Structures

There are actually two structures associated with window attributes. XWindow-Attributes is an internal, read-only structure that contains all the attributes, while XSet-WindowAttributes is a structure that contains only those attributes that a program is allowed to set. We won't show you XWindowAttributes until Section 4.4, since it is used in programming only for getting the values of the window attributes.

Example 4-1 shows the structure that is used to set the window attributes.

Example 4-1. The XSetWindowAttributes structure

```
typedef struct _XSetWindowAttributes {
    Pixmap background_pixmap;    /* pixmap, None, or ParentRelative */
    long background_pixel;       /* background pixel value */
    Pixmap border_pixmap;        /* pixmap, None, or CopyFromParent */
    long border_pixel;           /* border pixel value */
    int bit_gravity;             /* one of bit gravity symbols */
    int win_gravity;             /* one of the window gravity symbols */
    int backing_store;           /* NotUseful, WhenMapped, or Always */
    long backing_bitplanes;      /* planes to be preserved if possible */
    long backing_pixel;          /* value to use in restoring planes */
    Bool save_under;             /* should bits under window be saved */
    long event_mask;             /* events that should be queued */
    long do_not_propagate_mask;  /* events that shouldn't propagate */
    Bool override_redirect;      /* override redirected config. requests */
    Colormap colormap;           /* colormap associated with window */
    Cursor cursor;               /* cursor to be displayed or None */
} XSetWindowAttributes;
```

To set the window attributes, you need to set the elements of the XSetWindow-Attributes structure to the desired values, and then set a valuemask argument that represents which members are to be changed in the internal structure. A symbol specifying each member to be changed is combined with the bitwise OR operator (|). These symbols are shown in Table 4-1. They begin with the letters *CW* ("Create Window" or "Change Window") because the routines they are used in have those capital letters in their names.

Table 4-1. Window Attribute Mask Symbols

Member	Flag	Bit
background_pixmap	CWBackPixmap	0
background_pixel	CWBackPixel	1
border_pixmap	CWBorderPixmap	2
border_pixel	CWBorderPixel	3
bit_gravity	CWBitGravity	4
win_gravity	CWWinGravity	5
backing_store	CWBackingStore	6
backing_planes	CWBackingPlanes	7
backing_pixel	CWBackingPixel	8
override_redirect	CWOverrideRedirect	9
save_under	CWSaveUnder	10
event_mask	CWEventMask	11
do_not_propagate_mask	CWDontPropagate	12
colormap	CWColormap	13
cursor	CWCursor	14

For example, if you want to set the initial values of the background and border pixel values, you would follow the procedure shown in Example 4-2.

Example 4-2. Setting window attributes while creating a window

```
Display *display;
Window parent, window;
int x, y;
unsigned int width, height, border_width;
int depth;
Visual *visual;
unsigned int class;
XSetWindowAttributes setwinattr;
unsigned long valuemask;

/* (must open display) */

valuemask = CWBackPixel | CWBorderPixel;
setwinattr.background_pixel = WhitePixel(display, screen);
setwinattr.border_pixel = BlackPixel(display, screen);
window = XCreateWindow(display, parent, x, y, width, height,
        border_width, depth, class, visual, valuemask, &setwinattr);
```

If the window already exists, you can change those same attributes with the procedure shown in Example 4-3.

Example 4-3. Changing window attributes of existing window

```
Display *display;
Window window;
XSetWindowAttributes setwinattr;
unsigned long valuemask;

/* (must open display, create window) */

valuemask = CWBackPixel | CWBorderPixel;
setwinattr.background_pixel = WhitePixel(display, screen);
setwinattr.border_pixel = BlackPixel(display, screen);
XChangeWindowAttributes(display, window, valuemask, &setwinattr);
```

You can also use separate calls to XSetWindowBackground and XSetWindowBorder to set these particular attributes. These and a few other attributes have routines for setting them individually. (These routines are referred to as *convenience routines*. They are provided for the attributes that most often need to be set without modifying any other attributes.) Table 4-2 lists the attributes that can be set individually and the routines that set them. But it is important to realize that each of these routines would generate a separate protocol request to the server, so if more than one attribute is to be set, it is more efficient to use the procedures shown above in Examples 4-2 and 4-3.

Table 4-2. Attributes That Can Be Set Individually

Attribute	Routine for setting it
background_pixmap	XSetWindowBackgroundPixmap
background_pixel	XSetWindowBackground
border_pixmap	XSetWindowBorderPixmap
border_pixel	XSetWindowBorder
event_mask	XSelectInput
colormap	XSetWindowColormap
cursor	XDefineCursor or XUndefineCursor

Section 4.3 describes all of the attributes and the routines for setting them.

4.3 Program-settable Attributes

The sections that follow describe the options and default values for each member of the XSetWindowAttributes structure. The attributes control a wide variety of ways for a window to act. They can be grouped loosely to help you understand when you might want to set each attribute.

One group of attributes controls the appearance of a window. These are background_pixmap, background_pixel, border_pixmap, border_pixel, colormap, and cursor. Most clients will set the border, background, and cursor, but use the default colormap.

A second group is provided to allow clients to improve their redrawing performance under certain conditions. These are bit_gravity, backing_store, backing_bitplanes, backing_pixel, and save_under. These attributes don't affect the appearance or operation of a client. It is advisable to consider bit_gravity when designing a client, but the code for using these attributes can be added after a client's functionality is complete.

The event_mask and do_not_propagate_mask attributes control the selection and propagation of events. These attributes are described briefly in this chapter but also in much more detail in Chapter 8, *Events*.

The win_gravity attribute provides a means for relocating a window automatically when its parent is resized. Applications can take advantage of this feature to simplify the code that positions their subwindows when they are resized.

The override_redirect attribute controls whether requests to map or reconfigure the window can be intercepted by the window manager. override_redirect is meant to be set for the most temporary types of windows such as pop-up menus.

`InputOutput` windows have all of the attributes described in the sections below. `InputOnly` windows have only the following subset of attributes:

- `win_gravity`
- `event_mask`
- `do_not_propagate_mask`
- `override_redirect`
- `cursor`

4.3.1 The Window Background

The background of a window is the drawing surface on which other graphics are drawn. It may be a solid color or may be patterned with a pixmap. This choice is mostly an aesthetic decision for the programmer. However, users expect to be able to specify the background color on the command line or in the user defaults. Therefore, if a pixmap is used, the code for creating the pixmap should use the color specified by the user.

The two attributes that control the background are `background_pixmap` and `background_pixel`, and `XSetWindowBackgroundPixmap` and `XSetWindow-Background` set them.

These two attributes are not independent since they affect the same pixels. Either attribute can take precedence over the other, the winner being the one that is set last. If both are set in the same call to `XCreateWindow` or `XChangeWindowAttributes`, the `background_pixel` value is used.

The background of exposed areas of windows is automatically repainted upon receipt of `Expose` events. The background is redrawn on exposed areas regardless of the selection of `Expose` events. but any change in background attributes will not take effect until the next `Expose` event is received, or `XClearWindow` is called and the output buffer is flushed.

4.3.1.1 background_pixmap

If the background is set to a pixmap, the background is *tiled* with the pixmap. *Tiling* is the laying out of a pixmap to cover an area. The first pixmap is applied at the origin of the window (or its parent's origin if using the parent's background pixmap by specifying `ParentRelative`, as described below). Another copy of the same pixmap is applied next to that one and another below it, and so on until the window is filled.

The pixmap may be any size, though some sizes may be tiled faster than others. To find the most efficient tile size for a particular screen, call `XQueryBestTile`.

A pixmap must be created with `XCreatePixmap` or `XCreatePixmapFromBitmap-Data` before being set as the `background_pixmap` attribute. The pixmap must have the same depth as the window, and be created on the same screen. These attributes are assigned to a pixmap as it is created. (For more information on creating pixmaps for tiles, see Section 6.1.5.)

The `background_pixmap` attribute has the following possible values.

None (default)   specifies that the window has no defined background pixmap. The window initially will be invisible and will share the bits of its parent, but only if the `background_pixel` attribute is not set. When anything is drawn by any client into the area enclosed by the window, the contents will remain until the area is explicitly cleared with `XClearWindow`. The background is not automatically refreshed after exposure.

a pixmap ID   the background will be tiled with the specified pixmap. The background tile origin is the window origin. If the pixmap is not explicitly referenced again, it can be freed, since a copy is maintained in the server.

ParentRelative   specifies that the parent's background is to be used, and that the origin for tiling is the parent's origin (or the parent's parent if the parent's `background_pixmap` attribute is also Parent-Relative, and so on). The difference between setting Parent-Relative and explicitly setting the same pixmap as the parent is the origin of the tiling. The difference between Parent-Relative and None is that for ParentRelative the background is automatically repainted on exposure.

The window must have the same depth as the parent, or a Bad-Match error will occur. If the parent has background None, then the window will also have background None. The parent's background is re-examined each time the window background is required (when it needs to be redrawn due to mapping or exposure). The window's contents will be lost when the window is moved relative to its parent, and the contents will have to be redrawn.

Changing the `background_pixmap` attribute of the root window to None or Parent-Relative restores the default background, which is server-dependent.

By the way, the symbol `CopyFromParent` is not used for setting the background, but it will not cause an error since its value is the same as None.

4.3.1.2 background_pixel

If the background pixel value is specified, the entire background will take on the color (or shade of gray) indicated for that pixel value in the current colormap.*

---

* I should inform you here that a pixel value is not something you choose yourself; it is returned to you from `BlackPixel` or `WhitePixel` or one of the routines that allocate colors. We go into this subject in detail in Chapter 7, *Color*.

The `background_pixel` attribute has the following possible values.

undefined (default)   indicates that the background is as specified in the `background_pixmap` attribute. This value is possible only by creating a window with `XCreateWindow` and not setting the `background_pixel` attribute.

a pixel value   the background is filled with the specified pixel value.

4.3.2 The Window Border

Like the window background, the window border may have a solid color or may be tiled with a pixmap. This choice is again up to the programmer, though the user should be allowed to determine the color.

Unlike changes to the window background, changes to a window's border attributes are reflected immediately. No call to `XClearWindow` or call to flush the output buffer is necessary. This feature makes it tempting to use the border for indicating a client's state. But this is not recommended, since some window managers manipulate the border to indicate the keyboard focus window (see Section 8.3.2.1 for a description of the keyboard focus).

The design of a pattern for the border will be different from the background, because the border width is usually narrow (at most four pixels).

The two attributes that affect the border are `border_pixmap` and `border_pixel`. `XSetWindowBorder` and `XSetWindowBorderPixmap` can be used to set these attributes. Like the window background, whenever one of these routines is called, it overrides the previous setting of the border. If they are both set simultaneously with `XCreate-Window` or `XChangeWindowAttributes`, the `border_pixel` attribute takes precedence.

4.3.2.1 border_pixmap

If the `border_pixmap` is set to a pixmap, the border is tiled with the pixmap. Tiling is performed as described previously for the background pixmap.

The `border_pixmap` attribute has the following possible values.

`CopyFromParent` (default)
specifies that the border pixmap is to be copied from the parent. Subsequent changes to the parent's border do not affect the child.

`None`   specifies that the window has no border pixmap. If the window has no border pixel value either, then it uses the same border pixel value as the parent.

a pixmap ID   specifies a pixmap to be tiled in the border. The border tile origin is always the window origin; it is not taken from the background tile origin. If the pixmap is not explicitly referenced again, it can be freed since a copy is maintained in the server.

For the root window, CopyFromParent indicates that the default border will be inherited by subsequently created children of the root window, instead of any other border that was set for the root window.

4.3.2.2 border_pixel

If a border pixel value is specified, the entire background will take on the color (or shade of gray) indicated for that pixel value in the current colormap.

The border_pixel attribute has the following possible values.

undefined (default)
> indicates that the border is as specified in the border_pixmap attribute. This value is possible only by creating a window with XCreateWindow and not setting the border_pixel attribute.

a pixel value overrides the default and any border_pixmap given, and fills the border with the specified pixel value.

4.3.3 Bit Gravity

When an unobscured window is moved, its contents are moved with it, since none of the pixel values need to be changed. But when a window is enlarged or shrunk, the server has no idea where in the resulting window the old contents should be placed, so it normally throws them out. The bit_gravity attribute tells the server where to put the existing bits in the larger or smaller window. By instructing the server where to place the old contents, bit gravity allows some clients (not all can take advantage of it) to avoid redrawing parts of their windows.

Bit gravity is never *necessary* in programs. It does not affect the appearance or functionality of the client. It is used to improve performance in certain cases. Some X servers may not implement bit gravity, and may throw out the window contents on resizing regardless of the setting of this attribute. This response is the default for all servers. That is, the default bit gravity is ForgetGravity, which means that the contents of a window are always lost when the window is resized, even if they are maintained in backing store or because of a save_under (to be described in Sections 4.3.5 and 4.3.6).

The window is tiled with its background in the areas that are not preserved by the bit gravity, unless no background is defined, in which case the existing screen is not altered.

There is no routine to set the bit_gravity individually; it can only be set with XChangeWindowAttributes.

The `bit_gravity` attribute has eleven possible values.

`ForgetGravity` (default)

specifies that window contents should always be discarded after a size change. Note that some X servers may not implement bit gravity, and may use `ForgetGravity` in all cases.

`StaticGravity`

specifies that window contents should not move relative to the origin of the root window. This means that the area of intersection between the original extent of the window and the final extent of the window will not be disturbed.

Each constant below specifies where the old window contents should be placed in the resized window.

`NorthWestGravity`	upper-left corner of the resized window.
`NorthGravity`	top center of the resized window.
`NorthEastGravity`	upper-right corner of the resized window.
`WestGravity`	left center of the resized window.
`CenterGravity`	center of the resized window.
`EastGravity`	right center of the resized window.
`SouthWestGravity`	lower-left corner of the resized window.
`SouthGravity`	bottom center of the resized window.
`SouthEastGravity`	lower-right corner of the resized window.

Here are two examples of applications that could take advantage of bit gravity. Figure 4-1 shows a fictional application that draws a two-axis graph in a window, with the origin at the lower-left corner. If that window were resized, the application would want the old contents to be placed against the new lower-left corner, no matter which sides of the window were moved in or out. That application would set the `bit_gravity` attribute of this window to `SouthWestGravity`. Figure 4-1 shows the response of this window to resizing with this bit gravity setting.

Each compass constant such as `SouthWestGravity` indicates the placement of the retained region in the window after resizing. In this case, the lower-left corner of the existing pixels is placed against the lower-left corner of the resulting window. When an `Expose` event arrives, the application need only redraw the two new strips of the window at the top and right side. No `Expose` event will be generated on the area that was saved because of `bit_gravity`.

For another example, think of a window containing centered text. If that window were resized either larger or smaller, we would still like the text to be centered. In this case, the `bit_gravity` should be set to `CenterGravity`. Then, only if the window is resized smaller than the length of the text would we have to redraw the area, and only then to break the line or use a shorter message. We could see whether redrawing would be necessary by looking at the `ConfigureNotify` event that occurs as a result of the resize (see *basicwin* in Chapter 3, *Basic Window Program*). The window would still have to be redrawn if it were obscured and then exposed, of course—bit gravity only saves *some* of the redrawing that would otherwise have to be done.

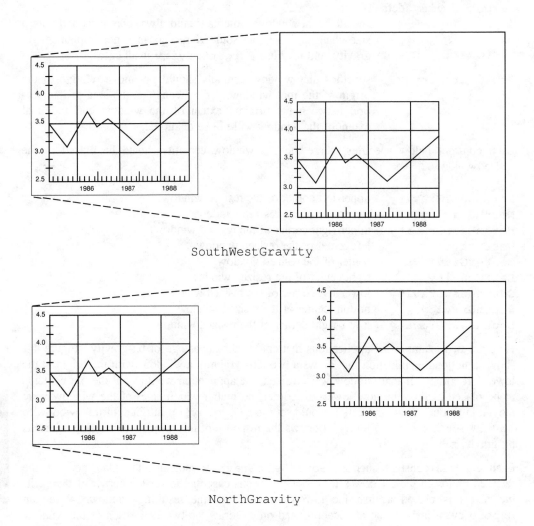

SouthWestGravity

NorthGravity

Figure 4-1. bit_gravity for a graphing application

If the constant were `NorthGravity`, the top center of the pixels in the window before the resize would be placed against the top center of the resulting window. This would be appropriate if we had a line of text centered at the top of the window that we wished to preserve when possible.

4.3.4 Window Gravity

The `win_gravity` attribute controls the repositioning of subwindows when a parent window is resized. Normally, each child has a fixed position measured from the origin of the parent window. Window gravity can be used to tell the server to unmap the child, or to move the child an amount depending on the change in size of the parent. The constants used to set `win_gravity` are similar to those for bit gravity, but their effect is quite different.

`NorthGravity` specifies that the child window should be moved horizontally by an amount one-half as great as the amount the window was resized in the horizontal direction. The child is not moved vertically. That means that if the window was originally centered along the top edge of the window, it will also be centered along the top edge of the window after resizing. If it was not originally centered, its relative distance from the center may be accentuated.

Window gravity is only useful for children placed against or very near the outside edges of the parent or directly in its center. Furthermore, the child must be centered along one of the outside edges or in a corner. Figure 4-2 shows the nine child positions where window gravity can be useful.

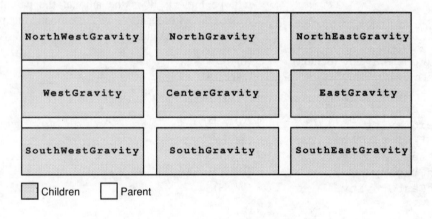

NorthWestGravity	NorthGravity	NorthEastGravity
WestGravity	CenterGravity	EastGravity
SouthWestGravity	SouthGravity	SouthEastGravity

Children Parent

Figure 4-2. Child positions where window gravity is useful

Otherwise, the window gravity may move the child outside the resized parent since there are no checks to prevent this. The application can try to prevent it by getting the new position of the child from a `ConfigureNotify` event (see Section 3.2.16) and moving the child inside if necessary. But this will cause a flash when the child window is automatically placed incorrectly and then moved to the correct position by the application. And if an application has to go to the trouble to check the position and move the child, it might as well just forget about window gravity and place the child itself.

`NorthWestGravity` (the default) indicates that the child (for which this attribute is set) is not moved relative to its parent.

`UnmapGravity` specifies that the subwindow should be unmapped when the parent is resized. This might be used when a client wishes to recalculate the positions of its children. Normally, the children would appear in their old positions before the client could move them into their recalculated positions. This can be confusing to the user. By setting the `win_gravity` attribute to `UnmapGravity`, the server will unmap the windows. They can be repositioned at the client's leisure, and then the client can remap them (with `XMap-Subwindows`) in their new locations.

There is no routine to set the `win_gravity` attribute individually; it can only be set with `XChangeWindowAttributes` or when the window is created.

The `win_gravity` attribute has the following possible values.

`UnmapGravity`	specifies that the child is unmapped (removed from the screen) when the parent is resized, and an `UnmapNotify` event is generated.
`StaticGravity`	specifies that window contents should not move relative to the origin of the root window.
One of the compass constants below	The list below shows the distance the child window will be moved; *W* is the amount the parent was resized in width, and *H* is the amount the parent was resized in height:

`NorthWestGravity` (default)	(0, 0)
`NorthGravity`	(W/2, 0)
`NorthEastGravity`	(W, 0)
`WestGravity`	(0, H/2)
`CenterGravity`	(W/2, H/2)
`EastGravity`	(W, H/2)
`SouthWestGravity`	(0, H)
`SouthGravity`	(W/2, H)
`SouthEastGravity`	(W, H)

4.3.5 Backing Store

A *backing store* automatically maintains the contents of a window while it is obscured, or even while it is unmapped. Backing is like having a copy of the window saved in a pixmap, automatically copied to the screen whenever necessary to keep the visible contents up-to-date. Backing store is only available on some servers, usually on high-performance workstations.

These servers can be instructed when to back up a window, and which planes to save, through the backing store attributes. Even when it is available, the backing store should be avoided since it may carry a heavy performance penalty on the server. You can find out whether backing is supported on a particular screen with the `DoesBackingStore` macro.

A client might use this feature to back up a window it is incapable of redrawing for some reason, or to be able to draw into a window that is obscured or unmapped.

Three separate attributes control backing: `backing_store`, `backing_planes`, and `backing_pixel`. There are no routines for setting these attributes individually. The `backing_store` attribute determines when and if a window's contents are preserved by the server. The `backing_planes` attribute specifies which planes must be preserved, and `backing_pixel` specifies the pixel value used to fill planes not specified in `backing_planes`.

When the backing store feature is active, and the window is larger than its parent, the server maintains complete contents, not just the region within the parent's boundaries. If the server is maintaining the contents of a window, `Expose` events will not be generated when that window is exposed.

Use of the backing store does not make a window immune to the other window attributes. If the `bit_gravity` is `ForgetGravity`, the contents will still be lost whenever the window is resized.

The `backing_store` attribute determines when and if a window's contents are preserved by the server when the window is unmapped or obscured.

The `backing_store` attribute has the following possible values.

`NotUseful` (default) advises the server that maintaining contents is unnecessary. A server may still choose to maintain contents.

`WhenMapped` advises the server that it would be beneficial to maintain contents of obscured regions when the window is mapped.

`Always` advises the server that it would be beneficial to maintain contents even when the window is unmapped.

The `backing_planes` attribute specifies a mask (default all 1's) that indicates which planes of the window hold dynamic data that must be preserved in the backing store.

The `backing_pixel` attribute specifies a pixel value (default 0) to be used in planes not specified in the `backing_plane` attribute.

The X server is free to save only the bit planes specified in `backing_planes`, and to regenerate the remaining planes with the specified pixel value.

4.3.6 Saving Under

The `save_under` attribute controls whether the contents of the screen beneath a window should be preserved just before the window is mapped and replaced just after it is unmapped. This attribute is most useful for pop-up windows, which need to be on the screen only briefly. No `Expose` events will be sent to the windows that are exposed when the pop-up window is unmapped, saving the time necessary to redraw their contents.

Setting `save_under` is never necessary, but it can improve the performance of clients that frequently map and unmap temporary windows. The user would otherwise have to wait for the area under the menu to be redrawn when the menu was unmapped.

There is no routine for setting the `save_under` attribute individually; it can only be set with `XChangeWindowAttributes` or when the window is created.

The `save_under` attribute is different from the backing store; `save_under` may save portions of several windows beneath a window for the duration of the appearance of the window on the screen, while the backing store saves the contents of a single window while it is mapped or even when unmapped, depending on the attributes.

Not all servers are capable of saving under windows. You can find out whether this feature is supported on a particular screen with the `DoesSaveUnders` macro.

The `save_under` attribute has the following possible values.

`False` (default) specifies that covered clients should be sent `Expose` events when the window is unmapped, even if they are preserved in the backing store.

`True` specifies that the server should save areas under the window, and replace them when the window is unmapped. `Expose` events are generated on covered areas only if they have the `bit_gravity` attribute set to `ForgetGravity`.

Setting the `save_under` attribute to `True` does not prevent all `Expose` events on the area underneath. For example, assume there is a window whose `bit_gravity` is `ForgetGravity`, and this window lies under a window that has the `save_under` attribute set to `True`. The contents of the obscured window will be lost if that window is resized while partially obscured, and `Expose` events will be generated even on the saved area.

4.3.7 Event Handling

The `event_mask` and `do_not_propagate_mask` attributes control the propagation of events through the window hierarchy. The `event_mask` attribute is normally set with `XSelectInput`, but it can also be set directly with `XChangeWindowAttributes`.

The `event_mask` attribute specifies which event types should be queued for this window. The `do_not_propagate_mask` specifies which types of events are not sent to ancestors. Both masks are made by combining the constants listed in Table 8-3 using the bitwise OR operator (|). Much more information on setting the event masks, including examples, is presented in Chapter 8, *Events*. This is a very important topic.

The `event_mask` attribute specifies which event types are queued for the window when they occur. The `do_not_propagate_mask` attribute defines which events should not be propagated to ancestor windows when the event type is not selected in this window.

The `event_mask` and `do_not_propagate_mask` attributes are specified with the bit-wise OR of any of the event mask symbols below:

NoEventMask	Button5MotionMask
KeyPressMask	ButtonMotionMask
KeyReleaseMask	KeymapStateMask
ButtonPressMask	ExposureMask
ButtonReleaseMask	VisibilityChangeMask
EnterWindowMask	StructureNotifyMask
LeaveWindowMask	ResizeRedirectMask
PointerMotionMask	SubstructureNotifyMask
PointerMotionHintMask	SubstructureRedirectMask
Button1MotionMask	FocusChangeMask
Button2MotionMask	PropertyChangeMask
Button3MotionMask	ColormapChangeMask
Button4MotionMask	OwnerGrabButtonMask

4.3.8 Substructure Redirect Override

A feature called *substructure redirect* allows a window manager to intercept any requests to map, move, resize, or change the border width of windows. This allows the window manager to modify these requests, if necessary, to ensure that they meet its window layout policy. `SubstructureRedirectMask` must be selected by the window manager for the parent of a window; this is usually done for the root window, in effect placing all windows under the control of the window manager.

Setting the `override_redirect` attribute `True` for a window allows a window to be mapped, moved, resized, or its border width changed without the intervention of the window manager. This override is usually done for menus and other pop-up windows that are frequently mapped and almost immediately unmapped again. However, under properly designed window managers, there is a property you can set to tell the window manager to allow a window to pop up without intervention (`XA_WM_TRANSIENT_FOR`). This more polite solution to the problem is described in Section 10.2.3.6.

There is no routine for setting the `override_redirect` attribute individually; it must be set with `XChangeWindowAttributes` or when creating the window.

The `override_redirect` attribute has the following possible values.

`False` (default) specifies that map, move, and resize requests may be processed by the window manager.

`True`   specifies that map, move, and resize requests are to be done verbatim, bypassing any window manager involvement.

4.3.9 Colormap

The `colormap` attribute specifies which colormap should be used to interpret the pixel values in a window.

For the large majority of clients without special color needs, this attribute can be left in its default state. By default, the `colormap` attribute from the parent is taken, which, if all ancestors of the window have used the default, will be the default colormap. This means that the default colormap for the screen will be used to translate into colors the pixel values drawn into this window.

If the client requires its own colormap for some reason, the client can create a colormap, and set the `colormap` attribute to the ID of this colormap. A colormap ID is of type `Colormap`.

The window manager should read this attribute and install the specified colormap into the hardware colormap when the user indicates that the application should be active. If the system only has one hardware colormap, all other applications will appear in false colors. This is one good reason that applications are encouraged not to create their own colormaps but to use the default colormap instead.

To understand this process you need to know more about colormaps in X, and for that, see Chapter 7, *Color*.

`XSetWindowColormap` sets the `colormap` attribute, which has the following possible values.

CopyFromParent (default)
: specifies that the colormap attribute is to be copied from the parent (subsequent changes to the parent's attribute do not affect the child), but the window must have the same visual type as the parent and the parent must not have a colormap of `None` (otherwise a `BadMatch` error occurs).

a colormap ID
: the specified colormap will be used for all operations in this window. You can obtain a list of the installed colormaps with `XListInstalledColormaps`. There is no way to get a list of virtual colormaps that are not installed.

None
: specifies that the default colormap for the screen should be used for this window.

4.3.10 Cursor

The cursor is the object that tracks the pointer on the screen. In X, a *cursor* is an X resource which defines a cursor pattern and its colors. The ID of a cursor is of type `Cursor`.

Most clients will define a suitable cursor for their top-level window, and other cursors for each subwindow if needed. For example, *xterm* specifies the thin text cursor for the main window and a vertical bi-directional arrow for the scroll bar.

A cursor can be associated with any `InputOutput` or `InputOnly` window using the `cursor` attribute. Then the specified cursor will track the pointer while the pointer is within the window's borders.

A primary purpose for having a different cursor in a window is to indicate visually to the user that something different will happen to keyboard or button input while in the window. Another reason might be to change a cursor's color to maintain its visibility over the background of certain windows (although there are other ways to obtain contrast, with the cursor mask). These are probably other uses for a separate cursor.

A call to `XDefineCursor` sets this attribute to a `Cursor`, and a call to `XUndefine-Cursor` sets it back to `None`, which means that the cursor of the parent is used. The resource `Cursor` must be created before calling `XDefineCursor`. This can be done with `XCreateFontCursor`, `XCreateGlyphCursor`, or `XCreatePixmapCursor`; the cursor resource can be freed with `XFreeCursor` when no further explicit references to it are to be made.

The `cursor` attribute has the following possible values.

None (default)   specifies that the parent's cursor will be used when the pointer is in the window.

a cursor ID   specifies a cursor that will be used whenever the pointer is in the window.

The cursor of the root window is initially a large X, but this may be changed like the cursor in any other window if desired.

4.3.11 Default Attributes

Table 4-3 summarizes the default attributes for an `InputOutput` window. Only five of the attributes are relevant for `InputOnly` windows: `win_gravity`, `event_mask`, `do_not_propagate_mask`, `override_redirect`, and `cursor`. These attributes have the same defaults as for `InputOutput` windows.

Table 4-3. Default Window Attributes

Member	Default Value
background_pixmap	None
background_pixel	Undefined
border_pixmap	CopyFromParent
border_pixel	Undefined
bit_gravity	ForgetGravity
win_gravity	NorthWestGravity
backing_store	NotUseful
backing_planes	All 1's (ones)
backing_pixel	0 (zero)
save_under	False
event_mask	0

Table 4-3. Default Window Attributes (continued)

Member	Default Value
do_not_propagate_mask	0
override_redirect	False
colormap	CopyFromParent
cursor	None

4.4 Information from the XWindowAttributes Structure

We've been describing the programmable window attributes stored in the XSetWindow-Attributes structure. Many of the other window characteristics described in Chapter 2, *X Concepts*, including the window configuration, are stored in the XWindowAttributes structure. However, these structure members are not changed through the attribute mechanisms. Programs cannot change these characteristics directly. For example, depth, class, and visual are assigned at window creation, are stored in XWindowAttributes, and cannot be changed. Other hidden attributes such as the window size, position, and border width must be changed with the cooperation of the window manager.

However, the current values of these attributes can be useful. You can get any member of the XWindowAttributes structure with a call to XGetWindowAttributes. All the window configuration values can be read this way to find out the current position, size, and border width of a window.

Example 4-4 shows the piece of the XWindowAttributes structure that contains the members that are not present in XSetWindowAttributes.

Example 4-4. Read-only XWindowAttributes members

```
typedef struct {
    /* members writable with XChangeWindowAttributes omitted */
    .
    .
    .

    /* window geometry — set by window configuration functions in
     * cooperation with window manager. */
    int x, y;              /* location of window */
    int width, height;     /* width and height of window */
    int border_width;      /* border width of window */

    /* this is the event_mask attribute set by XSelectInput */
    long your_event_mask; /* my event mask */

    /* set when the window is created, not changeable */
    Visual *visual;        /* the associated visual structure */
    int class;             /* InputOutput, InputOnly*/
```

Example 4-4. Read-only XWindowAttributes members (continued)

```
    int depth;              /* depth of window */
    Screen *screen;         /* pointer to screen the window is on */

    /* server sets these members */
    Window root;            /* root of screen containing window */
    Bool map_installed;     /* Boolean, is colormap currently installed*/
    int map_state;          /* IsUnmapped, IsUnviewable, or IsViewable */
    long all_event_masks;   /* events all clients have interest in*/
}   XWindowAttributes;
```

As you can see, the members of XWindowAttributes that cannot be directly written with XChangeWindowAttributes are separated into four groups.

The first group provides a way to get the window geometry. This information is also returned by XGetGeometry, but it might be useful to use XGetWindowAttributes instead if you need both the geometry and a few attributes.

The your_event_mask member can be useful if you want to add event mask symbols to those already selected. In a call to XSelectInput, you must always specify all the desired event masks. If you don't know which event masks are already selected, or don't want to bother passing an event_mask argument into one of your routines, you could read the existing event mask here. Then you could OR in any additional event mask symbols before calling XSelectInput or XSetWindowAttributes. See Chapter 8, *Events*, for more information on the use of event masks.

The depth, class, visual, and screen members are set when the window is created. If the window was created with XCreateSimpleWindow, they were inherited from the parent. If the window was created with XCreateWindow, these members were specified as arguments, except screen, which is indirectly specified by the *parent* argument. The screen member points to a structure that tells you about the screen this window was created on. This is one of the Screen structures from the list in the Display structure, and therefore the information it contains can also be gotten from the macros as described in Section 3.2.3 and Volume Two, Appendix C, *Macros*. Again, these should only be needed for convenience to avoid having to pass around these values as arguments or global variables.

The root member can be returned by the RootWindow macro.

The map_installed member can be monitored to tell your application whether the colormap it has set in its colormap attribute is currently installed. If not, the application will be displayed in false colors. See Chapter 7, *Color*, for more details. The map_state member can be monitored by a program and used to turn off processing while a window is unviewable. Some applications that continuously poll for input can stop doing so and save processor cycles when there is no chance of getting input.

The all_event_masks member tells you all the event types that are selected by all clients on the window requested. This is the OR of all the event_mask attributes for that window for all clients. Contrast your_event_mask, which specifies only the events selected by *your* client.

5
The Graphics Context

The graphics primitives supplied with X are quite simple. Most of the details about the graphics to be generated are stored in a resource called a graphics context (GC). GCs are stored in the server, thus reducing the amount of information that needs to be transmitted for each graphics request. This chapter describes how to use the GC, and provides details on each member of the XGCValues structure. Everyone should read this chapter.

In This Chapter:

GC

In This Chapter (continued):

5
The Graphics Context

The routines that draw graphics are called *graphics primitives*. They draw dots, lines, text, images, and tile or fill areas. But a given graphics primitive does not contain all the information needed to draw a particular graphic. A resource called the *graphics context* (GC) specifies many variables that apply to each graphic request. The appearance of everything that is drawn within a window (except the border and background of a window, which are window attributes) is controlled by the GC that is specified with each graphics request. What is drawn into a pixmap is also controlled by the GC used in the drawing to the pixmap, and again, possibly with a different GC, if the pixmap is copied into a window.

There are two performance-related reasons for having GCs. First, they reduce the traffic between Xlib and the server because the GC information is held in the server and only needs to be sent once before the first graphics request. Each subsequent primitive that specifies the same GC will use the same values. When a few settings of the GC need to be changed, only the selected few need to be sent, not the entire GC. Second, you can create several GCs, and then simply specify which GC you want applied to each graphic request. This has important performance benefits on servers that are capable of caching multiple GCs in their display hardware.

The GC also allows for more convenient programming, since to provide the same flexibility without the GC you would need to specify an absurd number of arguments every time you called a graphics primitive.

Before we can go on to describe what the GC does in particular, you must understand what a primitive does in general.

You should think of a graphics primitive as specifying which pixels in a *source rectangle* are to be drawn, and where this rectangle should be placed in the *destination drawable*. Note that the source rectangle does not correspond to any area of the screen (except for in XCopyArea and XCopyPlane, which are not really primitives). The source is an internal entity that is drawn as an intermediate stage in the drawing process. Primitives select pixels in the source rectangle by generating a bitmap with bits set for the pixels to be drawn. In the case of XFillPolygon, this bitmap might look like Figure 5-1.

Information in the GC is then applied to this bitmap to give it pixel values (which represent colors, and are returned by BlackPixel or WhitePixel or a routine that allocates colors), and perhaps a pattern (tile) or other features.

GC

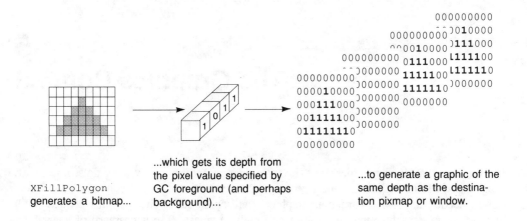

XFillPolygon generates a bitmap...

...which gets its depth from the pixel value specified by GC foreground (and perhaps background)...

...to generate a graphic of the same depth as the destination pixmap or window.

Figure 5-1. A "source" for a filled polygon

This modified source may then go through a number of other transformations before it appears on the screen. A graphics primitive does not draw on the screen as if it were simply a blank sheet of paper. Remember that there are multiple bits per pixel (multiple planes); a mask can be used to define which planes can be affected by the graphics request. Furthermore, those bits have existing values; while it is possible simply to overwrite them with new values, a wide range of other logical functions can be applied to combine the pixel values generated by the graphics request with what is already on the screen. It is also possible to define a clip mask that limits the effect of a graphics request to a particular area in a window. This is just the beginning of the possibilities controlled by the GC.

The following list gives an overview of the characteristics controlled by the GC, which are described in detail in the following sections. Some of these characteristics are specified by more than one member of the GC.

- The source* and old destination pixel values can be combined to compute the new destination pixel values, according to a *logical function*.

- In all primitives, the foreground determines the pixel value of set bits in the source. In a few primitives, the background of the GC specifies the pixel value for unset bits in the source. For example, the characters in a font would be drawn with the foreground pixel value by both XDrawString and XDrawImageString. However, the latter also fills the bounding rectangle of the string with the background pixel value.

- Line characteristics determine the width, dot pattern, and line-end type for lines.

- Fill characteristics determine the tile and fill style for filled areas and lines.

---

* Later in this chapter, when we discuss logical functions, we will use the term *source* to refer to the actual pixels selected by a graphics request plus the pixel values specified by the GC's foreground and background members.

- `GraphicsExpose` and `NoExpose` events can be selected to indicate when visibility affects `XCopyArea` and `XCopyPlane` requests.

- The font used for text-drawing requests may be specified.

- Subwindows may or may not obscure graphics drawn on the parent.

Now we'll discuss how to create and set the GC, before moving on to details of individual members of the GC.

5.1 Creating and Setting a Graphics Context

Before a GC can be used, you must create it by calling `XCreateGC`. `XCreateGC` requires only four arguments: *display*, *drawable*, *valuemask*, and *values*.

- The *display* argument (pointer to a `Display` structure) should be familiar by now; it specifies the connection to the X server. The *display* argument is used in virtually every Xlib routine.

- The *drawable* argument is a window or pixmap ID. You might think that the *drawable* argument specifies which window or pixmap the GC is to be used in, but this is not necessarily the case. It really indicates which screen the GC resource is associated with, and the depth of windows it can be used with. A GC can be used on any window or pixmap of the same depth and on the same screen as the drawable specified. Drawables are introduced in Section 2.3.5.

- The *values* argument is an `XGCValues` structure (shown in Example 5-1) filled with the desired settings for the GC.

- The *valuemask* argument specifies which members of the `XGCValues` structure are actually read. The members not represented by a bit set to 1 in the *valuemask* are given the default values listed in Section 5.11. The symbols used to make this bitmask correspond to the members of `XGCValues`, and are shown in Table 5-1.

The GC is set very much like the window attributes, as described in Section 4.2. Of course there is a different structure, and there are different masks for specifying which members are to be set. One other difference in practice is that every member of the GC can be set with an individual "convenience routine." Therefore, it can be preferable to create a default GC, and then modify it with the individual routines, rather than to set all the members in both the structure and mask before calling `XCreateGC` or `XChangeGC`. Both of these approaches are demonstrated below.

Example 5-1 and Table 5-1 present the `XGCValues` structure and the masks used when calling `XCreateGC` or `XChangeGC`.

GC

Example 5-1. The GCValues structure

```
/* Data structure for setting graphics context.   */

typedef struct {
    int function;           /* logical function */
    unsigned long plane_mask; /* plane mask */
    unsigned long foreground; /* foreground pixel */
    unsigned long background; /* background pixel */
    int line_width;         /* line width */
    int line_style;         /* LineSolid, LineOnOffDash, LineDoubleDash */
    int cap_style;          /* CapNotLast, CapButt, CapRound, CapProjecting */
    int join_style;         /* JoinMiter, JoinRound, JoinBevel */
    int fill_style;         /* FillSolid, FillTiled, FillStippled,
                             * FillOpaqueStippled */
    int fill_rule;          /* EvenOddRule, WindingRule */
    int arc_mode;           /* ArcChord, ArcPieSlice */
    Pixmap tile;            /* tile pixmap for tiling operations */
    Pixmap stipple;         /* pixmap of depth 1 */
    int ts_x_origin;        /* offset for tile or stipple operations */
    int ts_y_origin;
    Font font;              /* font for text operations (except XDrawText) */
    int subwindow_mode;     /* ClipByChildren, IncludeInferiors */
    Bool graphics_exposures; /* should events be generated on
                             * XCopyArea, XCopyPlane   */
    int clip_x_origin;      /* origin for clipping */
    int clip_y_origin;
    Pixmap clip_mask;       /* bitmap for clipping */
    int dash_offset;        /* patterned/dashed line information */
    char dashes;
} XGCValues;
```

The meaning and possible values for each member are described in Sections 5.3 through 5.9.

Table 5-1 shows the symbols used to specify which members of the XGCvalues structure actually contain meaningful values. The *valuemask* is made up of these symbols combined by means of a bitwise OR (|) .

Table 5-1. Symbols for Setting the XGCValues Structure

Member	Mask	Set Bit	Default
function	GCFunction	0	GXcopy
plane_mask	GCPlaneMask	1	all 1's
foreground	GCForeground	2	0
background	GCBackground	3	1
line_width	GCLineWidth	4	0
line_style	GCLineStyle	5	LineSolid
cap_style	GCCapStyle	6	CapButt
join_style	GCJoinStyle	7	JoinMiter
fill_style	GCFillStyle	8	FillSolid
fill_rule	GCFillRule	9	EvenOddRule

Table 5-1. Symbols for Setting the XGCValues Structure (continued)

Member	Mask	Set Bit	Default
tile	GCTile	10	pixmap filled with foreground pixel
stipple	GCStipple	11	pixmap filled with 1's
ts_x_origin	GCTileStipXOrigin	12	0
ts_y_origin	GCTileStipYOrigin	13	0
font	GCFont	14	(implementation dependent)
subwindow_mode	GCSubwindowMode	15	ClipByChildren
graphics_exposures	GCGraphicsExposures	16	True
clip_x_origin	GCClipXOrigin	17	0
clip_y_origin	GCClipYOrigin	18	0
clip_mask	GCClipMask	19	None
dash_offset	GCDashOffset	20	0
dashes	GCDashList	21	4 (i.e., the list [4, 4])
arc_mode	GCArcMode	22	ArcPieSlice

A *valuemask* composed of the symbols shown in Table 5-1 is used in XCreateGC, XCopyGC, and XChangeGC. In XCopyGC, though, the *valuemask* indicates which members are copied from the source GC to the destination GC, and the rest of the members in the destination are left unchanged. In XChangeGC, the specified members are changed and the rest are left unchanged.

5.1.1 Example of Creating and Setting a GC

Example 5-2 shows a simple way of setting some of the values for a GC before creating it. This example uses the default values except for the foreground and background pixel values.

Example 5-2. Example of setting a GC while creating it

```
GC gc;
XGCValues values;
unsigned long valuemask;
          .
          .
/* Open display, create window, etc. */
          .
          .
values.foreground = BlackPixel(display,screen);
values.background = WhitePixel(display,screen);

gc = XCreateGC(dpy, RootWindow(display, screen),
          (GCForeground | GCBackground), &values);

/* now you can use gc in drawing routines */
```

GC

In Example 5-2, the foreground pixel value is set to the value returned by the `BlackPixel` macro. This will result in a color of black if the default colormap is installed (more on this in Chapter 7, *Color*). To obtain a pixel value that represents any color other than black or white, you will need to allocate the color as described in Chapter 7.

Convenience functions are also available to change most elements of a GC after it is created. These functions are listed in Sections 5.3 through 5.9, which describe each GC element in detail. Example 5-3 performs the same functions as Example 5-2, but by creating a default GC and then modifying the contents with convenience functions.

Example 5-3. Example of setting default GC, then changing it

```
GC gc;
      .
      .
      .
/* Open display, create window, etc. */
      .
      .
      .
gc = XCreateGC(dpy, RootWindow(display, screen), 0, NULL);
SetForeground(display, gc, BlackPixel(display,screen));
SetBackground(display, gc, WhitePixel(display,screen));

/* now you can use gc in drawing routines */
```

You may wonder which of these two ways is more efficient, setting the `XGCValues` and `valuemask`, or calling the convenience functions. Actually, there isn't much difference, since in both cases, the individual requests to change the same GC are packaged into a single protocol request before being sent to the server. The method chosen is mainly a matter of personal preference.

5.2 Switching between Graphics Contexts

One purpose of the GC is to store information about how to interpret graphics requests so that the same information doesn't have to be sent with every request. Another useful feature of this approach is that you can create several GCs with the different characteristics you need and then switch between them. Example 5-4 demonstrates how this is done. It creates two slightly different GCs with swapped foreground and background pixel values.

Example 5-4. Example of switching graphics contexts

```
GC gc1, gc2;
XGCValues values;
unsigned long valuemask;
      .
      .
      .
/* Open display, create window, etc. */
```

Example 5-4. Example of switching graphics contexts (continued)

```
values.foreground = BlackPixel(display,screen);
values.background = WhitePixel(display,screen);

gc1 = XCreateGC(dpy, RootWindow(display, screen),
    (GCForeground | GCBackground), &values);

values.foreground = WhitePixel(display,screen);
values.background = BlackPixel(display,screen);

gc2 = XCreateGC(dpy, RootWindow(display, screen),
    (GCForeground | GCBackground), &values);

/* now you can use either gc in drawing routines */
/* thereby quickly swapping the foreground and background colors */
```

Whether it is faster to switch between GCs or to modify a few values of a single GC depends on the particular server implementation. On some types of display hardware, several or many GCs can be cached. On these systems it is faster to change between GCs than to change members of them. On systems that don't cache, or that cache only one GC, it is faster to change one or two elements of the GC than to switch between two slightly different GCs.

Now that you know how to create, set, and modify the GC, and how to set up multiple GCs, we can go into more detail about each element of the GC. The following sections describe each member of the graphics context. A useful quick-reference to the graphics context is provided inside the back cover of Volume Two.

5.3 Controlling the Effect of a Graphics Primitive

The GC provides a flexible way to control exactly which pixels and which planes are affected by graphics requests, and how the source and old destination pixel values are used to compute the new destination pixel values. As mentioned earlier, the bitmap generated by a graphics request (the source) has pixel values applied to it by the foreground and background members of the GC, and is then transformed by a logical operation between it and the existing value of the pixels (the destination), as well as by a plane mask and a clip mask.

As shown in Example 5-5, the logical operation, the plane mask, the clip mask, and the origin of the clip mask are all components of the GC.

GC

Example 5-5. Members of XGCValues that control combining of source and destination pixels

```
int function;              /* logical function */
unsigned long plane_mask; /* plane mask */
int clip_x_origin;         /* origin for clipping */
int clip_y_origin;
Pixmap clip_mask;    /* bitmap clipping; other calls for rects */
```

The source and existing destination pixels are combined by performing a logical function on the corresponding bits for each pixel. The `plane_mask` restricts the operation to a subset of planes, so that some bits in the source may be excluded from the computation. The `clip_mask` restricts the operation to a subset of the pixels, likewise eliminating some from the result.

The source, destination, `clip_mask`, and `plane_mask` are combined using the algorithm shown below to yield the new destination pixel values. For each bit in each pixel of the destination drawable, if the corresponding bit in `clip_mask` is set, the following expression defines whether that bit is set.

```
((src FUNC dst) AND plane_mask) OR (dst AND (NOT plane_mask))
```

That is, if the `plane_mask` bit is set, the source and existing destination pixels are combined using the logical function represented by `FUNC`. If the `plane_mask` bit is not set, the existing bit in the destination is not changed. Note that the `clip_mask` is placed relative to the drawable with the `clip_x_origin` and `clip_y_origin` members of the GC, which are described in Section 5.3.3.

Range checking is not performed on the values for `foreground`, `background`, or `plane_mask`; they are simply truncated to the appropriate number of bits. The program must make sure that the pixel values generated are less than or equal to the number of cells in the colormap, (see Chapter 7, *Color*) and that the `plane_mask` has no more bits than the depth of the drawable.

In the next three sections we'll look at the actual values that can be specified for each of these members.

5.3.1 Logical Function

The `function` member of the GC selects a logical function. *Logical functions* control how the *source* pixel values generated by a graphics request are combined with the *old destination* pixel values already present on the screen or drawable, to result in the *final destination* pixel values. Logical functions are also sometimes called *raster operations*, *raster ops*, or *display functions*. The logical function can be changed by a call to `XSetFunction`.

The *source* is the output of a graphics primitive, or an area of the screen or drawable (for an `XCopyArea`); the *destination* is the area of the drawable or window that is to receive the output. The 16 logical functions defined in *<X11/X.h>* are shown in Table 5-2.

Table 5-2. Logical Functions in the GC

Logical Function	Hex Code	Definition
GXclear	0x0	0
GXand	0x1	src AND dst
GXandReverse	0x2	src AND (NOT dst)
GXcopy	0x3	src
GXandInverted	0x4	(NOT src) AND dst
GXnoop	0x5	dst
GXxor	0x6	src XOR dst
GXor	0x7	src OR dst
GXnor	0x8	(NOT src) AND (NOT dst)
GXequiv	0x9	(NOT src) XOR dst
GXinvert	0xa	(NOT dst)
GXorReverse	0xb	src OR (NOT dst)
GXcopyInverted	0xc	(NOT src)
GXorInverted	0xd	(NOT src) OR dst
GXnand	0xe	(NOT src) OR (NOT dst)
GXset	0xf	1

Figure 5-2 illustrates the effect of the three logical functions on a 12-plane screen given a particular set of source and destination bit values for a single pixel.

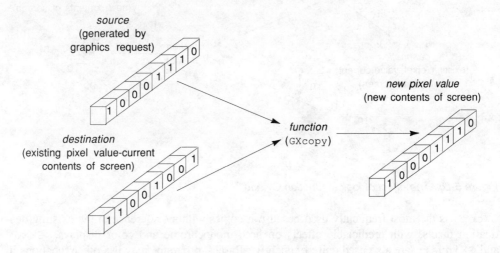

Figure 5-2a. The effect of logical function GXcopy

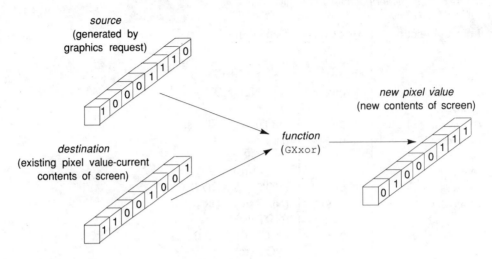

Figure 5-2b. The effect of logical function GXxor

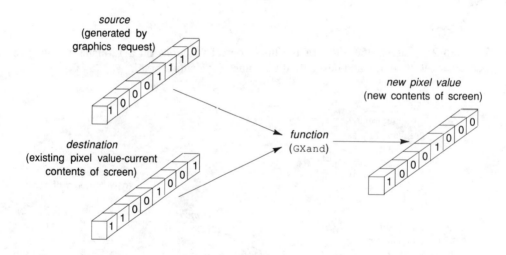

Figure 5-2c. The effect of logical function GXand

GXcopy is the most frequently used because it copies without reference to the existing destination pixels, with predictable effects on both monochrome and color displays. GXxor and GXinvert are also used quite frequently. Rarely, programs may use other functions in concert with particular planes of a color display. Here's some more detail on the most frequently-used logical functions:

GXcopy   ignores the bits already in the destination drawable. It is used for both monochrome and color.

GXinvert   ignores the source and inverts the old destination. This logical function is used to change black to white and vice versa when modifying only one plane (simulating a monochrome display). It is not normally used on color screens.

GXxor   combines the source and existing bits in such a way that if the operation is repeated, the drawable is returned to its initial condition. It is important that these two operations occur without intervening manipulation of the selected bits (for windows, the server should be grabbed, but for a very short time).* Otherwise the second XOR operation will not leave the drawable unchanged. GXxor has these properties on both monochrome and color screens.

5.3.2 Plane Mask

The plane_mask member of XGCValues determines which planes of the destination drawable are modified. The plane_mask can be changed by a call to XSetPlaneMask.

Destination planes represented by a bit set to 1 in the plane_mask can be changed by the graphics command, and the others cannot. The defined constant AllPlanes provides a plane_mask with all bits set, which should be used when every plane is to be affected. A plane_mask of 0 cancels the effect of the graphics primitive. A plane_mask of 1 affects only the first plane of the drawable, and is useful if you want a program to work in monochrome on both color and monochrome displays. The macro DisplayPlanes returns the number of planes available on the screen. However, the depth of the window is the upper limit on the number of meaningful bits in the plane_mask. Figure 5-3 illustrates the use of the plane_mask.

5.3.3 Clip Mask

Clipping allows you to limit the effect of graphics requests to a particular area of the display. The clip_mask member of XGCValues is a bitmap that indicates which pixels of the destination drawable are to be affected by graphics requests.

Pixels outside this area will not be drawn. The clip_mask can be set with XSetClip-Mask, XSetClipRectangles, or XSetRegion. XSetClipMask sets a clip mask composed of an arbitrary set of bits, as shown in Figure 5-4. XSetClipRectangles specifies an array of rectangles that will collectively be used as a clip mask. XSetRegion is another way to set the clip mask to a set of rectangles, sometimes more convenient that XSetClipRectangles. In Release 2, XUnionRectWithRegion can be used to add the rectangle from an Expose event into a region. Then XSetRegion sets the GC to clip output to those areas. This is useful for redrawing only the areas that have been exposed. See Example 3-16 which uses this technique. See Chapter 8, *Events*, for more information on Expose events.

GC

---

*When the server is grabbed, the client that grabbed it has sole control over the server and the screen. All other clients are put on hold; the server saves up events queued for them and does not change the screen on their behalf until the server grab is released. The server is grabbed and released with XGrabServer and XUngrabServer, but this should be done only when really necessary.

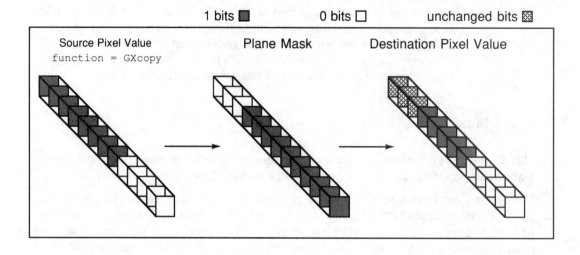

1 bits ■   0 bits □   unchanged bits ▨

Source Pixel Value
function = GXcopy

Plane Mask

Destination Pixel Value

Figure 5-3. The effect of the plane_mask on a 12-plane display

If the `clip_mask` is set manually with `XSetClipMask` or while creating the GC, a pixmap of depth 1 must be created. Then, the only pixels drawn are those for which the `clip_mask` has a set bit. This pixmap must have the same root as the GC, or a Bad-Match error will be generated.

The clip origin, which places the `clip_mask` relative to the destination drawable, is specified by two other members of the GC structure: `clip_x_origin` and `clip_y_origin`. Figure 5-4 shows how these coordinates specify the upper-left corner of the clip mask relative to the upper-left corner of the destination drawable specified in the graphics request. The origin of the `clip_mask` can be set with `XSetClipOrigin`. The gray area in the figure represents the data to be drawn. The lighter gray at the bottom shows the area outside the clip mask; this data will not be drawn.

5.4 Foreground and Background

The `foreground` and `background` elements of the GC specify the pixel values to be applied to the source. These are the "colors" used when drawing graphics.* They can be set by `XSetForeground` and `XSetBackground`.

---

* For practical purposes, you can loosely think of a pixel value as the "color" in which an object will be drawn, though it applies to both color and monochrome systems. Even on a color system, the actual color resulting from the specified foreground or background pixel value will depend on the plane mask and logical function in effect, as well as the values stored in the colormap entry to which the resulting value points! Later references in this chapter to drawing in the "foreground color" should be interpreted in this light.

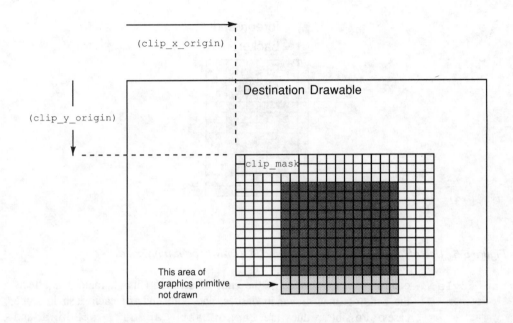

Figure 5-4. Use of clip origin to locate the clip_mask relative to drawable

The foreground member in the GC is used as the pixel value for set bits in the source in all primitives. The background is used for unset bits in the source in just four situations: using XDrawImageString (see Section 6.2.4), using XCopyPlane (see Section 6.1.6), drawing with line_style of LineDoubleDash (see Section 5.5.2), and filling with fill_style of FillOpaqueStippled (see Section 5.6.4).

Figure 5-5 shows the use of the foreground and background values when drawing a character with XDrawImageString. This primitive draws both the character and its bounding box. The character itself is drawn in the foreground pixel value; the remainder of the pixels in the bounding box are drawn with the background pixel value.

5.5 Line Characteristics

There are six line characteristics that are part of the graphics context and members of XGCValues:

line_width   specifies the width of the line in pixels. Zero means to draw using the server's fastest algorithm with a line width of one pixel.

line_style   specifies whether the line is solid in foreground, dashed in foreground, or alternating foreground and background. Possible values are LineSolid, LineOnOffDash, or LineDoubleDash.

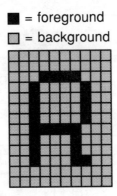

■ = foreground
□ = background

Figure 5-5. Use of foreground and background in XDrawImageString character

cap_style   controls the appearance of the ends of a line. This characteristic affects
             the ends of lines drawn in dashes, and both ends of each dash in some
             cases. Possible values are CapNotLast, CapButt, CapRound, and
             CapProjecting.

join_style   controls the appearance of joints between consecutive lines drawn by the
             same line-drawing routine. Possible values are JoinMiter, Join-
             Round, and JoinBevel.

dashes   specifies the length of the dashes for custom-designed dashed lines.

dash_offset specifies the starting point of the dash pattern for custom-designed dashed
             lines.

The line_width, line_style, cap_style, and join_style can be set using
XSetLineAttributes, while the dashes and dash_offset can be set with XSet-
Dashes. Now we'll describe each of these line characteristics in more detail, followed by
an example that sets them.

5.5.1 Line Width

The line_width member of XGCValues is measured in pixels. The line width can be
set with XSetLineAttributes.

A line_width greater than or equal to 1 is considered a *wide* line, and the value 0 is a
special case, considered a *thin* line. Wide and thin lines often use different drawing algorithms. The thin line is intended to be a fast algorithm for drawing a line of width 1.

Wide lines are drawn centered on the path described by the graphics request. A wide line drawn from [x1,y1] to [x2,y2] always draws the same pixels as a wide line drawn from [x2,y2] to [x1,y1], not counting cap and join styles. This is not necessarily the case for thin lines.

Unless otherwise specified by the join or cap style, the bounding box of a wide line with endpoints [x1,y1], [x2,y2] and width *w* is a rectangle with vertices at the following real coordinates:

Lower Left:	[x1-(w*sin(θ)/2), y1+(w*cos(θ)/2)]
Upper Right:	[x1+(w*sin(θ)/2), y1-(w*cos(θ)/2)]
Lower Left:	[x2-(w*sin(θ)/2), y2+(w*cos(θ)/2)]
Lower Right:	[x2+(w*sin(θ)/2), y2-(w*cos(θ)/2)]

where θ is the angle of the line measured from horizontal.

A pixel is drawn if the center of the pixel is fully inside the bounding box (which is viewed as having infinitely thin edges). If the center of the pixel is exactly on the bounding box, it is part of the line only if the interior of the box is immediately to the pixel's right. Pixels with centers on a horizontal edge are part of the line only if the interior of the box is immediately below the pixel.

Thin lines (line_width==0) are one-pixel-wide lines drawn using an unspecified, device-dependent fast algorithm. The set of points comprising this type of a line won't be affected by clipping.

A line_width of 1 and a thin line with line_width 0 may not be exactly alike. In general, drawing a thin line should be faster than drawing a wide line of width 1. However, because of their different drawing algorithms, thin lines may not mix well with wide lines, aesthetically speaking. For precise and uniform results across all displays, use a line_width of 1 rather than 0. If speed is the goal, use a line_width of 0.

5.5.2 Line Style

The line_style member of XGCValues defines which sections of a line are drawn, and in which pixel value, as shown in Figure 5-6. The line style can be set with XSetLine-Attributes. The actual length of each dash and gap is set by the dashes member of XGCValues, described in Section 5.5.5. The constants used to set line_style are as follows:

LineSolid	specifies that the full path of the line is drawn using the foreground pixel value.
LineOnOffDash	specifies that only the dashes are drawn with the foreground pixel value, and cap_style applies to each dash (except that Cap-NotLast is treated as CapButt for internal caps).
LineDoubleDash	specifies that the full path of the line is drawn, dashes with the foreground pixel value, gaps with the background pixel values, with CapButt style used where dashes and gaps meet.

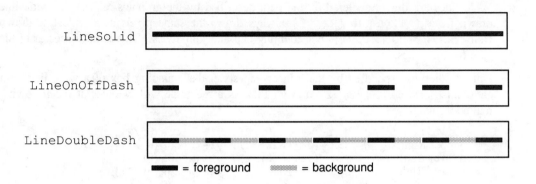

LineSolid

LineOnOffDash

LineDoubleDash

▬▬ = foreground   ░░░░ = background

Figure 5-6. The line styles

5.5.3 Cap Style

The cap_style member of XGCValues defines how the endpoints of lines are drawn, as shown in Figure 5-7. The cap style can be set with XSetLineAttributes. The constants used to set cap_style are as follows:

CapNotLast   is equivalent to CapButt, except that for a line_width of 0 or 1, the final endpoint is not drawn. If specified with line_style LineOnOffDash or LineDoubleDash, the ends of the dashes or where even and odd dashes meet are treated as CapButt.

CapButt   specifies that lines will be square at the endpoint with no projection beyond. The end is perpendicular to the slope of the line.

CapRound   specifies that lines will be terminated by a circular arc with the diameter equal to the line_width, centered on the endpoint (equivalent to CapButt for line_width of 0 or 1).

CapProjecting   specifies that lines will be square at the end, but with the path continuing beyond the endpoint for a distance equal to half the line_width (equivalent to CapButt for line_width of 0 or 1).

5.5.4 Join Style

The join_style member of XGCValues defines how corners are drawn for wide lines, as shown in Figures 5-8 and 5-9. The join style can be set with XSetLineAttributes.

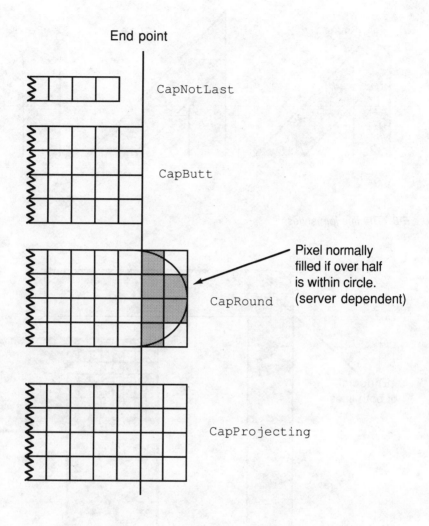

End point

CapNotLast

CapButt

CapRound

Pixel normally
filled if over half
is within circle.
(server dependent)

CapProjecting

Figure 5-7. The line cap (end) styles

The constants used to set `join_style` are as follows:

JoinMiter   specifies that the outer edges of the two lines should extend to meet at an angle.

JoinRound   specifies that lines should be joined by a circular arc with diameter equal to the `line_width`, centered on the join point.

JoinBevel   specifies `CapButt` endpoint styles, with the triangular notch filled.

GC

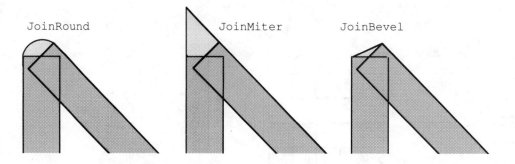

Figure 5-8. The line join styles

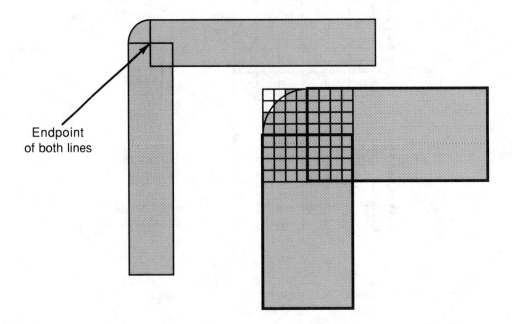

Endpoint
of both lines

Figure 5-9. Detail of JoinRound for 8-pixel-wide lines

5.5.5 Dash List and Offset

The `dashes` member of `XGCValues` must be a single, nonzero value specifying the length in pixels of both the dashes and the gaps. `XGCValues.dashes` is a simplified form of the more general patterns that can be set with `XSetDashes`.

In `XSetDashes`, the *dash_list* argument is a real list, with each value representing the length of a single dash or gap in the line. The initial and alternating members of *dash_list* are the length of the *even* dashes; the others are the *odd* dashes (gaps). All members must be nonzero. The length of the *dash_list* is also an argument to `XSet-Dashes`. The `dashes` element of `XGCValues` is equivalent to specifying a two-member *dash_list* [N, N] in `XSetDashes`, where *N* is the single value specified in `XGCValues.dashes`.

The `dash_offset` for `XSetDashes` defines the phase of the pattern, specifying how many pixels into the pattern the line should actually begin.

Example 5-6 shows a code segment that creates and sets the line dashes of five GCs. Figure 5-10 shows the lines that might result from drawing with these GCs.

Example 5-6. Code segment specifying five styles of dashed line in five GCs

```
#define NUMLINES 5
#define DOTTED_LIST_LENGTH 2
#define DOT_DASHED_LIST_LENGTH 4
#define SHORT_DASHED_LIST_LENGTH 2
#define LONG_DASHED_LIST_LENGTH 2
#define ODD_DASHED_LIST_LENGTH 3

void main(argc, argv)
int argc;
char **argv;
{
    GC gc[NUMLINES];
      .
      .
      .
    /* open display, create windows, etc. */

    set_dashes(gc);
    draw_lines(gc);
}


set_dashes(gc)
GC *gc[];
{
    XGCValues gcv;
    int i;
    static int dash_list_length[] = {
        DOTTED_LIST_LENGTH,
        DOT_DASHED_LIST_LENGTH,
        SHORT_DASHED_LIST_LENGTH,
        LONG_DASHED_LIST_LENGTH,
```

```
        ODD_DASHED_LIST_LENGTH
};

/* must be at least one element in each list */
static unsigned char dotted[DOTTED_LIST_LENGTH] =
        {3, 1};
static unsigned char dot_dashed[DOT_DASHED_LIST_LENGTH] =
        {3, 4, 3, 1};
static unsigned char short_dashed[SHORT_DASHED_LIST_LENGTH] =
        {4, 4};
static unsigned char long_dashed[LONG_DASHED_LIST_LENGTH] =
        {4, 7};
static unsigned char odd_dashed[ODD_DASHED_LIST_LENGTH] =
        {1, 2, 3};

static unsigned char *dash_list[] = {
    dotted,
    dot_dashed,
    short_dashed,
    long_dashed,
    odd_dashed,
};

int dash_offset = 0;

/* Open display, create window, etc. */

gcv.line_style = LineOnOffDash;
for (i = 0 ; i < NUMLINES; i++) {
    *gc[i] = XCreateGC(display, RootWindow(display, screen),
            GCLineStyle, &gcv);
    XSetDashes(display, *gc[i], dash_offset, dash_list[i],
            dash_list_length[i]);
}
}

draw_lines(gc)
GC *gc[];
{
    /* draw lines, using *gc[i] to specify which dash style */
}
```

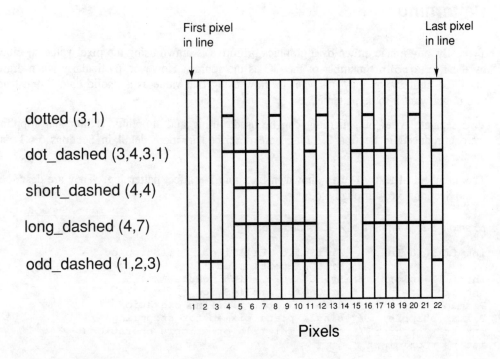

First pixel
in line

Last pixel
in line

dotted (3,1)

dot_dashed (3,4,3,1)

short_dashed (4,4)

long_dashed (4,7)

odd_dashed (1,2,3)

1 2 3 4 5 6 7 8 9 10 11 12 13 14 15 16 17 18 19 20 21 22

Pixels

Figure 5-10. Lines drawn with GCs set in Example 5-6

5.5.6 **Example of Setting Line Characteristics**

Example 5-7 demonstrates how to set the line characteristics with XSetLine-Attributes. This routine and XSetDashes (which sets dashes, demonstrated in Example 5-6) are the only ways to set line characteristics, other than with XCreateGC or XChangeGC.

Example 5-7. Setting line characteristics in a GC

```
set_line_attributes(gc)
GC gc;
{
    unsigned int line_width = 3; /* 0 would be fast line of width 1 */
    int line_style = LineSolid;  /* if LineOnOffDash or LineDoubleDash,
                                  * must set dashes */
    int cap_style = CapRound;    /* else CapNotLast, CapButt, or
                                  * CapProjecting */
    int join_style = JoinRound;  /* else JoinMiter or JoinBevel */

    XSetLineAttributes(display, gc, line_width, line_style,
            cap_style, join_style);
}
```

5.6 Patterning

Typically, any image drawn by a graphics primitive is drawn using the pixel value specified by the `foreground` member of the GC as the source. However, particularly when drawing filled figures, you may not want to draw using that value as a "solid color"—instead, you might want it to be patterned.

Two separate types of patterning can be used: tiling and stippling. Tiling and stippling were introduced in Section 2.3.7 and are described in more detail in Sections 5.6.1 and 5.6.2.

The members of `XGCValues` shown in Example 5-8 affect patterning. They are described in the Sections 5.6.4 through 5.6.6.

Example 5-8. Members of XGCValues affecting filling

```
int fill_style;    /* FillSolid, FillTiled, FillStippled,
                    * FillOpaqueStippled */
int fill_rule;     /* EvenOddRule, WindingRule */
int arc_mode;      /* ArcChord, ArcPieSlice */
Pixmap tile;       /* tile pixmap for tiling operations */
Pixmap stipple;    /* single plane pixmap for stippling */
int ts_x_origin;   /* offset for tile or stipple operations */
int ts_y_origin;
```

5.6.1 Tiles

A *tile* is a pixmap used to pattern the pixels specified by set bits in the source bitmap. The `tile` member of the GC can be set with `XSetTile`.

Tiles are so named because they are laid out next to each other in an array like bathroom tile. The origin of the first tile is specified with `ts_x_origin` and `ts_y_origin`, which are relative to the origin of the destination drawable. These members of the GC are set with `XSetTSOrigin`. Only pixels specified by set bits in the source bitmap are tiled. Figure 5-11 shows how tiles are used to pattern an area. Instead of being filled with a solid color (or shade of gray), the area is filled with the tile pattern. Creating a tile is described in Section 6.1.5. The tile pixmap must be created on the same root window and have the same depth as the destination drawable. If these conditions are not satisfied, a `BadMatch` error is generated. If a pixmap is used simultaneously in a graphics request both as a destination and as a tile, the results are not defined.

If the depth of the drawable and tile is 1, tiling is identical to stippling with `fill_style` `FillOpaqueStippled`, which we'll describe next.

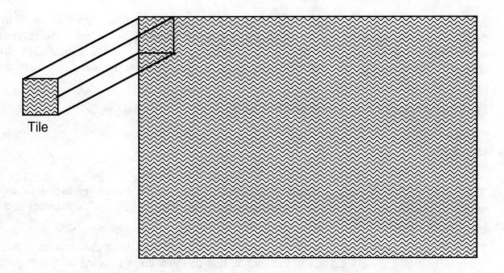

Tile

Figure 5-11. Tiling an area

5.6.2 Stipples

Stippling is similar to tiling, except that a stipple is a pixmap of depth 1, not of the depth of the drawable. The pixel values used to draw the pattern are the `foreground` and `background` in the GC.

There are two styles of *stippling*, selected by the `fill_style` of the GC: `FillStippled` and `FillOpaqueStippled`. For a `fill_style` of `FillOpaqueStippled`, the `foreground` pixel value in the GC is used for bits set in the stipple and the source, and the `background` pixel value is used for bits unset in the stipple but set in the source. For a `fill_style` of `FillStippled`, only the `foreground` pixel value is drawn for set bits in the stipple, and other pixels are not affected.

When the depth of the drawable is one, there is no difference between tiling with `fill_style` of `FillTiled` and stippling with `fill_style` of `FillOpaqueStippled`.

The `stipple` member of the GC may be changed with `XSetStipple`. If both the `stipple` and `tile` members of the GC are set, the `fill_style` determines which is used. Both cannot be used in a single graphics request.

GC

5.6.3 Tile and Stipple Sizes

A pixmap of any size can be used for tiling or stippling, but on some types of hardware, particular tile or stipple sizes run much faster than arbitrary sizes. XQueryBestSize returns the closest tile or stipple size to the one you specify, and also the largest allowable cursor. XQueryBestTile and XQueryBestStipple perform the same functions, but only for tiles and stipples, respectively.

For how to create a tile or stipple, see Section 6.1.5.

5.6.4 Fill Style

The fill_style member of XGCValues controls whether the source graphics are drawn with a solid color, a tile, or one of the two stipple styles. The fill_style member of the GC may be changed with XSetFillStyle.

The fill_style affects all line, text, and fill requests except lines drawn with line-width 0. It affects only set bits in the source; that is, those areas selected by the graphics request. Possible values are:

FillSolid   specifies that graphics should be drawn using the foreground pixel value.

FillTiled   specifies that graphics should be drawn using the tile pixmap.

FillStippled   specifies that graphics should be drawn using the foreground pixel value masked by stipple. In other words, bits set in the source and stipple are drawn in the foreground pixel value.

FillOpaqueStippled
                     specifies that graphics should be drawn using stipple, using the foreground pixel value for set bits in stipple and the background pixel value for unset bits in stipple.

Odd dashes in dotted lines are a special case. For the gaps (odd dashes) in lines with line_style of LineDoubleDash, FillSolid means to draw the gaps in the background pixel value, and FillStippled means to draw in the background pixel value masked by stipple. With a line_style of LineDoubleDash, FillTiled and FillStippled have the effect of wiping out the odd dashes, so that the line looks like LineOnOffDash with the specified fill style.

Figure 5-12 demonstrates the four fill styles.

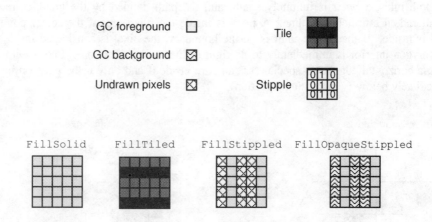

Figure 5-12. fill_style demonstrated on small pixmaps

5.6.5 Fill Rule

The fill_rule member of XGCValues defines what pixels are drawn for paths given in XFillPolygon requests. The *fill_rule* is also an argument to XPolygonRegion, which is described in Section 6.3. The fill_rule in the GC is set with XSetFill-Rule. The fill_rule may be EvenOddRule (the default in the GC) or Winding-Rule.

As shown in Figure 5-13, EvenOddRule means that if areas overlap an odd number of times, they are not drawn. Technically, it specifies that a point is drawn if an infinite ray with the point as origin crosses the path an odd number of times.

WindingRule, also shown in Figure 5-13, means that overlapping areas are always filled, regardless of how many times they overlap. Technically, this rule specifies that a point is inside the filled area if an infinite ray with the point as origin crosses an unequal number of clockwise- and counterclockwise-directed path segments.

Since polygons are drawn as a series of points connected by lines, the order of the points determines the direction of each line. A clockwise-directed path segment is one which crosses the ray from left to right as observed from the point. A counterclockwise-directed segment is one which crosses the ray from right to left as observed from the point. The case where a directed line segment is coincident with the ray is uninteresting because you can simply choose a different ray that is not coincident with a segment.

All calculations are performed on infinitely small points, so that if any point within a pixel is considered inside, the entire pixel is drawn. Pixels with centers exactly on boundaries are considered inside only if the filled area is to the right, except that on horizontal boundaries, the pixel is considered inside only if the filled area is below the pixel.

For both rules, a *point* is infinitely small, and the path defined by the graphics request is considered an infinitely thin line. A pixel is inside the filled area if the center point of the pixel is inside. If the center point is on the boundary, the pixel is considered inside only if the polygon interior is immediately to its right (x increasing direction). Pixels with centers along a horizontal edge are a special case and are inside if and only if the polygon interior is immediately below (y increasing direction).

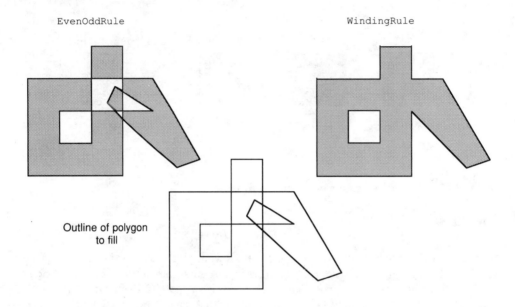

EvenOddRule   WindingRule

Outline of polygon to fill

Figure 5-13. fill_rule constants for filling closed polygons

5.6.6 Arc Mode (for Filling)

The `arc_mode` member of `XGCValues` controls filling of arcs drawn with `XFillArc` and `XFillArcs`. The `arc_mode` is set with `XSetArcMode`.

An arc is specified for `XFillArc` or `XFillArcs` as follows:

- The arc is bounded by a rectangle whose center is the center of the arc.

- The position of the upper-left corner of the rectangle is relative to the origin of the destination drawable.

- Two angles indicate the starting and stopping position of the arc. These are measured in sixty-fourths of a degree starting from the three-o'clock position, with positive angles indicating counterclockwise measurement.

The arc_mode can be either ArcPieSlice or ArcChord. Figure 5-14 demonstrates the two modes. For ArcChord, the arc and the single line segment joining the endpoints of the arc create a closed figure to fill. For ArcPieSlice, the arc and the two line segments joining the endpoints of the arc with the center point are used.

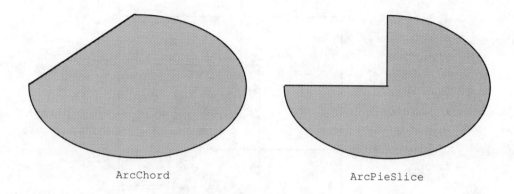

ArcChord   ArcPieSlice

Figure 5-14. arc_mode constants for filling arcs

5.7 Graphics Exposure

When using XCopyArea and XCopyPlane to copy data from one drawable to another, it is possible that certain portions of the source region will be obscured, unmapped, or otherwise unavailable. If this is the case, it may be desirable to generate an event to signal the client that one or more areas in the destination window could not be copied to and should be redrawn some other way.

The graphics_exposure flag in the GC specifies whether or not events should be generated in such a case. There are actually two possible event types that can be generated:

- One or more GraphicsExpose events are sent when a destination region cannot be completely drawn because the source region was obscured, unmapped, or otherwise unavailable.

- A single NoExpose event occurs when the specified source region is completely available.

These event types are not selected by XSelectInput or in the event_mask attribute; setting graphics_exposure to True is the only way to select them. The graphics_exposure member of the GC is set with XSetGraphicsExposures.

Figure 5-15 shows a typical XCopyArea request where the source region is obscured. It shows the areas that would be specified in the GraphicsExpose events generated. As shown in Figure 5-15, a single XCopyPlane or XCopyArea can result in more than one

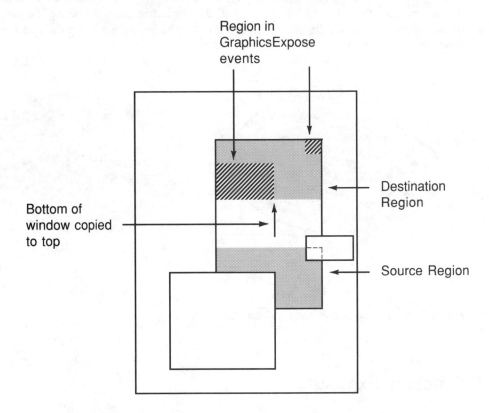

Region in
GraphicsExpose
events

Destination
Region

Source Region

Bottom of
window copied
to top

Figure 5-15. Copying a partially unavailable area

GraphicsExpose event, since the resulting area to be redrawn may be composed of several rectangles. A copy such as the one shown in Figure 5-15 would generate two GraphicsExpose events. One rectangle is specified by each event.

When graphics_exposure is False, neither of these events is sent under any circumstances. By default, graphics_exposure is True.

5.8 The Font

The font member of the GC specifies which font to use in graphics requests. If the specified font hasn't been loaded by this client, a graphics primitive that tries to draw text won't fail; it just won't draw. Therefore you should make sure you load the font.

The X server actually loads a requested font into memory only when XLoadFont or XLoadQueryFont is called and if the specified font has not already been loaded by another client. A font is unloaded when the last program using the font exits or unloads it. Duplicate copies of a font are never stored in the server.

There are several ways to deal with fonts. Most programs will use `XLoadQueryFont` to load a font and get information about the dimensions of each character. `XLoadQuery-Font` returns a pointer to an `XFontStruct`. The font in the GC can then be set to `XFontStruct.fid`. See Chapter 6, *Drawing Graphics and Text*, for details.

5.9 Subwindow Mode

The `subwindow_mode` member of `XGCValues` controls whether subwindows obscure their parent. This member is set with `XSetSubwindowMode`.

The value `ClipByChildren` sets the default condition, in which drawing into the area of a window obscured by its visible children produces no effect.

If the `subwindow_mode` is set to `IncludeInferiors`, drawing appears through visible children even when they have opaque backgrounds. The use of `IncludeInferiors` on a window of depth 1 with mapped inferiors of differing depth is not illegal, but the results are not defined in standard Xlib.

One familiar application of `IncludeInferiors` is the window manager's "rubber banding" of window outlines while they are being moved or resized. The outline is drawn on the root window with the GC set to `IncludeInferiors`.

5.10 Sharing GCs Between Clients

Despite the fact that a GC is a resource, and theoretically shareable, separate clients should not attempt to share GCs, because of the way GCs are implemented.

5.11 The Default Graphics Context

Table 5-3 shows the default values for all members of a graphics context.

Table 5-3. The Default Graphics Context

Component	Value
function	GXcopy
plane_mask	all 1's
foreground	0
background	1
line_width	0
line_style	LineSolid
cap_style	CapButt
join_style	JoinMiter
fill_style	FillSolid

GC

Table 5-3. The Default Graphics Context (continued)

Component	Value
fill_rule	EvenOddRule
arc_mode	ArcPieSlice
tile	pixmap filled with foreground pixel
stipple	pixmap filled with 1's
ts_x_origin	0
ts_y_origin	0
font	(implementation dependent)
subwindow_mode	ClipByChildren
graphics_exposures	True
clip_x_origin	0
clip_y_origin	0
clip_mask	None
dash_offset	0
dashes	4 (i.e., the list [4, 4])

A useful quick-reference to the graphics context is provided inside the back cover of Volume Two, *Xlib Reference Manual*.

6
Drawing Graphics and Text

This chapter describes the routines used to draw lines, geometrical figures, and text. It also discusses the use of pixmaps, images, and regions. You should be familiar with the use of the graphics context before attempting to use these routines.

In This Chapter:

Drawing

In This Chapter (continued):

6

Drawing Graphics and Text

Drawing with computers is a little like drawing by hand. Holding the pencil is not hard, but getting anything recognizable to appear on the page is a different matter. Similarly, drawing with X is quite easy, but designing what to draw and where can be a challenge. We can do little more in this chapter than tell you how to hold the pencil; the rest is up to you.

This chapter describes various techniques that have to do with drawing: drawing lines, rectangles and arcs; using bitmaps; placing and drawing text; using regions; creating and using cursors; and using images.

The `draw_text` and `draw_graphics` routines called in the *basicwin* program in Chapter 3, *Basic Window Program*, are used as examples in this chapter. Also described here are various versions of the `draw_box` routine, which is called in the simple window manager *winman* described in Chapter 14, *Window Management*.

Note that before you draw anything, you must set up a graphics context to specify, at minimum, the foreground and background pixel values for drawing. For monochrome applications, you should set these values using the `BlackPixel` and `WhitePixel` macros described in Chapter 3, *Basic Window Program*. For color applications, you should use one of the color allocation routines described in Chapter 7, *Color*. While the foreground and background values in the default GC *may* work on some servers, they are hardcoded (0 and 1), and should *not* be relied upon by any client, since they will give inconsistent results on color displays.

6.1 Drawing

The X drawing primitives are easy-to-use routines capable of drawing points, connected lines (polylines), disconnected lines (disjoint polylines), rectangles, and circles, ellipses, or arcs.

`XDrawPoint` requires only the coordinates of the point to be drawn. `XDrawPoints` requires a pointer to an array of coordinates for the points, the number of points, and a mode flag which controls whether the coordinates are interpreted relative to the origin of the drawable or relative to the previous point drawn.

Drawing

XDrawLine is similar to XDrawPoint but requires two points, a beginning and an end. XDrawLines works just like XDrawPoints but draws lines between consecutive points in the list. If the first and last points coincide, the lines will be joined properly according to the joining specifications in the GC.

XDrawSegments draws lines that are not necessarily connected end-to-end. It requires an array of pairs of endpoints. There is no mode flag for XDrawSegments, so the coordinates are always relative to the origin of the drawable.

XDrawRectangle draws the outline of a rectangle when given the upper-left corner and the height and width. XDrawRectangles draws multiple rectangles from an array of corner coordinates and dimensions. The actual width and height of a rectangle is one pixel larger than the dimensions specified, according to the X protocol (see Figure 6-2). These actual dimensions maintain consistency with the definition of a filled rectangle or a clipping region, which are exactly the size specified.

XDrawArc is similar to XDrawRectangle, except that it draws an arc that fits inside the rectangle. This function can draw circles and ellipses (or parts thereof) whose axes are parallel to the window coordinates. An elliptical arc occurs if the rectangle is not a square. The extent of the arc is specified by two angles: the first is the starting angle relative to the three-o'clock position, and the second is the angle relative to the starting position. The angles are signed integers in sixty-fourths of a degree (0 to 360 * 64 is a complete circle), with positive values drawing the arc counterclockwise. This scale factor is required so that angles can be specified more accurately than allowed by integral values between 0 and 360 degrees. Figure 6-1 demonstrates the arguments needed for XDrawArc.

These primitives select the source pixels that will be operated on according to the graphics context to supply the foreground and background colors, line and fill style, etc. The GC is described in Chapter 5, *The Graphics Context.*

X Version 11 also supports the XDraw and XDrawFilled routines that were available in X Version 10, though the performance of these is low. These routines are described in Appendix B, *X10 Compatibility.*

Xlib does not provide routines for drawing Bezier or cubic spline curves, but extensions for drawing these are publicly available.

6.1.1 Scaling Graphics

All drawing measurements in X are made in pixels. The positions you specify are relative to the origin (upper-left corner inside border) of the window specified in the drawing request. The width and height of a rectangle or bounding box for an arc are also specified in pixels.

Basing scaling on pixels has a weakness caused by the fact that pixels are not always the same size on the screen. Imagine a desktop publishing application. Its goal is to make everything drawn on the screen as close as possible to what will appear on the printed page. People may run the application from a PC which has a 9.5" by 7.25" screen with an 640 by 480 array of pixels, or from a workstation which has a 13.5" by 10.5" screen with an array of perhaps 1152 by 900 pixels. The ruler lines drawn by the application would look much

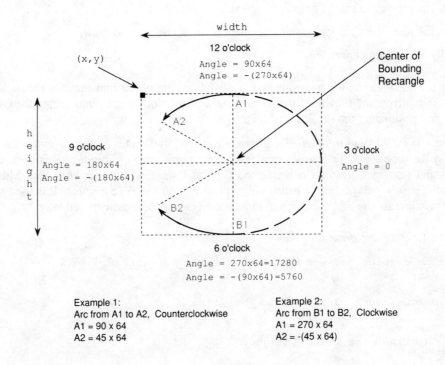

width

12 o'clock
Angle = 90x64
Angle = -(270x64)

(x,y)

Center of
Bounding
Rectangle

A1

A2

height

9 o'clock
Angle = 180x64
Angle = -(180x64)

3 o'clock
Angle = 0

B2

B1

6 o'clock
Angle = 270x64=17280
Angle = -(90x64)=5760

Example 1:
Arc from A1 to A2, Counterclockwise
A1 = 90 x 64
A2 = 45 x 64

Example 2:
Arc from B1 to B2, Clockwise
A1 = 270 x 64
A2 = -(45 x 64)

Figure 6-1. Angle measurement for XDrawArc or XDrawArcs

different on the two screens if their sizes were not adjusted accordingly. The application should calculate the ratio of the size in millimeters of the screen to its size in pixels, in both directions. The required information is returned by the `DisplayHeight`, `Display-HeightMM`, `DisplayWidth`, and `DisplayWidthMM` macros.

This correction of size distortion also solves a second, smaller problem. The relative density of pixels in the x and y directions on the screen may vary. For example, a square drawn with equal width and height may appear rectangular on the screen, since some (but fortunately not many) screens have more space between rows of pixels than between columns. By correcting for size variation this problem goes away. It is also possible to allow size variations but correct for the aspect ratio distortion, by multiplying the height measurements in pixels by the ratio:

$$\frac{DisplayHeight \div DisplayHeightMM}{DisplayWidth \div DisplayWidthMM}$$

or by multiplying the width measurements in pixels by the inverse of this ratio. Do not multiply both the width and height measurements.

Drawing

6.1.2 Example of Drawing Graphics

All drawing routines are used in essentially the same way:

- First, you create and set the graphics context.

- Then, calculate the dimensions and placement of what you want to draw.

- Finally, do the actual drawing.

Example 6-1 shows a routine named `draw_graphics` that places and draws a rectangle. As you can tell from the brevity of the routine, most of the trouble goes into setting the GC properly and positioning the item to be drawn. The actual drawing is very simple.

This routine is called from the *basicwin* program described in Chapter 3, *Basic Window Program*. By the time it is called, we have already done many things. The display is opened, windows and resources created (including the GC), and window manager hints set. Most importantly, `draw_graphics` is called only in response to `Expose` events. It is used to draw the window for the first time, and to redraw the contents of areas exposed later.

Example 6-1. The draw_graphics routine

```
draw_graphics(win, gc, window_width, window_height)
Window win;
GC gc;
unsigned int window_width, window_height;
{
        int x, y;
        unsigned int width, height;

        height = window_height/2;
        width = 3 * window_width/4;
        x = window_width/2 - width/2;   /* center */
        y = window_height/2 - height/2;
        XDrawRectangle(display, win, gc, x, y, width, height);
}
```

The calling routine gets the `window_width` and `window_height` arguments from `ConfigureNotify` events because the window being drawn into is a top-level window which might get resized by the window manager. Routines to draw into descendents of the top-level window may also require size arguments if the sizes of the windows will be adjusted in response to a resized top-level window.

6.1.3 The draw_box Routine

The `draw_box` routine shown in Example 6-2 creates a GC and draws a box. It uses a different technique for creating the GC and raises some interesting issues since it draws on the root window. It is called from the simple window manager program *winman* described in Chapter 14, *Window Management*. Its purpose is to draw an outline of a window. The program also calls this routine to erase the box and to redraw the box to show the current position or size of a window as it is moved.

Example 6-2. The draw_box routine

```
Display *display;
int screen;

draw_box(gcontext, x, y, width, height)
GC gcontext;
int x, y,
unsigned int width, height;
{
    /* set foreground pixel value - default may be white on white */
    XSetForeground(display, gcontext, BlackPixel(display,screen));

    /* drawing on root window - through all windows */
    XSetSubwindowMode(display, gcontext, IncludeInferiors);

    /* Logical function is XOR, so that double drawing erases box
     * on both color and monochrome screens. */
    XSetFunction(display, gcontext, GXxor);

    XDrawRectangle(display, RootWindow(display,screen), gcontext, x,
            y, width, height);
}
```

This routine uses a couple of tricks that need explanation. Notice that the GC is created with its default values and then three elements of the GC are changed, and that the drawing request draws on the root window. Since the box may be moved anywhere on the screen during a move operation (by the window manager), the box must be drawn on the root window. We set the foreground color to black so that the box will be visible over the default backgrounds of most windows (white). By default, the `subwindow_mode` member is set to `ClipByChildren`, specifying that graphics drawn to a window do not show through child windows. Because we want the entire box to be visible anywhere on the screen, we set the `subwindow_mode` to `IncludeInferiors`.

We are using a logical operation of `GXxor` so that the box can be drawn again to erase itself. This logical operation has the unique feature of returning the pixels to their original state in monochrome or color if the box is drawn twice, as long as none of the pixels were changed between the first and second drawings. To make sure nothing else is drawn in between, the program that calls `draw_box` grabs the server for the brief period of the window manipulation. Avoid grabbing the server unless absolutely necessary. This process is described further in Chapter 14, *Window Management*.

Drawing

6.1.4 Filling

The XFillRectangle, XFillRectangles, XFillArc, XFillArcs, and XFill-Polygon commands act much like the drawing routines described at the start of Section 6.1 except that they fill an area instead of drawing the outline.

To be more precise, the filling and drawing versions of the rectangle routines don't draw even the same outline if given the same arguments. The routine that fills a rectangle draws an outline one pixel shorter in width and height than the routine that just draws the outline, as shown in Figure 6-2. It is easy to adjust the arguments for the rectangle calls so that one draws the outline and another fills a completely different set of interior pixels. Simply add 1 to *x* and *y* and subtract 1 from *width* and *height*. In the case of arcs, however, this is a much more difficult proposition (probably impossible in a portable fashion).

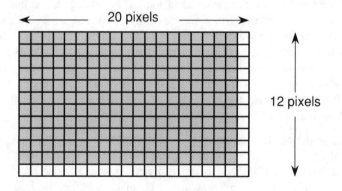

XDrawRectangle(display, drawable, gc, 0, 0, 19, 11);

← 20 pixels →

12 pixels

XFillRectangle(display, drawable, gc, 0, 0, 19, 11);

← 20 pixels →

12 pixels

Figure 6-2. The pixels affected by XFillRectangle vs. XDrawRectangle with the same arguments

The XFillPolygon routine is somewhat different from the other filling routines, since there is no directly analogous routine that draws a polygon with lines (though XDraw-Lines can be used to draw a closed polygon). Like the other routines, XFillPolygon uses an array of points to specify the nodes to be connected, but it connects the first and last points to form a closed figure, and then fills the resulting shape. The shape flag (which can be one of the symbols Complex, Convex, or Nonconvex) is a hint that may enable the server to improve the performance of the filling operation. The mode argument indicates whether the coordinates of the vertices are interpreted relative to the origin of the drawable or relative to the previous point.

The fill_rule member of the GC controls how complex, self-intersecting polygons are filled. The WindingRule setting of the fill_rule specifies that areas that are overlapped by two areas of the same polygon are filled. With EvenOddRule, overlapping areas are not filled. See Section 5.6.5 for more information.

6.1.5 Creating a Tile or Stipple

Tile and stipple patterns can be included in a program at compile time, or read in at run time if the user needs to be able to change the bitmap between invocations of the client. Normally the data is in the form of a bitmap, and if a tile (with depth greater than 1) is needed, the program then specifies the foreground and background pixel values in a call to the XCreatePixmapFromBitmapData routine described in Section 6.5. In Release 1, XCreatePixmapFromBitmapData was not available.

Example 6-3 shows two subroutines, one that creates a stipple from included data, and the other that reads the bitmap data from a file.

Example 6-3. Creating a stipple from included data

```
#define name_width 16
#define name_height 16
#define name_x_hot 8
#define name_y_hot 8
static char name_bits[] = {
    0xf81f, 0xe3c7, 0xcff3, 0x9ff9,
    0xbffd, 0x33cc, 0x7ffe, 0x7ffe,
    0x7e7e, 0x7ffe, 0x37ec, 0xbbdd,
    0x9c39, 0xcff3, 0xe3c7, 0xf81f };


void main(argc, argv)
int argc;
char **argv;
{
    .
    .
    .

    Pixmap stipple;
    unsigned int stip_width, stip_height;
    char *filename = "bitmaps/icon_bitmap";
```

Drawing

Example 6-3. Creating a stipple from included data (continued)

```
        if (create_included_stipple(&stipple, &stip_width,
                &stip_height) == False)
        fprintf(stderr, "basic: couldn't create included bitmap\n");
        printf("stipple is %dx%d\n", stip_width, stip_height);
        if (create_read_stipple(&stipple, filename, &stip_width,
                &stip_height) ! = BitmapSuccess)
        fprintf(stderr, "basic: can't read bitmap\n");
        printf("stipple is %dx%d\n", stip_width, stip_height);
            .
            .
            .
}

create_included_stipple(stip, width, height)
Pixmap *stip; /* returned created stipple */
unsigned int *width, *height;  /* returned */
{
        if (*stip = XCreateBitmapFromData(display, RootWindow(display,
                screen), name_bits, name_width, name_height) == NULL)
            return(False);
        *width = name_width;
        *height = name_height;
        return(True);
}

create_read_stipple(stip, filename, width, height)
Pixmap *stip;  /* returned created stipple */
char *filename;
unsigned int *width, *height;  /* returned */
{
        int depth = 1;
        int value;
        int x_hot, y_hot;  /* don't care about these unless for cursor */

        value = XReadBitmapFile(display, RootWindow(display, screen),
                filename, width, height, stip, &x_hot, &y_hot);
        if (value == BitmapFileInvalid)
            fprintf(stderr, "Filename %s contains invalid bitmap data\n",
                    filename);
        else if (value == BitmapOpenFailed)
            fprintf(stderr, "Filename %s could not be opened\n",
                    filename);
        else if (value == BitmapNoMemory)
            fprintf(stderr, "Not enough memory to allocate pixmap\n");
        return(value);
        /* returns BitmapSuccess if everything worked */
}
```

6.1.6 Copying and Clearing Areas

XClearWindow clears an entire window. If the window has a background_pixmap attribute, then the window is redrawn with this tile. If the window has background_pixmap or background_pixel attribute None, then the contents of the window are not changed. No exposure events are generated by XClearWindow, since the usual intent of this command is to clear the window so that new graphics may be drawn, not to refresh the old contents (which would be the normal response to an exposure event). Conversely, XClearWindow is not needed to clear a window before redrawing it due to an Expose event, because the exposure processing automatically draws the exposed area with the background pixel value or pixmap.

XClearArea is like XClearWindow but acts on a particular area within a window defined by the call's x, y, height, and width arguments. If the height or width argument is 0 then some special rules take effect that clear an area to the right and/or the bottom of the window, as shown in Figure 6-3. If the width argument is 0, the left edge of the cleared area is x and the right edge is the right border of the window. If the height is 0, the top is y and the bottom is the bottom of the window. If both height and width are 0, then the area between x and y and the bottom and right sides of the window are cleared. The exposures argument indicates whether an Expose event is generated on the cleared area.

XCopyArea is used for many purposes, including copying off-screen pixmaps to the screen and copying one screen area to another. You need to specify the source and destination drawables, the upper-left corner of the source and destination locations, and the width and height of the area.

Areas of the source that are not visible, not preserved in the backing store, or outside the boundaries of the source drawable are not copied. If the destination has a background tile attribute other than None, the destination areas corresponding to the uncopyable areas of the source are filled or tiled according to the background attributes.

The operation of XCopyPlane is quite different from XCopyArea. A single plane of the source region is given "depth" by "coloring" it with the foreground and background pixel values from the GC, before being written into the destination drawable. In other words, set bits in the source plane are given the foreground pixel value in the destination drawable, while unset bits are given the background pixel value. Therefore, XCopyPlane is useful for translating a pixmap of depth 1 (a bitmap) into a pixmap of the same depth as a window where it can be displayed.

If the graphics_exposure member of the GC is True, then one or more Graphics-Expose events are generated on the destination region when part of the source region could not be copied, or a single NoExpose event is generated if all the source region could be copied. This is the case for both XCopyArea and XCopyPlane requests.

That is about all there is to say about simple drawing, filling, and copying. Now we'll move on to drawing text.

Drawing

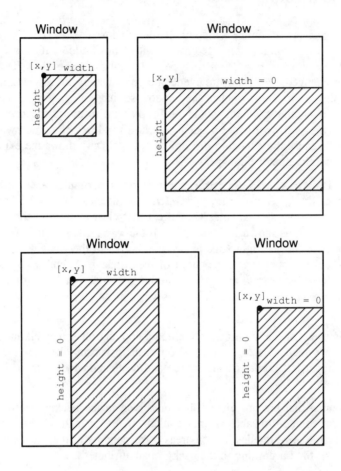

Figure 6-3. XClearArea — centered area cleared when width or height arguments are 0

6.2 Fonts and Text

A font in X is a set of bitmaps, and may represent text, a set of cursor shapes, or perhaps some other set of shapes for some other purpose.

The following sections describe the character format, loading fonts, character metrics, the XFontStruct and XCharStruct structures, placing text, font properties, and more.

6.2.1 Character Format

Every X function that draws text has two versions: one that handles single-byte (8-bit) fonts and one for two-byte (16-bit) fonts. The difference between these two is that a single-byte font is limited to 256 characters, while a two-byte font may have up to 256 rows each with 256 characters, a total of 65,536 characters. Large numbers of characters are necessary for Oriental languages.

On many servers, only single-byte fonts can be used with the routines whose names don't end in 16, and only two-byte fonts may be used with the routines that do end in 16. However, some servers may handle either type in either routine. At the moment, there is only one two-byte font on the standard X distribution, the Kanji font used by the *kterm* program, a terminal emulator for Japanese.

6.2.2 Loading Fonts

A font must be loaded before being used. If one or more clients are using the same font, they share the same copy in the server but each must request that the font be loaded, if only to get the font ID.

The available fonts are stored in a database that is accessible with the XListFonts and XListFontsWithInfo commands.

XListFonts lists the fonts that match the specified pattern (with wildcards) that are available on the current server. The list of font names generated by XListFonts can be freed when no longer needed using XFreeFontNames.

Once the desired font name is found, it can be used as a string in XLoadFont. Some fonts, such as "9x15," are almost always available and should not require a search through the list of fonts. The XLoadFont command loads a font and returns the font ID, which is used in all subsequent references to that font. The font ID is used in XSetFont to associate the font with a GC to be used in drawing text.

If the font is constant width, then it is ready for use as soon as it is loaded. If the font is proportionally spaced, and your program needs to calculate the extent of many strings in the same font, then you may want to get the table of the extents of the font characters and perform this calculation locally in order to save repeated round trip requests to the server. This information is stored in an XFontStruct, which is filled by calling the XQueryFont routine (that structure is described in Section 6.2.3.2). Both the XLoadFont and XQueryFont operations may be done together with XLoadQueryFont. If the font ID passed to the XQueryFont routines is of type GContext, the information about the font associated with the specified GC is returned.

The load_font routine shown in Example 6-4 is called in the *basicwin* program described in Chapter 3, *Basic Window Program*. It loads a font and gets the font information structure for later use in the routines that actually draw the text.

Drawing

Example 6-4. The load_font routine

```
load_font(font_info)
XFontStruct **font_info;
{
    char *fontname = "9x15";

    /* Access font */
    if ((*font_info = XLoadQueryFont(display,fontname)) == NULL)
    {
        (void) fprintf( stderr, "Basic: Cannot open 9x15 font\n");
        exit( -1 );
    }
}
```

In a more general client, the font name should be an argument to load_font and provision should be made to read it from the command line or user defaults.

XListFontsWithInfo returns a list of the loaded fonts matching a font name (with wildcards) and returns the information structure associated with each loaded font. The information returned is identical to that returned by XQueryFont except that per-character metrics are not returned. Only the maximum metrics over the entire font are returned. If XFontStruct.min_byte1 and XFontStruct.min_byte2 are 0, the font is a single-byte font.

XFreeFontInfo should be used to free the font information structure when the font is no longer needed but before the font is unloaded using XUnloadFont. XFreeFont combines XFreeFontInfo and XUnloadFont.

6.2.3 Character Metrics

Before going on to the structures that specify characters and fonts, we should go over some terminology. The measurements shown in Figure 6-4 are some of the *font metrics* that are the measurements in pixels that describe both a font as a whole and each character in the font. The names shown for the metrics are members of the font information structures.

Notice that the origin is not at the upper-left corner of each character, as in most of the rest of X. The origin of each character is on the *baseline*, which is a row of pixels somewhere near the lower middle of some characters. This part of X has been written to conform closely to the existing standards for fonts provided by companies like Adobe.

Notice that two structures are mentioned in Figure 6-4, XFontStruct and XCharStruct. XFontStruct holds information about the entire font, while XCharStruct (itself the type of several members of XFontStruct) holds information about a single character. These two structures have some common member names but their meanings are different.

There is a difference between the font ascent and descent members in XFontStruct and the ascent and descent members in each individual XCharStruct. The former specifies the largest of each measurement in any character in the font, and the latter specifies the measurements of single characters.

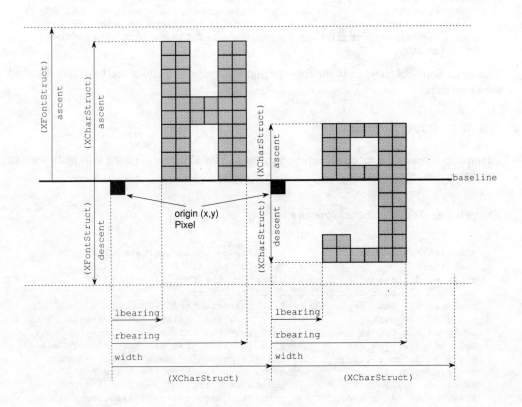

Figure 6-4. The metrics of two characters

Figure 6-4 assumes that the character bitmaps do not contain any padding zeros. If they do, then the bitmap dimensions above can extend beyond the visible glyph.

6.2.3.1 The XCharStruct Structure

One `XCharStruct` structure contains the metrics of a single character in a font. `XChar-Struct` is shown in Example 6-5. Refer back to Figure 6-4 for the meaning of each of its members.

Example 6-5. The XCharStruct structure

```
/*
 * per character font metric information.
 */
typedef struct {
    short lbearing;            /* origin to left edge of character */
    short rbearing;            /* origin to right edge of character */
```

Drawing

Example 6-5. The XCharStruct structure (continued)

```
    short width;               /* advance to next char's origin */
    short ascent;              /* baseline to top edge of raster */
    short descent;             /* baseline to bottom edge of raster */
    unsigned short attributes; /* per char flags (not predefined) */
} XCharStruct;
```

The `attributes` member is for font-specific information. It does not have any standard use or meaning.

6.2.3.2 The XFontStruct Structure

Example 6-6 shows the `XFontStruct` structure. This structure contains information about the font as a whole.

Example 6-6. The XFontStruct structure

```
typedef struct {
    XExtData *ext_data;        /* hook for extension to hang data */
    Font fid;                  /* font ID for this font */
    unsigned direction;        /* direction the font is painted */
    unsigned min_char_or_byte2; /* first character */
    unsigned max_char_or_byte2; /* last character */
    unsigned min_byte1;        /* first row that exists (for two-byte fonts) */
    unsigned max_byte1;        /* last row that exists (for two-byte fonts) */
    Bool all_chars_exist;      /* flag if all characters have nonzero size*/
    unsigned default_char;     /* char to print for undefined character */
    int n_properties;          /* how many properties there are */
    XFontProp *properties;     /* pointer to array of additional properties*/
    XCharStruct min_bounds;    /* minimum bounds over all existing char*/
    XCharStruct max_bounds;    /* maximum bounds over all existing char*/
    XCharStruct *per_char;     /* first_char to last_char information */
    int ascent;                /* max extent above baseline for spacing */
    int descent;               /* max descent below baseline for spacing */
} XFontStruct;
```

`XFontStruct` includes three members of type `XCharStruct`: one describes the smallest measurement for each character metric among all the characters in the font; one describes the largest; and one points to a list of structures, one for every character in the font. Note that the minimum character metrics do not describe the smallest character in the font, but the smallest of every measurement found anywhere in the font.

The following list describes in detail each member of the `XFontStruct` structure. Only font developers need to learn all these members. In general, an application programmer will use only the `ascent` and `descent` members and occasionally the `min_bounds`, `max_bounds`, `min_byte1`, and `min_byte2` members. These members are placed first so you can just scan the rest if you are interested. Refer back to Figure 6-4 for a visual representation of `ascent` and `descent`.

- The `min_bounds` and `max_bounds` are structures containing the minimum and maximum extents of the characters in the font, ignoring nonexistent characters. The bounding box of the font (the smallest rectangle that could contain any character bitmap in the font), by superimposing all of the characters at the same origin (specified by x, y), has its upper-left coordinate at:

```
[x + min_bounds.lbearing, y - max_bounds.ascent]
```

The bounding box's width is:

```
max_bounds.rbearing - min_bounds.lbearing
```

Its height is:

```
max_bounds.ascent + max_bounds.descent
```

- `ascent` is the logical extent of the font above the baseline, and is used for determining line spacing. Specific character bitmaps may extend beyond this ascent.

- `descent` is the logical extent of the font below the baseline, and is used for determining line spacing. Specific character bitmaps may extend beyond this descent. If the baseline is at absolute y-coordinate y, then the logical extent of the font is between the y-coordinates (`y - XFontStruct.ascent`) and (`y + XFontStruct.descent - 1`), inclusive.

- `direction` can be either `FontLeftToRight` or `FontRightToLeft`. This member is a hint about whether most `XCharStruct` members have a positive (`FontLeftToRight`) or a negative (`FontRightToLeft`) character-width metric, indicating the preferred direction of drawing the font.

- `min_byte1` and `max_byte1` are both 0 for single-byte fonts, since the second byte is not used. These members can be tested to see if a font is single- or two-byte. If single-byte, `min_char_or_byte2` specifies the index of the first member of the `per_char` array, and `max_char_or_byte2` specifies the index of the last member.

  `min_byte1` and `max_byte1` represent the first and last rows that exist in the font. There may be up to 256 rows in a font, but no normal font is likely to need all 256 rows (256 * 256 characters). For two-byte fonts, both `min_char_or_byte2` and `max_char_or_byte2` will be less than 256, and the two-byte character index values corresponding to `per_char` array member N (counting from 0) are:

$byte1 = N/D$ – `min_byte1`	/* row offset */
$byte2 = N\%D$ – `min_char_or_byte2`	/* column offset */

  where:

  D = number of characters per row
       (`max_char_or_byte2` - `min_char_or_byte2` + 1)
  $/$ = integer division
  $\%$ = integer modulus

- If the `per_char` pointer is `NULL`, then all glyphs (characters in the font) between the first and last character inclusive have the same extent and other information, as given by both `min_bounds` and `max_bounds`.

- If `all_chars_exist` is `True`, then all characters in the `per_char` array have nonzero bounding boxes.

Drawing

- `default_char` specifies the index that will be used when an undefined or nonexistent index is used. `default_char` is a single-byte character. For a font using two-byte matrix format, `default_char` has `byte1` in the most significant byte, and `byte2` in the least significant byte. If `default_char` itself specifies an undefined or nonexistent character, then no printing is performed for undefined or nonexistent index values.

The `XFontProp` member of `XFontStruct` is provided to allow additional properties (over and above the predefined properties) to be associated with a font. See Section 6.2.7 for a description of predefined and additional font properties.

6.2.4 Positioning of Text

All the routines that draw text require the same basic positioning techniques for positioning text on the screen.

Let's consider a string drawn with `XDrawImageString`. `XDrawImageString` draws the entire rectangle described by the `max_bounds` of the font, with the character drawn in the `foreground` pixel value and the rest drawn in the `background` pixel value (both from the GC). Figure 6-5 demonstrates the drawing of three strings. The origin of the baseline of each text line is specified in the `XDrawImageString` call. The offset of the first line of text in Figure 6-5 is (20 + ascent). Subsequent lines are placed (ascent + descent) below the origin of the first line. For routines other than `XDrawImage-String*`, these coordinates still position the background rectangle even though that rectangle is not drawn.

- If you want the upper-left corner of the background rectangle to be at pixel coordinate `(x,y)` then pass `(x, y+ascent)` as the baseline origin coordinates to the text routines. The ascent is the font ascent as given in `XFontStruct`.

- If you want the lower-left corner of the background rectangle to be at pixel coordinate `(x,y)` then pass `(x, y-descent+1)` as the baseline origin coordinates to the text routines. `descent` is the font descent as given in `XFontStruct`.

To position text vertically using the returned extents, normally you should use the font `ascent` and `descent` (rather than the string `ascent` and `descent`) if you will be drawing other strings that you want lined up. If you are seriously pressed for space, it is possible to save a few pixel rows with certain strings by using the string `ascent` and `descent` measurements.

It is important to find out how wide a given string is going to be in the chosen font. This width must be smaller than the width of the drawable if you want to be able to read the end of the text!

Listed below are several routines that return either a string width or its extent. Both types of routines return the width of the specified string in pixels. The routines that return an extent also provide vertical size information in the form of ascent and descent measurements for the particular string in question and for the font as a whole.

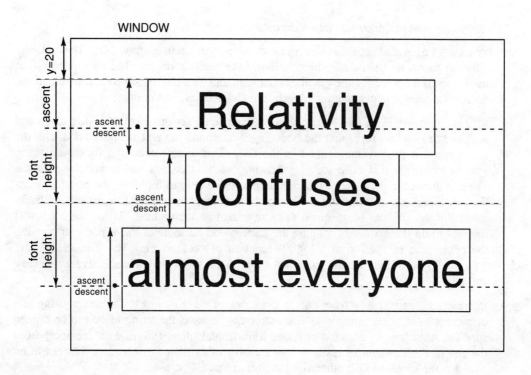

Figure 6-5. The vertical positioning of strings

- `XTextWidth` and `XTextWidth16` return the width in pixels of a string in a particular font.

- `XTextExtents` and `XTextExtents16` return string and font metrics, which include the width and height of the bounding box containing the string in the specified font. Use these routines if making repeated calls with the same `XFontStruct`.

- `XQueryTextExtents` and `XQueryTextExtents16` perform the same function as `XTextExtents` and `XTextExtents16` but they query the server instead of requiring a filled `XFontStruct` and performing the computation locally. Use these routines if you only need to calculate metrics once (or so) for a given font.

Whether you center, left justify, or right justify text is completely up to you. The only crucial test is to see that there is enough room for the height and width of the string at the chosen position.

6.2.5 Text-drawing Routines

The following routines draw text into a drawable:

- XDrawString and XDrawString16 draw a string into a drawable. They require only the string, its length, and the position of the baseline origin. The font in the GC is used both as a source for the graphics operation and as a clip mask, so that pixels in the destination drawable that are not in each font character are not drawn.

- XDrawImageString and XDrawImageString16 act just like XDrawString and XDrawString16 except that the bounding box around the text string is filled with the background pixel value defined in the GC. This avoids annoying flicker on many screens in clients that do a lot of redrawing, such as editors and terminal emulators. These routines are very useful when you need to be able to highlight the text for selections or to indicate that a menu choice has been made, because the foreground and background of the GC can be swapped to redraw the text highlighted. Using the other text routines to do this requires changing the background attribute of the window or copying the entire area to itself with a logical function of GXinvert. The function and fill_style in the GC are ignored for this request, but they are effectively GXcopy and FillSolid.

- XDrawText and XDrawText16 can draw one or more strings to the screen using one or more XTextItem structures. Each structure contains the string of text to be drawn, specifies what font to use, and provides a horizontal offset (the delta member) from the end of the last item of text. A font member other than None causes the font to be stored in the specified GC; otherwise the font in that GC is used.

  Accented or overstruck characters can be drawn in this manner. These functions can also be used to draw complex arrangements of text in one call instead of having to call XDrawString several times, changing the position, text, and font in between each call.

Example 6-7 displays the XTextItem structures used by XDrawText and XDraw-Text16.

Example 6-7. The XTextItem and XChar2b structures

```
typedef struct {
    char *chars;            /* pointer to string */
    int nchars;             /* number of characters */
    int delta;              /* delta between strings */
    Font font;              /* font to print it in, None don't change */
} XTextItem;

typedef struct {
    XChar2b *chars;         /* two-byte characters */
    int nchars;             /* number of characters */
    int delta;              /* delta between strings */
    Font font;              /* font to print it in, None don't change */
} XTextItem16;
```

Example 6-7. The XTextItem and XChar2b structures (continued)

```
typedef struct {          /* normal 16 bit characters are two-bytes */
    unsigned char byte1;
    unsigned char byte2;
} XChar2b;
```

The `font` member of `XTextItem` is stored in the GC for use in subsequent text requests.

A `delta` member specifies a change in horizontal position before the string is drawn. The delta is always added to the character origin and is not dependent on the draw direction of the font. For example, if `x = 40`, `y = 20`, and `items[0].delta = 8`, then the string specified by `items[0].chars` would be drawn starting at `x = 48`, `y = 20`. If `items[0].chars` pointed to two characters with a combined width of 16 pixels, the next delta, `items[1].delta`, would begin at `x = 64`. The next text item would begin at the end of this delta. The `delta` member can be used to backspace for overstriking characters.

6.2.6 The draw_text Routine

Example 6-8 shows the `draw_text` routine, called from the *basicwin* program described in Chapter 3, *Basic Window Program*. `draw_text` draws three strings in different locations in the window. It demonstrates how to calculate the vertical position of a string using the font ascent. In general there are three ways to set the `y` argument to a text-drawing routine to position text vertically:

- If you want the baseline (the first pixel in descent) to be at `y`, then pass `y` itself.

- If you want the upper-left corner of the string to be at `y`, then pass
  `(y + font_info->ascent)`.

- If you want the lower-left corner of the string to be at `y`, then pass
  `(y - font_info->descent + 1)`.

This example uses the second approach, setting `y` for the first line at:

```
20 + font_info->ascent,
```

and adding the font height:

```
font_info->ascent + font_info->descent
```

for each subsequent line.

Example 6-8. The draw_text routine

```
draw_text(win, gc, font_info, win_width, win_height)
Window win;
GC gc;
XFontStruct *font_info;
unsigned int win_width, win_height;
{
    int y = 20;   /* offset from corner of window*/
```

Drawing

Example 6-8. The draw_text routine (continued)

```
char *string1 = "Hi! I'm a window, who are you?";
char *string2 = "To terminate program; Press any key";
char *string3 = "or button while in this window.";
char *string4 = "Screen Dimensions:";
int len1, len2, len3, len4;
int width1, width2, width3;
char cd_height[50], cd_width[50], cd_depth[50];
int font_height;
int initial_y_offset, x_offset;

/* need length for both XTextWidth and XDrawString */
len1 = strlen(string1);
len2 = strlen(string2);
len3 = strlen(string3);

/* get string widths for centering */
width1 = XTextWidth(font_info, string1, len1);
width2 = XTextWidth(font_info, string2, len2);
width3 = XTextWidth(font_info, string3, len3);

/* output text, centered on each line */
XDrawString(display,win,gc,(win_width - width1)/2,y,string1,len1);
XDrawString(display,win,gc,(win_width - width2)/2,
        (int)(win_height - 35),string2,len2);
XDrawString(display,win,gc,(win_width - width3)/2,
        (int)(win_height - 15),string3,len3);

/* copy numbers into string variables */
(void) sprintf(cd_height, " Height - %d pixels",
        DisplayHeight(display,screen));
(void) sprintf(cd_width, " Width  - %d pixels",
        DisplayWidth(display,screen));
(void) sprintf(cd_depth, " Depth  - %d plane(s)",
        DefaultDepth(display, screen));

/* reuse these for same purpose */
len4 = strlen(string4);
len1 = strlen(cd_height);
len2 = strlen(cd_width);
len3 = strlen(cd_depth);

font_height = font_info->max_bounds.ascent +
        font_info->max_bounds.descent;

/* To center strings vertically, we place the first string
 * so that the top of it is two font_heights above the center
 * of the window.  Since the baseline of the string is what we
 * need to locate for XDrawString, and the baseline is one
 * font_info->max_bounds.ascent below the top of the chacter,
 * the final offset of the origin up from the center of the
 * window is one font_height + one descent. */

initial_y_offset = win_height/2 - font_height -
        font_info->max_bounds.descent;
x_offset = (int) win_width/4;
```

Example 6-8. The draw_text routine (continued)

```
    XDrawString(display, win, gc, x_offset, (int) initial_y_offset,
            string4,len4);

    XDrawString(display, win, gc, x_offset, (int) initial_y_offset +
            font_height,cd_height,len1);
    XDrawString(display, win, gc, x_offset, (int) initial_y_offset +
            2 * font_height,cd_width,len2);
    XDrawString(display, win, gc, x_offset, (int) initial_y_offset +
            3 * font_height,cd_depth,len3);
}
```

Note that this routine may be called repeatedly in response to `Expose` events. That's why the font is loaded, a GC is created, and its font member is set to the loaded font in separate routines before the event loop. The font information structure (containing the font ID) and GC resource ID are passed to `draw_text` as arguments.

6.2.7 Font Properties

A font is not guaranteed to have any properties. When possible, fonts should have at least the properties listed in Table 6-1. The property atoms shown in Table 6-1 can be found in *<X11/atom.h>*. `XGetFontProperty` returns the value of a property given the atom for that property. In the descriptions in Table 6-1, the data associated with a property is referred to with the same name as the property, but in mixed case. For example, the property atom `XA_SUPERSCRIPT_X` contains a value that is referred to as `SuperscriptX` in the description.

Applications that make heavy use of text may use these properties to space various characters properly.

Table 6-1. Font Properties

Property Name	Type	Description
XA_MIN_SPACE	unsigned int	The minimum interword spacing.
XA_NORM_SPACE	unsigned int	The normal interword spacing.
XA_MAX_SPACE	unsigned int	The maximum interword spacing.
XA_END_SPACE	unsigned int	The additional spacing at the end of sentences.
XA_SUPERSCRIPT_X	int	Offset (in pixels) from the character origin where superscripts should begin. If the origin is at [x,y], then superscripts should begin at [x + SuperscriptX, y - SuperscriptY].

Drawing

Table 6-1. Font Properties (continued)

Property Name	Type	Description
XA_SUPERSCRIPT_Y	int	Offset (in pixels) from the character origin where superscripts should begin. If the origin is at [x,y], then superscripts should begin at [x + SuperscriptX, y - SuperscriptY].
XA_SUBSCRIPT_X	int	Offset (in pixels) from the character where subscripts should begin. If the origin is at [x,y], then subscripts should begin at [x + SubscriptX, y + SubscriptY].
XA_SUBSCRIPT_Y	int	Offset (in pixels) from the character where subscripts should begin. If the origin is at [x,y], then subscripts should begin at [x + SubscriptX, y + SubscriptY].
XA_UNDERLINE_POSITION	int	Y offset (in pixels) from the baseline to the top of an underline. If the baseline is y-coordinate y, then the top of the underline is at [y + UnderlinePosition].
XA_UNDERLINE_THICKNESS	unsigned int	Thickness in pixels from the baseline to the top of an underline.
XA_STRIKEOUT_ASCENT	int	Vertical extents (in pixels) for boxing or voiding characters. If the baseline is at y-coordinate y, then the top of the strikeout box is at [y - StrikeoutAscent], and the height of the box is [StrikeoutAscent + StrikeoutDescent].
XA_STRIKEOUT_DESCENT	int	Vertical extents (in pixels) for boxing or voiding characters. If the baseline is at y-coordinate y, then the top of the strikeout box is at [y - StrikeoutAscent], and the height of the box is [StrikeoutAscent + StrikeoutDescent].
XA_ITALIC_ANGLE	int	The angle of the dominant staffs of characters in the font, in degrees scaled by sixty-four, relative to the three-o'clock position from the character origin, with positive indicating counterclockwise motion (as in XDrawArc).
XA_X_HEIGHT	int	"1 ex" as in TeX, but expressed in units of pixels. Often the height of lowercase *x*.
XA_QUAD_WIDTH	int	"1 em" as in TeX, but expressed in units of pixels. The width of an *m* in the current font and point size.

Table 6-1. Font Properties (continued)

Property Name	Type	Description
XA_WEIGHT	unsigned	The weight or boldness of the font, expressed as a value between 0 and 1000.
XA_POINT_SIZE	unsigned	The point size, expressed in tenths of a point, of this font at the ideal resolution. There are 72.27 points to the inch.
XA_RESOLUTION	unsigned	The number of pixels per point, expressed in hundredths, at which this font was created.

It is also possible for fonts to have properties not in this predefined list. If there are such properties, they will be stored in a list of XFontProp structures in the XFontStruct for the font. Example 6-9 shows the XFontProp structure.

Example 6-9. The additional Font property structure

```
/*
 * Additional properties to allow
 * arbitrary information with fonts.
 */
typedef struct {
    Atom name;
    unsigned long card32;
} XFontProp;
```

6.2.8 Setting the Font Path

XSetFontPath, XGetFontPath, and XFreeFontPath are available to set or get the current search path for fonts. These functions are very rarely needed but you should know that they exist. Their purpose is to allow for additional directories of fonts besides the default */usr/lib/X11/fonts*. The font path is common to all clients of the server, so it should be modified with care. If the directory that contains the standard fonts is removed from the path, neither any client nor the server can access fonts.

6.3 Regions

An X *region* is an arbitrary set of pixels on the screen. But usually, a region is either a rectangular area, several overlapping or adjacent rectangular areas, or a general polygon. Regions are chiefly used to set the clip_mask member of the GC. XSetRegion sets the clip_mask to a region so that output will occur only within the region. Using XSetRegion is a lot easier than defining a single-plane pixmap with the desired size and shape and then using that bitmap to set the clip_mask with XSetClipMask, and it is more flexible than the clip_mask you can set with XSetClipRectangles.

The most common use of setting the clip_mask to a region is to combine the rectangle from each of multiple Expose events and a single window into a single region and clip the redrawing to that region. This provides a performance improvement in some situations. See Section 3.2.13.1 for more information and an example.

A region has an x and y offset, which is used internally when making calculations with regions (offsets for all regions have a common origin). The offset has an effect if the region is used as a clip_mask. When making a graphics request with the clip_mask of the GC set with XSetRegion, the offset of the region is added to clip_x_origin and clip_y_origin to determine the placement of the region relative to the destination drawable.

Regions can be created with XCreateRegion or XPolygonRegion. XCreateRegion creates an empty region, which rectangles can be added to with XUnionRectWithRegion and various other functions that perform mathematical operations on regions. XCreateRegion and XPolygonRegion return a pointer to the opaque type Region, whose definition a program does not need to know. Just the pointer is used to refer to the region. XPolygonRegion creates a region of the same shape as XDrawLines would draw given the same arguments (except that XPolygonRegion does not require a drawable or a GC, and therefore interprets the lines as thin lines). It specifies a list of points, and has a flag that indicates whether areas overlapping an odd number of times should be included or not included in the region (like the fill_rule in the GC).

Internally, regions are used extensively throughout the server, and each region is implemented as a group of nonoverlapping rectangles. Therefore, performance will be best if the regions you use have sides parallel to the coordinate axes. Nonrectangular regions can be created with XPolygonRegion.

Empty regions are created with XCreateRegion, and are used with the following functions to store the results of operations on regions: XXorRegion, XUnionRegion, XSubtractRegion, XIntersectRegion, and in Release 2, XUnionRectWithRegion.

A region is destroyed with XDestroyRegion.

XClipBox returns the size and position of the smallest rectangle that completely encloses the given region. This function returns an XRectangle structure that contains the coordinates of the upper-left corner and the width and height of the rectangle enclosing a region.

6.3.1 Moving and Resizing Regions

XOffsetRegion changes the offset of the specified region by the number of pixels specified by its arguments *dx* and *dy*. XShrinkRegion reduces the size of the given region by the number of pixels specified by *dx* and *dy*, with positive values indicating that the region is to be increased in size. XShrinkRegion also modifies the offset of the region to keep the center of the region near its original position.

6.3.2 Computations with Regions

Several functions are available to combine two regions in various ways. Each function takes three regions as arguments: two operands and a region in which to place the result.

- XIntersectRegion computes the intersection (overlapping area) of two regions.

- XUnionRegion computes the union (total of both areas) of two regions.

- XSubtractRegion subtracts two regions. The result is the region listed first minus the intersection of the two regions.

- XXorRegion computes the difference between the union and the intersection of two regions.

- XUnionRectWithRegion computes the union of a rectangle and region and sets the region to the result.

6.3.3 Returning Region Information

This group of region functions makes logical determinations about regions. All of these routines return nonzero if their conditions are satisfied.

- XRectInRegion determines whether a given rectangle is completely inside, completely outside, or overlapping a given region.

- XEmptyRegion determines whether there is any area in the specified region.

- XEqualRegion determines whether two regions have the same offset, size, and shape.

- XPointInRegion determines whether a specified point resides in a region.

- XRectInRegion determines whether a rectangle specified by *x*, *y*, *width*, and *height* occurs in the specified region. It returns RectangleIn if the rectangle is completely inside the region, RectanglePart if the rectangle overlaps the edge of a region, and RectangleOut if the rectangle and the region are nonintersecting.

Drawing

6.4 Images

Xlib provides an image structure that is capable of storing all the data corresponding to a screen area or pixmap. Supported operations on this structure include creating and destroying the image, getting a pixel, storing a pixel, extracting a subimage of an image, and adding a constant to an image.

All of the image manipulation functions discussed in this section use the XImage data structure, shown in Example 6-10:

Example 6-10. The XImage structure

```
struct _XImage {
    int width, height;   /* size of image */
    int xoffset;         /* number of pixels offset in x direction */
    int format;          /* XYBitmap, XYPixmap, ZPixmap */
    char *data;          /* pointer to image data */
    int byte_order;      /* data byte order, LSBFirst, MSBFirst */
    int bitmap_unit;     /* quant. of scan line 8, 16, 32 */
    int bitmap_bit_order;/* LSBFirst, MSBFirst */
    int bitmap_pad;      /* 8, 16, 32 either XY or Z format */
    int depth;           /* depth of image */
    int bytes_per_line;  /* accelerator to next line */
    int bits_per_pixel;  /* bits per pixel (ZPixmap format) */
    unsigned long red_mask;      /* bits in z arrangement */
    unsigned long green_mask;
    unsigned long blue_mask;
    char *obdata;        /* hook for the object routines to hang on */
    struct funcs {       /* image manipulation routines */
        struct _XImage *(*create_image)();
        int (*destroy_image)();
        unsigned long (*get_pixel)();
        int (*put_pixel)();
        struct _XImage *(*sub_image)();
        int (*add_pixel)();
        } f;
} XImage;
```

The XImage structure describes an image as it exists in the client's memory. You may notice that several of these members match members of the Display and Screen structures, allowing the program to compare these values and convert images accordingly. When there are differences in byte_order and bitmap_unit between the image and the server, XPutImage (which places an image in a window or pixmap) makes the appropriate conversions. However, it does not convert images of different depths.

* The height, width, and xoffset are set when an image is created. The offset is used to align an image to even-addressable boundaries.

* The format member may be XYBitmap, XYPixmap, or ZPixmap.

    In XYBitmap, the bitmap is represented in scan line order, with each scan line made up of multiples of the bitmap_unit and padded with meaningless bits. Within each bitmap_unit the bit order depends on bitmap_bit_order.

In XYPixmap, each plane is represented as a bitmap, and the planes appear in most-significant to least-significant bit order, with no padding between planes.

In ZPixmap, the pixels (instead of bits) are listed in scan line order. Each pixel has bits_per_pixel bits, and the bits in the pixel that are allocated to red, green, and blue for DirectColor and TrueColor are specified by red_mask, blue_mask, and green_mask. See Chapter 7, *Color*, for more information. At the end of each scan line a pad is used as for XYBitmap.

- The byte_order is the data byte order, either LSBFirst or MSBFirst. The bitmap_bit_order is the bit order within each byte, again either LSBFirst or MSBFirst. The bitmap_unit specifies how many bits make up a unit of image data (usually the same as the word size), and it can be 8, 16, or 32. Together, these members determine the exact arrangement of bits in memory, as shown in Figure 6-6. VAXes use byte_order of LSBFirst while 68000-family systems use MSBFirst. The XImageByteOrder macro returns which byte order is used on the machine you are using.

- The bitmap_pad member can be 8, 16, or 32, and it specifies the quantum of the scan line. In other words, the start of one scan line and the start of the next are separated by an integer multiple of this number.

- The depth of an image is assigned as the image is created. The depth of a window from which image data is read must match this depth.

- The bytes_per_line member specifies how many bytes make up a scan line.

- The bits_per_pixel member is for ZPixmap images only. This member of the XImage structure must match the member of the same name in the ScreenFormat structure (itself a member of Display).

- The red_mask, green_mask, and blue_mask members are for ZPixmap only, and specify the number of bits in the pixel that are allocated to red, green, and blue. This implies that the visual is DirectColor or TrueColor. See Chapter 7, *Color*, for more information.

6.4.1 Manipulating Images

These are the available functions that operate on images:

- XCreateImage allocates enough memory for an XImage structure.

- XGetImage fills an XImage structure with data corresponding to a visible area of the screen or a pixmap.

- XPutImage dumps an XImage structure with data into an area of a window or a pixmap.

- XDestroyImage frees that storage.

- XGetPixel gets a single pixel value specified by an x,y location from an image.

Drawing

```
byte_order = LSBFirst, bitmap_bit_order = LSBFirst
    0  1  2  3  4  5  6  7  8  9 10 11 12 13 14 15 16      Pixel #
    0  1  2  3  4  5  6  7  8  9 10 11 12 13 14 15 16      Bit #
    0                             1                        Byte #

byte_order = LSBFirst, bitmap_bit_order = MSBFirst
   16 15 14 13 12 11 10 9  8  7  6  5  4  3  2  1  0       Pixel #
    0  1  2  3  4  5  6  7  8  9 10 11 12 13 14 15 16      Bit #
    0                             1                        Byte #

byte_order = MSBFirst, bitmap_bit_order = LSBFirst
   16 15 14 13 12 11 10 9  8  7  6  5  4  3  2  1  0       Pixel #
   16 15 14 13 12 11 10 9  8  7  6  5  4  3  2  1  0       Bit #
    0                      1                               Byte #

byte_order = MSBFirst, bitmap_bit_order = MSBFirst
    0  1  2  3  4  5  6  7  8  9 10 11 12 13 14 15 16      Pixel #
   16 15 14 13 12 11 10 9  8  7  6  5  4  3  2  1  0       Bit #
    0                      1                               Byte #
```

Figure 6-6. Bit and byte order for images, for bitmap_unit = 16

- XPutPixel puts a single pixel value into an image in a specified location.

- XAddPixel increments each pixel in a pixmap by a constant value.

- XSubImage creates a new image that is a subset of an existing one. It executes XCreateImage and then performs multiple executions of XGetPixel and XPut-Pixel, so it may be slow.

- XGetSubImage creates an image from a subsection of a drawable.

The functions to read and write images to and from disk files have not yet been defined by the X Consortium.

Example 6-11 demonstrates the use of images. See Volume Two, *Xlib Reference Manual*, for more information on the image-handling functions.

6.4.2 Examples Using Images

Images are one of the areas of X that has not yet been extensively used. Therefore, there are few examples available that use images to their potential. The unique feature of images is that all the data is stored and is directly accessible in Xlib, rather than in the server like Pixmap and Window resources. Since images completely represent a screen area, you can do anything you want to any of the pixel values in the image. Applications like image processing and machine vision would probably use images.

Example 6-11 shows a routine using images. This routine reads an image from the screen, manipulates it, and puts a reflected version of the contents in a new window of the same size. It uses XGetImage, XPutImage, and XPutPixel.

Example 6-11. Example using images — reflect_window

```
/* window and newwindow must have the same size and depth,
 * and window must be visible */
reflect_window (window, newwindow, gc, width, height)
Window window, newwindow;
GC gc;
unsigned int width, height;
{
XImage *xi;
unsigned long pixelvalue1, pixelvalue2;
int y;
int left_x, right_x;

xi = XGetImage(display, window, 0,0, width, height, AllPlanes, XYPixmap);
printf("calculating reflection -- this may take awhile...\n");

for (left_x=0 ; left_x<width/2 ; left_x++)
        {
        for (y=0 ; y<height ; y++)
                {
                pixelvalue1 = XGetPixel(xi, left_x, y);
                right_x = width - left_x;
                if (left_x != right_x)
                        {
                        pixelvalue2 = XGetPixel(xi, right_x, y);
                        XPutPixel(xi, left_x, y, pixelvalue2);
                        }
                XPutPixel(xi, right_x, y, pixelvalue1);
                }
        }
printf("putting image\n");
XPutImage(display, newwindow, gc, xi, 0, 0, 0, 0, width, height);
}
```

With sufficient understanding of the format of image data, this routine could be rewritten without XGetPixel and XPutPixel, which would speed it up substantially. However, there would have to be separate code for the three image formats to make the code as portable as the version shown.

6.5 Bitmap Handling

Bitmaps are used for creating icon patterns, cursors, and tiles. A bitmap may be created in two ways—by reading the data directly from a file or by including data in your program.

In the first method, you must have a bitmap file created with XWriteBitmapFile or the *bitmap* application. Then you create a single-plane Pixmap with XCreatePixmap, and call XReadBitmapFile to fill the Pixmap with the data from the file. Then if you want a pixmap with depth for the background of a window or for a tile, you can call XCreate-PixmapFromBitmapData.

Drawing

In the second method, you use an #include statement to read in a bitmap file created in X Version 10 or X Version 11 format, and then call XCreateBitmapFromData.

Both these methods are demonstrated in Section 6.1.5. The format for X Version 10 bitmap include files is shown in Example 6-12.

Example 6-12. X Version 10 bitmap file format

```
#define name_width 16
#define name_height 16
#define name_x_hot 8
#define name_y_hot 8
static short name_bits[] =
    {
    0xf81f, 0xe3c7, 0xcff3, 0x9ff9,
    0xbffd, 0x33cc, 0x7ffe, 0x7ffe,
    0x7e7e, 0x7ffe, 0x37ec, 0xbbdd,
    0x9c39, 0xcff3, 0xe3c7, 0xf81f
    };
```

The X Version 11 bitmap format (Example 6-13) is slightly different in that it uses the char type instead of short. XWriteBitmapFile always writes in X Version 11 format.

Example 6-13. X Version 11 bitmap file format

```
#define name_width 16
#define name_height 16
#define name_x_hot 8
#define name_y_hot 8
static char name_bits[] = {
    0xf8, 0x1f, 0xe3, 0xc7, 0xcf, 0xf3, 0x9f, 0xf9, 0xbf, 0xfd, 0x33, 0xcc,
    0x7f, 0xfe, 0x7f, 0xfe, 0x7e, 0x7e, 0x7f, 0xfe, 0x37, 0xec, 0xbb, 0xdd,
    0x9c, 0x39, 0xcf, 0xf3, 0xe3, 0xc7, 0xf8, 0x1f};
```

6.6 Cursors

The cursor is different from other types of output to the screen since it is transient, passing over the screen without permanently changing it. The cursor is drawn where the pointer is pointing and removed as soon as the pointer moves.

Each window can have a different cursor defined in its window attributes (using XDefine-Cursor). Whenever the pointer is in a visible window, the cursor is set to the cursor defined for that window. If no cursor was defined for that window, the cursor will be the one that was defined for the parent window unless otherwise specified in the attributes.

From X's perspective, a cursor consists of a cursor shape, mask, foreground and background colors, and *hotspot*:

• The cursor bitmap determines the shape of the cursor.

• The mask bitmap determines the pixels on the screen that will be modified by the cursor.

- The pixel values determine the foreground color (the 1 bits in the cursor bitmap) and the background color (the 0 bits in the cursor bitmap).

- The *hotspot* defines the point on the cursor that will be reported when a pointer event occurs. The hotspot is the actual tracking position—for example, the center for a crosshair cursor, or the point of an arrow.

There usually are limitations imposed by the hardware on cursors as to size, shape, and whether a mask is implemented. XQueryBestCursor is used to find out what sizes are possible.

You need to create a Cursor resource to call XDefineCursor. Read on for a description of the various ways to create cursors.

6.6.1 The Standard Cursor Font

Many popular cursor shapes are provided in the standard cursor font, *<X11/cursorfont.h>*. Each of these cursor shapes can be turned into a Cursor resource using XCreateFont-Cursor. Example 6-14 demonstrates this process.

The cursor font is shown in Volume Two, Appendix I, *The Cursor Font*, and on the reference page for XCreateFontCursor in Volume Two. Each of these cursors uses two characters in the cursor font. One determines the shape of the cursor, and the other is a mask which selects which pixels on the screen are disturbed by the cursor. You will notice that the mask for each standard cursor is very similar to the shape for that cursor, but one pixel wider in all directions. This means that when the cursor is black, and over a black background, this one pixel outline of the cursor will appear in white around the cursor, making the cursor visible over any background.

Example 6-14. Creating a Cursor from the standard cursor font

```
#include <X11/cursorfont.h>
int cursor_shape = XC_arrow;
Window window;
Cursor cursor;
cursor = XCreateFontCursor(display, cursor_shape);
XDefineCursor(display, window, cursor);
/* now cursor will appear when pointer is in window */
```

If your client is operating on a color screen and it allows the user to specify window background colors, it should allow the user to specify cursor colors, since otherwise there might be problems with lack of contrast between the window background and cursor. These pixel values may be specified in the calls to XCreatePixmapCursor and XCreateGlyph-Cursor, or XRecolorCursor may be called for an existing cursor.

XCreateGlyphCursor allows you to do the same thing as is done with the standard cursors, but using font characters you specify from any font. The hotspot of these cursors and those created by XCreateFontCursor is the origin of each font character (just as if it were text). Usually the hotspot is placed in a logical location, but it is not possible to determine where the hotspot is from within the program, or to change its location.

Drawing

XCreatePixmapCursor allows you to create a cursor from shape and mask pixmaps and foreground and background pixel values. XQueryBestCursor should be called to determine the allowed cursor sizes before preparing the pixmaps.

You can free the cursor with XFreeCursor right after the XDefineCursor call if no further explicit references to it are made.

6.6.2 Loading and Changing Cursors

The following routines are used to manipulate cursors:

XCreateFontCursor	creates a cursor from the font of standard cursors. This is the easiest way to create a cursor.
XCreateGlyphCursor	creates a cursor from a font character (glyph) and a mask.
XCreatePixmapCursor	creates a cursor from pixmap data.
XDefineCursor	associates a cursor with a window, so that the specified cursor is displayed in the window whenever the pointer is in the window.
XUndefineCursor	reverses XDefineCursor, so that the window uses the cursor assigned to its parent.
XFreeCursor	frees memory associated with a cursor.
XQueryBestCursor	returns the supported cursor sizes on the given display.
XRecolorCursor	changes the foreground and background color of a cursor.

See Volume Two, *Xlib Reference Manual*, for more information on these routines.

7
Color

This chapter describes how to use color in your programs. Color handling in X can be more complex than in other graphics systems because of the need for portability to many different types of displays. Certain advanced topics in color handling are still poorly defined in the X standard. This chapter starts with the basics, which everyone working with color should read, and gradually moves to more advanced topics. Pick and choose from the later sections as appropriate.

In This Chapter:

In This Chapter (continued):

A typical X application allows the user to specify colors for the background and border of each of its windows, colors for the cursor, and foreground and background colors to be set in GCs for drawing text and graphics. More complex applications (such as Computer Aided Design) might use color to distinguish physical or logical layers. Still more complex applications, such as imaging, might use fine gradations of color to represent real-world data. Yet in discussing window attributes, and how to set the foreground and background members of the GC, we have spoken only of pixel values.

How are these pixel values translated to colors? And how must an X client manage color if it is to run successfully on the wide variety of display hardware available in the X environment?

Because X must support a wide variety of systems with differing display hardware, the Xlib color-handling mechanisms are fairly complex. Even programmers who have previously written color graphics applications will find there are some new concepts to learn.

This chapter starts out by describing the different types of displays that an X application may run on, and the mechanisms Xlib provides for determining the display type. It then describes the simplest color-allocation mechanisms, which could be used by applications whose principal use of color is for decoration. It proceeds to discuss more complex color applications, and concludes with a section on writing applications that will be portable across different types of color and monochrome displays.

7.1 Basic Color Terms and Concepts

Most color displays on the market today are based on the RGB color model. Each pixel on the screen is actually made up of three phosphors: one red, one green, and one blue. Each of these three phosphors is sensitive to a separate electron beam. When all three phosphors are fully illuminated, the pixel appears white to the human eye. When all three are dark, the pixel appears black. When the illumination of each primary color varies, the three phosphors generate a subtractive color that might seem surprising. For example, equal portions of red and green, with no admixture of blue, make yellow.

You no doubt know that a color display uses multiple bits per pixel (also referred to as multiple planes) to specify colors. There is a type of display (which we'll discuss later) in which these bits are used directly to control the illumination of the red, green and blue phosphors that make up each pixel. Far more commonly, though, a *colormap* is used to translate each pixel's bit value into the visible colors you see on the screen.

A colormap is no more than a lookup table. Any given pixel value is used as an index into this table—for example, a pixel value of 16 will select the sixteenth element, or *colorcell*.

On the most common type of color system, each colorcell contains separate intensity values for each of the three primary colors. Depending on the display hardware, these values can be anywhere from 1 to 16 bits each, and are most commonly 8 bits each.

As shown in Figure 7-1, a pixel value uniquely identifies a particular colorcell. Each pixel value in the visible portions of a window is continuously read out of display memory and looked up in the colormap. The RGB values in the specified colorcell control the intensity of the three primary colors and thus determine the color that is displayed on the screen.

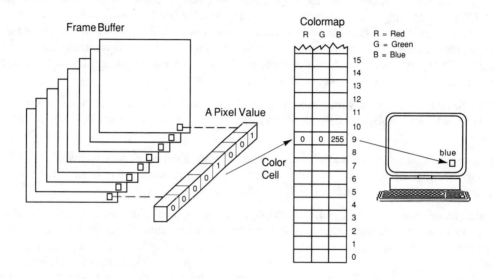

Figure 7-1. Pixel value to RGB mapping with the colormap on a color display

The range of colors possible on the display is a function of the number of bits available in the colormap for RGB specification. If eight bits is available for each primary, then the range of possible colors is 256^3 (about 16 million colors).

However, the number of different colors that can be displayed on the screen at any one time is a function of the number of planes. A four-plane system could index 2^4 colorcells (16 distinct colors); an eight-plane system could index 2^8 colorcells (256 distinct colors); and a 24-plane system could index 2^{24} colorcells (over 16 million distinct colors).

7.2 Differences in Display Hardware

The description of color mapping given in the previous section was actually somewhat over-simplified. There are significant differences in how the colormap is used on mid-range color displays, monochrome and gray-scale displays, and high performance color displays.

7.2.1 Mid-range Color Displays

The most common type of color display has between 4 and 8 planes, and uses the colormap indexing technique described above. This type of display is so widespread because it provides a flexible color system while being moderately priced. The mapping of pixel values to colorcells, with arbitrary RGB values stored in each colorcell, allows a very large gamut of possible colors, even though a more limited number can be shown on the screen at any one time.

If the colormap is predefined, and cannot be modified, this type of display is referred to as a *static color* display. Realistically, a static color display is unlikely to exist, since the main advantage of a read-only, predefined colormap is the predictability of the mapping between pixel values and colors, but displays with a relatively small number of simultaneous colors don't lend themselves to applications that use this mapping (such as 3-D rendering).

7.2.2 Monochrome and Gray Scale

Monochrome (black and white) displays have only a single plane of display memory. Each pixel is made up of a single phosphor, which can be either on or off.

Gray scale displays are sometimes used for publishing applications, since pixels made up of a single phosphor are smaller than those made up of three phosphors, and the resolution is therefore better. As shown in Figure 7-2, a gray scale display works by looking up the intensity of the pixel in the colormap, which for this display type contains only a single value. This controls the intensity of a single electron beam. Gray scale can be simulated on a color display by making the red, green, and blue values equal in a given colorcell to determine the brightness of gray pixels on the screen.

A gray scale display might have a read-only colormap, so that the gray levels in each cell could not be changed. A monochrome display is an example of this type; it is a single-plane display with a two-element colormap.

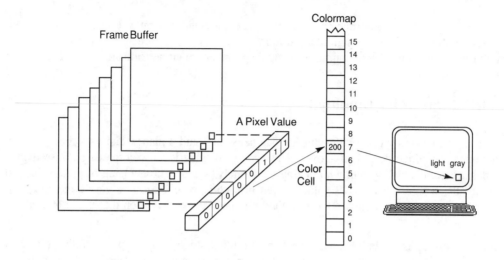

Figure 7-2. Pixel value to RGB mapping: gray scale and monochrome displays

7.2.3 High Performance Color Displays

As memory has become cheaper, and applications more advanced, workstations with up to 24 planes have become more common. With 24 bits per pixel, it is possible to display many more distinct colors at the same time. This makes it possible to do smooth shading and other applications that use a large number of closely-spaced colors.

The problem with so many planes is that a colormap of the style used in mid-range color displays would be impossibly large: it would contain over sixteen million entries. Instead, the available bits per pixel are broken down into three separate colormap indices, one for each primary color, as shown in Figure 7-3. This approach still allows the full range of colors to be generated, but makes the job of loading the colormap much more manageable.

In high-performance displays, having a read-only colormap makes just as much sense as having it read/write, because nearly every color imaginable can be simultaneously available. With a read-only colormap there is a fixed relationship between the pixel values used to select a color and the actual RGB values generated. This makes possible applications that want to calculate pixel values directly instead of having to calculate colors and then determine which pixel value represents that color as is necessary when the colormap is read/write.

In reality, most displays in this class let you use the color resources in either fashion. How this is done is our next topic.

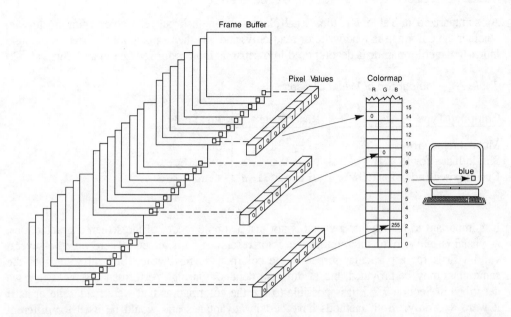

Figure 7-3. Pixel value to RGB mapping: high-performance color displays

7.2.4 How X Manages Different Display Types

X describes the color capabilities of the display hardware with a visual. A *visual* is actually a structure containing information about a way of using a particular display. A visual must be specified when creating a colormap or a window, and the same visual must be used in creating a window as was used to create the colormap to be used in that window. A window can inherit its parent's visual, and since the root window is created with a default visual, windows will often share this default visual. If you need to get the default visual, you can do so with the `DefaultVisual` macro.

The `Visual` structure is intended to be opaque; programs are not supposed to access its contents directly. The reason for this is so that Xlib's authors have the ability to change the structure without breaking existing clients. However, the procedure used to avoid accessing its members directly is cumbersome, and most programmers compromise by flagging their code where they break the rules so that if `Visual` ever does change, they will be able to fix the code quickly.

The members of the `Visual` structure that are important to understand are `map_entries` and `class`. The other members are only used in advanced color handling. The `map_entries` member specifies how many colorcells there are in a colormap created with this visual. On high-performance color screens with the colormap composed of separate maps for each primary color, `map_entries` is the largest of the three submaps. The `class` member contains a constant specifying one of six different visual classes,* corresponding to the different types of screen: `GrayScale`, `StaticGray`, `Pseudo-Color`, `StaticColor`, `DirectColor`, or `TrueColor`.

As summarized in Table 7-1, the visual classes distinguish between color or monochrome, whether the colormap is read/write or read-only, and whether a pixel value provides a single index to the colormap or is decomposed into separate indices for red, green and blue values.

Table 7-1. Comparison of Visual Classes

Colormap Type	Read/Write	Read-only
Monochrome/Gray	GrayScale	StaticGray
Single Index for RG&B	PseudoColor	StaticColor
Decomposed Index for RG&B	DirectColor	TrueColor

It is important to realize that a visual is not just a simple record of the screen characteristics. A visual is *one way* of interpreting the color resources on a screen. There may be several valid visuals for a particular screen if the colormap is read/write. Several visuals of the same class may be provided, but at different depths. On high-performance screens that we described in Section 7.2.3, it is possible to use the colormap as if it were read/write or as if it were read/only. Both methods have certain advantages and would be used for different applications. There would be a separate visual for each of these ways of using the display hardware. One of these visuals would be `TrueColor` and the other `DirectColor`. Some 24-plane displays allow the screen to be treated as two separate 12-plane `Pseudo-Color` visuals. (This allows for "double-buffering," a technique useful for animation, or for storing distance data to simplify hidden line and plane calculations in 3-D applications.) In fact, on some advanced workstations you can use a different visual in each window.

Figure 7-4 schematically represents the visual classes that can be supported by each type of display. A display that supports the `DirectColor` class can theoretically support any of the six visual classes. A `PseudoColor` display can support `PseudoColor`, `Static-Color`, `GrayScale`, or `StaticGray` visuals. A `GrayScale` display can support `GrayScale` or `StaticGray`. The three types of screen with read-only colormaps can only support visuals of their own class. But remember that just because a certain visual class can theoretically be supported by a certain display hardware doesn't mean that the server implementors will decide to support that class.

---

*Do not confuse *visual* class with *window* class. While both are represented in certain structures as the `class` member, and both are set when a window is created and cannot be changed, they are quite different. The window class is `InputOutput` or `InputOnly`. The visual class is only part of the overall visual, which is the way color is represented for a window.

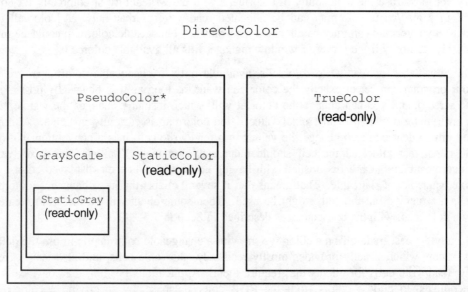

* `PseudoColor` can also mimic `DirectColor`, but only with a small number of colorcells.

Figure 7-4. Hierarchy of visual classes

7.2.5 Shareability vs. Changeability

Notice that `PseudoColor`, `DirectColor`, and `GrayScale` visuals have changeable colormaps, but `StaticColor`, `TrueColor`, and `StaticGray` have immutable colormaps. Within the changeable colormaps, it is possible to have both read-only and read/write colorcells, while in the immutable colormaps, you are limited to only read-only cells.

One advantage of immutable colormaps is that all the cells are read-only, and can be shared between clients, so all the cells are available to every client. Immutable colormaps make it possible to calculate pixel values from the colors desired, since the mapping between pixel values and colors is predictable. This technique is necessary for smooth shading and 3-D rendering algorithms. The disadvantage of immutable colormaps are that there may not be the exact color you desire (if there are a small number of planes), and you cannot change the colorcell to change the color of existing pixels on the screen. To change a color, you have to redraw the graphics with a new pixel value.

In general, the advantages of changeable colormaps are that you can have both private read/write cells and shareable read-only cells. That is why `PseudoColor` and `Direct-Color` are the most useful visuals, when a screen supports them. `PseudoColor` and `DirectColor` allow you to decide whether your client really needs read/write cells, or whether it can use read-only cells. Read-only usage is preferred since these cells can be shared by all clients, which means that the colormap is less likely to run out of free cells.

Try not to confuse the writeability of colormaps with the writeability of colorcells. A colorcell in a read/write colormap can be allocated read/write or read-only. A colorcell in a read-only colormap can only be allocated read-only. A changeable colormap could be made entirely read-only if the server or window manager fills all available colorcells.

The advantages of read/write colorcells, available only in changeable colormaps, are that your program can select exactly the color you want (as long as it is physically possible on the screen), and you can change the color at will, which instantly changes the visible color of everything drawn with that pixel value if the colormap is currently installed. Although any other client can also change the values in a read/write cell, it is a convention that only the client that allocated the cell should change its contents. You *own* that pixel value. Since most clients can't be satisfied with having no control over their displayed colors, this pixel value is not shareable. That means that if several clients that use changeable colormap cells are running, all the cells might be used. Then some client will be forced to create its own colormap, with the consequences described in Section 7.5.

Usually the best trade-off on a color system with a changeable colormap is to use the default colormap, which usually provides mostly read-only, shareable cells, and also leaves free a few read/write cells for clients that require them. Applications needing read-only cells are encouraged to choose colors from the RGB color database, by specifying a color name instead of RGB values. Using color names will maximize the chance of clients requesting the same RGB values. Otherwise, clients might waste cells by allocating very close, but not identical, RGB values for certain colors.

7.2.6 The Default Visual

A window is created with a certain visual, which cannot be changed. The root window is created with a default visual when the server initializes. All windows which inherit the visual from the root window will use the default visual; this includes all top-level windows created with `XCreateSimpleWindow`, and all top-level windows created with `XCreateWindow` using `CopyFromParent` for the *visual* argument. With `XCreateSimpleWindow`, the visual is automatically inherited from the parent. The default visual can also be specified for a window using `XCreateWindow` and specifying the `DefaultVisual` macro as the *visual* argument.

The default visual usually specifies the visual that the server implementors expect most of the clients running on their machine to want to use. Therefore, most programs should use it unless they have color needs that can't be satisfied by it. Programs that require only a small number of colors, and don't depend on the colors being exactly as specified can use the default visual.

On most color systems, the default visual is a `PseudoColor` visual. On black and white systems, the default visual class doesn't really matter, because the mere fact that there is only one display plane determines that a program should use only `BlackPixel` and `WhitePixel` for pixel values.

7.2.7 The Default Colormap

Some displays support multiple hardware colormaps. Most workstations support only one. In any case, X can manage multiple *virtual colormaps*. If the hardware colormap is read/write, then it is possible to swap virtual colormaps in and out of the hardware colormap.

A virtual colormap is created with a call to XCreateColormap. Like the call to create a window, this routine takes a visual as an argument. In order to be used with a window, a colormap must be created using the same visual as the window.

When the server initializes, it creates one virtual colormap called the default colormap, sets the colormap attribute of the root window, and installs this colormap.

Each window can have its own colormap as a window attribute (see Chapter 4, *Window Attributes*). Because the hardware colormap is a limited resource that must be shared by all clients, it should generally be left to the window manager to install colormaps (although we will tell you how to do this later in the chapter). Unless they have special color needs, clients should plan to use the default colormap.

Table 7-2 shows a typical visual type for the default colormap for each type of display hardware (color, gray scale, and monochrome) and for each type of hardware colormap (immutable or changeable). The default visual type for color servers varies widely. It is likely to be PseudoColor on 4-to-8-plane systems, and it could be TrueColor, DirectColor, or PseudoColor on high-performance systems.

Table 7-2. Visual Class of Default Colormaps for Various Servers

Hardware Colormap Type	Display Type		
	Color	Gray Scale	Monochrome
Changeable	varies	GrayScale	GrayScale
Immutable	StaticColor	StaticGray	StaticGray

The contents of the default colormap are server-dependent. For servers whose default visual is a PseudoColor visual, some of the colormap cells will be initially unallocated cells, and some will probably be read-only sharable cells. Someday, the default colormap may be allocated with the XA_RGB_DEFAULT_MAP standard colormap described in Section 7.6, but few if any servers or window managers do this today.

On an eight-plane color display, the default colormap would have read-only cells allocated with evenly distributed colors produced from any combination of six levels of red, six of green, and six of blue. This yields 216 colors that can be shared by all clients, and still leaves 40 colorcells to be allocated by clients as read/write, private cells.

Since the default colormap is of the same visual type as the root window, it can be used only in windows which have the same visual as the root window.

Monochrome clients should use the default colormap and select the pixel values returned by the `BlackPixel` and `WhitePixel` macros. They should not normally create windows with a `StaticGray` visual unless it is the default, because having multiple virtual colormaps would cause an installation problem on servers with a single hardware colormap.

7.3 Allocating Shared Colors

On `PseudoColor`, `DirectColor` and `GrayScale` displays, the colormap is read-write, and clients can store their own RGB values into colorcells, or even swap entire virtual colormaps in and out of the hardware colormap. Even when the colormap is read/write, though, the server or the window manager could load a default colormap with a reasonable distribution of predefined colors, leaving a percentage of the colorcells free for private color storage by clients that require exact colors. The default colormap is returned by the `Default-Colormap` macro.

Since free colorcells can quickly become a scarce resource when clients store private color values, simple clients that mainly use color for decoration are encouraged always to allocate from the pool of predefined colors.

A client attempting to allocate a shared, read-only colorcell doesn't *specify* a pixel value in order to draw in a given color. Instead, it requests a color, and is *returned* a pixel value that will point to the closest available color. Colors can be specified either as actual RGB values, or as names that will be looked up in a predefined color database. The returned pixel value can be used to set the `background_pixel` or `border_pixel` attribute of a window, or to set the `foreground` or `background` member of a GC, which are used by drawing requests. (See Chapter 4, *Window Attributes*, and Chapter 5, *The Graphics Context*, for more information.)

Read-only colorcells can be allocated with the following routines:

XAllocColor Returns the index of the colorcell (a pixel value) that contains the RGB values closest to those requested.

XAllocNamedColor
             Returns the index of the colorcell that contains the RGB values closest to those associated with a specified color name from the ASCII color name database.

XParseColor Parses either an ASCII color name or a hexadecimal color specification into RGB values that can be used with XAllocColor.

By convention, clients should allow users to specify colors from the command line or in the resource database, using either a color name or a hexadecimal specification. Since XAlloc-NamedColor can interpret only color names, the combination of XParseColor and XAllocColor is preferred for clients that allocate read/write cells (where sharing is not an issue). XParseColor parses both forms the user may specify.

If you want to find out about the composition of the default colormap before allocating colors, you can tell how many colorcells it has from the information in the Visual structure, or if you wish to respect that this is intended to be an opaque structure, using XGet-

VisualInfo or XMatchVisualInfo as described in Section 7.7.3. Using XQuery-
Color and XQueryColors you can find out what RGB values are in each colorcell. But
there is no way to determine whether a given cell is read-only or read/write, or how many
cells are currently unallocated.

Applications must allocate colors by trial and error. The routines that allocate colorcells all
have Status return values. If the call to allocate colorcells returns False, the client may
modify the arguments and try again. If repeated attempts fail, the client can settle with
BlackPixel and WhitePixel, or if these colors are inadequate, create a new virtual
colormap if the screen has changeable hardware colormap, or if not, decide that its color
needs can't be met and exit. For more information, see Section 7.7.

7.3.1 The XColor Structure

Both XAllocColor and XAllocNamedColor (as well as other functions that manipulate colorcells) take as an argument an XColor structure. This structure is used to specify
the desired RGB values, as well as to return the pixel value.

The XColor structure is shown in Example 7-1. The information it contains closely
matches the information in each cell of the colormap.

Example 7-1. The XColor structure

```
typedef struct {
    unsigned long pixel;        /* pixel value */
    unsigned short red, green, blue;    /* RGB values */
    char flags;                 /* DoRed, DoGreen, and/or DoBlue */
    char pad;                   /* unused; pads structure to
                                 * even word boundary */
} XColor;
```

The pixel member indicates which cell in the colormap is being set or is having its RGB
values queried. This member is used to set the pixel value in the GC or window attributes.

The red, green, and blue members are 16-bit values, even though many colormaps only
use eight bits to specify each primary color. The server will automatically scale the values.
Full brightness in a color would be a value of 65535, half-brightness would be 32767, and
off would be 0.

When allocating colors, the exact values requested and the closest available values are not
the same in most cases, because there would have to be 65535 [3] different colormap entries to
cover every possible triple of red, green, and blue. Even in more reasonable cases, many of
the nonshared colormap entries will have been taken by other programs. This means that a
client that requires precise colors should check the returned RGB values to make sure the
values meet its specifications.

The flags member of the XColor structure is a bitwise OR of the symbols DoRed, Do-
Green, and DoBlue. These flags are used to specify which of the red, green, and blue
values should be read while changing the RGB values in a read/write colorcell.

7.3.2 The Color Name Database

In order to simplify color specification and to promote sharing of colors, X provides an ASCII color name database. By using names from this database, you are reasonably sure of getting a color close to the one you request. Server implementors will change the RGB values corresponding to each color name to make sure that the appropriate color appears on their screen. If they haven't done this, the colors that appear may be off.

It is also important to note that the color names are not specified by the X11 protocol or Xlib. Therefore, server implementors may change them, but more often they will simply add to the list. (Note that some servers allow users to customize this file. For more information, see Volume Three, *X Window System User's Guide*.)

Table 7-3 shows the color names and corresponding RGB values in the default color database. The text version of this database in the standard distribution on a UNIX system is in the file */usr/lib/X11/rgb.txt*. The location of this file may vary.

The color names in the color database are strings in which each character uses the ISO Latin-1 encoding. The ISO (International Standards Organization) encoding is used by virtually all workstations manufacturers. What this means is that the first 127 character codes correspond to 7-bit ASCII, and are the normal English characters that appear on U.S. keyboards. But ISO characters are 8-bit, and the characters from 128 to 255 are used for characters with accents and other variations, necessary for other western languages.

Server vendors should be able to supply a color database file for each foreign language. The RGB values would be the same, but the names would be different. In the English file, the entry for green is encoded with the ISO character codes 103 (g), 114 (r), 101 (e), 101 (e), 110 (n). In German, the same entry would be for *grün*, encoded with the ISO codes 103 (g), 114 (r), 252 (ü), 110 (n). In a workstation configured for German, this string will be just as easy to type as *green* is in English, because there will be a keyboard key for *ü*.

Note that keysyms also use the ISO Latin standard (see Chapter 8, *Events*). Therefore, should you need the code for any character, you can get it from the 8 least significant bits of the keysym value for that character, listed in *<X11/keysymdef.h>*.

Table 7-3. The Color Database

English Words	Red	Green	Blue	English Words	Red	Green	Blue
aquamarine	112	219	147	medium aquamarine	50	204	153
black	0	0	0	medium blue	50	50	204
blue	0	0	255	medium forest green	107	142	35
blue violet	159	95	159	medium goldenrod	234	234	173
brown	165	42	42	medium orchid	147	112	219
cadet blue	95	159	159	medium sea green	66	111	66
coral	255	127	0	medium slate blue	127	0	255
cornflower blue	66	66	111	medium spring green	127	255	0
cyan	0	255	255	medium turquoise	112	219	219
dark green	47	79	47	medium violet red	219	112	147
dark olive green	79	79	47	midnight blue	47	47	79
dark orchid	153	50	204	navy	35	35	142
dark slate blue	107	35	142	navy blue	35	35	142
dark slate gray	47	79	79	orange	204	50	50
dark slate grey	47	79	79	orange red	255	0	127
dark turquoise	112	147	219	orchid	219	112	219
dim gray	84	84	84	pale green	143	188	143
dim grey	84	84	84	pink	188	143	143
firebrick	142	35	35	plum	234	173	234
forest green	35	142	35	red	255	0	0
gold	204	127	50	salmon	111	66	66
goldenrod	219	219	112	sea green	35	142	107
gray	192	192	192	sienna	142	107	35
green	0	255	0	sky blue	50	153	204
green yellow	147	219	112	slate blue	0	127	255
grey	192	192	192	spring green	0	255	127
indian red	79	47	47	steel blue	35	107	142
khaki	159	159	95	tan	219	147	112
light blue	191	216	216	thistle	216	191	216
light gray	168	168	168	turquoise	173	234	234
light grey	168	168	168	violet	79	47	79
light steel blue	143	143	188	violet red	204	50	153
lime green	50	204	50	wheat	216	216	191
magenta	255	0	255	white	252	252	252
maroon	142	35	107	yellow	255	255	0
				yellow green	153	204	50

7.3.3 Hexadecimal Color Specification

It is also possible to specify colors using a hexadecimal string.

The hexadecimal form of color specification is necessary since you may want the user to be able to specify an exact color, not just the rough approximation allowed by an ASCII name. The hexadecimal specification must be in one of the following formats:

```
#RGB            (4 bits each of red, green, and blue)
#RRGGBB         (8 bits each of red, green, and blue)
#RRRGGGBBB      (12 bits each of red, green, and blue)
#RRRRGGGGBBBB   (16 bits each of red, green, and blue)
```

Each of the letters represents a hexadecimal digit. For example, #3a7 and #0003000a0007 are equivalent.

XParseColor returns a zero status if the color specification begins with # but does not match this form, or does not begin with # and cannot be found in the color database.

7.3.4 Code to Allocate Standard Colors

Example 7-2 shows code to allocate a color using a name from the ASCII color name database. The same calls would be used to parse a hexadecimal color string. (Pink could be specified in the call to XParseColor as "#bc8f8f" instead of "pink".) Because simple allocation of colors should work on all types of color system, the program doesn't need to do any checking of the visual class. Instead, it simply needs to take into account the possibility that it might be running on a black-and-white system. It does this by testing the return values of the functions used to allocate colors, and if they fail, setting a flag that will cause the program to use the BlackPixel and WhitePixel macros instead.

Example 7-2. Allocating a read-only colorcell

```c
#include <X11/Xlib.h>
#include <X11/Xutil.h>
#include <X11/Xos.h>
#include <stdio.h>

extern Display *display;
extern int screen;
extern unsigned long foreground_pixel, background_pixel, border_pixel;

#define MAX_COLORS 3

get_colors()
{
    int depth;
    Visual *visual;
    static char *name[] = {"Red", "Yellow", "Green"};
    XColor exact_def;
    Colormap cmap;
    int ncolors = MAX_COLORS;
    int colors[MAX_COLORS];
```

Example 7-2. Allocating a read-only colorcell (continued)

```
    int i;

    printf("in get colors\n");

    depth  = DisplayPlanes(display, screen);
    visual = DefaultVisual(display, screen);
    cmap   = DefaultColormap(display, screen);
    if (depth == 1)  {   /* one-plane monochrome */
        /* Use BlackPixel and WhitePixel only.
         * We must do this first if depth is 1, since
         * it may allocate colors succesfully but
         * the colors might all be black */;
        border_pixel = BlackPixel(display, screen);
        background_pixel = WhitePixel(display, screen);
        foreground_pixel = BlackPixel(display, screen);
        }
    else {
        for (i = 0; i < MAX_COLORS; i++) {
        printf("allocating %s\n", name[i]);
            if (!XParseColor (display, cmap, name[i], &exact_def)) {
                fprintf(stderr, "basic: color name %s not in \
                        database", name[i]);
                exit(0);
            }
            printf("The RGB values from the database are \
                    %d, %d, %d\n", exact_def.red,
                    exact_def.green, exact_def.blue);
            if (!XAllocColor(display, cmap, &exact_def)) {
                fprintf(stderr, "basic: all colorcells allocated \
                        and read/write\n");
                exit(0);
            }
            printf("The RGB values actually allocated are \
                    %d, %d, %d\n", exact_def.red,
                    exact_def.green, exact_def.blue);
            colors[i] = exact_def.pixel;
        }

        printf("basic: allocated %d read/write colorcells\n",
                ncolors);

        border_pixel = colors[0];
        background_pixel = colors[1];
        foreground_pixel = colors[2];
    }
}
```

7.3.5 Specifying Explicit RGB Values

If you are using read-only colorcells, you should most likely use XParseColor to convert
a color name or hexadecimal string to an RGB value. However, it is also possible to specify
the desired RGB values explicitly. Simply declare an XColor structure, and set its red,
green and blue members to the desired RGB values. Example 7-3 shows a brief code
fragment that demonstrates how to allocate a color using explicit RGB values:

Example 7-3. Explicit RGB specification

```
Display *display;
int screen;
Colormap colormap;
Window window;
XColor pink;

/* Open Display, etc. */

colormap = DefaultColormap (display, screen);

/* allocate using RGB values */
pink.red = 45000; pink.green = 65536; pink.blue = 65536;
if (XAllocColor (display, colormap, &pink) == 0)
    /* handle failure */

/* Now you can use pink.pixel as the value for a window
    background or border, or to set the foreground or
    background member of a GC  */
```

There are several ways of specifying an explicit RGB value. In Example 7-2, we use an
integral value. Table 7-4 shows four ways to specify pink as explicit individual RGB
values.

Table 7-4. Four ways to specify pink

	pink.red	pink.green	pink.blue
Integer	48128	36608	36608
Shifted Int	(188<<8)	(143<<8)	(143<<8)
Hexadecimal	0xbc00	0x8f00	0x8f00
Shifted Hex	(0xbc<<8)	(0x8f<<8)	(0x8f<<8)

As described in Section 7.3.3, there is also a combined hexadecimal format that can be used
to specify colors on the command line or in the user's resource database file. In this format,
pink would be #bc8f8f. And, as we have said, it is better to use color names when allocating read-only colorcells than to use any of these explicit RGB values.

7.3.6 Choosing Default Colors

Usually a client should allow the user to specify the preferred colors, either on the command line or in the resource database or both. The resource manager (described in Chapter 11, *Managing User Preferences*) can be used to merge these preferences with the defaults of the program. However, the client needs to have reasonable default colors in case the user doesn't specify any preferences.

Follow these guidelines for your application's default colors:*

• Use ASCII color names for read-only colorcells if possible, since this maximizes the chance of sharing cells.

• Use colors with large contributions from two or all three primary colors—they light the screen more brightly.

• Avoid shades of pure blue—the human eye is relatively insensitive to and unable to focus on images made of pure blue light. Mix blue shades with white (white contains equal parts of all three primary colors).

• Remember that some users are color-blind. Don't use the same intensity of green and red for "safe" and "danger"—use colors with differing intensity.

7.4 Storing Private Colors

On a system with a read/write colormap, a client that requires exact colors can allocate read/write cells and then store colors into them.

For read/write cells the steps of allocation and setting of colors are separate, since the colors may be changed at will. The colors in the allocated colorcells are not defined until they are stored.

XAllocColorCells at its simplest allows you to allocate read/write cells so you can change the RGB values dynamically. You specify as arguments *ncolors* and *nplanes* and it allocates *ncolors* ^{nplanes} pixel values. It returns the pixel values in two arrays, *pixels* and *plane_masks*, which you have to combine with OR in various permutations in order to calculate all the pixel values. To be more precise, each plane mask has one bit for GrayScale and PseudoColor, or three bits for DirectColor or TrueColor, and none of the masks have bits in common. The real reason for this style of arguments will become clear in Section 7.4.1. But to simply allocate just a few cells, you set the *ncolors* argument to the number of colorcells desired, and *nplanes* to 0, and all the pixel values you need will be returned in the *pixels* array. The RGB values of the allocated cells are set with XStoreColor, XStoreColors or XStoreNamedColor.

---

*Courtesy Oliver Jones, Apollo Computer.

XAllocColorPlanes, on the other hand, is only used when you want to be able to vary a primary color component of graphics already drawn without redrawing them. It allocates read/write cells, so that a preset number of bits are reserved for each primary color. Primarily for DirectColor, it also allows you to simulate a small DirectColor colormap on a PseudoColor visual, but uses up colorcells quickly. It treats the colormap as three separate lookup tables, allocating $ncolors * 2^{nreds}$ entries in the red lookup table, $ncolors * 2^{ngreens}$ entries in the green lookup table, and $ncolors * 2^{nblues}$ entries in the blue lookup table.

The following routines are used to actually store colors into read/write colorcells once they are allocated:

XStoreColor

> Changes the read/write colormap cell corresponding to the specified pixel value to the hardware color that most closely matches the RGB values specified.* The flags Do-Red, DoGreen, and DoBlue in the XColor structure indicate which primary colors in the cell are to be changed.

XStoreColors

> Like XStoreColor, except it does multiple cells per call. Changes the read/write colormap cell corresponding to the specified pixel value to the hardware color that most closely matches the RGB values specified. The flags DoRed, DoGreen, and DoBlue in each XColor structure indicate which primary colors in each cell are to be changed.

XStoreNamedColor

> Performs the same function as StoreColor, except that it stores the RGB values associated with an ASCII color name in the RGB database. This call would be useful for loading a private colormap with each of the default named colors.

7.4.1 Allocating Read/Write Colorcells for Overlays

XAllocColorCells allows you to nondestructively overlay one set of graphics over another. The underlying graphics won't be visible, but they can be refreshed by simply setting or clearing one or more planes in the drawable. This technique can improve the performance of a client by reducing the amount of complicated graphics that have to be redrawn. It can be useful for highlighting text or graphics for selection.

The trick that allows drawing without destroying what is already drawn relies on the fact that we can draw in one plane of the drawable, changing the pixel values and therefore the color, without changing any another plane. It is these other planes that contain the information about the drawing that was already there. The disadvantage of this approach is that we have to allocate more colorcells than we would normally need in order to be able to save the

---

*Even when storing explicit RGB values, you may not get the precise color you specify. For example, if the hardware colormap only supports four bits of intensity in each primary, and you specify eight-bit values, the server will scale the values you provide to the closest possible equivalent on the hardware.

information already there. Some of the colorcells will need to be loaded with duplicate RGB values.

To illustrate this trick, we're going to draw in one color, with the background in a second color, and then draw something temporary over the top with a third color. To do this we need to allocate four colorcells with XAllocColorCells. The pixel values allocated will look something like this:

Color	Important Bits	Other bits
foreground:	----0--0-----------------------	*all other bits don't care*
background:	----0--1-----------------------	*all other bits don't care*
highlighting:	----1--0-----------------------	*all other bits don't care*
highlighting:	----1--1-----------------------	*all other bits don't care*

The bits indicated could have been any bits, but it is significant that only two bits distinguish the four pixel values. The first pixel value is used for the foreground, and the second for the background. We draw overlays in the third pixel value, that has a 0 for the bit that distinguishes foreground and background. Since we don't want to erase what was drawn in the foreground and background pixel values, we use a plane mask to restrict the drawing of the highlighting pixel value to a single plane, the one where bits in the highlighting pixel value are set to 1. When the entire plane indicated by the 1 in the third and fourth pixel values is cleared, anything drawn in the third pixel value disappears and anything that was drawn in the foreground or background will reappear. The color in the cell indicated by the fourth pixel value must be the same as the color of the third for the same color to appear regardless of the value of the bit set or not set in the foreground and background pixel values.

XAllocColorCells doesn't return these four pixel values directly. Instead, it returns the arrays *pixels* and *plane_masks* that are more convenient for actually using the overlays than a single array of pixel values. (Each of these arrays has the number of members that was specified in the *ncolors* and *nplanes* arguments.) Both arrays consist of unsigned long values like pixel values. One array contains the plane masks of the overlay planes, and the other contains the pixel values that can be used for drawing independent of the overlay planes. Here are the values in each array when we call XAllocColorCells with *ncolors* = 2 and *nplanes* = 1.

Array Members		Significant Bits	Remaining Bits
pixels[0]	=	-----0-0-----------------------	*all other bits don't care*
pixels[1]	=	-----0-1-----------------------	
plane_masks[0]	=	-----1-------------------------	*all other bits 0*

The two members of the *pixels* array are used for the foreground and background. The pixel values used for drawing in the highlighting color are composed by combining with a bitwise OR each item in the *pixels* array with each item in the *plane_masks* array. In this case, the highlighting pixel value is (pixels[0] | plane_mask[0]) and the overwriting pixel value is (pixels[1] | plane_mask[0]). When highlighting, the plane mask in the GC should be set to the OR of the members of *plane_masks* used to make the highlighting pixel value. In this simplest case, highlighting should be done with the plane mask set to plane_mask[0].

We have been hinting at the fact that this overlay technique can be used with more than two colors and more than one plane. *ncolors* specifies the number of colors than can be drawn in and preserved while drawing in the overlays. *nplanes* specifies how many separate overlays you may have, or how many bits of color are available in a single overlay. By ORing together each *pixels* with any combination of *plane_masks*, a total of *ncolors* $\ast$ $2^{nplanes}$ colorcells are allocated. Each plane mask has one bit for Gray-Scale and PseudoColor, or three bits for DirectColor or TrueColor, and none of the masks have bits in common. But remember that the chances of success in allocating the colorcells you request decreases rapidly as you request more colors and planes, not only because of the number of cells, but because of the special requirements for the significant bits in each cell.

XAllocColorCells takes a *contig* argument that specifies whether the planes returned in *plane_masks* must be contiguous. The *contig* argument is normally set to False, specifying that the allocated planes need not be contiguous, because then the chances of success of the XAllocColorCells call are greater. There are more likely to be a number of non-contiguous planes available than the same number of contiguous planes. The *contig* argument may have to be set to True for imaging applications that want to be able to perform mathematical operations on the pixel values. It is easier to perform operations by shifting bits with contiguous planes than to acheive the same effect with random planes.

Your code should always have a backup plan in case you can't get the overlay scheme you prefer. In most cases, the underlying graphics can be redrawn if the overlays that would preserve them cannot be allocated.

Example 7-4 demonstrates allocating the read-write cells for a single overlay plane. It allocates two *pixels* and one *plane_masks*, or in other words, four read/write colorcells. The third and fourth are both set to the highlighting color. If this overlay plan fails, it allocates three colors so that a highlight can still be implemented even though the underlying graphics will have to be redrawn. If the color allocation fails completely, it uses black and white, which can be highlighted using the GXxor logical function to invert the color.

Example 7-4. XAllocColorCells allocating read/write colorcells for overlay plane

```
#include <X11/Xlib.h>
#include <X11/Xutil.h>
#include <X11/Xos.h>
#include <stdio.h>

extern Display *display;
extern int screen;
extern unsigned long foreground, background_pixel;
extern unsigned long overlay_pixel_1, overlay_pixel_2;
extern int overlay_plane;

#define MAX_COLORS 3
```

```
#define MAX_PLANES 1
#define CANNOT_OVERLAY 0
#define CAN_OVERLAY 1

int
get_colors()
{
    int depth;
    static char *name[] = {"Red", "Yellow", "Green", "Green"};
    XColor exact_defs[MAX_COLORS];
    Colormap cmap;
    int ncolors = 4;
    int plane_masks[MAX_PLANES];
    int colors[MAX_COLORS];
    int i;

    depth = DisplayPlanes(display, screen);
    cmap   = DefaultColormap(display, screen);
    if (depth == 1)  {  /* one-plane monochrome */
        /* use BlackPixel and WhitePixel only */;
        background_pixel = WhitePixel(display, screen);
        foreground = BlackPixel(display, screen);
        printf("using black and white\n");
        return(CANNOT_OVERLAY);
    }
    else {
        /* allocate our colorcells */
        if (XAllocColorCells (display, cmap, False, plane_masks, 1,
                colors, 2) == 0) {
            /* Can't get enough read/write cells to overlay.
             * Try at least to get three colors. */
            if (XAllocColorCells (display, cmap, False, plane_masks,
                    0, colors, 3) == 0) {
                /* Can't even get that.  Give up and
                 * use black and white */
                background_pixel = WhitePixel(display, screen);
                foreground = BlackPixel(display, screen);
                printf("using black and white\n");
            }

            ncolors = 3;
            printf("got only three colors\n");
        }

        /* allocated colorcells succesfully,
         * now set their colors - three and four
         * are set to the same RGB values */
        for (i = 0; i < ncolors; i++)
        {
            if (!XParseColor (display, cmap, name[i],
                    &exact_defs[i])) {
                fprintf(stderr, "basic: color name %s not \
                        in database", name[i]);
                exit(0);
            }
```

```
                /* set pixel value in struct to the allocated one */
                exact_defs[i].pixel = colors[i];
        }
        printf("set RGB values\n");

        /* this sets the color of read/write cell */
        XStoreColors (display, cmap, exact_defs, ncolors);
        printf("stored colors\n");
        background_pixel = colors[0];
        foreground = colors[1];
        if (ncolors == 4) {
            overlay_pixel_1 = colors[0] | plane_masks[0];
            overlay_pixel_2 = colors[1] | plane_masks[0];
            overlay_plane = plane_masks[0];
            return(CAN_OVERLAY);
        }
        else {
            overlay_pixel_1 = colors[2];
            return(CANNOT_OVERLAY);
        }
    }
}
```

7.4.2 Using XAllocColorPlanes

XAllocColorPlanes is used when you want to be able to change the amount of a primary color in graphics without having to redraw them. In other words, perhaps you are looking at an image and would like to increase the redness of it. The best way to do this is to increase the amount of red in every pixel value. XAllocColorPlanes would be the way to allocate colors to allow this. It is rarely used except in imaging applications and 3-D graphics, and will rarely work except on 24-plane workstations.

Note that for applications like a paint mixing program, in which you have three bars for the three primary colors and a palette that shows the mixed color, you would not use XAlloc-ColorPlanes. The correct way to implement this is to allocate a single read/write color for the palette and to change it dynamically. (The primary colors should be allocated using read-only colors.)

The next piece of code, Example 7-5, is similar to Example 7-4, but it uses XAlloc-ColorPlanes. It is somewhat sketchy because real applications that use XAllocColor-Planes are complicated.

After allocating colors with XAllocColorPlanes, you can then use XStoreColors to set the colors (the other calls for setting colors set only one cell at a time). When *nred*, *ngreen*, and *nblue* are each 8, only one call to XAllocColorPlanes and one call to XStoreColors are necessary to allocate and set all 16 million colors of an entire 24-plane colormap.

Example 7-5. Using XAllocColorPlanes to allocate colorcells for DirectColor

```
#define PIXELS 256
Display *display;
int screen;
int contig = False;           /* non-contiguous planes */
unsigned long pixels[PIXELS];   /* return of pixel values */

/* number of independent pixel values allocate */
unsigned int ncolors = PIXELS;

XColor defs[2048]; /* PIXELS * 2^maxplanes where maxplanes
        * is the largest of nred, ngreen, and nblue */

/* number of planes to allocate for each primary */
unsigned int nreds = 3, ngreens = 3, nblues = 2;

/* returned masks, which bits of pixel value for each primary */
unsigned long red_mask, green_mask, blue_mask;

Colormap colormap;
Status status;

/* open display, etc. */
/* get or create large DirectColor colormap */

while (status = XAllocColorPlanes(display, colormap,
        contig, pixels, ncolors, nreds, ngreens, nblues,
        &red_mask, &green_mask, &blue_mask) == 0) {
    {
    /* Make contig False if it was True,
     * reduce value of ncolors,
     * reduce value of nreds, ngreens and/or nblues,
     * or try allocating new map,
     * break when you give up */
    break;
    }
if (status == 0)
    {
    fprintf(stderr, "%s: couldn't allocate requested colorcells",
            argv[0]);
    exit(-1);
    }

/* define desired colors in defs */

while (status = XStoreColors(display, colormap, defs,
        ncolors) == 0)
    {
    fprintf(stderr, "%s: can't store colors", argv[0]);
    /* try to fix problem here, exit or break */
    exit(-1);
    }

/* draw your shaded stuff! */
```

7.4.3 Highlighting in Monochrome

It is easy to highlight monochrome graphics. The simplest way is to set the GC to the GXxor logical function, and draw your graphics once to draw them, and again to undraw them. You must grab the server between the drawing and undrawing so that no other client change the same pixels in between. This can be made slightly more efficient on some servers by setting the foreground used in drawing to the exclusive OR of BlackPixel and WhitePixel, or by setting the logical function to GXinvert and using a plane mask which is the exclusive OR of WhitePixel and BlackPixel.

On a color screen, these techniques will draw in pixel values you didn't allocate, and therefore the color may not necessarily contrast against the background. A more controlled approach is called for. Probably it is best to allocate a read-only color to draw in, or highlight using overlays as described in Section 7.4.1.

7.5 Creating and Installing Colormaps

In discussing colormaps earlier in this chapter, we have sidestepped the distinction between *hardware colormaps* and *virtual colormaps*.

A hardware colormap is a physical register from which the display hardware reads the RGB intensity values that generate the colors on the screen. Most workstations have only one hardware colormap, in which case all windows on the screen are interpreted using the same colormap. Some high-performance workstations have multiple hardware colormaps, in which case separate windows may have their own independent colormaps.

If the hardware colormap cannot be changed, it is termed *immutable*. The StaticColor, TrueColor, and StaticGray visuals are the only visuals that can possibly work on systems that have immutable hardware colormaps. In immutable colormaps, no client can allocate private colorcells and all RGB values are preset.

Monochrome systems normally have an immutable colormap, since it does little good to swap the two entries or make them both black or white. Immutable colormaps are uncommon on color systems, but they might be present on some low-cost workstations.

On most color workstations, you can write new values into the hardware colormap or colormaps to change that mapping. These hardware colormaps are termed *changeable*. The PseudoColor, DirectColor, and GrayScale visuals have changeable colormaps.

If you can write into the hardware colormap, you can also copy an entire separate colormap into the hardware colormap. X manages multiple colormaps by keeping a copy of each colormap called a virtual colormap. X allows any virtual colormap to be modified by clients if the colormap has a visual that indicates it is writable. X copies these colormaps into the hardware colormap as needed and as instructed by the window manager or applications.

On the most common color workstations, with 4 to 8 planes, it is quite easy for clients that require precise colors to allocate all the available colorcells. Virtual colormaps are one response to the realization that the color needs of all the clients cannot always be satisfied.

When a client can't get the colorcells it needs from the installed colormap, it can create a new one.

Note, however, that hardware colormaps are a limited resource that must be shared by all the clients using a server. Particularly when there is only one hardware colormap, this resource must be carefully managed.

When a virtual colormap is installed and there is only one hardware colormap, any colormap that is currently installed in the hardware will be uninstalled (made virtual again), and the new colormap will be installed into the hardware. When the new colormap is installed, all the clients that used the old colormap will be displayed in false colors, since the pixel values in their windows will be interpreted according to the new colormap. This is true assuming that only one hardware colormap is allowed (on all but high-performance workstations).

The window manager should ideally have the responsibility to mediate the desires of all the different clients displaying on a screen that want to modify the colormap. Unfortunately, the initial crop of window managers (including *uwm*) don't do this, leading to an unfortunate catch-22 for current applications.*

By now you should be getting the idea that it is much better to arrange to share the default colormap with the other applications than to try to create one of your own. The only time when you should really need to create a special colormap is when you are doing smooth shading, or similar applications that need many, strangely distributed colors. But if you are doing that, you will probably be resigned to the fact that it will only run on a high-performance workstation. Since those often allow multiple hardware colormaps, you can create your own colormap and you may be able to install it without affecting other applications.

7.5.1 Functions for Manipulating Colormaps

The following functions should be used primarily by window managers, and by applications only if they need a special purpose colormap.

XCreateColormap
        Creates a virtual colormap resource, either with no allocated entries, or with all allocated writable, that matches the passed visual. If no entries are allocated, they can be allocated either as read/write or as read-only cells. If all entries are allocated writable, the colormap is completely private, does not need to be allocated, but just needs its colors set with XStoreColors.

---

*According to the current conventions for interclient communication, it is the window manager's responsibility to install and uninstall (at times of its choosing) the colormaps specified in the window attributes of the top-level windows. The colormaps specified in the window attributes of subwindows must be installed by the application itself, as described in the section regarding colormaps in Appendix F. Unfortunately, most current window managers don't install colormaps yet. While this is another incentive to use the default colormap that is usually installed anyway, your application may need to install its own colormap until better window managers become available.

`XInstallColormap`

A window manager function to install a colormap. Any window using that colormap ID as an attribute receives a `ColormapNotify` event. Only the default colormap is initially installed.

`XUninstallColormap`

Removes a virtual colormap from the set of installed hardware colormaps. Sends `ColormapNotify` event to windows that are using the specified map.

`XFreeColormap`

Uninstalls the specified virtual colormap and frees the resources associated with the colormap. Sends a `ColormapNotify` event to any windows that were using the colormap.

`XListInstalledColormaps`

Lists the installed colormaps.

`XCopyColormapAndFree`

Moves all the client's existing colormap entries to a new colormap and frees those entries of the old colormap. This is used when read/write colorcell allocation fails, either because all the cells in the old colormap are already in use, or because the number of planes requested were not available.

`XSetStandardColormap`

Creates a standard colormap, one of `XA_RGB_DEFAULT_MAP`, `XA_RGB_BEST_MAP`, `XA_RGB_RED_MAP`, `XA_RGB_GREEN_MAP`, `XA_RGB_BLUE_MAP`, or `XA_RGB_GRAY_MAP`. (See Section 7.6 for details.)

`XGetStandardColormap`

Gets a structure containing information about the standard colormap specified by a atom. Once this is done, you can find out what pixel values are represented by various RGB values. This call does not install the colormap.

`XSetWindowColormap`

Sets the colormap attribute of a window.

7.5.2 The ColormapNotify Event

`ColormapNotify` events herald changes relating to the colormap specified in the colormap attribute for a particular window, or changes to the attribute itself.

If your application might be adversely affected by changes to the colormap, you should watch for these events and act accordingly. To receive `ColormapNotify` events, pass `ColormapChangeMask` to `XSelectInput`. Example 7-6 shows the structure for the `XColormapEvent`.

Example 7-6. The ColormapEvent structure

```
typedef struct {
    int type;
    unsigned long serial;    /* # of last request processed by server */
```

Example 7-6. The ColormapEvent structure (continued)

```
    Bool send_event;      /* true if this came from SendEvent request */
    Display *display;     /* display the event was read from */
    Window window;
    Colormap colormap;    /* Colormap or None */
    Bool new;
    int state;            /* ColormapInstalled, ColormapUninstalled */
} XColormapEvent;
```

Here is a brief explanation of each member of the XColormapEvent structure:

window   The window this event was selected for, whose colormap attribute or colormap was changed.

colormap   The colormap associated with the window, either a colormap ID or the constant None. It will be None only if this event was in response to an XFreeColormap call.

new   True when the colormap attribute has been changed, or False when the colormap is installed or uninstalled.

state   Either ColormapInstalled or ColormapUninstalled; it indicates whether the colormap is installed or uninstalled.

XFreeColormap, XInstallColormap, and XUninstallColormap generate this event for windows that have their colormap attribute set to the colormap that was affected. From the information in the structure, you can tell which of these calls generated the event, and what the current status of the colormap is. The conventions for what the applications should do in response to each of these contingencies has not yet been determined. See Chapter 10, *Interclient Communication* and Appendix F, *Proposed Interclient Communication Conventions* for additional details.

7.5.3 The Required Colormap List

The X Protocol specifies that each server can specify a required list of colormaps, which affects what happens when other colormaps are installed or uninstalled. Here is what the Protocol specification says about the required list (translated into Xlib terms):

> At any time, there is a subset of the installed maps, viewed as an ordered list, called the required list. The length of the required list is at most min_maps, where min_maps is a member of the Display structure. The required list is maintained as follows. When a colormap is an explicit argument to XInstallColormap, it is added to the head of the list, and the list is truncated at the tail if necessary to keep the length of the list to at most min_maps. When a colormap is an explicit argument to XUninstallColormap and it is in the required list, it is removed from the list. A colormap is not added to the required list when it is installed implicitly by the server, and the server cannot implicitly uninstall a colormap that is in the required list.

In less precise words, the `min_maps` most recently installed maps are guaranteed to be installed. This number will often be one; clients needing multiple colormaps should beware.

7.6 The Standard Colormaps

X defines a set of standard colormap properties that refer to a set of commonly-used colormaps. Their purpose is to increase the sharing of color resources between applications. At this point, however, few if any servers or window managers create the standard colormaps, so it is unclear if or when standard colormaps will begin to play a major part in the design of color handling in applications. Applications that create their own colormaps should create standard colormaps if one exists that fit their needs. Then it is possible that other applications creating the same standard colormap could cooperate without the help of a window manager. If your application does not create or use a custom colormap, you can skip this section if pressed for time.

Even though they don't exist as predefined virtual colormaps, standard colormaps are useful, because applications that share these colormap conventions display true colors more often, especially on displays with severely limited hardware colormaps.

Applications can also use the knowledge about the structure of a standard colormap to optimize the process of figuring out which existing pixel values correspond to required colors, and which colors must be allocated and set from scratch. One of the standard colormaps is the default colormap.

7.6.1 The Standard Colormap Properties

This section describes the standard colormap properties. These colomaps may have been created by the server, or they may have to be created by the application. Either way, the application can get information about them by calling `XGetStandardColormap`. You specify an atom like `XA_RGB_BEST_MAP` and this function returns an `XStandard-Colormap` structure.

The following list names the atoms and describes the colormap associated with each one.

`XA_RGB_DEFAULT_MAP`
> This property defines part of the system default colormap, as described in Section 7.2.7. These colorcells are normally read-only and shareable. A typical allocation of the `XA_RGB_DEFAULT_MAP` on 8-plane displays is all the colors produced from any combination of 6 reds, 6 greens, and 6 blues. This gives 216 uniformly distributed colors, and leaves 40 for other programs or for special-purpose colors for text, borders, and so on. A typical allocation for the `XA_RGB_DEFAULT_MAP` on 24-plane displays is 64 reds, 64 greens, and 64 blues. This gives about one million uniformly distributed colors (64 intensities of 4096 different hues) and leaves lots of colorcells available for other purposes.

XA_RGB_BEST_MAP

This property defines the "best" RGB colormap available on the display. Of course, this is a subjective evaluation. Many image-processing and 3-D programs need to use all available colormap cells and to distribute as many perceptually distinct colors as possible over those cells. In this case there may be more green values available than red, and more green or red than blue.

On an 8-plane DirectColor visual, XA_RGB_BEST_MAP is a 3/3/2 allocation. On a 24-plane DirectColor visual, XA_RGB_BEST_MAP is an 8/8/8 allocation. On other displays, XA_RGB_BEST_MAP is purely up to the implementor of the display.

XA_RGB_RED_MAP
XA_RGB_GREEN_MAP
XA_RGB_BLUE_MAP

These properties define all-red, all-green, and all-blue colormaps, respectively. These maps are used by programs that make color-separated images. For example, a user might generate a full-color image on an 8-plane display by rendering an image once with high color resolution in red, once with green, and once with blue, and exposing a single frame in a camera with three images.

XA_RGB_GRAY_MAP

This property describes the "best" gray-scale colormap available on the display. As previously mentioned, only the colormap, red_max, red_mult, and base_pixel fields of the XStandardColormap structure are used for gray-scale colormaps.

7.6.2 The XStandardColormap Structure

An application that wants to use a standard colormap must get the structure that contains the specification for the colormap using XGetStandardColormap. Some servers, particularly on high-performance workstations, create some or all of the standard colormaps when they initialize. If the desired colormap has already been created, it is returned in the colormap member of the XStandardColormap structure shown in Example 7-7. If the colormap does not yet exist, the colormap member will be 0. In that case, the application can create a colormap and allocate entries to match the specification in the remaining members of XStandardColormap.

Example 7-7. The XStandardColormap structure

```
typedef struct _XStandardColormap {
    Colormap colormap;
    unsigned long red_max, green_max, blue_max;
    unsigned long red_mult, green_mult, blue_mult;
    unsigned long base_pixel;
} XStandardColormap;
```

The members of the XStandardColormap structure are as follows:

- The colormap member is the ID of a colormap created by the XCreateColormap function or the default colormap. This ID can be used to install a virtual colormap into the hardware colormap.

- The red_max, green_max, and blue_max fields give the maximum red, green, and blue values, respectively. A typical allocation that provides 6 * 6 * 6 = 216 read-only, shareable colors in a PseudoColor colormap on a standard 8-plane workstation is red_max = 5, green_max = 5, and blue_max = 5. This leaves 40 cells available for special colors and private, nonshareable purposes. On a 24-plane workstation, there would be 8 bits available for each color in a TrueColor visual, which would allow 256 shades of each primary color. In this case, red_max = 255, green_max = 255, and blue_max = 255. This map would include 256 x 256 x 256 = 16.38 million total colors.

- The red_mult, green_mult, and blue_mult fields scale each pixel subfield into the proper range in the 16-bit RGB value in the colorcell with the range 0 to 65535. The red pixel subfield is moved red_mult bits toward the most significant bit of the pixel value.

  For a 3/3/2 DirectColor allocation (8 reds, 8 greens, 4 blues), red_mult might be 32, green_mult might be 4, and blue_mult might be 1. These effectively move the red value into the most significant bits of the RGB value in the colorcell, the green into the middle, and the blue into the least significant bits. This arrangement is arbitrary but useful. For a 6-colors-each allocation, which must be PseudoColor since the planes can't be evenly allocated to separate primaries, red_mult might be 36, green_mult might be 6, and blue_mult might be 1.

- The base_pixel field gives the base value that is added to the pixel value calculated from the RGB values and scale factors. Usually, the base_pixel is obtained from a call to the XAllocColorPlanes function.

7.6.3 The 3/3/2 Standard Colormap

Now let's look at a typical standard colormap. The following example describes the 3/3/2 DirectColor standard colormap used on eight-plane displays. Three planes are used for red, three planes for green, and two planes for blue. This 3/3/2 allocation allows values in the range of:

```
red      0-7   thus   red_max    = 7
green    0-7          green_max  = 7
blue     0-3          blue_max   = 3
```

To obtain the pixel value, these RGB values must be shifted to their corresponding planes. If the red value is contained in the three most significant planes or bits, the green values in the three next most significant planes or bits, and the blue value in the two least significant planes or bits, then the pixel can be constructed as shown in Figure 7-5.

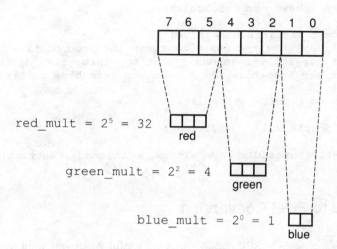

red_mult = 2^5 = 32

green_mult = 2^2 = 4

blue_mult = 2^0 = 1

Figure 7-5. Shifting pixel subfields into pixel value

In a `DirectColor` system like this, the multiples are equal to 2^n, where n is their lowest plane or bit position. If the red, green, and blue were stored in a different order, the multiples would not be 32, 4, 1, but would still be calculated from the above description and formula. The 3/3/2 standard colormap allocation is fairly standard.

7.6.4 Installing a Standard Colormap

Example 7-8 installs the XA_RGB_BEST_MAP standard colormap. This example assumes a `PseudoColor` visual, but you should check the visual class of the root window to be sure.

Example 7-8. Code to install and use XA_RGB_BEST_MAP

```
Display *display;
int screen;
XStandardColormap best_map_info;    /* structure to fill */
unsigned long whitepixel;       /* computed pixel value for white */
Colormap colormap;
Window window;
Status status;
XSetWindowAttributes attrib;            /* so we can set colormap */
unsigned long attribmask;

/* Open Display, etc. */

if (status = XGetStandardColormap(display, RootWindow(display,
        screen), &best_map_info, XA_RGB_BEST_MAP) == 0);
    printf("%s: can't get standard colormap", argv[0]);
```

Example 7-8. Code to install and use XA_RGB_BEST_MAP (continued)

```
attrib.colormap = best_map_info.colormap;

whitepixel = best_map_info.base_pixel   +
        (best_map_info.red_max * best_map_info.red_mult) +
        (best_map_info.green_max * best_map_info.green_mult) +
        (best_map_info.blue_max * best_map_info.blue_mult);

attrib.background_pixel = whitepixel;

attribmask = CWBackPixel | CWColormap;

XChangeWindowAttributes(display, window, attribmask, &attrib);
```

7.6.5 Examples of RGB to Pixel Conversion

The standard colormaps such as XA_RGB_BEST_MAP are useful when you want to calculate pixel values from RGB values.

Consider a 3-D display program that draws a smoothly shaded sphere. At each pixel in the image of the sphere, the program computes the intensity and color of light reflected to the viewer. The result of each computation is a triple of red, green, and blue coefficients in the range 0.0 to 1.0. To draw the sphere, the program needs a colormap that provides a large range of uniformly distributed colors. The colormap must be arranged so that the program can convert its RGB triples into pixel values very quickly, because drawing the entire sphere will require many such conversions. An example of one such calculation is shown in Example 7-9.

Example 7-9. Calculating pixel values from floating point RGB values

```
XStandardColormap best_map_info;
float red, green, blue;
unsigned long pixelvalue;
int status;

status = XGetStandardColormap(display, RootWindow(display,
    screen), &best_map_info, XA_RGB_BEST_MAP);

if (!status)
    {
    printf("%s: specified standard colormap not available", argv[0]);
    exit(-1);
    }

pixelvalue = best_map_info.base_pixel +
    ((unsigned long)(0.5 + (red * best_map_info.red_max)) *
        best_map_info.red_mult) +
    ((unsigned long)(0.5 + (green * best_map_info.green_max)) *
        best_map_info.green_mult) +
```

Example 7-9. Calculating pixel values from floating point RGB values (continued)

```
((unsigned long) (0.5 + (blue * best_map_info.blue_max)) *
       best_map_info.blue_mult);
```

Example 7-9 demonstrated how to translate colors represented by real numbers between zero and one. The next example, Example 7-10, demonstrates how to do it for integer primary colors.

Example 7-10. Calculating pixel values from integer RGB values

```
XStandardColormap best_map_info;
unsigned long red, green, blue;
unsigned long pixelvalue;
int status;

status = XGetStandardColormap(display, RootWindow(display,
     screen), &best_map_info, XA_RGB_BEST_MAP);

if (!status)
     {
     printf("%s: specified standard colormap not available",
            argv[0]);
     exit(-1);
     }

pixelvalue = best_map_info.base_pixel +
         (red * best_map_info.red_mult) +
         (green * best_map_info.green_mult) +
         (blue * best_map_info.blue_mult);
```

For gray scale colormaps, only the `colormap`, `red_max`, `red_mult`, and `base_pixel` fields of the `XStandardColormap` structure are defined. The other fields are ignored. Pixel values for a `StaticGray` or `GrayScale` visual must be in the range `base_pixel < pixel_value < (red_max * red_mult) + base_pixel`. To compute a gray pixel value, use the following expression:

```
pixel_value = gray * red_mult + base_pixel
```

where:

gray = the gray value you desire (0 to `red_max`).

`red_mult` = value from `XStandardColormap` structure

`base_pixel` = the offset in the colormap.

7.7 Writing Portable Color Programs

As we've shown in previous sections, basic color allocation and storage is fairly simple. Even virtual colormaps are fairly easy to create and install. But because X supports so many different types of equipment, you must take special care to make sure that your program will run on both black-and-white and color displays, and that it makes intelligent decisions about whether or not it is possible for it to run on a particular type of color display.

Unless your application has special color needs, tailor it to run on any type of screen. The way to do that is to determine the characteristics of the default visual, and modify your application's color allocation accordingly. On all but high-performance workstations, the macros `DisplayCells`, `DisplayPlanes`, `DefaultVisual`, `DefaultColormap`, and `DefaultDepth` provide you with all the information you need. (For more information on these macros, see Volume Two, *Xlib Reference Manual*.)

An application with special color needs can determine all the types of visuals that are available on a screen, and then choose the best one. `XMatchVisualInfo` and `XGetVisualInfo` are used to get this information and select one visual from those available. How to use these routines is described in Section 7.7.3. Some high-performance displays support more than one visual, and in fact allow the applications to choose the visual and depth on a window-by-window basis.

The default visual is returned by the `DefaultVisual` macro. On color workstations with four to eight planes, this is usually a `PseudoColor` visual, associated with the default colormap (whose ID is returned by `DefaultColormap`), containing read-only cells corresponding to the colors in the RGB database, plus a few unallocated read/write cells. The initial contents of the default colormap are server-dependent. Most programs without special color requirements can use this colormap and visual without further ado.

A window is created with a depth, window class, and visual class that can't be changed during the lifetime of the window. If `XCreateSimpleWindow` was used to create the window, all of these are inherited from the parent.

7.7.1 Monochrome vs. Color

A simple color client may work on a monochrome workstation, simply by virtue of the fact that `XAllocColor` returns the nearest realizable color to the one you ask for, which on single-plane workstations will always either be black or white. A problem arises if the closest colors to those specified are both black or both white when they are supposed to contrast. You can avoid this by checking the returned pixel values to make sure they are not the same—but it is probably better to code defensively, and test explicitly the number of planes on the screen to distinquish black and white from color.

Example 7-2 takes this defensive approach to supporting color or monochrome. Example 7-11 below uses a more concise approach. It tests that the number of colorcells is greater than 2, and if not, it sets the appropriate black and white values on the spot. It also defaults to black and white if either of the routines to parse or allocate colors fail. I had to hit a C reference manual to understand this one, not having seen the ? or : operators before. If the returned value of iscolor, XParseColor, and XAllocColor are 1, gc.foreground is set to blue.pixel. If any of them are 0, gc.foreground is set to BlackPixel.

Example 7-11. A code fragment to use color or monochrome as appropriate

```
Bool iscolor;
XColor blue;

iscolor = (XDisplayCells (display, screen) > 2);
gc.foreground = (iscolor &&
    XParseColor (display, cmap, "blue", &blue) &&
    XAllocColor (display, cmap, &blue))
        ? blue.pixel : BlackPixel (display, screen));
```

When you design an application to run on black and white workstations, you can easily make it run on color units (in black and white) too. Use the BlackPixel and White-Pixel macros to find the appropriate pixel values; never assume hardcoded values of 0 and 1. However, these pixel values will only result in predictably contrasting colors when the default colormap is installed. When the default colormap is not installed, you are at the mercy of the window manager, and your application can do nothing constructive about it. (It will not work to use XAllocColor to explicitly allocate cells for black and white from the currently installed colormap. This might temporarily get you the colors you want, but you have no control over which colormap is installed, and it is even more likely to be uninstalled since it is not the default colormap. Furthermore, you don't own that colormap, and you may break the application that created it.)

You should also be careful using logical functions in the GC other than GXcopy on color screens, since these have unpredictable results unless the colormap is preset or a plane mask is set in the GC. You can still use the functions like GXinvert that are useful on monochrome screens, but you need to limit the effect of the operation to a single plane with the GC's plane mask.

On a gray scale workstation, a color application should still work correctly. If a Pseudo-Color visual is available, use it. You don't need to set the red, green and blue values to be equal, but instead you can expect the resultant gray scale intensities to be described by the following formula:

    intensity = (.30 * red) + (.59 * green) + (.11 * blue)

If only a GrayScale visual is available, the red value only will be used for gray scale intensity.

Again, it is probably safer to explicitly test the visual class, and modify your color handling accordingly.

7.7.2 Finding the Visual Class

Example 7-12 shows a sample of code that tests the default visual, and branches accordingly. Within each branch the application would call routines to allocate colors appropriate for that visual class.

Example 7-12. Finding the default visual

```
unsigned long foreground;
unsigned long background;
Display *display;
int screen;
int depth;
Visual *visual;

/* open display, get default screen, etc. */

depth = DisplayPlanes(display, screen);
visual =DefaultVisual(display, screen);
if (depth == 1)   {   /* one-plane monochrome */
    /* use BlackPixel and WhitePixel only */;
    foreground = BlackPixel(display, screen);
    background = WhitePixel(display, screen);
}
else {
    switch (visual->class) {
        case PseudoColor:
            /* read/write, limited colors */
            break;
        case StaticColor:
            /* read-only, limited colors */
            break;
        case DirectColor:
            /* read/write, many colors */
            break;
        case TrueColor:
            /* read-only, many colors */
            break;
        case GrayScale:
            /* read/write, monochrome shades */
            break;
        case StaticGray:
            /* read-only, monochrome shades */
            break;
    }
}
```

However, this routine takes a short-cut that is not strictly correct. Members of the `Visual` structure are not supposed to be referenced in programs, so that changes to the `Visual` structure won't make programs nonportable.

7.7.3 Getting Information about Visuals

The correct way to access the contents of a `Visual` structure is to use `XGetVisualInfo` or `XMatchVisualInfo`. Only programs that need to do something different depending on the characteristics of the available visuals need to get visual information. As demonstrated in Section 7.3.4, programs with simple color needs can simply allocate colors or use black and white based on the number of planes the screen has. The `DisplayCells`, `DisplayPlanes`, and `DefaultDepth` macros can give you a quick idea of what is available on a screen without getting visual information, except that you can't tell the difference between color and gray scale.

Applications that require a particular visual type or particular qualities of a certain visual type can use `XGetVisualInfo` to find the appropriate visual if it exists. `XGetVisualInfo` returns a list of visual structures that match the attributes specified by template and mask arguments. The template is an `XVisualInfo` structure with members set to the required values, and the mask indicates which members are matched with the list of available visuals. `XMatchVisualInfo` returns a single visual that matches the required visual class and depth.

The `XVisualInfo` structure returns information about the the available visuals. It is used both to select a visual type from those available and as a source of information while using a particular visual.

The `XVisualInfo` structure is shown in Example 7-13.

Example 7-13. The XVisualInfo structure

```
typedef struct {
    Visual *visual;
    VisualID visualid;
    int screen;
    unsigned int depth;
    int class;
    unsigned long red_mask;
    unsigned long green_mask;
    unsigned long blue_mask;
    int colormap_size; /* same as map_entries member of Visual */
    int bits_per_rgb;
} XVisualInfo;
```

The `visual` member is a pointer to the internal `Visual` structure. This pointer is used as the *visual* argument of `XCreateWindow` and `XCreateColormap`.

The `visualid` member is not normally needed by applications.

As discussed earlier, the `class` member specifies whether the screen is to be considered color or monochrome and changeable or immutable. The `class` member can be one of the constants `StaticGray`, `GrayScale`, `StaticColor`, `PseudoColor`, `TrueColor`, or `DirectColor`.

The red_mask, green_mask, and blue_mask members are used only for the Direct-Color and TrueColor visual classes, where there is a separate map for each primary color. They define which bits of the pixel value index into the colormap for each primary color. Each mask has one contiguous set of bits, with no bits in common with the other masks. These values are zero for monochrome and most four- to eight-plane color systems.

The colormap_size member of the structure tells you how many different pixel values are valid with this visual. For a monochrome screen, this value is two. For the default visual of an eight-plane color system, this value is typically 254 or 256 (two colors are often reserved for the cursor). For DirectColor and TrueColor, colormap_size will be the number of cells for the biggest individual pixel subfield. The colormap_size member is the same as map_entries member of the visual structure.

The bits_per_rgb member specifies how many bits in each of the Red, Green, and Blue values in a colorcell are used to drive the RGB gun in the display. For a monochrome screen, this value is one. For the default visual of an eight-plane color system, this value is typically eight. The pixel subfields (the red, green, and blue values in each colorcell) are 16-bit unsigned short values, but only the highest bits_per_rgb bits are used to drive the RGB gun in the screen. This number corresponds the number of bits of resolution in the Digital to Analog Converter (DAC) in the display hardware.

7.7.3.1 Example of Choosing a Visual

Example 7-14 shows a routine that uses XGetVisualInfo to get all the visuals of depth 8 on the current screen, as defined by the X server, and then creates a colormap and window.

Example 7-14. Code to match visuals

```
#include <X11/Xlib.h>
#include <X11/Xutil.h>

visual()
{
Display *display;
Colormap colormap;
Window window;
int screen;
     .
     .
     .

XVisualInfo vTemplate;    /* template of the visual we want */
XVisualInfo *visualList;  /* list of XVisualInfo structs that match */
int visualsMatched;       /* number of visuals that match */
     .
     .
     .

/*
 * Set up the XVisualInfo template so that it returns
 * a list of all the visuals of depth 8 defined on the
 * current screen by the X server
 */
```

Example 7-14. Code to match visuals (continued)

```
vTemplate.screen = screen;
vTemplate.depth = 8;
visualList = XGetVisualInfo (display, VisualScreenMask |
        VisualDepthMask, &vTemplate, &visualsMatched);
if ( visualsMatched == 0 )
    fatalError ("No matching visuals\n");

/*
 * Create a colormap for a window using the first of the visuals
 * in the list ov XVisualInfo structs returned by XGetVisualInfo.
 */
colormap = XCreateColormap (display, RootWindow(display, screen),
    visualList[0].visual, AllocNone);
    .
    .
    .

window = XCreateWindow (display, RootWindow(display, screen),
    x, y, width, height, border_width, vTemplate.depth,
    InputOutput, visualList[0].visual, mask, &attributes);
XSetWindowColormap(display, window, colormap);

/* All done with visual information.  Free it.  */

XFree(visualList);
    .
    .
    .

} /* end routine */
```

7.8 Miscellaneous Color Handling Functions

The following miscellaneous functions provide additional ways to use the color database, to find out the RGB values in a colormap cell, and to free cells that are no longer needed.

XLookupColor   Looks up an ASCII color name in the color database and returns separate color structures containing the exact RGB values specified in the database for that name and the closest RGB values available on the hardware. This function does not look at any cells in the colormap, even though it has a *colormap* argument! This argument specifies which screen the color should be looked up on. The difference between XLookupColor and XParseColor is that XParseColor accepts the hexadecimal color specification (which XLookupColor does not), while XLookupColor returns the closest colors available on the hardware (which XParseColor does not).

XQueryColor   Fills an XColor structure with the RGB values corresponding to the colormap cell indicated by a pixel value. Also sets the flags member of the structure to (DoRed | DoGreen | DoBlue).

XQueryColors Fills multiple XColor structures with the RGB values and flags corresponding to the colormap cells indicated by a pixel values. Also sets each flags member to (DoRed | DoGreen | DoBlue).

XFreeColors Frees the colormap cells associated with the given pixel values, and/or frees the given planes. Since all the colorcells an application allocates are freed when the application exits, this routine is needed only when an application is finished with cells before it exits. Freeing a read/write colorcell makes that cell available to other applications. Freeing a read-only cell may make the cell unallocated, but only if no other application is sharing that cell.

8
Events

This chapter is another must-read. Events are central to X. The fundamental framework for handling events was given in Chapter 3, but this chapter gives much more detail, both on selecting events for a window, and on handling them when they arrive. It discusses each of the masks used to select events; for a description of the event structures themselves, see Appendix E.

In This Chapter:

8
Events

An event, to quote the Oxford English Dictionary, is an "incident of importance," or a "consequence, result, or outcome." This definition holds for X. An event reports some device activity, or is generated as a side effect of an Xlib routine.

From a programmer's point of view, an event reports:

- Something that your program needs to know about, such as user input, or information available from other clients;

- Something your program is doing that other clients need to know about, such as making text available for pasting to another client;

- Something the window manager needs to know, such as a request by your program for a change to the layout of the screen by mapping a window.

Programming with events is quite different from traditional methods of programming for input. You cannot simply wait for a user to type something, and expect nothing else to happen in the meantime. Other programs are running concurrently and sharing the same system resources including the screen. They can affect your program. What happens if another window is placed over yours in the middle of the instruction your user is typing? The program must be able to listen to several types of events at once, and jump back and forth when acting on them. Events imply a philosophy that the program should respond to the user's actions, not the other way around. Events make this type of programming straightforward.

Events occur asynchronously and get queued for each client that requested them. It is possible for more than one client to get copies of the same event. Usually a program handles each one in turn and performs the appropriate action before reading the next one. But there is usually no way for a program to predict in what order it will find the events on the queue.

This chapter covers events in detail, going further than the introduction to events in Chapter 2, *X Concepts*. Here we discuss the event union and structure types, the selection and propagation of events, how each event type is usually used, how events are received and handled in a program, and how they are sent by one client to another.

After you have read and understood this chapter, see Chapter 9, *The Keyboard and Pointer*, which demonstrates how to use events to handle the user's input, and Appendix E, *Event Reference*, which describes all the event types in a reference format.

8.1 Overview of Event Handling

There are three important steps in a program's handling of events. First, the program selects the events it wants for each window. Then it maps the window. Finally, it provides an event loop which reads events from the event queue as they occur.

This process is quite simple, the only complication being the variety of events that may occur, each perhaps having a different meaning when it occurs in a different window. You have to know every circumstance in which a particular event is generated, and make sure that your program does the right thing with it. But you won't need to understand the details of every event in order to begin using the most important ones.

To select events, you call `XSelectInput` for each window that you want to receive events. You specify a mask which specifies which event types you want, combining any number of the event mask symbols with the bitwise OR operator (|).

You must make sure that every window that is to receive events appears on the screen after the events are selected for that window, but before the event loop begins. Otherwise, the client will miss the first `Expose` event that triggers the drawing of the window's contents. For top-level windows, the client might also miss the `ConfigureNotify` event that reports the size of the window granted by the window manager. For a window to appear on the screen it must be mapped and all its ancestors must be mapped. It is permissible to map all the windows except the top-level ones at any time, but the mapping of children of the root window must be done between the `XSelectInput` call and the routine that gets events for the event loop.

A simple event loop was shown in Chapter 3, *Basic Window Program*. The only difference between this loop and the loops in real clients is in the number of different event types handled, and the complexity of each branch.

Even though selection of events must be done first, we're going to start by describing how to handle events once you've got them, because there are fewer details involved. We'll return to the exact procedure for selecting events and the meaning of each event mask symbol in Section 8.3.

8.2 Event Processing

This section describes what an event type is and what an event structure contains, reviews how the event queue stores events and how a program reads events from it, and summarizes all the routines that can be used to get events.

8.2.1 The Event Structures

An event is implemented as a packet of information stored in a structure. The simplest event structure is shown in Example 8-1.

Example 8-1. The XAnyEvent structure

```
typedef struct {
    int type;               /* the type of event */
    unsigned long serial;   /* # of last request processed by server */
    Bool send_event;        /* true if send from a SendEvent request */
    Display *display;       /* display the event was read from */
    Window window;          /* window that receives event */
} XAnyEvent;
```

There are thirty different event structures. Virtually all of them have the members shown in the XAnyEvent structure. Most of the event structures also contain additional members that provide useful information for clients. The first member of every event structure, type, indicates the type of event. We'll come back to the type in Section 8.2.2. The serial member identifies the last protocol request processed by the server, for use in debugging. The send_event flag indicates whether this event was sent from the server (False) or from another client (True). Other clients can send events with XSendEvent, as described in Section 8.4.

Many of the event structures also have a display or root member, or both. The display member identifies the connection to the server that is active. The root member indicates the screen to which the event window is linked. Most programs only use a single screen and therefore don't need to worry about the root member. The display member can be useful for passing the display variable into routines by simply passing a pointer to the event structure.

Most event structures also have a window member, which indicates the window that selected and received the event. This is the window where the event arrives if it is a keyboard or pointer event and has propagated through the hierarchy as described in Section 8.3.2. One event type may have two different meanings to a client, depending on which window the event appears in.

8.2.2 Event Types and XEvent Union

The XEvent union contains all the event structures, as shown in Example 8-2.* The first member of the XEvent union is the type of event. Each event structure within the XEvent union also begins with the type of event. A client determines the type of event by looking at the type member of XEvent. Then the client branches to specific code for that event type. After the initial determination of the event type, only the event structure containing the specific information for each event type should be used in each branch. For

---

* See a C language tutorial or reference manual if you are unfamiliar with unions.

example, assuming you've declared an XEvent variable called report, the report.xexpose structure should be used within the branch for Expose events.

The value of type is any one of the constants listed in the center column of Table 8-3. After determining the event type; you know which event structure from the XEvent union contains specific information about the event. You can then use the appropriate event structure name, such as xkey, to access the specific information unique to that event structure. The event structure name is shown on each event reference page in Appendix E, *Event Reference*.

Example 8-2. The XEvent union

```
typedef union _XEvent {
      int type;              /* must not be changed; first member */
      XAnyEvent xany;
      XKeyEvent xkey;
      XButtonEvent xbutton;
      XMotionEvent xmotion;
      XCrossingEvent xcrossing;
      XFocusChangeEvent xfocus;
      XKeymapEvent xkeymap;
      XExposeEvent xexpose;
      XNoExposeEvent xnoexpose;
      XGraphicsExposeEvent xgraphicsexpose;
      XVisibilityEvent xvisibility;
      XCreateWindowEvent xcreatewindow;
      XDestroyWindowEvent xdestroywindow;
      XUnmapEvent xunmap;
      XMapEvent xmap;
      XMappingEvent xmapping;
      XMapRequestEvent xmaprequest;
      XReparentEvent xreparent;
      XConfigureEvent xconfigure;
      XGravityEvent xgravity;
      XResizeRequestEvent xresizerequest;
      XConfigureRequestEvent xconfigurerequest;
      XCirculateEvent xcirculate;
      XCirculateRequestEvent xcirculaterequest;
      XPropertyEvent xproperty;
      XSelectionClearEvent xselectionclear;
      XSelectionRequestEvent xselectionrequest;
      XSelectionEvent xselection;
      XColormapEvent xcolormap;
      XClientMessageEvent xclient;
} XEvent;
```

8.2.3 The Event Queue

The event structures are placed on an event queue in the order they occur, so that the program can read them and act accordingly. As described in Section 2.1.2 and shown in Figure 8-1, the server maintains one event queue, on which all events are placed, and Xlib maintains one event queue for each client, on which the events for that client are placed. The events in the server's queue are periodically transferred over the network to the Xlib queues. Two clients can receive copies of the same events if they each select them.

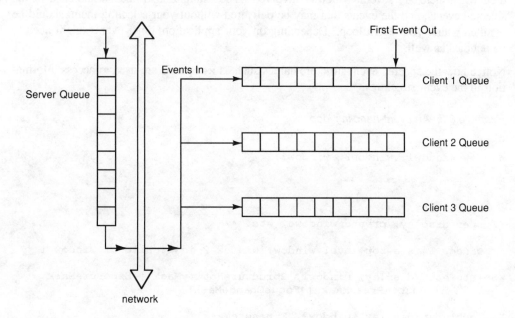

Figure 8-1. The server's event queue and each client's event queue

The client sets up an event-receiving loop to handle the events that arrive on its event queue. There are several routines a client can use to get events. They differ in how many windows they monitor, how many types of events they look for, and whether they wait for events to appear before returning. For a description of the event-getting routines, see Section 8.2.6.

8.2.4 Handling Events

In *basicwin* (the example program in Chapter 3, *Basic Window Program*), you have already seen the structure of the code you should write to handle events. In a more complex application, the code for each event type will simply be divided according to the members in each event structure. Usually, the next branch after the event type will test the window in which the event occurred.

The branch for `Expose` events in Example 8-3 demonstrates how an event might be handled when there are several windows involved. The example also notes when each of the selected events, and the events that may be delivered without your selecting them, should be handled within your event loop. Depending on your application, other events might need to be handled as well.

Notice how the specific event structure names such as `xexpose` are used to access information in the event structures.

Example 8-3. An event-handling loop

```
XEvent report;
Window window1, window2, window3;
    .
    .
    .

/* open display, create windows, etc. */

/* window 1 is a top-level window, window 2 is a child of window 1 */

XSelectInput(display, window1, StructureNotifyMask | ExposureMask
        | ButtonPressMask | FocusChangeMask);

XSelectInput(display, window2, ExposureMask);
XSelectInput(display, window3, ExposureMask);

XMapWindow(display, window1);
XMapWindow(display, window2);
XMapWindow(display, window3);

/* get events, use first to display text and graphics */
while (1)
{
    /* Get any type of event on any window.
     * This gets events on every window for which
     * we have selected events (2 in this case). */
    XNextEvent(display, &report);

    switch (report.type) {
    case Expose:
        printf("got an Expose event\n");
        /* Redraw contents of windows.
         * Note: can't use switch because
         * window IDs are not constant */
        if (report.xexpose.window = window1)
```

Example 8-3. An event-handling loop (continued)

```
                /* redraw window 1 */;
        else if (report.xexpose.window = window2)
                /* redraw window 2 */;
        else (report.xexpose.window = window3)
                /* redraw window 3 */;
        break;
    case ButtonPress:
        printf("got a ButtonPress event\n");
        /* respond to buttonpress, probably
         * depending on which window is reported
         * in report.xbutton.window          */
        break;
    case FocusOut:
        printf("got a FocusOut event\n");
        /* Some other client got the keyboard focus.
         * This client can no longer expect input,
         * and it should go into inactive mode. */
        break;
    case FocusIn:
        printf("got a FocusIn event\n");
        /* This client got the keyboard focus back.
         * Normal operation may resume. */
        break;
    case MappingNotify:
        printf("got a MappingNotify event\n");
        /* Keyboard or Pointer mapping was changed
         * by another client.  If keyboard,
         * should call XRefreshKeyboardMapping, unless
         * keyboard events are not used. */
        break;
    case ClientMessage:
        printf("got a ClientMessage event\n");
        /* Primarily used for transfering selection
         * data.  Also might be used in a private
         * interclient protocol.  Otherwise, not
         * needed in event loop */
        break;
    case SelectionClear:
        printf("got a SelectionClear event\n");
        /* If this application previously called
           XSetSelectionOwner, it may get this event.
           Otherwise, you don't need it in your
           event loop */
        break;
    case SelectionNotify:
        printf("got a SelectionNotify event\n");
        /* If this application calls
           XConvertSelection, it will get this event.
           Otherwise, you don't need it in your
           event loop */
        break;
    case SelectionRequest:
        printf("got a SelectionRequest event\n");
        /* If this application previously called
           XSetSelectionOwner, it may get this event.
```

Example 8-3. An event-handling loop (continued)

```
                  Otherwise, you don't need it in your
                  event loop */
          break;
      case GraphicsExpose:
          /* fall through into NoExpose */
      case NoExpose:
          printf("got a GraphicsExpose or NoExpose event\n");
          /* If this application calls XCopyArea or XCopyPlane,
           * and the graphics_exposure member of the GC is True,
           * and the source is a window,
           * these events may be generated.  Handle
           * GraphicsExpose like Expose */
      case default:
          printf("Unexpected event or event to be thrown away\n");
           * Put a print statement here, to be safe */
          break;
      }   /* end switch on event type */
} /* end while (1)
```

The XNextEvent routine gets the next event on the queue for our client, or waits until one appears before returning. There are many other routines that get events of particular types, in particular windows, with or without waiting for the event to appear. These routines are described in Section 8.2.6.

The first member of the XEvent report contains the type of event. This information is used in an ''if-else'' chain, or in a ''switch'' statement to branch according to the event type. Once the type is known, the specific event structure is known and its contents can be accessed. For example, the width of the exposed area in the window is contained in the XExposeEvent structure as report.xexpose.width, where report is the XEvent variable, xexpose is the member of the XEvent union, and width is a member of the XExposeEvent structure type. The report.xfocus structure should be used within the branch for FocusIn and FocusOut events. The detail member of the focus event structures would be report.xfocus.detail.

8.2.5 Printing the Event Type

I recommend that you print the event type and perhaps other event information in each branch of the event loop while you are in the application debugging stage. Be very careful that the loop handles all the events that can occur, and that the Xlib routine you choose to get events is capable of getting all the events you need. If your program hangs and can't be interrupted with Control-C, it is probably waiting for an event that you did not select. For example, you may have called XMaskEvent with a mask of ButtonReleaseMask but you didn't select ButtonReleaseMask in the XSelectEvent call. The event-getting routines don't check to make sure you have selected the events you are requesting.

Instead of printing the event type as a number which you then have to interpret using the <X11/X.h> include file, you can have your program print the real name of the event. Example 8-4 creates an include file containing an array of strings spelling out the event type names. Example 8-5 then prints the correct event name.

Example 8-4. An include file for printing the event type — eventnames.h

```
static char *event_names[] = {
    "",
    "",
    "KeyPress",
    "KeyRelease",
    "ButtonPress",
    "ButtonRelease",
    "MotionNotify",
    "EnterNotify",
    "LeaveNotify",
    "FocusIn",
    "FocusOut",
    "KeymapNotify",
    "Expose",
    "GraphicsExpose",
    "NoExpose",
    "VisibilityNotify",
    "CreateNotify",
    "DestroyNotify",
    "UnmapNotify",
    "MapNotify",
    "MapRequest",
    "ReparentNotify",
    "ConfigureNotify",
    "ConfigureRequest",
    "GravityNotify",
    "ResizeRequest",
    "CirculateNotify",
    "CirculateRequest",
    "PropertyNotify",
    "SelectionClear",
    "SelectionRequest",
    "SelectionNotify",
    "ColormapNotify",
    "ClientMessage",
    "MappingNotify"
};
```

Note that *eventnames.h* is not a standard include file, but one we have written for the purpose of printing the event type more legibly. You could use a similar method to identify windows, but since their IDs are not constants, you would need to load the array dynamically after you have created the windows.

Example 8-5 demonstrates printing an event using the include file shown in Example 8-4.

Example 8-5. Printing the event type

```
#ifdef DEBUG
#include "eventnames.h"
#endif

XEvent event;
XNextEvent(display, &event);
```

Example 8-5. Printing the event type (continued)

```
#ifdef DEBUG
fprintf(stderr, "winman: unexpected %s event\n", event_name[event.type]);
#endif
```

8.2.6 Routines That Get Events

There are several functions that get event structures from the queue. They differ in the following respects:

- The number of windows they monitor (whether they inspect the `window` member).
- Whether they look for particular event types.
- Whether the event is removed from the queue when it is read.
- Whether a routine you write is used to determine whether the event should be returned.
- Whether Xlib waits until an event meeting the criteria arrives or immediately returns a success or failure code.
- Whether the connection to the server is flushed to see if any more events are available.

The following is a list of the event-handling routines and their differences. In all of these routines, you pass a pointer to an XEvent structure to be filled.

XNextEvent	gets the next event of any type on any window. This function flushes the output buffer if Xlib's queue does not contain an event, and waits for an event to arrive from the server connection.
XMaskEvent	gets the next event matching the specified mask on any window. This function flushes the output buffer if Xlib's queue does not contain a matching event, and waits for a matching event to arrive from the server connection.
XCheckMaskEvent	behaves like XMaskEvent but immediately returns False if there is no matching event in Xlib's queue and none could be read from the server connection after flushing the output buffer. Returns True if a matching event was found.
XWindowEvent	gets the next event matching both the specified mask and specified window. This function flushes the output buffer if Xlib's queue does not contain a matching event, and waits for a matching event to arrive from the server connection.
XCheckWindowEvent	behaves like XWindowEvent but immediately returns False if there is no matching event in Xlib's queue and none could be read from the server connection after flushing the output buffer. Returns True if a matching event was found.

XIfEvent	looks for an event on the queue that matches the conditions set by a user-supplied predicate procedure. This function flushes the output buffer if Xlib's queue does not contain a matching event, and waits for a matching event to arrive from the server connection.
XCheckIfEvent	behaves like XIfEvent but immediately returns False if there is no matching event in Xlib's queue and none could be read from the server connection after flushing the output buffer. Returns True if a matching event was found.
XPeekEvent	gets the next event of any type from any window without removing the event from the queue. This function flushes the output buffer if Xlib's queue is empty, and waits for an event to arrive from the server connection.
XPeekIfEvent	gets the next event that matches the specified predicate procedure, without removing the event from the queue. This function flushes the output buffer if Xlib's queue does not contain a matching event, and waits for a matching event to arrive from the server connection.
XCheckTypedEvent	searches the queue from the oldest event for the desired event type, without discarding all those searched that don't match. If no matching event is found in Xlib's queue, this function flushes the output buffer and returns False.
XCheckTypedWindowEvent	searches the queue from the oldest event for the desired window and event type, without discarding those searched that don't match. If no matching event is found in Xlib's queue, this function flushes the output buffer and returns False.
XEventsQueued	returns the number of events on the queue, but has three modes that specify what else is done. All three modes count the events already in Xlib's queue, and return if there are any. QueuedAlready returns even if there aren't any events in the queue. QueuedAfterFlush flushes the output buffer and attempts to read more events from the connection before returning. QueuedAfterReading attempts to read more events from the connection without flushing the buffer. Not available in Release 1.
XPending	returns the number of events on the queue. This is identical to XEventsQueued with mode QueuedAfterFlush.
XPutBackEvent	puts an event you supply back on Xlib's queue, so that it will be the next to be received by XNextEvent.
XGetMotionEvents	gets all the motion events that occurred on the specified window in a specified time period. This function won't work if there is no motion history buffer, which is true if display->

`motion_buffer = 0`. There is no macro available for accessing this member of the display structure.

You may notice that there are two broad categories of routines that get input: those that wait for a matching event and those that do not wait. The latter may be used in porting applications that use the "polling" style of programming, which checks to see if input has arrived at regular intervals by continuously calling a "polling" function in a loop. Given the choice, however, it is much better to use the routines that wait for events as much as possible, since this technique does not waste processor cycles. This is true event-*driven* programming.

Table 8-1 organizes the event-receiving functions according to whether they wait for events if none are present on Xlib's queue.

Table 8-1. Event-getting routines

Event Specifications	Desired Result		
	Wait if necessary	Return `False` immediately if none queued	Leave in queue (may wait)
Any event	XNextEvent	n/a	XPeekEvent
With predicate	XIfEvent	XCheckIfEvent	XPeekIfEvent
For window	XWindowEvent	XCheckWindowEvent	n/a
For event mask	XMaskEvent	XCheckMaskEvent	n/a
For type	n/a	XCheckTypedEvent	n/a
For window and type	n/a	XCheckTypedWindow-Event	n/a

Note that most of the routines apparently missing from Xlib according to Table 8-1 can be simulated with other routines and fairly simple code. The hole on the top row can be filled by calling XCheckMaskEvent with a mask set to all 1's. For the three routines missing in the last column, you can write a predicate procedure and call XPeekIfEvent. An example predicate procedure is shown in Example 8-6. The two routines missing the the first column can also be replaced with a predicate procedure and XIfEvent.

The event-getting routines with Check in their names are useful for programs that need to poll for input to handle interrupts. To illustrate the handling of interrupts, let's say you have a routine in a program that performs a complex, lengthy calculation like a Fourier transform. You want to be able to abort the calculation in case you change your mind. Therefore you need to be able to check the keyboard to see if a Control-C or other interrupt character has been typed. You also might want to provide for exposure events during the long wait, though you might be able to get away without this provision. This would be a good application for XCheckTypedEvent or XCheckTypedWindowEvent, since these routines poll without waiting if no events can be read. When an event does arrive, you can decide from the type or window whether to bother processing it.

Release 2 has a small bug in the types of the event_mask argument to XWindowEvent and XCheckWindowEvent. This argument should be unsigned long, but in XWindowEvent it is long and in XCheckWindowEvent it is int. This bug appears only on machines where the int or long type is less than 32 bits, since the masks require 24 bits.

8.2.7 Predicate Procedures

The routines XIfEvent, XCheckIfEvent, and XPeekIfEvent allow you to supply a procedure that returns True or False depending on some characteristic of the event. You would use one of these routines if you have a matching algorithm that is complicated, or simply to enable you to clear up the code by putting some of the event processing in a separate routine.

Your predicate procedure is called with the same arguments as the event-getting routine (except for the predicate procedure, of course). Example 8-6 shows a predicate procedure and the XIfEvent call that uses it. This code would normally use XNextEvent, but we have substituted XIfEvent so that we can filter out button events on buttons other than button 1. This predicate procedure returns True for all events except the undesirable button events.

Example 8-6. A predicate procedure and XIfEvent call

```
void main(argc, argv)
int argc;
char **argv;
{
        .
        .
        .
    Bool predproc();
    static char *stuff = "do this or that";
        .
        .
        .
    XSelectInput(display, wint, ExposureMask | ButtonPressMask
        | ButtonReleaseMask | ButtonMotionMask
        | PointerMotionHintMask);
        .
        .
        .
    while (1)  {
          XIfEvent(display, &report, predproc, stuff);
          switch  (report.type) {
    /* NOTE: no code here for eliminating button events on
     * other buttons, because only button one events
     * are returned by XIfEvent */
```

Example 8-6. A predicate procedure and XIfEvent call (continued)

```
                        case ButtonPress:
                                points[index].x = report.xbutton.x;
                                points[index].y = report.xbutton.y;
                                break;
                        case ButtonRelease:
                                index++;
                                points[index].x = report.xbutton.x;
                                points[index].y = report.xbutton.y;
                                break;


                            .
                            .
                            .

                }
        }
}

Bool predproc(display, event, arg)
Display *display;
XEvent *event;
char *arg;
{
        printf("The arg is %s\n", arg);
        switch (event->type) {
                case Expose:
                case MotionNotify:
                case ConfigureNotify:
                case KeyPress:
                        return(True);
                        break;
                case ButtonPress:
                case ButtonRelease:
                        if (event->xbutton.button == Button1)
                                return(True);
                        else
                                return(False);
                        break;
                default:
        }
}
```

8.3 Selecting Events

For each window, a client must select which event types it wants placed in its queue when
they occur in that window. This is normally done with XSelectInput, which sets the
event_mask attribute of a window. The client need not select events on all of its windows, only those in which it wants to see the events that occur.

To select event types for a window, pass an `event_mask` as an argument to `XSelect-Input`, or set the `event_mask` member of the `XSetWindowAttributes` structure and call `XChangeWindowAttributes`. (For more information on the `XSetWindow-Attributes` structure, see Section 4.1.)

The `event_mask` is formed by combining with the bitwise OR operator (|) the event mask symbols listed in the first column of Table 8-2. Each mask symbol sets a bit in the `event_mask`.

Table 8-2 also describes briefly the circumstances under which you would want to specify each symbol. You will need to read about each mask in Section 8.3.3; see the examples using the events in Chapter 9, *The Keyboard and Pointer*, and throughout the book; and look at the event structures in Appendix E, *Event Reference*, before you will really understand when to use each of these symbols.

Table 8-2. Event Mask Definitions

Event Mask Symbol	Circumstances
NoEventMask	No events
KeyPressMask	Keyboard down events
KeyReleaseMask	Keyboard up events
ButtonPressMask	Pointer button down events
ButtonReleaseMask	Pointer button up events
EnterWindowMask	Pointer window entry events
LeaveWindowMask	Pointer window leave events
PointerMotionMask	All pointer motion events
PointerMotionHintMask	Fewer pointer motion events
Button1MotionMask	Pointer motion while button 1 down
Button2MotionMask	Pointer motion while button 2 down
Button3MotionMask	Pointer motion while button 3 down
Button4MotionMask	Pointer motion while button 4 down
Button5MotionMask	Pointer motion while button 5 down
ButtonMotionMask	Pointer motion while any button down
KeymapStateMask	Any keyboard state change on `EnterNotify`, `LeaveNotify`, `FocusIn` or `FocusOut`
ExposureMask	Any exposure (except `GraphicsExpose` and `NoExpose`)
VisibilityChangeMask	Any change in visibility
StructureNotifyMask	Any change in window configuration.
ResizeRedirectMask	Redirect resize of this window
SubstructureNotifyMask	Notify about reconfiguration of children
SubstructureRedirectMask	Redirect reconfiguration of children
FocusChangeMask	Any change in keyboard focus
PropertyChangeMask	Any change in property
ColormapChangeMask	Any change in colormap
OwnerGrabButtonMask	Modifies handling of pointer events

The `do_not_propagate_mask` window attribute is formed in the same way as `event_mask` but can only be set with `XChangeWindowAttributes`. Its function is described in Section 8.3.2.

Example 8-7 shows how to set the `event_mask` and call `XSelectInput`.

Example 8-7. An example of selecting input

```
Display display;
Window window;
unsigned long event_mask;
   .
   .
   .
/* must open display, create window, etc. */

/* select key events */
event_mask = ExposureMask | KeyPressMask | KeyReleaseMask;
XSelectInput(display, window, event_mask);

/* map window after selecting */

/* get events */
```

In Example 8-7, events are selected *before* the window is mapped. This sequence is important, since otherwise the window will not receive the first `Expose` event that occurs after a new window is mapped, and it will not know when to redraw the window. You will remember from *basicwin* that an `Expose` event signifies that a window has become visible and needs to be redrawn. Every `Expose` event, including the first, should trigger the drawing of the window's contents.

Also, note that you cannot add to the selected events by calling `XSelectInput` with a single additional mask. You must specify all the desired event masks every time you call it.

8.3.1 Correspondence Between Event Masks and Events

Each event mask symbol indicates that a certain type of event, or group of event types, should be queued when it occurs. For example, when used alone as an *event_mask* argument to `XSelectInput`, a `KeyPressMask` symbol indicates that only `KeyPress` events are desired. A `FocusChangeMask` symbol, on the other hand, indicates an interest in two types of events: `FocusIn` and `FocusOut`.

On the other hand, there is more than one event mask symbol for `MotionNotify` events; the different masks specify the conditions under which pointer motion events are desired. For example, if both `Button1MotionMask` and `Button3MotionMask` symbols are combined to form an `event_mask` argument to `XSelectInput`, only one event type is requested: `MotionNotify` events. However, this event type will be queued only if the pointer moves while the first or third button (or both) is held down.

Table 8-3 lists each event mask, its associated event types, and the associated structure definition. The structures for each event type are described in Appendix E, *Event Reference*.

Table 8-3. Event Masks, Event Types, and Event Structures

Event Mask	Event Type	Structure
KeyPressMask	KeyPress	XKeyPressedEvent
KeyReleaseMask	KeyRelease	XKeyReleasedEvent
ButtonPressMask	ButtonPress	XButtonPressedEvent
ButtonReleaseMask	ButtonRelease	XButtonReleasedEvent
OwnerGrabButtonMask	n/a	n/a
KeymapStateMask	KeymapNotify	XKeymapEvent
PointerMotionMask PointerMotionHintMask ButtonMotionMask Button1MotionMask Button2MotionMask Button3MotionMask Button4MotionMask Button5MotionMask	MotionNotify	XPointerMovedEvent
EnterWindowMask	EnterNotify	XEnterWindowEvent
LeaveWindowMask	LeaveNotify	XLeaveWindowEvent
FocusChangeMask	FocusIn FocusOut	XFocusInEvent XFocusOutEvent
ExposureMask	Expose	XExposeEvent
selected in GC by graphics_expose member)	GraphicsExpose NoExpose	XGraphicsExposeEvent XNoExposeEvent
ColormapChangeMask	ColormapNotify	XColormapEvent
PropertyChangeMask	PropertyNotify	XPropertyEvent
VisibilityChangeMask	VisibilityNotify	XVisibilityEvent
ResizeRedirectMask	ResizeRequest	XResizeRequestEvent
StructureNotifyMask	CirculateNotify ConfigureNotify DestroyNotify GravityNotify MapNotify ReparentNotify UnmapNotify	XCirculateEvent XConfigureEvent XDestroyWindowEvent XGravityEvent XMapEvent XReparentEvent XUnmapEvent

Table 8-3. Event Masks, Event Types, and Event Structures (continued)

Event Mask	Event Type	Structure
SubstructureNotifyMask	CirculateNotify	XCirculateEvent
	ConfigureNotify	XConfigureEvent
	CreateNotify	XCreateWindowEvent
	DestroyNotify	XDestroyWindowEvent
	GravityNotify	XGravityEvent
	MapNotify	XMapEvent
	ReparentNotify	XReparentEvent
	UnmapNotify	XUnmapEvent
SubstructureRedirectMask	CirculateRequest	XCirculateRequestEvent
	ConfigureRequest	XConfigureRequestEvent
	MapRequest	XMapRequestEvent
(always selected)	MappingNotify	XMappingEvent
(always selected)	ClientMessage	XClientMessageEvent
(always selected)	SelectionClear	XSetSelectClearEvent
(always selected)	SelectionNotify	XSelectionEvent
(always selected)	SelectionRequest	XSelectionRequestEvent

There is no event mask for several of the event types listed at the end of this table, because the X server or another client can send them to any client without them being selected. For example, MappingNotify indicates that the keyboard mapping (see Section 9.1.2.3) or pointer mapping has changed. This event is reported to all clients by the server when any client changes those mappings. The selection events are a means of interclient communication, where one client announces with an event that it has a selection of text or graphics available for pasting, and another client responds with an event specifying in what format it would like the information. Similarly, ClientMessage events are always selected because they are sent from one client directly to another using the XSendEvent routine.

8.3.2 Propagation of Device Events

The fifth member in almost every event structure, window, contains the ID of the window in which the event appears to have occurred. This is called the *event window*. For ButtonPress, ButtonRelease, KeyPress, KeyRelease, and MotionNotify events, the event window is not necessarily the window in which the event originally happened, which is called the *source window*.

Which window is reported in the event on the queue depends on the results of propagation up through the window hierarchy, and is controlled by the event_mask and do_not_propagate_mask window attributes.

The source window is the *lowest* visible window in the hierarchy that encloses the pointer when the device event occurs. It is also the *smallest* visible window enclosing the pointer. The window member of the event in the queue (the event window) will be the source window only if the event_mask attribute (set with XSelectInput) of the source window selected the event's type.

If the event was not selected for the source window, then the event is sent to the parent, and so on until the event arrives at an ancestor window that has selected the right event type. The ID of this window is then placed in the window member of the event structure and that structure is placed on the queue for this client. Once a window that has selected the event is found, the event no longer propagates. If no window selected the event anywhere in the hierarchy up to and including the root window, the event is thrown away.

The do_not_propagate_mask window attribute also gets involved in this process. When an event arrives at a window, but finds it has not been selected, the do_not_propagate_mask determines whether the event will be sent to ancestor windows. By default, all events that can propagate, do. If the mask for the event type that occurred is included in the do_not_propagate_mask, the event is thrown away.

Figure 8-2 demonstrates the propagation of an event through the hierarchy, given three different event_mask and do_not_propagate attribute settings.

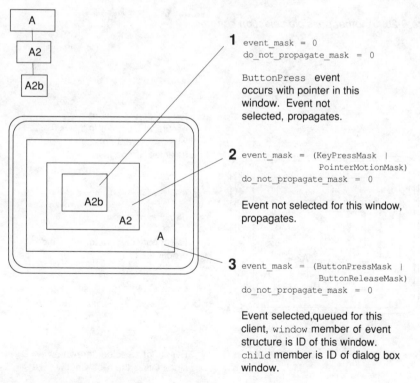

Figure 8-2a. One possible selection scheme

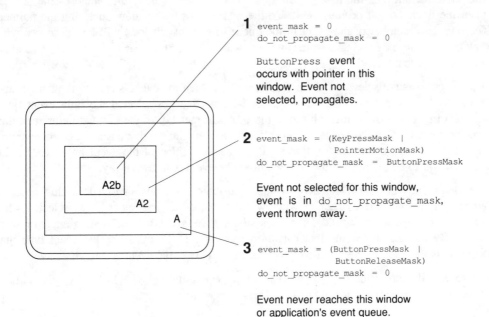

1 `event_mask = 0`
`do_not_propagate_mask = 0`

`ButtonPress` event
occurs with pointer in this
window. Event not
selected, propagates.

2 `event_mask = (KeyPressMask |`
`                    PointerMotionMask)`
`do_not_propagate_mask = ButtonPressMask`

Event not selected for this window,
event is in `do_not_propagate_mask`,
event thrown away.

3 `event_mask = (ButtonPressMask |`
`                    ButtonReleaseMask)`
`do_not_propagate_mask = 0`

Event never reaches this window
or application's event queue.

Figure 8-2b. Another possible selection scheme

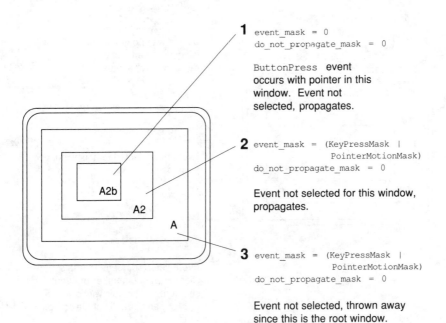

1 `event_mask = 0`
`do_not_propagate_mask = 0`

`ButtonPress` event
occurs with pointer in this
window. Event not
selected, propagates.

2 `event_mask = (KeyPressMask |`
`                    PointerMotionMask)`
`do_not_propagate_mask = 0`

Event not selected for this window,
propagates.

3 `event_mask = (KeyPressMask |`
`                    PointerMotionMask)`
`do_not_propagate_mask = 0`

Event not selected, thrown away
since this is the root window.

Figure 8-2c. Yet another possible selection scheme

For brevity, we need conventions for describing the distribution of events. We'll say that an event is *sent* to a window when it is generated in that window either because of device action or as a side effect to an Xlib routine. A window *receives* an event sent to it only if the window has selected that event type or if the event type is always selected. Only when a window *receives* an event is it placed on the queue for that client.

Another convention is helpful in describing the selection of events. We'll say that "the window has selected that event type" rather than the more cumbersome "the program has called XSelectInput, specifying the window and the mask that selects that event type."

We've described the way device events propagate normally. But two other actions can modify this operation: changing the keyboard focus window, or grabbing the keyboard or pointer. Not only do these change the distribution of normal events, they create new events as side effects. We'll just introduce these here and return to them in Chapter 9, *The Keyboard and Pointer*.

8.3.2.1 The Keyboard Focus Window

The keyboard focus window affects the distribution of KeyPress and KeyRelease events. Normally, the window manager allows the user to specify which window, if any, should be the keyboard focus. Only the focus window and its descendants receive keyboard input, and within them event propagation occurs normally. Events occurring outside the focus window are delivered to the focus window. By default, the focus window is the root, and keyboard events are normally distributed to all windows on the screen, since all the windows on a screen are descendants of the root.

The keyboard focus is set to a window with XSetInputFocus. The focus window must be viewable.* If it is not viewable, or later becomes not viewable, the focus reverts to another window specified in the XSetInputFocus call, the *revert_to* window.

The current focus window can be read with XGetFocusWindow.

FocusOut events are delivered to the old focus window and FocusIn events to the window which receives the focus. Windows in between these two windows in the hierarchy are said to be virtually crossed and receive focus change events depending on the relationship and direction of transfer between the origin and destination windows. Some or all of the windows between the window containing the pointer at the time of the focus change and that window's root can also receive focus change events. By checking the detail member of FocusIn and FocusOut events, a client can tell which of its windows can receive input. See Chapter 9, *The Keyboard and Pointer*, for more information about tracking the keyboard focus.

---

* For a window to be viewable, it must be mapped and all its ancestors must be mapped, but it may be obscured.

Applications should set the keyboard focus to one of their own windows only when absolutely necessary, because this will prevent other clients from receiving keyboard events. It is permissible for clients to set the focus window when the mouse enters their top-level window, as long as they set it back to the root window when the pointer leaves again. A client might want to do this to send all keyboard input to one of its subwindows. See Chapter 10, *Interclient Communication*, for more information about what a client should do regarding the keyboard focus.

8.3.2.2 Keyboard and Pointer Grabbing

The keyboard and/or the pointer can be grabbed when their input should not be allowed to be interrupted by other clients. As the name implies, grabbing prevents other clients from receiving input, and therefore can be antisocial. It should not be done unless absolutely necessary. Grabbing the pointer is particularly troublesome, because there is no event to announce to other clients that this has happened (see Appendix F, *Proposed Interclient Communication Conventions*).

In general, grabbing is an advanced topic that you do not need to understand in detail until you find a reason to use it. But there are two exceptions to this rule. You do need to know what will happen when other clients grab, so that your client can prepare for it. Secondly, an automatic grab takes place between `ButtonPress` and `ButtonRelease` events if your client has selected both. You must understand grabbing to understand the implications of this automatic grab.

An *active grab* causes pointer and keyboard events to be sent to the grabbing window regardless of the current position of the pointer. Active grabs are invoked directly by calling `XGrabPointer` and `XGrabKeyboard`. A *passive grab* (invoked by calling `XGrabKey` or `XGrabButton`) causes an active grab to begin when a certain key or button combination is pressed.

When you grab a device, you have the option of confining the pointer to any window within the grabbing client, and of controlling the further processing of both keyboard and pointer events.

Grabbing the keyboard effectively selects all keyboard events, whether you selected them previously or not. Grabbing the keyboard also causes `FocusIn` and `FocusOut` events to be sent to the old and new focus windows, but they must be selected by each window to be received. In the call to grab the pointer, however, you specify what types of pointer, button, and enter/leave events you want.

Grabs take precedence over the keyboard focus window. Grabs of the keyboard generated `FocusIn` and `FocusOut` events, so that if your client selects these, it can determine whether or not it can get keyboard events. Pointer grabbing is more problematic, since no event notifies other clients when one client has grabbed it. Basicly, there is nothing a client can do if it can't even find out when the pointer is grabbed.

For more on keyboard and pointer grabbing, see Section 9.4. For a description of server grabbing, which is a different topic though still related to events, see Chapter 14, *Window Management*.

8.3.3 Event Masks

This section describes the event masks and the events they select. After reading this section you should have a good idea of what types of events exist, what they are for, how to select them, and when to use them. Chapter 9, *The Keyboard and Pointer* and the sections listed in Table 8-5 provide practical examples and describe the use of some of the more commonly-used events in more detail.

8.3.3.1 KeyPressMask and KeyReleaseMask

`KeyPress` and `KeyRelease` events report when a keyboard key has been pressed or released. Most, but not all, servers are capable of generating `KeyRelease` events. Shift, Control, and other modifier keys generate events just like the main keyboard.

The `KeyPress` and `KeyRelease` events provide a keycode that identifies the key, but the keycodes are server-dependent and should not be used to interpret the event. Instead, you can use `XLookupString` to translate the keycode into a portable symbol called a keysym, which represents the symbol on the cap of the key, and into an ASCII character string. Both the mapping between keycodes and keysyms and the mapping between keysyms and ASCII strings can be modified.

In `XLookupString`, the main routine used for interpreting `KeyPress` and `KeyRelease` events, there is a provision for a special Compose key which is available on some keyboards, so that multikey sequences, usually used to type characters for languages other than English, can be entered and translated into the appropriate keysym. The Compose key feature, however, is not implemented in Release 2.

The events selected by `KeyPressMask` and `KeyReleaseMask` are used in the examples in Section 9.1.1.

8.3.3.2 ButtonPressMask, ButtonReleaseMask, and OwnerGrabButtonMask

`ButtonPress` and `ButtonRelease` events occur when the pointer buttons are pressed. There are generally between three and five buttons on the pointer, and the event structure specifies not only the button that caused the event, but also the current state of all the pointer buttons and the modifier keys on the keyboard. The mapping between the bits in the button mask and the physical buttons can be changed with `XSetPointerMapping` and read with `XGetPointerMapping`, and is global to the server.

The pointer is automatically grabbed between the `ButtonPress` and `ButtonRelease` events, on behalf of the client for whose window the `ButtonPress` was selected. This way, you always expect to receive button events in pairs since the release will be sent to your client regardless of the position of the pointer at that time. Only one client can select button events on any one window at one time, due to the grab that automatically takes place.

The `OwnerGrabButtonMask` does not select any event by itself, but it controls the distribution of button events to your client during the automatic grab between the `ButtonPress` and `ButtonRelease` (and during any grab your client might make). If it is selected, the automatic grab has the same effect as an `XGrabButton` call with the owner_events argument set to True, so that the ButtonRelease event is sent to whichever of the client's windows the pointer is in. If the ButtonRelease occurs outside the client's windows, or if OwnerGrabButtonMask is not selected, all events will be sent only to the window where the ButtonPress occurred. Current wisdom suggests that you should always select OwnerGrabButtonMask with ButtonPressMask.

The events selected by ButtonPressMask and ButtonReleaseMask are discussed in Section 9.2.2 and demonstrated in Examples 9-9, 14-1, and 14-6.

8.3.3.3 The Pointer Motion Masks

There are eight pointer motion masks: PointerMotionMask, PointerMotion-HintMask, ButtonMotionMask, Button1MotionMask, Button2MotionMask, Button3MotionMask, Button4MotionMask, and Button5MotionMask. Up to five pointer buttons are supported, even though most mice have only three buttons and some have only one.

* PointerMotionMask selects motion events that occur when any or none of the pointer buttons are pressed. Each event includes the position of the pointer within the event window, and the position relative to the origin of the root window. All motion events contain a mask that gives the current status of the modifier keys and pointer buttons, and the current server time. MotionNotify events occur in large numbers while the pointer is moving steadily. Therefore, this mask is selected alone only by clients that require a complete record of pointer position, such as painting programs.

* PointerMotionHintMask is used in concert with other pointer motion masks to reduce the number of events generated. By itself, it doesn't select any events. PointerMotionHintMask specifies that the server should send only one Motion-Notify event when the pointer moves, until a key or button state changes, the pointer leaves the window, or the client calls XQueryPointer or XGetMotionEvents. The idea is that instead of processing hundreds of pointer motion events, the client gets only one event per movement and then queries the pointer position or examines the motion history buffer (the latter may not exist on some servers) for the current position. This approach is suitable for clients that need the pointer position at particular times, but that don't need all the intermediate positions. Even though each query for the pointer position is a round-trip request, the performance of this approach is better than that of selecting all the events with PointerMotionMask, because of the reduced network traffic.

* ButtonMotionMask selects any pointer motion events that occur when at least one button is pressed.

* Button1MotionMask, Button2MotionMask, Button3MotionMask, Button4MotionMask, and Button5MotionMask select pointer motion events that occur when the specified button is pressed. If two or more of these masks are used, events with any combination of the specified buttons (except both released) will be selected.

Handling the events selected by these masks is described in Section 9.2.1, and demonstrated in three examples in that section.

8.3.3.4 FocusChangeMask

FocusIn and FocusOut events occur when the keyboard focus window is changed. A window that selects FocusChangeMask receives a FocusOut event if it was the old focus window or is in the same branch of the hierarchy as the old focus window. It receives a FocusIn event if it is the new focus window or is in the same branch of the hierarchy as the new focus window. The detail member in the event tells the relationship of the window to the new or old focus window. With this information, it is possible to tell whether the window can receive keyboard input. You can read the details of what events are delivered in Appendix E, *Event Reference*.

EnterNotify, LeaveNotify, FocusIn, and FocusOut events are often used together to track whether the pointer is in a window and whether the client has the keyboard focus. If the focus is the root, EnterNotify and LeaveNotify events are used. With any other focus, the FocusIn and FocusOut events take precedence.

FocusIn and FocusOut events are described and used in Section 9.3.

8.3.3.5 EnterWindowMask and LeaveWindowMask

EnterNotify and LeaveNotify events are typically used to inform a client that the pointer just entered or just left one of its windows. If the client receives a LeaveNotify event in its top-level window, the client won't be receiving any more key, button, or motion events until it gets an EnterNotify event, unless it is the keyboard focus window or has grabbed the keyboard or pointer.

An EnterNotify event is also generated when a window is mapped over the current position of the pointer, and a LeaveNotify is generated when a window containing the pointer is unmapped.

EnterNotify and LeaveNotify events are described and used in Section 9.3.

8.3.3.6 KeymapStateMask

KeymapNotify events notify the client about the keyboard state when the pointer or keyboard focus enters a window. The keyboard state is represented (in the event structure) by 32 bytes of data called a *keyboard vector*, with one bit for each keyboard key. The number of a bit in the vector for a particular key is the same as the key's keycode. This vector is the same as the vector returned by XQueryKeymap.

This event type, if it is selected, always follows immediately after an EnterNotify or FocusIn event. It allows a client to find out which keys were pressed when the pointer or the keyboard focus entered the window. Since the state of the modifier keys is already reported in EnterNotify and FocusIn events, the KeymapNotify event is only useful for reporting the state of other keys.

`KeymapState` events are not used in the examples in this manual, because they are rarely needed. For more information about them, see Appendix E, *Event Reference.*

8.3.3.7 ExposureMask

An `Expose` event tells a client which window, or area within a window, has just become visible. The usual response is to redraw the contents of the area, or of the entire window if that is easier and comparably fast. Figure 8-3 shows a typical window hierarchy before and after window *C* is lowered. Two `Expose` events are sent to window *A* specifying areas *E1* and *E2*, and one `Expose` event is sent to window *B* specifying area *E3*.

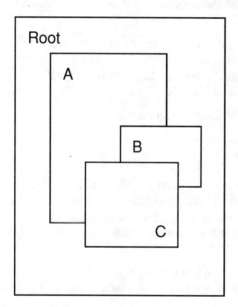 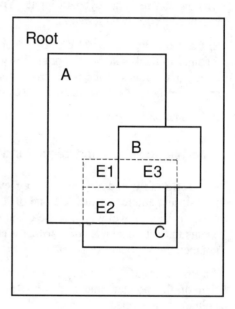

Figure 8-3. Expose events generated by lowering of window C

The handling of `Expose` events is fully described and demonstrated in Section 3.2.13.1.

8.3.3.8 VisibilityChangeMask

A `VisibilityNotify` event is sent when a window makes any change in visibility (Table 8-4), except when the window becomes not viewable. (Becoming not viewable means that the window or one of its ancestors was unmapped, which generates an `Unmap-Notify` event.) This event might be used by a client that must be completely visible in order to be useful.

The symbol returned in the state flag of the event is shown in the third column of the table.

Table 8-4. Visibility Transitions Causing VisibilityNotify Events

Beginning State	Final State	state Flag
unobscured	partially obscured	VisibilityPartiallyObscured
unobscured	fully obscured	VisibilityFullyObscured
partially obscured	unobscured	VisibilityUnobscured
partially obscured	fully obscured	VisibilityFullyObscured
fully obscured	unobscured	VisibilityUnobscured
fully obscured	partially obscured	VisibilityPartiallyObscured
not viewable	unobscured	VisibilityUnobscured
not viewable	partially obscured	VisibilityPartiallyObscured
not viewable	fully obscured	VisibilityFullyObscured

VisibilityNotify events are not demonstrated in this book. For more information on them, see Appendix E, *Event Reference*.

8.3.3.9 ColormapChangeMask

ColormapNotify events report when the colormap attribute of the window (for which this mask was selected) changes, and when the colormap specified by the attribute is installed, uninstalled, or freed. XChangeWindowAttributes can generate this event when the colormap window attribute is changed. XFreeColormap, XInstall-Colormap, and XUninstallColormap generate this event if called on the colormap specified in the attribute of the window. From the information in the structure, you can tell which of these calls generated the event, and what the current status of the colormap is. The conventions for what the client should do in response to each of these contingencies has not yet been determined. See Chapter 10, *Interclient Communication*.

ColormapNotify events are dicussed in Section 7.5.2.

8.3.3.10 PropertyChangeMask

A PropertyNotify event indicates that a property of a certain window was changed or deleted. This event is generated when XChangeProperty, XDeleteProperty, or XRotateWindowProperties is called, or when XGetWindowProperty is called with certain arguments. Beyond its normal purpose, this event can be used to get the current server time. This is done by appending zero-length data to a property using XChange-Property, which generates a PropertyNotify event containing the time.

The uses of PropertyNotify events are described in Chapter 10, *Interclient Communication*.

8.3.3.11   StructureNotifyMask and SubstructureNotifyMask

`StructureNotifyMask` selects a group of event types that report when the state of a window has changed. This includes the window's configuration (size, position, border width, stacking order), whether it was destroyed, whether it was moved due to its `win_gravity` window attibute, whether it was mapped or unmapped, and whether it was reparented.

`SubstructureNotifyMask` selects the same events plus one that indicates that a window has been created; it monitors all the *subwindows* of the window specified in the `XSelectInput` call that used this mask. Only `SubstructureNotifyMask` selects `CreateNotify` events, because the window does not exist beforehand and therefore no ID exists to use in a call to `XSelectInput` using `StructureNotifyMask`.

Applications often select `StructureNotifyMask` to be notified that they have been manipulated by the window manager or some other client, so that they can act accordingly.

The following list describes the events selected by `StructureNotifyMask` and `SubstructureNotifyMask`:

- A `CirculateNotify` event reports a call to change the stacking order, and includes whether the final position is on top or on bottom. This event is generated by `XCirculateSubwindows`, `XCirculateSubwindowsUp`, or `XCirculate-SubwindowsDown`.

- A `ConfigureNotify` event reports changes to a window's configuration, including its size, position, border width, and stacking order. This event is generated by `XConfigureWindow`, `XRaiseWindow`, `XLowerWindow`, `XRestackWindows`, `XMoveWindow`, `XResizeWindow`, `XMoveResizeWindow`, `XMapRaised`, and `XSetWindowBorderWidth`.

- A `CreateNotify` event reports that a new window has been created with either `XCreateSimpleWindow` or `XCreateWindow`.

- A `DestroyNotify` event reports that a window has been destroyed with `XDestroy-Window` or `XDestroySubwindows`. When a window is destroyed, this event is delivered to all subwindows of the window before it is delivered to the window itself, unless the subwindows are in another client's save-set (see Chapter 14, *Window Management*, for a description of save-sets).

- A `GravityNotify` event reports when a window is moved because its parent was resized and had its window gravity attribute set.

- A `MapNotify` event reports when a window is mapped. This event is generated by `XMapWindow`, `XMapRaised`, and `XMapSubwindows`.

- A `ReparentNotify` event reports when a client successfully reparents a window (see Chapter 14, *Window Management*, for a description of window reparenting).

- An `UnmapNotify` event reports when a mapped window is unmapped. This event also indicates whether the unmapping of a child window was due to the fact that the parent window was resized and the child had a window gravity attribute of `UnmapGravity`.

The `ConfigureNotify` event is used in the *basicwin* application described in Chapter 3, *Basic Window Program*. The rest of these events are used in a similar fashion by applications that need detailed knowledge of their state.

8.3.3.12 SubstructureRedirectMask

The three event types selected by `SubstructureRedirectMask`: `Circulate-Request`, `ConfigureRequest`, and `MapRequest`, can be used by a client (virtually always the window manager) to intercept and cancel window-configuration-changing requests made by other clients to change the window configuration. Only one client at a time can select `SubstructureRedirectMask` on a particular window. Normally, `SubstructureRedirectMask` is selected on the root window, to allow the window manager to intercept layout-changing requests for the top-level windows of each application. When these events are selected, the Xlib requests noted in the paragraphs below do not perform their usual function, but instead simply generate these events. The window manager is then able to modify the requests according to its layout policy before repeating the requests itself with its modified arguments.

These events differ from `CirculateNotify`, `ConfigureNotify`, and `MapNotify`, in that the `*Request` events† deliver the parameters of the request before the requests are carried out, and indicate that the original request has been canceled. The `*Notify` requests indicate the final outcome of such requests, unhindered.

Each of the event structures associated with the following event types includes an `override_redirect` member, which is either `True` or `False`. If it is `True`, the window manager should ignore the event, since this indicates that the client has set the `override_redirect` attribute to indicate that this is a temporary window. (For more information, see Section 14.2.)

- `CirculateRequest` events report when an Xlib function, such as `XRestack-Windows`, `XCirculateSubwindows`, `XCirculateSubwindowsDown`, or `XCirculateSubwindowsUp`, is called to change the stacking order of a group of children.

- `ConfigureRequest` events report when an Xlib function, such as `XConfigure-Window`, `XRaiseWindow`, `XLowerWindow`, `XMoveWindow`, `XResizeWindow`, `XMoveResizeWindow`, or `XSetWindowBorderWidth`, is called to resize, move, restack, or change the border width of a window.

- `MapRequest` events report when `XMapWindow` or `XMapSubwindows` is called to map a window.

The uses of the event types selected by `SubstructureRedirectMask` are described in Chapter 14, *Window Management*.

---

† The * (wildcard) notation is used occasionally in this book to indicate a number of events or routines with similar names.

8.3.3.13 ResizeRedirectMask

The `ResizeRequest` event is generated when some other client (usually the window manager) attempts to resize the window on which `ResizeRedirectMask` is selected. `XConfigureWindow`, `XResizeWindow`, and `XMoveResizeWindow` generate this event. Only one client can select `ResizeRedirectMask` at a time on a particular window.

This event includes the *requested* size. The final size may be adjusted by the window manager, and can be found from the resulting `ConfigureNotify` event, or, if the window is visible, from the `Expose` event.

A client might wish to select this mask if it has only one acceptable size. Then when any client attemped to resize the window, the request would be sent as an event and can be safely ignored. However, if some client (say, the window manager) has selected `SubstructureRedirectMask` for the parent of the window on which `Resize-RedirectMask` was selected, the substructure redirect takes precedence. Therefore, this usually won't work. `ResizeRedirectMask` is not very useful given that most window managers select `SubstructureRedirectMask`.

8.3.3.14 Automatically Selected Events

Seven types of event can be sent to your program even if you don't explicitly select them. Your client must handle or throw away `MappingNotify` events regardless of whether the client reads the keyboard. All the others are generated in response to your own actions (either by the server or other clients), and therefore you should know that you are going to get them. Example 8-3 describes when each of these events should be present in your event loop.

- `MappingNotify` events are caused by `XSetPointerMapping`, `XChange-KeyboardMapping`, and `XSetModifierMapping` calls that set the pointer button, keyboard key, and keyboard modifier key mappings. Since these mappings are global to the server, each client must call the correct function to refresh its knowledge of the mappings.

  If the changed mapping is of the keyboard, a receiving client should call `XRefresh-KeyboardMapping`, which updates a client's knowledge of the server's mapping between keycodes and keysym.

  If the changed mapping is of the pointer, the client can call `XGetPointerMapping` to update its knowledge. Most current clients don't do this, however, because it is assumed that the button mappings were intentionally changed by the user. That means that the client should not attempt to adjust its operation so that the buttons have their old meanings.

- `ClientMessage` events are sent as a result of a call to `XSendEvent` by a client to a particular window. They contain data described by an `Atom`. These events are normally used to transfer selection data. The `send_event` member of the event structure will always be set.

- SelectionClear, SelectionNotify, and SelectionRequest events are used to communicate back and forth between two applications that are transferring information. This process is described in Section 10.3.

- GraphicsExpose and NoExpose events are selected not by an event mask but by the graphics_exposure member of the GC. One or the other of them (or both) is generated by each XCopyArea or XCopyPlane request when the GC specified for the request has this member set to True. Otherwise, the events are not generated. The GraphicsExpose event indicates that a source area could not be completely copied into a destination because the source was partially or fully obscured. The NoExpose event indicates that the copy was not affected by an obscured source. More than one GraphicsExpose event can be generated by a single XCopy* request, depending on the number and position of the obscuring windows, but only one NoExpose is possible as a result of a single copy. GraphicsExpose events are often handled just like Expose events.

8.4 Sending Events

The XSendEvent function may be used to send a ClientMessage event or any other event type to a particular window, to the current keyboard focus window, or to the window in which the pointer is located. Sending events is necessary in selection processing, as described in Section 10.3. It also may be useful for designing test procedures for your input handling or for making demonstration programs that simulate user input.

In Release 2, the send_event member of each event structure indicates the origin of the event. If True, it was sent from another client rather from the server. Note that unless this flag is explicitly checked, events from the server and from other clients will appear the same to your application.

In Release 1, the send_event flag was not present, but instead the highest bit of the type member indicated whether the event originated from the server or another client. If you are using Release 1, and you want events sent by other clients to be treated like any other event, use the code shown in Example 8-8 on all incoming events. It masks the high bit so that comparisons with the event type symbols will work.

Example 8-8. Masking the high bit (Release 1 only)

```
XEvent report;

XNextEvent(display, &report);
report.type &= 0x7f;
/* now all events will appear the same
 * whether sent by server or XSendEvent */
    switch (event.type) {
    case MotionNotify:
        break;
    ...
    }
```

8.5 Where to Find More on Each Event

All event types are described in reference format in Appendix E, *Event Reference*. The information on each page includes the event structure definition, description of each event structure member, XEvent union name, how to select the event, when it is generated, and notes on its use. Table 8-5 shows other places in this manual where you can find information about using certain event types.

Table 8-5. Where Events Are Described Further

Event Type	Section
KeyPress KeyRelease	9.1.1.1
ButtonPress ButtonRelease	9.2.2
KeymapNotify	9.3.1
MotionNotify	9.2.1
EnterNotify LeaveNotify	9.3
FocusIn FocusOut	9.3
Expose	3.2.13.1
GraphicsExpose NoExpose	5.7
ColormapNotify	7.5.2
PropertyNotify	10.1
ConfigureNotify	3.2.16
CirculateRequest ConfigureRequest MapRequest	14.2
MappingNotify	9.1.2.3
SelectionClear	10.3*
SelectionNotify	10.3*
SelectionRequest	10.3*

* Also in Appendix F, *Proposed Interclient Communication Conventions*

9

The Keyboard and Pointer

This chapter describes how to handle keyboard and pointer events, but also describes many other topics related to these two input devices. In particular, it discusses X's use of keysyms as portable symbols for character encoding, keyboard remapping, keyboard and pointer "grabs," and keyboard and pointer preferences.

In This Chapter:

The Keyboard and Pointer

In Chapter 3, *Basic Window Program*, we showed you quite thoroughly how to deal with
Expose events. But all we did with pointer and keyboard events was to exit the program.
As you can guess, there can be more to it than that. This chapter describes and demonstrates the handling of keyboard and pointer events, describes keyboard and pointer mapping, and describes how to set keyboard preferences.

9.1 The Keyboard

The keyboard is an area like color, where X clients have to be made portable across systems
with different physical characteristics. In the case of the keyboard, these variations are in
two areas: whether the keyboard provides KeyPress and KeyRelease events or just
KeyPress events, and the symbols on the caps of the keys.

Almost all serious workstations provide both KeyPress and KeyRelease events. Some
personal computers, however, may not. Therefore, avoid depending on KeyRelease
events if you want your client to be portable to the lowest classes of machines.

The second problem is adjusting for variations in the keys available on each keyboard and
the codes they generate. We'll start explaining how this problem is solved by describing the
contents of a key event.

KeyPress and KeyRelease events are stored in XKeyEvent structures, shown in
Example 9-1. Each key event contains the keycode of the key that was pressed, and
state, a mask which indicates which modifier keys and pointer buttons were being held
down just before the event. A *modifier key* is a key like Shift or Control that can modify the
meaning of a key event. In addition to their effect on the processing of other keys, the
modifier keys also generate key events with unique keycodes.

Example 9-1. The XKeyEvent structure

```
typedef struct {
    int type;                    /* of event */
    unsigned long serial;        /* last request processed by server */
    Bool send_event;             /* true if from a SendEvent request */
    Display *display;            /* server connection */
    Window window;               /* "event" window reported in */
```

Example 9-1. The XKeyEvent structure (continued)

```
    Window root;                /* root window event occurred on */
    Window subwindow;           /* child window */
    Time time;                  /* milliseconds */
    int x, y;                   /* coordinates in event window */
    int x_root, y_root;         /* coordinates relative to root */
    unsigned int state;         /* key or button mask */
    unsigned int keycode;       /* detail */
    Bool same_screen;           /* same screen flag */
} XKeyEvent;
typedef XKeyEvent XKeyPressedEvent;
typedef XKeyEvent XKeyReleasedEvent;
```

The keycode member of XKeyEvent is a number between 7 and 255. The keycode is the same regardless of whether a key is pressed or released. The keycode for each physical key never changes on a particular server, but the key with the same symbol on it on different brands of equipment may generate different keycodes. For portability reasons, and because the keycode by itself without the state of the modifier keys does not provide enough information to interpret an event, clients can't use keycodes by themselves to determine the meaning of key events.

Instead of using the keycode alone, X clients call XLookupString to translate the key event into a keysym. A *keysym* is a defined constant that corresponds to the meaning of a key event. For example, the translation of the keycode generated by the ''a'' key on any system would be XK_a if no other keys were being held and XK_A if the Shift key were being held or if Shift Lock was in effect (all keysyms begin with XK_). The translation of the keycode for the Return key (which is labeled Enter or just ⏎ on some keyboards) would be XK_Return. The Enter key on the keypad, if any, would have the keysym XK_KP_Enter. Example 9-2 shows some keysym definitions. All keysyms are defined in *<X11/keysymdef.h>*.

Example 9-2. Some sample keysym definitions

```
#define XK_BackSpace     0xFF08    /* back space, back char,... */
#define XK_Left          0xFF51    /* Move left, left arrow */
#define XK_Undo          0xFF65    /* Undo, oops */
#define XK_Num_Lock      0xFF7F
#define XK_KP_Multiply   0xFFAA
#define XK_Shift_L       0xFFE1    /* Left shift */
#define XK_space         0x020     /* space */
#define XK_numbersign    0x023     /* # */
#define XK_3             0x033
#define XK_question      0x03f     /* "?" */
#define XK_A             0x041
#define XK_e             0x065
```

XLookupString also provides an ASCII string that corresponds to the keysym, or NULL if there is no associated string. By default, all the keys that have ASCII values will have that value as their string. For example, XK_A would have the string ''A,'' XK_ampersand would have the string ''&,'' and XK_4 would have the string ''4.'' XK_Return, XK_Escape, and XK_Delete have ASCII values but they are not printable.

XK_Shift_L (the Shift key on the left side of the keyboard) would not normally have an associated string.

The ASCII value for a particular keysym as returned by XLookupString can be changed by the client using XRebindKeysym, and it can be a string of any length, not just a single character. Even though keysyms like XK_F1 (the F1 key) have no default ASCII mapping, they can be given strings. This mapping would apply only to the client that calls XRebindKeysym.

With these introductory comments, we'll move right to the examples that handle keyboard input. Then we'll return to discuss keysyms in more detail and the various keyboard mappings and how they can be changed.

9.1.1 Simple Keyboard Input

Example 9-3 shows the framework of the code for translating a keyboard event into both a keysym and an ASCII string. You'll need the keysym to determine what the keystroke means, and the ASCII string if the keystroke is a printable character. If the keystroke is printable, the program would append the ASCII interpretation of the key event to the end of the result string (and display it). If the keystroke is a modifier key being pressed, the event can normally be ignored since the modifier status of events on other keys is already dealt with by XLookupString. But XK_Delete or XK_Backspace would indicate that a character should be removed from the string.

The function keys are not initially mapped to ASCII strings and can be ignored, but if the client allows the user to map them to an arbitrary string, it should treat them like any other printable character.

You may notice in Example 9-3 that XLookupString returns something called an XComposeStatus. Some keyboards provide a Compose key, which is used to type characters not found on the keyboard keys. It's purpose is to make it possible to type characters from other languages without disturbing the normal operation of the keyboard. As it usually works, you press the Compose key followed by some other key to generate characters like é. A table is usually provided which tells you which keys correspond to each foreign character. Processing of multikey sequences using the Compose key may one day be provided by XLookupString, but it is not supported in Release 2, even though the XCompose-Status argument is already present.*

Example 9-3. Translating a key event to keysym and ASCII

```
Display *display;
XEvent event;
char buffer[20];
int bufsize = 20;
KeySym key;
XComposeStatus compose;
```

---

* If your *lint* program complains about the variable compose which is declared but not used, you may be able to trick it with a line such as compose=compose;.

Example 9-3. Translating a key event to keysym and ASCII (continued)

```
int charcount;
    .
    .
    .
    /*  open display, create window, select, map */

XNextEvent(display, &event);
switch( event.type ) {
    .
    .
    .
case KeyPress:
    charcount = XLookupString(&event, buffer, bufsize, &keysym,
            &compose);
    /* branch according to keysym, then use buffer if the key
     * is printable */
    break;
case MappingNotify:
    XRefreshKeyboardMapping(&event);
    break;
}
```

Keysyms for accented vowels, tildes, and most combinations found in western languages are provided in the LATIN1 set. If you want to display an accented *e*, for example, the keysym is XK_eacute. If the desired character is not present in the desired font, the client can prepare two or more text items for XDrawText for displaying the desired overstrike character, and use the delta member to move the second character back over the first. XDrawText is capable of drawing in a different font for each text item, in case the desired accent is in a separate font from the desired character.

9.1.1.1 Getting a String — A Dialog Box

Let's say you are porting a non-event-driven program to X, and you have a routine called get_string that gets an ASCII string from the user. It gets the entire string before returning. But under X, the user might stop typing midway through, pop some other window on top to check some bit of information, then pop the original application back on top. That means you need to handle exposure in the middle of the input string, which in turn means you need a function that remembers the string's state so that it can be redrawn in the get_string routine. You also have to be prepared in case the keyboard gets remapped by some other client. Suddenly, an event loop appears in your tiny subroutine to get a string. Every subroutine that gets input will need an event loop of some sort, though all clients can be written to reduce the number of loops to manageable proportions.

Example 9-4 is a modification to the *basicwin* program described in Chapter 3, *Basic Window Program* that puts up a pop-up dialog box. If the user presses a button in the *basicwin* window, the application puts up a dialog box, which the user can type into until a carriage return is typed. All the printable characters except Tab are supported, and Delete or Backspace operate as would be expected. The code allows the user to type the string while also handling the other events that might occur.

Example 9-4. Implementing a dialog box

```
/* other include files */
#include <X11/keysym.h>

/* other defined constants */
#define MAX_POPUP_STRING_LENGTH 40
#define MAX_MAPPED_STRING_LENGTH 10

/* global variables display and screen */

void main(argc, argv)
int argc;
char **argv;
{
     /* declarations from basicwin */
       .
       .
       .

     /* the following are for pop-up window */
     static Window pop_win;
     char buffer[MAX_MAPPED_STRING_LENGTH];
     int bufsize=MAX_MAPPED_STRING_LENGTH;
     int start_x, start_y;
     KeySym keysym;
     XComposeStatus compose;
     int totalcount;
     unsigned int pop_width, pop_height;
     char string[MAX_POPUP_STRING_LENGTH];
     int popped = False;
     int length;

     /* create main window (win) and select its events */
       .
       .
       .


     XMapWindow(display, win);

     /* get events, use first to display text and graphics */
     while (1)  {
         XNextEvent(display, &report);
         switch  (report.type) {
         case Expose:
             if (report.xexpose.window == pop_win) {
                 if (popped)
                     XDrawString(display, pop_win, gc, start_x,
                         start_y, string, strlen(string));
             }
             else { /* it's the main window */
                 /* refresh main window as in basicwin */
             }
             break;
         case ConfigureNotify:
             /* same as in basicwin */
```

Example 9-4. Implementing a dialog box (continued)

```
                     .
                     .
                     .
              break;
         case ButtonPress:
              /* put up popup window, create if necessary */
              if (!pop_win) {   /* create it */
              /* determine popup box size from font info */
              pop_width = MAX_POPUP_XA_STRING_LENGTH *
                        font_info->max_bounds.width + 4;
              pop_height = font_info->max_bounds.ascent +
                        font_info->max_bounds.descent + 4;
              pop_win = XCreateSimpleWindow(display, win, x, y, pop_width,
                        pop_height, border_width, BlackPixel(display,
                        screen), WhitePixel(display, screen));
              /* calculate starting position of string in window */
              start_x = 2;
              start_y = font_info->max_bounds.ascent + 2;
              XSelectInput(display, pop_win, ExposureMask | KeyPressMask);
              }
              /* if window is already mapped, this won't do anything */
              XMapWindow(display, pop_win);
              popped = True;
              break;
              /* trickle down into KeyPress (no break) */
         case KeyPress:
              if (report.xkey.window == win) {
                   /* key on main window indicates exit */
                   XUnloadFont(display, font_info->fid);
                   XFreeGC(display, gc);
                   XCloseDisplay(display);
                   exit(1);
              }
              else {
                   /* Get characters until you encounter
                    * a carriage return.  Deal with
                    * backspaces, etc. */
                   count = XLookupString(&report, buffer, bufsize,
                             &keysym, &compose);
                   /* now do the right thing with
                    * as many keysyms as possible. */
                   if ((keysym == XK_Return) || (keysym == XK_KP_Enter)
                             || (keysym == XK_Linefeed)) {
                        XUnmapWindow(display, pop_win);
                        popped = False;
                        printf("string is %s0, string);
                        break;
                   }
                   else if (((keysym >= XK_KP_Space)
                             && (keysym <= XK_KP_9))
                             || ((keysym >= XK_space)
                             && (keysym <= XK_asciitilde)))
                        {
                        if ((strlen(string) + strlen (buffer)) >=
                        MAX_POPUP_STRING_LENGTH)
```

Example 9-4. Implementing a dialog box (continued)

```
                        XBell(display, 100);
                else
                        strcat(string, buffer);
                }
        else if ((keysym >= XK_Shift_L)
                && (keysym <= XK_Hyper_R))
                ;/* do nothing because its a modifier key */
        else if ((keysym >= XK_F1)
                && (keysym <= XK_F35))
                if (buffer == NULL)
                        printf("Unmapped function key0);
        else if ((strlen(string) + strlen (buffer)) >=
                MAX_POPUP_STRING_LENGTH)
                XBell(display, 100);
                else
                        strcat(string, buffer);

        else if ((keysym == XK_BackSpace) ||
                (keysym == XK_Delete)) {
                if ((length = strlen(string)) > 0) {
                        string[length - 1] = NULL;
                        XClearWindow(display, pop_win);
                }
                else
                        XBell(display, 100);
                }
                else {
                        printf("keysym %s is not handled0,
                                XKeysymToString(keysym));
                        XBell(display, 100);
                }
                XDrawString(display, pop_win, gc, start_x,
                        start_y, string, strlen(string));
                break;
                }
        case MappingNotify:
                XRefreshKeyboardMapping(&report);
                break;
        default:
                /* all events selected by StructureNotifyMask
                 * except ConfigureNotify are thrown away here,
                 * since nothing is done with them */
                break;
        } /* end switch */
    } /* end while */
}
```

Example 9-4 takes advantage of the fact that the keysyms are constants arranged in groups with consecutive values. By looking for any keysym in a given range, you don't need to specify every keysym you intend to match.

Notice that the program uses keysyms to match all the keystrokes, and then does different things depending on whether the keysym is a normal key, a modifier key, a function key, a delete key, or an enter key. If the key is printable, it copies the ASCII values returned by `XLookupString` into the result string.

This program does have some weaknesses.* One of them is that it redraws the entire string instead of just the character being changed. Using `XTextItem` structures for each character and calling `XDrawText` instead of `XDrawString` would improve its performance. A second advantage of the `XTextItem` approach is that it would support Tab characters and functions keys mapped to strings. Since a tab has to be expanded into a number of spaces before being drawn, and function keys may be mapped to arbitrary strings, it is difficult to properly implement them with the approach we have used in Example 9-4.

9.1.2 The Keyboard Mappings

As we've said, there are several translations that take place between the pressing of a key and its interpretation within a program. The first, the mapping between physical keys and keycodes, is server-dependent and can't be modified. A client can't determine anything about this first mapping, and it is just a fact that certain physical keys generate certain keycodes. The second mapping, keycodes to keysyms, can be modified by clients but is server-wide so it usually isn't modified. The specification of which keycodes are modifiers is also part of the second level of mapping, because it affects the mapping of keycodes to keysyms. The third mapping, from keysyms to strings, is local to a client. This is the mapping with which a client can allow the user to map the function keys to strings for convenience of typing.

We're going to describe the mapping between keysyms and strings first, because this is the mapping that applications are most likely to change. Following that, we'll describe what you need to know about the keycode to keysym mapping and modifier mapping to write normal applications. These mappings are normally only changed by clients run from the user's startup script that do nothing else, because they change the keyboard mapping for all applications.

After that, Sections 9.1.3.1 and 9.1.3.2 are optional reading. They describe the background and development of keysyms, and how to write special-purpose programs to change the server-wide mapping of keycodes to keysyms and the modifier mapping. These techniques are not needed in normal applications.

---

* I could say I left it this way because it is simpler, and it is, but that's not why I wrote it this way. I didn't realize the other way would be better until the program was already done. I'll leave it as an exercise for you to modify it as described!

9.1.2.1 Keysyms to Strings

The default mapping of keysyms to ASCII is defined by the server. The ASCII representation of the keys on the main keyboard are the ASCII codes for the single characters on the caps of the keys. Keysyms that don't have ASCII representations, such as the function keys, initially have mappings to NULL, but they can sometimes be mapped to strings, as we'll describe. However, the modifier keys on some machines can't be mapped to strings at all.

Any client in which the user is expected to type a large amount of text should support remapping of the function keys to strings. XRebindKeysym is the only function that can change this string, the one returned by XLookupString. The string can be any length. This change affects only the client that calls XRebindKeysym.

Example 9-5 is a short code sample that demonstrates how to remap function keys to strings. It binds the string "STOP" to Shift-F1 and "ABORT" to Control-Shift-F1. Since keyboards may have two Shift and two Control keys, one on each side, the process has to be done for both. Mapping the function keys combined with modifiers won't work on all servers. (On the Sun sample server, this code results in STOP being generated when F1 is pressed with any modifiers, and ABORT is never generated.) However, mapping of unmodified function keys should work on all servers.

Example 9-5. Mapping keys to strings

```
#include <X11/keysym.h>
    .
    .
    .
Display *display;

KeySym modlist[2];    /* array of modifier keysyms */
unsigned int string_length;
unsigned int list_length;
    .
    .
    .
/* open display */
    .
    .
    .
/* map Shift-F1 to "STOP"  */
string_length = 4;
list_length = 1;
modlist[1] = XK_Shift_R;    /* Do right shift key */
XRebindKeysym(display, XK_F1, modlist, list_length, "STOP",
        string_length);
modlist[1] = XK_Shift_L;    /* Do left shift key */
XRebindKeysym(display, XK_F1, modlist, list_length, "STOP",
        string_length);

/* map Control-Shift-F1 to "ABORT"  */
string_length = 5;
list_length = 2;

/* Both Right Pressed */
modlist[1] = XK_Shift_R; modlist[2] = XK_Control_R;
XRebindKeysym(display, XK_F1, modlist, list_length, "ABORT",
        string_length);
```

Example 9-5. Mapping keys to strings (continued)

```
/* Left Shift, Right Control */
modlist[1] = XK_Shift_L; modlist[2] = XK_Control_R;
XRebindKeysym(display, XK_F1, modlist, list_length, "ABORT",
        string_length);

/* Right Shift, Left Control */
modlist[1] = XK_Shift_R; modlist[2] = XK_Control_L;
XRebindKeysym(display, XK_F1, modlist, list_length, "ABORT",
        string_length);

/* Both Left Pressed */
modlist[1] = XK_Shift_L; modlist[2] = XK_Control_L;
XRebindKeysym(display, XK_F1, modlist, list_length, "ABORT",
        string_length);
```

9.1.2.2 The Modifier Keys

A keysym represents the meaning of a certain combination of a key and modifier keys such
as Shift and Control. For example, XK_A represents the letter "a" pressed while the shift
key is held down or while shift-lock is on. As in this example, the keysym depends on what
modifier key is being held.

Although Shift is present on all keyboards and Control on most, the remaining modifier keys
are not standardized. There may be Meta, Hyper, Super, Left, Right, or Alternate keys. X
however, has a fixed set of logical modifiers, listed in the first column of Table 9-1. Each of
these logical modifier symbols correspond to a bit in the state member of the XKey-
Event structure. On each keyboard, there is a mapping between the physical modifier keys
and these logical modifiers. Table 9-1 also shows the keysyms of the keys that are by
default mapped to the logical modifiers on a Sun-3 system, and the corresponding keycodes
for that system. You can use the *xmodmap* command without arguments to find out the
default modifier mapping on any system.

Table 9-1. Logical modifiers and a typical modifier key mapping

Logical Modifier	Default Keycodes of Physical Keys (Sun-3)	Modifier Keysym
ShiftMask	(0x6a), (0x75)	XK_Shift_L, XK_Shift_R
ShiftLockMask	(0x7e)	XK_Caps_Lock
ControlMask	(0x53)	XK_Control_L
Mod1Mask	(0x7f), (0x81)	XK_Meta_L, XK_Meta_R
Mod2Mask	(unmapped)	
Mod3Mask	(unmapped)	
Mod4Mask	(unmapped)	
Mod5Mask	(unmapped)	

Each keycode may have a list of keysyms, one for every logical modifier. Each list, of varying length, conveys the set of meanings for the key with each of the modifier keys pressed. This array of keysyms for each keycode is initially defined by the server. In most cases, only two keysyms are defined for the keys that represent single printable characters, and only one for the rest.

9.1.2.3 Keycodes to Keysyms

Clients can change the mapping of keycodes to keysyms (with XChangeKeyboard-Mapping), but they rarely do because this mapping is global to the server. This change would affect every client operating on the server. Every client would receive a Mapping-Notify event (regardless of whether they selected it or whether they actually use keyboard input), and must then get a new keysym table from the server with XRefreshKeyboard-Mapping. (This table is stored in the Display structure and is used by XLookup-String and the other routines that return keysyms.) XRefreshKeyboardMapping works by erasing the copy of the keyboard and/or modifier mappings that are present in the Display structure (the keysyms and modifiermap members). The next time that an Xlib call is made that requires either of these mappings, a request is made to the server, the new mappings are transferred to Xlib, and the pointers in the Display structure are reset to the new mapping data. Subsequent calls to access this data use the Display structure instead of querying the server.

One of few applications that might change the mapping between keycodes and keysyms would be an application that converted between QWERTY and DVORAK keyboard layout. These are the nicknames for two different layouts for the alphabetic characters on English-language keyboards. The QWERTY keyboard in common use was originally designed to be slow enough so that mechanical typesetting machine operators would not be able to type fast enough to jam their machines. The DVORAK keyboard, on the other hand, was designed to place the most common letters in the English language under the home row of keys and is much faster.

Let's say a user wanted to use the DVORAK layout instead of the default, which is QWERTY. This application would not even need to create a window, but it would change the mapping of keycodes to keysyms with XChangeKeyboardMapping. The user could then move the keycaps around on the keyboard or label them somehow. Except for calling XRefreshKeyboardMapping, other applications would operate as usual. From then on, while the server was running, all applications would work properly with the DVORAK layout.

9.1.3 Background on Keysyms

Keysyms are a concept developed especially for X. It may help you to understand them better to read about how they were designed. But this is optional reading and you can skip to Section 9.2 if you don't plan to write programs that change the mapping of keycodes to keysyms.

The keysyms are defined in two include files, *<X11/keysym.h>* and *<X11/keysymdef.h>*. Together these files define several sets of keysyms for different languages and purposes. There are sets for Latin, Greek, Cyrillic, Arabic, and so on, intended to allow for internationalization of programs. There are also sets for publishing and technical purposes because these fields have their own "languages." *<X11/keysym.h>* defines which character sets are active, and *<X11/keysymdef.h>* defines the symbols in all the sets. Only *<X11/keysym.h>* needs to be included in application because it includes *<X11/keysymdef.h>*.

By default, the enabled sets of defined keysyms include the ISO Latin character sets (1-4), a set of Greek characters, and a set of miscellaneous symbols common on keyboards (Return, Help, Tab, and so on). These are sufficient for making an application work in any western language. Symbols for Katakana, Arabic, Cyrillic, Technical, Special, Publishing, APL, and Hebrew character sets are defined in *<X11/keysymdef.h>* but are not enabled in *<X11/keysym.h>*, and may not be available on all servers. This is because some C compilers have a limit to the number of allowable defined symbols.

Many of the keysym sets share keysyms with sets earlier in the *<X11/keysymdef.h>* include file. For example, there is only one XK_space keysym because a space is common to all languages. XK_space is in LATIN1 so that it is always available. The LATIN2 and LATIN3 sets are quite short because they share most of their symbols with the previous sets.

9.1.3.1 The Design of Keysyms

English-language keyboards tend to be quite standard in the alphanumeric keys, but they differ radically in the miscellaneous function keys. Many function keys are left over from early timesharing days or are designed for a specific application. Keyboard layouts from large manufacturers tend to have lots of keys for every conceivable purpose, whereas small workstation manufacturers often have keys that are solely for support of some unique function.

There are two ways of thinking about how to define keysyms given such a situation: the *Engraving* approach and the *Common* approach.

The Engraving approach is to create a keysym for every unique key engraving. This is effectively taking the union of all key engravings on all keyboards. For example, some keyboards label function keys across the top as F1 through F*n*, others label them as PF1 through PF*n*. These would be different keys under the Engraving approach. Likewise, "Lock" would differ from "Shift Lock," which is different from the up-arrow symbol that has the effect of changing lower case to upper case. There are lots of other aliases such as "Del," "DEL," "Delete," "Remove," and so forth. The Engraving approach makes it easy to decide if a new entry should be added to the keysym set: if it does not exactly match an existing one, then a new one is created. One estimate is that there would be on the order of 300-500 miscellaneous keysyms using this approach, not counting foreign translations and variations.

The Common approach tries to capture all of the keys present on a number of common keyboards, folding likely aliases into the same keysym. For example, "Del," "DEL," and "Delete" are all merged into a single keysym. Vendors would be expected to augment the keysym set (using the vendor-specific encoding space) to include all of their unique keys that were not included in the standard set. Each vendor decides which of its keys map into the standard keysyms. It is more difficult to implement this approach, since a judgement is required whether a sufficient set of keyboards implement an engraving to justify making it a keysym in the standard set and which engravings should be merged into a single keysym. Under this scheme, there are an estimated 100-150 keysyms for an English-language keyboard.

While neither scheme is perfect, the Common approach has been selected because it makes it easier to write a portable application. Having the Delete functionality merged into a single keysym allows an application to implement a deletion function and expect reasonable bindings on a wide set of workstations. Under the Common approach, application writers are still free to look for and interpret vendor-specific keysyms, but, because they are in an extended set, application developers should be more conscious that they are writing applications in a nonportable fashion.

9.1.3.2 Conventions for Keysym Meaning

For each keycodes, the server defines a list of keycodes, corresponding to the key pressed while various modifier keys are being held. There are conventions for the meanings of the first two keysyms in the list. The first keysym in the list for a particular key should be construed as the symbol corresponding to a `KeyPress` when no modifier keys are down. The second keysym in the list, if present, usually should be construed as the symbol when the Shift or Shift-Lock modifier keys are down. However, if there is only one keysym for a particular keycode, if it is alphabetic, and if case distinction is relevant for it, then the appropriate case should be based on the Shift and Lock modifiers. For example, if the single keysym is an uppercase A, you have to use the `state` member of `XKeyEvent` to determine if the Shift key is held. `XLookupString` should translate the event into the correct ASCII string anyway.

X does not suggest an interpretation of the keysyms beyond the first two, and does not define any spatial geometry of the symbols on the key by their order in the keysym list. This is because the list of modifier keys varies widely between keyboards. However, when programming, it should be safe to assume that the third member in the keysym list would correspond to the key pressed with the next most common modifier available on the keyboard, which might be Control.

For keyboards with both left-side and right-side modifier keys (for example, Shift keys on each side that generate different keycodes), the bit in the `state` member in the event structure defines the OR of the keys. If electronically distinguishable, these keys can have separate keycodes and up/down events generated, and your program can track their individual states manually.

9.1.4 Changing the Server-Wide Keyboard Mappings

Both the keycode-to-keysym mapping and the modifier mapping affect all clients when they are changed by any client. That's why normal applications won't change them. Special-purpose programs, however, can be written to change these mappings, usually to be run from a user's startup script. These sections describe how to write such programs. If you don't plan to write one, you can skip ahead to Section 9.1.5.

9.1.4.1 Changing the Keycode to Keysym Mapping

XChangeKeyboardMapping changes the current mapping of the specified range of keycodes to keysyms.

Example 9-6 shows a simple program called *mapkey* that changes the keyboard mapping for all the applications running on the server. This application takes pairs of arguments that are keysyms, and maps the keycode associated with the first keysym to the second keysym. In other words, you could use it to map the F1 key to be Escape and Home to be a Control key on the right side of the keyboard by typing the following:

```
$   mapkey F1 Escape Home Control_R
```

Example 9-6. An application for server-wide keymapping

```c
#include <stdio.h>
#include <X11/Xlib.h>
#include <X11/Xutil.h>
#include <X11/Xatom.h>
#include <X11/keysym.h>

main(argc, argv)
int argc;
char **argv;
{
     KeySym old, new;
     int old_code;
     Display *dpy;

     if (!(dpy = XOpenDisplay(""))) {
          fprintf(stderr,"Cannot open display '%s'\n",
                    XDisplayName(""));
          exit(1);
     }
     argv++, argc--;

     if (argc & 0x1) {
          fprintf(stderr,"Usage:  Keysymfrom Keysymto Keysymfrom \
                    Keysymto ...\n");
          exit(1);
     }
     while (argc > 1) {
          old = XStringToKeysym(*argv++);
          new = XStringToKeysym(*argv++);
```

Example 9-6. An application for server-wide keymapping (continued)

```
            argc--, argc--;
            old_code = XKeysymToKeycode(dpy, old);
            XChangeKeyboardMapping(dpy, old_code, 1, &new, 1);
        }
    XFlush(dpy);
    XCloseDisplay(dpy);
    exit(0);
}
```

The application in Example 9-6 could be rewritten on a larger scale to change a keyboard from QWERTY to DVORAK layout as described in Section 9.1.2.3. Since the keycodes are server-dependent, the QWERTY-to-DVORAK conversion program would not be portable between machines unless it used XGetKeyboardMapping to get the current mapping of keycodes to keysyms and then remapped them.

XGetKeyboardMapping returns an array of keysyms that represent the current mapping of the specified range of keycodes. If you just want to inspect the mapping but not free or modify it, the Display.keysyms member is a pointer to the same data returned by XGetKeyboardMapping, except that it may be NULL if a client has just changed the mapping. Also, you should realize that the Display structure is private and may change between releases of X, so that accessing this member directly may lead to a portability problem. In Release 2 there is no macro to access this member.

9.1.4.2 Changing Modifier Mapping

X allows you to control which physical keys are considered modifier keys. Normal applications won't do this. The modifier mapping might be changed for a left-handed user if by default there was only one Control key on the left side of the keyboard and the user preferred to have a Control key on the right side. In that case, a conveniently placed key on the right side could be mapped to a logical Control key. Like keycode-to-keysym remapping, this would typically be done by a special-purpose application run from the user's startup script.

While modifier keys generate KeyPress and KeyRelease events like other keys, modifier keys are the only keys reported in the state member of every key, button, motion, or border crossing event structure. The state member is a mask that indicates which logical modifiers were pressed when the event occurred. Each bit in state is represented by a constant such as ControlMask. state is used by XLookupString to generate the correct keysym from a key event. Note that the state member of events other than key, button, motion, and border crossing events does not have the meaning described here.

XInsertModifiermapEntry and XDeleteModifiermapEntry provide the easiest ways by far to add or delete a few keycodes for a modifier. However, they are only available in Release 2. If you are using Release 1, read Section 9.1.4.3; the technique you should use is described there.

Using XInsertModifiermapEntry and XDeleteModifiermapEntry is straight-forward. You get the current modifier mapping stored in an XModifierKeymap structure with a call to XGetModifierMapping. You specify this structure, a keycode, and one of the eight modifier symbols as the three arguments to XInsertModifiermapEntry or XDeleteModifiermapEntry. Both routines return a new XModifierKeymap structure suitable for calling XSetModifierMapping. You should add or delete all the key-codes you intend to change before calling XSetModifierMapping.

You should not need to understand how the modifiers are stored to use the procedure described above for adding or deleting keycodes. To change the modifier map without the aid of XInsertModifiermapEntry or XDeleteModifiermapEntry, read Section 9.1.4.3.

XSetModifierMapping is the routine that actually changes the mapping. As such, it is when calling XSetModifierMapping that any errors appear, even though they are usually caused by an invalid XModifierKeymap structure that was set earlier.

These are the requirements for the XModifierKeymap structure specified to XSet-ModifierMapping:

- Zero keycodes are ignored.

- No keycode may appear twice anywhere in the map (otherwise, a BadValue error is generated).

- All nonzero keycodes must be in the range specified by min_keycode and max_keycode in the Display structure (else a BadValue error).

- A server can impose restrictions on how modifiers can be changed. For example, certain keys may not generate up transitions in hardware, or multiple modifier keys may not be supported. If a restriction is violated, then the status reply is MappingFailed, and none of the modifiers are changed.

If the new keycodes specified for a modifier differ from those currently defined and any (current or new) keys for that modifier are in the down state, then the status reply is MappingBusy, and none of the modifiers are changed.

XSetModifierMapping generates a MappingNotify event on a MappingSuccess status.

When finished mapping the keyboard, you can free the XModifierKeymap structures by calling XFreeModifiermap.

9.1.4.3 Changing Release 1 Modifier Mapping

Skip to Section 9.1.5 unless you are using Release 1.

Because Release 1 does not include XInsertModifiermapEntry and XDelete-ModifiermapEntry, mapping the modifiers is more difficult. The first step is the same. An XModifierKeymap structure (Example 9-7) is created using XGetModifier-Mapping (or XNewModifiermap, though this is rarely done because filling the structure is complicated).

Example 9-7. The XModifierKeymap structure

```
typedef struct {
    int max_keypermod;      /* server's max # of keys per modifier */
    KeyCode *modifiermap;   /* an 8 by max_keypermod array */
} XModifierKeymap;
```

The `modifiermap` element of the structure is an array of keycodes. There are eight by `max_keypermod` keycodes in this array: eight because there are eight modifiers, and `max_keypermod` because that is the number of keycodes that must be reserved for each modifier.

The eight modifiers are represented by the constants `ShiftMapIndex`, `LockMapIndex`, `ControlMapIndex`, `Mod1MapIndex`, `Mod2MapIndex`, `Mod3MapIndex`, `Mod4Map-Index`, and `Mod5MapIndex`. These are not actually used as arguments, but they are convenient for referring to each row in the `modifiermap` structure while filling it.

Now you can interpret the `modifiermap` array. For each modifier in a given `modifier-map`, the corresponding keycodes are from

modifiermap[index * max_keypermod]

to

modifiermap[[(index + 1) * max_keyspermod] -1]

where `index` is the appropriate modifier index definition (`ShiftMapIndex`, `LockMap-Index`, etc.). You must set the `mod_map` array up properly before calling `XSet-ModifierMapping`. Now you know why `XInsertModifiermapEntry` and `XDeleteModifiermapEntry` were added in Release 2!

9.1.5 Other Keyboard Handling Routines

Several routines in addition to `XLookupString` provide ways to translate key events. None of these routines are commonly needed in applications.

You might think that `XKeysymToString` and `XStringToKeysym` describe the mapping between keysyms and strings, but they don't. `XKeysymToString` doesn't return the same string as is placed in the *buffer* argument of `XLookupString`, when `XKeysym-ToString` is given the keysym that `XLookupString` returns. `XKeysymToString` changes the symbol form of a keysym (`XK_Return`), which is a number, into a string form of the symbol (''Return''), and `XStringToKeysym` does the reverse. `XKeysym-ToString(XK_F1)` would return ''F1'' regardless of what string is currently mapping to the F1 key. Only `XLookupString` returns the string mapped to a particular keysym with `XRebindKeysym`.

`XKeycodeToKeysym` and `XKeysymToKeycode` make the mapping between single key-codes and keysyms more accessible. (`XLookupKeysym` actually takes a key event, extracts the keycode, and calls `XKeycodeToKeysym`.) For `XKeycodeToKeysym` and `XLookupKeysym`, you must specify which keysym you want from the list for the keycode, with the *index* argument. Remember that the list of keysyms for each keycode represents the key with various combinations of modifier keys pressed. The meaning of the keysym list beyond the first two (unmodified, Shift or Shift Lock) is not defined. Therefore, the *index* values of 0 and 1 are the most commonly used.

9.2 The Pointer

The pointer generates events as it moves, as it crosses window borders, and as its buttons are pressed. It provides position information that can define a path in the two-dimensional space of the screen, tell you which window the pointer is in, and allow the user to "point and click," generating input without using the keyboard. In fact, the pointer is the most unique feature of a window system.

This section describes how to track the pointer and how to handle the pointer buttons. Border crossing events are discussed in Section 9.3 because they must be handled in concert with keyboard focus change events.

9.2.1 Tracking Pointer Motion

There are three ways of handling pointer motion events:

* Getting all motion events. The program simply receives and processes every motion event. This option is suitable for applications that require all movements to be reported, no matter how small. Since many motion events are generated, and reporting the processing of the events may lag behind the pointer, this approach is not suitable for applications that require the most current information about pointer position.

* Getting hints and querying pointer position. This method greatly reduces the number of motion events sent, but requires that XQueryPointer be called to get the current pointer position. This option is suitable for applications that require only the final position of the mouse after each movement.

* Reading the motion history buffer. After checking that the buffer exists, call XGet-MotionEvents when you want the array of events occurring between two specified times. This option is not available on all servers, but it is suitable for detailed pointer position reporting. Its advantage over getting all motion events is that the list of pointer positions in the motion history buffer can be used for undoing or responding to exposure events in drawing applications.

Let's look at each of these methods in detail.

9.2.1.1 Getting All Motion Events

The most obvious way to handle motion events is to get all motion events. The only complication is that you must keep the processing of each event to a minimum so that the feedback loop to the user is reasonably fast.

Example 9-8 shows another modification to *basicwin*, the program described in Chapter 3, *Basic Window Program*. It creates a child window of the top-level window of the application, and allows the user to draw into it by moving the pointer with any button held down.

Example 9-8. Getting all motion events

```
/* global declarations of display and screen */
  .
  .
  .

#define BUF_SIZE 2000

void main(argc, argv)
int argc;
char **argv;
{
    /* declarations from basicwin */
    .
    .
    .

    Window wint;
    int xpositions[BUF_SIZE], ypositions[BUF_SIZE];
    int i;
    int count = 0;
    Bool buffer_filled = False;

    /* open display and create window win */
    .
    .
    .

    wint = XCreateSimpleWindow(display, win, 20, 20, 50, 50,
            border_width, BlackPixel(display, screen),
            WhitePixel(display,screen));

    XSelectInput(display, wint, ExposureMask | ButtonMotionMask);

    XMapWindow(display, wint);
    .
    .
    .

    /* select events for and map win */

    while (1)   {
        XNextEvent(display, &report);
        switch (report.type) {
        case MotionNotify:
```

Example 9-8. Getting all motion events (continued)

```
                printf("got a motion event\n");
                xpositions[count] = report.xmotion.x;
                ypositions[count] = report.xmotion.y;
                XDrawPoint(display, wint, gc,
                        report.xmotion.x, report.xmotion.y);
                /* The following implements a fast ring buffer.
                 * when count reaches buffer size */
                if (count <= BUF_SIZE)
                    count++;
                else {
                    count = 0;
                    buffer_filled = True;
                }
                break;
        case Expose:
                printf("got expose event\n");
                if (report.xexpose.window == wint) {
                    while (XCheckTypedWindowEvent(display,
                            wint, Expose, &report));
                    /* This redraws the right number of points.
                     * If the ring buffer is not
                     * yet filled, it draws count points.
                     * Otherwise, it draws all the points. */
                    for (i=0 ; i < (buffer_filled ?
                            BUF_SIZE : count) ; i++)
                        XDrawPoint(display, wint, gc, xpositions[i],
                                ypositions[i]);
                }
                else {
                    while (XCheckTypedWindowEvent(display,
                            win, Expose, &report));
                    if (window_size == SMALL)
                        TooSmall(win, gc, font_info);
                    else {
                        /* place text in window */
                        place_text(win, gc, font_info, width, height);

                        /* place graphics in window, */
                        place_graphics(win, gc, width, height);
                    }
                }
            break;
            /* other event types handled same as basicwin */
             .
             .
             .
        } /* end switch */
    } /* end while */
}
```

The program keeps a record of the points drawn so that they can be redrawn in case of an
Expose event. The event record is a ring buffer so that the latest BUF_SIZE pointer positions are always maintained.

The program requires that one or more of the pointer buttons must be held down while drawing. (Most drawing applications require a button to be held because otherwise it is impossible to move the pointer into a different application without drawing a trail of points to the edge of the window.) Therefore, drawing applications normally select `Button-MotionMask`.

It would be quite easy to extend this program by giving each button a different meaning. Drawing with button 1 could mean drawing in black, button 2 could mean drawing in white, and button 3 could mean toggling the previous state of the drawn pixels. The only change necessary to implement this would be code that changes the foreground pixel value and logical operation in a GC or creates three GCs with these variations. The routine would determine which button was pressed from the `state` member of the event structure and determine what to do if more than one button was pressed.

9.2.1.2 Using Pointer Motion Hints

If you do not need a record of every point the pointer has passed through, but only its current position, using motion hints is the most efficient method of handling pointer motion events. This method could be used for dragging in menus or scroll bars, in a window manager when it moves the outlines of windows, or in a drawing application in a line-drawing mode. We'll demonstrate the technique in a line-drawing application.

To use this method, select `PointerMotionHintMask` in addition to the specific event masks you desire. `PointerMotionHintMask` is a modifier; it does not select events by itself.

Example 9-9 demonstrates how to read pointer events with `PointerMotionHintMask` selected. The code shown in the example draws lines between the series of points the user specifies with button clicks. The `ButtonPress` event indicates the beginning of a line, `MotionNotify` events allow the application to draw a temporary line to the current pointer position, and `ButtonRelease` events indicate that the line should be drawn permanently, between the points indicated by the `ButtonPress` and `ButtonRelease` events.

Example 9-9. Using pointer motion hints

```
/* declare global variables display and screen */
    .
    .
    .

void main(argc, argv)
int argc;
char **argv;
{
    /* declarations from basicwin */
       .
       .
       .
    Window wint;
    XPoint points[BUF_SIZE];
```

Example 9-9. Using pointer motion hints (continued)

```
    int index = 1;
    int pos_x, pos_y;
    int prev_x, prev_y;
    GC gcx;

    wint = XCreateSimpleWindow(display, win, 20, 20, 50, 50,
            border_width, BlackPixel(display, screen),
            WhitePixel(display,screen));

    XSelectInput(display, wint, ExposureMask | ButtonPressMask
            | ButtonReleaseMask | ButtonMotionMask
            | PointerMotionHintMask);

    gcx = XCreateGC(display, win, 0, NULL);
    XSetFunction(display, gcx, GXxor);
    XSetForeground(display, gcx, BlackPixel(display, screen));

    XMapWindow(display, wint);
    while (1)  {
        XNextEvent(display, &report);
        switch  (report.type) {
        case ButtonPress:
            points[index].x = report.xbutton.x;
            points[index].y = report.xbutton.y;
            break;
        case ButtonRelease:
            index++;
            points[index].x = report.xbutton.x;
            points[index].y = report.xbutton.y;
            break;
        case MotionNotify:
            printf("got a motion event\n");
            while (XCheckMaskEvent(display,
                    ButtonMotionMask, &report));
            if (!XQueryPointer(display, report.xmotion.window,
                    &root, &child, &root_x, &root_y,
                    &pos_x, &pos_y, &keys_buttons))
                /* pointer is on other screen */
                break;

            /* undraw previous line, only if not first */
            if (index != 1)
                XDrawLine(display, wint, gcx, points[index].x,
                        points[index].y, prev_x, prev_y);

            /* draw current line */
            XDrawLine(display, wint, gcx, points[index].x,
                    points[index].y, pos_x, pos_y);
            prev_x = pos_x;
            prev_y = pos_y;
            break;
        case Expose:
            printf("got expose event\n");

            if (report.xexpose.window == wint) {
```

Example 9-9. Using pointer motion hints (continued)

```
                while (XCheckTypedWindowEvent(display,
                        wint, Expose, &report));
                XSetFunction(display, gcx, GXcopy);
                XDrawLines(display, wint, gcx, points,
                        index, CoordModeOrigin);
                XSetFunction(display, gcx, GXxor);
            }
            else {
                /* same code as basicwin */
            }
            break;
        } /* end switch */
    } /* end while */
}
```

In some applications you don't need to track pointer motion events to know where the pointer is at particular times. The pointer position is given in ButtonPress, Button-Release, KeyPress, KeyRelease, EnterNotify and LeaveNotify events. You can use any of these events to locate objects in a window.

9.2.1.3 Motion History

If the motion history buffer exists on the server (display->motion_buffer > 0), all selected motion events are placed in a list of XTimeCoord structures. There is no macro for accessing this member of the display structure. You specify the desired range of times to XGetMotionEvents, and it returns a pointer to a list of XTimeCoord structures, representing all the pointer positions during the range of times.

The XTimeCoord structure is shown in Example 9-10.

Example 9-10. The XTimeCoord structure

```
typedef struct _XTimeCoord {
    unsigned short x,y;  /* position relative to root window */
    Time time;
} XTimeCoord;
```

Example 9-11 shows another version of the program used to demonstrate getting all motion events. (This code has not been tested because few if any existing servers have the motion history buffer.) An application that uses motion history should also support the all-motion-events approach for use on servers that don't have the buffer.

Example 9-11. Reading the motion history buffer

```
/* global declarations of display and screen */
    .
    .
    .

#define BUF_SIZE 2000
```

Example 9-11. Reading the motion history buffer (continued)

```
void main(argc, argv)
int argc;
char **argv;
{
    /* declarations from basicwin */
        .
        .
        .

    Window wint;
    int xpositions[BUF_SIZE], ypositions[BUF_SIZE];
    int i;
    int count = 0;
    Bool buffer_filled = False;

    /* open display and create window win */
        .
        .
        .

    if (display->motion_buffer <= 0)
        {
        printf("%s: motion history buffer not provided on server",
                argv(0));
        exit(-1);   /* or use all events method instead */
        }

    wint = XCreateSimpleWindow(display, win, 20, 20, 50, 50,
            border_width, BlackPixel(display, screen),
            WhitePixel(display,screen));

    XSelectInput(display, wint, ExposureMask | ButtonMotionMask
            | PointerMotionHintMask);

    XMapWindow(display, wint);
        .
        .
        .

    /* select events for and map win */

    while (1)  {
        XNextEvent(display, &report);
        switch  (report.type) {
        case MotionNotify:
                printf("got a motion event\n");
            while (XCheckTypedEvent(display, MotionNotify, &report));
            start = prevtime;
            stop = report.xmotion.time;
            xytimelist = XGetMotionEvents(display, window, start,
                    stop, &nevents);
            for (i=0;i<nevents;i++)
                XDrawPoint(display, window, gc, xytimelist[i]->x,
                        xytimelist[i]->y);
```

Example 9-11. Reading the motion history buffer (continued)

```
                break;
        case Expose:
            printf("got expose event\n");
            if (report.xexpose.window == wint) {
                while (XCheckTypedWindowEvent(display,
                        wint, Expose, &report));
                xytimelist = XGetMotionEvents(display, window,
                        0, CurrentTime, &nevents);
                for (i=0 ; i < nevents ; i++)
                    XDrawPoint(display, window, gc, xytimelist[i]->x,
                            xytimelist[i]->y);
            }
            else {
                while (XCheckTypedWindowEvent(display,
                        win, Expose, &report));
                if (window_size == SMALL)
                    TooSmall(win, gc, font_info);
                else {
                    /* place text in window */
                    place_text(win, gc, font_info, width, height);

                    /* place graphics in window, */
                    place_graphics(win, gc, width, height);
                }
            }
            break;
        /* other event types handled same as basicwin */
            .
            .
            .

        } /* end switch */
    } /* end while */
}
```

Keyboard/
Pointer

9.2.2 Handling Pointer Button Events

The examples of tracking pointer motion in Section 9.2.1 use the buttons to some extent, but they don't tell you the whole story. There is the subject of automatic button grabs, and there are issues involved in making each button perform a different function. Let's tackle grabs first.

When a pointer button is pressed, an active grab is triggered automatically (as described in Section 8.3.2.2, an active grab means that all button events before the matching Button-Release event on the same button always goes to the same application, or sometimes the same window, as the ButtonPress). The automatic grab does not take place if an active grab already exists or a passive grab on the present key and button combination exists for some window higher level in the hierarchy than the window in which the ButtonPress occurred.

The OwnerGrabButtonMask that you can specify in calls to XSelectInput controls the distribution of the ButtonRelease event (and any other pointer events that occur between the ButtonPress and ButtonRelease). If OwnerGrabButtonMask is selected, the ButtonRelease event will be sent to whichever window in the application the pointer is in when the event occurs. If the pointer is outside the application, or if OwnerGrabButtonMask is not selected, the event is sent to the window in which the ButtonPress occurred.

OwnerGrabButtonMask should be selected when an application wants to know which window ButtonRelease events occur in. This information is useful when you require that both the ButtonPress and matching ButtonRelease events occur in the same window in order for an operation to be executed. In practice, it doesn't hurt to select OwnerGrabButtonMask even if you don't need the response it provides. If you do not select OwnerGrabButtonMask, any changes you try to make to the event mask of the grabbing window before the ButtonRelease will not take effect, unless done with XChangeActivePointerGrab.

The automatic grabs affect only the window to which button events are sent. To be more precise, they affect the value of the window member in the button event structures in the application's event queue. And for the event to be placed on the queue in the first place, it must have been selected on the window specified in the window member.

Now let's talk about distinguishing which pointer button was pressed. Two members of the XButtonEvent structure contain information about the button state. The button member specifies the button that changed state to trigger the event. The state member gives the state of all the buttons and modifier keys just before the event. You'll need the state member only if you require that certain key or button combinations be pressed to trigger an operation.

Especially if you require that the same button must be pressed and released in a certain window, be sure to account for the case where, for example, button 1 is pressed, then buttons 2 and 3 are pressed and released (perhaps repeatedly) or pressed and held, before button 1 is again released. You must be careful if you structure your code as shown in Example 9-12, to handle ButtonPress and ButtonRelease events in pairs.* There is no case for ButtonRelease in the example. Instead, the code for ButtonPress looks for the matching ButtonRelease event. The matching ButtonRelease might not be the next button event, so intervening events must be dealt with. This problem appears only if you are trying to distinguish the button that was pressed.

Example 9-12. Accepting button events in pairs

```
    case ButtonPress:
        /* draw pane in white on black */
        paint_pane(event.xbutton.window, panes, gc, rgc,
                font_info, BLACK);

        /* keep track of which button was pressed */
```

---

* This code is an excerpt from *winman*, the simple window manager described in Chapter 14, *Window Management*.

Example 9-12. Accepting button events in pairs (continued)

```
        button = event.xbutton.button;

        /* keep track of which window press occurred in */
        inverted_pane = event.xbutton.window;

        /* get the matching ButtonRelease on same button */
        while (1) {
            /* get rid of presses on other buttons */
            while (XCheckTypedEvent(display, ButtonPress,
                    &event));
            /* wait for release; if on correct button exit */
            XMaskEvent(display, ButtonReleaseMask, &event);
            if (event.xbutton.button == button)
                break;
        }

        /* all events are sent to the grabbing window
         * regardless of whether this is True or False,
         * because owner_events only affects the
         * distribution of events when the pointer is
         * within this application's windows.  We don't
         * expect it to be for a window manager.  */
        owner_events = True;

        /* we don't want pointer or keyboard events
         * frozen in the server */
        pointer_mode = GrabModeAsync;
        keyboard_mode = GrabModeAsync;

        /* we don't want to confine the cursor */
        confine_to = None;

        XGrabPointer(display, menuwin, owner_events,
                ButtonPressMask | ButtonReleaseMask,
                pointer_mode, keyboard_mode,
                confine_to, hand_cursor, CurrentTime);

        /* if press and release occurred in same window,
         * do command, if not, do nothing */
        if (inverted_pane == event.xbutton.window)
            {
            /* convert window ID to
             * window array index   */
            for (winindex = 0; inverted_pane !=
                    panes[winindex]; winindex++)
                ;
            switch (winindex)
                {
            case 0:
                raise_lower(display, screen,
                        RAISE);
                break;
            .
            .
            .
```

Example 9-12. Accepting button events in pairs (continued)

```
                        case 9: /* exit */
                            XSetInputFocus(display,
                                RootWindow(display,screen),
                                RevertToPointerRoot,
                                CurrentTime);
                            /* turn all icons back into windows */
                            /* must clear focus highlights */
                            XClearWindow(display, RootWindow(display, screen));
                            /* need to change focus border
                             * width back here */

                            XFlush(display);
                            XCloseDisplay(display);
                            exit(1);
                        default:
                            (void) fprintf(stderr,
                                    "Something went wrong\n");
                            break;
                        } /* end switch */
                    } /* end if */

            /* Invert Back Here (logical function is GXcopy) */
            paint_pane(event.xexpose.window, panes, gc, rgc,
                    font_info, WHITE);

            inverted_pane = NONE;
            draw_focus_frame();
            XUngrabPointer(display, CurrentTime);
            XFlush(display);
            break;
        case DestroyNotify:
              .
              .
              .
```

9.2.3 Changing the Pointer Button Mapping

Some applications may allow the user to modify the mapping between the physical pointer
buttons and the logical buttons that are reported when a button is pressed. In other words, if
physical button 1 were mapped to logical button 3, then when either button 3 or button 1
were pressed, it would appear to all applications that only button 3 were pressed.

There are five logical buttons, but the number of physical buttons may range from one up to
and perhaps greater than five. Mapping the pointer buttons might be done, for example, to
simulate buttons 4 and 5 on a system with a three button mouse. However, while physical
buttons 1 and 2 were mapped to logical 4 and 5, no buttons would be mapped to logical 1
and 2. Therefore, there would have to be a way of toggling between the modes, perhaps
using a function key.

The mapping of pointer buttons is analogous to the mapping between keycodes and keysyms in that it is global to the server and affects all clients. However, since the translation of a pointer event takes place in the server, unlike key event processing routines that use information stored in Xlib whenever possible, no routine is necessary to update the pointer mapping like `XRefreshKeyboardMapping` updates the keyboard mapping.

`XGetPointerMapping` returns the current mapping between physical and logical pointer buttons. `XSetPointerMapping` sets this mapping.

9.2.4 Moving the Pointer

The `XWarpPointer` routine moves the pointer to a relative or global position. Its use should be minimized and constrained to particular predictable circumstances because it often confuses the user.

`XWarpPointer` has various features for moving only in certain situations. See the reference page in Volume Two, *Xlib Reference Manual*, for details.

Warping the pointer generates `MotionNotify` and border crossing events just as if the user moved the pointer.

9.3 Border Crossing and Keyboard Focus Change Events

`LeaveNotify` and `EnterNotify` events are generated when the pointer crosses a window border. If the window manager is of the real-estate-driven variety (as *uwm* is), you might be tempted to assume that a `LeaveNotify` event indicates that the window will not receive keyboard input until it receives a matching `EnterNotify`. However, this assumption is not true if the user has been allowed to set a keyboard focus window. It is also not true if the window manager is of the listener variety (see Chapters 1, 10, and 14). Ideally, you should be prepared to deal with either type of window manager.

Pointer input can only be delivered to a window when the pointer is inside the window (unless the window grabs the pointer). Therefore, an application that depends on pointer input can expect to be idle when the pointer leaves the window and to be active again when the pointer enters. Notice that keyboard input can be diverted with the keyboard focus or grabs, while pointer input can only be diverted by grabs.

`FocusIn` and `FocusOut` events occur when the keyboard focus window changes (when some client calls `XSetInputFocus`). By using focus events together with the border crossing events, an application should be able to determine whether or not it can get keyboard input. If it cannot get keyboard input, it may change its behavior somewhat. If it polls for keyboard input to allow for interrupts, it can stop polling. If it normally highlights a window when the pointer enters it, it should not do so if the keyboard focus is not the root window.

In general, to determine if it will get keyboard input, an application should first check `FocusIn` and `FocusOut` events. If the focus window is the root window, then the application should check `LeaveNotify` and `EnterNotify` to see if keyboard events are possible.

Additional focus change and border crossing events are generated when the origin and destination of the focus or pointer crossing do not have a parent-child relationship. These events are called *virtual crossing* events. See Appendix E, *Event Reference*, for a description of when these events are generated and how to distinguish them from normal crossing events.

Example 9-13 shows the code that would be used to monitor whether the application will receive keyboard input. When `keyboard_active` is `True` in this code, the application could highlight its main window.

Example 9-13. Monitoring whether keyboard input will be available

```
Bool keyboard_active;
Bool focus;

/* open display, create window, select input */

/* select input before setting keyboard focus, if application does */

while (1)  {
    XNextEvent(display, &report);
    switch  (report.type) {

      .
      .
      .

    case EnterNotify:
        printf("enter\n");
        /* make sure focus is an ancestor */
        (report.xcrossing.focus) ?
                  (keyboard_active = True)
                : (keyboard_active = False);
        break;
    case LeaveNotify:
        printf("leave\n");
        /* we get input only if we have the focus */
        (focus) ? (keyboard_active = True)
                : (keyboard_active = False);
        break;
    case FocusIn:
        /* we get keyboard input for sure */
        printf("focus in\n");
        focus = True;
        keyboard_active = True;
        break;
    case FocusOut:
        /* we lost focus, get no keyboard input */
        printf("focus out\n");
        focus = False;
        keyboard_active = False;
        break;
```

```
          .
          .
          .
      }
} /* end while */
```

Example 9-13 could be used as a basis for code that highlights a portion of an application when it can get keyboard input. It would be in *active* mode when the keyboard_active flag is True. When an EnterNotify event is received, the focus member of the event structure is checked to see that the focus window is an ancestor of the window in question. If so, keyboard_active is True. When a LeaveNotify event is received, keyboard_active is True only if the application has the focus. On FocusIn events, keyboard_active is True, and a flag (focus) is set to indicate whether the keyboard will be active after LeaveNotify events.

9.3.1 The KeymapNotify Event

The KeymapNotify event, when selected, always follows on the queue immediately after a FocusIn or EnterNotify event. Its purpose is to allow the application to easily determine which combination of keys were pressed when the focus was transferred to the window or the pointer entered it. The KeymapNotify event contains a keyboard *vector*, which is an 32 element array of type char, in which each bit represents a key. For a given key, its keycode is its position in the keyboard vector.

The XQueryKeymap function also returns this keyboard vector. Keyboard vectors are always independent of all the keyboard mapping and reading functions, since the bits in the vector correspond to keycodes that can't be changed. This way of reading the keyboard is just like reading the pointer buttons. It can be useful for applications that treat the keyboard not as characters but, for example, as piano keys or drum pads.

Since XQueryKeymap makes a routine-trip request, reading the keyboard this way could not acheive the same performance when operating over a network as the same program implemented using events.

9.4 Grabbing the Keyboard and Pointer

There are times when a program might want to bypass the normal keyboard or pointer event propagation path in order to get input independent of the position of the pointer. This is the purpose of grabbing the keyboard and pointer. There are routines to grab the keyboard (XGrabKeyboard) or the pointer (XGrabPointer), or to arrange that they become grabbed when a certain combination of keys and/or buttons is pressed (XGrabKey, XGrab-Button). There are corresponding calls to ungrab (XUngrabButton, XUngrabKey, XUngrabKeyboard, and XUngrabPointer), and there is one call to change the charac-teristics of a pointer grab (XChangeActivePointerGrab).

One of the most common situations where grabbing takes place is with button events. Most applications want both a ButtonPress and a ButtonRelease, so that they can compare the two positions. Since this is such a common desire, the server *automatically* grabs the pointer between the ButtonPress and ButtonRelease if both are selected, so that you don't have to make an explicit grab.

One reason for grabbing a device is so that you can handle a series of events contiguously without fear of intervening events. But when you grab a device, no other application can receive input from that device. Therefore it is something to do only when absolutely necessary.

The routines that grab take several arguments that tailor the input response in these ways:

- When the pointer is grabbed, the cursor may be confined to any window (the *confine_to* argument).

- The distribution of events to windows within the application can be modified by the *owner_events* argument. If *owner_events* is True, then the grabbed events will be sent to the window within the application that the pointer indicates. If *owner_events* is False, or the pointer is outside the applications, then the events are always sent only to window specified by *window*.

- A window called the *grab_window* is specified. All events that occur outside the calling application's windows are reported to the grab window. All events within the application's windows will be sent to the grab window if the *owner_events* argument is False, or they will be reported normally within the application (to the window indicated by the pointer, or propagating from that window if it did not select the event) if *owner_events* is True.

- For events that occur outside the calling application's windows, and events that occur inside when *owner_events* is False, the *event_mask* argument specifies which types of events are selected for the grab window. This *event_mask* overrules the existing *event_mask* for the grab window unless *owner_events* is True.

- Event processing for either keyboard or pointer events or both may be halted altogether during the grab until a releasing XAllowEvents call is invoked by setting the *pointer_mode* or *keyboard_mode* arguments to GrabModeSync.

- The *cursor* argument specifies a particular Cursor to be displayed while the grab is active. This cursor indicates to the user that input is going to the grabbing window, since the cursor will not change when moved across the screen as it normally would.

- Grabbing calls may specify a time when the grab should take place (the *time* argument).

You can change several of the conditions of an active pointer grab, namely the *event_mask*, *cursor*, and *time*, using XChangeActivePointerGrab.

XGrabKey and XGrabButton arrange for a grab to take place when a certain combination of keys or buttons is pressed. After one of these routines is called, a passive grab is said to be in effect, until the specified keys and buttons are pressed. At that time, the grab is active and is indistinguishable from a grab generated by a call to XGrabKeyboard or

XGrabPointer. After a passive grab, an active pointer grab will take effect when the following four conditions are met:

- The specified button is pressed when an optional set of modifier keyboard keys is pressed, and no other keys or buttons are pressed.

- The pointer is contained in the grab window specified in the grabbing call.

- The cursor-confining window (specified in the confine_to argument of XGrab-Pointer or XGrabButton) must be visible, if one is specified.

- These conditions are not satisfied by any ancestor.

Grabbing the keyboard is similar to setting the keyboard focus window, but grabbing is more flexible since there are more arguments to modify the effect. Focus changes and keyboard grabs and ungrabs all generate the same FocusIn and FocusOut events.

If pointer grabs and ungrabs cause the pointer to move in or out of a window, they generate EnterNotify and LeaveNotify events.

The XAllowEvents routine is used only when the *pointer_mode* or *keyboard_mode* in previous grabbing calls were set to GrabModeSync. Under these conditions, the server queues any events that occur (but does not send them to the Xlib event queues for each application) and the keyboard or pointer is considered "frozen." XAllowEvents releases the events that are queued in the server for the frozen device. After the call, the device is still frozen, and the server again queues any events that occur on that device until the next XAllowEvents or Ungrab* call. In effect, XAllowEvents allows events to come in a batch through the network to the event queues for each application in Xlib.

The pointer modes have no effect on the processing of keyboard events, and vice versa.

Both a pointer grab and a keyboard grab may be active at the same time, by the same or different clients. If a device is frozen on behalf of either grab, no event processing is performed for the device. It is possible for a single device to be frozen by both grabs. In this case, the freeze must be released on behalf of both grabs before events can again be processed.

9.5 Keyboard Preferences

Xlib provides routines to control beep pitch and volume, key click, Shift Lock mode, mouse acceleration, keyboard lights and keyboard auto-repeat. Not all servers will actually be able to control all of these parameters.

There are five routines that deal with the keyboard and pointer preferences. XGetKeyboardControl and XChangeKeyboardControl are the primary routines for getting or setting all these preferences at once. XAutoRepeatOff and XAutoRepeatOn set the global keyboard autorepeat status but are not able to control the autorepeat of individual keys as XChangeKeyboardControl can.

9.5.1 Setting Keyboard Preferences

XChangeKeyboardControl uses the standard X method of changing internal structure members. The *values* argument to XChangeKeyboardControl specifies the structure containing the desired values; the *value_mask* argument specifies which members in the structure specified in *values* should replace the current settings. See the reference page for XChangeKeyboardControl in Volume Two, *Xlib Reference Manual*, for a list of the mask symbols.

Example 9-14 shows the XKeyboardControl structure.

Example 9-14. The XKeyboardControl structure

```
typedef struct {
    int key_click_percent;
    int bell_percent;
    int bell_pitch;
    int bell_duration;
    int led;
    int led_mode;              /* LedModeOn or LedModeOff */
    int key;
    int auto_repeat_mode;      /* AutoRepeatModeOff, AutoRepeatModeOn,
                                * AutoRepeatModeDefault */
} XKeyboardControl;
```

The following list describes each member of the XKeyboardControl structure:

* key_click_percent sets the volume for key clicks between 0 (off) and 100 (loud) inclusive.

* bell_percent sets the base volume for the bell (or beep) between 0 (off) and 100 (loud) inclusive.

* bell_pitch sets the pitch (specified in Hz) of the bell.

* bell_duration sets the duration (specified in milliseconds) of the bell.

* led_mode controls whether the keyboard LEDs are to a be used. If led is not specified and led_mode is LedModeOn, the state of all the lights are changed. If led_mode is LedModeOff, then the states of the lights are not changed. If led is specified, the light specified in led is turned on if led_mode is LedModeOn, or turned off if led_mode is LedModeOff.

* led is a number between 1 and 32 inclusive which specifies which light is turned on or off, depending on led_mode.

* auto_repeat_mode specifies how to handle auto-repeat when a key is held down. If only auto_repeat_mode is specified, then the global auto-repeat mode for the entire keyboard is changed, without affecting the per key settings. If the auto_repeat_mode is AutoRepeatModeOn, the keys that are set to auto-repeat will do so. If it is set to AutoRepeatModeOff, no keys will repeat. If it is set to AutoRepeatModeDefault, all the keys or the specified key will operate in the default mode for the server. Normally the default mode is for all nonmodal keys to

repeat (everything except Shift Lock and similar keys). The `auto_repeat_mode` can also be set using the `XAutoRepeatOn` and `XAutoRepeatOff` routines. None of the other members of the `XKeyboardControl` structure have convenience routines for setting them.

- `key` specifies the keycode of a key whose auto-repeat status will be changed to the setting specified by `auto_repeat_mode`. If this value is specified, `auto_repeat_mode` affects only the key specified in `key`. This is the only way to change the mode of a single key.

Setting any of `key_click_percent`, `bell_percent`, `bell_pitch`, or `bell_duration` to −1 restores the default value for that member.

The initial state of many of these parameters may be determined by command line arguments to the X server. On systems that operate only under the X Window System, the server is executed automatically during the boot procedure, and you can determine if any of the defaults have been modified by looking in *letc/ttys*.

Table 9-2 shows the default values and ranges for each member when no command line arguments are specified for the server.

Table 9-2. Keyboard Preference Settings — Default and Ranges

Parameter	Range
`key_click_percent`	0 – 100
`bell_percent`	0 – 100
`bell_pitch`	hertz (20 – 20K)
`bell_duration`	milliseconds
`led`	1 – 32
`led_mode`	`LedModeOff`, `LedModeOn`
`key`	7 – 255
`auto_repeat_mode`	`AutoRepeatModeOn`, `AutoRepeatModeOff`, `AutoRepeatModeDefault`

9.5.2 Getting Keyboard Preferences

To obtain the current state of the user preferences, use `XGetKeyboardControl`. This routine returns an `XKeyboardState` structure as shown in Example 9-15.

Example 9-15. The XKeyboardState structure

```
typedef struct {
    int key_click_percent;
    int bell_percent;
    unsigned int bell_pitch, bell_duration;
    unsigned long led_mask;
    int global_auto_repeat;
    char auto_repeats[32];
} XKeyboardState;
```

Except for `led_mask`, `auto_repeats`, and `global_auto_repeat`, these members have the same range of possible values listed in Table 9-2.

The `led_mask` member is not directly analogous to any member of `XKeyboard-Control`. Each bit set to 1 in `led_mask` indicates a lit LED. The least significant bit of `led_mask` corresponds to LED zero.

The `global_auto_repeat` member is either `AutoRepeatModeOn` or `AutoRepeat-ModeOff`. It reports the state of the parameter set by the `auto_repeat_mode` member of `XKeyboardControl`.

The `auto_repeats` member is a key vector like the one in `KeymapNotify` events and returned by `XQueryKeymap`. Each bit set to 1 in `auto_repeats` indicates that auto-repeat is enabled for the corresponding key. The vector is represented as 32 bytes. Byte *N* (from 0) contains the bits for keycodes *8N* to *8N+7*, with the least significant bit in the byte representing keycode *8N*. Every key on the keyboard is represented by a bit in the vector.

9.6 Pointer Preferences

`XSetPointerControl` sets the parameters that control pointer acceleration, and `XGet-PointerControl` gets them. *Pointer acceleration* is a feature that allows the user to move the cursor more quickly across the screen. If pointer acceleration is active, when the pointer moves more that a certain *threshold* amount in a single movement, the cursor will move a *multiple* of the amount the physical pointer moved. The effect of acceleration is that you can have detailed control over the pointer for fine work and, by flicking the wrist, you can also move quickly to the far reaches of the screen.

`XSetPointerControl` takes three argument (in addition to the ubiquitous *display*): *accel_numerator*, *accel_denominator*, and *threshold*.

The *accel_numerator* and *accel_denominator* arguments make up a fraction that determines the multiple used to determine how many pixels to move the cursor based on how much the physical pointer moved. The *threshold* argument specifies how many pixels the physical pointer must have moved for acceleration to take effect.

10

Interclient Communication

As a multi-window environment, X must support a mechanism for communication between applications. There are three: properties, selections, and cut buffers, all of which are described in this chapter. The special case of communication between an application and the window manager is also covered here. Proposed conventions for additional aspects of interclient communication are covered in Appendix F.

In This Chapter:

10
Interclient Communication

Communication is necessary to make sure that all applications running under X cooperate properly with the window manager and share the system resources politely. Communication also allows applications to communicate with each other. Each application in an integrated computing environment must have the ability to transfer data to and accept data from other applications.

Communication between clients takes place through *properties*. Sometimes properties are set directly by one application and read by another. This is the case with most communication between the window manager and the clients.

There is also a simple but limited means of communication through properties called *cut buffers*. But the preferred and most powerful method of general communication between clients is called *selections*. Selections actually establish a dialog between the two applications, not just a one way communication. Both cut buffers and selections are ways of using properties for communication.

Succesful communication depends on conventions for the meanings of the data communicated through properties and selections. The conventions in this area that are firmly established are described in this chapter. However, this is not a complete set. A more complete but tentative set of conventions was proposed in Release 2 in David Rosenthal's *Inter-Client Communication Conventions Manual*, which is reprinted in Appendix F, *Proposed Interclient Communication Conventions*. These proposed conventions have been revised, and are currently being reviewed by the X Consortium. The "final" conventions should be decided upon by Release 3, expected in the fall of 1988. The X consortium promises that programs written using the proposals set forth in Release 2 will be compatible with the final conventions. However, anyone who can wait for Release 3 before programming in the elaborate conventions described in Appendix F should wait. O'Reilly & Associates, Inc. will prepare a document describing the official conventions when they become available.

Interclient
Communication

10.1 Properties and Atoms

Properties allow you to associate arbitrary information with windows, usually to make that data available to the window manager or other applications.

Each property has a unique integer ID, called an atom. An atom is just a nickname for a property, so that arbitrary length property name strings don't have to be transferred back and forth between Xlib and the server. The atom is assigned by the server, and will remain defined in the server even after the client that defined it terminates. The atoms for the predefined properties are constants defined in *<X11/Xatom.h>*; all of them begin with the prefix XA_. This naming conventions avoids name clashes with user defined symbols.

A property is uniquely identified by an atom and a window. Therefore, there may be one property on each window identified by a given atom. In other words, there can be a XA_WM_NAME property on each and every window, even though by convention this property is only set or read on the top-level windows of each application. A property on a window takes up space only once it is set.

Each property also has a name, which is an ASCII string. For the predefined properties, the name is never used in code. That is why we have chosen for this book to refer to all predefined properties by their atoms. But for properties defined by convention between related clients (not predefined), this string is used so that the applications can determine the correct atom for the property. The first client to call XInternAtom with the property name string as an argument gets a new atom. Subsequent clients that call XInternAtom with the same string will get the same atom. After each client has called XInternAtom, they use the atom rather than the string to refer to the property. They use this process because for properties defined by clients the actual number used for an atom may differ between invocations of the server.

Each property has a type, which itself is a property. There are several predefined properties for use as some of the more often needed types.

The data associated with a property can be stored as an array of 8-bit quantities, 16-bit quantities, or 32-bit quantities only. Properties can contain structures or raw data. New properties of complex type must be encoded and decoded into one of the three byte formats by the program before being sent to the server. The predefined property types have been carefully designed to match one of the data formats so that encoding and decoding is not necessary.

Release 2 of X has 68 predefined properties for window manager communication, selections, standard colormaps, and font specifications. The properties used for window manager communication and selections are described in this chapter. The standard colormap properties are described in Chapter 7, *Color*, and the font properties are described in Chapter 6, *Drawing Graphics and Text*.

Properties are set with XChangeProperty and read with XGetWindowProperty. Whenever XChangeProperty is called, a PropertyNotify event is generated.

10.2 Communicating with Window Managers

To permit window managers to perform their role of mediating the competing demands for resources such as screen space, the clients being managed must adhere to certain conventions, and must expect the window managers to do likewise. However, no complete set of these conventions has been agreed upon that deals with all the issues that application and window manager writers have thought of so far. Therefore, this section describes only those conventions that are established because Xlib has interfaces for them.

10.2.1 Client Actions

It has been accepted as a fundamental principle of client-window manager communication that a general client should not care which window manager is running, or indeed if one is running at all. The choice of window manager is up to the user or perhaps the system administrator, not the client. Clients are allowed to establish a private protocol with a particular window manager, but no claim of general utility for the features implemented that way should be made.

In general, the object of the X11 design is that clients should as far as possible do exactly what they would do in the absence of a window manager, except for:

- Hinting to the window manager about the hardware-limited resources they would like to obtain.

- Cooperating with the window manager by accepting the hardware-limited resources they are allocated, even if not those requested.

- Being prepared for some hardware-limited resource allocations to change at any time. These changes will be announced to the client through events.

The two most common hardware-limited resources are screen space and colormaps. Note that these procedures are not required for the virtually unlimited *X resources* such as windows or cursors.

10.2.1.1 Creating a Top-level Window

Clients may create one or more windows that are children of the root window. All these windows that are not temporary (like pop-up menus) are known as top-level windows. It is these windows that the window manager controls.

The window manager can change the border width, color, or pattern of an application's top-level window's border (usually to indicate the keyboard focus), so this window must be an `InputOutput` window.

Clients can be written to allow the user to override the choice of a root window and treat a non-root window as a pseudo-root. Since the pseudo-root concept has not yet been adopted as part of the interclient conventions, we will henceforth use the term *root* instead. If *pseudo-root* is adopted in a later release, you can then interpret the term *root* as *pseudo-root*.

10.2.2 Properties Set By Clients

Once the client has created one or more top-level windows, but before they are mapped, it must place properties on those windows to inform the window manager of their desired behavior. Some of these properties are mandatory (the *standard properties*), and some are optional.

XSetStandardProperties, which was introduced and used in *basicwin* in Chapter 3, sets all the required properties. The purpose of XSetStandardProperties is to provide a simple interface for the programmer who wants to code an application quickly. Other functions are provided to communicate to the window manager the optional information.

In order to work well with most window managers, every program should call both XSet-StandardProperties and XSetWMHints for each top-level window. These provide the window manager with the following information:

- Name of the program for title bar
- Name string for the icon
- Icon pixmap and/or window
- Preferred icon position
- Command and arguments used to invoke the program
- Size hints for window in normal state
- Startup state (normal or iconified)
- Keyboard focus model used by the application

The window manager, not Xlib, sets the defaults for all these properties. Also, they are only hints. A window manager determines what to do with this information and is allowed to ignore it. They will of course be ignored if no window manager is running.

The following sections describe the properties set by the client that indicate its preferences to the window manager. Table 10-1 shows all the predefined properties that clients can set, and the section in this chapter where they are described:

Table 10-1. The Window Manager Hints Property Atoms

Property	Property Type	C Type	Description	See Section
XA_WM_NAME	XA_STRING	char *	Application name	10.2.2.1
XA_WM_CLASS	XA_WM_CLASS	XClassHint	Application name and window name	10.2.2.2
XA_WM_ICON_NAME	XA_STRING	char *	Name to be used in icon	10.2.2.3

Table 10-1. The Window Manager Hints Property Atoms (continued)

Property	Property Type	C Type	Description	See Section
`XA_WM_COMMAND`	`XA_STRING`	`char *`	Command and arguments, separated by ASCII 0's, used to invoke application	10.2.2.4
`XA_WM_NORMAL_HINTS`	`XA_WM_SIZE_HINTS`	`XSizeHints`	Size hints for window in normal state (not iconified or zoomed)	10.2.2.5
`XA_WM_ZOOM_HINTS`	`XA_WM_SIZE_HINTS`	`XSizeHints`	Size hints for zoomed window	10.2.2.6
`XA_WM_HINTS`	`XA_WM_HINTS`	`XWMHints`	Additional hints set by client for use by window manager	10.2.2
`XA_WM_TRANSIENT_FOR_HINT`	`XA_STRING`	`char *`	Tells window manager which window is the real main window with which a temporary window is associated	10.2.3.6

Because all the data in a single property must be of the same format (8-, 16-, or 32-bit), and because the C structures representing property types cannot be guaranteed to be uniform in the same way, `Set*` and `Get*` functions which do the necessary marshalling of data are provided. These are referenced in the sections describing each property. See the relevant pages in Volume Two, *Xlib Reference Manual*, for full details on each function.

Calling the `Set*` function for a property with complex structure redefines all members in that property, even though only some of those members may have a specified new value.

10.2.2.1 XA_WM_NAME

Three properties are provided to allow the window manager to display appropriate text in the window title bar and icon. These are the `XA_WM_NAME`, `XA_WM_CLASS`, and `XA_WM_ICON_NAME` properties which represent the window name, window class, and icon name, respectively.

The `XA_WM_NAME` property is an uninterpreted string that the client wishes displayed in association with the window (for example, in a window title bar).

Window managers are expected to make an effort to display this information; simply ignoring `XA_WM_NAME` is not acceptable behavior. Clients can assume that at least the first part of this string is visible to the user, unless the user has made an explicit decision to make it invisible by placing the headline off-screen, or covering it by other windows. But `XA_WM_NAME` should not be used for application-critical information, nor to announce asynchronous changes of application state that require timely user response. The expected uses are:

- To permit the user to identify one of a number of instances of the same client.

- To provide the user with noncritical state information.

Even window managers that support headline bars will place some limit on the length of string that can be visible; brevity here is important.

The window name is stored by the client with XStoreName and read by the window manager with XFetchName.

10.2.2.2 XA_WM_CLASS

The XA_WM_CLASS property is a string containing two null-separated elements, res_class and res_name, that are meant to be used by clients both as a means of permanent identification, and as the handles by which both the client and the window manager obtain user defaults related to the window. res_class is meant to identify the client (such as *emacs*), while res_name is meant to more specifically identify the particular instance. The application should use res_name as a key for looking up user defaults with XGetDefault or with the resource manager routines described in Chapter 11, *Managing User Preferences*; if the user defaults are not found under res_name, the application should use res_class. The members should be set using the following rules (these may not be valid on non-UNIX systems):

- Set XA_WM_CLASS.res_class to the name of the client (for example, *emacs*).

- Set XA_WM_CLASS.res_name to the first of the following that applies:

  1. an optional command line argument (*-rn name*)

  2. the environment variable RESOURCE_NAME

  3. the trailing component of argv[0] (after the last /)

The XA_WM_CLASS property should only be written once and must be present when the window is mapped; window managers will ignore changes to it while the window is mapped.

The XA_WM_CLASS property contains a structure of type XClassHint. Example 10-1 shows the XClassHint structure.

Example 10-1. The XClassHint structure

```
typedef struct {
    char *res_name;
    char *res_class;
} XClassHint;
```

XA_WM_CLASS can be set by the client with XSetClassHint and read by the window manager with XGetClassHint.

10.2.2.3 XA_WM_ICON_NAME

The XA_WM_ICON_NAME property is an un-interpreted string that the client wishes displayed in association with its icon window when the client is iconified (for example, an icon label). In other respects, it is similar to XA_WM_NAME. Fewer characters will normally be visible in XA_WM_ICON_NAME than XA_WM_NAME, for obvious geometric reasons.

If the icon name is not specified, most window managers will attempt to use the window class (XA_WM_CLASS.res_class). If an icon pixmap has been specified in the standard properties or XA_WM_HINTS, it is normally displayed in the icon in addition to the icon name. The icon name is set by the application with XSetIconName and read by the window manager with XGetIconName.

10.2.2.4 Application Command and Arguments

The XA_WM_COMMAND property stores the shell command and arguments used to invoke the application, separated by NULL characters. This is especially useful for window managers that can store the status of the windows on the screen so that they can be recreated with the same size and position at the next login. This is also one of the possible functions of a session manager.

Applications use XSetCommand function to set the command property. There is no matching XGetCommand; window managers must use XGetWindowProperty to read this property.

Clients should ensure, by re-setting this property, that it always reflects a command that will restart them in their current state.

10.2.2.5 Window Size Hints — Normal and Zoom

A client must inform the window manager before attempting to make changes to the layout of the screen. A client does this by setting certain properties before mapping, moving, resizing, or changing the border width of its top-level windows. Since most clients leave all these operations up to the window manager except for mapping the top-level window for the first time, these properties are normally set only once just before mapping this window.

Size hints inform the window manager of the desired position and range of sizes that are preferable for each top-level window. If the application has a normal state and a zoomed state, two properties may be set to indicate different size preferences in the two states. XSetNormalHints sets the XA_WM_NORMAL_HINTS for a window in normal state, and XSetZoomHints sets the XA_WM_ZOOM_HINTS for a window in zoomed state.

Both the XA_WM_NORMAL_HINTS and XA_WM_ZOOM_HINTS properties are XSize-Hints structures, shown in Example 10-2.

Example 10-2. The XSizeHints structure

```
typedef struct {
    long flags;    /* marks defined members in structure */
    int x, y;
    int width, height;
    int min_width, min_height;
    int max_width, max_height;
    int width_inc, height_inc;
    struct {
            int x;   /* numerator */
            int y;   /* denominator */
    } min_aspect, max_aspect;
} XSizeHints;
```

- The `x`, `y`, `width`, and `height` members describe a desired position and size for the window. The coordinate system for `x` and `y` is the root window, irrespective of any reparenting that may have occurred.

- The `min_width` and `min_height` members specify the minimum size that the window can be for the application to be useful. The `max_width` and `max_height` members specify the maximum useful size.

- The `width_inc` and `height_inc` members define an arithmetic progression of sizes, from the minimum size to the maximum size, into which the window prefers to be resized. For example, *xterm* prefers size increments matching the dimensions of the font being used.

The following algorithm should be used by the window manager to calculate the displayed size of the top-level window. `i` and `j` are nonnegative integer loop variables within the window manager that would be incremented until a size that matches the window manager's window management policy is reached.

```
width = min_width + ( i * width_inc )
height = min_height + ( j * height_inc )
```

Window managers are encouraged to use `i` and `j` instead of `width` and `height` in reporting window sizes to users. Similarly, applications should interpret the command line or user default geometry using `width_inc` and `height_inc` pixels instead of single pixels as the unit. *xterm*, for example, interprets size specifications in terms of the font dimensions, not in pixels. A default *xterm* window has 24 rows and 80 columns of characters

The `min_aspect` and `max_aspect` members specify the desired range of ratios of width to height for the window, and are each expressed as a ratio of the `x` and `y` members of `min_aspect` and `max_aspect`.

The `flags` member of `XSizeHints` indicates which members in the structure contain important information. The constants in Table 10-2 can be combined with bitwise OR to set `flags`. The `USPosition` and `USSize` flags indicate that the user specified the desired values, while `PPosition` and `PSize` indicate that the program determined the values. This distinction is important since it supports the power structure where the user overrides the window manager and the window manager overrides the program in decisions about window layout. The window manager should override the program's choice of window location or geometry when PPosition or PSize respectively are set, but the user's choices should override the window manager's choice when USPosition or USSize are set.

Table 10-2. The XSizeHints Flags

Flag	Bit	Description
USPosition	0	user specified x, y
USSize	1	user specified width, height
PPosition	2	program specified position
PSize	3	program specified size
PMinSize	4	program specified minimum size
PMaxSize	5	program specified maximum size
PResizeInc	6	program specified resize increments
PAspect	7	program specified min and max aspect ratios
PAllHints	2-7	program specified all hints

XGetNormalHints is normally used by the window manager to read the hints for the normal state set by the program. There are actually three sets of Set* and Get* calls, one each to send and receive the hints for the program in normal state, one for zoomed state, and one for any state. .All these functions use the XSizeHints structure described above. Table 10-3 lists these functions.

Table 10-3. Functions to Set and Get Size Hints

Window State	To Set	To Get
Normal	XSetNormalHints	XGetNormalHints
Zoomed	XSetZoomHints	XGetZoomHints
Any State	XSetSizeHints	XGetSizeHints

XSetSizeHints and XGetSizeHints are only useful if an application and a window manager agree on a private protocol that defines a new type of size hint atom beyond the existing two.

10.2.3 Additional Window Manager Hints

The window manager hints stored in the XA_WM_HINTS property provide a means of communicating optional information from the client to the window manager. While not strictly required, setting this property is recommended. The window manager hints include:

• Whether the program sets the focus window independently or only when assigned by the window manager.

• Whether the program desires to begin life as a window or as an icon.

- The window to be used as an icon.

- The pixmap to be used to draw on the icon, and the mask that determines which pixels are modified.

- The initial position of the icon.

These choices are stored in a structure as the XA_WM_HINTS property of the top-level window of a program. This property is set by the client with XSetWMHints and read by the window manager with XGetWMHints. The XWMHints structure is shown in Example 10-3.

Example 10-3. The XWMHints structure

```
typedef struct {
    long flags;        /* marks defined members in structure */
    Bool input;        /* does application need window manager
                        * for keyboard input */
    int initial_state; /* see below */
    Pixmap icon_pixmap; /* pixmap to be used as icon */
    Window icon_window; /* window to be used as icon */
    int icon_x, icon_y; /* initial position of icon */
    Pixmap icon_mask;  /* pixmap to be used as mask for icon_pixmap */
    XID window_group;  /* ID of related window group */
    /* this structure may be extended in the future */
} XWMHints;
```

Note that a messages flag (of type unsigned int) may be added to the XWMHints structure in Release 3. See Appendix F, *Proposed Interclient Communication Conventions*, for more information.

The following sections describe the members of XWMHints.

10.2.3.1 Flags Field

The client must set the flags field to indicate which members of the XWMHints structure are to be read by the window manager. Table 10-4 shows the symbols used to set flags:

Table 10-4. Flags for Window Manager Hints

Member	Flag	Bit
input	InputHint	0
initial_state	StateHint	1
icon_pixmap	IconPixmapHint	2
icon_window	IconWindowHint	3
icon_x, icon_y	IconPositionHint	4
icon_mask	IconMaskHint	5
window_group	WindowGroupHint	6
all of the above	AllHints	0-6

10.2.3.2   Input Field and the Input Focus

The `input` member of `XWMHints` is used to communicate to the window manager the keyboard focus model used by the application. For the input hint to be read by the window manager, the `InputHint` constant should be specified in `flags`.

There are four input models:

- No Input

  The client never expects keyboard input. An example would be *xload*, or another output-only client.

- Passive Input

  The client expects keyboard input but never explicitly sets the keyboard focus. An example would be a simple client with a no subwindows, which will accept input in `PointerRoot` mode, or when the window manager sets the keyboard focus to its top-level window (in click-to-type mode).

- Locally Active Input

  The client expects keyboard input, and explicitly sets the keyboard focus, but only does so when one of its windows already has the focus.

  An example of a Locally Active style client would be a client with subwindows defining various data entry members. Such an application might use Next and Prev keys to move the keyboard focus between the members, once its top-level window has acquired the focus in `PointerRoot` mode, or when the window manager sets the keyboard focus to its top-level window (in click-to-type mode).

- Globally Active Input

  The client expects keyboard input, and explicitly sets the keyboard focus even when the focus is set to a window the client does not own. An example would be a client with a scroll bar, that wants to allow users to scroll the window without disturbing the keyboard focus even if it is in some other window. The client wants to acquire the keyboard focus when the user clicks in the scrolled region, but not when the user clicks in the scroll bar itself, and then set the focus back to its original window. Thus, the client wants to prevent the window manager setting the keyboard focus to any of its windows.

Clients using the Globally Active and No Input models should set the `input` flag to `False`. Clients using the Passive and Locally Active models should set the input flag to `True`.

10.2.3.3   Initial State Field

The `initial_state` member of `XWMHints` indicates to the window manager whether the application prefers to be in iconified, zoomed, normal, or inactive state. `initial_state` specifies the state the client prefers to be in at the time the top-level window is mapped. In addition, clients may ask the window manager to switch between states by setting the `initial_state` flag (its name has become somewhat misleading).

The `initial_state` flags are shown in Table 10-5.

Table 10-5. Initial State Hint Flags

Flag	Value	Description
DontCareState	0	Client doesn't care what state it is in.
NormalState	1	Client wants top-level normal window visible.
ZoomState	2	Client wants to be in zoomed state.
IconicState	3	Client wants to be iconified, whatever that means for this window manager. It can assume that at least one of its `icon_window` (if any), its `icon_pixmap` (if any), or its `XA_WM_ICON_NAME` will be visible.
InactiveState	4	Client wants to be inactive, whatever that means for each window manager. Inactive windows might be available from a pop-up menu, or some other means that doesn't involve permanently allocating screen space.
IgnoreState	5	Proposed for Release 3 (not in Release 2). Client wants the window manager to ignore this window, and in return agrees that attempts to map it (or its `icon_window`) will be ignored.

The `StateHint` constant set in the `flags` member of the `XWMHints` structure indicates that the `initial_state` member of that structure is read.

10.2.3.4 Icon Hints

Under X, icons are by convention controlled by the window manager, except that the client is allowed to provide a variety of pixmap patterns, names, and an icon window among which the window manager may pick and choose. The four members of `XWMHints` shown in Example 10-4 provide this information to the window manager.

Example 10-4. The icon hints elements of the XWMHints structure

```
Pixmap icon_pixmap;  /* pixmap for icon */
Pixmap icon_mask;    /* pixmap to be used as mask for icon_pixmap */
Window icon_window;  /* window to be used as icon */
int icon_x, icon_y;  /* initial position of icon */
```

`icon_pixmap` is the pattern to be used to distinguish the icon from other clients. This pixmap should be:

- One of the sizes specified in the `XA_WM_ICON_SIZE` property on the root, as described in section 10.2.3.1.

- 1 bit deep. The window manager will select suitable background (for the 0 bits) and foreground (for the 1 bits) colors. These user defaults can, of course, specify different colors for the icons of different clients.

The `icon_mask` is a bitmap that determines which pixels in `icon_pixmap` are drawn on the icon window. This allows for icons that appear to be nonrectangular. Most existing window managers (including *uwm*) use the icon pixmap as a background tile for the icon window, a method which does not allow for the use of a mask.

`icon_window` is a window created but not mapped by the client. Clients that need to know their icon's ID, or want to set more than a simple two-color bitmap as an icon background pixmap, should set this hint. For example, *xbiff* and *xmh* change their icon pixmap when mail arrives, and they need to know their icon's ID to do this. Normally this hint is not specified and the window manager creates the icon window itself. It is dangerous to depend on `icon_window` actually being the icon window since the window manager might not read `icon_window` hints and might map a different icon window. When `icon_window` is specified, the client can set an icon pixmap by setting the background pixmap attribute of the window, or it may specify the `icon_pixmap` hint. Window managers that support specified icon windows will expect that:

- The icon window is a child of the root.

- The icon window is one of the sizes specified in the `XA_WM_ICON_SIZE` property on the root (described in Section 10.2.3.1).

- The icon window uses the default visual and default colormap for the screen in question.

- The client will neither map nor unmap the icon window. If the client does map the icon window, it will be treated as if it had set the `initial_state` flag to `ClientIcon-State`. This treatment is not guaranteed to result in the icon window actually being mapped.

The preferred initial position of the icon is given as the `icon_x` and `icon_y` members of `XWMHints`, relative to the origin of the screen.

To summarize the client procedures regarding icons:

- Use `XSetIconName` to set a string in `XA_WM_ICON_NAME`. All clients should do this, since it provides a fall-back for window managers whose ideas about icons differ widely from those of the client.

- Use `XSetWMHints` to set a pixmap into the `icon_pixmap` member of the `XA_WM_HINTS` property, and possibly another into the `icon_mask` member. The window manager is expected to display the pixmap masked by the mask. The pixmap should be one of the sizes found in the `XA_WM_ICON_SIZE` property on the root. Window managers will normally clip or tile pixmaps which do not match `XA_WM_ICON_SIZE`.

or

- Use `XSetWMHints` to set a window into the `icon_window` member of the `XA_WM_HINTS` property. The window manager is expected to use that window instead of creating its own, and to map that window whenever the client is in `IconState` or `ClientIconState`. In general, the size of the icon window should be one of those specified in `XA_WM_ICON_SIZE` on the root, if that property exists. Window managers may resize icon windows.

Clients should not depend on being able to receive input events by selecting them on their icon windows. Some window managers may not support this.

10.2.3.5 Window Group

The `window_group` member of `XWMHints` lets the client specify that it has multiple top-level windows. Window managers may provide facilities for manipulating the group as a whole. For example, group leaders may have the full set of decorations, and other group members a restricted set.

One of the top-level windows is known as the group leader. The `window_group` member of the hints for each of the other top-level windows should be set to the ID of the group leader.

The window group leader may be a window which exists only for that purpose, and may never be mapped. Its `window_group` member should contain its own ID. The properties of the window group leader are those for the group as a whole (for example, the icon to be shown when the entire group is iconified). Every other top-level window may also have its own hints applicable only to itself.

10.2.3.6 Transient Windows

All temporary subwindows of the root should use `XSetTransientForHint` to specify the real top-level window of the application that is creating the temporary window. This allows the window manager to process the temporary window accordingly (perhaps by not decorating it), though it is not required to perform any special favors. The `XA_WM_TRANSIENT_FOR` property is the ID of another top-level window.

It is important not to confuse `XA_WM_TRANSIENT_FOR` with the `override_redirect` window attribute. `override_redirect` specifies that the window manager doesn't get the chance to intercept the mapping request. This should only be done on the most temporary of windows, or windows that the programmer wants to be mapped without window manager intervention such as automated demonstration programs. `XA_WM_TRANSIENT_FOR` should be used when other windows are allowed to be active while the transient window is visible, such as when the pointer is not grabbed while the window is popped up. If other windows must be frozen, use `override_redirect` and grab the pointer while the window is mapped.

Temporary windows that are popped up frequently should also set the `save_under` window attribute so that windows beneath the window may not need to redraw themselves quite so often.

To summarize, clients wishing to pop-up a window should do one of three things:

- They can create and map another normal top-level window, which will get decorated and managed as a separate client by the window manager. See the discussion of window groups in Section 10.2.3.5.

- If the window will be visible for a relatively short time, and deserves a somewhat lighter treatment, they can set the XA_WM_TRANSIENT_FOR property. They can expect less decoration, but should set all the normal window manager properties on the window. An example of an appropriate case would be a dialog box.

- If the window will be visible for a very short time, and should not be decorated at all, the client can set the override_redirect window attribute. In general, this should be done only if the pointer is grabbed while the window is mapped. The window manager will never interfere with these windows, which should be used with caution. An example of an appropriate use is a pop-up menu.

10.2.4 Properties Set by the Window Manager

The properties described above are those which the client is responsible for maintaining on its top-level windows. This section describes what the client should do with the property that the window manager places on clients' top-level windows. Right now there is only one, but in the future there may be more.

10.2.4.1 XA_WM_ICON_SIZE

The window manager may set the XA_WM_ICON_SIZE property on the root window to specify the icon sizes it allows. Clients should read this property using XGetIconSizes and provide an icon window or pixmap of an appropriate size as part of the XWMHints described in Section 10.2.3.4. This property is an XIconSize structure shown in Example 10-5.

Example 10-5. The XIconSize structure

```
typedef struct {
    int min_width, min_height;
    int max_width, max_height;
    int width_inc, height_inc;
} XIconSize;
```

The width_inc and height_inc members define an arithmetic progression of sizes, from the minimum size to the maximum size, representing the supported icon sizes. XGetIconSizes actually returns a list of these structures, in case the window manager needs more than one to specify all of its accepted icon sizes.

This property is not of much use until a few standard window managers become available that actually set this property. At that time, clients will probably have an icon pixmap prepared to fit the hints of each of the standard window managers, and use the hints to determine which window manager is in operation.

10.2.5 Client Responses to Window Manager Actions

The window manager performs a number of operations on client resources, primarily on their top-level windows. Clients must not try to fight this, but may elect to receive notification of the window manager's operations.

The client may receive notification that its window has been moved, resized, raised, lowered, or that its border width has been changed by selecting `StructureNotifyMask` on its top-level window.

The response of the client to being resized should be to accept the size it has been given, and to do its best with it. If the size is impossible to work with, clients can change the `initial_state` member in their `XA_WM_HINTS` property thereby asking to be iconified, and they can display a message in the window indicating that the size is unacceptable.

Note that when a top-level window has been reparented by the window manager, which is common, the client will not receive events indicating that the window has moved relative to the root window. When the client's top-level window is moved, it does not move relative to it parent, which is the window manager's frame with title bar, resizing box, etc. The frame moves relative to the root window and the client's window remains fixed relative to the frame. Therefore, no `ConfigureNotify` event will be generated on the client's window by the move. A sophisticated window manager could select the same types of events on the frame window as are selected on the client's top-level window, and then on receipt send similar events with `XSendEvent` to the client's window, with the position members in the event adjusted to apply directly to the client's window. This would allow the client to get complete information about configuration changes while its top-level window is reparented. In the absence of that level of window manager sophistication, the client cannot depend on having knowledge of its configuration without querying the server.

There is a proposal in the Release 2 conventions for a way applications can determine their configuration while reparented. See Appendix F, *Proposed Interclient Communication Conventions*, for more information.

10.3 Selections

Selections are the primary mechanism X11 defines for clients that want to exchange information with other clients. A selection transfers arbitrary information between two clients. You can think of a selection as a piece of text or graphics that is highlighted in one application and can be pasted into another, though the information transferred can be almost anything. Clients are strongly encouraged to use this mechanism so that there is a uniform procedure in use by all applications.

The user may want to transfer information from an application, and at other times, to the application. Many applications need to be able to assume either role. In particular, clients should not display text in a permanent window without allowing the user to select it and convert it into a string, and any application that requires the user to type extensively should allow the user to paste in text from other applications.

Selections communicate between an *owner* client and a *requestor* client. The owner has the data representing the value of a selection, and the requestor wants it. The selection mechanism provides a way to notify other clients when useful data is placed in a property, and to allow the owner of the data to convert it to a type asked for by the requestor.

Note that in the X11 environment, *all* data transferred between clients must go via the server (unless they are running on the same host, but that is a special case). An X11 client can neither assume that another client can open the same files, nor communicate directly through IPC channels. The other client may be talking to the server via a completely different networking mechanism (for example, one client might be DECnet, and the other TCP/IP). Thus, passing indirect references to data such as file names, hostnames, port numbers, and so on is permitted only if both clients specifically agree.

10.3.1 The Selection Mechanism

Let's look how a typical selection transaction occurs, and then go into all the details of how to make it happen. From the user's point of view, it works like this:

1. The user highlights a selection of text or graphics in one application. For example, in *xterm*, selections are highlighted with the foreground and background colors reversed.

2. The user moves the pointer into another application, and presses the key or button that indicates that the selection should be pasted. The keys or buttons used for this purpose in all applications probably should be the ones used by *xterm*, since most users use the cutting and pasting feature of *xterm* frequently.

The desired result is that the text or graphics should appear in the application in which it was pasted. Now, how do two applications actually make this happen?

The application in which the text or graphics is being selected must first of all figure out what information is being selected, and be able to convert it into a format that can be transferred to other applications. If the selection is text, usually the selection is a string, and the selected area is highlighted, by having the user drag the pointer over the area. Then this application has to become the owner of a selection atom.

There are two built-in selection atoms: XA_PRIMARY and XA_SECONDARY. Unless the client foresees needing two simultaneous selections, it should use XA_PRIMARY. It calls XSetSelectionOwner, specifying the selection atom, any window that it created (this window is used by other applications to identify the owner), and the time. The time used should be from the event that triggered the bid to own the selection (not CurrentTime) because of race conditions that can otherwise occur. If the client does not already own the selection atom, then this call will generate a `SelectionClear` event for the old owner, telling it to un-highlight the old selection.

Each client that wants to be able to have a selection pasted into it must set aside a key or button combination to indicate that the user wishes to paste in the current selection. In response to the event that occurs when that key or button combination is pressed, the client calls `XConvertSelection`. This call specifies which selection the application wants (`XA_PRIMARY` until other conventions are established), the property to place the data in, the window on which to set this property, and the time. These arguments are quite clear. But the `XConvertSelection` call also specifies a target type that the application wants the data in. You need to understand what happens after the `XConvertSelection` call to understand the purpose of the target type property.

The server places all the arguments of the `XConvertSelection` call into an `XSelectionRequestEvent`, and sends the event to the selection owner. The owner then tries to convert the selection data into the format specified in the target type property. If the selection owner knows how to convert the data into the requested type, it puts the data in the property specified in the event, and returns the atom of this property in the `property` member of a `SelectionNotify` event. If the selection owner can't convert the selection into the requested type, it returns `None` as the `property` member in the `SelectionNotify` event. The owner sends this `SelectionNotify` event using `XSendEvent`.

When the requestor receives the `SelectionNotify` event, it either reads the property if it is set, repeats the request with a different target type if the owner returned `None`, or gives up on pasting data from that selection owner. It could be that the user is trying to do something like paste graphics into a text-only application.

Now you should understand the selection mechanism in general, let's look at a more tangible example of how it takes place.

10.3.2 An Example of Selection

Let's say a text editor is the owner of the selection `XA_PRIMARY`. The user is editing a C program and debugging the same C program in another window. The user would like to select a line in the source code and instruct the debugger to stop at that same line without having to type in the line number. Perhaps the debugger would have a button labeled "stop at" that, when pressed, would tell the debugger to request a value for the primary selection. The text editor would allow the user to select text on a line, and would be able to convert that selection into a string if it was pasted into another text editor, or into a line number if it was pasted into the debugger. Which type the text editor would choose would depend on the target type of the selection request.

Assuming the text editor already uses the selection mechanism to transfer text to other applications, adding the line number capability should be easy. It would simple need to look for a new target type that indicated to it to figure out what line number the selected text is on. It might choose the first line if more than one line were selected, or simply display an error message telling the user to select a single line.

The debugger application would then make the call shown in Example 10-6.

Example 10-6. Setting the primary selection to a line number

```
Display display;
Atom target;
Window debugger_window;
Time time;
Bool only_if_exists;
Atom data_prop;

/* we create atom for data to be put into */
data_prop = XInternAtom(display, "STOP_LINE_NUM",
        only_if_exists = False);

/* target type atom must have been created by owner */
target_type = XInternAtom(display, "LINE_NUMBER",
        only_if_exists = True);

if (target_type == None) {
    fprintf(stderr, "%s: selection owner did not create LINE_NUMBER \
            atom", argv[0]);
    return(False);
}

XConvertSelection(display, XA_PRIMARY, target_type,
        data_prop, debugger_window, time = triggering_event_time)

/* wait for a SelectionNotify event, and if the
 * property member is the same as data_prop, the
 * conversion went fine.  If the property member is
 * None, the conversion failed. */
```

The server sends all of the above information in a `SelectionRequest` event to the text editor client (which had previously made itself the owner of the selection with `XSet-SelectionOwner`).

The text editor stores the data in the property specified in the `SelectionRequest` event on `debugger_window`, then sends a `SelectionNotify` event (using `XSendEvent`) to the requesting application. Upon receiving this event, the debugger reads this property and uses its value to place a break point in the C program.

Now that you have seen a more practical application of selections, we'll more on to a more precise description of each step in the selection transfer process.

10.3.3 Acquiring Selection Ownership

When the user decides to select something in an application, the application needs to become the selection owner. Being the selection owner means that when any other application requests the value of the selection with XConvertSelection, the owner gets the resulting XSelectionRequest event. The transfer of selection ownership also makes sure that only one application at a time is attempting to set the properties. The previous application to call XSetSelectionOwner, if it was another application, receives a SelectionClear event, which indicates to it that it should clear any area it has highlighted.

Note that if the time in the XSetSelectionOwner request is in the future relative to the server's current time, or if it is in the past relative to the last time the selection concerned changed hands, the XSetSelectionOwner request appears to the client to succeed, but ownership is *not* actually transferred. To ensure that ownership has been transferred, a client must perform the sequence shown in Example 10-7:

Example 10-7. Code to ensure transfer of selection ownership

```
XSetSelectionOwner(display, selection_atom, owner, time);
if (XGetSelectionOwner(dpy, selection_atom) != owner) {
    /* We didn't get the selection */
}
```

If XGetSelectionOwner returns a window ID rather than None, then the selection ownership was successfully transferred.

10.3.4 Responsibilities of the Selection Owner

When a requestor wants the value of a selection, the owner receives a Selection-Request event. Example 10-8 shows the XSelectionRequestEvent structure.

Example 10-8. The XSelectionRequestEvent structure

```
typedef struct {
    int type;
    unsigned long serial;/* # of last request processed by server */
    Bool send_event;    /* true if this came from SendEvent request */
    Display *display;   /* display the event was read from */
    Window owner;       /* must be next after type */
    Window requestor;
    Atom selection;
    Atom target;
    Atom property;
    Time time;
} XSelectionRequestEvent;
```

The `owner` and the `selection` members will be the values specified in the `XSet-SelectionOwner` request, and therefore the selection owner is interested in them only if it owns more than one selection.

The owner should convert the selection into the type specified by the `target` member and set the property specified by the `property` member of the `SelectionRequest` event. Current conventions hold that all properties used to reply to `SelectionRequest` events should be placed on the requestor window. If the data comprising the selection cannot be stored on the requestor window (for example, because the server cannot provide sufficient memory), the owner must refuse the selection request as above.

The owner should also send the requestor a `SelectionNotify` event using `XSend-Event` with an *event_mask* of 0. The members of the `SelectionNotify` event should be set to the same values received in the `SelectionRequest` event, except that if the selection could not be converted to the requested type, set the `property` member to `None`. Example 10-9 shows the `XSelectionEvent` structure which is used for `SelectionNotify` events.

Example 10-9. The XSelectionEvent structure

```
typedef struct {
    int type;
    unsigned long serial;/* # of last request processed by server */
    Bool send_event;      /* true if this came from SendEvent request */
    Display *display;     /* display the event was read from */
    Window requestor;     /* must be next after type */
    Atom selection;
    Atom target;
    Atom property;        /* Atom or None */
    Time time;
} XSelectionEvent;
```

The `selection`, `target`, and `property` members should be set to the values received in the `SelectionRequest` event. Setting the `property` member to `None` indicates that the conversion requested could not be made.

The data stored in the property must eventually be deleted. According to the current conventions, selection requestors are responsible for deleting the converted properties whose names they receive in `SelectionNotify` events. Owners are responsible for deleting all other properties involved in communicating selections.

A selection owner may need confirmation that the data comprising the selection has actually been transferred. They should express interest in `PropertyNotify` events for the `requestor` window and wait until the property in the `SelectionNotify` event has been deleted before assuming that the selection data has been transferred.

10.3.5 Giving Up Selection Ownership

When some other client becomes the owner of a particular selection, the previous owner receives a SelectionClear event. The XSelectionClearEvent structure is shown in Example 10-10.

Example 10-10. The XSelectionClearEvent structure

```
typedef struct {
  int type;
  unsigned long serial;     /* # of last request processed by server */
  Bool send_event;          /* true if from a SendEvent request */
  Display *display;         /* display the event was read from */
  Window window;
  Atom selection;
  Time time;
} XSelectionClearEvent;
```

The time member is the time at which the ownership changed hands, and the owner member is the window the new owner specified in its XSetSelectionOwner request.

If an owner loses ownership while it has a transfer in progress, that is to say before it receives notification that the requestor has received all the data, it must continue to service the ongoing transfer to completion.

To relinquish ownership of a selection voluntarily, a client should execute a XSet-SelectionOwner request for that selection atom, with *owner* specified as None, and *time* specified as CurrentTime. Alternatively, the client may destroy the window used as the owner value of the XSetSelectionOwner request, or it may exit. In both cases the ownership of the selection involved will revert to None.

10.3.6 Requesting a Selection

A client wishing to obtain the value of a selection in a particular form issues an XConvertSelection call. The arguments of the call are three atoms, a window, and the time. The first atom is the selection, usually XA_PRIMARY. The second atom is the target type, the type in which the requestor wants the data. The conventions will specify a standard list of target type atoms. The third atom specifies the property that the owner should set to the converted data. The window argument is the window on which the property containing the data is to be set. The time member should be set to the timestamp on the event triggering the request for the selection value. Note that the requestor of a selection does not need to know the owner of the selection or the window it specified in the XSet-SelectionOwner call.

The client that calls XConvertSelection call will get a SelectionNotify event, sent to it from the selection owner. The *requestor*, *selection*, *time*, and *target* arguments of this event will be the same as those on the XConvertSelection request.

If the `property` member is `None`, the conversion has been refused. This can mean that there is no owner for the selection, that the owner does not support the conversion implied by `target`, or that the server did not have sufficient space to accommodate the data.

If the `property` member is not `None`, then that property will exist on the `requestor` window. The value of the selection can be retrieved from this property using `XGet-WindowProperty`. When using `XGetWindowProperty` to retrieve the value of a selection, the *property* argument should be set to the `property` member in the `SelectionNotify` event. The `type` member should be set to `AnyPropertyType`, because the requestor has no way of knowing beforehand what type the selection owner will use.

The property in the `SelectionNotify` should be deleted by invoking `XGetWindow-Property` with the *delete* argument set to `True`. As discussed above, the owner has no way of knowing when the data has been transferred to the requestor unless the property is removed.

10.3.7 Large Data Transfers

Selections can get large, and this poses two problems:

- Transferring large amounts of data to the server is expensive, and it would be beneficial to be able to reuse the data once it has been sent to answer further `XConvert-Selection` requests.

- All servers will have limits on the amount of data that can be stored in a single property. Exceeding this limit will result in a `BadAlloc` error on the `XChangeProperty` call that the selection owner uses to store the data.

The proposed conventions for dealing with these problems are given in Appendix F, *Proposed Interclient Communication Conventions*.

10.3.8 More on Selection Properties and Types

A given selection has a *type* associated with it. Built-in property types that might apply to selections are `XA_BITMAP`, `XA_INTEGER`, `XA_CARDINAL`, `XA_POINT`, `XA_RECTANGLE`, `XA_PIXMAP`, and `XA_STRING`. Other types that clients could define might be `XA_FILE_NAME` or `XA_PICTURE` (a sequence of graphics primitives to reproduce a picture—the Macintosh uses this type of selection to cut and paste graphics into text applications, and vice versa).

It is important to observe that defining a new atom consumes resources in the server, and they are not released until the server re-initializes. Thus, it must be a goal to reduce the need for newly minted atoms.

The selection named by `XA_PRIMARY` is used for all commands which take only a single argument. It is the principal means of communication between clients which use the selection mechanism.

It is suggested that the selection named by XA_SECONDARY be used:

- As the second argument to commands taking two arguments. For example, it might be used when exchanging the primary and secondary selections, or

- As a means of obtaining data when there is a primary selection, and the user does not wish to disturb it.

A CLIPBOARD selection has been proposed for deleted data, but an atom with this name is not defined in Release 2. The owner of the CLIPBOARD selection would be a single, special client implemented for the purpose.

10.3.8.1 Target Atoms

The atom that a requestor supplies as the *target* argument of XConvertSelection determines the form of the data supplied. The set of such atoms is extensible, but a generally accepted base set of *target* atoms is needed. Such a set is proposed but not yet accepted, and is shown in Appendix F, *Proposed Interclient Communication Conventions*. However, some types are already predefined properties, and these can safely be used.

These properties describe types of data. They contain the C language types of the structures that are used for many of the Xlib functions. The built-in property types are shown in Table 10-6.

Table 10-6. Built-in Property Types

Type Atom	C Language Type
XA_ARC	XArc
XA_POINT	XPoint
XA_ATOM	Atom
XA_RGB_COLOR_MAP	Atom (standard colormap)
XA_BITMAP	Pixmap (of depth 1)
XA_RECTANGLE	XRectangle
XA_CARDINAL	int (dimensionless)
XA_STRING	char *
XA_COLORMAP	Colormap
XA_VISUALID	VisualID
XA_CURSOR	Cursor
XA_WINDOW	Window
XA_DRAWABLE	Drawable
XA_WM_HINTS	XWMHints
XA_FONT	Font
XA_INTEGER	int
XA_WM_SIZE_HINTS	XSizeHints
XA_PIXMAP	Pixmap

The owner should not translate the selection into some arbitrary fallback target type (such as XA_STRING), and return the fallback target to the requestor in the SelectionNotify event, because this might confuse the requestor. The conversion should simply fail. The proposed conventions specify a target type that indicates to the owner that it should return a property containing the list of target types it supports.

One proposed target atom is XA_INDIRECT. This property would itself specify a list of property/window pairs that would contain the selection data.

10.4 Cut Buffers

Cut buffers are provided as a simple but limited method of interclient communication. Cut buffers are sometimes used by applications that use the Andrew toolkit. The concept (but not the implementation) of cut buffers was inherited from Version 10 of X. The selection mechanism is superior for many applications since it allows communication regarding the type of the data transferred. Selections are described in Section 10.3. If, for some reason, you prefer not to use selections, read on.

The cut buffers are eight properties on the root window of screen 0 of a display. The buffers are numbered 0 to 7. Cut buffers rely on a prior agreement between the two clients regarding the format of the data to be placed in the cut buffers. The data that can be placed in a single cut buffer is limited to the maximum size of a single property, which is server-dependent.

Because the cut buffers are properties, it is possible to be notified when they have been written into. PropertyNotify events can assist applications in timing their communication. These are selected with PropertyChangeMask.

The functions that are used to read and write to cut buffers are XStoreBuffer, XStore-Bytes, XFetchBuffer, and XFetchBytes. XRotateBuffers moves the contents of the eight buffers any number of positions. The routines with Bytes in the name use cut buffer 0 only, while the others may use any of the eight.

11

Managing User Preferences

It is a fundamental part of the X philosophy that the user, not the application, should be in control of the way things work. For this reason, applications should allow the user to specify window geometry and many other characteristics both via command-line options and in a file that specifies their default preferences. This chapter discusses the use of the resource manager, which helps an application to evaluate and merge its own defaults with user preferences. While the information in this chapter is not essential for X programming, it is essential for writing programs that will work in ways that users will come to expect. For additional information on the resource manager at work, see Chapter 12.

In This Chapter:

Resource
Manager

11
Managing User Preferences

Applications can and should be made customizable by the user. Every application should provide command-line options that allow users to set colors or patterns for the window border and background, set foreground colors for drawing, start the application at a desired size, position and configuration, select fonts, and so on. Furthermore, an application must allow users to specify their own default values for each of these options. These are the *user preferences*.

Prior to X11 Release 2, users stored default values for their preferences in a file in their home directory called *.Xdefaults*. Additional defaults could be stored in a file pointed to by the shell environment variable XENVIRONMENT, or in a system-specific file called *.Xdefaults-system*. However, experience showed that this approach caused problems for users running clients from multiple machines across the network. A separate *.Xdefaults* file had to be maintained on each machine.

For this reason, in Release 2, the *xrdb* program was designed to install the user's preferences in a property on the root window of the current server, called the XA_RESOURCE_MANAGER property. In this way, all clients running on the same server share the same user preferences. The Release 2 mechanisms support the old mechanism for compatibility, but look at *.Xdefaults* only if the XA_RESOURCE_MANAGER property has not be set by *xrdb*. *xrdb* also allows for dynamic changing of defaults without editing files.

To make things more complicated, application-specific defaults can also be stored in a file in the directory */usr/lib/X11/app-defaults*. (Each file should have the same name as the application itself.)

As a result, there are three and sometimes four sets of options that need to be read and merged: the program's defaults, the user's defaults stored in the root window's XA_RESOURCE_MANAGER property or in the user's *.Xdefaults* file, and the command line arguments.

Furthermore, the order in which the various options are merged is important. A value for an option in the user's defaults should override the program's default for that option, but a value on the command line would override both the program's and the user's default value.

The routines and database structures used for managing user preferences are collectively referred to as the *resource manager*.

Release 1 of X11 provided a routine called XGetDefault for reading user preferences from the *.Xdefaults* file. In Release 2, the XGetDefault routine has been updated to use the more flexible server-based approach, and can still be used. However, there is also another set of resource manager routines, which were originally developed for the Xt Toolkit. The Xt Toolkit resource manager was merged into Xlib because the task of managing user preferences is common to all X applications. By making the resource manager part of Xlib, the developers ensured that all toolkits layered on Xlib will use the same mechanism, providing users with a consistent interface.

The resource manager routines are part of Xlib as of Release 2 (though some additional routines are still only available in the X Toolkit.) Since all of these routines have names beginning with *Xrm*, they are conveniently grouped together in Volume 2, *Xlib Reference Manual*. You must include *<X11/Xresource.h>* to use XGetDefault or the other resource manager functions.

In the following sections, we'll talk about handling user preferences using both XGetDefault and the resource manager routines. We'll also talk about how to use XParseGeometry, which parses window size and placement preferences (whether specified on the command line or in *.Xdefaults*).

After that, we'll discuss the format of the data in the resource manager database. The rules for specifying preferences are fairly complex, although for most current applications, using them is quite simple.

Finally, we'll talk briefly about some more advanced resource manager routines. Typical application developers can skip these sections.

11.1 Using XGetDefault

XGetDefault allows a program to read a single entry from the resource manager database. It reads the defaults from the XA_RESOURCE_MANAGER property in the server, or if that is not set, the user's *.Xdefaults* file. Next, if there is an XENVIRONMENT environment variable, then the file specified in it is loaded as well. The value returned by XGetDefault for a particular program/option key will be the last match found in this list.

Actually, the XA_RESOURCE_MANAGER property is automatically copied from the server into the Display structure returned by XOpenDisplay. Therefore, each call to XGetDefault does not really read that property directly, but instead a local copy of it. Therefore, XGetDefault does not require a round-trip request and is quite fast.

Unfortunately, XGetDefault does not do the whole job of handling program options. XGetDefault does not parse the command line options, or read the application-specific defaults database. Normally, the command line options are read one at a time, and if a command line argument is present for a particular option, it overrides any default value and XGetDefault does not need to be called. But if no value for a particular option is found, XGetDefault must be called. If XGetDefault returns a non-null string, that is the option value, which usually has to be converted into a useful type for the program. If XGetDefault returns NULL, your program needs a default value, which it can read from a database file in the *app-defaults* directory using XrmGetFileDatabase and XrmGetResource or, less desirable, it can hardcode the default values.

The sequence of operation for using XGetDefault is shown in Figure 11-1.

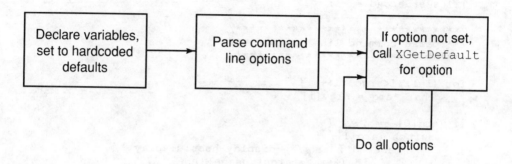

Figure 11-1. Procedure for processing user defaults with XGetDefault

Example 11-1 shows the code for one way to handle program options using XGet-
Default. It is taken without modification from the X demo *puzzle*.*

Example 11-1. Handling program options with XGetDefault

```
#define DEFAULT_SPEED          2
int     PuzzleSize = 4;
int     PuzzleWidth=4, PuzzleHeight=4;
char    *ProgName;
int     UsePicture = 0;
int     CreateNewColormap = 0;
char    *PictureFileName;
int     TilesPerSecond;

/* other global declarations */

main(argc,argv)     /* this is complete */
int argc;
char *argv[];
{
    int i, count;
    char *ServerName, *Geometry;
```

---

* Be sure to try the puzzle program using the mandrill face picture (*puzzle -picture mandrill.cm*) on an 8-plane color
screen. It's the most visually impressive X application I've seen, and the program is very well written, too.

Example 11-1. Handling program options with XGetDefault (continued)

```
char *puzzle_size = NULL;
char *option;

ProgName = argv[0];

ServerName = "";
Geometry   = "";
TilesPerSecond = -1;

/********************************/
/** parse command line options **/
/********************************/

for (i=1; i<argc; i++) {
    char *arg = argv[i];

if (arg[0] == '-') {
    switch (arg[1]) {
        case 'd':       /* -display host:display */
            if (++i >= argc) usage ();
            ServerName = argv[i];
            continue;
        case 'g':       /* -geometry geom */
            if (++i >= argc) usage ();
            Geometry = argv[i];
            continue;
        case 's':       /* -size WxH or -speed n */
            if (arg[2] == 'i') {
                if (++i >= argc) usage ();
                puzzle_size = argv[i];
                continue;
            } else if (arg[2] == 'p') {
                if (++i >= argc) usage ();
                TilesPerSecond = atoi (argv[i]);
                continue;
            } else
                usage ();
            break;
        case 'p':       /* -picture filename */
            if (++i >= argc) usage ();
            UsePicture++;
            PictureFileName = argv[i];
            continue;
        case 'c':       /* -colormap */
            CreateNewColormap++;
            continue;
        default:
            usage ();
        }                       /* end switch */
    } else
        usage ();
}                       /* end for */

/* open display here */
SetupDisplay (ServerName);
```

Example 11-1. Handling program options with XGetDefault (continued)

```
    if (!Geometry) {
        Geometry = XGetDefault (display, ProgName, "Geometry");
    }

    if (!puzzle_size) {
        option = XGetDefault (display, ProgName, "Size");
        puzzle_size = option ? option : "4x4";
    }

    if (TilesPerSecond <= 0) {
        option = XGetDefault (display, ProgName, "Speed");
        TilesPerSecond = option ? atoi (option) : DEFAULT_SPEED;
    }

    if (!UsePicture) {
        option = XGetDefault (display, ProgName, "Picture");
        if (option) {
        UsePicture++;
        PictureFileName = option;
        }
    }

    if (!CreateNewColormap) {
        option = XGetDefault (display, ProgName, "Colormap");
        if (option) {
        CreateNewColormap++;
        }
    }

    sscanf (puzzle_size, "%dx%d", &PuzzleWidth, &PuzzleHeight);
    if (PuzzleWidth < 4 || PuzzleHeight < 4) {
        fprintf (stderr, "%s:  Puzzle size must be at least 4x4\n",
                ProgName);
    exit (1);
    }
    PuzzleSize = min((PuzzleWidth/2)*2,(PuzzleHeight/2)*2);

    Setup (Geometry,argc,argv);
    ProcessInput();
    exit (0);
}

static char *help_message[] = {
"where options include:",
"    -display host:display           X server to use",
"    -geometry geom                  geometry of puzzle window",
"    -size WxH                       number of squares in puzzle",
"    -speed number                   tiles to move per second",
"    -picture filename               image to use for tiles",
"    -colormap                       create a new colormap",
NULL};

usage()
{
```

Resource
Manager

Example 11-1. Handling program options with XGetDefault (continued)

```
        char **cpp;

        fprintf (stderr, "usage:  %s [-options ...]\n0, ProgName);
        for (cpp = help_message; *cpp; cpp++) {
            fprintf (stderr, "%s\n", *cpp);
        }
        fprintf (stderr, "\n");
        exit (1);
}
```

In Example 11-1, as in most existing applications, the program default values are hardcoded. Ideally, they should be taken from a file so that the code does not have to be recompiled to change them. Example 11-2 shows how this could be added to the code in Example 11-1. Only the processing of a single option is shown.

Example 11-2. Processing geometry option using program defaults file

```
}
    XrmDatabase applicationDB;
    char *classname = "puzzle";
    char name[255];            /* would be 15 for System V */
    char Geometry[20];
    char Geostr[20];
    char *str_type[20];
    XrmValue value;
    unsigned int border_width;
    unsigned int font_width, font_height;
    int pad_x, pad_y;

    /* width and height are *not* type unsigned when returned
     * from XGeometry.  Don't ask me why... */
    int x, y, width, height;

    for (i=1; i<argc; i++) {
        char *arg = argv[i];
        if (arg[0] == '-') {
            switch (arg[1]) {
                .
                .
                .
                case 'g':/* -geometry geom */
                    if (++i >= argc) usage ();
                    Geometry = argv[i];
                    continue;
                .
                .
                .
            }
        }
        else
            usage ();
    }
```

```
if (!Geometry) {
    Geometry = XGetDefault (display, ProgName, "Geometry");
}

(void) strcpy(name, "/usr/lib/X11/app-defaults/");
(void) strcat(name, classname);
/* get application defaults file, if any */
if ((applicationDB = XrmGetFileDatabase(name)) == NULL)
    fprintf(stderr, "%s: program default file not found",
            ProgName);

/* Get the program default geometry string regardless of
 * whether it has been specified on command line or in
 * resource database, because those specifications may
 * be partial.  We're going to use XGeometry to fill in the
 * gaps. */
if (XrmGetResource(applicationDB, "puzzle.geometry",
        "Puzzle.Geometry",
        str_type, &value) == True) {
(void) strncpy(Geostr, value.addr, (int) value.size);
} else {
    fprintf(stderr, "%s: default geometry option not found",
            ProgName);
Geostr[0] = NULL;
}

XGeometry(display, screen, Geometry, Geostr, (border_width = 0),
        (font_width = 1), (font_height = 1),
        (pad_x = 0), (pad_y = 0), &x, &y, &width, &height);
/* Now x, y, width, and height are the specs to use
 * when creating the window, and nothing has been hardcoded. */
```

11.2 Using the Release 2 Resource Manager in an Application

As you can see, handling program options properly with XGetDefault is not trivial, even though XGetDefault is supposed to be the simple interface to the resource manager. Whether it is any easier to use the resource manager calls is debatable, but the resource manager calls do have certain advantages.

For one, there is a single routine that takes care of parsing the command line. Secondly, you can mechanize the whole process of handling program options by turning every set of options into a database, merging them into a single database, and then extracting the correct values. The resulting code is easier to expand or modify than code that uses XGet-Default.

The basic routines that every application should use include:

XrmInitialize

> Initializes the resource manager database. Must be called before any other routines.

`XrmParseCommand`

Parses command line options into a data structure compatible with other resource manager routines. Various styles of command line options (with or without arguments, and with various styles of arguments) are supported.

`XrmGetFileDatabase`

Reads preferences from a file and stores them in a resource manager database structure. This routine can be used to read the *Xdefaults* file, the *default-app/** file, and the file (if any) pointed to by the XENVIRONMENT environment variable.

`XrmGetStringDatabase`

Reads preferences from a string. This routine can be used to read already-defined preferences from the copy of the XA_RESOURCE_MANAGER property from the root window.

`XrmMergeDatabases`

Merges databases created with other routines into a single combined database. This routine is used to combine the separate preference databases created with the functions described immediately above. The order in which the various databases are merged determines which databases take precedence.

`XrmGetResource`

Extract a resource definition from the database so that it can be used to set program variables appropriately.

The sequence of operations for a typical application is shown in Figure 11-2.

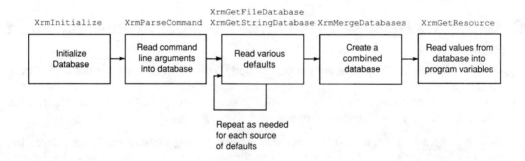

Figure 11-2. Procedure for processing defaults with resource manager functions

Examples of routines that use these functions can be found in Chapter 12, *A Complete Application*.

11.3 Standard Geometry

One of the preferences that must be handled by clients is the preferred size and placement of a window or icon. By convention, rather than having the user specify various elements of the size and placement with separate options, clients accept a single *standard geometry string*, which has the following format:

```
=<width>x<height>{+-}<xoffset>{+-}<yoffset>
```

Items enclosed in <> are integers, and items enclosed in { } are a set from which one item is allowed. The `xoffset` and `yoffset` values are optional. They determine the position of the window or icon—for the top-level window they are, by convention, interpreted relative to the origin of the root window. When `xoffset` and `yoffset` are interpreted relative to the root window, the sign has no relevence. But an application could set up a convention whereby if the sign was negative, the offsets were interpreted relative to the bottom right corner of the screen, or some other reference point.

After being read in from the command line or from a preference file, this string can be separated into separate `x`, `y`, `width`, and `height` values with `XParseGeometry`. See Chapter 12, *A Complete Application*, for an example that uses `XParseGeometry`.

In addition, there is a function called `XGeometry` that can be used to parse a partial geometry specification from the user. `XGeometry` takes two geometry strings, one specified (presumably) by the user, which might be complete, and the other, a default geometry string specified by the program. If the user-specified string specifies an element of the geometry, that value is used; otherwise, the corresponding value from program's default geometry string is used. Most current applications use `XParseGeometry` rather than `XGeometry` because they hard code the default geometry values, and therefore they don't have a second geometry string to pass to `XGeometry`.

`XGetGeometry` gets the current geometry string, border width, depth, and root window of the specified window.

11.4 Managing User Preferences Database

Most current clients allow users to specify preferences using a fairly simple mechanism. A preference string consists of the name of a client, followed by one or more predefined variables that indicate the preference to set. This is followed by a colon, optional white space, and the actual value of the preference.*

---

*Thanks to Jim Fulton of the X Consortium for providing an explanation of the resource manager on the *comp.window.x* network news group, from which portions of this section are excerpted.

The format of these preference strings is most easily seen by looking at a resource database file, such as the one shown in Example 11-3.

Example 11-3. A simple resource database file

```
.font:                      fixed
.borderWidth:               2

xterm.scrollBar:            on
xterm.title:                xterm
xterm.windowName:           xterm
xterm.boldFont:             8x13
xterm.curses:               off
xterm.internalBorder:       2
xterm.iconStartup:          off
xterm.jumpScroll:           on
xterm.reverseWrap:          true
xterm.saveLines:            700
xterm.visualBell:           off
```

The options which begin with a period apply to all programs unless overruled by a program-specific entry with the same option name.

This simple example demonstrates the rules as commonly practiced. However, there are a number of additional rules that will come increasingly into play as more complex, object-oriented applications are developed.

First of all, the information may apply only to a particular application or to an entire group of applications.

Secondly, preferences need not apply just to some attribute of the top-level window. They may apply only to a particular subwindow within an application. For example, the *xmh* mail handler allows the user to set preferences for multiple levels of windows. These levels can be specified explicitly, or using a kind of "wildcard" syntax.

As a result, you should think of the syntax for preference specifications not as:

> *client.keyword: value*

but as:

> *object ... subobject ... attribute: value*

where the hierarchy of objects and subobjects usually corresponds to major structures within an application (such as windows, panels, menus, scrollbars, and so on), but also can be a class of such objects. The final term is frequently an attribute of an object (such as its background color.)

Individual elements in the hierarchy of objects and subobjects are called *components*. Component names can be either *instance names* or *class names*. By convention, instance names always begin with a lowercase letter, while class names always begin with an uppercase letter.

Both types of name may include either uppercase or lowercase letters anywhere but in the starting position; in fact, for clarity, a component name is often made up of multiple words concatenated without spaces, with an initial capital serving as the word delimiter. For example, `buttonBox` might be the instance name for a window containing command buttons, while `ButtonBox` would be the corresponding class name.

For example, consider a hypothetical mail-reading program called *xmail*, which is similar to the current *xmh* application.* As shown in Figure 11-3, *xmail* is designed in such a manner that it uses a complex window hierarchy, all the way down to individual command buttons which are small subwindows. If each window is properly assigned a name and class, it becomes easy for the user to specify attributes of any portion of the application.

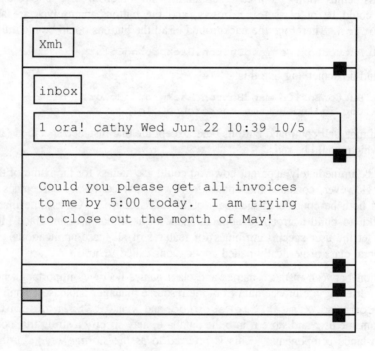

```
Xmh

inbox

1 ora! cathy Wed Jun 22 10:39 10/5

Could you please get all invoices
to me by 5:00 today.  I am trying
to close out the month of May!
```

Figure 11-3. The hypothetical xmail display

The top-level window is called `xmail`. It contains a series of vertically-stacked windows (panes), one of which contains all the command buttons controlling the program's functions. This control pane is named `toc` (table of contents). One of the command buttons is used to include (fetch) new mail.

---

*We don't discuss the actual *xmh* application, even though it does use an object-oriented approach, because speaking hypothetically gives us greater freedom to set up illustrative examples.

This button needs the following resources:

- Label string
- Font
- Foreground color
- Background color
- Foreground color for its active state
- Background color for its active state

A full instance name specifying the background color of the include button might be:

```
xmail.toc.includeButton.backgroundColor
```

Defining class names allows the user to set default values more freely. The pane containing the buttons could be of class `ButtonBox`, and the buttons themselves are all of class `CommandButton`. Therefore, the background of all the buttons could be identified with:

```
Xmail.ButtonBox.CommandButton.BackgroundColor
```

The user could do something like this:

```
Xmail.ButtonBox.CommandButton.BackgroundColor:   blue
xmail.toc.includeButton.backgroundColor:         red
```

which would make all command buttons blue, except the one instance specified (include-Button), which would be red.

It might not be immediately apparent how you could use a class for the name of the application itself. However, consider the emacs family of text editors. Microemacs and GNU emacs could both be considered members of the class `Emacs`. Or assume that you were using a toolkit to build a group of applications with a similar user interface. It might be desirable to let the user specify attributes for features of all these applications. You might define a general class of vertically paned applications called `Vpane`.

The distinction between instance names and class names becomes important when you are storing and retrieving preference data from the resource manager database. Routines such as `XrmParseCommand`, `XrmGetFileResource`, and `XrmGetStringResource`, which take data from the user and store it into the database, may specify a string that contains both class and instance components. (This is referred to as the *storage key*.) Furthermore, as we'll see below, this string may contain "loose bindings" (wildcards) rather than a fully-specified resource name.

Routines such as `XrmGetResource` that retrieve data from the database, on the other hand, must specify two separate strings (*retrieval keys*), one made up completely of instance names, and the other of class names. Both strings must be fully specified.

The reason for the difference becomes obvious if you consider these routines in practice. It is desirable for the user to be able to state preferences in as flexible a way as possible. But when the program goes to intepret those preferences, and to merge separate sets of preferences, it must end up making a specific determination of exactly what option to set.

11.4.1 Tight Bindings and Loose Bindings

The components in a resource name can be bound together in two ways: by a tight binding (a dot "."") or by a loose binding (an asterisk "*"). Thus `xmail.toc.background` has three name components tightly bound together, while `Vpane*Command.foreground` uses both a loose and a tight binding.

Bindings can precede the first component, but may not follow the last component. By convention, if no binding is specified before the first component, a tight binding is assumed. For example, `xmail.background` and `.xmail.background` both begin with tight bindings before the `xmail`, while `*xmail.background` begins with a loose binding.

The difference between tight and loose bindings comes when a function like `XrmGet-Resource` is comparing two keys. A tight binding means that the components on either side of the binding must be sequential. A loose binding is a sort of wildcard, meaning that there may be unspecified components between the two components that are loosely bound together. For example, `xmail.toc.background` would match `xmail*background` and `*background` but not `xmail.background` or `background`.

Because loose bindings are flexible, they are very useful for defining defaults. They allow defaults to match many specific applications, and will still match if the applications are slightly changed (for example, if an extra level is inserted into the hierarchy.)

A key used to store data into the database can use both loose and tight bindings. This allows the user to specify a data value which can match many different retrieval keys. In contrast, keys used to retrieve data from the database can use only tight bindings. You can only look up one item in the database at a time.

Remember also that a storage key can mix name and class components, while the retrieval keys are a pair of keys, one consisting purely of name (first character lower case) components and one consisting purely of class (first character upper case) components.

11.4.2 The -name Option

If you set up your defaults to use the class name for a program instead of an instance name, users can then list instance resources under an arbitrary name that they specify with the *-name* option to a program. For example, if *xterm* were set up this way, with the following resources defined:

```
XTerm*Font:              6x10
smallxterm*Font:         3x5
smallxterm*Geometry:     80x10
bigxterm*Font:           9x15
bigxterm*Geometry:       80x55
```

the user could use the following commands to create *xterm*'s of different sizes:

```
xterm &                  (create a normal xterm)
xterm -name smallxterm   (create a small xterm)
xterm -name bigxterm     (create a big xterm)
```

11.4.3 Storage/Access Rules

The algorithm for determining which resource name or names match a given query is the heart of the database. The key idea is that resources may be stored with only a partially specified instance and/or class name, while they are accessed with a completely specified instance and class name pair. The lookup algorithm then searches the database for the instance that most closely matches this full instance and class name pair.

The resource manager must solve the problem of how to compare the pair of retrieval keys to a single storage key. (Actually, it must compare the pair of retrieval keys to many single storage keys, since the resource manager will compare the retrieval keys against every key in the database, but one at a time.)

The solution of comparing a pair of keys to a single key is simple. The resource manager compares component by component, matching a component from the storage key against both the corresponding component from the instance retrieval key, and the corresponding component from the class retrieval key. If the storage key component matches either retrieval key component, then that component is considered to match. For example, the storage key `xmail.toc.Foreground` matches the instance name key `xmail.toc.foreground` and the class name key `Vpane.Box.Foreground`.

Because the resource manager allows loose bindings (wildcards) and mixing names and classes in the storage key, it is possible for many storage keys to match a single instance/class retrieval key pair. To solve this problem, the resource manager uses the following precedence rules to determine which is the best match (and only the value from that match will be returned). The precedence rules are, in order of preference:

1. The attribute of the name and class must match. For example, assuming that Xterm allowed multiple levels of resource specification, queries for

        xterm.scrollbar.background   (name)
        XTerm.Scrollbar.Background   (class)

    will not match the following database entry:

        xterm.scrollbar: on

2. Database entries with instance or class prefixed by a dot (".") are more specific than those prefixed by an asterisk ("*"). For example, the entry `xterm.geometry` is more specific than entry `xterm*geometry`.

3. Instances are more specific than classes. For example, the entry `*scrollbar.-background` is more specific than the entry `*Scrollbar.Background`.

4. An instance or class name that is explicitly stated is more specific than one that is omitted. For example, the entry `Scrollbar*Background` is more specific than the entry `*Background`.

5. Left components are more specific than right components. For example, the entry `xterm*background` is more specific than the entry `scrollbar*background`.

As an example of these rules, assume the following user preference specifications:

```
xmail*background:          red
*command.font:             8x13
*command.background:       blue
*Command.Foreground:       green
xmail.toc*Command.activeForeground:   black
xmail.toc.border:          3
```

A query for the name

```
xmail.toc.messageFunctions.include.activeForeground
```

and class

```
Vpane.Box.SubBox.Command.Foreground
```

would match `xmail.toc*Command.activeForeground` and return "black." However, it also matches `*Command.Foreground` but with lower preference, so it would not return "green."

The programmer should think carefully when deciding what classes to use. For example, many text applications have some notion of background, foreground, border, pointer, and cursor or marker color. Usually the background is set to one color, and all of the other attributes are set to another so that they may be seen on a monochrome display. To allow users of color displays to set any or all of them, the colors might be organized into classes as follows:

Table 11-1. Setting Classes

Instance	Class
background	Background
foreground	Foreground
borderColor	Foreground
pointerColor	Foreground
cursorColor	Foreground

Then, to configure the application to run in "monochrome" mode, but using two colors, the user would only have to use two specifications:

```
obj*Background:  blue
obj*Foreground:  red
```

Then, if the user decided to make the cursor yellow, but have the pointer and the border remain the same as the foreground, you would only need one new resource specification:

```
obj*cursorColor: yellow
```

11.4.4 Resource Manager Values and Representation Types

The resource manager stores character strings in a structure called an `XrmValue`. Physically, database values consist of a size and an address. The size is specified in machine-dependent units, while the address is a machine-dependent pointer to the character string in uninterpreted machine memory.

The declaration of the `XrmValue` is shown in Example 11-4:

Example 11-4. The XrmValue structure

```
typedef struct {
    unsigned int size;
    caddr_t addr;
} XrmValue, *XrmValuePtr;
```

In addition, a representation type is stored along with each value in the data structure. The corresponding representation type is returned along with the data value when the database is accessed. The type provides a way to distinguish between different representations of the same information. For example, a color may be specified by a color name ("red"), or be coded in a hexadecimal string ("#4f6c84"), or by a pixel value, or by RGB values. Representation types are user-defined character strings describing the way the data is represented. You specify them when you store data, and you interpret them when you access data. Previous releases of X contained programs to perform automatic type conversion. These converter routines and types were found to be insufficiently general, and were removed from Xlib. However, similar conversion functions are now being implemented in the X Toolkit.

You create representation types from simple character strings by using the macro `Xrm-StringToRepresentation`. For example,

```
XrmStringToRepresentation("RGB_value")
```

might be used if the data to be stored was a color represented as an RGB value. Certain functions let you store data without specifying a representation type. These functions always take data in the form of a `char[]`, and automatically assign it the representation type `String`. The type `XrmRepresentation` is internally represented as an `Xrm-Quark`, since it is an ID for a string. (See Section 11.5.2 for details.)

11.5 Other Resource Manager Routines

The resource manager includes a number of other routines that will be of limited use to most application developers. They are discussed briefly here for the sake of completeness.

11.5.1 Putting Resources into the Database

While all most applications will need to do is to read various sources of user preferences and merge them into a database, routines also exist for putting explicit resource values into the database or writing out the database into a file. For example, the *xrdb* program allows a user to write out the current contents of the resource manager database into a file. An application could allow users to modify the application defaults file and would then need those routines.

Routines for putting resources include:

`XrmPutResource`
>   Stores preference data into a resource database.

`XrmPutLineResource`
>   Stores a single line of preference data into a resource database.

`XrmPutStringResource`
>   Stores a preference string into a resource database.

`XrmPutFileDatabase`
>   Writes a resource database into a file.

The resource manager only frees or overwrites entries when new data is stored into a database with `XrmMergeDatabases`, or `XrmPutResource` and related routines. A client that does not use these functions should be safe using the addresses to strings returned by routines like `XrmGetResource`.

11.5.2 Quarks

A special data type called a *quark* is used internally by the resource manager to represent strings. They were created to improve the efficiency of the resource manager. The resource manager needs to make many comparisons of strings when it gets data from the database. It must compare, component by component, the name and class specification of the requested resource to each stored key in the database. Quarks are simple identifiers (presently represented as integers) for strings. Thus, instead of comparing strings, the resource manager converts each component of the string into the corresponding quark, and compares the quarks instead. This converts lengthy string comparisons into quick numeric comparisons, with the obvious savings in efficiency. The price is the overhead needed to convert back and forth between strings and quarks, but this is a small price for avoiding multiple string comparisons in a large database.

In summary then, a quark is to a string as an atom is to a property. Quarks, however, are local to the application.

Quarks are implemented using an internal table of strings. The function `XrmString-ToQuark` returns a pointer to the quark for a given string. Clients that do more than just access their defaults once might consider calling `XrmStringToQuark` for each string and then using the quark form of the routines that get resources.

The following functions convert between strings and quarks:

- `XrmQuarkToString`
- `XrmStringToQuark`
- `XrmStringToBindingQuarkList`
- `XrmStringToQuarkList`
- `XrmUniqueQuark`

The following routines can be used to work directly on quarks rather than strings when retrieving or storing resources:

- `XrmQGetResource`
- `XrmQGetSearchList`
- `XrmQGetSearchResource`
- `XrmQPutResource`
- `XrmQPutStringResource`

All of the quark routines are unlikely to be used by application developers. However, they will be of use to toolkit developers. See Volume Two, *Xlib Reference Manual*, for more information.

You will need to use a group of special macros with the routines that handle quarks. They are described in Volume Two, Appendix C, *Macros*, and listed below. Unfortunately, they don't follow the normal naming convention for macros since they begin with *Xrm* (no other macros begin with *X*), possibly because the resource manager used to be part of a separate library.

- `XrmStringToName`
- `XrmStringToClass`
- `XrmStringToRepresentation`
- `XrmNameToString`
- `XrmClassToString`
- `XrmRepresentationToString`

12
A Complete Application

*While the simple application in Chapter 3 demonstrated the most important X pro-
gramming techniques, it was far from a complete application. This chapter describes
a calculator program that provides for calculations in a number of different bases.
This program has a more robust event loop than the simple application in Chapter 3,
and demonstrates the use of the resource manager routines for integrating user
preferences.*

In This Chapter:

12
A Complete Application

Our basic window program in Chapter 3 did not do all the things an application normally should do. We should have more complete communication with the window manager, parse the command line, and merge these options with the user's defaults to set up user-preferred colors and miscellaneous options. This chapter describes and demonstrates these techniques with a real application, *basecalc*.

The *basecalc* application is a programmer's calculator that allows integer calculations in binary, octal, decimal, and hexadecimal, and conversions between these bases. It is not quite as complicated as *xcalc*, the standard calculator for X, but it demonstrates X techniques just as well. *basecalc* also does base conversions, which *xcalc* does not.

Only the sections of the program that illustrate X concepts are shown and described in this chapter. The entire program is shown in Appendix D, *The* basecalc *Application*.

This program has one characteristic that is not strictly correct in the X environment. It has only one allowable size. If the window manager refuses its request for that size or its main window is reduced in size by the user, it should print a message indicating that it can't operate in that space. Luckily, the standard window manager *uwm* honors the application's size hints and refuses to resize the window. Other window managers might not be so cooperative.

12.1 Description of basecalc

Figure 12-1 shows *basecalc* on the screen. It is a calculator which can perform integer math in decimal, octal, hexadecimal, or binary, and can convert values between any of these bases. The calculator may be operated with the pointer by pressing any pointer button on the calculator pads, or with the keyboard by typing the same symbols shown on the calculator face.

Code for *basecalc* is available on the diskette of example programs available from O'Reilly and Associates, Inc. See the *Preface* for ordering information. The long horizontal window along the top of the calculator is the display, in which the values punched on the calculator and results are displayed. The digits (0-9) and letters (A-F) in the left-hand portion of the calculator keypad are for entering values. The top row of the right-hand portion of the keypad is for base selection. These can be used either to set the current base of calculations,

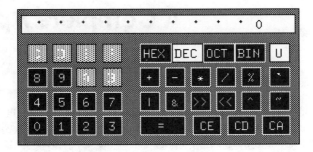

Figure 12-1. The basecalc application on the screen

or to convert a value between bases. Only one of the base indicators is highlighted at a time.

Only valid numbers in the current base are allowed to be entered. Valid pads are black while invalid ones are light gray. When a pad is triggered by pressing a pointer button, it flashes white, and the operation or value indicated by the pad is executed if the pointer button is released in the same pad. The pad also responds to the pointer entering or leaving the window while a pointer button is pressed.

The calculator also operates from the keyboard. Numbers, letters, and special characters can be typed in (or pasted from another application) to represent all the functions except Clear Entry (CE). The Backspace key also performs this function.

This application runs on any X system, since it uses only the colors black and white. It achieves the appearance of different levels of gray by creating a pattern with differing amounts of black and white. It could easily be modified to use color on color systems.

Here is the list of available functions and how they are used. If you don't plan to be using *basecalc*, skip to Section 12.2 because you won't need to know how to use *basecalc* from the desktop.

All operations work in all bases. You may shift bases at any point in any calculation. The last of any series of consecutive operators pressed will be acted upon.

+,-,*,/   Normal addition, subtraction, multiplication, and division. A number is entered, then one of these operators, then another number, and finally the equals sign, Enter key, or any operator. The result will then be displayed in the window. If the last character entered was an operator, you can continue specifying numbers and operators in alternation.

, &	AND and OR. Used just like the addition operator. The ''	'' and ''&'' symbols on the keyboard trigger this function.
<< , >>	Shift Left and Shift Right. Used just like the addition operator. Enter the number to be shifted, then the ''>>'' or ''<<'' pad (or the ''>'' or ''<'' keys), and then the number of bits to shift the number, followed by the ''='' or Enter key.
^	Exclusive OR. Used just like the addition operator. Sets all bits that are in either number but not both. Available from the ^ (caret) key.
%	Mod (remainder after division). Used like the addition operator. Available on the % (percent) key.
'	Change sign. This is a unary operator, since it performs its function immediately on the current contents of the display. Its results depend on whether the calculator is in signed or unsigned mode. If in unsigned mode, the result is the unsigned equivalent of a negative number. This function is available from the left single-quote key.
~	Two's complement. This is a unary operator. It changes all the bits in the value.
CE	Clear Entry. Erases the last value entered. The Backspace key also performs this function.
CD	Clear Digit. Erases the last digit entered.
CA	Clear All. Clears all operator and value registers.
U or S	Unsigned or Signed. Specifies whether all other operations should be performed in signed or unsigned mode.
=	Compute. The Return key also performs this function.

These mathematical operations have nothing to do with X, and how they are implemented is not described here. They are provided so that you can use the program if you have the code, and so you can more easily understand the complete code in Appendix D, *The* basecalc *Application*. In this chapter, we're going to concentrate on the aspects of the program that are standard to X applications. On that note...

12.2 Include Files

The include files used in this program are the standard ones, except for the few needed to perform system calls to get the user's home directory, current Rubout key, etc. The *<X11/Xresource.h>* file is necessary to use the resource manager.

Example 12-1. basecalc — include files

```
#include <X11/Xlib.h>
#include <X11/Xutil.h>
#include <X11/Xresource.h>
#include <X11/cursorfont.h>

#include <stdio.h>
#ifdef SysV
#include <termio.h>
#else
#include <sgtty.h>
#include <sys/ttychars.h>
#endif SysV
#include <ctype.h>
#include <pwd.h>

/* global declarations file for this application */
#include "basecalc.h"
```

The constant definitions and global variables declared or defined in *./basecalc.h* are shown above the routines in which they are used in the *basecalc* example program. You can take a look at the entire include file in Appendix D, *The* basecalc *Application.*

12.3 The Main of basecalc

The main is a very short and straightforward outline for the major routines to follow.

Example 12-2. basecalc — the main

```
char myDisplayName[256];

/*
 * X11 Release 2 Integer Programmer's Calculator with base conversions
 */

main (argc, argv)
int argc;
register char *argv[];
{
    /* so we can use the resource manager data merging functions */
    XrmInitialize();

    /* parse command line first so we can open display, store any
     * options in a database */
    parseOpenDisp (&argc, argv);

    /* get server defaults, program defaults, .Xdefaults; merge them */
    getUsersDatabase();

    /* merge user defaults and command line options and convert
     * into a form usable by this program */
    mergeOpts ();
```

Example 12-2. basecalc — the main (continued)

```
        /* load font, make pixmaps, set up arrays of windows */
        initCalc ();

        /* get keyboard settings for interrupt, delete, etc. */
        initTty ();

        /* make a standard cursor */
        makeCursor ();

        /* set standard properties, create and map windows */
        makeWindows (argc, argv);

        /* get events */
        takeEvents ();

        /* bow out gracefully */
        XCloseDisplay(display);
        exit (1);
}
```

`initTty` is not shown in this chapter, but it is included in Appendix D. It simply performs a few system calls to determine which keys are being used for erase, delete, and interrupt.

The following sections describe each routine called in the main. Each section will begin with a brief description of the routine, followed by the declarations from *./basecalc.h* that are needed with that routine, and then the code.

12.4 Getting User Preferences

This section describes and demonstrates the use of the resource manager in a typical application. For a more complete but less practical description of the resource manager, see Chapter 11, *Managing User Preferences.*

12.4.1 User Defaults for Basecalc

As described in Chapter 11, *Managing User Preferences*, the user's default values for options are normally found in the XA_RESOURCE_MANAGER property on the root window. That property is normally set by the user with the *xrdb* program. For compatibility, if there is no XA_RESOURCE_MANAGER property defined (either because *xrdb* was not run or if the property was removed), your program should assume that the defaults can be found in a file called *.Xdefaults* in the user's home directory.

Note that XGetDefault, described in Chapter 11, *Managing User Preferences*, only deals with some of this complexity. It does not read the XA_RESOURCE_MANAGER property and it does not merge in the command line arguments. That is why, in this example, we've used a different, more thorough technique, using the native resource manager calls.

Here is a sample resource database file with a few options for *basecalc*.

Example 12-3. A sample .Xdefaults file

```
basecalc.iconStartup      on
basecalc.base             2
basecalc.signed           on
```

For a complete description of preference matching rules, see Chapter 11, *Managing User Preferences*. The basecalc.iconStartup preference indicates whether the application will start as an icon. It is turned on in this case. The basecalc.base preference sets the base which the calculator will start with, and is here specified as binary (base 2). The basecalc.signed preference specifies whether the calculator should start up in signed mode or unsigned mode.

12.4.2 Parsing the Command Line

XrmInitialize must be called before any other resource manager function. (It simply sets up a default XrmRepresentation type for strings, but that fact doesn't affect how the resource manager is used in applications.) After that, the first thing to be done is to parse the command line so that we can read the display argument out of it before opening the display. parseOpenDisp does this, loading all the command line options that match resources in the option table into a database for later merging with the user's defaults. Take a look at the code and then we'll explain it.

Example 12-4. The parseOpenDisp routine

```
/* global variables */
Display *display;
int screen;
char myDisplayName[256];

/* Command line options table.  We don't do anything with many of
 * these resources, but the program is ready for expansion to allow
 * variable sizes, fonts, etc. */

#define GEOMETRY          "*geometry"
#define ICONGEOMETRY      "*iconGeometry"
#define UNSIGNED          "*unsigned"
#define BASE              "*base"
#define ICONSTARTUP       "*iconStartup"

static int opTableEntries = 25;
static XrmOptionDescRec opTable[] = {
{"=",             GEOMETRY,                 XrmoptionIsArg,  (caddr_t) NULL},
{"#",             ICONGEOMETRY,             XrmoptionIsArg,  (caddr_t) NULL},
{"-s",            UNSIGNED,                 XrmoptionNoArg,  (caddr_t) "off"},
{"-x",            BASE,                     XrmoptionNoArg,  (caddr_t) "16"},
```

Example 12-4. The parseOpenDisp routine (continued)

```
{"-h",             BASE,                          XrmoptionNoArg,  (caddr_t) "16"},
{"-d",             BASE,                          XrmoptionNoArg,  (caddr_t) "10"},
{"-o",             BASE,                          XrmoptionNoArg,  (caddr_t) "8"},
{"-b",             BASE,                          XrmoptionNoArg,  (caddr_t) "2"},
{"-background",    "*background",                 XrmoptionSepArg, (caddr_t) NULL},
{"-bd",            "*borderColor",                XrmoptionSepArg, (caddr_t) NULL},
{"-bg",            "*background",                 XrmoptionSepArg, (caddr_t) NULL},
{"-borderwidth",   "*TopLevelShell.borderWidth",  XrmoptionSepArg, (caddr_t) NULL},
{"-bordercolor",   "*borderColor",                XrmoptionSepArg, (caddr_t) NULL},
{"-bw",            "*TopLevelShell.borderWidth",  XrmoptionSepArg, (caddr_t) NULL},
{"-display",       ".display",                    XrmoptionSepArg, (caddr_t) NULL},
{"-fg",            "*foreground",                 XrmoptionSepArg, (caddr_t) NULL},
{"-fn",            "*font",                       XrmoptionSepArg, (caddr_t) NULL},
{"-font",          "*font",                       XrmoptionSepArg, (caddr_t) NULL},
{"-foreground",    "*foreground",                 XrmoptionSepArg, (caddr_t) NULL},
{"-geometry",      ".TopLevelShell.geometry",     XrmoptionSepArg, (caddr_t) NULL},
{"-iconic",        ".TopLevelShell.iconic",       XrmoptionNoArg,  (caddr_t) "on"},
{"-ic",            ICONSTARTUP,                   XrmoptionNoArg,  (caddr_t) "on"},
{"-name",          ".name",                       XrmoptionSepArg, (caddr_t) NULL},
{"-title",         ".TopLevelShell.title",        XrmoptionSepArg, (caddr_t) NULL},
{"-xrm",           NULL,                          XrmoptionResArg, (caddr_t) NULL},
};

static XrmDatabase commandlineDB;

/*
 * Get command line options
 */
parseOpenDisp (argc, argv)
int *argc;
register char *argv[];
{
    XrmValue value;
    char *str_type[20];

    myDisplayName[0] = ' ';

    XrmParseCommand(&commandlineDB, opTable, opTableEntries, argv[0],
            argc, argv);

    /*
     * Check for any arguments left
     */
    if (*argc != 1) Usage();

    /* get display now, because we need it to get other databases*/
    if (XrmGetResource(commandlineDB, "basecalc.display",
            "Basecalc.Display", str_type, &value)== True) {
        (void) strncpy(myDisplayName, value.addr, (int) value.size);
    }

    /*
     * Open display
     */
```

basecalc

Example 12-4. The parseOpenDisp routine (continued)

```
    if (!(display = XOpenDisplay(myDisplayName))) {
        (void) fprintf(stderr, "%s: Can't open display '%s'\n",
            argv[0], XDisplayName(myDisplayName));
    exit(1);
    }

    screen = DefaultScreen(display);
}
```

The large options table (opTable) defines all the command line arguments that Xrm-ParseCommand is going to look for. It describes not only what flag to look for, but also the style of each option. Some options are a simple flag, others are a flag followed by a value with no space or with a space, and so on. The options table also specifies what to call each option when searching for it in the database.

Example 12-5 shows the structure that defines the options table.

Example 12-5. XrmOptionDescRec, XrmOptionDescList, and XrmOptionKind declarations

```
typedef struct {
    char *option;            /* option specification string in argv */
    char *resourceName;      /* binding & resource name (without
                              * application name) */
    XrmOptionKind argKind;   /* which style of option it is */
    caddr_t value;           /* value to provide if XrmoptionNoArg */
} XrmOptionDescRec, *XrmOptionDescList;

typedef enum {
    XrmoptionNoArg,     /* value is specified in OptionDescRec.value */
    XrmoptionIsArg,     /* value is the option string itself */
    XrmoptionStickyArg,/* value is chars immediately following option */
    XrmoptionSepArg,    /* value is next argument in argv */
    XrmoptionResArg,    /* resource & value in next argument in argv */
    XrmoptionSkipArg,   /* ignore this option & next argument in argv */
    XrmoptionSkipLine   /* ignore this option & the rest of argv */
} XrmOptionKind;
```

The styles of command line arguments allowed are as follows:

XrmoptionNoArg

> If this flag is present, take the value in the value member (the last column) of the options table. For example, the *-s* (signed) option for the calculator indicates that the value should be off and the calculator should begin in unsigned mode.

XrmoptionIsArg

> The flag itself indicates something without any additional information. In the case of the calculator, *-x* or *-h* indicates that it should start up in hexadecimal mode.

XrmoptionStickyArg

> The value is the characters immediately following the option with no white space intervening. This is not used in the calculator, but it is like the arguments for *uucico* where *-sventure* means to call system *venture*.

XrmoptionSepArg

> The next item after the white space after this flag is the value of the option. For example, the option *-fg blue* would be of this type, and would indicate that blue is the value for the resource specified by *-fg*.

XrmoptionResArg

> The resource name and its value are the next argument in `argv` after the white space after this flag. For example, the flag might be *-res* and the resource name/value might be `basecalc*background:white`.

XrmoptionSkipArg

> Ignore this option and the next argument in `argv`.

XrmoptionSkipLine

> Ignore this option and the rest of `argv`.

As `XrmParseCommand` parses the command line, it removes arguments that it finds in the options table from `argv` and `argc`. Therefore, if `argc` is non-zero after `XrmParse-Command`, at least one of the command line arguments was illegal. The best thing to do is print both the illegal options (by printing `argv`) and the correct option syntax.

If all the options were correctly parsed, then it is time to extract the display name so that we can connect with the display. We need to connect now because we want to get the user's resource database from the server to merge with the command line arguments we already have. If there was no display specified on the command line, we use `NULL` as usual to connect to the server indicated in the UNIX environment variable DISPLAY. We set the global variable `screen` to the default screen so that we can use it in future macro calls.

It would be possible (and actually preferable) to search the other local databases, namely the *app-defaults/** and *.Xdefaults* files, for a display name before connecting to the display. This wasn't done in *basecalc* because of an oversight.

12.4.3 Getting the Databases

The `GetUsersDataBase` routine shown in Example 12-6, reads in options from four possible sources: the program's defaults, the user's defaults stored in a property on the server with *xrdb*, the user's defaults in a file specified by the environment variable XENVIRON-MENT, or if these are not present, the user's *.Xdefaults* file. It merges all these together into one database and then merges in the database obtained from the command line.

Let's look at the global declarations and the routine. This routine is quite similar to the routine in the Xt toolkit that performs the same function (that was its origin).

basecalc

Example 12-6. The GetUsersDataBase routine

```
Display *display;
XrmDatabase rDB;   /* for final merged database */

/*
 * Get program's and user's defaults
 */
getUsersDatabase()
{
    XrmDatabase homeDB, serverDB, applicationDB;

    char filenamebuf[1024];
    char *filename = &filenamebuf[0];
    char *environment;
    char *classname = "Basecalc";
    char name[255];

    (void) strcpy(name, "/usr/lib/X11/app-defaults/");
    (void) strcat(name, classname);
    /* get application defaults file, if any */
    applicationDB = XrmGetFileDatabase(name);
    (void) XrmMergeDatabases(applicationDB, &rDB);

    /* Merge server defaults, created by xrdb, loaded as a
     * property of the root window when the server initializes, and
     * loaded into the display structure on XOpenDisplay.  If not
     * defined, use .Xdefaults  */
    if (display->xdefaults != NULL) {
        serverDB = XrmGetStringDatabase(display->xdefaults);
    } else {
        /* Open .Xdefaults file and merge into existing database */
        (void) GetHomeDir(filename);
        (void) strcat(filename, ".Xdefaults");

        serverDB = XrmGetFileDatabase(filename);
    }
    XrmMergeDatabases(serverDB, &rDB);

    /* Open XENVIRONMENT file, or if not defined, the .Xdefaults,
     * and merge into existing database */
    if ((environment = getenv("XENVIRONMENT")) == NULL) {
        int len;
        environment = GetHomeDir(filename);
        (void) strcat(environment, ".Xdefaults");
        len = strlen(environment);
        (void) gethostname(environment+len, 1024-len);
    }
    homeDB = XrmGetFileDatabase(environment);
    XrmMergeDatabases(homeDB, &rDB);
}
```

XrmGetFileDatabase reads the application defaults file and loads it into a database, returning a pointer to the database. This database should contain the default values for each configurable variable used in the program. This file should look just like a user preference file, and it should parallel every option in the command line options table. In case this file is unavailable, the application should also have hardcoded defaults for all these values, but it should not have to use them.

Note that Example 12-6 gets the user's database set by *xrdb* from display->xdefaults. The xdefaults member of the Display structure is set by XOpen-Display to the value of the XA_RESOURCE_MANAGER property on the root window of screen 0. This database is in the form of a single string, but it can easily be read into a database with XrmGetStringDatabase.

Note, however, that applications should not access members of the Display structure directly like this, because the member names might be changed in later releases. They should only use the macros provided for this purpose. Unfortunately, no macro was provided in Release 1 or Release 2 to read display->xdefaults. Such a macro is promised in Release 3. In the meantime, you have the choice of cheating a little, or you can read the property directly as shown in Example 12-7. Reading the property when the information is already available in Xlib is only a little bit wasteful, since it requires only a single round-trip request.

Example 12-7. Reading the XA_RESOURCE_MANAGER property

```
char *resource_database_string;
/*
 * Get the resource manager database off the root window
 */
{
Atom actual_type;
int actual_format;
unsigned long nitems;
unsigned long leftover;
if (XGetWindowProperty(display, RootWindow(display, 0),
        XA_RESOURCE_MANAGER, 0L, 100000000L, False, XA_STRING,
        &actual_type, &actual_format, &nitems, &leftover,
        (unsigned char **) &resource_database_string) != Success) {
        /* the property isn't set */
    resource_database_string = (char *) NULL;
    }
}
```

12.4.4 Getting Options from the Database

The mergeOpts routine performs the final merging of the defaults database with the command line database, and then reads options out of the database and sets program variables appropriately. The program does not take advantage of all the options supported in the options table, but it is ready to be expanded to do so.

basecalc

Example 12-8. basecalc — the mergeOpts routine

```
mergeOpts()
{
    char *str_type[20];
    char buffer[20];
    long flags;
    XrmValue value;
    int x, y, width, height;
    XColor screen_def;

    /* command line takes precedence over everything */
    XrmMergeDatabases(commandlineDB, &rDB);

    /* get geometry */
    if (XrmGetResource(rDB, "basecalc.geometry",
            "Basecalc.Geometry", str_type, &value)== True) {
        (void) strncpy(Geostr, value.addr, (int) value.size);
    } else {
        Geostr[0] = NULL;
    }

    if (XrmGetResource(rDB, "basecalc.iconGeometry",
            "Basecalc.IconGeometry", str_type, &value)== True) {
        (void) strncpy(iconGeostr, value.addr, (int) value.size);
    } else {
        iconGeostr[0] = NULL;
    }

    if (XrmGetResource(rDB, "basecalc.signed", "Basecalc.Signed",
            str_type, &value)== True)
        if (strncmp(value.addr, "False", (int) value.size) == 0)
            Unsigned = False;

    if (XrmGetResource(rDB, "basecalc.base", "Basecalc.Base",
            str_type, &value)== True) {
        (void) strncpy(buffer, value.addr, (int) value.size);
        buffer[value.size] = NULL;
        Base = atoi(buffer);
    } else Base = 10;

    if (XrmGetResource(rDB, "basecalc.foreground",
            "Basecalc.Foreground", str_type, &value)== True) {
        (void) strncpy(buffer, value.addr, (int) value.size);
        if (XParseColor(display, DefaultColormapOfScreen(screen),
                buffer, &screen_def) == 0) {
            (void) fprintf(stderr, "basecalc: fg color specification
                %s invalid", buffer);

            foreground = BlackPixel(display, screen);
        } else {
            foreground = screen_def.pixel;
            AllocateColor(&screen_def);
        }
    } else {
        foreground = BlackPixel(display, screen);
    }
```

Example 12-8. basecalc — the mergeOpts routine (continued)

```
        if (XrmGetResource(rDB, "basecalc.background",
                "Basecalc.Background", str_type, &value)== True) {
            (void) strncpy(buffer, value.addr, (int) value.size);
            if (XParseColor(display, DefaultColormapOfScreen(screen),
                    buffer, &screen_def) == 0)   {
                (void) fprintf(stderr, "basecalc: bg color specification \
                    %s invalid", buffer);
                background = BlackPixel(display, screen);
            }  else {
                background = screen_def.pixel;
                AllocateColor(&screen_def);
            }
        } else {
            background = WhitePixel(display, screen);
        }

    /*
     * Get window geometry info
     */
    if (Geostr != NULL) {
        flags = XParseGeometry(Geostr,
                &x, &y, &width, &height);
        if ((WidthValue|HeightValue) & flags)
            Usage ();
        if (XValue & flags) {
            if (XNegative & flags)
                x = DisplayWidth(display, screen) +
                        x - sizehints.width;
            sizehints.flags |= USPosition;
            sizehints.x = x;
        }
        if (YValue & flags) {
            if (YNegative & flags)
                y = DisplayHeight(display, screen) +
                        x - sizehints.width;
            sizehints.flags |= USPosition;
            sizehints.y = y;
        }
    }


    /*
     * Get icon geometry info
     */
    if (iconGeostr != NULL) {
        iconGeostr[0] = '=';
        flags = XParseGeometry(iconGeostr,
                &x, &y, &width, &height);
        if ((WidthValue|HeightValue) & flags)
            Usage ();
        if (XValue & flags) {
            if (XNegative & flags)
                x = DisplayWidth(display, screen) +
                        x - iconsizehints.width;
            iconsizehints.flags |= USPosition;
```

basecalc

Example 12-8. basecalc — the mergeOpts routine (continued)

```
                    wmhints.flags |= IconPositionHint;
                    wmhints.icon_x = x;
                    iconsizehints.x = x;
            }
        if (YValue & flags) {
                if (YNegative & flags)
                    y = DisplayHeight(display, screen) +
                            x - iconsizehints.width;
                iconsizehints.flags |= USPosition;
                wmhints.flags |= IconPositionHint;
                wmhints.icon_y = y;
                iconsizehints.y = y;
            }
        }
    }
}
```

The variables that are used to access the data returned from the database are Geostr,
iconGeostr, Unsigned, Base, iconOnly, foreground, and background. The
routine then calls XrmGetResource for each resource, which places the data which
resulted from the combination of the command line and the resource database into user-
accessible variables. Geostr and iconGeostr are used to set up the window manager
size hints. Later in the code, the variables Unsigned, Base, iconOnly, foreground,
and background will also be used.

The next step is to get the standard geometry strings from the database, parse them, and use
these or the defaults to set the window manager hints to match. This program repeats this
process for the main window and for the icon. Strictly speaking, it is not necessary to set
window manager hints for the icon, and they are not used for that purpose in this program.

XParseGeometry returns a bitmask which indicates which parts of the geometry string
were actually set on the command line or in the resource database. There are symbols to
indicate each bit in this mask, and they are:

XValue, YValue	position of window or icon.
WidthValue, HeightValue	dimensions of window or icon.
XNegative, YNegative	indicates whether XValue or YValue are negative.

12.5 Printing a Usage Message

GetOpts calls Usage when the user tries to specify dimensions for the main window or
icon, since this program can't deal with that complexity.

Example 12-9. basecalc — the Usage routine

```
/* Print message to stderr and exit */
Usage ()
{
    fprintf (stderr,
        "%s: [=+X+Y] [#+X+Y] [-ic] [-s] [-h|x|d|o|b] [<display>]\n",
        calcName ? calcName : "basecalc");
    exit (1);
}
```

12.6 Initializing the Calculator

The `initCalc` routine performs three major functions. It loads the font to be used in all text, creates GCs for foreground and background of the calculator, and then sets the initial pixmaps for all pads. The windows for each pad do not exist yet.

Again, we'll begin with the declarations that are used in the routine:

Example 12-10. basecalc — declarations for initCalc

```
/* Background pattern for calculator (Light Gray) */
#define lgray_width 16
#define lgray_height 16
static char lgray_bits[] = {
    0x88, 0x88, 0x22, 0x22, 0x88, 0x88, 0x22, 0x22,
    0x88, 0x88, 0x22, 0x22, 0x88, 0x88, 0x22, 0x22,
    0x88, 0x88, 0x22, 0x22, 0x88, 0x88, 0x22, 0x22,
    0x88, 0x88, 0x22, 0x22, 0x88, 0x88, 0x22, 0x22};

/* pattern for disabled buttons (Dark Gray) */
#define gray_width 16
#define gray_height 16
static char gray_bits[] = {
    0xaa, 0xaa, 0x55, 0x55, 0xaa, 0xaa, 0x55, 0x55,
    0xaa, 0xaa, 0x55, 0x55, 0xaa, 0xaa, 0x55, 0x55,
    0xaa, 0xaa, 0x55, 0x55, 0xaa, 0xaa, 0x55, 0x55,
    0xaa, 0xaa, 0x55, 0x55, 0xaa, 0xaa, 0x55, 0x55};

#define   WHITE      0
#define   BLACK      1
#define   DARKGRAY   2
#define   LIGHTGRAY  3

int pressedColor = WHITE;
int unpressedColor =    BLACK;
int disabledColor =     LIGHTGRAY;
int displayColor = WHITE;

#define NBUTTONS 38

struct windata {
    int   color;    /* color */
```

basecalc

Example 12-10. basecalc — declarations for initCalc (continued)

```
        char *text;    /* pointer to the text string */
        int x;         /* x coordinate of text */
        int y;         /* y coordinate of text */
        int value;     /* 0 - 16 for number, symbol for operator */
        int type;      /* digit, operator, conversion, or special */
} windata[NBUTTONS] = {
        { 1, "                        0 ", 2, 3, 0, WTYP_DISP },

        { 0, "C", 5, 3, 12, WTYP_DIGIT },
        { 0, "D", 5, 3, 13, WTYP_DIGIT },
        { 0, "E", 5, 3, 14, WTYP_DIGIT },
        { 0, "F", 5, 3, 15, WTYP_DIGIT },

        { 0, "8", 5, 3,  8, WTYP_DIGIT },
        { 0, "9", 5, 3,  9, WTYP_DIGIT },
        { 0, "A", 5, 3, 10, WTYP_DIGIT },
        { 0, "B", 5, 3, 11, WTYP_DIGIT },

        { 0, "4", 5, 3,  4, WTYP_DIGIT },
        { 0, "5", 5, 3,  5, WTYP_DIGIT },
        { 0, "6", 5, 3,  6, WTYP_DIGIT },
        { 0, "7", 5, 3,  7, WTYP_DIGIT },

        { 0, "0", 5, 3,  0, WTYP_DIGIT },
        { 0, "1", 5, 3,  1, WTYP_DIGIT },
        { 0, "2", 5, 3,  2, WTYP_DIGIT },
        { 0, "3", 5, 3,  3, WTYP_DIGIT },

        { 0, "CA", 6, 3, OPR_CLRA, WTYP_SPECIAL },
        { 0, "CE", 6, 3, OPR_CLRE, WTYP_SPECIAL },
        { 0, "CD", 6, 3, OPR_CLRD, WTYP_SPECIAL },
        { 0, "=", 17, 2, OPR_ASGN, WTYP_OPERATOR },

        { 0, "+", 5, 3, OPR_ADD, WTYP_OPERATOR },
        { 0, "-", 5, 3, OPR_SUB, WTYP_OPERATOR },
        { 0, "*", 5, 4, OPR_MUL, WTYP_OPERATOR },
        { 0, "/", 5, 3, OPR_DIV, WTYP_OPERATOR },
        { 0, "%", 5, 3, OPR_MOD, WTYP_OPERATOR },

        { 0, "|", 5, 3, OPR_OR,  WTYP_OPERATOR },
        { 0, "&", 5, 3, OPR_AND, WTYP_OPERATOR },
        { 0, ">>",1, 3, OPR_SHR, WTYP_OPERATOR },
        { 0, "<<",0, 3, OPR_SHL, WTYP_OPERATOR },
        { 0, "^", 5, 3, OPR_XOR, WTYP_OPERATOR },

        { 0, "HEX", 2, 3, 16, WTYP_CONVERSION },
        { 0, "DEC", 2, 3, 10, WTYP_CONVERSION },
        { 0, "OCT", 2, 3,  8, WTYP_CONVERSION },
        { 0, "BIN", 2, 3,  2, WTYP_CONVERSION },

        { 0, "U",  5, 3, OPR_UNS, WTYP_SPECIAL },
        { 0, "`",  5, 3, OPR_NEG, WTYP_OPERATOR },
        { 0, "~",  5, 3, OPR_NOT, WTYP_OPERATOR },
};
```

Example 12-10. basecalc — declarations for initCalc (continued)

```
/* font for all numbers and text */
char *myFontName =    "8x13";

/* for keeping track of colors */
GC   fgGC;
GC   bgGC;
```

The data in `lgray` and `gray` are for making pixmaps for tiling in various shades of gray. This program is written to operate correctly on any kind of display. If the display is simple monochrome without grays, you can still get gray shades by creating different pixmaps with slightly different ratios of black and white pixels. The light gray pixmap is used for disabled pads, which are not valid in the current base. The dark gray pixmap is used for the background of the calculator. Simple pixel values of `BlackPixel` and `WhitePixel` are used for valid and selected pads. The symbols WHITE, BLACK, LIGHTGRAY, and DARK-GRAY are defined to clarify the code. If foreground and background colors are specified on the command line, they will also be used in the pixmaps and their colors will be mixed.

The `windata` structure provides information about each subwindow on the calculator: the color, text, position relative to the individual pad subwindows, value (digit or symbol), and type of pad. The first window in the list of data is the display window, where the entered values and results are shown. As you can see, the data for all the windows is initialized, except for the color, which is set in `initCalc`. None of these values change during the operation of the program except the color and the value in the display window.

The `type` member of `windata` indicates which of the four major classes of pads the window fits in. These are WTYP_DIGIT, WTYP_OPERATOR, WTYP_CONVERSION, and WTYP_SPECIAL, and represent digits, operators, conversions (bases), and special keys. The special keys are Clear Entry (CE), Clear All (CA), Clear Digit (CD), and Unsigned (U). Each pad within each type is identified with the `value` member of `windata`. For digits, this is the digit itself, and for operators, conversions, and special keys, it is a symbol representing each key.

Last but not least, `fgGC` and `bgGC` are two GCs which are used to save the colors between which the pads are changed. The pads have to change back and forth between black and white frequently and having one GC for each reduces the traffic to the server.

Without further ado, here is the `initCalc` routine.

Example 12-11. basecalc — the initCalc routine

```
/*
 * Initialize calculator options
 */
initCalc ()
{
    register int win;
    register int found = -1;
    XGCValues values;
    extern char lgray_bits[];

    if ((theFont = XLoadQueryFont (display, myFontName)) == NULL) {
```

basecalc

Example 12-11. basecalc — the initCalc routine (continued)

```
        (void) fprintf(stderr, "basecalc: can't open font %s\n",
                myFontName);
        exit(-1);
}

/*
 * Make the utility pixmaps
 */
grayPixmap = makePixmap(gray_bits, gray_width, gray_height);
lgrayPixmap = makePixmap(lgray_bits, lgray_width, lgray_height);

/*
 * Make the utility gc's
 */
values.font = theFont->fid;
values.foreground = foreground;
fgGC = XCreateGC(display, DefaultRootWindow(display),
        GCForeground|GCFont, &values);
values.foreground = background;
values.function = GXcopy;
bgGC = XCreateGC(display, DefaultRootWindow(display),
        GCForeground|GCFont|GCFunction, &values);

/*
 * Loop through buttons, setting disabled buttons
 * to Color Light Gray.  Also, find the window
 * which corresponds to the starting dsplay base.
 * Also add ascent to y position of text.
 */
for (win = 1; win < NBUTTONS; win++) {
    if (windata[win].type == WTYP_CONV &&
            windata[win].value == Base) {
        found = win;
    } else
        if (windata[win].type == WTYP_DIG &&
                windata[win].value >= Base) {
            windata[win].color = disabledColor;
        } else
        if (windata[win].type == WTYP_SPEC &&
                windata[win].value == OPR_UNS) {
            if (Unsigned)
                windata[win].text = "U";
            else
                windata[win].text = "S";
            windata[win].color = pressedColor;
        }
        else
            windata[win].color = unpressedColor;
    windata[win].y += theFont->max_bounds.ascent;
}
windata[0].y += theFont->max_bounds.ascent;
if (found >= 0) {
    winBase = found;
    windata[found].color = pressedColor;
} else {
```

Example 12-11. basecalc — the initCalc routine (continued)

```
            (void) fprintf(stderr, "basecalc: can't use base %d\n",
                    Base);
        exit(-1);
        }
        windata[0].color = displayColor;
}
```

The first action in this routine is to load the font. The process of loading and using a font should be familiar to you from the discussion and examples in Chapter 6, *Drawing Graphics and Text*.

The routine then calls makePixmap to make pixmaps out of the lgray and gray data in the include file. This routine calls XCreatePixmapFromBitmapData to convert a single plane pixmap into a pixmap with depth suitable for tiling.

Then initCalc creates two GCs, each with a different foreground color. These are used later in drawButton.

Now initCalc begins a loop through all the window data set up in the array of structures called windata. The first operation within the loop is to adjust the position of text in each button according to the font information. Then the pad colors are set according to the Base and Unsigned variables. These variables have default values (10 and U) but they may have been updated according to the command line or the resource database.

Finally, initCalc sets the color of the display window and the current base pad. If the base is not valid this will not have been caught until now, so the routine prints out a message and exits.

12.7 Making Windows

The makeWindows routine creates a cursor, sets up attributes, and creates the main window, all the pad windows, and the display window. It also creates the icon pixmap from data, and then uses it as the background attribute for creating the icon window. The icon will be tiled with this pixmap independent of the icon size. Finally all the standard properties and window manager hints are sent.

There is nothing in makeWindows that you haven't seen in previous examples, so we won't show it here. Look at the code in Appendix D, *The basecalc Application*, if you are interested.

basecalc

12.8 Selecting Events

`selectEvents` selects events for all the windows of the application.

Example 12-12. basecalc — the selectEvents routine

```
selectEvents ()
{
    int win;

    /* window behind calculator */
    XSelectInput (dpy, calcWin, KeyPressMask|KeyReleaseMask);

    /* where results are drawn */
    XSelectInput (dpy, dispWin, ExposureMask);

    /* pad windows */
    for (win = 1; win < NBUTTONS; win++)
        XSelectInput (dpy, Buttons[win].ID,
            ExposureMask|ButtonPressMask|ButtonReleaseMask|
            EnterWindowMask|LeaveWindowMask);
}
```

The entire calculator window requires key events because we want to be able to operate the calculator from the keyboard as well as with the pointer.

The display window (`dispWin`) requires exposure events because it must be able to refresh itself for the usual reasons.

All other windows (pads) require exposure events for refresh, button events for selection, and border crossing event so that the button only needs to be released within a pad to activate the pad. This last feature makes it easier to work quickly with the calculator.

12.9 Processing Events

This routine processes events. The top portion of `takeEvents` converts key events to the corresponding button event and then the bottom sets the colors and flags and draws the button in the new color. Key codes are mapped to ASCII with `XLookupString`, and `key-ToWin` is called to get the offset into `windata` that is represented by this key. When key events occur the appropriate pad is flashed.

Example 12-13. basecalc — the takeEvents routine

```
takeEvents ()
{
    XEvent Event;
    register int win;
    register int Pressed = FALSE;
    register int inWindow = FALSE;
    char buffer[10];
    register char *keyChars = buffer;
```

Example 12-13. basecalc — the takeEvents routine (continued)

```
register int keyDown = FALSE;
int i, nbytes;

while (1) {
    /* get event if key not down */
    if (!keyDown)
        XNextEvent (dpy, &Event);
    else
        Event.type = KeyRelease;

    /* Map keyboard events to Window Events */
    if (Event.type == KeyPress || Event.type == KeyRelease) {
        nbytes = XLookupString (&Event, buffer,
            sizeof(buffer), NULL, NULL);
        if (Event.type == KeyPress)
            {
            Event.type = ButtonPress;
            keyDown = TRUE;
            }
        else
            {
            for (i=0; i<60000; i++)
                ; /* wait */
            Event.type = ButtonRelease;
            }
        if ((Event.xbutton.window =
            keyToWin (keyChars, nbytes)) == None){
            keyDown = FALSE;
            continue;
        }
    }
    for (win=0; win < NBUTTONS; win++)
        if (Buttons[win].ID == Event.xbutton.window)
            break;
    switch (Event.type) {
    case ButtonPress:
        if (windata[win].color == disabledColor)
            break;
        Pressed = win;
        if (!keyDown)
            inWindow = TRUE;
        windata[win].color = pressedColor;
        drawButton (win, 0);
        break;
    case LeaveNotify:
        if (Pressed != win)
            break;
        inWindow = FALSE;
        windata[win].color = unpressedColor;
        drawButton (win, 0);
        break;
    case EnterNotify:
        if (Pressed != win)
            break;
        inWindow = TRUE;
```

Example 12-13. basecalc — the takeEvents routine (continued)

```
                windata[win].color = pressedColor;
                drawButton (win, 0);
                break;
        case ButtonRelease:
                if (windata[win].color == disabledColor ||
                    Pressed != win) {
                     keyDown = FALSE;
                     break;
                }
                Pressed = 0;
                windata[win].color = unpressedColor;
                if (keyDown || inWindow)
                     winPressed (win);
                keyDown = FALSE;
                inWindow = FALSE;
                drawButton (win, 0);
                break;
        case Expose:
                drawButton (win, 1);
                break;
        }
        XFlush(dpy);
    }
}
```

12.10 Drawing a Pad

This routine simply sets colors and draws the text in a pad. Example 12-14 shows the
drawButton routine.

Example 12-14. basecalc — the drawButton routine

```
/* Draw a single pad with its text */
drawButton (win, exposeEvent)
register int win;
{
    register char *string;
    register int x, y;
    struct windata *winp;
    char *Measure;
    XSetWindowAttributes attributes;
    unsigned long valuemask;
    GC gc;

    winp = &windata[win];
    x = winp->x;
    y = winp->y;
    string = winp->text;

    switch (windata[win].color) {
```

Example 12-14. basecalc — the drawButton routine (continued)

```
        case WHITE:
            gc = fgGC;
            attributes.background_pixel = background;
            attributes.border_pixel = foreground;
            valuemask = CWBackPixel|CWBorderPixel;
            break;
        case BLACK:
            gc = bgGC;
            attributes.background_pixel = foreground;
            attributes.border_pixel = background;
            valuemask = CWBackPixel|CWBorderPixel;
            break;
        case LIGHTGRAY:
            gc = bgGC;
            attributes.background_pixmap = lgrayPixmap;
            attributes.border_pixel = foreground;
            valuemask = CWBackPixmap|CWBorderPixel;
            break;
    }
    if (!exposeEvent){
        XChangeWindowAttributes(display, Buttons[win].self,
                valuemask, &attributes);
        XClearWindow(display, Buttons[win].self);
    }
    XDrawString (display, Buttons[win].self, gc, x, y, string,
            strlen (string));
    if (win == 0) {
        switch (Base) {
            case 10:
            case 8:
                Measure = Octmeasure;
                break;
            default:
            case 16:
            case  2:
                Measure = Hexmeasure;
                break;
        }
        XDrawString (display, dispWin, gc, 7, 6, Measure, 31);
    }
}
```

12.11 Routines Not Shown

The following is a brief description of all the subroutines of *basecalc* that were not shown in this chapter. All of these can be seen in full in Appendix D, *The* basecalc *Application*.

initTty   performs system calls to get user's current erase, delete, and interrupt
                   characters.

basecalc

makePixmap	makes a pixmap from bitmap data, shown and described in Chapter 6, *Drawing Graphics and Text*.
Sprintf	a modified version of `sprintf`, the standard C utility, which doesn't print in binary. `Sprintf` calls `printInBase`.
printInBase	composes the string that should be displayed. Called from `Sprintf`.
convButton	changes the current base and converts a value if any.
digitButton	gets a digit and assigns it to `Value`.
specButton	clears a digit, an entry, or all, or toggles unsigned mode.
operButton	an operation. Either does it or waits for next value and = .
displayVal	calculates appropriate format string for base.
keyToWin	translates a keycode as if a pad had been selected.
winPressed	determines whether pad pressed was a digit, an operator, a conversion, or a special pad.

13
Other Programming Techniques

As its title implies, this chapter discusses a few orphaned techniques that didn't quite fit in anywhere else. This chapter is important if you want to use one of these techniques, but most readers may just want to skim it.

In This Chapter:

13
Other Programming Techniques

This chapter covers a few obscure but occasionally necessary programming techniques. The routines and techniques described here will not be needed in most programs.

The end of the chapter contains information about porting programs from X Version 10 to X Version 11 and from other graphics environments to X Version 11.

13.1 Screen Saver

Screen-saver routines are provided to control the blanking of the screen when it has been idle for a time. XSetScreenSaver sets the operation of the screen-saver, including:

- How long the display remains idle before it is blanked.

- The time between random pattern motions.

- Whether the application prefers screen blanking or not (regardless of whether the screen is capable of it).

- Whether exposures are generated when the screen is restored.

XActivateScreenSaver and XResetScreenSaver turn the screen saver on and off respectively, and XForceScreenSaver can turn it on or off according to a flag. XGet-ScreenSaver returns the current settings of the screen saver.

13.2 Access from Other Hosts and Nodes

X does not provide any protection from unauthorized access to individual windows, pixmaps, or other resources. If a program finds out the resource ID, it can manipulate or even destroy the resource. To provide some minimal level of protection, however, connections are only permitted from machines which are listed on a *host access list*. This is adequate on single user workstations, but obviously breaks down on machines running more than one server. While provisions exist in the server for proper connection authentication, no standard has yet been developed.

The initial access control list is read at startup and reset time. The initial set of hosts allowed to open connections consists of:

- The host the window system is running on.

- On UNIX systems, each host listed in the */etc/X?.hosts* file, where ''?'' indicates the number of the server (the number between : and . in the display_name argument to XOpenDisplay that would connect to the server). This file should consist of host names separated by newlines. DECnet nodes must terminate in ''::'' to distinguish them from internet hosts.

If a host is not in the access control list when the access control mechanism is enabled and the host attempts to establish a connection, the server refuses the connection.

13.2.1 Adding, Removing, or Listing Hosts

You can add, get, or remove hosts with XAddHost, XAddHosts, XListHosts, XRemoveHost, and XRemoveHosts. All the host access control functions use the XHostAddress structure. The members in this structure are:

Example 13-1. The XHostAddress structure

```
typedef struct {
     int family;        /* for example FamilyInternet */
     int length;        /* length of address, in bytes */
     char *address;     /* pointer to where to find the bytes */
} XHostAddress;
```

family	Specifies which address family to use (for example, TCP/IP or DECnet). The family symbols FamilyInternet, FamilyDECnet, and FamilyChaos are defined in *<X11/X.h>*.
length	Specifies the length of the address in bytes.
address	Specifies a pointer to the address.

For these functions to execute successfully, the client application must run on the same host as the X server and must have permission in the initial authorization at connection setup before calling these functions.

13.2.2 Enabling and Disabling Access Control

Normally, the access control list determines whether a client succeeds in connecting to the server. Sometimes it is more convenient (though less safe) to allow a client or *any* host to have access. In this case, a client running on the same host as the server can call XDisableAccessControl. Thereafter, the host access list will no longer be used to filter connection requests. To reset the server to its default condition with access control, use XEnableAccessControl. XSetAccessControl performs either of these functions according to a flag.

13.3 Getting the Window Hierarchy

XQueryTree lets you get the IDs of the windows in a sizeable portion of the window hierarchy with a single call. This is the only way to find out the IDs of windows created by other clients except through events with the help of the user. XQueryTree gets the root window ID, the parent window ID, and the list of child window IDs given a window. It also returns the number of children.

13.4 Close Down Mode

Normally, all resources associated with a client will be destroyed when the connection between the client and the server closes. This can happen without prior warning to either the server or the client when, for example, the network cable is accidentally pulled out of one of the machines. Therefore, robust applications need a way of recovering from that occurrence. XSetCloseDownMode helps implement one method of recovery.

Clients in the default DestroyAll close down mode will have all their resources killed when the connection to the server dies. XSetCloseDownMode can set two other modes, RetainPermanent and RetainTemporary, which allow client resources to live on for a time. A client may want its resources to live on to assist in the process of recovering from a broken connection with the server, usually caused by a network failure. When next run after the problem has been corrected, the application could somehow determine which resources were its own and continue operating where it left off. The "somehow" is the crux of the problem. The only way I can think of to allow the client to find out the ID's of its resources after the client is resurrected is for the client to save all the resource ID's in a file (or perhaps in a property) immediately after they are created. Then upon startup it can read this information and see if the specified resources still exist. If they do, it can skip creating them.

A dying connection between the server and client raises other problems, too. Even if a client's resources are put on life support, there is no longer any "brain" behind them. The user's instructions will go unanswered and there will be no visible warning on the screen that the client is no longer connected. The window manager or some other program, if running on the same machine as the server, could conceivably detect this situation and print a message. However, this kind of functionality in a window manager hasn't been demonstrated up to now. Otherwise, the user can only be warned that the connection could die and that this would cause the window to freeze (if the client's resources were preserved; the window would disappear if the close down mode had not been set). The user could then restart the client to reactivate the window.

XKillClient can kill resources that remain alive after the connection closes. It can kill resources associated with a single client by specifying any resource ID associated with that client, or it can kill all resources of all clients that terminated with mode Retain-Temporary if given the argument AllTemporary. XKillClient might be used by the window manager or conceivably by a separate client to save space in the server by cleaning up resources after clients die that have requested that their resources be kept alive.

This should not be done unless the user agrees with it because it could upset an application's attempt to recover from a broken connection with the server.

13.5 Connection Close Operations

This section describes what happens when a client or a display is disconnected from the server and the functions that control that behavior.

When the connection between the X server and the display hardware is closed, either by a call to XCloseDisplay or by an exiting process, the X server performs these automatic operations:

- Disowns all selections made by the program.

- Releases all passive grabs made by the program.

- Performs an XUngrabPointer and XUngrabKeyboard if the client application had actively grabbed the pointer or the keyboard.

- Performs an XUngrabServer if the client had grabbed the server.

- Marks all resources (including colormap entries) allocated by the client application as permanent or temporary, according to whether the closedown mode is Retain-Permanent or RetainTemporary (see Section 13.4).

The X server performs these operations when the closedown mode is DestroyAll:

- The *save-set* is a list of other client's windows, referred to as save-set windows (see Section 14.4 for a complete description of save-sets). If any window in the client's save-set is an inferior of a window created by the client, the X server reparents the save-set window to the closest ancestor so that the save-set window is not an inferior of a window created by the client.

- Performs an XMapWindow request on the save-set window, if the save-set window is unmapped. The X server does this even if the save-set window was not an inferior of a window created by the client.

- Destroys all windows created by the client, after examining each window in the client's save-set.

- Performs the appropriate free request on all nonwindow resources (Font, Pixmap, Bitmap, Cursor, Colormap, and GC) created by the client.

Additional processing occurs when the *last* connection to the X server closes with close down mode DestroyAll. The X server:

- Resets its state, as if it had just been started. The X server destroys all lingering resources from clients that have terminated in RetainPermanent or Retain-Temporary mode.

- Deletes all but the predefined atom IDs.

- Deletes all properties on all root windows.

- Resets all device attributes (key click, bell volume, acceleration) and the access control list.

- Restores the standard root tiles, cursors, default pointing device, and default font path.

- Restores the keyboard focus to `PointerRoot`.

13.6 Data Management

Xlib provides two ways to help you manage data within an application: the context manager and association tables. The former saves you the trouble of creating arrays and dynamically allocating memory for data to be used only within your application. The latter is a fast lookup table useful for lists that require frequent searching.

13.6.1 The Context Manager

Four routines are provided to let you associate data with a window locally in Xlib, rather than in the server as in properties. The context manager routines store and retrieve untyped data according to the display, a window ID, and an assigned context ID. The display argument to the context manager routine (returned from `XOpenDisplay`) is used as an additional dimension to the array, not as a pointer to the display structure. No requests to the server are made.

First you call `XUniqueContext` to obtain an ID for a particular type of information you want to assign to windows. `XUniqueContext` just provides a unique integer ID every time you call it (you can also make up your own if you wish). This ID indicates to the application what type of information is stored, but none of the calls require you to specify the data type. Then use `XSaveContext` to store information into the context manager, and `XFindContext` reads it. If you plan to rewrite a particular piece of data corresponding to a window ID and context ID, it is better in terms of time and space to erase the current entry with `XDeleteContext` before calling `XSaveContext` again. `XDeleteContext` does not make the context ID invalid.

If you have many different pieces of data of the same type, such as an array, that must be associated with each window, you have the option of packing it in a single chunk of data and storing it by context, or creating a different context ID for each member of the array. The context ID indicates the *meaning* of the data (how you interpret it), not necessarily the C language type.

13.6.2 Association Tables

Association tables provide a fast lookup table for data that must be searched frequently. They are implemented as a linked list of structures. To use these functions, you must link in the *-loldX*, the X10 compatibility library.

Association tables associate arbitrary information with resource IDs. This is similar to the context manager, but the resource IDs used with association tables are existing resources, not created for the purpose of storing data for later retrieval.

Application programs often need to be able to easily refer to their own data structures when an event arrives. The association table system provides users of the X library with a method of associating their own data structures with X resources (Pixmap, Font, Window, and so on).

An XAssocTable can be used to type X resources. For example, the user may wish to have three or four "types" of windows, each with different properties. This can be accomplished by associating each X window ID with a pointer to a window property data structure defined by the programmer. The generic type for resource IDs is XID.

There are a few guidelines that should be observed when using an XAssocTable:

• All XIDs are relative to the currently active display. Therefore, if you are using multiple displays you need to be sure the correct display is active before performing an XAssocTable operation. XAssocTable imposes no restrictions on the number of XIDs per table, the number of XIDs per display or the number of displays per table.

• Because of the hashing scheme used by the association mechanism the following rules for determining the size of XAssocTables should be followed. Associations will be made and looked up more efficiently if the table size (number of buckets in the hashing system) is a power of two and if there are not more than 8 XIDs per bucket.

XCreateAssocTable creates an association table. To create an entry in a specific XAssocTable, use XMakeAssoc. Some size suggestions might be: use 32 buckets per 100 objects; a reasonable maximum number of object per buckets is 8. XMakeAssoc inserts data into an XAssocTable keyed on an XID. XDeleteAssoc deletes an association in an XAssocTable keyed on its XID. Data is inserted into the table only once. Redundant inserts are meaningless and cause no problems. The queue in each association bucket is sorted from the lowest XID to the highest XID. Redundant deletes (and deletes of nonexistent XIDs) are meaningless and cause no problems. Deleting associations in no way impairs the performance of an XAssocTable.

XLookUpAssoc retrieves the data stored in an XAssocTable by its XID. If an appropriately matching XID can be found in the table the routine will return the data associated with it. If the XID cannot be found in the table the routine will return NULL.

XDestroyAssocTable frees the memory associated with a specific XAssocTable. Using an XAssocTable after it has been destroyed is guaranteed to have unpredictable and probably disastrous consequences!

13.7 The After Function

Every protocol request calls an *after function* just before it returns. This function is normally `NoOp`, but the program may specify the name of any function using `XSetAfter-Function`.

13.8 Coordinate Transformation

`XTranslateCoordinates` translates coordinates relative to one window into the coordinates relative to a second, and determines whether the resulting position relative to the second window is in a subwindow of the second window.

Because the window-based coordinate system is so convenient, this function is rarely needed. Since `XTranslateCoordinates` makes a round-trip request, it cannot be used heavily to port to X programs that use global coordinates.

13.9 Porting Programs to X

Any program that runs on an ASCII terminal can be run directly under the terminal emulator *xterm*. The only problem is how to deal with changing the size of the window while the application is running. The application may read the termcap definition to determine the original window size. Look at the X application *resize*, which can be used to change the physical size of the *xterm* window and make corresponding changes to TERMCAP all at once. The *resize* reference page (see Volume Three, *X Window System User's Guide*) suggests a couple of C-shell aliases for commands to resize *xterm* windows.

If you have a Berkeley 4.3-compatible tty driver and at least *xterm 2.2*, *xterm* sets the tty driver's row and column attributes when its top-level window is resized. *vi* and *more* and several other programs also look at those attributes when figuring out the terminal size. Also, *xterm* will send a SIGWINCH signal to the controlling process, which, if it is *vi* or *more*, will understand this signal and change its own notion of screen size, repainting the window in the process. This is the best way to deal with window resizing under *xterm*.

Graphics programs face a more difficult porting path. They must be rewritten to use the X library. In the case of programs that are already based on an event-driven window system (such as SunTools, or the Mac), the port should be quite straightforward.

Programs written for single user systems such as PCs will be a little more difficult, since they must be converted to respond to events instead of asking for one type of input at a time. They must also be modified to work in a multitasking environment.

Byte order is another traditionally thorny issue in porting. Byte order refers to the order in which bytes of data are stored in memory. There are actually four ways for two-byte data to be ordered, since the direction of each byte has two variations and the position of the most significant byte is also variable.

For X pixmaps, byte order is defined by the server, and clients with different native byte ordering must swap bytes as necessary. For all other parts of the protocol, the byte order is defined by the client, and the server swaps bytes as necessary.

13.9.1 Porting from X10 to X11

X Version 11 is very much different from X Version 10, though it still uses some of the same concepts. It has nearly twice as many routines, and has several major completely new concepts such as virtual colormaps, the graphics context, and window manager hints. Porting most X Version 10 programs will essentially require translating all the function calls, adding the window manager communication, setting of the graphics context, and treatment of colors. However, because of the added functionality, there are now better ways to do things in many cases. You should consider carefully whether to do a minimal translation or to do a more extensive rewrite that might achieve better performance.

Release 2 includes an X10-to-X11 conversion program (*X10toX11*) that allows X10 clients to run under X11 without even recompiling by translating their X10 requests into X11 requests and tailoring the return values back to X10 format. This program has a performance penalty of 20% according to its authors.

Some of the existing X11 applications are minimal rewrites of X10 programs. Take care before using the existing programs as examples.

Some X10 functions are still supported. They are described in Appendix B, *X10 Compatibility*. The functionality of the X10 XDraw and its variations that fill and tile are supported, but are implemented with the X11 drawing routines. Therefore, they are likely to be slow. The association table functions are also available. Both groups of functions can be used by including the file *<X11/X10.h>* at the top of each source file, and linking with the *-loldX* library. Reference pages for the X10 compatibility routines are provided in Volume Two, *Xlib Reference Manual*.

13.10 Using Extensions to X

An extension is a set of routines and capabilities that a hardware vendor has provided for use on a particular machine, in addition to the standard X library.

Extensions to X are not second-class citizens and there should be very little to distinguish the use of an extension from that of the core protocol. The only difference is that the application should check to make sure the extension exists, and then query the extension to find out the major opcode, additional event types, and additional error types so that the extension can be integrated properly. If the extensions have been written properly so that they initialize themselves when first called, they should be usable just like other X library functions.

XListExtensions returns a list of all extensions supported by the server. Once the name of the desired extension is known, XQueryExtension should be called to get specific information about the extension. XFreeExtensionList should then be used to free the memory allocated by XListExtensions.

14
Window Management

X programs may be expected to cooperate with any one of a number of different window managers. This chapter discusses the design of a simple window manager, not so that you will be able to write one, but so that you will know what to expect from one. As it turns out, some of the techniques used in this program (such as menus) could be adapted for other clients as well. Everyone should at least look through this chapter.

In This Chapter:

In This Chapter (continued):

14
Window Management

A window manager is a program implemented with Xlib to control the layout of windows on the screen, responding to user requests to move, resize, raise, lower, or iconify windows. The window manager may also enforce a policy for window layout (such as mandating a standard window or icon size and placement), and provide a menu for commonly used shell commands.

This chapter is not primarily for window manager writers, as these are a rare breed. Before long, there will be several good customizable window managers available, and there will be very little reason for users or application writers to want to write their own. Only a few people in the X community are going to be actively involved in writing window managers, and chances are good they will already know most of what is described here. This chapter is presented for two reasons: so that application writers will get a better understanding of how to cooperate with the window manager; and so we can describe and demonstrate the Xlib routines that are provided mainly for the purpose of window management. As it turns out, the examples in this chapter also have elements (such as menus) that are useful in ordinary applications as well.

We'll begin by describing the features and routines in Xlib that are provided mainly to give window managers the authority they need to control window layout, and the flexibility to provide a good user interface. These features include the following:

- Substructure redirection, which allows the window manager to intercept requests to change the screen layout. This enables a window manager to enforce a window layout policy.

- Reparenting, which lets the window manager build a frame or other "decoration" around each top-level window. The frame could possibly contain boxes which could be used to move or resize the window.

- The save-set, which ensures that the windows the window manager iconifies or reparents are returned to their original state if the window manager dies unexpectedly.

Then we'll describe what the window manager can do with the properties set by clients, building on the description of interclient communication presented in Chapter 10, *Interclient Communication*.

Finally, we'll describe a simple window manager program. You should find this program helpful not only in demonstrating window management techniques, but also for showing Xlib programming in a more complex setting than *basicwin* in Chapter 3, *Basic Window*

Program, or *basecalc* in Chapter 12, *A Complete Application*. You should understand both those programs before tackling this one.

14.1 Layout Policy

A window manager may have a policy on how top-level windows will be placed on the screen.

The standard window manager *uwm* does not have a window layout policy, but some existing window managers do. For example, the Siemens RTL Tiled window manager mandates that only temporary pop-up windows can overlap. That policy makes exposure a rare occurrence but makes resizing much more common. A second simpler example is the window manager designed by Stellar Computer for its high-performance workstations. The Stellar window manager aligns icons along the top edge of the screen, along with the Stellar logo. Since the window manager creates the icons or is passed their IDs through hints, it can distinguish them from other windows on the screen.

Within its window layout policy, the window manager should honor the window size and position hints returned by XGetNormalHints and XGetWMHints as closely as possible (each application sets these hints). Under the window manager *uwm*, the user selects the size of a newly created window by moving a flashing outline of a window. The size hints provided by the application determine the minimum dimensions, maximum dimensions, and desired increment for the window size, and these are indicated in the motion of the outline. For example, *uwm* the minimum size hints take priority over the user's input, so that the user can't resize the window smaller than the minimum size.

Applications are free to resize or move the children of their top-level windows as necessary. The window manager has no control over them in this respect.

14.2 Substructure Redirection

The window manager enforces its window layout policy using substructure redirection. When the window manager selects SubstructureRedirectMask on the root window, an attempt by any other client to change the configuration of any child of the root window will fail. Instead, an event describing the layout change request will be sent to the window manager. The window manager then reads the event and determines whether to honor the request, modify it, or deny it completely. If it decides to honor the request, it calls the routine that the client called that triggered the event, with the same arguments. If it decides to modify the request, it calls the same routine but with modified arguments.

The *structure*, as we are using the term here, is the location, size, stacking order, border width, and mapping status of a window. The *substructure* is all these statistics about the children of a particular window. This is the complete set of information about screen layout that the window manager might need in order to implement its policy. *Redirection* means that an event is sent to the client selecting redirection (usually the window manager), and the original structure-changing request will not be executed at all.

The events that are selected by SubstructureRedirectMask and the routines that are intercepted are as follows:

- CirculateRequest events report when an Xlib function, such as XRestack-Windows, XCirculateSubwindows, XCirculateSubwindowsDown, or XCirculateSubwindowsUp, is called to change the stacking order of a group of children.

- ConfigureRequest events report when an Xlib function, such as XConfigure-Window, XRaiseWindow, XLowerWindow, XMoveWindow, XResizeWindow, XMoveResizeWindow, or XSetWindowBorderWidth, is called to resize, move, restack, or change the border width of a window.

- MapRequest events report when XMapWindow or XMapSubwindows is called to map a window.

ResizeRedirectMask also selects ConfigureRequest events when a client has called XMoveResizeWindow, XResizeWindow, or XConfigureWindow. However, if any client has selected SubstructureRedirectMask on the parent of the window for which ResizeRedirectMask is selected, the SubstructureRedirectMask takes precedence.

When SubstructureRedirectMask is selected on the root window, the only time that a configuration request on a child of the root window is not intercepted is when the override_redirect attribute of that child window has been set to True. This is intended for temporary pop-up windows that should not be reparented or affected by the window manager's layout policy.

Only one window manager at a time can select SubstructureRedirectMask or ResizeRedirectMask on a particular window.

Substructure redirect allows the window manager to separate the portion of itself that moves and resizes windows from the portion that enforces window policy. While the window reconfiguration section is driven by the user, the policy section can be completely driven from the *Request events that signal that the user has proposed a change to the window layout. And since applications will only attempt to resize or move their top-level windows in direct response to a user request, those requests are just as valid as the ones from the window reconfiguration section of the window manager.

14.3 Reparenting

A window manager can decorate windows on the screen with title bars, and place little boxes on the title bar with which the window can be moved or resized. This is only one possibility, modelled on the user interface on the Macintosh™.

To do this the window manager creates a child of the root somewhat larger than the top-level window of the application. Then it calls XReparentWindow specifying the top-level window of the application as *win* and the new parent as *parent*. *win* and all its descendants will then be descendants of *parent*.

In the area where the new parent is visible around the top-level window of the application, the window manager can put anything it wants. This could include text, graphics, and small windows which perform certain functions when a button is clicked in them.

The window manager can decorate all top-level windows, but it should ignore windows that are mapped with their override_redirect attribute set. This is indicated in the *Request events, so there is no need to query the attributes. The window manager should also not decorate windows that have set the XA_WM_TRANSIENT_FOR property, but it may apply its window layout policy to them. The window manager calls XGetTransient-ForHint for each window to get this property.

By the way, it is impossible (except by luck) for the window manager to match the colors of the decoration to the colors of the window it is decorating. A window manager cannot find out what colors a window uses for its border or background because these values are hidden in the server and are not accessible from Xlib.

14.3.1 Shadows

Window shadows can be imperfectly implemented by reparenting top-level windows. The shadow would appear to be the same size as the corresponding window but slightly offset diagonally (see Figure 14-1).

What happens if we try to accomplish the following style of background with two windows: one InputOutput window slightly larger in both dimensions than the application's top-level window, and one InputOutput shadow window the same size as the application window, offset into the corner of the InputOnly window? The larger window would have its background_pixmap attribute set to ParentRelative so that it looked invisible, and the smaller window would have its background set to black or gray to make the shadow. Figure 14-2 shows how the layers are lined up.

When the window with the shadow is moved around the screen when no other applications are on the screen, the shadow looks good. But when the window is moved over other applications, a strange thing happens. The background of the root window shows itself in the "invisible" corner of the shadow, as shown in Figure 14-3.

It turns out that a perfect shadow is not possible, because the server clips regions of the screen in rectangles, not in the complex shape required by a shadow. However, if the shadow is only two pixels wide, this approach might look good enough.

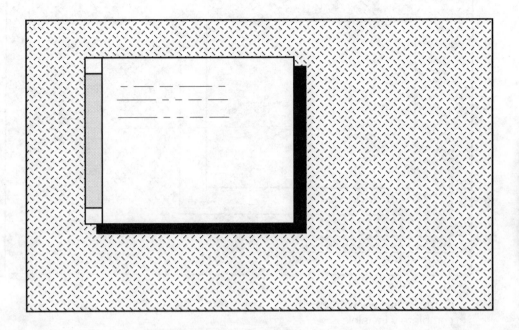

Figure 14-1. Goal of background shadow

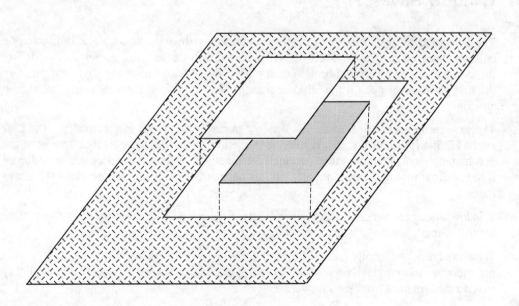

Figure 14-2. Window layering for background shadow

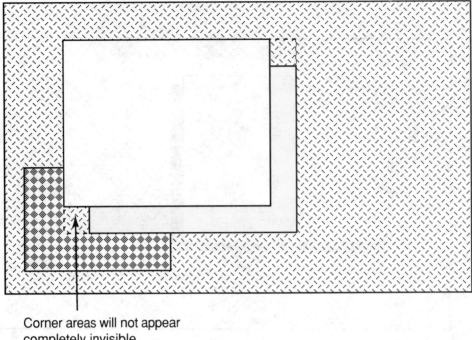

Corner areas will not appear
completely invisible

Figure 14-3. Actual effect of shadow attempt

14.4 Window Save-set

The save-set is a list of windows, usually maintained by the window manager, but including only windows created by other clients. If the window manager dies, all windows listed in the save-set will be reparented back to their closest living ancestor if they were reparented in the first place, or mapped if the window manager has unmapped them so that it could map an icon.

The save-set is necessary because the window manager might not exit normally. The user might kill it with Control-C if it is running in the foreground, or more likely, the user might get the process number and kill it. Actually, the actions of the save-set are performed even if the window manager exits normally, so less code is needed if the save set does the cleaning up.

Window managers almost always place in the save-set all the windows they reparent or iconify, using XAddToSaveSet.

Windows are automatically removed from the save-set when they are destroyed. If this were not the case, the program would have to monitor DestroyNotify events and explicitly remove the windows from the save-set.

The routines XRemoveFromSaveSet and XChangeSaveSet are available, but they are not often needed even in window managers. XChangeSaveSet adds or removes a window from the save-set.

14.5 Window Manager – Client Communications

There is no point in reiterating all that was said in Chapter 10, *Interclient Communication*, about the properties that applications set for the window manager. As described there, these properties are hints that the window manager may use or ignore as the programmer sees fit. There is a large amount of flexibility and variety in what window managers can do with the information provided in these hints. Its actions are to some extent constrained by the inter-client communication conventions described in Appendix F, *Proposed Interclient Communication Conventions*, even though these conventions are not fully developed.

However, even though a window manager could ignore all these hints and be strictly correct, most users and applications are expecting a bit more. These hints allow the window manager to smooth the user interface so that the system appears integrated. Any good window manager will read most if not all of the properties described in this section and try to do with them what is most helpful to applications and users.

14.5.1 Reading the Hints

Hints help the window manager conform to the needs of the application while at the same time letting it control window layout and policy. The window manager gets the hints with the routines shown in Table 14-1:

Table 14-1. Window Manager Hints

Hint	Set (by Application)	Get (by Window Manager)
Window Name	XStoreName	XFetchName
Icon Name	XSetIconName	XGetIconName
Shell Command and Arguments	XSetCommand	use XGetWindowProperty to get XA_WM_COMMAND
Icon Pixmap	XSetStandardProperties or XSetWMHints	XGetWMHints
Normal Size Hints	XSetNormalHints	XGetNormalHints
Above Five (Minimum Properties)	XSetStandardProperties	(Above Five Functions)
WM Hints	XSetWMHints	XGetWMHints
Zoom Hints	XSetZoomHints	XGetZoomHints
Transient Window	XSetTransientForHint	XGetTransientForHint
Class Hint	XSetClassHint	XGetClassHint

winman

Getting all of this information within the window manager as described above is simple, with the exception of getting the shell command and arguments. The property must be read with XGetWindowProperty since no convenience function is defined.

14.5.2 Setting Icon Sizes

The icon size property is the only hint that the window manager should set for applications to read. The window manager may prefer particular sizes of icons to yield a consistent appearance for all icons on the screen. The window manager calls XSetIconSizes (which sets the XA_WM_ICON_SIZE property on the root window), indicating the preferred sizes. The icon size hints include maximum and minimum dimensions and size increments. Once standard window managers evolve that set this property (*uwm* doesn't), applications may have one icon pixmap prepared for each standard window manager.

14.6 Window Management Functions

The functions described in this section are used primarily by the window manager on top-level windows. Applications might want to be prepared to use them on their top-level windows in case a window manager isn't running, but conventions for doing so have not yet been determined. Applications can use them on their subwindows.

XConfigureWindow is the most general routine for changing the configuration of a window, namely its size, position, border width, and stacking position.

The routines to move and resize windows are XMoveWindow, XMoveResizeWindow, and XResizeWindow. The routine to change the border width of a window is XSetWindowBorderWidth.

Quite a variety of routines are provided to change the stacking order of windows. These operations affect only a single group of siblings. Furthermore, they affect only overlapping siblings. If any of the siblings specified do not overlap, their stacking order is not changed.

XCirculateSubwindowsDown
        moves the lowest mapped sibling to the top of the stacking order.

XCirculateSubwindowsUp
        moves the highest mapped sibling to the bottom of the stacking order.

XCirculateSubwindows
        performs either XCirculateSubwindowsDown or XCirculate-
        SubwindowsUp according to a flag.

XRestackWindows
        specifies a list of siblings in the desired stacking order.

XRaiseWindow   moves a window to the top of the stacking order among its siblings.

XMapRaised	maps a window, placing it on top of the stacking order of its siblings. For a window mapped for the first time, this is equivalent to XMapWindow. But when an already mapped window is unmapped, it retains its stacking order when mapped again with XMapWindow.
XLowerWindow	moves a window to the bottom of the stacking order among its siblings.
XConfigureWindow	
	restacks the window according to a stack_mode and relative to a particular sibling. This function is also capable of moving, resizing, and changing the border width of a window.

All these functions have the ability to change the screen layout, and therefore can be monitored and intercepted by the window manager. They are also commonly used by the window manager itself to allow the user to change the screen layout.

The stack_mode of the XConfigureWindow routine has five possible values: Above, Below, BottomIf, TopIf, and Opposite. If the window is simultaneously being moved or resized, this calculation is performed with respect to the window's final size and position, not its initial position. If a sibling and a stack_mode is specified, the window is restacked as described in Table 14-2.

Table 14-2. Meaning of Stacking Mode with Sibling Specified

Window Stack Mode	Description
Above	window is placed just above sibling
Below	window is placed just below sibling
TopIf	if sibling obscures window, then window is placed at the top of the stack
BottomIf	if window obscures sibling, then window is placed at the bottom of the stack
Opposite	if any sibling occludes window, then window is placed at the top of the stack, else if window occludes any sibling, then window is placed at the bottom of the stack

If a stack_mode is specified but no sibling is specified, the window is restacked as described in Table 14-3.

Table 14-3. Meaning of Stacking Mode without Sibling

Window Stack Mode	Description
Above	window is placed at the top of the stack
Below	window is placed at the bottom of the stack
TopIf	if any sibling obscures window, then window is placed at the top of the stack
BottomIf	if window obscures any sibling, then window is placed at the bottom of the stack
Opposite	if any sibling occludes window, then window is placed at the top of the stack, else if window occludes any sibling, then window is placed at the bottom of the stack

Another set of routines that are usually only used by the window manager are the ones that grab and ungrab the server. XGrabServer and XUngrabServer are used when a program requires total control of the screen, so that output requests from other programs are queued but not displayed. One application of grabbing is to draw temporary, moving objects on the screen such as the outline of a window being moved. The outline (or grid) is drawn with logical function GXxor, which when drawn twice, leaves the screen as it was initially. If the server were not grabbed in between the first drawing and the second of the same line, some other program might update the same part of the display, resulting in glitches after the second drawing.

14.7 A Basic Window Manager

This section describes the design of a simple window manager called *winman*. This example window manager should be helpful in several ways. It demonstrates many of the Xlib routines that are intended to be used only by window managers. It also shows what a window manager might do with the properties that applications set, and how window managers implement icons. This window manager also demonstrates the use of the save-set to make sure that if it dies the windows it has iconified will be restored. It doesn't, however, demonstrate substructure redirection or reparenting. See the code for *uwm* for an example of substructure redirection, and *wm* or *twm* for examples of reparenting.

The *winman* program also demonstrates some techniques that may be helpful in ordinary applications, such as how to implement a menu using Xlib. (Most applications will ultimately do this with a toolkit.)

If you have the diskette of example programs from O'Reilly and Associates, you can compile and run *winman* to see how it works (ordering information appears in the *Preface*). Be sure to stop or kill any other window managers running before running *winman*. Both *winman* and the other window manager may get confused because they are not designed to cooperate with each other. The following explanations will be easier to follow if you have used the program.

14.7.1 Operation of the Program

The *winman* program creates a menu composed of horizontal bars and places it in the upper-right corner of the screen, as shown in Figure 14-4. (This figure is a screen dump made with the X utilities *xwd* and *xpr*).

Figure 14-4. The menu created by winman

The menu provides a number of basic functions for manipulating windows on the screen:

`Raise`	brings a window to the top of the stack, so that it is fully visible.
`Lower`	lowers a window to the bottom so that the area formerly hidden is made visible.
`Move`	changes the position of a window on the screen, and raises it.
`Resize`	changes the size of a window, and raises it.
`CirculateDn`	moves the window on the bottom to the top.
`CirculateUp`	moves the window on the top to the bottom.
`(De)Iconify`	turns a window into a small marker window, or vice versa.
`Keybrd Focus`	assigns all keyboard input to the selected window, regardless of the position of the pointer.

New Xterm	creates a new xterm window and places it at the upper-left corner of the screen. You can subsequently move or resize the new window with the Move and Resize functions.
Exit	It is good practice for all programs to provide a way to quit. (*uwm* requires the user to look up the process number and kill the process.) Since this window manager is primarily for demonstration purposes, this choice is provided to make it easy to kill the program.

All input for the window manager is supplied through the pointer. A cursor (which tracks the pointer) is assigned to the menu to indicate that input in this area selects a menu item. Choices are made from the menu by pressing a pointer button in the appropriate region of the menu. When a menu choice is made, the menu bar and its label change to inverse video. In other words, everything that was black in the bar changes to white and vice versa (*winman* works in black and white on all systems, even those with color). After the choice is made but before the operation is complete, the pointer is grabbed, so that all pointer input is directed to the menu window independent of the position of the pointer. While the pointer is grabbed, *winman*'s cursor changes to a hand and tracks the pointer anywhere on the screen. This reminds you that the window manager is expecting the next pointer input even though the pointer is no longer on the menu. When the chosen operation is complete, the menu is returned to its initial condition and the pointer grab is released.

If CirculateDn, CirculateUp, or New Xterm is chosen, selection of a window is not necessary. The circulation operations act on all overlapping windows that are children of the root. The New Xterm choice simply creates a new *xterm* window.

If Raise, Lower, (De)Iconify or Kybrd Focus is chosen, the user must press a pointer button to select a window. (*winman*'s own menu can't be iconified because this would make it impossible to recover the window manager menu.) Kybrd Focus sets the keyboard focus window and highlights that window with a white background behind the window.

If Move or Resize is chosen, the user must press a pointer button on the window to be manipulated, drag the pointer with the button held until the outline of the window is in the chosen size or position, and then release the button. (*winman*'s own menu can be moved but not resized.) A moving outline of the window is used to indicate the intended dimensions or position of the window.

14.7.2 Description of the Code of main

Example 14-1 shows the main for the *winman* window manager. The isIcon routine that is called in main is described in Section 14.7.14 below. The draw_box routine, also called in main, is described in Section 6.1.3. All the rest of *winman*'s code is described in sections following main.

Instead of breaking up the code in little pieces as we have done in earlier examples, this time we'll show you main together in one place. By this point in the manual, you should know enough to understand most of this code. Any questions you may have should be answered by the description immediately following the code.

Example 14-1. winman — main C program

```c
#include <X11/Xlib.h>
#include <X11/Xutil.h>
#include <X11/Xatom.h>
#include <X11/Xos.h>
#include <X11/cursorfont.h>

#include <stdio.h>
#include <signal.h>

#include "bitmaps/focus_frame_bi"        /* name must be <= 14 chars for
                                          * system V compatibilty */

#define MAX_CHOICE 10
#define DRAW 1
#define ERASE 0
#define RAISE 1
#define LOWER 0
#define MOVE 1
#define RESIZE 0
#define NONE 100
#define NOTDEFINED 0
#define BLACK 1    /* this is not a pixel value; this is a flag */
#define WHITE 0    /* this is not a pixel value; this is a flag */

Window focus_window;
Window inverted_pane = NONE;

static char *menu_label[] =
    {
    "Raise",
    "Lower",
    "Move",
    "Resize",
    "CirculateDn",
    "CirculateUp",
    " (De) Iconify",
    "Kybrd Focus",
    "New Xterm",
    "Exit",
    };

Display *display;
int screen;

main()
    {
    Window menuwin;
    Window panes[MAX_CHOICE];
    int menu_width, menu_height, x = 0, y = 0, border_width = 4;
    int winindex;
    int cursor_shape;
    Cursor cursor, hand_cursor;
    char *font_name = "9x15";
    XFontStruct *font_info;
    int direction, ascent, descent;
```

Example 14-1. winman — main C program (continued)

```
int char_count;
char *string;
XCharStruct overall;
Bool owner_events;
int pointer_mode;
int keyboard_mode;
Window confine_to;
GC gc, rgc;
int pane_height;
Window assoc_win = NOTDEFINED;          /* ID of associated icon */
XEvent event;
char icon_name[8];
unsigned int button;


if ( (display=XOpenDisplay(NULL)) == NULL )
    {
    (void) fprintf( stderr, "winman: cannot connect to \
            X server %s\n", XDisplayName(NULL));
    exit( -1 );
    }

screen = DefaultScreen(display);

/* Access font */
font_info = XLoadQueryFont(display,font_name);

if (font_info == NULL)
    {
    (void) fprintf( stderr, "winman: Cannot open font %s\n",
            font_name);
    exit( -1 );
    }

string = menu_label[6];
char_count = strlen(string);

/* determine the extent of each menu pane based
 * on the font size */
XTextExtents(font_info, string, char_count, &direction, &ascent,
        &descent, &overall);

menu_width = overall.width + 4;
pane_height = overall.ascent + overall.descent + 4;
menu_height = pane_height * MAX_CHOICE;

/* place the window in upper-right corner*/
x = DisplayWidth(display,screen) - menu_width - (2*border_width);
y = 0;    /* appears at top */

/* create opaque window */
menuwin = XCreateSimpleWindow(display, RootWindow(display,
        screen), x, y, menu_width, menu_height,
        border_width, BlackPixel(display,screen),
        WhitePixel(display,screen));
```

Example 14-1. winman — main C program (continued)

```
     /* create the choice windows for the text */
     for (winindex = 0; winindex < MAX_CHOICE; winindex++) {
         panes[winindex] = XCreateSimpleWindow(display, menuwin, 0,
                 menu_height/MAX_CHOICE*winindex, menu_width,
                 pane_height, border_width = 1,
                 BlackPixel(display,screen),
                 WhitePixel(display,screen));
             XSelectInput(display, panes[winindex], ButtonPressMask
                     | ButtonReleaseMask | ExposureMask);
     }

     XSelectInput(display, RootWindow(display, screen),
             SubstructureNotifyMask);

     /* these don't appear until parent (menuwin) is mapped */
     XMapSubwindows(display,menuwin);

     /* create the cursor for the menu */
     cursor = XCreateFontCursor(display, XC_left_ptr);
     hand_cursor = XCreateFontCursor(display, XC_hand2);

     XDefineCursor(display, menuwin, cursor);

     focus_window = RootWindow(display, screen);

     /* Create two graphics contexts for inverting panes (white and
      * black).  We invert the panes by changing the background
      * pixel, clearing the window, and using the GC with the
      * contrasting color to redraw the text.  Another way is
      * using XCopyArea.  The default is to generate GraphicsExpose
      * and NoExpose events to indicate whether the source area
      * was obscured.  Since the logical function is GXinvert
      * the destination is also the source.   Therefore if other
      * windows are obscuring parts of the exposed pane, the
      * wrong area will be inverted.  Therefore we would need to
      * handle GraphicsExpose and NoExpose events.  We'll do it the
      * easier way. */

     gc = XCreateGC(display, RootWindow(display, screen), 0, NULL);
     XSetForeground(display, gc, BlackPixel(display, screen));
     rgc = XCreateGC(display, RootWindow(display, screen), 0, NULL);
     XSetForeground(display, rgc, WhitePixel(display, screen));

     /* map the menu window (and its subwindows) to the screen */
     XMapWindow(display, menuwin);

     /* Force child processes to disinherit the TCP file descriptor.
      * This helps the shell command (creating new xterm) forked and
      * exec'ed from the menu to work properly.  */
     if ((fcntl(ConnectionNumber(display), F_SETFD, 1)) == -1)
         fprintf(stderr, "winman: child cannot disinherit TCP fd");

     /* loop getting events on the menu window */
     while (1)
```

Example 14-1. winman — main C program (continued)

```
    {
    /* wait for an event */
    XNextEvent(display, &event);

    /* if expose, draw text in pane if it is pane */
    switch (event.type) {
    case Expose:
        if (assoc_win == event.xexpose.window)   /* if icon */
            XDrawString(display, assoc_win, gc, 2, ascent + 2,
                        icon_name, strlen(icon_name));
        else /* it's a pane, might be inverted */
            {
            if (inverted_pane == event.xexpose.window)
                paint_pane(event.xexpose.window, panes, gc,
                           rgc, font_info, BLACK);
            else
                paint_pane(event.xexpose.window, panes, gc,
                           rgc, font_info, WHITE);
            }
        break;
    case ButtonPress:

        paint_pane(event.xbutton.window, panes, gc, rgc,
                   font_info, BLACK);

        button = event.xbutton.button;
        inverted_pane = event.xbutton.window;

        /* get the matching ButtonRelease on same button */
        while (1) {
            /* get rid of presses on other buttons */
            while (XCheckTypedEvent(display, ButtonPress,
                    &event));
            /* wait for release; if on correct button exit */
            XMaskEvent(display, ButtonReleaseMask, &event);
            if (event.xbutton.button == button)
                break;
        }

        /* all events are sent to the grabbing
         * window regardless of
         * whether this is True or False.
         * owner_events only affects the distribution of
         * events when the pointer is within this
         * application's windows. */
        owner_events = True;

        /* we don't want pointer or keyboard events
         * frozen in the server */
        pointer_mode = GrabModeAsync;
        keyboard_mode = GrabModeAsync;

        /* we don't want to confine the cursor */
        confine_to = None;
```

Example 14-1. winman — main C program (continued)

```
        XGrabPointer(display, menuwin, owner_events,
                ButtonPressMask | ButtonReleaseMask,
                pointer_mode, keyboard_mode,
                confine_to, hand_cursor, CurrentTime);

    /* if press and release occurred in same window,
     * do command, if not, do nothing */
    if (inverted_pane == event.xbutton.window)
        {
        /* convert window ID to
         * window array index  */
        for (winindex = 0; inverted_pane !=
                panes[winindex]; winindex++)
            ;
        switch (winindex)
            {
        case 0:
            raise_lower(display, screen,
                    RAISE);
            break;
        case 1:
            raise_lower(display, screen,
                    LOWER);
            break;
        case 2:
            move_resize(display, screen,
                menuwin, hand_cursor, MOVE);
            break;
        case 3:
            move_resize(display, screen,
                menuwin, hand_cursor, RESIZE);
            break;
        case 4:
            circup(display, screen);
            break;
        case 5:
            circdn(display, screen);
            break;
        case 6:
            iconify(display, screen, menuwin,
                font_info, &assoc_win,
                icon_name);
            break;
        case 7:
            focus_window = focus(display, screen,
                    font_info, &assoc_win);
            break;
        case 8:
            execute("xterm&");
            break;

        case 9: /* exit */
            XSetInputFocus(display,
                RootWindow(display,screen),
                RevertToPointerRoot,
```

Example 14-1. winman — main C program (continued)

```
                            CurrentTime);
                    /* save-set turns all icons
                     * back into windows */

                    /* must clear focus highlights */
                    XClearWindow(display, RootWindow(display ,
                        screen));
                    XFlush(display);
                    XCloseDisplay(display);
                    exit(1);
                default:
                    (void) fprintf(stderr,
                            "Something went wrong\n");
                    break;
                } /* end switch */
            } /* end if */

        /* Invert Back Here (logical function is copy) */
        paint_pane(event.xexpose.window, panes, gc, rgc,
                font_info, WHITE);

        inverted_pane = NONE;
        draw_focus_frame();
        XUngrabPointer(display, CurrentTime);
        XFlush(display);
        break;
    case DestroyNotify:
        /* window we have iconified has died, remove its icon.
         * Don't need to remove window from save-set
         * because that is done automatically */
        removeIcon(event.xdestroywindow.window);
        break;
    case CirculateNotify:
    case ConfigureNotify:
    case UnmapNotify:
        /* all these uncover areas of screen */
        draw_focus_frame();
        break;
    case CreateNotify:
    case GravityNotify:
    case MapNotify:
    case ReparentNotify:
        /* don't need these but get them automatically
         * since we need DestroyNotify and UnmapNotify
         */
        break;
    default:
        fprintf(stderr, "winman: got unexpected event %s\n",
                event.type);
    } /* end switch */
    } /* end menu loop (while) */
} /* end main */
```

14.7.3 Window Layering

The first issue that comes up when writing a menu is how to layer the windows that contain each menu item. It would be possible to write a menu that only used one window, placing the text within the window in the right places and highlighting areas when the pointer coordinates in the ButtonPress events indicated that an item was chosen. This is a hard way, because it doesn't take advantage of X's windowing capabilities. It would also be possible to make each menu panel a subwindow of the root window. While this would simplify the event handling and highlighting, we would have to define a cursor for each of the windows. More importantly, the user would have to move all the windows separately if the menu were to be moved, unless we monitored movement of any one of the windows and made the rest follow. There are also other ramifications, including that it would be difficult to identify the menu as a whole to make sure it wasn't iconified; this would require comparing the IDs in events with the IDs of all the windows. The best solution is a combination of the above approaches.

The menu is created by superimposing ten small InputOutput child windows (defs[ ]) on one large InputOutput parent window (menuwin), as shown in Figure 14-5. This has the advantage that there is a single parent window for the application, which we can use to locate the panes of the menu, and to identify the menu as a whole. You can also assign a cursor to the larger window, and since the smaller windows are its children, the same cursor appears in all of them. This avoids nine cursor assignments.

The nine smaller windows do three other convenient things; their borders make a neat division between areas of the menu, they determine which area of the menu the user chooses, and they define a convenient area to invert from black on white to white on black to indicate which menu choice was made.

14.7.4 Selecting Input

Now that we've decided how to layer the windows to best advantage, it's time to plan what events are going to be needed. The menuwin window requires no events since it is chiefly there to tie together the menu panes. ButtonPress, ButtonRelease, and Expose events are required for the panes, so they can accept a choice, and redraw the pane in case anything obscures and then exposes part or all of the menu. ButtonRelease events are selected so that we can verify menu choices by making sure the ButtonRelease happens in the same window as the ButtonPress. Since the pointer is grabbed during the selection of a window on the screen to be manipulated (a window not associated with the window manager), we don't need to select input on any of these windows. However, we need to know when applications that *winman* has iconified have been killed, so that we can remove the icon. This requires selecting SubstructureNotifyMask on the root window.

Some of the other events selected by SubstructureNotifyMask also come in handy for triggering the redrawing of the highlighting background drawn around the focus window by *winman*. This background is drawn on the root window and might have to be redrawn whenever a new area of the root window becomes exposed. It has to be redrawn when

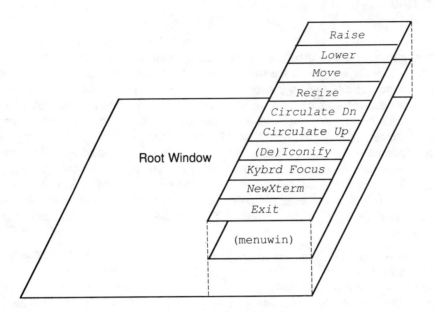

Root Window

Raise
Lower
Move
Resize
Circulate Dn
Circulate Up
(De)Iconify
Kybrd Focus
NewXterm
Exit
(menuwin)

Figure 14-5. Window layering for the menu

ConfigureNotify, CirculateNotify, or UnmapNotify events arrive. This could also have been done by selecting Expose events on the root window, but since we have already selected these other events and they will be sent from the server to Xlib anyway, it improves performance slightly to use them instead of Expose events on the root window.

14.7.5 Handling Input

There are numerous commands available for getting input. The routines used in main are XMaskEvent, XCheckTypedEvent and XNextEvent.

- XNextEvent is used to get any type of event that occurs in any window. It waits until an event arrives.

- XMaskEvent allows you to choose which the event masks of the events to look for, monitoring all windows. It waits until an event arrives.

- XCheckTypedEvent allows you to choose the types of events to look for, monitors all windows, and doesn't wait even if no matching event is on the queue.

These routines were described and most of them demonstrated in Chapter 8, *Events* and Chapter 9, *The Keyboard and Pointer*. But the way they are used in main might need some explanation. Consider the excerpt from main shown in Example 14-2.

Example 14-2. Use event-getting routines together

```
    /* get the matching ButtonRelease on same button */
    while (1) {
        /* get rid of presses on other buttons */
        while (XCheckTypedEvent(display, ButtonPress,
                &event));
        /* wait for release; if on correct button exit *

        XMaskEvent(display, ButtonReleaseMask, &event);
        if (event.xbutton.button == button)
            break;
    }
```

Here, we have already gotten a ButtonPress event and are waiting for a Button-Release on the same button. This cannot be done with XMaskEvent alone because we might get a ButtonRelease on a different button first, and there is no way to select or get only the button events on a single button (except by writing a predicate procedure as shown in Example 8-6). Therefore, XMaskEvent must be called in a loop and the button member in each event must be checked. Furthermore, the CheckTypedEvent call is necessary to make sure that Xlib's queue doesn't fill up with ButtonPress events that are not wanted since the routine is waiting for a button release. XCheckTypedEvent is used again in the routine that actually move or resize a window, to throw away excess Motion-Notify events.

The Expose event processing in main doesn't throw away excess events to avoid multiple repaints. It probably should, but it is not that easy to do. There is a problem with just throwing out all the Expose events. Any of the menu panes or any icon can receive Expose events, and we wouldn't want to throw away all the Expose events on one just because the other has been redrawn. That makes it necessary to check the window in each Expose event before throwing it away. XCheckTypedWindowEvent does a great job for the icon window branch, but won't work for the menu pane branch because the panes are actually nine different windows. A loop that checks the window member in each Expose event against the IDs of each of the menu pane windows will work, but may take more time than the multiple repaints would have in the first place. As it is, we have already minimized redrawing in another way by redrawing only the panes that are exposed instead of the entire menu.

14.7.6 Inverting an Area

There are at least four possible strategies for inverting a menu pane containing text. They are not all equally good.

One is to use XCopyArea to copy the pane to itself using GXinvert as the logical function in the GC. This approach is weak because GXinvert would not achieve the desired effect on a color system, even though it would work fine on a monochrome system.

The second strategy, adopted in main, is to change the background pixel value of the window and change the foreground pixel value in the GC to draw the text in a contrasting color. In *winman* the colors are black and white, but this approach will work correctly with any two contrasting colors.

The third approach would be to use XDrawImageString to draw the text. XDraw-ImageString draws a complete rectangle, with the text in the foreground pixel value from the GC and the rest of the rectangle in the background pixel value. If this rectangle were the same size as the menu pane, the entire pane could be inverted in color simply by swapping the foreground and background pixel values in the GC. The one weakness of this approach is that the rectangle drawn by XDrawImageString might not leave as much space around the text as you would like. However, this is a very fast approach, useful in menus and for the selection of text.

The fourth approach involves a trick using colors allocated by XAllocColorCells. It is possible to allocate colors so that the two contrasting colors in the drawable are swapped by setting to 1 or 0 all the bits in a plane of the drawable. In this technique the text does not need drawing at all for highlighting, because the plane that the text is drawn on is not modified by the operation to set or clear the bits in the other plane. You would need to allocate four colorcells, two of which contained the foreground RGB values and two the background. This would not work on a monochrome system, since you could not allocate four colorcells. This technique is described in Section 7.4.1.

14.7.7 Cursors

The main creates two cursors: one an arrow for selecting from the menu and the other a hand for manipulating windows. It uses the call to grab the pointer to change the cursor to the hand. That has the nice side effect that the cursor will automatically change back when the grab is released, so that the cursor window attribute does not need to be changed with XDefineCursor.

14.7.8 Grabbing the Pointer

XGrabPointer is called to allow the user to select a window anywhere on the screen to be manipulated. While the pointer is grabbed, all pointer input is sent to the menu. Note that keyboard input is still sent normally to the application the pointer is in.

The arguments to XGrabPointer can be confusing. The *owner_events* argument affects the distribution of events when the pointer is within this application's windows. Therefore, it doesn't affect our application because we are using the grab to get input from outside the menu windows. The *pointer_mode* and *keyboard_mode* arguments also don't apply to the job at hand, so they are set to GrabModeAsync which doesn't affect the processing of events. Their other settings cause event to be held in the server until a releasing XAllowEvents call. Finally, the *confine_to* argument also doesn't fit our job because we want the pointer to be able to roam around the screen rather than be confined to a window.

That about wraps up the new techniques used in main that haven't been used earlier in this book. Now we'll move on to some of the routines that main calls, beginning with paint_pane.

14.7.9 Painting the Menu

The `paint_pane` routine displays text in a menu pane. It is called when an exposure event occurs on a pane. When the menu is exposed, all of the exposure events are sent contiguously, refreshing each of the panes that was exposed. When the menu is first mapped, the `Expose` events trigger the drawing of all the panes for the first time.

Each call of this routine puts the text in one choice window. The first operation compares the window ID from the event with the IDs in the `panes` array to determine which string from the `menu_label` array to use.

Windows are cleared automatically when exposure occurs. But `paint_pane` is not always called in response to Expose events; it is also used to invert the pane when a choice is made. Therefore, the output buffer will not necessarily be flushed before the next call to draw the area. the `XClearWindow` call is necessary.

Example 14-3. winman — the paint_pane routine

```
static char *menu_label[] = {
    "Raise",
    "Lower",
    "Move",
    "Resize",
    "CirculateDn",
    "CirculateUp",
    "(De)Iconify",
    "Kybrd Focus",
    "New Xterm",
    "Exit",
};

paint_pane(window, panes, ngc, rgc, font_info, mode)
Window window;
Window panes[];
GC ngc, rgc;
XFontStruct *font_info;
int mode;
{
    int win;
    int x = 2, y;
    GC gc;

    if (mode == BLACK) {
        XSetWindowBackground(display, window, BlackPixel(display,
                screen));
        gc = rgc;
    }
    else {
        XSetWindowBackground(display, window, WhitePixel(display,
                screen));
        gc = ngc;
    }
    /* clearing repaints the background */
    XClearWindow(display, window);
```

Example 14-3. winman — the paint_pane routine (continued)

```
    /* find out index of window for label text */
    for (win = 0; window != panes[win]; win++)
        ;

    y = font_info->max_bounds.ascent;

    /* the string length is necessary because strings for
          XDrawString may not be NULL terminated */
    XDrawString(display, window, gc, x, y, menu_label[win],
            strlen( menu_label[win]));
}
```

14.7.10 Circulating Windows

The `circup` and `circdn` routines are simple, because they have no arguments and they require no user input. They simply take all overlapping top-level windows and move the bottom one to the top, or the top one to the bottom.

Example 14-4. winman — the circle up and circle down routines

```
circup(display,screen)
Display *display;
int screen;
    {
    XCirculateSubwindowsUp(display, RootWindow(display,screen));
    }

circdn(display,screen)
Display *display;
int screen;
    {
    XCirculateSubwindowsDown(display, RootWindow(display,screen));
    }
```

14.7.11 Raising and Lowering Windows

The `raise_lower` routine gets a `ButtonPress` event, finds out which window it occurred in, and raises or lowers the window unless it was the root.

The `XQueryPointer` call is used to get the window ID of the window that the button is pressed in. This call is necessary because the program did not create or select input on the windows that it is going to manipulate.

Example 14-5. winman — the raise and lower routines

```
raise_lower( display, screen, raise_or_lower )
Display *display;
int screen;
Bool raise_or_lower;
{
    XEvent report;
    int root_x,root_y;
    Window child, root;
    int win_x, win_y;
    unsigned int mask;
    unsigned int button;

    /* wait for ButtonPress, find out which subwindow of root */
    XMaskEvent(display, ButtonPressMask, &report);
    button = report.xbutton.button;
    XQueryPointer(display, RootWindow(display,screen), &root,
            &child, &root_x, &root_y, &win_x, &win_y,
            &mask);

    /* if not RootWindow, raise */
    if (child != NULL)
    {
        if (raise_or_lower == RAISE)
            XRaiseWindow(display, child);
        else
            XLowerWindow(display, child);
    }

    /* get the matching ButtonRelease on same button */
    while (1)  {
        XMaskEvent(display, ButtonReleaseMask, &report);
        if (report.xbutton.button == button) break;
    }
}
```

14.7.12 Moving and Resizing Windows

The move_resize routine is similar to raise_lower, but uses the difference in position between a ButtonPress and a ButtonRelease event to determine the change in position or size of the window. It also uses MotionNotify events to draw an outline of the window during the move or resize. During resizing, the upper-left corner of the window stays in place, while the lower-right corner moves the same way the pointer does between the press and the release. The code could be expanded to allow any corner of the window to be resized.

The routine that draws the box for the temporary window outline was described in Chapter 6, *Drawing Graphics and Text*.

If there is an icon associated with the moved window, that icon is not moved. Similarly, if the window moved is an icon, its associated main window is not moved. This is an arbitrary window manager policy decision. Some window managers might legislate a certain relationship between the position of a window and its icon.

Example 14-6. winman — the move and resize routines

```
move_resize(display, screen, menuwin, hand_cursor, move_or_resize)
Display *display;
int screen;
Window menuwin;
Cursor hand_cursor;
Bool move_or_resize;
{
    XEvent report;
    XWindowAttributes win_attr;
    int press_x, press_y, release_x, release_y, move_x, move_y;
    static int box_drawn = False;
    int left, right, top, bottom;
    Window root, child;
    Window win_to_configure;
    int win_x, win_y;
    unsigned int mask;
    unsigned int pressed_button;
    XSizeHints size_hints;
    Bool min_size, increment;
    unsigned int width, height;
    int temp_size;
    static GC gc;
    static int first_time = True;

    if (first_time) {
        gc = XCreateGC(display, RootWindow(display,screen), 0, NULL);
        XSetSubwindowMode(display, gc, IncludeInferiors);
        XSetForeground(display, gc, BlackPixel(display, screen));
        XSetFunction(display, gc, GXxor);
        first_time = False;
        }

    /* wait for ButtonPress choosing window to configure */
    XMaskEvent(display, ButtonPressMask, &report);
    pressed_button = report.xbutton.button;

    /* which child of root was press in? */
    XQueryPointer(display, RootWindow(display,screen), &root,
            &child, &press_x, &press_y, &win_x,
            &win_y, &mask);
    win_to_configure = child;

    if ((win_to_configure == NULL)  ||
            ((win_to_configure == menuwin)
            && (move_or_resize == RESIZE)))  {
        /* if in RootWindow or resizing menuwin get
         * release event and get out */
        XMaskEvent(display, ButtonReleaseMask, &report);
        return;
    }

    /* button press was in a valid subwindow of root */
```

Example 14-6. winman — the move and resize routines (continued)

```
/* get original position and size of window */
XGetWindowAttributes(display, win_to_configure,
        &win_attr);

/* get size hints for the window */
XGetNormalHints(display, win_to_configure, &size_hints);
if (size_hints.flags && PMinSize)
    min_size = True;
if (size_hints.flags && PResizeInc)
    increment = True;

/* now we need pointer motion events. */
XChangeActivePointerGrab(display, PointerMotionHintMask |
        ButtonMotionMask | ButtonReleaseMask |
        OwnerGrabButtonMask, hand_cursor, CurrentTime);

/* don't allow other display operations during move,
 * because the moving outline drawn with
 * Xor won't work properly otherwise. */
XGrabServer(display);

/* move outline of window until button release */
while  (1) {
    XNextEvent(display, &report);
    switch (report.type) {
        case ButtonRelease:
            if (report.xbutton.button == pressed_button) {
                if (box_drawn)
                    undraw_box(gc, left, top, right, bottom);

                /* this may seem premature,
                 * but actually ButtonRelease
                 * indicates that the
                 * rubber-banding is done */
                XUngrabServer(display);

                /* get final window position */
                XQueryPointer(display, RootWindow(display,
                        screen), &root, &child, &release_x,
                        &release_y, &win_x, &win_y, &mask);

                /* move or resize window */
                if (move_or_resize == MOVE)
                    XMoveWindow(display, win_to_configure,
                        win_attr.x + (release_x - press_x),
                        win_attr.y + (release_y - press_y));
                else
                    XResizeWindow(display, win_to_configure,
                        win_attr.width + (release_x - press_x),
                        win_attr.height + (release_y - press_y));

                XRaiseWindow(display, win_to_configure);
                XFlush(display);
                box_drawn = False;
                return;
```

Example 14-6. winman — the move and resize routines (continued)

```
            }
            break;

    case MotionNotify:
        if (box_drawn == True)
            undraw_box(gc, left, top, right, bottom);

        /* can get rid of all MotionNotify events in queue,
         * since otherwise the round-trip  delays caused by
         * XQueryPointer may cause a backlog
         * of MotionNotify events, which will cause additional
         * wasted XQueryPointer calls. */
        while (XCheckTypedEvent(display, MotionNotify,
                &report));

        /* get current mouse position */
        XQueryPointer(display, RootWindow(display,screen),
                &root, &child, &move_x, &move_y,
                &win_x, &win_y, &mask);

        if (move_or_resize == MOVE) {
            left = move_x - press_x + win_attr.x;
            top = move_y - press_y + win_attr.y;
            right = left + win_attr.width;
            bottom = top + win_attr.height;
        }
        else
            {
            if (move_x < win_attr.x) move_x = 0;
            if (move_y < win_attr.y ) move_y = 0;
                left = win_attr.x;
                top = win_attr.y;
                right = left + win_attr.width + move_x
                        - press_x;
                bottom = top + win_attr.height + move_y
                        - press_y;
            /* must adjust size according to size hints */
            /* enforce minimum dimensions */
            width = right - left;
            height = bottom - top;

            /* make sure dimension are increment of
             * width_inc and height_inc and at least
             * min_width and min_height */
            for (temp_size = size_hints.min_width;
                    temp_size < width;
                    temp_size += size_hints.width_inc)
                ;
            right = left + temp_size + 2;

            for (temp_size = size_hints.min_height;
                    temp_size < height;
                    temp_size += size_hints.height_inc)
                ;
            /* most applications (xterm included)
```

Example 14-6. winman — the move and resize routines (continued)

```
                            * pad their right and bottom
                            * dimensions by 2 pixels */
                           bottom = top + temp_size + 2;
                           }

                      draw_box(gc, left, top, right, bottom);
                      box_drawn = True;
                      break;
                default:
                      /* StructureNotify events shouldn't appear here,
                       * because of the ChangeActivePointerGrab
                       * call, but they do for some reason. */
                      /* Anyway, it doesn't matter */
                      /* fprintf(stderr, "unexpected event type %s\n",
                               report.type); */
                      ;
            } /* end switch */
      } /* end outer while */
} /* end move */
```

Figure 14-6 shows an example of the screen during a move operation.

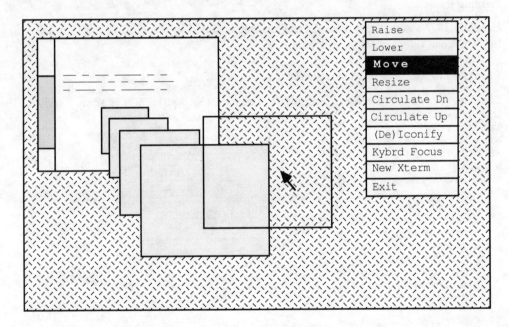

Figure 14-6. Dragging a window outline

The XChangeActivePointerGrab function is used to narrow the types of events that are received. In other terms, it changes the events that are selected for the window for the duration of the grab. This makes it unnecessary to throw away ButtonPress events that are used early in the program but not needed in this routine.

The server is grabbed in this example to make sure that no other program displays output on the screen while the box is being dragged. This is necessary because the box is drawn and then undrawn with the same command and GC using the GXxor logical function. Graphics drawn twice with Exclusive OR will appear as they started, but only if the pixels affected are not changed by any other application in between. If any other client were allowed to draw between the draw and the undraw, the screen might not be returned to normal.

Note that the actual color of the rubber-banded line is unpredictable on a color system, because the pixel value is simply the Exclusive OR of what was already there. If a particular color of rubber-banded line is desired, you will have to use the overlay technique described in Section 7.4.1.

14.7.13 (De)Iconifying Windows

The iconify routine must be able to turn a window into an icon, or turn an icon back into a window. It is completely up to the window manager to keep track of the association between windows and icons. Therefore, a substantial portion of *winman*'s code is devoted to maintaining a list of the main windows and their associated icon windows. We'll look at the code for the routine that main calls, iconify, and then delve into the details of implementing icons.

Example 14-7 shows the iconify routine that is called in response to the user selecting the (De)Iconify item on *winman*'s menu.

Example 14-7. winman — the iconify routine

```
iconify(display, screen, menuwin, font_info, assoc_win, icon_name)
Display *display;
int screen;
Window menuwin;
XFontStruct *font_info;
Window *assoc_win;
char *icon_name;
    {
    XEvent report;
    extern Window focus_window;
    int press_x,press_y;
    Window child;
    Window root;
    int win_x, win_y;
    unsigned int mask;
    unsigned int button;

    /* wait for ButtonPress, any win */
    XMaskEvent(display, ButtonPressMask, &report);
    button = report.xbutton.button;

    /* find out which subwindow the mouse was in */
    XQueryPointer(display, RootWindow(display,screen), &root,
        &child, &press_x, &press_y, &win_x, &win_y, &mask);

    /* Can't iconify rootwindow or menu window */
```

Example 14-7. winman — the iconify routine (continued)

```
    if ((child == NULL) || (child == menuwin))
        {
        /* wait for ButtonRelease before exiting */
        while (1)  {
            XMaskEvent(display, ButtonReleaseMask, &report);
            if (report.xbutton.button == button) break;
            }
        return;
        }

    /* returned value of isIcon not used here, but it
     * is elsewhere in the code */
    isIcon(child, press_x, press_y, assoc_win, font_info, &icon_name);
    /* window selected is unmapped, whether it is icon
     * or main window.  The other is then mapped. */
    XUnmapWindow(display, child);
    XMapWindow(display, *assoc_win);

    /* wait for ButtonRelease before exiting */
    /* get the matching ButtonRelease on same button */
    while (1)  {
        XMaskEvent(display, ButtonReleaseMask, &report);
        if (report.xbutton.button == button) break;
    }
}
```

If the window is not an icon, the window is unmapped and an icon window is created and mapped. If the window is an icon, it is unmapped and the associated main window is remapped. The `iconify` routine guards against iconifying the menu, since there is no way in this program to undo that operation.

The `iconify` routine calls the `isIcon` routine. If the window selected is not an icon, `isIcon` creates an icon window, enters it into a linked list, and returns the icon window's ID. If the window selected is an icon, the associated main window's ID is returned. Either way, the window selected is unmapped and the associated window is mapped.

The routines underlying `isIcon` are a simplified version of the icon-handling code from *uwm*. Notice that these routines are in a separate source file, so they must include the standard include files and declare as `extern` the global variables set in *winman.c*.

Example 14-8. winman — the isIcon routine

```
#include <X11/Xlib.h>
#include <X11/Xatom.h>
#include <X11/Xutil.h>
#include <X11/cursorfont.h>

#include <stdio.h>

extern Display *display;
extern int screen;
```

Example 14-8. winman — the isIcon routine (continued)

```
/* for linked list containing window ID, icon ID, and icon_name.
 * own indicates whether winman created the icon window (True) or was
 * passed it through the WMHints (False) */
typedef struct _windowList {
    struct _windowList *next;
    Window window;
    Window icon;
    Bool own;
    char *icon_name;
} WindowListRec, *WindowList;

WindowList Icons = NULL;

Bool isIcon(win, x, y, assoc, font_info, icon_name)
Window win;
int x, y;
Window *assoc;
XFontStruct *font_info;
char **icon_name;
{
    WindowList win_list;
    Window makeIcon();

    /* go through linked list of window-icon structures */
    for (win_list = Icons; win_list; win_list = win_list->next) {
        if (win == win_list->icon) { /* win is icon */
            *assoc = win_list->window;
            icon_name = &win_list->icon_name;
            return(True);
        }
        if (win == win_list->window) { /* win is main window */
            *assoc = win_list->icon;
            icon_name = &win_list->icon_name;
            return(False);
        }
    }
    /* window not in list means icon not created yet.
     * Create icon and add main window to save-set
     * in case window manager dies */
    *assoc = makeIcon(win, font_info, x, y, *icon_name);
    XAddToSaveSet(display, win);
    return(False);
}
```

The isIcon routine looks through the linked list of structures, of which there is one for each top-level window that has ever been iconified.

- If win is found in the structures, and it is an icon, isIcon returns True.

- If win is found and it is a main window, isIcon returns False.

- If win is not found at all, isIcon calls makeIcon to create an icon for the window and then calls XAddToSaveSet to add the window to *winman*'s save-set. This code only gets called when an application is being iconified for the first time. Since it is possible that *winman* will get killed before it has a chance to remap the main windows of the applications it has iconified, these windows must be automatically remapped when *winman* dies. That's what the save-set does. (*winman* can be killed by typing Control-C in the window it was invoked from if it has been run in the foreground, or with the Exit choice from *winman*'s menu.)

14.7.14 Creating The Icons

winman

The `makeIcon` routine called in `isIcon` is used to read the hints that the application has specified for the icon. As you'll recall, the window manager has the option of honoring or ignoring these hints. *winman* honors them to the greatest extent possible. It allows an application to specify an icon pixmap or icon window, an icon name, and the icon's position.

If some or all of these hints are not set, *winman* does the best it can. If no icon window is specified, *winman* creates one. If no icon pixmap is specified, *winman* uses a white background and writes the icon name on it in black.

Example 14-9. winman — the makeIcon routine

```
Window makeIcon(window, font_info, x, y, icon_name_return)
Window window;      /* associated window. */
XFontStruct *font_info;
int x, y; /* current mouse position. */
char *icon_name_return;
{
    int icon_x, icon_y;      /* Icon U. L. X and Y coordinates. */
    int icon_w, icon_h;      /* Icon width and height. */
    int icon_bdr; /* Icon border width. */
    int depth;      /* for XGetGeometry */
    Window root;   /* for XGetGeometry */
    XSetWindowAttributes icon_attrib;      /* for icon creation */
    unsigned long icon_attrib_mask;
    XWMHints *wmhints; /* see if icon position provided */
    XWMHints *XGetWMHints();
    Window finishIcon();
    char *icon_name;

    /*
    * Process window manager hints.
    * If icon window hint exists, use it directly
    * If icon pixmap hint exists, get its size
    * otherwise, get default size.
    * If icon position hint exists, use it
    * otherwise, use the position passed (current mouse position)
    */
    if (wmhints = XGetWMHints(display, window)) {
        if (wmhints->flags&IconWindowHint)
            /* icon window was passed; use it as is */
            return(finishIcon(window, wmhints->icon_window,
                False, icon_name));
        else if (wmhints->flags&IconPixmapHint)
```

Example 14-9. winman — the makeIcon routine (continued)

```
        {
             /* Pixmap was passed.
              * Determine size of icon
              * window from pixmap. Only
              * icon_w and icon_h are significant. */
             if (!XGetGeometry(display, wmhints->icon_pixmap,
                     &root, &icon_x, &icon_y,
                     &icon_w, &icon_h, &icon_bdr, &depth)) {
                 fprintf(stderr, "winman: client passed invalid \
                         icon pixmap." );
                 return( NULL );
             }
             else {
                 icon_attrib.background_pixmap = wmhints->icon_pixmap;
                 icon_attrib_mask = CWBorderPixel|CWBackPixmap;
             }
        }
        /* else no window or pixmap passed */
        else {
             icon_name = getDefaultIconSize(window, font_info,
                     &icon_w, &icon_h);
             icon_attrib_mask = CWBorderPixel | CWBackPixel;
             icon_attrib.background_pixel = (unsigned long)
                     WhitePixel(display,screen);
        }
    }
    /* else no hints at all exist */
    else {
        icon_name = getDefaultIconSize(window, &font_info,
                &icon_w, &icon_h);
        icon_attrib_mask = CWBorderPixel | CWBackPixel;
    }
    /* Pad sizes. */
    icon_w += 2;
    icon_h += 2;

    strcpy(icon_name_return, icon_name);

    /* Set the icon border attributes.   */
    icon_bdr = 2;
    icon_attrib.border_pixel = (unsigned long)
            BlackPixel(display,screen);

    /* If icon position hint exists, get it.
     * This also checks to see if wmhints is NULL,
     * which it will be if WMHints were never set at all */
    if (wmhints && (wmhints->flags&IconPositionHint))
    {
        icon_x = wmhints->icon_x;
        icon_y = wmhints->icon_y;
    }
    else
    {
        /* put it where the mouse was */
        icon_x = x;
```

Example 14-9. winman — the makeIcon routine (continued)

```
        icon_y = y;
    }

    /* Create the icon window.  */
    return(finishIcon(window, XCreateWindow(display,
            RootWindow(display, screen),
            icon_x, icon_y, icon_w, icon_h,
            icon_bdr, 0, CopyFromParent, CopyFromParent,
            icon_attrib_mask, &icon_attrib),
            True, icon_name));
}
```

14.7.15 Getting the Icon Size

We'll show you getDefaultIconSize (which calls getIconName) and then
finishIcon, the two routines called from makeIcon. getDefaultIconSize and
getIconName are shown in Example 14-10.

Example 14-10. winman — the getDefaultIconSize and getIconName routines

```
char *
getDefaultIconSize(window, font_info, icon_w, icon_h)
Window window;
XFontStruct *font_info;
int *icon_w, *icon_h;
{
    /* Determine the size of the icon window.  */
    char *icon_name;

    if (!(icon_name = getIconName(window)))
        /* if no icon or program name set */
        strcpy(icon_name, "Icon");

    *icon_h = font_info->ascent + font_info->descent + 4;
    *icon_w = XTextWidth(font_info, icon_name, strlen(icon_name));

    return(icon_name);
}

char *
getIconName(window)
Window window;
{
    char *name;

    if (XGetIconName( display, window, &name )) return( name );

    /* get program name if set */
    if (XFetchName( display, window, &name )) return( name );

    return( NULL );
}
```

The routines in Example 14-10 simply get the icon name and determine a size for the icon from the name, given the font dimensions. If no icon name is available, they use the program name, and if that is not available, they use the string "Icon." However, this should never happen if the applications *winman* manages are written properly.

14.7.16 Updating the Icon List

Now we'll turn to `finishIcon`, which is called from `makeIcon`. `finishIcon` creates and defines a cursor for the icon, selects `Expose` events for it, and updates the linked list of structures to include the new icon and its associated window. (Actually, the cursor should have been created in another routine, because here it is executed every time a new icon is created.)

Example 14-11. winman — The finishIcon routine

```
Window finishIcon(window, icon, own, icon_name)
Window window, icon;
Bool own; /* whether winman created the icon window */
char *icon_name;
{
    WindowList win_list;
    Cursor manCursor;


    /* if icon window didn't get created, return failure */
     if (icon == NULL) return(NULL);

    /*
     * Use the man cursor whenever the mouse is in the icon window.
     */
    manCursor = XCreateFontCursor(display, XC_man);
    XDefineCursor(display, icon, manCursor);

     /* Select events for the icon window */
    XSelectInput(display, icon, ExposureMask);

    /*
     * Set the event window's icon window to be the new icon window.
     */
    win_list = (WindowList) malloc(sizeof(WindowListRec));
    win_list->window = window;
    win_list->icon = icon;
    win_list->own = own;
    win_list->icon_name = icon_name;
    win_list->next = Icons;
    Icons = win_list;

    return(icon);
}
```

One nice user interface possibility is suggested by the code for `finishIcon`. We could let the user turn an icon back into a main window by pressing some key or button in the icon. To do this we would select button or key events on the icon, and then look for them in one of the event loops in main. If button events were chosen, we would need to identify which window the button event appeared in to distinguish between events from the menu and events in the icon, but this would be easy.

14.7.17 Removing Icons

Finally, we need a way to remove icons for applications that have been iconified but exit while the window manager is running. The main selects StructureNotifyMask to be notified when top-level windows are destroyed, and responds by calling removeIcon, which is shown in Example 14-12.

Example 14-12. winman — the removeIcon routine

```
removeIcon(window)
Window window;
{
    WindowList win_list, win_list1;

    for (win_list = Icons; win_list; win_list = win_list->next)
        if (win_list->window == window) {
            if (win_list->own)
                XDestroyWindow(display, win_list->icon);
            break;
        }
    if (win_list) {
        if (win_list==Icons) Icons = Icons->next;
        else
            for (win_list1 = Icons; win_list1->next;
                    win_list1 = win_list1->next)
                if (win_list1->next == win_list) {
                    win_list1->next = win_list->next;
                    break;
                };
    }
}
```

Whether *winman* exits graciously (through the Exit choice on the menu) or by being killed, all the main windows it has iconified have already been placed in the save-set, so that they will automatically be mapped. Therefore, no routine to clear the icons is necessary.

14.7.18 Changing Keyboard Focus

Setting the keyboard focus allows the user to stop worrying about whether the pointer is in the window to be typed into. The underlying function here is XSetInputFocus. It causes keyboard input to go to the selected window regardless of the position of the pointer. When the root window is selected, keyboard events are distributed normally according to the position of the pointer (this is the default situation).

winman highlights the focus window by increasing the width of the border and drawing a white outline around the window. This is necessary because it would not be obvious which application had the focus unless the application itself was programmed to indicate when it has the focus. Of course, applying the keyboard focus to a window that does not use keyboard input, like the main window of *xclock*, would cause your input to be just thrown away and the only indication of what is happening would be the highlighting drawn around the focus window.

The focus routine selects a window much like the raise_lower function does. If the subwindow returned by XQueryPointer is NULL, the pointer must be on the root window, and the focus can be set to the ID of the root window. Otherwise we need to find out if the subwindow is an icon. The focus should be on the real window as opposed to the icon, since the icon is controlled by the window manager and doesn't accept keyboard input for the application.

To change the border width of the new focus window, we need to get the old width with XGetWindowAttributes, and save it so it can be replaced when the focus is changed again.

Example 14-13. winman — the focus routine

```
focus(display, screen, font_info, assoc_win)
Display *display;
int screen;
XFontStruct *font_info;
Window *assoc_win;
{
    XEvent report;
    int x,y;
    Window child;
    Window root;
    extern Window focus_window;
    int win_x, win_y;
    unsigned int mask;
    char *icon_name;
    unsigned int button;
    XWindowAttributes win_attr;
    static int old_width;
    static Window old_focus;
    int status;

    /* wait for ButtonPress, any win */
    XMaskEvent(display, ButtonPressMask, &report);
    button = report.xbutton.button;

    /* find out which subwindow the mouse was in */

    XQueryPointer(display, RootWindow(display,screen), &root,
            &child, &x, &y, &win_x, &win_y, &mask);

    if ((child == NULL) || (isIcon(child, x, y, assoc_win,
            font_info, &icon_name)))
        focus_window = RootWindow(display, screen);
    else
```

Example 14-13. winman — the focus routine (continued)

```
            focus_window = child;

    if (focus_window != old_focus)  { /* if focus changed */
        /* if not first time set, set border back */
        if   (old_focus != NULL)
            XSetWindowBorderWidth(display, old_focus, old_width);

        XSetInputFocus(display, focus_window, RevertToPointerRoot,
                CurrentTime);
        if (focus_window != RootWindow(display, screen)) {
            /* get current border width and add one */
            if (!(status = XGetWindowAttributes(display,
                    focus_window, &win_attr)))
                fprintf(stderr, "winman: can't get attributes for \
                        focus window\n");
            XSetWindowBorderWidth(display, focus_window,
                    win_attr.border_width + 1);
            /* keep record so we can change it back */
            old_width = win_attr.border_width;
        }
    }

    /* get the matching ButtonRelease on same button */
    while (1)   {
        XMaskEvent(display, ButtonReleaseMask, &report);
        if (report.xbutton.button == button) break;
    }

    old_focus = focus_window;
    return(focus_window);
}
```

winman

14.7.19 Drawing the Focus Frame

The focus routine calls draw_focus_frame to further highlight the focus window.
There are several ways to do this, ranging from almost trivial to fairly complex. The easiest
way is to change the border width and/or color to indicate which window is the focus.
Another way is to draw on the root window behind the focus window. This has a slightly
different effect in that no highlight would appear on windows where they did not contact the
root window. We do both, to be absolutely sure the current focus window is well indicated.
The window is highlighted by increasing its border width and by tiling a region underneath
the current focus window with a pixmap.

A third and more complicated way is to reparent the focus window into a background frame
as described above in Section 14.3. This would work well if the windows already had been
reparented to add a title bar.

The draw_focus_frame routine shown in Example 14-14 also demonstrates the two-step process of creating a useful pixmap from the data in an include file generated by the bitmap program. You must create a bitmap from the data before making a pixmap from the bitmap.

Example 14-14. winman — the draw_focus_frame routine

```
draw_focus_frame()
{
    XWindowAttributes win_attr;
    int frame_width = 4;
    Pixmap focus_tile;
    GC gc;
    int depth = 1;
    int foreground = BlackPixel(display, screen);
    int background = WhitePixel(display, screen);
    extern Window focus_window;
    Bool first_time = True;

    if (first_time) {
        /* make Bitmap from bitmap data */
        focus_tile = XCreatePixmapFromBitmapData(display,
                RootWindow(display,screen),
                focus_frame_bi_bits, focus_frame_bi_width,
                focus_frame_bi_height, foreground,
                background, depth);

        /* Create graphics context */
        gc = XCreateGC(display, RootWindow(display,screen), 0, NULL);
        XSetTile(display, gc, focus_tile);
        first_time = False;
    }

    /* get rid of old frames */
    XClearWindow(display, RootWindow(display,screen));

    /* if focus is RootWindow, no frame drawn */
    if (focus_window == RootWindow(display,screen)) return;

    /* get dimensions and position of focus_window*/
    XGetWindowAttributes(display, focus_window, &win_attr);

    XFillRectangle(display, RootWindow(display,screen), gc,
        win_attr.x - frame_width, win_attr.y - frame_width,
        win_attr.width + 2 * (win_attr.border_width + frame_width),
        win_attr.height + 2 * (win_attr.border_width + frame_width));
}
```

14.7.20 Executing a Shell Command

The menu item to create a new *xterm* window uses execute, which is a routine taken directly from the code for *uwm*. This routine can be used to execute any shell command, and therefore may come in handy in virtually any application, not just a window manager. Example 14-15 shows the execute routine.

Example 14-15. winman — the execute routine

```
#ifdef SYSV
#ifndef hpux
#define vfork() fork()
#endif /* hpux */
#endif /* SYSV */

/* the following procedure is a copy of the implementation of
 * system, modified to reset the handling of SIGINT, SIGQUIT,
 * and SIGHUP before exec-ing */
execute(s)
char *s;
{
    int status, pid, w;
    register int (*istat)(), (*qstat)();

    if ((pid = vfork()) == 0) {
        signal(SIGINT, SIG_DFL);
        signal(SIGQUIT, SIG_DFL);
        signal(SIGHUP, SIG_DFL);
        execl("/bin/sh", "sh", "-c", s, 0);
        _exit(127);
    }
    istat = signal(SIGINT, SIG_IGN);
    qstat = signal(SIGQUIT, SIG_IGN);
    while ((w = wait(&status)) != pid && w != -1)
        ;
    if (w == -1)
        status = -1;
    signal(SIGINT, istat);
    signal(SIGQUIT, qstat);
    return(status);
}
```

There is some code in main that helps execute do its thing. It makes sure that the new process does not inherit any open files from the parent process, our window manager. Without this call, the child process might affect the operation of the client instead of being completely separate. All routines that execute shell commands should include the code shown in Example 14-16 in the routine that calls execute.

Example 14-16. winman — code for assisting execution of shell commands

```
/* Force child processes to disinherit the TCP file descriptor.
 * This helps the shell command (creating new xterm) forked and
 * exec'ed from the menu to work properly.  */
if ((fcntl(ConnectionNumber(display), F_SETFD, 1)) == -1)
        fprintf(stderr, "winman: child cannot disinherit TCP fd");
```

14.8 Unresolved Issues in Window Management

There are many unresolved issues in window management under X. One large area concerns communication with clients. As described in Chapter 10, *Interclient Communication*, the conventions for communication in both directions between the window manager and clients are still being developed. Window managers will change greatly once conventions are fully established.

Another question concerns when a window manager should install client-created colormaps. The current convention is that the window manager should install the colormap specified by the colormap attribute of the top-level window, and the client should be responsible for installing colormaps for children of its top-level window, but only when its top-level colormap is installed. Unfortunately, no current window managers follow this convention, which leaves application writers in a bit of a bind.

                                                        Xlib Programming Manual

A
Glossary

X uses many common terms in unique ways. A good example is "children." While most, if not all, of these terms are defined where they are first used in this book, you will undoubtedly find it easier to refresh your memory by looking for them here.

A
Glossary

This glossary is an expanded version of the glossary in the *Xlib–C Language X Interface*, by Jim Gettys, Ron Newman, and Bob Scheifler.

access control list

X maintains lists of hosts that are allowed access to each server controlling a display. By default, only the local host may use the display, plus any hosts specified in the *access control list* for that display. This access control list can be changed by clients on the local host. Some server implementations may implement other authorization mechanisms in addition or instead of this one. The list can currently be found in */etc/X#.hosts* where # is the number of the display. The access control list is also known as the host access list.

active grab

A grab is *active* when the pointer or keyboard is actually owned by a single grabbing client. See also **grab**.

ancestor

If window *W* is an inferior of window *A*, then *A* is an *ancestor* of *W*. The parent window, the parent's parent window, and so on are all ancestors of the given window. The root window is the ancestor of all windows on a given screen.

atom

An *atom* is a unique numeric ID corresponding to a string name. Atoms are used to identify properties, types, and selections in order to avoid the overhead of passing arbitrary-length property-name strings.

background

Windows may have a *background*, consisting of either a solid color or a tile pattern. If a window has a background, it will be repainted automatically by the server whenever there is an Expose event on the window. If a window does not have a background, it will be transparent. See also **foreground**.

backing store

When a server maintains the contents of a window, the off-screen saved pixels are known as a *backing store*. This feature is not available on all servers. Use the `DoesBackingStores` macro to determine if this feature is supported.

bit gravity

When a window is resized, the contents of the window are not necessarily discarded. It is possible to request the server (though no guarantees are made) to relocate the previous contents to some region of the resized window. This attraction of window contents for some location of a window is known as *bit gravity*. For example, an application that draws a graph might request that the contents be moved into the lower-left corner, so that the origin of the graph will still appear in the lower-left corner.

bit plane

On a color or gray scale display, each pixel has more than one bit defined. Data in display memory can be thought of either as pixels (multiple bits per pixel) or as bit planes (one bit plane for each usable bit in the pixel). The *bit plane* is an array of bits the size of the screen.

bitmap

A *bitmap* is a pixmap with a depth of one bit. There is no bitmap type in X11. Instead, use a pixmap of depth 1.

border

A window can have a border that is zero or more pixels wide. If a window has a border, the border can have a solid color or a tile pattern, and it will be repainted automatically by the server whenever its color or pattern is changed or an `Expose` event occurs on the windows.

button grabbing

A pointer grab that occurs only when a specified set of keys and/or buttons are held down is referred to as a *button grab*.

byte order

The order in which bytes of data are stored in memory is hardware-dependent. For pixmaps and bitmaps, *byte order* is defined by the server, and clients with different native byte ordering must swap bytes as necessary. For all other parts of the protocol, the byte order is defined by the client, and the server swaps bytes as necessary.

children

The *children* of a window are its first-level subwindows. All of these windows were created with the same window as parent. A client creates its top-level window as a child of the root window.

class

There are two uses of the term *class* in X: window class and visual class. The window class specifies whether a window is InputOnly or InputOutput (which see). The visual class specifies the color model that is used by a window See the classes **DirectColor, GrayScale, PseudoColor, StaticColor, StaticGray,** and **TrueColor.**

client

An application program connects to the window system server by an interprocess communication (IPC) path, such as a TCP connection or a shared memory buffer. This program is referred to as a *client* of the window system server. More precisely, the client is the IPC path itself; a program with multiple paths open to the server is viewed as multiple clients by the protocol. X Resources are available only as long as the connection remains intact, not as long as a program remains running. Normally the connection and the program terminate concurrently, but the client's resources may live on if XChangeClosedownMode has been called.

clipping regions

In many graphics routines, a bitmap or list of rectangles can be specified to restrict output to a particular region of the window. The image defined by the bitmap or rectangles is called a *clipping region*, or clip mask. Output to child windows is automatically clipped to the borders of the parent unless subwindow_mode of the GC is IncludeInferiors. Therefore the borders of the parent can be thought of as a clipping region.

colorcell

An entry in a colormap is known as a *colorcell*. An entry contains three values specifying red, green and blue intensities. These values are always 16-bit unsigned numbers, with zero being minimum intensity. The values are truncated or scaled by the server to match the display hardware. See also **colormap.**

colormap

A *colormap* consists of a set of colorcells. A pixel value indexes into the colormap to produce intensities of Red, Green, and Blue to be displayed. Depending on hardware limitations, one or more colormaps may be installed at one time, such that windows associated with those maps display with true colors. Regardless of the number of installable colormaps, any number of virtual colormaps can be created. When needed, a virtual colormap can be installed and the existing installed colormap might have to be deinstalled. The colormap on most systems is a limited resource that should be conserved by allocating read-only colorcells whenever possible, and selecting RGB values from the predefined color database. Read-only cells may be shared between clients. See also **colorcell, DirectColor, GrayScale, PseudoColor, StaticColor, StaticGray,** and **TrueColor.**

connection

The IPC path between the server and client is known as a *connection*. A client usually (but not necessarily) has one connection to the server over which requests and events are sent.

containment

A window *contains* the pointer if the window is viewable and the hotspot of the cursor is within a visible region of the window or a visible region of one of its inferiors. The border of the window is included as part of the window for containment. The pointer is in a window if the window contains the pointer but no inferior contains the pointer.

coordinate system

The *coordinate system* has x horizontal and y vertical, with the origin (0, 0) at the upper-left. Coordinates are discrete, and in terms of pixels. Each window and pixmap has its own coordinate system. For a window, the origin is inside the border, if there is one.

cursor

A *cursor* is the visible shape of the pointer on a screen. It consists of a hotspot, a shape bitmap, a mask bitmap, and a pair of pixel values. The cursor defined for a window controls the visible appearance of the pointer when the pointer is in that window.

depth

The *depth* of a window or pixmap is the number of bits per pixel.

descendants

See **inferiors**.

device

Keyboards, mice, tablets, track-balls, button boxes, etc. are all collectively known as input *devices*.

DirectColor

DirectColor is a visual class in which a pixel value is decomposed into three separate subfields for colormap indexing. One subfield indexes an array to produce red intensity values; the second subfield indexes a second array to produce blue intensity values; and the third subfield indexes a third array to produce green intensity values. The RGB (red, green, and blue) values in the colormap entry can be changed dynamically. This visual class is normally found on high-performance color workstations.

display

A *display* is a set of one or more screens that are driven by a single X server. The Xlib `Display` structure contains all information about the particular display and its screens as well as the state that Xlib needs to communicate with the display over a particular connection.

drawable

Both windows and pixmaps may be used as destinations in graphics operations. These are collectively known as *drawables*.

event

Clients are informed of device input or client request side effects asynchronously via *events*. Events are grouped into types; events are never sent to a client by the server unless the client has specifically asked to be informed of that type of event. However, other clients can force events of any type to be sent to any clients. Events are typically reported relative to a window.

event mask

Events are requested relative to a window. The set of event types a client requests relative to a window is described using an *event mask*. The `event_mask` is a window attribute, which can be set with `XSelectInput`, and is also specified in calls that grab the pointer or keyboard. The `do_not_propagate_mask` attribute is also an event mask, and it specifies which events should not be propagated to ancestor windows.

event propagation

Device-related events *propagate* from the source window to ancestor windows until a window that has selected that type of event is reached, or until the event is discarded explicitly in a `do_not_propagate_mask` attribute.

event source

The smallest window containing the pointer is the *source* of a device related event.

exposure

Window *exposure* occurs when a window is first mapped, or when another window that obscures it is unmapped, resized, or moved. Servers do not guarantee to preserve the contents of windows when windows are obscured or reconfigured. `Expose` events are sent to clients to inform them when contents of regions of windows have been lost and need to be regenerated.

extension

Named *extensions* to the core protocol can be defined to extend the system. Extension to output requests, resources, and event types are all possible, and expected. Extensions can perform at the same level as the core Xlib.

font
> A *font* is an array of characters or other bitmap shapes such as cursors. The protocol does no translation or interpretation of character sets. The client simply indicates values used to index the font array. A font contains additional metric information to determine intercharacter and interline spacing.

foreground
> The pixel value that will actually be used for drawing pictures or text is referred to as the *foreground*. The foreground is specified as a member of a graphics context.

frozen events
> Clients can *freeze* event processing while they change the screen, by grabbing the keyboard or pointer with a certain mode. These events are queued in the server (not in Xlib), until an `XAllowEvents` call with a counteracting mode is given.

GC
> The term *GC* is used as a shorthand for graphics context. See **graphics context**.

glyph
> A *glyph* is an image, usually of a character in a font, but also possibly a cursor shape or some other shape.

grab
> Keyboard keys, the keyboard, pointer buttons, the pointer, and the server can be *grabbed* for exclusive use by a client, usually for a short time period. In general, these facilities are not intended to be used by normal applications, but are intended for various input and window managers to implement various styles of user interfaces.

graphics context
> Various information for graphics output is stored in a *graphics context* (GC), such as foreground pixel, background pixel, line width, clipping region, etc. Everything drawn to a window or pixmap is modified by the GC used in the drawing request.

gravity
> See **bit gravity** and **window gravity**.

GrayScale
> `GrayScale` is a visual class in which the red, green, and blue values in any given colormap entry are equal, thus producing shades of gray. The gray values can be changed dynamically. `GrayScale` can be viewed as a degenerate case of `PseudoColor`.

hint
> Certain properties, such as the preferred size of a window, are referred to as *hints*, since the window manager makes no guarantee that it will honor them.

host access list

See **access control list**.

hotspot

A cursor has an associated *hotspot* that defines the point in the cursor which corresponds to the coordinates reported for the pointer.

identifier

Each resource has an *identifier* or *ID*, a unique value that clients use to name the resource. Any client can use a resource if it knows the resource ID.

inferiors

The *inferiors* of a window are all of the subwindows nested below it: the children, the children's children, etc. The term *descendants* is a synonym.

input focus

See **keyboard focus**.

InputOnly window

A window that cannot be used for graphics requests is called an `InputOnly` window. `InputOnly` windows are invisible and can be used to control such things as cursors, input event generation, and grabbing. `InputOnly` windows cannot have `InputOutput` windows as inferiors.

InputOutput window

The normal kind of window that is used both for input and output is called an `InputOutput` window. It usually has a background. `InputOutput` windows can have both `InputOutput` and `InputOnly` windows as inferiors.

input manager

Control over keyboard input may be provided by an *input manager* client. This job may also be done by the window manager.

key grabbing

A keyboard grab that occurs only when a certain key or key combination is pressed is called a *key grab*. This is analogous to button grabbing.

keyboard focus

The *keyboard focus* is the window that receives main keyboard input. By default the focus is the root window, which has the effect of sending input to the window that is being pointed to by the mouse. It is possible to attach the keyboard input to a specific window with `XSetInputFocus`. Events are then sent to the window independent of the pointer position, or if the `owner_events` argument is `True`, to the window containing the pointer if it is owned by the same client as the focus window.

keyboard grabbing

All keyboard input is sent to a specific window (or client, depending on `owner_events`) when the keyboard is grabbed. This is analogous to mouse grabbing. This is very much like a temporary keyboard focus window.

keycode

A *keycode* is a code in the range [8, 255] inclusive that represents a physical or logical key on the keyboard. The mapping between keys and keycodes cannot be changed. A list of keysyms is associated with each keycode.

keysym

A *keysym* is a #defined symbol which is a portable representation of the symbol on the cap of a key. Each key may have several keysyms, corresponding to the key when various modifier keys are pressed. You should interpret key events according to the keysym returned by `XLookupString` or `XLookupKeysym`, since this translates server-dependent keycodes into portable keysyms.

listener

A *listener* style window manager sets the keyboard focus to a particular window when that window is clicked on with a pointer button. This is the window manager style used with the Apple Macintosh™.

mapping

A window is said to be *mapped* if a `XMapWindow` or `XMapRaised` call has been performed on it. Unmapped windows are never viewable. Mapping makes a window eligible for display. The window will actually be displayed if the following conditions are met:

1. All its ancestors are mapped.
2. It is not obscured by siblings.

modifier keys

Shift, Control, Meta, Super, Hyper, Alt, Compose, Apple, Caps Lock, Shift Lock, and similar keys are called *modifier keys*.

monochrome

A *monochrome* screen has only two colors: black and white. Monochrome is a special case of the `StaticGray` visual class, in which there are only two colormap entries.

obscures

Window *A obscures* window *B* if *A* is higher in the global stacking order, and the rectangle defined by the outside edges of *A* intersects the rectangle defined by the outside edges of *B*.

occludes

Window *A occludes* window *B* if both are mapped, if *A* is higher in the global stacking order, and if the rectangle defined by the outside edges of *A* intersects the rectangle defined by the outside edges of *B*. The (fine) distinction between the terms *obscures* and *occludes* is that for *obscures*, the windows have to be mapped, while for *occludes* they don't. Also note that window borders are included in the calculation. Note that InputOnly windows never obscure other windows but can occlude other windows.

padding

Some bytes are inserted in the data stream to maintain alignment of the protocol requests on natural boundaries. This *padding* increases ease of portability to some machine architectures.

parent window

Each new window is created with reference to another previously-created window. The new window is referred to as the child, and the reference window as the *parent*. If *C* is a child of *P*, then *P* is the parent of *C*. Only the portion of the child that overlaps the parent is viewable.

passive grab

A key or button grab is a *passive grab*. The grab becomes active when the key or button is actually pressed. Before the active grab takes place, nothing has changed.

pixel value

A *pixel value* is an N-bit value, where *N* is the number of bit planes used in a particular window or pixmap. For a window, a pixel value indexes a colormap to derive an actual color to be displayed. For a pixmap, a pixel value will be interpreted as a color in the same way when it is copied into a window.

pixmap

A *pixmap* is a three-dimensional array of bits. A pixmap is normally thought of as a two-dimensional array of pixels, where each pixel can be a value from 0 to $(2^N - 1)$, where *N* is the depth (z-axis) of the pixmap. A pixmap can also be thought of as a stack of *N* bitmaps.

plane

When a pixmap or window is thought of as a stack of bitmaps, each bitmap is called a *plane*.

plane mask

Graphics operations can be restricted to affect only a subset of bit planes in a drawable. A *plane mask* is a bit mask describing which planes are to be modified.

pointer

The *pointer* is the pointing device currently attached to the cursor, and tracked on the screens. This may be a mouse, tablet, track-ball or joystick, among other things.

pointer grabbing

A client can actively *grab* control of the pointer, causing button and motion events to be sent to that client rather than the client the pointer indicates.

pointing device

A *pointing device* is typically a mouse or tablet, or some other device with effective two-dimensional motion. There is only one visible cursor defined by the core protocol, and it tracks whatever pointing device is currently attached as the pointer.

property

Windows may have associated *properties*, each consisting of a name, a type, a data format, and some data. The protocol places no interpretation on properties; they are intended as a general-purpose data storage and intercommunication mechanism for clients. There is, however, a list of predefined properties and property types so that clients might share information such as resize hints, program names, and icon formats with a window manager via properties. In order to avoid passing arbitrary-length property-name strings, each property name is associated with a corresponding integer value known as an atom. See also **atom**.

property list

The *property list* of a window is the list of properties that have been defined for the window.

PseudoColor

A visual class in which a pixel value indexes the colormap entry to produce independent red, green, and blue values. That is, the colormap is viewed as an array of triples (RGB values). The RGB values can be changed dynamically.

quark

A *quark* is an integer ID that identifies a name, class, or type string for the resource manager. Like atoms and resource IDs, quarks eliminate the need to pass strings of arbitrary length over the network. The quark type is XrmQuark, and the types XrmName, XrmClass, and XrmRepresentation are also defined to be XrmQuark.

raise

Changing the stacking order of a window so as to occlude all sibling windows is to *raise* that window.

real estate

A window management style characterized by the input being sent to whichever window the pointer is in. This is the most common style of input management used in X.

rectangle

A *rectangle* specified by [x,y,w,h] has an (infinitely thin) outline path with corners at [x,y], [x+w,y], [x+w,y+h] and [x, y+h]. When a rectangle is filled, the lower-right edges are not drawn. For example, if w=h=0, nothing would be drawn. For w=h=1, a single pixel would be drawn.

redirect

Window managers (or other clients) may wish to enforce window layout policy in various ways. When a client attempts to change the size or position of a window, the operation may be *redirected* to the window manager, rather than actually being performed. Then the window manager (or other client that redirected the input) is expected to decide whether to allow, modify, or deny the requested operation before making the call itself.

reparenting

The window manager often *reparents* the top-level windows of each application in order to add a title bar and perhaps resize boxes. In other words, a window with a title bar is inserted between the root window and each top-level window. See also **save-set.**

reply

Information requested by a client, by routines whose names include the word Query, is sent back to the client with a *reply*. Both events and replies are multiplexed on the same connection. Requests that require replies are known as round-trip requests, and should be avoided when possible since they introduce network delays. Most requests do not generate replies. Some requests generate multiple replies.

request

A command to the server is called a *request*. It is a single block of data sent over the connection to the server.

resource

Windows, pixmaps, cursors, fonts, graphics contexts, and colormaps are known as *resources*. They all have unique identifiers (IDs) associated with them for naming purposes. The lifetime of a resource is bounded by the lifetime of the connection over which the resource was created.

RGB values

Red, green, and blue intensity values are used to define a color. These values are always represented as 16-bit unsigned numbers, with 0 the minimum intensity and 65535 the maximum intensity. The X server scales these values to match the display hardware.

root

The *root* of a window, pixmap or graphics context (GC) is the same as the root of whatever drawable was used when the window, pixmap or GC was created. These resources can only be used on the screen indicated by this window. See **root window**.

root window

Each screen has a *root window* covering it. It cannot be reconfigured or unmapped, but otherwise acts as a full fledged window. A root window has no parent.

round-trip request

A request to the server that generates a reply is known as a *round-trip request*. See **reply**.

save-set

The *save-set* of a client is a list of other clients' windows which, if they are inferiors of one of the client's windows at connection close, should not be destroyed, and which should be reparented and remapped if the client is unmapped. Save-sets are typically used by window managers to avoid lost windows if the manager should terminate abnormally. See **reparenting** for more background information.

scan line

A *scan line* is a list of pixel or bit values viewed as a horizontal row (all values having the same y coordinate) of an image, with the values ordered by increasing x-coordinate values.

scan line order

An image represented in *scan line order* contains scan lines ordered by increasing y-coordinate values.

screen

A server may provide several independent *screens*, which may or may not have physically independent monitors. For instance, it is possible to treat a color monitor as if it were two screens, one color and the other black and white. There is only a single keyboard and pointer shared among the screens. A Screen structure contains the information about that screen and is a member of the Display structure.

selection

Selections are a means of communication between clients using properties and events. From the user's perspective, a selection is an item of data which can be highlighted in one instance of an application and pasted into another instance of the same or a different application. The client that highlights the data is the owner, and the client into which the data is pasted is the requestor. Properties are used to store the selection data and the type of the data, while events are used to synchronize the transaction and to allow the requestor to indicate the type it prefers for the data and to allow the owner to convert the data to the indicated type if possible.

server

The *server* provides the basic windowing mechanism. It handles IPC connections from clients, demultiplexes graphics requests onto the screens, and multiplexes input back to the appropriate clients. It controls a single keyboard and pointer and one or more screens that make up a single display.

server grabbing

The server can be *grabbed* by a single client for exclusive use. This prevents processing of any requests from other client connections until the grab is complete. This is typically a transient state for such tasks as rubber-banding and pop-up menus, or to execute requests indivisibly.

sibling

Children of the same parent window are known as *sibling* windows.

stacking order

Sibling windows may stack on top of each other, obscuring lower windows. This is similar to papers on a desk. The relationship between sibling windows is known as the *stacking order*. The first window in the stacking order is the window on top.

StaticColor

The `StaticColor` visual class represents a multiplane color screen with a predefined and read-only hardware colormap. It can be viewed as a degenerate case of `PseudoColor`. See **PseudoColor**.

StaticGray

The `StaticGray` visual class represents a multiplane monnochrome screen with a predefined and read-only hardware colormap. It can be viewed as a degenerate case of `GrayScale`, in which the gray values are predefined and read-only. Typically, the values are linearly increasing ramps. See **GrayScale**.

stipple

A *stipple* is a single plane pixmap that is used to tile a region. Bits set to 1 in the stipple are drawn with a foreground pixel value; bits set to 0, with a background pixel value. The stipple and both pixel values are members of the GC.

status

Many Xlib functions return a *status* of `True` or `False`. If the function does not succeed, its return arguments are not disturbed.

tile

A pixmap can be replicated in two dimensions to *tile* a region. The pixmap itself is also known as a *tile*.

time

A *time* value in X is expressed in milliseconds, typically since the last server reset. Time values wrap around (after about 49.7 days). One time value, represented by the constant `CurrentTime`, is used by clients to represent the current server time.

top-level window

A child of the root window is referred to as a *top-level window*.

TrueColor

The `TrueColor` visual class represents a high-performance multiplane display with predefined and read-only RGB values in its hardware colormap. It can be viewed as a degenerate case of `DirectColor`, in which the subfields in the pixel value directly encode the corresponding RGB values. Typically, the values are linearly increasing ramps. See **DirectColor**.

type property

A *type property* is used to identify the interpretation of property data. Types are completely uninterpreted by the server; they are solely for the benefit of clients.

viewable

A window is *viewable* if it and all of its ancestors are mapped. This does not imply that any portion of the window is actually visible, since it may be obscured by other windows.

visible

A region of a window is *visible* if someone looking at the screen can actually see it; that is, the window is viewable and the region is not obscured by any other window.

visual

> The specifications for color handling for a drawable, including visual class, depth, RGB/pixel, etc., are collectively referred to as a *visual*, and are stored in a structure of type `Visual`.

visual class

> One of `PseudoColor`, `GrayScale`, etc. A definition of the colormap type but not its depth.

window gravity

> When windows are resized, subwindows may be repositioned automatically relative to an edge, corner, or center of the window. This attraction of a subwindow to some part of its parent is known as *window gravity*.

window manager

> Manipulation of windows on the screen is provided by a *window manager* client. The window manager has authority over the arrangement of windows on the screen, and the user interface for selecting which window receives input. See also **redirect**.

XYPixmap

> The data for an image is said to be in `XYPixmap` format if it is organized as a set of bitmaps representing individual bit planes. This applies only to the server's internal data format for images. It does not affect normal programming with pixmaps.

ZPixmap

> The data for an image is said to be in `ZPixmap` format if it is organized as a set of pixel values in scan line order. This applies only to the server's internal data format for images. It does not affect normal programming with pixmaps.

zoomed window

> Some applications have not only a normal size for their top-level window and an icon, but also a *zoomed window* size. This could be used in a painting program (similar to the MacPaint™ fat bits). The zoomed window size preferences can be specified in the window manager hints.

B
X10 Compatibility

X11 includes a conversion library, so that X10.4 applications can be easily ported to X11, albeit with a loss of performance. In addition, there are a few X10 routines that provide functionality missing in X11, which may still be used. This appendix discusses XDraw and related commands, and association table routines for data management.

In This Chapter:

B
X10 Compatibility

These functions are provided in a separate library in both Release 1 and Release 2, for compatibility with X Version 10. They can be used by including the file *<X11/X10.h>* and linking with the *-loldX* library.

X Version 11 XDraw now provides all the functionality of the X Version 10 routines XDraw, XDrawPatterned, and XDrawDashed. X Version 11 XDrawFilled now provides the functionality of the old XDrawFilled and XDrawTiled. These routines now use the GC to specify the fill, tile or stipple, line styles, etc.

The association table routines described in Chapter 13, *Other Programming Techniques*, are also carried over from X10, but there are no performance penalties for using them, and they provide functionality not available otherwise in the X11 Xlib.

XDraw and XDrawFilled

XDraw and XDrawFilled call other Xlib routines, not the server directly. If you just have straight lines to draw, using XDrawLines or XDrawSegments is much faster. If you want to draw spline curves in a portable fashion, you currently have no choice but to use XDraw until a standard spline extension is adopted.

XDraw draws an arbitrary polygon or curve. The figure drawn is defined by a list of vertices (*vlist*). The points are connected by lines as specified in the flags in the vertex structure. In X Version 11, XDraw provides all the functionality of the X Version 10 routines XDraw, XDrawPatterned, and XDrawDashed. XDrawFilled now provides the functionality of the old XDrawFilled and XDrawTiled. The fill, pattern, line_style, and tile are all controlled by the graphics context. Lines are properly joined according to the GC if they connect and make a closed figure.

The error status returned is the opposite of what it was under X Version 10, conforming to the X Version 11 standard that 0 indicates failure. The VertexDrawLastPoint flag and the routines XAppendVertex and XClearVertexFlag from X Version 10 are not supported.

The *vlist* and *vcount* arguments of XDraw and XDrawFilled control the line or area that is drawn.

vlist   Specifies a pointer to the list of vertices which indicate what to draw.

vcount   Specifies how many vertices are in *vlist*.

Each Vertex, as defined in *<X11/Xlib.h>*, is a structure with the following members:

Example B-1. The Vertex structure for XDraw

```
typedef struct _Vertex {
    short x,y;
    unsigned short flags;
} Vertex;
```

The x and y members are the coordinates of the vertex. These coordinates are interpreted according to the flags.

The flags member, as defined in Xlib.h, is a mask made by ORing the following symbols:

Table B-1. Vertex Flags

Flag	Bit	If not set
VertexRelative	0	absolute
VertexDontDraw	1	draw
VertexCurved	2	straight
VertexStartClosed	3	not closed
VertexEndClosed	4	not closed

XDraw fails (returns 0) only if it runs out of memory or is passed a Vertex list which has a vertex with VertexStartClosed set not followed by a vertex with VertexEnd-Closed set. The x and y coordinates in Vertex are relative to the upper-left inside corner of the drawable if VertexRelative is not specified in flags or to the previous vertex if VertexRelative is specified. The first vertex must be an absolute vertex.

If VertexDontDraw is specified in flags, no line or curve is drawn from the previous vertex to this one. This is analogous to picking up the pen and moving it to another place before drawing another line.

If VertexCurved is specified in flags, a spline algorithm is used to draw a smooth curve from the previous vertex, through the current one, to the next vertex. Otherwise, a straight line is drawn from the previous vertex to the current one. You should set Vertex-Curved in flags only if a previous and next vertex are both defined, either explicitly or through the definition of a closed curve. If VertexStartClosed is specified, then this point marks the beginning of a closed curve. This vertex must be followed later in the array by another vertex whose absolute coordinates are identical and which has VertexEnd-Closed specified in its flags.

It is permissible for both the `VertexDontDraw` and `VertexCurved` bits to be 1. This is useful to define the previous point for the smooth curve, without drawing until the current point.

Example B-2 shows a routine that draws a box on the root window for use by the window manager described in Chapter 14, *Window Management*. Of course, you would want to create the GC in the calling routine if `draw_box` were to be called more than once.

Example B-2. draw_box implemented with X Version 10 XDraw

```
draw_box(display, screen, left,top,right,bottom)
Display *display;
int screen;
int left,top,right,bottom;
    {
    Vertex corner[5];
    int vertexcount = 5;
    int planes = FIRST_PLANE;
    GC gc;

    /* Create graphics context */
    /* ignore XGCvalues and use defaults */
    gc = XCreateGC(display, RootWindow(display, screen), 0, NULL);

    /* Set graphics context to include font */
    XSetFunction(display, gc, GXxor);

    XSetForeground(display, gc, BlackPixel(display,screen));

    XSetPlaneMask(display, gc, planes);

    corner[0].x = left;
    corner[0].y = top;
    corner[0].flags = 0;

    corner[1].x = left;
    corner[1].y = bottom;
    corner[1].flags = 0;

    corner[2].x = right;
    corner[2].y = bottom;
    corner[2].flags = 0;

    corner[3].x = right;
    corner[3].y = top;
    corner[3].flags = 0;

    corner[4].x = left;
    corner[4].y = top;
    corner[4].flags = 0;

    XDraw(display, RootWindow(display, screen), gc, corner, vertexcount);
    XFlush();
    }
```

C

Writing Extensions to X

Extensibility is an important part of X. Hooks are provided into Xlib and the protocol so that extensions will have the same performance as the core routines. This appendix provides information on how to write extensions and integrate them into X.

In This Chapter:

Extensions

C
Writing Extensions to X

Because X can only evolve by extension to the core protocol, it is important that extensions not be perceivable as second class citizens. At some point, some extensions may be adopted as parts of the "X Standard."

Therefore, there should be little to distinguish the use of an extension from that of the core protocol. To avoid having to initialize extensions explicitly in application programs, extensions should perform "lazy evaluations" and automatically initialize themselves when called for the first time.

Extensions written according to these instructions will run at essentially the same performance as the core protocol requests.

It is expected that a given extension to X will consist of multiple requests. Defining ten new features as ten separate extensions is very bad practice. Rather, they should be packaged into a single extension and should use minor opcodes to distinguish the features.

Basic Protocol Support Routines

The basic protocol requests for extensions are `XQueryExtension` and `XList-Extensions`. `XQueryExtension` has the following format:

```
Bool XQueryExtension(display, name, major_opcode, first_event,
        first_error)
    Display *display;
    char *name;
    int *major_opcode; /* RETURN */
    int *first_event;  /* RETURN */
    int *first_error;  /* RETURN */
```

`XQueryExtension` determines if the named extension is present. If so, the major opcode for the extension is returned (if it has one). Otherwise, `False` is returned. Any minor opcode and the request formats are specific to the extension. If the extension involves

---

*As of this printing, Appendix C is only lightly edited and reformatted from the original MIT material. Before attempting to write extensions, you should be intimately familiar with the *X Window System Protocol, Version 11*, by Robert Scheifler and Ron Newman.

Appendix C: Writing Extensions to X

additional event types, the base event type code is returned. Otherwise, `False` is returned. The format of the events is specific to the extension. If the extension involves additional error codes, the base error code is returned. Otherwise, zero is returned. The format of additional data in the errors is specific to the extension.

The extension name should be in ISO LATIN1 encoding. Upper and lower case are distinguished.

`XListExtensions` returns a list of all extensions supported by the server. It has the following format:

```
char **XListExtensions(display, nextensions)
    Display *display;
    int *nextensions;
```

`XFreeExtensionList` frees the memory allocated by `XListExtensions`. It has the following format:

```
XFreeExtensionList(list)
    char **list;
```

Hooking into Xlib

The functions described in this section allow one to hook into the library. They are not normally used by application programmers but are used by people who need to extend the core X protocol and the X library interface. The functions, which generate protocol requests for X, are typically called "stubs."

In extensions, stubs first should check to see if they have initialized themselves on a connection. If they have not, they then should call `XInitExtension` to attempt to initialize themselves on the connection.

If the extension needs to be informed of GC/font allocation or deallocation, or if the extension defines new event types, there are several functions that allow an extension to be called when these events occur.

Initializing the Extension

In *<X11/Xlib.h>*, the following structure is defined to return the information from `XInit-Extension`.

Example C-1. The XExtCodes structure

```
typedef struct _XExtCodes { /* public to extension, cannot be changed */
    int extension;      /* extension number */
    int major_opcode;   /* major opcode assigned by server */
    int first_event;    /* first event number for the extension */
    int first_error;    /* first error number for the extension */
} XExtCodes;
```

XInitExtension has the following format:

```
XExtCodes *XInitExtension(display, name)
    Display *display;
    char *name;
```

XInitExtension first determines if the extension exists. Then, it allocates storage for maintaining the information about the extension on the connection, chains this onto the extension list for the connection, and returns the information the stub implementor will need to access the extension. If the extension does not exist, XInitExtension returns NULL.

In particular, the extension number in the XExtCodes structure is needed in other calls below. This extension number is unique only to a single connection.

Hooks into the Library

The functions described in the following sections allow you to define procedures that are to be called when various circumstances occur. The procedures include creating a new GC for a connection, copying a GC, freeing a GC, creating and freeing fonts, converting events defined by extensions to and from wire format, and error handling.

All of these functions return the previous routine defined for this extension.

XESetCloseDisplay

You use this procedure to define a procedure to be called whenever XCloseDisplay is called. This procedure returns any previously defined procedure, usually NULL. XESet-CloseDisplay has the following format:

```
int (*XESetCloseDisplay(display, extension, proc))()
    Display *display;  /* display */
    int extension;     /* extension number */
    int (*proc)();     /* routine to call when display closed */
```

When XCloseDisplay is called, your routine is called with these arguments:

```
(*proc)(display, codes)
    Display *display;
    XExtCodes *codes;
```

XESetCreateGC

You use this procedure to define a procedure to be called whenever a new GC is created. This procedure returns any previously defined procedure, usually NULL. XESetCreateGC has the following format:

```
int (*XESetCreateGC(display, extension, proc))()
    Display *display;  /* display */
    int extension;     /* extension number */
    int (*proc)();     /* routine to call when GC created */
```

When a GC is created, your routine will be called with these arguments:

```
(*proc)(display, gc, codes)
    Display *display;
    GC gc;
    XExtCodes *codes;
```

XESetCopyGC

You use this procedure to define a procedure to be called whenever a GC is copied. This procedure returns any previously defined procedure, usually NULL. XESetCopyGC has the following format:

```
int (*XESetCopyGC(display, extension, proc))()
    Display *display;  /* display */
    int extension;     /* extension number */
    int (*proc)();     /* routine to call when GC copied */
```

When a GC is copied, your routine will be called with these arguments:

```
(*proc)(display, gc, codes)
    Display *display;
    GC gc;
    XExtCodes *codes;
```

XESetFreeGC

You use this procedure to define a procedure to be called whenever a GC is freed. This procedure returns any previously defined procedure, usually NULL. XESetFreeGC has the following format:

```
int (*XESetFreeGC(display, extension, proc))()
    Display *display;  /* display */
    int extension;     /* extension number */
    int (*proc)();     /* routine to call when GC freed */
```

When a GC is freed, your routine will be called with these arguments:

```
(*proc)(display, gc, codes)
    Display *display;
    GC gc;
    XExtCodes *codes;
```

XESetCreateFont

You use this procedure to define a procedure to be called whenever XLoadQueryFont and XQueryFont are called. This procedure returns any previously defined procedure, usually NULL. XESetCreateFont has the following format:

```
int (*XESetCreateFont(display, extension, proc))()
    Display *display;  /* display */
    int extension;     /* extension number */
    int (*proc)();     /* routine to call when font created */
```

When XLoadQueryFont or XQueryFont is called, your routine will be called with these arguments:

```
(*proc)(display, fs, codes)
    Display *display;
    XFontStruct *fs;
    XExtCodes *codes;
```

XESetFreeFont

You use this procedure to define a procedure to be called whenever XFreeFont is called. This procedure returns any previously defined procedure, usually NULL. XESetFreeFont has the following format:

```
int (*XESetFreeFont(display, extension, proc))()
    Display *display;  /* display */
    int extension;     /* extension number */
    int (*proc)();     /* routine to call when font freed */
```

When XFreeFont is called, your routine will be called with these arguments:

```
(*proc)(display, fs, codes)
    Display *display;
    XFontStruct *fs;
    XExtCodes *codes;
```

The next two functions allow you to define new events to the library.

XESetWireToEvent

There is an implementation limit such that your host event structure size cannot be bigger than the size of the `XEvent` union of structures. There is also no way to guarantee that more than 24 elements or 96 characters in the structure will be fully portable between machines.

You use `XESetWireToEvent` to define a procedure to be called when an event needs to be converted from wire format (`xEvent`) to host format (`XEvent`). `XESetWire-ToEvent` has the following format:

```
int (*XESetWireToEvent(display, event_number, proc))()
    Display *display;  /* display */
    int event_number;  /* event routine to replace */
    Bool (*proc)();    /* routine to call when converting event */
```

The event number defines which protocol event number to install a conversion routine for. This procedure returns any previously defined procedure.

You can replace a core event conversion routine with one of your own, though this is not encouraged. It would, however, allow you to intercept a core event and modify it before it was queued or otherwise examined.

When Xlib needs to convert an event from wire format to natural host format, your routine will be called with these arguments:

```
(*proc)(display, re, event)
    Display *display;
    XEvent *re;
    xEvent *event;
```

Your routine must return status to indicate if the conversion succeeded. The `re` argument is a pointer to where the host format event should be stored, while the event argument is the 32-byte wire event structure. In the `XEvent` structure you are creating, `type` must be the first member and `window` must be the second member. You should fill in the `type` member with the type specified for the `xEvent` structure. You should copy all other members from the `xEvent` structure (wire format) to the `XEvent` structure (host format). Your conversion routine should return `True` if the event should be queued or `False` if it should not be queued.

XESetEventToWire

You use `XESetEventToWire` to define a procedure to be called when an event needs to be converted from host format (`XEvent`) to wire format (`xEvent`) form. `XESetEvent-ToWire` has the following format:

```
int (*XESetEventToWire(display, event_number, proc))()
    Display *display;  /* display */
    int event_number;  /* event routine to replace */
    int (*proc)();     /* routine to call when converting event */
```

The event number defines which protocol event number to install a conversion routine for. This procedure returns any previously defined procedure. It returns 0 if the conversion fails or nonzero otherwise.

You can replace a core event conversion routine with one of your own, though this is not encouraged. It would, however, allow you to intercept a core event and modify it before being sent to another client.

When Xlib needs to convert an event from wire format to natural host format, your routine will be called with these arguments:

```
(*proc)(display, re, event)
    Display *display;
    XEvent *re;
    xEvent *event;
```

The *re* argument is a pointer to the host format event, while the *event* argument is a pointer to where the 32-byte wire event structure should be stored. In the XEvent structure you are forming, type must be the first member, and window must be the second. You then should fill in type with the type from the xEvent structure. All other members then should be copied from the wire format to the XEvent structure.

XESetError

You use this procedure when you want to suppress the calling of the external error handling when an error occurs. This allows status to be returned on a call at the cost of the call being synchronous (though most such routines are query operations in any case, and are typically programmed to be synchronous). XESetError has the following format:

```
int (*XESetError(display, extension, proc))()
    Display *display;   /* display */
    int extension;      /* extension number */
    int (*proc)();      /* routine to call when X error happens */
```

When Xlib detects an protocol error in _XReply, it will call your procedure with these arguments:

```
int (*proc)(display, err, codes, ret_code)
    Display *display;
    xError *err;
    XExtCodes *codes;
    int *ret_code;
```

The *err* argument is a pointer to the 32-byte wire format error. The *codes* argument is a pointer to the extension codes structure. The *ret_code* argument is the return code you may want _XReply returned to.

If your routine returns a value 0, the error is not be suppressed, and the client's error handler is called. If your routine returns nonzero, the error is suppressed, and _XReply returns the value of *ret_code*.

XESetErrorString

The Xlib XGetErrorText function returns a string to the user for an error. This procedure allows you to define a routine to be called which should return a pointer to the error message. XESetErrorString has the following format:

```
char *(*XESetErrorString(display, extension, proc))()
    Display *display;    /* display */
    int extension;       /* extension number */
    char *(*proc)();     /* routine to call when I/O error happens */
```

The following is an example.

```
char *(*proc)(display, code, codes)
    Display *display;
    int code;
    XExtCodes *codes;
```

Your procedure is called with the error code detected. You should return a pointer to a null-terminated string containing the error message.

XESetFlushGC

The XESetFlushGC procedure is identical to XSetCopyGC, except that XESetFlush-GC is called when a GC cache needs to be updated in the server. XESetFlushGC has the following format:

```
int (*XESetFlushGC(display, extension, proc))()
    Display *display;    /* display */
    int extension;       /* extension number */
    char *(*proc)();     /* routine to call when I/O error happens */
```

Hooks onto Xlib Data Structures

Various Xlib data structures have provisions for extension routines to chain extension-supplied data onto a list. These structures are: GC, Visual, Screen, ScreenFormat, Display, and XFontStruct. Because the list pointer is always the first member in the structure, a single set of routines can be used to manipulate the data on these lists.

The structure in Example C-2 is used in the routines in this section and is defined in *<X11/Xlib.h>*.

Example C-2. The XExtData structure

```
typedef struct _XExtData {
    int number;                /* number returned by XRegisterExtension */
    struct _XExtData *next;/* next item on list of data for structure */
    int (*free)();             /* if defined, called to free private */
    char *private;             /* data private to this extension */
} XExtData;
```

When any of the data structures listed above (GC, Visual, Screen, ScreenFormat, Display, and XFontStruct) are freed, the list is walked, and the *free* routine (if any) is called. If *free* is NULL, then the library will free the data pointed to by *private* and the structure itself.

XAddToExtensionList

XAddToExtensionList is used to add extension data onto an Xlib data structure. It has the following format:

```
XAddToExtensionList(structure, ext_data)
    struct _XExtData **structure; /* pointer to structure to add */
    XExtData *ext_data;           /* extension data structure to add */
```

The *structure* argument is a pointer to one of the data structures listed above (GC, Visual, Screen, ScreenFormat, Display, and XFontStruct).

You must initialize ext_data->number with the extension number before calling this routine.

XFindOnExtensionList

XFindOnExtensionList returns the first extension data structure for the extension numbered *number*. It has the following format:

```
XExtData *XFindOnExtensionList(structure, number)
    struct _XExtData **structure;
    int number;    /* extension number from XInitExtension */
```

It is expected that an extension will add at most one extension data structure to any single data structure's extension data list. There is no way to find additional structures.

Allocating a Resource ID

The XAllocID macro, which allocates and returns a resource ID, is defined in <X11/Xlib.h>.

```
XAllocID(display)
    Display *display;
```

This macro is a call through the Display structure to the internal resource ID allocator. It returns a resource ID that you can use when creating new resources.

GC Caching

GCs are cached by the library, to allow merging of independent change requests to the same GC into single protocol requests. This is typically called a *write back* cache. Any extension routine whose behavior depends on the contents of a GC must flush the GC cache, to make sure the server has up-to-date contents in its GC.

If you extend the GC to add additional resource ID components, you should ensure that the library stub immediately sends the change request. This is because a client can free a resource immediately after using it, so if you only stored the value in the cache without forcing a protocol request, the resource might be destroyed before being set into the GC. You can use the _XFlushGCCache procedure to force the cache to be flushed. The _XFlushGCCache procedure is defined as follows:

```
_XFlushGCCache (display, gc)
    Display *display;
    GC gc;
```

The FlushGC macro checks the dirty bits in the library's GC structure and calls _XFlush-GCCache if any members have changed. The FlushGC macro is defined as follows:

```
FlushGC (display, gc)
    Display *display;
    GC gc;
```

Graphics Batching

If you extend X to add more poly graphics primitives, you may be able to take advantage of facilities in the library that allow back-to-back single calls to be transformed into poly requests. This may dramatically improve performance of programs that are not written using poly requests. In the Display structure is a pointer to an xReq called last_req which is the last request being processed. By checking that the last request type, drawable, gc, and other options are the same as the new one, and that there is enough space left in the buffer, you may be able to just extend the previous graphics request by extending the length field of the request and appending the data to the buffer. This can improve naive programs five times or more. For example, here is the source for the XDrawPoint stub.

Example C-3. Example of graphics batching

```
#include "copyright.h"
#include "Xlibint.h"

/* precompute the maximum size of batching request allowed */

static int size = sizeof(xPolyPointReq) + EPERBATCH * sizeof(xPoint);

XDrawPoint(dpy, d, gc, x, y)
    register Display *dpy;
```

Example C-3. Example of graphics batching (continued)

```
    Drawable d;
    GC gc;
    int x, y; /* INT16 */
{
    xPoint *point;
    LockDisplay(dpy);
    FlushGC(dpy, gc);
    {
    register xPolyPointReq *req = (xPolyPointReq *) dpy->last_req;
    /* if same as previous request, with same drawable, batch requests */
    if (
            (req->reqType == X_PolyPoint)
        && (req->drawable == d)
        && (req->gc == gc->gid)
        && (req->coordMode == CoordModeOrigin)
        && ((dpy->bufptr + sizeof (xPoint)) <= dpy->bufmax)
        && (((char *)dpy->bufptr - (char *)req) < size) ) {
      point = (xPoint *) dpy->bufptr;
      req->length += sizeof (xPoint) >> 2;
      dpy->bufptr += sizeof (xPoint);
        }

    else {
        GetReqExtra(PolyPoint, 4, req); /* 1 point = 4 bytes */
        req->drawable = d;
        req->gc = gc->gid;
        req->coordMode = CoordModeOrigin;
        point = (xPoint *) (req + 1);
        }
    point->x = x;
    point->y = y;
    }
    UnlockDisplay(dpy);
    SyncHandle();
}
```

To keep clients from generating very long requests that may monopolize the server, there is
a symbol defined in *<X11/Xlibint.h>* called EPERBATCH that limits the number of requests
batched. Most of the performance benefit occurs in the first few merged requests. Note that
FlushGC is called *before* picking up the value of last_req, since it may modify this
field.

Writing Extension Stubs

All X requests always contain the length of the request, expressed as a 16-bit quantity of
32-bit entities. This means that a single request can be no more than 256K bytes in length.
Some servers may not support single requests of such a length. The value of:

```
    dpy->max_request_size
```

Extensions

contains the maximum length as defined by the server implementation. For further information, see the X Protocol documentation.

Requests, Replies, and Xproto.h

The following discussion may be easier to understand if you look at the *<X11/Xproto.h>* include file. The file contains three sets of definitions that are of interest to the stub implementor: request names, request structures, and reply structures.

You need to generate a file equivalent to *<X11/Xproto.h>* for your extension and need to include it in your stub routine. Each stub routine also must include *<X11/Xlibint.h>*.

The identifiers are deliberately chosen in such a way that, if the request is called X_Do-Something, then its request structure is xDoSomethingReq, and its reply is xDo-SomethingReply. The GetReq family of macros, defined in *<X11/Xlibint.h>*, takes advantage of this naming scheme.

For each X request, there is a definition in *<X11/Xproto.h>* that looks similar to this:

```
#define X_DoSomething   42
```

In your extension header file, this will be a minor opcode, instead of a major opcode.

Request Format

Every request contains an 8-bit major opcode and a 16-bit length field expressed in units of 4 bytes. Every request consists of 4 bytes of header (containing the major opcode, the length field, and a data byte) followed by zero or more additional bytes of data. The length field defines the total length of the request, including the header. The length field in a request must equal the minimum length required to contain the request. If the specified length is smaller or larger than the required length, the server should generate a Bad-Length error. Unused bytes in a request are not required to be zero.

Major opcodes 128 through 255 are reserved for extensions. Extensions are intended to contain multiple requests, so extension requests typically have an additional minor opcode encoded in the spare data byte in the request header, but the placement and interpretation of this minor opcode as well as all other fields in extension requests are not defined by the core protocol. Every request is implicitly assigned a sequence number (starting with one) used in replies, errors, and events.

Most protocol requests have a corresponding structure typedef in *<X11/Xproto.h>* which looks like this:

```
typedef struct _DoSomethingReq {
    CARD8 reqType;      /* X_DoSomething */
    CARD8 someDatum;    /* used differently in different requests */
    CARD16 length B16;  /* total # of bytes in request, divided by 4 */
    ...
    /* request-specific data */
    ...
} xDoSomethingReq;
```

If a core protocol request has a single 32-bit argument, you need not declare a request structure in your extension header file. Instead, such requests use *<X11/Xproto.h>*'s xResourceReq structure. This structure is used for any request whose single argument is of type Window, Pixmap, Drawable, GContext, Font, Cursor, Colormap, Device, Atom, or VisualID.

```
typedef struct _ResourceReq {
    CARD8 reqType;      /* the request type, e.g.  X_DoSomething */
    BYTE pad;           /* not used */
    CARD16 length B16;  /* 2 (total # of bytes in request,
                         * divided by 4) */
    CARD32 id B32;      /* Window, Drawable, Font, GContext, etc. */
} xResourceReq;
```

If convenient, you can do something similar in your extension header file.

In both of these structures, the reqType field identifies the type of the request (for example, X_MapWindow or X_CreatePixmap). The length field tells how long, in units of 4-byte "longwords," the request is. This length includes both the request structure itself and any variable length data, such as strings or lists, that follow the request structure. Request structures come in different sizes, but all requests are padded to be a multiple of 4 bytes long.

To help (but not cure) portability problems to certain machines, two macros, B16 and B32, ahve been defined. These macros can become bit field specifications on some machines. For example, on a Cray, these should be used for all 16-bit and 32-bit quantities, as shown in the structures above.

A few protocol requests take no arguments at all. Instead, they use *<X11/Xproto.h>*'s xReq structure, which contains only a reqType and a length (and a pad byte).

If the protocol request requires a reply, then *<X11/Xproto.h>* also contains a reply structure typedef:

```
typedef struct _DoSomethingReply {
    BYTE type;                  /* always X_Reply */
    BYTE someDatum;             /* used differently in different
                                 * requests */
    CARD16 sequenceNumber B16;  /* # of requests sent so far */
    CARD32 length B32;          /* # of additional bytes, divided by 4 */
    ...
    /* request-specific data */
    ...
} xDoSomethingReply;
```

Extensions

Most of these reply structures are 32 bytes long. If there are not that many reply values, then they contain a sufficient number of pad fields to bring them up to 32 bytes. The length field is the total number of bytes in the request minus 32, divided by 4. This length will be nonzero only if:

- The reply structure is followed by variable length data such as a list or string

- The reply structure is longer than 32 bytes

Only GetWindowAttributes, QueryFont, QueryKeymap, and GetKeyboard-Control have reply structures longer than 32 bytes in the core protocol.

A few protocol requests return replies that contain no data. *<X11/Xproto.h>* does not define reply structures for these. Instead, they use the xGenericReply structure, which contains only a type, length, and sequence number (and sufficient padding to make it 32 bytes long).

Starting to Write a Stub Routine

An Xlib stub routine should always start like this:

```
#include "Xlibint.h"

XDoSomething (arguments,... )
/* argument declarations */
{

/* variable declarations, if any */
... }
```

If the protocol request has a reply, then the variable declarations should include the reply structure for the request. The following is an example.

```
xDoSomethingReply rep;
```

Locking Data Structures

In order to lock the display structure, for systems that want to support multithreaded access to a single display connection, each stub will need to lock its critical section. Generally, this section is the point from just before the appropriate GetReq call documented below until all arguments to the call have been stored into the request. The precise instructions needed for this locking depend upon the machine architecture. Two calls, which are generally implemented as macros, have been provided.

```
LockDisplay(display)
     Display *display;

UnlockDisplay(display)
     Display *display;
```

Sending the Protocol Request and Arguments

After the variable declarations, a stub routine should call one of four macros defined in *<X11/Xlibint.h>*: `GetReq`, `GetReqExtra`, `GetResReq`, or `GetEmptyReq`. All of these macros take as their first argument the name of the protocol request as declared in *<X11/Xproto.h>*, except with the initial "X_" removed. Each one declares a `Display` structure pointer (called `dpy`) and a pointer to a request structure (called `req`) which is of the appropriate type. The macro then appends the request structure to the output buffer, fills in its type and length field, and sets `req` to point to it.

If the protocol request has no arguments (for instance, X_GrabServer), then use `GetEmpty-Req`:

```
GetEmptyReq (DoSomething);
```

If the protocol request has a single 32-bit argument (such as `Pixmap`, `Window`, `Drawable`, `Atom`, and so on), then use `GetResReq`. The second argument to the macro is the 32-bit object. X_MapWindow is a good example.

```
GetResReq (DoSomething, rid);
```

The *rid* argument is the pixmap ID, window ID, or other resource ID.

If the protocol request takes any other argument list, then call `GetReq`. After the `GetReq` call, you need to set all the other fields in the request structure, usually from arguments to the stub routine.

```
GetReq (DoSomething);
/* fill in arguments here */
req->arg1 = arg1;
req->arg2 = arg2;
...
```

A few stub routines (such as, `XCreateGC` and `XCreatePixmap`) return a resource ID to the caller but pass a resource ID as an argument to the protocol request. Such routines use the macro `XAllocID` to allocate a resource ID from the range of IDs that were assigned to this client when it opened the connection.

```
rid = req->rid = XAllocID();
...
return (rid);
```

Finally, some stub routines transmit a fixed amount of variable-length data after the request. Typically, these routines (such as `XMoveWindow` and `XSetWindowBackground`) are special cases of more general functions like `XMoveResizeWindow` and `XChangeGC`. These special case routines use `GetReqExtra`, which is the same as `GetReq`, except that it takes an additional argument (the number of extra bytes to allocate in the output buffer after the request structure). This number should always be a multiple of 4.

Extensions

Variable-length Arguments

Some protocol requests take additional variable length data that follow the `xDo-SomethingReq` structure. The format of this data varies from request to request. Some requests require a sequence of 8-bit bytes, others a sequence of 16- or 32-bit entities, and still others a sequence of structures.

It is necessary to add the length of any variable length data to the length field of the request structure. That length field is in units of 32-bit longwords. If the data is a string or other sequence of 8-bit bytes, then you must round the length up and shift it before adding:

```
req->length += (nbytes+3)>>2;
```

To transmit the variable length data, use the `Data` macro. If the data fits into the output buffer, then this macro copies it to the buffer. If it does not fit, however, the `Data` macro calls `_XSend`, which transmits first the contents of the buffer and then your data. The `Data` macro takes three arguments: the `Display`, a pointer to the beginning of the data, and the number of bytes to be sent.

```
Data(dpy, (char *) data, nbytes);
```

If the data are 16-bit entities, then use the `PackData` macro instead. It takes the same arguments and does the same things, but it does the right thing on machines where a short is 32 bits instead of the usual 16.

Both `Data` and `PackData` are macros which may use their last argument more than once, so that argument should be a variable, rather than an expression such as `nitems*sizeof(item)`. You should do that kind of computation in a separate statement before calling `Data`.

If the protocol request requires a reply, then call the procedure `_XSend` instead of the `Data` macro. `_XSend` takes the same arguments, but because it sends your data immediately instead of copying it into the output buffer (which would later be flushed anyway by the following call on `_XReply`), it is faster.

Replies

If the protocol request has a reply, then call `_XReply` after you have finished dealing with all the fixed and variable length arguments. `_XReply` flushes the output buffer and waits for an `xReply` packet to arrive. If any events arrive in the meantime, `_XReply` queues them for later use. `_XReply` has the following format:

```
Status _XReply(display, rep, extra, discard)
    Display *display;
    xReply *rep;
    int extra;    /* number of 32-bit words expected after the reply */
    Bool discard; /* should I discard data following "extra" words */
```

_XReply waits for a reply packet and copy its contents into the specified rep structure. _XReply handles error and event packets that occur before the reply is received. _XReply takes four arguments:

1. A Display* structure

2. A pointer to a reply structure (which must be cast to an xReply*)

3. The number of additional bytes (beyond sizeof(xReply) = 32 bytes) in the reply structure

4. A Boolean that tells _XReply to discard any additional bytes beyond those it was told to read

Because most reply structures are 32 bytes long, the third argument is normally 0. The only core protocol exceptions are the replies to X_GetWindowAttributes, X_QueryFont, X_QueryKeymap, and X_GetKeyboardControl, which have longer replies.

The last argument should be xFalse, if the reply structure is followed by additional variable length data (such as a list or string). It should be True if there is no variable-length data. This last argument is provided for upward-compatibility reasons—to allow a client to communicate properly with a hypothetical later version of the server which sends more data than the client expected. For example, some later version of XGetWindowAttributes might use a larger, but compatible, xGetWindowAttributesReply which contains additional attribute data at the end.

_XReply returns True if it received a reply successfully, or False if it received an XError or some other error condition.

For a request with a reply that is not followed by variable-length data, you write something like this:

```
_XReply (display, (xReply *)&rep, 0, True);
*ret1 = rep.ret1;
*ret2 = rep.ret2;
*ret3 = rep.ret3;
...
UnlockDisplay(dpy);
SyncHandle();
return (rep.ret4);
}
```

If there is variable-length data after the reply, change the True to False, and use _XRead to read the variable-length data.

Each protocol request is a little different. For further information, see the Xlib sources for examples.

Synchronous Calling

To ease debugging, just before returning to the user, each routine should have a call to a routine called `SyncHandle`. This routine generally is implemented as a macro. If synchronous mode is enabled (see the `XSynchronize` reference page in Volume Two, *Xlib Reference Manual*), the request is sent immediately. The library, however, waits until any error the routine could generate at the server has been handled.

Allocating and Deallocating Memory

To support the possible reentrancy of these routines, you must observe several conventions when allocating and deallocating memory. This is most often done when returning data to the user from the window system of a size the caller could not know in advance (for example, a list of fonts or a list of extensions). This occurs because the standard C library routines on many systems are not protected against signals or other multithreaded use. The following analogies to standard I/O library routines have been defined:

```
Xmalloc()      Replaces malloc()
Xfree()        Replaces free()
Xcalloc()      Replaces calloc()
```

These should be used in place of any calls you would make to the normal C library routines.

If you need scratch space inside a critical section (for example, to pack and unpack data to and from wire protocol), the general memory allocators may be too expensive for use (particularly in output routines, which are performance critical). The routine below returns a scratch buffer for your use:

```
char *_XAllocScratch(display, nbytes)
    Display *display;
    unsigned long nbytes;
```

This storage must only be used inside of the critical section of your stub.

Portability Considerations

Many machine architectures, including many of the more recent RISC architectures, will not correctly access data at unaligned locations; their compilers will pad out structures to preserve this characteristic. Many other machines capable of unaligned references pad inside of structures as well to preserve alignment, since accessing aligned data is usually much faster. Since the library and the server are using structures to access data at arbitrary points in a byte stream, all data in request and reply packets *must* be naturally aligned. That is, 16-bit data must start on 16-bit boundaries in the request, and 32-bit data must start on 32-bit boundaries. All requests *must* be a multiple of 32 bits in length, to preserve the natural alignment in the data stream. Pad structures out to 32-bit boundaries. Pad information does not have to be zeroed, unless you wish to preserve such fields for future use in your protocol requests. Floating point varies radically between machines and should be avoided completely if at all possible.

This code may run on machines with 16-bit int's. So, if any integer argument, variable, or return value either can take only nonnegative values or is declared as a CARD16 in the protocol, be sure to declare it as unsigned int and not as int. (This of course does not apply to Booleans or enumerations.)

Similarly, if any integer argument or return value is declared CARD32 in the protocol, declare it as an unsigned long and not as int or long. This also goes for any internal variables that may take on values larger than the maximum 16-bit unsigned int.

The library currently assumes that a char is 8 bits, a short is 16 bits, an int is 16 or 32 bits, and a long is 32 bits. The PackData macro is a half-hearted attempt to deal with the possibility of 32-bit short's. However, much more work is needed to make this really work properly.

Deriving the Correct Extension Opcode

The remaining problem a writer of an extension stub routine faces that the core protocol does not face is to map from the call to the proper major and minor opcodes. While there are a number of strategies, the simplest and fastest is outlined below.

1. Declare an array of pointers, _NFILE long, of type XExtCodes*. (_NFILE is defined in <stdio.h> and is the number of file descriptors supported on the system.) Make sure these are all initialized to NULL.

2. When your stub is entered, your initialization test is just to use the display pointer passed in to access the file descriptor, and an index into the array. If the entry is NULL, then this is the first time you are entering the routine for this display. Call your initialization routine and pass it the display pointer.

3. Enter your initialization routine, call XInitExtension, and if it succeeds, store the pointer returned into this array. Make sure to establish a close display handler to allow you to zero the entry. Do whatever other initialization your extension requires (for example, install event handlers, and so on). Your initialization routine would normally return a pointer to the XExtCodes structure for this extension, which is what would normally be found in your array of pointers.

4. After returning from your initialization routine, the stub can now continue normally, because it has its major opcode safely in hand in the XExtCodes structure.

Extensions

D
The *basecalc* Application

This appendix lists the complete source code for the basecalc application described in Chapter 12. Source code is available on high-density PC floppies for those who want to run this application. See the Preface for ordering information.

D
The basecalc Application

The X Programmer's Calculator (*basecalc*) was described in Chapter 12, *A Complete Application*.

This appendix presents the complete code for *basecalc*, including the following files and routines that were not shown in Chapter 12.

basecalc.h	include file for this application.
initTty	performs system calls to get users current erase, delete, and interrupt characters.
makePixmap	makes a pixmap from bitmap data, shown and described in Chapter 6, *Drawing Graphics and Text*.
Sprintf	a modified version of the standard C utility sprintf, which doesn't print in binary. Sprintf calls printInBase.
printInBase	composes the string that should be displayed. Called from Sprintf.
convButton	changes the current base and converts a value if any.
digitButton	gets a digit and assigns it to the variable Value.
specButton	clears a digit, an entry, or all, or toggles unsigned mode.
operButton	an operation, either does it or waits for next value and =.
displayVal	calculates appropriate format string for base.
keyToWin	translate a keycode as if a pad had been selected.
winPressed	determines whether pad pressed was a digit, an operator, a conversion, or a special pad.

Example D-1 shows the *basecalc.h* include file. This include file sets up the structures and global variables used in the calculator application.

Example D-1. The complete basecalc.h file

```
/*
 * Window flags
 */
#define WTYP_OPER     0x01       /* Operator, +, -, =, etc */
#define WTYP_DIG      0x02       /* Digit 0 - 9, A - F */
#define WTYP_DISP     0x04       /* Display Window */
#define WTYP_CONV     0x08       /* Converter - hex, oct, dec, bin */
#define WTYP_SPEC     0x10       /* Special, CE, CA, CD */

/*
 * Operators
 */
#define OPR_ADD       1
#define OPR_SUB       2
#define OPR_MUL       3
#define OPR_DIV       4
#define OPR_MOD       5
#define OPR_OR        6
#define OPR_AND       7
#define OPR_XOR       8
#define OPR_SHL       9
#define OPR_SHR       10
#define OPR_CLRE      11
#define OPR_CLRD      12
#define OPR_CLRA      13
#define OPR_ASGN      14
#define OPR_NEG       15
#define OPR_NOT       16
#define OPR_UNS       17

/*
 * Colors
 */
#define    WHITE 0
#define    BLACK 1
#define    DARKGRAY   2
#define    LIGHTGRAY  3

static XrmDatabase commandlineDB, rDB;

int pressedColor =   WHITE;
int unpressedColor = BLACK;
int disabledColor =  LIGHTGRAY;
int displayColor =   WHITE;

char myDisplayName[256];
char *myFontName =   "8x13";

char *calcName;

Display *display;
int screen;
XFontStruct *theFont;
Cursor theCursor;
Window calcWin;
```

```
Window iconWin;
Window dispWin;
Pixmap lgrayPixmap;
Pixmap grayPixmap;
Pixmap IconPixmap;

int foreground;
int background;

GC fgGC;
GC bgGC;

/*
 * Calculator variables
 */
int  Base = 10;            /* default base */
int  winBase;              /* windata offset for current base,
                            * set in initCalc, used in convButton */
int  Digit = 0;
long Value = 0;            /* current pressed value */
long Accum = 0;            /* current results */
Bool Unsigned = True;      /* default for U/S key */
int  lastOpt = OPR_ADD;    /* initial previous operator */
int  calcReset = 0;
char Hexmeasure[] = "  .   .    .    .    .    .   .    ";
char Octmeasure[] = "  .  .    .    .    .    .   .    .  ";


/*
 * Startup options
 */
Bool iconOnly = False;

char Geostr[20];
char iconGeostr[20];


/* Command line options table.  We don't do anything with many of
 * these resources, but the program is ready for expansion */

#define GEOMETRY         "*geometry"
#define ICONGEOMETRY     "*iconGeometry"
#define UNSIGNED         "*unsigned"
#define BASE             "*base"
#define ICONSTARTUP      "*iconStartup"

static int opTableEntries = 25;
static XrmOptionDescRec opTable[] = {
{"=",            GEOMETRY,          XrmoptionIsArg,  (caddr_t) NULL},
{"#",            ICONGEOMETRY,      XrmoptionIsArg,  (caddr_t) NULL},
{"-s",           UNSIGNED,          XrmoptionNoArg,  (caddr_t) "off"},
{"-x",           BASE,              XrmoptionNoArg,  (caddr_t) "16"},
{"-h",           BASE,              XrmoptionNoArg,  (caddr_t) "16"},
{"-d",           BASE,              XrmoptionNoArg,  (caddr_t) "10"},
{"-o",           BASE,              XrmoptionNoArg,  (caddr_t) "8"},
{"-b",           BASE,              XrmoptionNoArg,  (caddr_t) "2"},
```

basecalc
Code

```
{"-background",   "*background",                XrmoptionSepArg, (caddr_t) NULL},
{"-bd",           "*borderColor",               XrmoptionSepArg, (caddr_t) NULL},
{"-bg",           "*background",                XrmoptionSepArg, (caddr_t) NULL},
{"-borderwidth",  "*TopLevelShell.borderWidth", XrmoptionSepArg, (caddr_t) NULL},
{"-bordercolor",  "*borderColor",               XrmoptionSepArg, (caddr_t) NULL},
{"-bw",           "*TopLevelShell.borderWidth", XrmoptionSepArg, (caddr_t) NULL},
{"-display",      ".display",                   XrmoptionSepArg, (caddr_t) NULL},
{"-fg",           "*foreground",                XrmoptionSepArg, (caddr_t) NULL},
{"-fn",           "*font",                      XrmoptionSepArg, (caddr_t) NULL},
{"-font",         "*font",                      XrmoptionSepArg, (caddr_t) NULL},
{"-foreground",   "*foreground",                XrmoptionSepArg, (caddr_t) NULL},
{"-geometry",     ".TopLevelShell.geometry",    XrmoptionSepArg, (caddr_t) NULL},
{"-iconic",       ".TopLevelShell.iconic",      XrmoptionNoArg,  (caddr_t) "on"},
{"-ic",           ICONSTARTUP,                  XrmoptionNoArg,  (caddr_t) "on"},
{"-name",         ".name",                      XrmoptionSepArg, (caddr_t) NULL},
{"-title",        ".TopLevelShell.title",       XrmoptionSepArg, (caddr_t) NULL},
{"-xrm",          NULL,                         XrmoptionResArg, (caddr_t) NULL},
};

/*
 * Keyboard equivalents
 */
struct keyCode {
    int kc_char;
    char *kc_func;
    int kc_len;
} keyCodes[] = {
    { CERASE, "CD", 2 },
#ifdef SysV
    { 027, "CE", 2 },
#else
    { CWERASE, "CE", 2 },
#endif SysV
    { CKILL, "CE", 2 },
    { CINTR, "CA", 2 },
    { 0, 0, 0 },
};
char quitChar = CQUIT;

#include "bitmaps/basecalc.icon"
#include "bitmaps/lgray"
#include "bitmaps/gray"

/*
 * Placement variables
 */
XSizeHints sizehints = {
    PMinSize | PMaxSize | PPosition | PSize | USSize,
    400, 100,        /* x, y */
    300, 139,        /* width, height */
    300, 139,        /* min_width and min_height */
    300, 139,        /* max_width and max_height */
    0, 0,            /* width and height increments, not set */
    0, 0, 0, 0,      /* aspect ratio, not set */
};
```

```
XSizeHints iconsizehints = {
    PMinSize | PMaxSize | PPosition | PSize,
    150, 2,
    icon_width, icon_height,
    icon_width, icon_height,
    icon_width, icon_height,
    0, 0,
    0, 0, 0, 0,
};
XWMHints wmhints = {
    InputHint | StateHint | iconWindowHint,
    False,              /* Why not true? */
    IconicState,        /* starts up as icon */
    0,                  /* icon pixmap - set later */
    0,                  /* icon window - created later */
    150, 2,             /* icon position of icon */
    0,                  /* icon mask pixmap  - not used */
};


/*
 * Configuration of subwindows
 */
typedef struct _opaqueFrame {
    Window self;                    /* window ID, filled in later */
    int x, y;                       /* where to create the window */
    unsigned int width, height;     /* width and height */
} opaqueFrame;


#define NBUTTONS 38
opaqueFrame Buttons[NBUTTONS] = {
    { 0, 3, 5, 292, 18},            /* display area */

    { 0, 10, 35, 19, 18},           /* c d e f */
    { 0, 37, 35, 19, 18},
    { 0, 63, 35, 19, 18},
    { 0, 91, 35, 19, 18},

    { 0, 10, 60, 19, 18},           /* 8 9 a b */
    { 0, 37, 60, 19, 18},
    { 0, 63, 60, 19, 18},
    { 0, 91, 60, 19, 18},

    { 0, 10, 85, 19, 18},           /* 4 5 6 7 */
    { 0, 37, 85, 19, 18},
    { 0, 63, 85, 19, 18},
    { 0, 91, 85, 19, 18},

    { 0, 10, 110, 19, 18},          /* 0 1 2 3 */
    { 0, 37, 110, 19, 18},
    { 0, 63, 110, 19, 18},
    { 0, 91, 110, 19, 18},

    { 0, 261, 110, 28, 18},         /* ca ce, cd, = */
```

basecalc
Code

```
    { 0,  187, 110, 28, 18},
    { 0,  224, 110, 28, 18},
    { 0,  131, 110, 46, 18},

    { 0,  131,  60, 19, 18},            /* + - * / % */
    { 0,  158,  60, 19, 18},
    { 0,  185,  60, 19, 18},
    { 0,  212,  60, 19, 18},
    { 0,  239,  60, 19, 18},

    { 0,  131,  85, 19, 18},            /* | & << >> ^ */
    { 0,  158,  85, 19, 18},
    { 0,  185,  85, 19, 18},
    { 0,  212,  85, 19, 18},
    { 0,  239,  85, 19, 18},

    { 0,  131,  35, 32, 18},            /* hex oct bin dec */
    { 0,  165,  35, 31, 18},
    { 0,  198,  35, 32, 18},
    { 0,  232,  35, 31, 18},

    { 0,  269,  35, 20, 18},            /* UNS */
    { 0,  269,  60, 20, 18},            /* NEG */
    { 0,  269,  85, 20, 18},            /* NOT */
};

struct windata {
    int   color;                       /* color */
    char *text;                        /* pointer to the text string */
    int   x;                           /* x coordinate of text */
    int   y;                           /* y coordinate of text */
    int   value;                       /* 0 - 16 for number, symbol for operator */
    int   type;                        /* number, operator, display */
} windata[NBUTTONS] = {
    { 1, "                    0 ", 2, 3, 0, WTYP_DISP },

    { 0, "C", 5, 3, 12, WTYP_DIG },
    { 0, "D", 5, 3, 13, WTYP_DIG },
    { 0, "E", 5, 3, 14, WTYP_DIG },
    { 0, "F", 5, 3, 15, WTYP_DIG },

    { 0, "8", 5, 3,  8, WTYP_DIG },
    { 0, "9", 5, 3,  9, WTYP_DIG },
    { 0, "A", 5, 3, 10, WTYP_DIG },
    { 0, "B", 5, 3, 11, WTYP_DIG },

    { 0, "4", 5, 3, 4, WTYP_DIG },
    { 0, "5", 5, 3, 5, WTYP_DIG },
    { 0, "6", 5, 3, 6, WTYP_DIG },
    { 0, "7", 5, 3, 7, WTYP_DIG },

    { 0, "0", 5, 3, 0, WTYP_DIG },
    { 0, "1", 5, 3, 1, WTYP_DIG },
    { 0, "2", 5, 3, 2, WTYP_DIG },
    { 0, "3", 5, 3, 3, WTYP_DIG },
```

```
       { 0,  "CA",  6,  3,  OPR_CLRA, WTYP_SPEC },
       { 0,  "CE",  6,  3,  OPR_CLRE, WTYP_SPEC },
       { 0,  "CD",  6,  3,  OPR_CLRD, WTYP_SPEC },
       { 0,  "=",  17,  2,  OPR_ASGN, WTYP_OPER },

       { 0,   "+",  5,  3,  OPR_ADD, WTYP_OPER },
       { 0,   "-",  5,  3,  OPR_SUB, WTYP_OPER },
       { 0,   "*",  5,  4,  OPR_MUL, WTYP_OPER },
       { 0,   "/",  5,  3,  OPR_DIV, WTYP_OPER },
       { 0,   "%",  5,  3,  OPR_MOD, WTYP_OPER },

       { 0,   "|",  5,  3,  OPR_OR,  WTYP_OPER },
       { 0,   "&",  5,  3,  OPR_AND, WTYP_OPER },
       { 0,  ">>",1,  3,  OPR_SHR, WTYP_OPER },
       { 0,  "<<",0,  3,  OPR_SHL, WTYP_OPER },
       { 0,   "^",  5,  3,  OPR_XOR, WTYP_OPER },

       { 0, "HEX",  2,  3,  16, WTYP_CONV },
       { 0, "DEC",  2,  3,  10, WTYP_CONV },
       { 0, "OCT",  2,  3,   8, WTYP_CONV },
       { 0, "BIN",  2,  3,   2, WTYP_CONV },

       { 0,  "U",   5,  3,   OPR_UNS, WTYP_SPEC },
       { 0,  "`",   5,  3,   OPR_NEG, WTYP_OPER },
       { 0,  "~",   5,  3,   OPR_NOT, WTYP_OPER },
};
```

Example D-2 is the complete source for the calculator application described in Chapter 12.

Example D-2. Remaining code for basecalc

```
/*
 * X Version 11 Release 2 Integer Programmer's Calculator
 */
#include <X11/Xatom.h>
#include <X11/Xlib.h>
#include <X11/Xutil.h>
#include <X11/Xresource.h>
#include <X11/cursorfont.h>

#include <stdio.h>
#ifdef SysV
#include <termio.h>
#else
#include <sgtty.h>
#include <sys/ttychars.h>
#endif SysV
#include <ctype.h>
#include <pwd.h>

#include "basecalc.h"
```

basecalc
Code

```
/*
 * Programmer's calculator with
 * number base conversions
 */
main (argc, argv)
int argc;
register char *argv[];
{
     /* so we can use the resource manager data merging functions */
     XrmInitialize();

     /* parse command line first so we can open display, store any
      * options in a database   */
     parseOpenDisp (&argc, argv);

     /* get server defaults, program defaults, .Xdefaults, merge them */
     getUsersDatabase();

     /* merge user defaults and command line options and convert
      * into a form usable by this program */
     mergeOpts ();

     /* load font, make pixmaps, set up arrays of windows */
     initCalc ();

     /* get keyboard settings for interrupt, delete, etc. */
     initTty ();

     /* make a standard cursor */
     makeCursor ();

     /* set standard properties, create and map windows */
     makeWindows (argc, argv);

     /* get events */
     takeEvents ();

     /* bow out gracefully */
     XCloseDisplay(myDisplayName);
     exit (1);
}

static char *GetHomeDir( dest )
char *dest;
{
     int uid;
     extern char *getenv();
     extern int getuid();
     extern struct passwd *getpwuid();
     struct passwd *pw;
     register char *ptr;

     if((ptr = getenv("HOME")) != NULL) {
          (void) strcpy(dest, ptr);
```

```
      } else {
            if((ptr = getenv("USER")) != NULL) {
                  pw = getpwnam(ptr);
            } else {
                  uid = getuid();
                  pw = getpwuid(uid);
            }
            if (pw) {
                  (void) strcpy(dest, pw->pw_dir);
            } else {
                  *dest = ' ';
            }
      }
      return dest;
}



/*
 * Get program's and user's defaults
 */
getUsersDatabase()
{
      XrmDatabase homeDB, serverDB, applicationDB;

      char filenamebuf[1024];
      char *filename = &filenamebuf[0];
      char *environment;
      char *classname = "XCalc";
      char name[255];

      (void) strcpy(name, "/usr/lib/X11/app-defaults/");
      (void) strcat(name, classname);
      /* get application defaults file, if any */
      applicationDB = XrmGetFileDatabase(name);
      (void) XrmMergeDatabases(applicationDB, &rDB);

      /* MERGE server defaults, these are created by xrdb, loaded as a
       * property of the root window when the server initializes, and
       * loaded into the display structure on XOpenDisplay.  If not
       * defined, use .Xdefaults */
      if (display->xdefaults != NULL) {
            serverDB = XrmGetStringDatabase(display->xdefaults);
      } else {
            /* Open .Xdefaults file and merge into existing database */
            (void) GetHomeDir(filename);
            (void) strcat(filename, "/.Xdefaults");

            serverDB = XrmGetFileDatabase(filename);
      }
      XrmMergeDatabases(serverDB, &rDB);

      /* Open XENVIRONMENT file, or if not defined, the ~/.Xdefaults,
       * and merge into existing database */
      if ((environment = getenv("XENVIRONMENT")) == NULL) {
            int len;
```

```
            environment = GetHomeDir(filename);
            (void) strcat(environment, "/.Xdefaults-");
            len = strlen(environment);
            (void) gethostname(environment+len, 1024-len);
    }
    homeDB = XrmGetFileDatabase(environment);
    XrmMergeDatabases(homeDB, &rDB);
}


/*
 * Get command line options
 */
parseOpenDisp (argc, argv)
int *argc;
register char *argv[];
{
    XrmValue value;
    char *str_type[20];

    myDisplayName[0] = ' ';

    XrmParseCommand(&commandlineDB, opTable, opTableEntries, argv[0],
            argc, argv);

    /*
     * Check for any arguments left
     */
    if (*argc != 1) Usage();

    /* get display now, because we need it to get other databases*/
    if (XrmGetResource(commandlineDB, "basecalc.display",
            "Basecalc.Display", str_type, &value)== True) {
        (void) strncpy(myDisplayName, value.addr, (int) value.size);
    }

    /*
     * Open display
     */
    if (!(display = XOpenDisplay(myDisplayName))) {
        (void) fprintf(stderr, "%s: Can't open display '%s'\n",
                argv[0], XDisplayName(myDisplayName));
    exit(1);
    }

    screen = DefaultScreen(display);
}

mergeOpts()
{
    char *str_type[20];
    char buffer[20];
    long flags;
    XrmValue value;
    int x, y, width, height;
```

```
    XColor screen_def;

    /* command line takes precedence over everything */
    XrmMergeDatabases(commandlineDB, &rDB);

    /* get geometry */
    if (XrmGetResource(rDB, "basecalc.geometry", "XCalc.Geometry",
            str_type, &value)== True) {
        (void) strncpy(Geostr, value.addr, (int) value.size);
    } else {
        Geostr[0] = NULL;
    }

    if (XrmGetResource(rDB, "basecalc.iconGeometry",
            "XCalc.IconGeometry", str_type, &value)== True) {
        (void) strncpy(iconGeostr, value.addr, (int) value.size);
    } else {
        iconGeostr[0] = NULL;
    }

    if (XrmGetResource(rDB, "basecalc.signed", "XCalc.Signed",
            str_type, &value)== True)
        if (strncmp(value.addr, "False", (int) value.size) == 0)
            Unsigned = False;

    if (XrmGetResource(rDB, "basecalc.base", "XCalc.Base",
            str_type, &value)== True) {
        (void) strncpy(buffer, value.addr, (int) value.size);
        buffer[value.size] = NULL;
        Base = atoi(buffer);
    } else Base = 10;

    if (XrmGetResource(rDB, "basecalc.foreground",
            "XCalc.Foreground", str_type, &value)== True) {
        (void) strncpy(buffer, value.addr, (int) value.size);
        if (XParseColor(display, DefaultColormapOfScreen(screen), buffer,
            &screen_def) == 0)   {
            (void) fprintf(stderr, "basecalc: fg color \
                    specification %s invalid", buffer);
            foreground = BlackPixel(display, screen);
        }
        foreground = screen_def.pixel;
        /* must allocate this pixel value */
    } else {
        foreground = BlackPixel(display, screen);
    }

    if (XrmGetResource(rDB, "basecalc.background", "XCalc.Background",
            str_type, &value)== True) {
        (void) strncpy(buffer, value.addr, (int) value.size);
        XParseColor(display, DefaultColormapOfScreen(screen),
                buffer, &screen_def);
        background = screen_def.pixel;
        /* must allocate this pixel value */
    } else {
```

```
            background = WhitePixel(display, screen);
    }

    /* iconOnly[0] = NULL; */

/*
 * Get window geometry info
 */
    if (Geostr != NULL) {
        flags = XParseGeometry(Geostr,
            &x, &y, &width, &height);
        if ((WidthValue|HeightValue) & flags)
            Usage ();
        if (XValue & flags) {
            if (XNegative & flags)
                x = DisplayWidth(display, screen) +
                    x - sizehints.width;
            sizehints.flags |= USPosition;
            sizehints.x = x;
        }
        if (YValue & flags) {
            if (YNegative & flags)
                y = DisplayHeight(display, screen) +
                    x - sizehints.width;
            sizehints.flags |= USPosition;
            sizehints.y = y;
        }
    }


/*
 * Get icon geometry info
 */
    if (iconGeostr != NULL) {
        iconGeostr[0] = '=';
        flags = XParseGeometry(iconGeostr,
            &x, &y, &width, &height);
        if ((WidthValue|HeightValue) & flags)
            Usage ();
        if (XValue & flags) {
            if (XNegative & flags)
                x = DisplayWidth(display, screen) +
                    x - iconsizehints.width;
            iconsizehints.flags |= USPosition;
            wmhints.flags |= IconPositionHint;
            wmhints.icon_x = x;
            iconsizehints.x = x;
        }
        if (YValue & flags) {
            if (YNegative & flags)
                y = DisplayHeight(display, screen) +
                    x - iconsizehints.width;
            iconsizehints.flags |= USPosition;
            wmhints.flags |= IconPositionHint;
            wmhints.icon_y = y;
            iconsizehints.y = y;
```

```
                }
        }
}


/*
 * Print message to stderr and exit
 */
Usage ()
    {
    (void) fprintf (stderr,
        "%s: [=+X+Y] [#+X+Y] [-ic] [-s] [-h|x|d|o|b] [<display>]\n",
        calcName ? calcName : "basecalc");
    exit (1);
}


*
* Make a pixmap.
*/
Pixmap
makePixmap(data, width, height)
char *data;
unsigned int width, height;
{
    Pixmap pid;

    pid = XCreatePixmapFromBitmapData(display,
                DefaultRootWindow(display), data,
                width, height, foreground, background,
                DefaultDepth(display, screen));
    return(pid);
}


/*
 * Initialize calculator options
 */
initCalc ()
{
    register int win;
    register int found = -1;
    XGCValues values;
    extern char lgray_bits[];

    if ((theFont = XLoadQueryFont (display, myFontName)) == NULL) {
        (void) fprintf(stderr, "basecalc: can't open font %s\n", myFontName);
        exit(-1);
    }

/*
 * Make the utility pixmaps
 */
    grayPixmap = makePixmap(gray_bits, gray_width, gray_height);
    lgrayPixmap = makePixmap(lgray_bits, lgray_width, lgray_height);
```

```
/*
 * Make the utility GCs
 */
    values.font = theFont->fid;
    values.foreground = foreground;
    fgGC = XCreateGC(display, DefaultRootWindow(display),
        GCForeground|GCFont, &values);
    values.foreground = background;
    values.function = GXcopy;
    bgGC = XCreateGC(display, DefaultRootWindow(display),
        GCForeground|GCFont|GCFunction, &values);


/*
 * Loop through buttons, setting disabled buttons
 * to Color Light Gray. Also, find the window
 * which corresponds to the starting dsplay base.
 * Also add ascent to y position of text.
 */
    for (win = 1; win < NBUTTONS; win++) {
        if (windata[win].type == WTYP_CONV &&
                windata[win].value == Base) {
            found = win;
        } else
            if (windata[win].type == WTYP_DIG &&
                windata[win].value >= Base) {
                windata[win].color = disabledColor;
            }
            else
                if (windata[win].type == WTYP_SPEC &&
                    windata[win].value == OPR_UNS) {
                    if (Unsigned)
                        windata[win].text = "U";
                    else
                        windata[win].text = "S";
                    windata[win].color = pressedColor;
                }
                else
                    windata[win].color = unpressedColor;
        windata[win].y += theFont->max_bounds.ascent;
    }
    windata[0].y += theFont->max_bounds.ascent;
    if (found >= 0) {
        winBase = found;
        windata[found].color = pressedColor;
    } else {
        (void) fprintf(stderr, "basecalc: can't use base %d\n", Base);
        exit(-1);
    }
    windata[0].color = displayColor;
}
```

Example D-2. Remaining code for basecalc (continued)

```
/*
 * Get the user's tty special chars
 * This is currently 4.2 specific.
 */
initTty ()
{
      register struct keyCode *keyCodePtr;
      register int fd;
#ifdef SysV
      struct termio term;
#else
      struct sgttyb tty;
      struct tchars tchars;
      struct ltchars ltchars;
#endif SysV

      if (!isatty(0)) {
            if ((fd = open ("/dev/console", 0)) < 0)
                  return;
      } else
            fd = 0;
#ifdef SysV
      (void) ioctl  (fd, TCGETA,   &term);
#else
      (void) ioctl  (fd, TIOCGETP, &tty);
      (void) ioctl  (fd, TIOCGETC, &tchars);
      (void) ioctl  (fd, TIOCGLTC, &ltchars);
#endif SysV
      if (fd)
            (void) close (fd);

      keyCodePtr = keyCodes;
#ifdef SysV
      keyCodePtr++->kc_char = term.c_cc[VERASE];
      keyCodePtr++;
      keyCodePtr++->kc_char = term.c_cc[VKILL];
      keyCodePtr->kc_char = term.c_cc[VINTR];
      quitChar = term.c_cc[VQUIT];
#else
      keyCodePtr++->kc_char = tty.sg_erase;
      keyCodePtr++->kc_char = ltchars.t_werasc;
      keyCodePtr++->kc_char = tty.sg_kill;
      keyCodePtr->kc_char = tchars.t_intrc;
      quitChar = tchars.t_quitc;
#endif SysV
}


/*
 * Make the cursor
 */
makeCursor ()
{
      theCursor = XCreateFontCursor (display, XC_hand1);
}
```

The basecalc Application

basecalc Code

475

```
/*
 * Set up the selection of events
 */
InitEvents ()
{
     int win;

     XSelectInput (display, calcWin, KeyPressMask|KeyReleaseMask);
     XSelectInput (display, dispWin, ExposureMask);
     for (win = 1; win < NBUTTONS; win++)
          XSelectInput (display, Buttons[win].self,
               ExposureMask|
               ButtonPressMask|ButtonReleaseMask|
               EnterWindowMask|LeaveWindowMask);
}


/*
 * Get events and process them
 */
takeEvents ()
{
     XEvent Event;
     register int win;
     register int Pressed = 0;
     register int inWindow = 0;
     char buffer[10];
     register char *keyChars = buffer;
     register int wasKeyDown = 0;
     unsigned i, nbytes;

     while (1) {
          if (!wasKeyDown)
               XNextEvent (display, &Event);
          else
               Event.type = KeyRelease;

     /*
      * Map keyboard events
      * to Window Events
      */
          if (Event.type == KeyPress || Event.type == KeyRelease) {
               nbytes = XLookupString (&Event, buffer,
                    sizeof(buffer), NULL, NULL);
               if (Event.type == KeyPress) {
                    Event.type = ButtonPress;
                    wasKeyDown = 1;
               } else {
                    for (i=0; i<60000; i++)
                         ;
                    Event.type = ButtonRelease;
               }
               if ((Event.xbutton.window =
```

```
                    keyToWin (keyChars, nbytes)) == None){
                      wasKeyDown = 0;
                      continue;
                }
        }
        for (win=0; win < NBUTTONS; win++)
            if (Buttons[win].self == Event.xbutton.window)
                break;
        switch (Event.type) {
        case ButtonPress:
            if (windata[win].color == disabledColor)
                break;
            Pressed = win;
            if (!wasKeyDown)
                inWindow = 1;
            windata[win].color = pressedColor;
            drawButton (win, 0);
            break;
        case LeaveNotify:
            if (Pressed != win)
                break;
            inWindow = 0;
            windata[win].color = unpressedColor;
            drawButton (win, 0);
            break;
        case EnterNotify:
            if (Pressed != win)
                break;
            inWindow = 1;
            windata[win].color = pressedColor;
            drawButton (win, 0);
            break;
        case ButtonRelease:
            if (windata[win].color == disabledColor ||
                Pressed != win) {
                  wasKeyDown = 0;
                  break;
            }
            Pressed = 0;
            windata[win].color = unpressedColor;
                if (wasKeyDown || inWindow)
                winPressed (win);
            wasKeyDown = 0;
            inWindow = 0;
            drawButton (win, 0);
            break;
        case Expose:
            drawButton (win, 1);
            break;
        }
        XFlush(display);
    }
}
```

basecalc
Code

```
/*
 * Make the calculator windows
 */
makeWindows (argc, argv)
int argc;
char *argv[];
{
    register int i;
    XSetWindowAttributes attributes;

/*
 * Define the border and background for the main window.
 * - Black border and a patterned background.
 */
    attributes.border_pixel = foreground;
    attributes.background_pixmap = grayPixmap;
    /*
     * Create the main window (calculator frame) as a
     * child of the Root Window
     */
    attributes.cursor = theCursor;
    calcWin = XCreateWindow(display, DefaultRootWindow(display),
        sizehints.x, sizehints.y, sizehints.width, sizehints.height,
        1, DefaultDepth(display, screen), InputOutput,
        CopyFromParent, CWBorderPixel|CWBackPixmap|CWCursor,
        &attributes);
    XSetStandardProperties (display, calcWin, "basecalc", NULL,
        NULL, argv, argc, &sizehints);

    /*
     * Create the icon window and associate it with the calculator
     */
    IconPixmap = makePixmap(icon_bits, icon_width, icon_height);
    attributes.border_pixel = foreground;
    attributes.background_pixmap = IconPixmap;
    iconWin = XCreateWindow(display, DefaultRootWindow(display),
        iconsizehints.x, iconsizehints.y,
        iconsizehints.width, iconsizehints.height,
        1, DefaultDepth(display, screen), InputOutput,
        CopyFromParent, CWBorderPixel|CWBackPixmap,
        &attributes);
    wmhints.icon_window = iconWin;
    wmhints.initial_state = iconOnly ? IconicState : NormalState;
    XSetWMHints(display, calcWin, &wmhints);

/*
 * Create the buttons as subwindows
 */
    attributes.background_pixmap = lgrayPixmap;
    attributes.border_pixel = foreground;
    for (i = 0; i < NBUTTONS; i++)
        switch (windata[i].color) {
        case WHITE:
            Buttons[i].self = XCreateSimpleWindow(display, calcWin,
                Buttons[i].x, Buttons[i].y,
```

```
                        Buttons[i].width, Buttons[i].height,
                        1, foreground, background);
                break;
        case BLACK:
                Buttons[i].self = XCreateSimpleWindow(display, calcWin,
                        Buttons[i].x, Buttons[i].y,
                        Buttons[i].width, Buttons[i].height,
                        1, background, foreground);
                break;
        case LIGHTGRAY:
                Buttons[i].self = XCreateWindow(display, calcWin,
                        Buttons[i].x, Buttons[i].y,
                        Buttons[i].width, Buttons[i].height,
                        1, CopyFromParent, InputOutput, CopyFromParent,
                        CWBorderPixel|CWBackPixmap, &attributes);
                break;
        }

    /*
     * The display window is distinctive
     */
    dispWin = Buttons[0].self;

    /*
     * Initialize event catching
     */
    InitEvents ();

    /*
     * Map the calculator and subwindows
     */
    XMapSubwindows(display, calcWin);
    XMapWindow(display, calcWin);
}


/*
 * Draw a single button with its text
 */
drawButton (win, exposeEvent)
register int win;
{
    register char *string;
    register int x, y;
    struct windata *winp;
    char *Measure;
    XSetWindowAttributes attributes;
    unsigned long valuemask;
    GC gc;

    winp = &windata[win];
    x = winp->x;
    y = winp->y;
    string = winp->text;
```

basecalc
Code

```
        switch (windata[win].color) {
        case WHITE:
                gc = fgGC;
                attributes.background_pixel = background;
                attributes.border_pixel = foreground;
                valuemask = CWBackPixel|CWBorderPixel;
                break;
        case BLACK:
                gc = bgGC;
                attributes.background_pixel = foreground;
                attributes.border_pixel = background;
                valuemask = CWBackPixel|CWBorderPixel;
                break;
        case LIGHTGRAY:
                gc = bgGC;
                attributes.background_pixmap = lgrayPixmap;
                attributes.border_pixel = foreground;
                valuemask = CWBackPixmap|CWBorderPixel;
                break;
        }
        if (!exposeEvent){
                XChangeWindowAttributes(display, Buttons[win].self,
                        valuemask, &attributes);
                XClearWindow(display, Buttons[win].self);
        }
        XDrawString (display, Buttons[win].self, gc, x, y, string, strlen (string));
        if (win == 0) {
                switch (Base) {
                case 10:
                case 8:
                        Measure = Octmeasure;
                        break;
                default:
                case 16:
                case  2:
                        Measure = Hexmeasure;
                        break;
                }
                XDrawString (display, dispWin, gc, 7, 6, Measure, 31);
        }
}


static unsigned int lastDisp = 1;
/*
 * Do the operation corresponding to a key press
 */
winPressed (win)
{
        register int type;

        type = windata[win].type;
        switch (type) {
        case WTYP_CONV:
                convButton (win);
```

```
            displayVal (lastDisp == 1 ? Value : Accum);
            break;
    case WTYP_DIG:
            digitButton (win);
            displayVal (Value);
            lastDisp = 1;
            break;
    case WTYP_OPER:
            if (operButton (win) == 0) {
                    displayVal (Accum);
                    lastDisp = 2;
            } else {
                    displayVal (Value);
                    lastDisp = 1;
            }
            break;
    case WTYP_SPEC:
            specButton (win);
            displayVal (lastDisp == 1 ? Value : Accum);
            lastDisp = 1;
    }
}


/*
 * Handle a conversion button
 */
convButton (win)
{
    register int i, newBase, Diff, Digit;
    register int HiBase, lowBase;

    newBase = windata[win].value;
    windata[winBase].color = unpressedColor;
    drawButton (winBase, 0);
    windata[win].color = pressedColor;

    Diff = newBase - Base;
    if (Diff) {
        if (newBase > Base) {
            lowBase = Base;
            HiBase = newBase;
        } else {
            lowBase = newBase;
            HiBase = Base;
        }
        for (i = 1; i < NBUTTONS; i++) {
            if (windata[i].type == WTYP_DIG) {
                    Digit = windata[i].value;
                    if (Digit >= lowBase && Digit < HiBase) {
                        if (Diff < 0)
                                windata[i].color = disabledColor;
                        else
                                windata[i].color = unpressedColor;
                        drawButton (i, 0);
```

basecalc
Code

```
                        }
                    }
                }
        }
        winBase = win;
        Base = newBase;
}


/*
 * Handle a digit button
 */
digitButton (win)
{
        register unsigned long Temp;

        if (calcReset) {
                calcReset = 0;
                Accum = 0;
                Value = 0;
                lastOpt = OPR_ADD;
        }
        Digit = windata[win].value;
        if (Unsigned)
                Temp = (unsigned)Value * (unsigned)Base + Digit;
        else
                Temp = Value * Base + Digit;
        if ((unsigned)Temp/Base != (unsigned)Value) {   /* OverfLow? */
        /*
         * Flash the display since the character didn't register
         */
                windata[0].color =
                        (displayColor == WHITE) ? BLACK : WHITE;
                drawButton (0, 0);
                XFlush(display);
                Delay ();
                windata[0].color = displayColor;
                drawButton (0, 0);
                return;
        }
        Value = Temp;
}


/*
 * Handle a special operator
 */
specButton (win)
{
        register int oper;

        oper = windata[win].value;

        switch (oper) {
        case OPR_CLRD:
```

```
            if (lastOpt == OPR_ASGN)
                break;
            Value = (unsigned)Value / Base;
            break;
    case OPR_CLRE:
            Value = 0;
            break;
    case OPR_CLRA:
            Accum = 0;
            Value = 0;
            lastOpt = OPR_ADD;
            break;
    case OPR_UNS:
            Unsigned = !Unsigned;
            windata[win].text = Unsigned ? "U" : "S";
            windata[win].color = pressedColor;
            drawButton (win, 0);
            break;
    }
}


/*
 * Handle an operator
 */
operButton (win)
{
    register int oper;

    oper = lastOpt;
    lastOpt = windata[win].value;

    calcReset = 0;
    switch (lastOpt) {
        case OPR_NEG:
                Value = -Value;
                if ((lastOpt = oper) == OPR_ASGN)
                        Accum = Value;
                return 1;
        case OPR_NOT:
                Value = ~Value;
                if ((lastOpt = oper) == OPR_ASGN)
                    Accum = Value;
                return 1;
    }

    switch (oper) {
        case OPR_ADD:
                if (Unsigned)
                        Accum = (unsigned)Accum + (unsigned)Value;
                else
                        Accum += Value;
                break;
        case OPR_SUB:
                if (Unsigned)
```

```
                              Accum = (unsigned)Accum - (unsigned)Value;
                    else
                              Accum -= Value;
                    break;
            case OPR_MUL:
                    if (Unsigned)
                              Accum = (unsigned)Accum * (unsigned)Value;
                    else
                              Accum *= Value;
                    break;
            case OPR_DIV:
                    if (Value == 0)
                              break;
                    if (Unsigned)
                              Accum = (unsigned)Accum / (unsigned)Value;
                    else
                              Accum /= Value;
                    break;
            case OPR_MOD:
                    if (Unsigned)
                              Accum = (unsigned)Accum % (unsigned)Value;
                    else
                              Accum %= Value;
                    break;
            case OPR_OR:
                    Accum |= Value;
                    break;
            case OPR_AND:
                    Accum &= Value;
                    break;
            case OPR_SHR:
                    if (Unsigned)
                              Accum = (unsigned)Accum >> (unsigned)Value;
                    else
                              Accum >>= Value;
                    break;
            case OPR_SHL:
                    if (Unsigned)
                              Accum = (unsigned)Accum << (unsigned)Value;
                    else
                              Accum <<= Value;
                    break;
            case OPR_XOR:
                    Accum ^= Value;
                    break;
            case OPR_ASGN:
                    break;
    }
    if (lastOpt == OPR_ASGN) {
        Value = Accum;
        calcReset = 1;
        return 1;
    }
    Value = 0;
    return 0;
```

```
}


/*
 * Display a number in the display window
 */
displayVal (number)
register long number;
{
     register char *Fmt;
     register char *cp;
     register int i;

     switch (Base) {
     case 16:
          Fmt = "%32x";
          break;
     case 10:
          Fmt = "%32d";
          break;
     case 8:
          Fmt = "%32o";
          break;
     case 2:
          Fmt = "%032b";
          break;
     }
     cp = windata[0].text;
     for (i=32; --i >= 0; )
          *cp++ = ' ';
     *cp = ' ';
     Sprintf (windata[0].text, Fmt, number);
     drawButton (0, 0);
}


/*
 * Translate a key code to a corresponding window
 */
keyToWin (str, n)
register char *str;
register unsigned n;
{
     register int value = -1;
     register struct keyCode *keyCodePtr;
     register char ch;
     register int i;

     if (n > 0) {
          ch = *str;
          if (islower(ch) && isxdigit(ch))
               value = 10 + ch - 'a';
          else
               if (isdigit(ch))
                    value = ch - '0';
```

basecalc
Code

```
        if (value >= 0) {
            for (i = 1; i < NBUTTONS; i++)
                if (windata[i].type == WTYP_DIG &&
                    windata[i].value == value)
                    return Buttons[i].self;
        } else {
        /*
         * Do some translations - these should be driven
         * from the user's terminal erase, kill, etc
         */
            switch (ch) {
            case 'U':
                if (Unsigned)
                    return -1;
                str = "S";
                n = 1;
                break;
            case 'S':
                if (!Unsigned)
                    return -1;
                str = "U";
                n = 1;
                break;
            case ' '
            case '\n':
                str = "=";
                n = 1;
                break;
            default:
                if (ch == quitChar) {
                    XCloseDisplay(myDisplayName);
                    exit (1);
                }
                keyCodePtr = keyCodes;
                while ((n = keyCodePtr->kc_len) > 0) {
                    if (ch == keyCodePtr->kc_char) {
                        str = keyCodePtr->kc_func;
                        break;
                    }
                    keyCodePtr++;
                }
                if (n == 0)
                    n = 1;
                break;
            }
            for (i = 1; i < NBUTTONS; i++) {
                if (windata[i].type != WTYP_DIG &&
                    strncmp (windata[i].text, str, (int) n) == 0)
                    return Buttons[i].self;
            }
        }
    }
    return None;
}
```

```
/*
 * Specialized version of C Library sprintf.
 *
 * %s %c %u %d (==%u) %o %x %b (binary) are recognized.
 * %0W... - where 0 means pad with zeros otherwise blanks
 *        - if W, the minimum field width is larger than
 *        - the number
 */
Sprintf(cp, fmt, x1)
register char *cp;
register char *fmt;
unsigned x1;
{
     register int c, b, sign;
     register unsigned int     *adx;
     register char    *s;
     register unsigned short fw;
     char *printInBase();
     char pad;

     adx = &x1;
loop:
     while ((c = *fmt++) != '%') {
          if (c == ' ') {
               *cp = c;
               return;
          }
          *cp++ = c;
     }
     c = *fmt++;
     if (c == '0') {
          pad = '0';
          c = *fmt++;
     } else
          pad = ' ';

     /*
      * Calculate minimum field width
      */
     fw = 0;
     while (c >= '0' && c <= '9') {
          fw = fw * 10 + (c - '0');
          c = *fmt++;
     }
     switch (c) {
     case 's':
          s = (char *)*adx;
          while (c = *s++)
               *cp++ = c;
          break;
     case 'c':
          c = (int)*adx;
          *cp++ = c;
          break;
```

```
    default:
        sign = 0;
        switch (c) {
        case 'x':
            b = 16;
            break;
        case 'd':
            if (!Unsigned)
                sign = 1;
        case 'u':
            b = 10;
            break;
        case 'o':
            b = 8;
            break;
        case 'b':
            b = 2;
            break;
        default:
        /*
         * Unknown format
         */
            b = 0;
            break;
        }
        if (b)
            cp = printInBase (cp, (long)*adx, b, fw, pad, sign);
        break;
    }
    adx++;
    goto loop;
}

/*
 * Print a number n in base b into string cp.
 * Minimum field width = fw, pad character = pad
 */
char *
printInBase (cp, n, b, fw, pad, sign)
register char *cp;
register long n;
register b;
register int fw, pad;
{
    register i, nd, c;
    int   flag;
    int   plmax;
    char d[33];

    c = 1;
    if (sign)
        flag = n < 0;
    else
        flag = 0;
    if (flag)
```

```
            n = (-n);
    if (b==2)
            plmax = 32;
    else if (b==8)
            plmax = 11;
    else if (b==10)
            plmax = 10;
    else if (b==16)
            plmax = 8;
    if (b==10) {
            if (flag == 0)
                    sign = 0;
            flag = 0;
    }
    for (i=0;i<plmax;i++) {
            if (flag == 0)
                    nd = (unsigned)n%b;
            else
                    nd = n%b;
            if (flag) {
                    nd = (b - 1) - nd + c;
                    if (nd >= b) {
                            nd -= b;
                            c = 1;
                    } else
                            c = 0;
            }
            d[i] = nd;
            if (flag == 0)
                    n = (unsigned)n/b;
            else
                    n = n/b;
            if ((n==0) && (flag==0))
                    break;
    }
    if (i==plmax)
            i--;
    if (sign) {
            fw--;
            if (pad == '0')
                    *cp++ = '-';
    }
    if (fw > i+1) {
            for (fw -= i+1; fw > 0; fw--)
                    *cp++ = pad;
    }
    if (sign && pad != '0')
            *cp++ = '-';
    for (;i>=0;i--)
            *cp++ = "0123456789ABCDEF"[d[i]];
    *cp = ' ';
    return cp;
}
```

basecalc
Code

Example D-2. Remaining code for basecalc (continued)

```
/*
 * Delay a little while
 */
Delay ()
{
    int tic;

    for (tic = 0; tic < 50000; tic++)
        ;
}
```

E
Event Reference

This appendix provides a detailed description of each event type, in a reference page format. The information provided here is essential for a full understanding of the events, how they are selected and propogated, and the intricacies of their operation.

In This Chapter:

In This Chapter (continued):

Event Reference

This appendix describes each event structure in detail and briefly shows how each event type is used. It covers the most common uses of each event type, the information contained in each event structure, how the event is selected, and the side effects of the event, if any. Each event is described on a separate reference page.

Meaning of Common Structure Elements

Example E-1 shows the `XEvent` union and a simple event structure that is one member of the union. Several of the members of this structure are present in nearly every event structure. They are described here before we go into the event-specific members (see also Section 8.2.2).

Example E-1. XEvent union and XAnyEvent structure

```
typedef union _XEvent {
    int type;                  /* must not be changed; first member */
    XAnyEvent xany;
    XButtonEvent xbutton;
    XCirculateEvent xcirculate;
    XCirculateRequestEvent xcirculaterequest;
    XClientMessageEvent xclient;
    XColormapEvent xcolormap;
    XConfigureEvent xconfigure;
    XConfigureRequestEvent xconfigurerequest;
    XCreateWindowEvent xcreatewindow;
    XDestroyWindowEvent xdestroywindow;
    XCrossingEvent xcrossing;
    XExposeEvent xexpose;
    XFocusChangeEvent xfocus;
    XNoExposeEvent xnoexpose;
    XGraphicsExposeEvent xgraphicsexpose;
    XGravityEvent xgravity;
    XKeymapEvent xkeymap;
    XKeyEvent xkey;
    XMapEvent xmap;
    XUnmapEvent xunmap;
    XMappingEvent xmapping;
    XMapRequestEvent xmaprequest;
```

```
    XMotionEvent xmotion;
    XPropertyEvent xproperty;
    XReparentEvent xreparent;
    XResizeRequestEvent xresizerequest;
    XSelectionClearEvent xselectionclear;
    XSelectionEvent xselection;
    XSelectionRequestEvent xselectionrequest;
    XVisibilityEvent xvisibility;
} XEvent;

typedef struct {
    int type;
    unsigned long serial;/* # of last request processed by server */
    Bool send_event;       /* true if this came from SendEvent request */
    Display *display;      /* display the event was read from */
    Window window;         /* window on which event was requested in
                            * event mask */
} XAnyEvent;
```

The first member of the XEvent union is the type of event. When an event is received (with XNextEvent, for example), the application checks the type member in the XEvent union. Then the specific event type is known. and the specific event structure (such as xbutton) is used to access information specific to that event type.

Before the branching depending on the event type, only the XEvent union is used. After the branching, only the event structure which contains the specific information for each event type should be used in each branch. For example, if the XEvent union were called report, the report.xexpose structure should be used within the branch for Expose events.

You'll notice that each event structure also begins with a type member. This member is rarely used, since it is an identical copy of the type member in the XEvent union.

Most event structures also have a window member. The only ones that don't are selection events (SelectionNotify, SelectionRequest, and SelectionClear) and events selected by the graphics_exposures member of the GC (GraphicsExpose and NoExpose). The window member indicates the event window that selected and received the event. This is the window where the event arrives if it has propagated through the hierarchy as described in Section 8.3.2. One event type may have two different meanings to an application, depending on which window it appears in.

Many of the event structures also have a display and/or root member. The display member identifies the connection to the server that is active. The root member indicates which screen the window that received the event is linked to in the hierarchy. Most programs only use a single screen and therefore don't need to worry about the root member. The display member can be useful since you can pass the display variable into routines by simply passing a pointer to the event structure, eliminating the need for a separate display argument.

All event structures include a `serial` member, that gives the number of the last protocol request processed by the server. This is useful in debugging, since an error can be detected by the server but not reported to the user (or programmer) until the next routine that gets an event. That means several routines may execute successfully after the error occurs. The last request processed will often indicate the request that contained the error.

All event structures also include a `send_event` flag, which if `True` indicates that the event was sent by `XSendEvent` (i.e., by another client rather than by the server).

The following pages describe each event type in detail. The events are presented in alphabetical order, each on a separate page. Each page describes the circumstances under which the event is generated, the mask used to select it, the structure itself, its members, and useful programming notes. Note that the description of the structure members does not include those members common to many structures. If you need more information on these members, please refer to this introductory section.

ButtonPress, ButtonRelease

When Generated

There are two types of pointer button events: `ButtonPress` and `ButtonRelease`. Both contain the same information.

Select With

May be selected separately, using `ButtonPressMask` and `ButtonReleaseMask`.

XEvent Structure Name

```
typedef union _XEvent {
    . . .
    XButtonEvent xbutton;
    . . .
} XEvent;
```

Event Structure

```
typedef struct {
    int type;              /* of event */
    unsigned long serial;  /* # of last request processed by server */
    Bool send_event;       /* true if this came from a SendEvent request */
    Display *display;      /* display the event was read from */
    Window window;         /* event window it is reported relative to */
    Window root;           /* root window that the event occurred under */
    Window subwindow;      /* child window */
    Time time;             /* when event occurred, in milliseconds */
    int x, y;              /* pointer coords relative to receiving window */
    int x_root, y_root;    /* coordinates relative to root */
    unsigned int state;    /* mask of all buttons and modifier keys */
    unsigned int button;   /* button that triggered event */
    Bool same_screen;      /* same screen flag */
} XButtonEvent;
typedef XButtonEvent XButtonPressedEvent;
typedef XButtonEvent XButtonReleasedEvent;
```

Event Structure Members

subwindow   If the source window is the child of the receiving window, then the `subwindow` member is set to the ID of that child.

time   The server time when the button event occurred, in milliseconds. `Time` is declared as `unsigned long`, so it wraps around when it reaches the maximum value of a 32 bit number (every 49.7 days).

x, y   If the receiving window is on the same screen as the root window specified by `root`, then `x` and `y` are the pointer coordinates relative to the receiving window's origin. Otherwise, `x` and `y` are zero.

When active button grabs and pointer grabs are in effect (see Section 9.4), the coordinates relative to the receiving window may not be within the window (they may be negative or greater than window height or width).

`x_root, y_root`
> The pointer coordinates relative to the root window which is an ancestor of the event window. If the pointer was on a different screen, these are zero.

`state`
> The state of all the buttons and modifier keys just before the event, represented by a mask of the button and modifier key symbols: `Button1Mask`, `Button2Mask`, `Button3Mask`, `Button4Mask`, `Button5Mask`, `Shift-Mask`, `ControlMask`, `LockMask`, `Mod1Mask`, `Mod2Mask`, `Mod3Mask`, `Mod4Mask`, and `Mod5Mask`. If a modifier key is pressed and released when no other modifier keys are held, the `ButtonPress` will have a `state` member of 0 and the `ButtonRelease` will have a nonzero `state` member indicating that itself was held just before the event.

`button`
> A value indicating which button changed state to trigger this event. One of the constants: `Button1`, `Button2`, `Button3`, `Button4`, or `Button5`.

`same_screen`
> Indicates whether the pointer is currently on the same screen as this window. This is always `True` unless the pointer was actively grabbed before the automatic grab could take place.

Notes

Unless an active grab already exists, or a passive grab on the button combination that was pressed already exists at a higher level in the hierarchy than where the `ButtonPress` occured, an automatic active grab of the pointer takes place when a `ButtonPress` occurs. Because of the automatic grab, the matching `ButtonRelease` is sent to the same application that received the `ButtonPress` event. If `OwnerGrabButtonMask` has been selected, the `ButtonRelease` event is delivered to the window which contained the pointer when the button was released, as long as that window belongs to the same client as the window in which the `ButtonPress` event occurred. If the `ButtonRelease` occurs outside or the client's windows, or `OwnerGrabButtonMask` was not selected, the `ButtonRelease` is delivcred to the window in which the `ButtonPress` occurred. The grab is terminated when all buttons are released. During the grab, the cursor associated with the grabbing window will track the pointer anywhere on the screen.

If the application has invoked a passive button grab on an ancestor of the window in which the `ButtonPress` event occurs, then that grab takes precedence over the automatic grab, and the `ButtonRelease` will go to that window, or it will be handled normally by that client depending on the `owner_events` flag in the `XGrabButton` call.

CirculateNotify

When Generated

CirculateNotify events are generated when a window is actually restacked from a call to either XCirculateWindowUp or XCirculateWindowDown. If the window manager prevents such an operation, then no XCirculateNotify event is generated.

Select With

This event type is selected using StructureNotifyMask in the XSelectInput call for the window to be raised, or by selecting SubstructureNotifyMask for the parent of the window to be raised.

XEvent Structure Name

```
typedef union _XEvent {
    . . .
    XCirculateEvent xcirculate;
    . . .
} XEvent;
```

Event Structure

```
typedef struct {
    int type;
    unsigned long serial;/* # of last request processed by server */
    Bool send_event;        /* true if this came from SendEvent request */
    Display *display;       /* display the event was read from */
    Window event;
    Window window;
    int place;              /* PlaceOnTop, PlaceOnBottom */
} XCirculateEvent;
```

Event Structure Members

event   The window receiving the event. If the event was selected by Structure-NotifyMask, event will be the same as window. If the event was selected by SubstructureNotifyMask, event will be the parent of window.

window   The window that was restacked.

place   Either PlaceOnTop or PlaceOnBottom. Indicates whether the window was raised to the top or bottom of the stack.

CirculateRequest

When Generated

CirculateRequest events report when another client calls XCirculateSubwindows, XCirculateSubwindowsUp or XCirculateSubwindowsDown for a specified parent window, and the stacking order is actually changed. If this event type is selected, the window is not moved in the stacking order. This gives the client that selects this event (usually the window manager) the opportunity to review the request in the light of its window management policy, before executing the circulate request itself, or deny the request.

Select With

This event type is selected for the parent window with the SubstructureRedirectMask.

XEvent Structure Name

```
typedef union _XEvent {
    . . .
    XCirculateRequestEvent xcirculaterequest;
    . . .
} XEvent;
```

Event Structure

```
typedef struct {
    int type;
    unsigned long serial;/* # of last request processed by server */
    Bool send_event;        /* true if this came from SendEvent request */
    Display *display;       /* display the event was read from */
    Window parent;
    Window window;
    int place;              /* PlaceOnTop, PlaceOnBottom */
} XCirculateRequestEvent;
```

Event Structure Members

parent   The parent of the window that was restacked. This is the window that selected the event.

window   The window being restacked.

place   PlaceOnTop or PlaceOnBottom. Indicates whether the window was to be placed on top or on the bottom of the stacking order.

ClientMessage

When Generated

ClientMessage events are generated only when a client calls the function XSendEvent. Any type of event can be sent with XSendEvent, but it will be distinguished from normal events by the the send_event member being set to True. If your program wants to be able to treat events sent with XSendEvent as different from normal events, you can read this member.

Select With

There is no event mask for ClientMessage events and they are not selected with XSelectInput. Instead, XSendEvent directs them to a specific window, which is given as a window ID: the PointerWindow or the InputFocus.

XEvent Structure Name

```
typedef union _XEvent {
    ...
    XClientMessageEvent xclient;
    ...
} XEvent;
```

Event Structure

```
typedef struct {
    int type;
    unsigned long serial;/* # of last request processed by server */
    Bool send_event;      /* true if this came from SendEvent request */
    Display *display;     /* display the event was read from */
    Window window;
    Atom message_type;
    int format;
    union {
        char b[20];
        short s[10];
        int l[5];
    } data;
} XClientMessageEvent;
```

Event Structure Members

message_type
> An atom that specifies how the data is to be interpreted by the receiving client. The X server places no interpretation on the type or the data, but it must be a list of 8-bit, 16-bit, or 32-bit quantities, so that the X server can correctly swap bytes as necessary. The data always consists of twenty 8-bit values, ten 16-bit values, or five 32-bit values, although each particular message might not make use of all of these values.

format
> Specifies the format of the property specified by message_type. This will be on of the values 8, 16, or 32.

ColormapNotify

When Generated

ColormapNotify events herald changes relating to the colormap specified in the colormap attribute for a particular window, or changes to the attribute itself.

Select With

To receive this event type, pass ColormapChangeMask to XSelectInput.

XEvent Structure Name

```
typedef union _XEvent {
    ...
    XColormapEvent xcolormap;
    ...
} XEvent;
```

Event Structure

```
typedef struct {
    int type;
    unsigned long serial;/* # of last request processed by server */
    Bool send_event;      /* true if this came from SendEvent request */
    Display *display;     /* display the event was read from */
    Window window;
    Colormap colormap;    /* Colormap or None */
    Bool new;
    int state;            /* ColormapInstalled, ColormapUninstalled */
} XColormapEvent;
```

Event Structure Members

window   The window whose associated colormap or attribute changes.

colormap   The colormap associated with the window, either a colormap ID or the constant None. It will be None only if this event was generated due to an XFree-Colormap call.

new   True when the colormap attribute has been changed, or False when the colormap is installed or uninstalled.

state   Either ColormapInstalled or ColormapUninstalled; it indicates whether the colormap is installed or uninstalled.

When Generated

ConfigureNotify events announce actual changes to a window's configuration (size, position, border, stacking order).

Select With

To receive this event type for a single window, specify the window ID of that window and pass StructureNotifyMask as the event_mask argument to XSelectInput. To receive this event for all children of a window, specify the parent window ID and pass SubstructureNotifyMask.

XEvent Structure Name

```
typedef union _XEvent {
    . . .
    XConfigureEvent xconfigure;
    . . .
} XEvent;
```

Event Structure

```
typedef struct {
    int type;
    unsigned long serial;/* # of last request processed by server */
    Bool send_event;      /* true if this came from SendEvent request */
    Display *display;      /* display the event was read from */
    Window event;
    Window window;
    int x, y;
    int width, height;
    int border_width;
    Window above;
    Bool override_redirect;
} XConfigureEvent;
```

Event Structure Members

event   The window that selected the event. The event and window members are identical if the event was selected with StructureNotifyMask.

window   The window whose configuration was changed.

x, y   The final coordinates of the reconfigured window relative to its parent.

width, height
     The width and height in pixels of the window after reconfiguration.

border_width
     The width in pixels of the border after reconfiguration.

above   If this member is None, then the window is on the bottom of the stack with respect to its siblings. Otherwise, the window is immediately on top of the specified sibling window.

override_redirect
The override_redirect attribute of the reconfigured window. If True, it indicates that the client wants this window to be immune to interception by the window manager of configuration requests. Window managers normally should ignore this event if override_redirect is True.

ConfigureRequest

When Generated

`ConfigureRequest` events announce another client's attempt to change a window's size, position, border, and/or stacking order. The X server generates this event type when another client attempts to reconfigure the window with `XConfigureWindow` or another configuration control function. If this event type is selected, the window is not reconfigured. This gives the client that selects this event (usually the window manager) the opportunity to revise the requested configuration before executing the `XConfigureWindow` request itself, or to deny the request.

Select With

To receive this event type for any window in a group of children, specify the parent window and pass `SubstructureRedirectMask` to `XSelectInput`.

XEvent Structure Name

```
typedef union _XEvent {
    . . .
    XConfigureRequestEvent xconfigurerequest;
    . . .
} XEvent;
```

Event Structure

```
typedef struct {
    int type;
    unsigned long serial;/* # of last request processed by server */
    Bool send_event;      /* true if this came from SendEvent request */
    Display *display;     /* display the event was read from */
    Window parent;
    Window window;
    int x, y;
    int width, height;
    int border_width;
    Window above;
    int detail;           /* Above, Below, TopIf, BottomIf, Opposite */
    unsigned long value_mask;
} XConfigureRequestEvent;
```

Event Structure Members

parent   The window that selected the event. This is the parent of the window being configured.

window   The window that is being configured.

x, y   The requested position for the upper-left pixel of the window's border relative to the origin of the parent window.

width, height
    The requested width and height in pixels for the window.

border_width

        The requested border width for the window.

above   None, Above, Below, TopIf, BottomIf, or Opposite. Specifies the sibling window on top of which the specified window should be placed. If this member has the constant None, then the specified window should be placed on the bottom.

Notes

The geometry is derived from the XConfigureWindow request that triggered the event.

CreateNotify

When Generated

The X server reports CreateNotify events to clients when windows are created.

Select With

To receive this event type on children of a window, specify the parent window ID and pass SubstructureNotifyMask. Note that this event type cannot selected by Structure-NotifyMask.

XEvent Structure Name

```
typedef union _XEvent {
    ...
    XCreateWindowEvent xcreatewindow;
    ...
} XEvent;
```

Event Structure

```
typedef struct {
    int type;
    unsigned long serial;/* # of last request processed by server */
    Bool send_event;       /* true if this came from SendEvent request */
    Display *display;      /* display the event was read from */
    Window parent;         /* parent of the window */
    Window window;         /* window ID of window created */
    int x, y;              /* window location */
    int width, height;     /* size of window */
    int border_width;      /* border width */
    Bool override_redirect;   /* creation should be overridden */
} XCreateWindowEvent;
```

Event Structure Members

parent   The ID of the created window's parent.

window   The ID of the created window.

x, y   The coordinates of the created window relative to its parent.

width, height   The width and height in pixels of the created window.

border_width   The width in pixels of the border of the created window.

override_redirect

The override_redirect attribute of the created window. If True, it indicates that the client wants this window to be immune to interception by the window manager of configuration requests. Window managers normally should ignore this event if override_redirect is True.

Notes

For descriptions of these members, see the XCreateWindow function and the XSet-WindowAttributes structure.

DestroyNotify

When Generated

`DestroyNotify` events announce that a window has been destroyed.

Select With

To receive this event type on children of a window, specify the parent window ID and pass `SubstructureNotifyMask` as part of the *event_mask* argument to `XSelectInput`. This event type cannot be selected with `StructureNotifyMask`.

XEvent Structure Name

```
typedef union _XEvent {
    ...
    XDestroyWindowEvent xdestroywindow;
    ...
} XEvent;
```

Event Structure

```
typedef struct {
    int type;
    unsigned long serial;/* # of last request processed by server */
    Bool send_event;       /* true if this came from SendEvent request */
    Display *display;      /* display the event was read from */
    Window event;
    Window window;
} XDestroyWindowEvent;
```

Event Structure Members

event   The window that selected the event.

window   The window that was destroyed.

EnterNotify, LeaveNotify

When Generated

`EnterNotify` and `LeaveNotify` events occur when the pointer enters or leaves a window.

When the pointer crosses a window border, a `LeaveNotify` event occurs in the window being left and an `EnterNotify` event occurs in the window being entered. Whether or not each event is queued for any application depends on whether any application selected the right event on the window in which it occured.

In addition, `EnterNotify` and `LeaveNotify` events are delivered to windows that are *virtually crossed*. These are windows that are between the origin and destination windows in the hierarchy but not on the screen. Further explanation of virtual crossing is provided two pages following.

Select With

Each of these events can be selected separately with `XEnterWindowMask` and `XLeaveWindowMask`.

XEvent Structure Name

```
typedef union _XEvent {
    ...
    XCrossingEvent xcrossing;
    ...
} XEvent;
```

Event Structure

```
typedef struct {
    int type;               /* of event */
    unsigned long serial;   /* # of last request processed by server */
    Bool send_event;        /* true if this came from SendEvent request */
    Display *display;       /* display the event was read from */
    Window window;          /* event window it is reported relative to */
    Window root;            /* root window that the event occurred on */
    Window subwindow;       /* child window */
    Time time;              /* milliseconds */
    int x, y;               /* pointer x, y coordinates in receiving window */
    int x_root, y_root;     /* coordinates relative to root */
    int mode;               /* NotifyNormal, NotifyGrab, NotifyUngrab */
    int detail;             /* NotifyAncestor, NotifyVirtual, NotifyInferior,
                             * NotifyNonLinear, NotifyNonLinearVirtual */
    Bool same_screen;       /* same screen flag */
    Bool focus;             /* Boolean focus */
    unsigned int state;     /* key or button mask */
} XCrossingEvent;
typedef XCrossingEvent XEnterWindowEvent;
typedef XCrossingEvent XLeaveWindowEvent;
```

Event Structure Members

The following list describes the members of the `XCrossingEvent` structure.

`subwindow`   In a `LeaveNotify` event, if the pointer began in a child of the receiving window then the `child` member is set to the window ID of the child. Otherwise, it is set to `None`. For an `EnterNotify` event, if the pointer ends up in a child of the receiving window then the `child` member is set to the window ID of the child. Otherwise, it is set to `None`.

`time`   The server time when the crossing event occurred, in milliseconds. `Time` is declared as `unsigned long`, so it wraps around when it reaches the maximum value of a 32 bit number (every 49.7 days).

`x, y`   The point of entry or exit of the pointer relative to the event window.

`x_root, y_root`
    The point of entry or exit of the pointer relative to the root window.

`mode`   Normal crossing events or those caused by pointer warps have mode `NotifyNormal`; events caused by a grab have mode `NotifyGrab`; and events caused by a released grab have mode `NotifyUngrab`.

`detail`   The value of the `detail` member depends on the hierarchical relationship between the origin and destination windows and the direction of pointer transfer. Determining which windows receive events and with which `detail` members is quite complicated. This topic is described in the next section.

`same_screen`
    Indicates whether the pointer is currently on the same screen as this window. This is always `True` unless the pointer was actively grabbed before the automatic grab could take place.

`focus`   If the receiving window is the focus window or a descendant of the focus window, the `focus` member is `True`; otherwise it is `False`.

`state`   The state of all the buttons and modifier keys just before the event, represented by a mask of the button and modifier key symbols: `Button1Mask`, `Button2Mask`, `Button3Mask`, `Button4Mask`, `Button5Mask`, `ShiftMask`, `ControlMask`, `LockMask`, `Mod1Mask`, `Mod2Mask`, `Mod3Mask`, `Mod4Mask`, and `Mod5Mask`.

Virtual Crossing and the detail Member

Virtual crossing occurs when the pointer moves between two windows that do not have a parent-child relationship. Windows between the origin and destination windows in the hierarchy receive `EnterNotify` and `LeaveNotify` events. The `detail` member of each of these events depends on the hierarchical relationship of the origin and destination windows and the direction of pointer transfer.

Virtual crossing is an advanced topic that you shouldn't spend time figuring out unless you have an important reason to use it. I have never seen an application that uses this feature, and I know of no reason for its extreme complexity. With that word of warning, proceed.

Let's say the pointer has moved from one window, the origin, to another, the destination. First we'll specify what types of events each window gets, and then the detail member of each of those events.

The window of origin receives a `LeaveNotify` event and the destination window receives an `EnterNotify` event, if they have requested this type of event. If one is an inferior of the other, the `detail` member of the event received by the inferior is `NotifyAncestor` and the detail of the event received by the superior is `NotifyInferior`. If the crossing is between parent and child, these are the only events generated.

However, if the origin and destination windows are not parent and child, other windows are *virtually crossed* and also receive events. If neither window is an ancestor of the other, ancestors of each window up to but not including the least common ancestor receive `LeaveNotify` events if they are in the same branch of the hierarchy as the origin and `EnterNotify` events if they are in the same branch as the destination. These events can be used to track the motion of the pointer through the hierarchy.

- In the case of a crossing between a parent and a child of a child, the middle child receives a `LeaveNotify` with detail `NotifyVirtual`.

- In the case of a crossing between a child and the parent of its parent, the middle child receives a `EnterNotify` with detail `NotifyVirtual`.

- In a crossing between windows whose least common ancestor is two or more windows away, both the origin and destination windows receive events with detail `NotifyNonlinear`. The windows between the origin and the destination in the hierarchy, up to but not including their least common ancestor, receive events with detail `NotifyNonlinearVirtual`. The least common ancestor is the lowest window from which both are descendants.

- If the origin and destination windows are on separate screens, the events and details generated are the same as for two windows not parent and child, except that the root windows of the two screens are considered the least common ancestor. Both root windows also receive events.

Table E-1 shows the event types generated by a pointer crossing from window *A* to window *B* when window *C* is the least common ancestor of *A* and *B*.

Table E-1. Border Crossing Events and Window Relationship

LeaveNotify	EnterNotify
Origin window (*A*)	Destination window (*B*)
Windows between *A* and *B* exclusive if *A* is inferior	Windows between *A* and *B* exclusive if *B* is inferior
Windows between *A* and *C* exclusive	Windows between *B* and *C* exclusive
Root window on screen of origin if different from screen of destination	Root window on screen of destination if different from screen of origin

Table E-2 lists the `detail` members in events generated by a pointer crossing from window *A* to window *B*.

Table E-2. Event detail Member and Window Relationship

detail Flag	Window Delivered To
NotifyAncestor	Origin or destination when either is descendant
NotifyInferior	Origin or destination when either is ancestor
NotifyVirtual	Windows between *A* and *B* exclusive if either is descendant
NotifyNonlinear	Origin and destination when *A* and *B* are two or more windows distant from least common ancestor *C*
NotifyNonlinearVirtual	Windows between *A* and *C* exclusive and between *B* and *C* exclusive when *A* and *B* have least common ancestor *C*. Also on both root windows if *A* and *B* are on different screens.

For example, Figure E-1 shows the events that are generated by a movement from a window (window *A*) to a child (window *B1*) of a sibling (window *B*). This would generate three events: a LeaveNotify with detail NotifyNonlinear for the window *A*, an EnterNotify with detail NotifyNonlinearVirtual for its sibling window *B*, and an EnterNotify with detail NotifyNonlinear for the child (window *B1*).

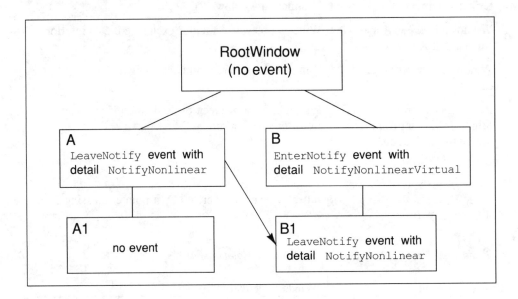

Figure E-1. Events generated by a move between windows

EnterNotify and LeaveNotify events are also generated when the pointer is grabbed, if the pointer was not already inside the grabbing window. In this case, the grabbing window receives an EnterNotify and the window containing the pointer receives a LeaveNotify event, both with mode NotifyUngrab. The pointer position in both events is the position before the grab. The result when the grab is released is exactly the same except that the two windows receive EnterNotify instead of LeaveNotify and vice versa.

Figure E-2 demonstrates the events and details caused by various pointer transitions, indicated by heavy arrows.

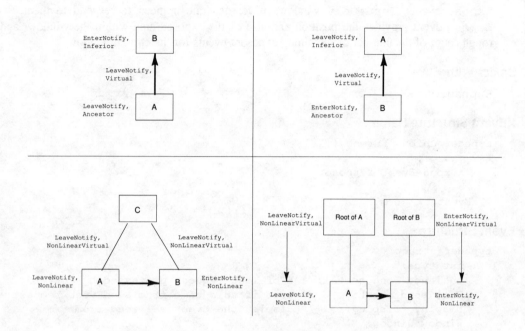

Figure E-2. Border crossing events and detail member for pointer movement from window A to window B, for various window relationships

Expose

When Generated

Expose events are generated when a window becomes visible or a previously invisible part of a window becomes visible. Only InputOutput windows generate or need to respond to Expose events; InputOnly windows never generate or need to respond to them. The Expose event provides the position and size of the exposed area within the window, and a rough count of the number of remaining exposure events for the current window.

Select With

ExposureMask

XEvent Structure Name

```
typedef union _XEvent {
    ...
    XExposeEvent xexpose;
    ...
} XEvent;
```

Event Structure

```
typedef struct {
    int type;
    unsigned long serial;/* # of last request processed by server */
    Bool send_event;       /* true if this came from SendEvent request */
    Display *display;      /* display the event was read from */
    Window window;
    int x, y;
    int width, height;
    int count;             /* if nonzero, at least this many more */
} XExposeEvent;
```

Event Structure Members

x, y   The coordinates of the upper-left corner of the exposed region relative to the origin of the window.

width, height   The width and height in pixels of the exposed region.

count   The approximate number of remaining contiguous Expose events that were generated as a result of a single function call.

Notes

A single action such as a window movement or a function call can generate several exposure events on one window or on several windows. The server guarantees that all exposure events generated from a single action will be sent contiguously, so that they can all be handled before moving on to other event types. This allows an application to keep track of the rectangles specified in contiguous Expose events, set the clip_mask in a GC to the areas specified in the rectangle using XSetRegion or XSetClipRectangles, and then finally redraw the window clipped with the GC in a single operation after all the Expose events have arrived.

The last event to arrive is indicated by a `count` of 0. In Release 2, `XUnionRectWith-Region` can be used to add the rectangle in `Expose` events to a region before calling `XSet-Region`.

If your application is able to redraw partial windows, you can also read each exposure event in turn and redraw each area.

FocusIn, FocusOut

When Generated

`FocusIn` and `FocusOut` events occur when the keyboard focus window changes, as a result of an `XSetInputFocus` call. They are much like `EnterNotify` and `LeaveNotify` events except that they track the focus rather than the pointer.

Select With

`FocusIn` and `FocusOut` events are selected with `FocusChangeMask`. They cannot be selected separately.

XEvent Structure Name

```
typedef union _XEvent {
    . . .
    XFocusChangeEvent xfocus;
    . . .
} XEvent;
```

Event Structure

```
typedef struct {
    int type;               /* FocusIn or FocusOut */
    unsigned long serial;   /* # of last request processed by server */
    Bool send_event;        /* true if this came from SendEvent request */
    Display *display;       /* display the event was read from */
    Window window;          /* window of event */
    int mode;               /* NotifyNormal, NotifyGrab, NotifyUngrab */
    int detail;             /* NotifyAncestor, NotifyVirtual, Notify-
                             * Inferior, NotifyNonLinear, NotifyNonLinear-
                             * Virtual, NotifyPointer, NotifyPointerRoot,
                             * NotifyDetailNone */
} XFocusChangeEvent;
typedef XFocusChangeEvent XFocusInEvent;
typedef XFocusChangeEvent XFocusOutEvent;
```

Event Structure Members

mode   For events generated when the keyboard is not grabbed, mode is `Notify-Normal`; when the keyboard is grabbed, mode is `NotifyGrab`; and when a keyboard is ungrabbed, mode is `NotifyUngrab`.

detail The `detail` member identifies the relationship between the window that receives the event and the origin and destination windows. It will be described in detail after the description of which windows get what types of events.

Notes

The *keyboard focus* is a window that has been designated as the one to receive all keyboard input irrespective of the pointer position. Only the keyboard focus window and its descendants receive keyboard events. By default, the focus window is the root window. Since all windows are descendants of the root, the pointer controls the window that receives input.

Most window managers allow the user to set a focus window, to avoid the problem where the pointer sometimes gets bumped into the wrong window and your typing doesn't go to the intended window. If the pointer is pointing at the root window, all typing is usually lost since there is no application for this input to propagate to. Some applications may set the keyboard focus so that they can get all keyboard input for a given period of time, but this practice is not encouraged.

Focus events are used when an application wants to act differently when the keyboard focus is set to another window or to itself. `FocusChangeMask` is used to select `FocusIn` and `FocusOut` events.

`FocusOut` events are delivered to the old focus window and `FocusIn` events to the window which receives the focus. Windows in between in the hierarchy are virtually crossed and receive focus change events depending on the relationship and direction of transfer between the origin and destination windows. Some or all of the windows between the window containing the pointer at the time of the focus change and that window's root can also receive focus change events. By checking the `detail` member of `FocusIn` and `FocusOut` events, an application can tell which of its windows can receive input.

The `detail` member gives clues about the relationship of the event receiving window to the origin and destination of the focus. The `detail` member of `FocusOut` and `FocusIn` events is analogous to the `detail` member of `LeaveNotify` and `EnterNotify` events, but with even more permutations to make life complicated.

Virtual Focus Crossing and the detail Member

We will now embark on specifying the types of events sent to each window and the `detail` member in each event, depending on the relative position in the hierarchy of the origin window (old focus), destination window (new focus), and the pointer window (window containing pointer at time of focus change). Don't even try to figure this out unless you have to.

Table E-3 shows the event types generated by a focus transition from window A to window B when window C is the least common ancestor of A and B, and P is the window containing the pointer. This table includes most of the events generated, but not all of them. It is quite possible for a single window to receive more than one focus change event from a single focus change.

Table E-3. FocusIn and FocusOut Events and Window Relationship

FocusOut	FocusIn
origin window (A)	destination window (B)
windows between A and B exclusive if A is inferior	windows between A and B exclusive if B is inferior
windows between A and C exclusive	windows between B and C exclusive
root window on screen of origin if different from screen of destination	root window on screen of destination if different from screen of origin
pointer window up to but not including origin window if pointer window is descendant of origin	pointer window up to but not including destination window if pointer window is descendant of destination
pointer window up to and including pointer window's root if transfer was from `PointerRoot`	pointer window up to and including pointer window's root if transfer was to `PointerRoot`

Table E-4 lists the detail members in events generated by a focus transition from window *A* to window *B*, with *P* being the window containing the pointer.

Table E-4. Event detail Member and Window Relationship

detail Flag	Window Delivered To
NotifyAncestor	Origin or destination when either is descendant
NotifyInferior	Origin or destination when either is ancestor
NotifyVirtual	Windows between *A* and *B* exclusive if either is descendant
NotifyNonlinear	Origin and destination when *A* and *B* are two or more windows distant from least common ancestor *C*
NotifyNonlinearVirtual	Windows between *A* and *C* exclusive and between *B* and *C* exclusive when *A* and *B* have least common ancestor *C*. Also on both root windows if *A* and *B* are on different screens
NotifyPointer	Window *P* and windows up to but not including the origin or destination windows
NotifyPointerRoot	Window *P* and all windows up to its root, and all other roots, when focus is set to or from Pointer-Root
NotifyNone	All roots, when focus is set to or from None

The following two pages show all the possible combinations of focus transitions and of origin, destination, and pointer windows and shows the types of events that are generated and their detail member. Solid lines indicate branches of the hierarchy. Dotted arrows indicate the direction of transition of the focus. At each end of this arrow are the origin and destination windows, windows *A* to *B*. Arrows ending in a bar indicate that the event type and detail described are delivered to all windows up to the bar.

In any branch, there may be windows that are not shown. Windows in a single branch between two boxes shown will get the event types and details shown beside the branch.

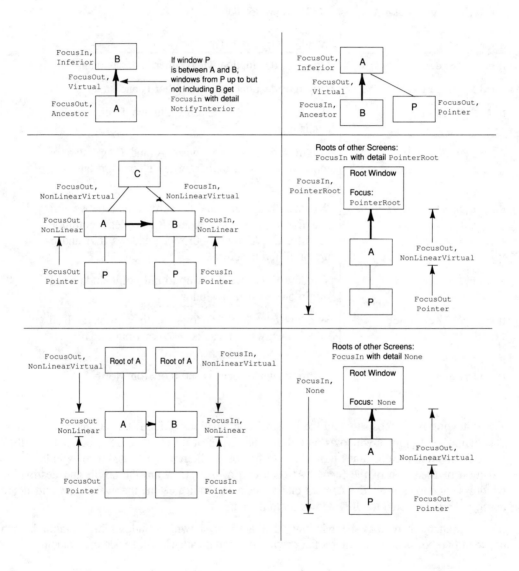

Figure E-3. FocusIn and FocusOut event schematics

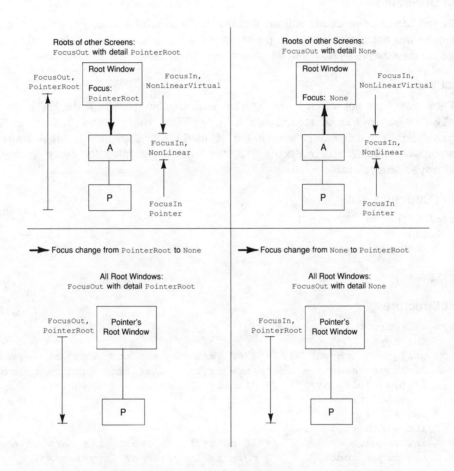

Figure E-3. FocusIn and FocusOut event schematics (cont'd)

FocusIn and FocusOut events are also generated when the keyboard is grabbed, if the focus was not already assigned to the grabbing window. In this case, all windows receive events as if the focus was set from the current focus to the grab window. When the grab is released, the events generated are just as if the focus was set back.

When Generated

GraphicsExpose events indicate that the source area for a XCopyArea or XCopyPlane request was not available because it was outside the source window or obscured by a window. NoExpose events indicate that the source region was completely available.

Select With

These events are not selected with XSelectInput, but are sent if the GC in the XCopy-Area or XCopyPlane request had its graphics_exposures flag set to True. If graphics_exposures is True in the GC used for the copy, either one NoExpose event or one or more GraphicsExpose events will be generated for every XCopyArea or XCopyPlane call made.

XEvent Structure Name

```
typedef union _XEvent {
    ...
    XNoExposeEvent xnoexpose;
    ...
} XEvent;
```

Event Structure

```
typedef struct {
    int type;
    unsigned long serial;/* # of last request processed by server */
    Bool send_event;       /* true if this came from SendEvent request */
    Display *display;      /* display the event was read from */
    Drawable drawable;
    int x, y;
    int width, height;
    int count;             /* if nonzero, at least this many more */
    int major_code;        /* core is CopyArea or CopyPlane */
    int minor_code;        /* not defined in the core */
} XGraphicsExposeEvent;

typedef struct {
    int type;
    unsigned long serial;/* # of last request processed by server */
    Bool send_event;       /* true if this came from SendEvent request */
    Display *display;      /* display the event was read from */
    Drawable drawable;
    int major_code;        /* core is CopyArea or CopyPlane */
    int minor_code;        /* not defined in the core */
} XNoExposeEvent;
```

Event Structure Members

drawable   A window or an off-screen pixmap. This specifies the destination of the graphics request that generated the event.

x, y   The coordinates of the upper-left corner of the exposed region relative to the origin of the window.

width, height The width and height in pixels of the exposed region.

count   The approximate number of remaining contiguous GraphicsExpose events that were generated as a result of the XCopyArea or XCopyPlane call.

major_code   The graphics request used. This may be one of the symbols CopyArea or CopyPlane, or a symbol defined by a loaded extension.

minor_code   Zero unless the request is part of an extension.

Notes

Expose events and GraphicsExpose events both indicate the region of a window that was actually exposed (x, y, width, and height). Therefore they can often be handled similarly.

When Generated

GravityNotify events report when a window is moved because of a change in the size of its parent. This happens when the win_gravity attribute of the child window is something other than StaticGravity or UnmapGravity.

Select With

To receive this event type for a single window, specify the window ID of that window and use StructureNotifyMask as part of the event_mask argument to XSelectInput. To receive notification of movement due to gravity for a group of siblings, specify the parent window ID and use SubstructureNotifyMask.

XEvent Structure Name

```
typedef union _XEvent {
    ...
    XGravityEvent xgravity;
    ...
} XEvent;
```

Event Structure

```
typedef struct {
    int type;
    unsigned long serial;/* # of last request processed by server */
    Bool send_event;      /* true if this came from SendEvent request */
    Display *display;     /* display the event was read from */
    Window event;
    Window window;
    int x, y;
} XGravityEvent;
```

Event Structure Members

event   The window that selected the event.

window   The window that was moved.

x, y   The new coordinates of the window relative to its parent.

KeymapNotify

When Generated

KeymapNotify events are reported immediately after EnterNotify or FocusIn events.

This is a way for the application to read the keyboard state as the application is "woken up," since the two triggering events usually indicate that the application is about to receive user input.

Select With

KeymapStateMask

XEvent Structure Name

```
typedef union _XEvent {
    . . .
    XKeymapEvent xkeymap;
    . . .
} XEvent;
```

Event Structure

```
typedef struct {
    int type;
    unsigned long serial;/* # of last request processed by server */
    Bool send_event;      /* true if this came from SendEvent request */
    Display *display;     /* display the event was read from */
    Window window;
    char key_vector[32];
} XKeymapEvent;
```

Event Structure Members

window   Reports the window which was reported in the window member of the preceeding EnterNotify or FocusIn event.

key_vector A bit vector or mask, each bit representing one physical key, with a total of 256 bits. For a given key, its keycode is its position in the keyboard vector. You can also get this bit vector by calling XQueryKeymap.

Notes

The serial member of KeymapNotify does not contain the serial number of the most recent Protocol Request processed, because this event always follows immediately after FocusIn or EnterNotify events in which the serial member is valid.

KeyPress, KeyRelease

When Generated

KeyPress and KeyRelease events are generated for all keys, even those mapped to modifier keys such as Shift or Control.

Select With

Each type of keyboard event may be selected separately with KeyPressMask and Key-ReleaseMask.

XEvent Structure Name

```
typedef union _XEvent {
    ...
    XKeyEvent xkey;
    ...
} XEvent;
```

Event Structure

```
typedef struct {
    int type;               /* of event */
    unsigned long serial;   /* # of last request processed by server */
    Bool send_event;        /* true if this came from SendEvent request */
    Display *display;       /* display the event was read from */
    Window window;          /* event window it is reported relative to */
    Window root;            /* root window that the event occurred on */
    Window subwindow;       /* child window */
    Time time;              /* milliseconds */
    int x, y;               /* pointer coords relative to receiving window */
    int x_root, y_root;     /* coordinates relative to root */
    unsigned int state;     /* modifier key and button mask */
    unsigned int keycode;   /* server-dependent code for key */
    Bool same_screen;       /* same screen flag */
} XKeyEvent;
typedef XKeyEvent XKeyPressedEvent;
typedef XKeyEvent XKeyReleasedEvent;
```

Event Structure Members

subwindow   If the source window is the child of the receiving window, then the subwindow member is set to the ID of that child.

time   The server time when the button event occurred, in milliseconds. Time is declared as unsigned long, so it wraps around when it reaches the maximum value of a 32-bit number (every 49.7 days).

x, y   If the receiving window is on the same screen as the root window specified by root, then x and y are the pointer coordinates relative to the receiving window's origin. Otherwise, x and y are zero.

When active button grabs and pointer grabs are in effect (see Section 9.4), the coordinates relative to the receiving window may not be within the window (they may be negative or greater than window height or width).

x_root, y_root
: The pointer coordinates relative to the root window which is an ancestor of the event window. If the pointer was on a different screen, these are zero.

state
: The state of all the buttons and modifier keys just before the event, represented by a mask of the button and modifier key symbols: `Button1Mask`, `Button2Mask`, `Button3Mask`, `Button4Mask`, `Button5Mask`, `ShiftMask`, `ControlMask`, `LockMask`, `Mod1Mask`, `Mod2Mask`, `Mod3Mask`, `Mod4Mask`, and `Mod5Mask`.

keycode
: The `keycode` member contains a server-dependent code for the key that changed state. As such it should be translated into the portable symbol called a keysym before being used. It can also be converted directly into ASCII with `XLookupString`. For a description and examples of how to translate key-codes, see Section 9.1.1.

Notes

Remember that not all hardware is capable of generating release events, and that only the main keyboard (a-z, A-Z, 0-9), Shift, and Control keys are always found.

Keyboard events are analogous to button events, though of course there are many more keys than buttons, and the keyboard is not automatically grabbed between press and release.

All the structure members have the same meaning as described for `ButtonPress` and `ButtonRelease` events except that `button` is replaced by `keycode`.

When Generated

The X server generates `MapNotify` and `UnmapNotify` events when a window changes state from unmapped to mapped or vice versa.

Select With

To receive these events on a single window, use `StructureNotifyMask` in the call to `XSelectInput` for the window. To receive these events for all children of a particular parent, specify the parent window ID and use `SubstructureNotifyMask`.

XEvent Structure Name

```
typedef union _XEvent {
    . . .
    XMapEvent xmap;
    XUnmapEvent xunmap;
    . . .
} XEvent;
```

Event Structure

```
typedef struct {
    int type;
    unsigned long serial;/* # of last request processed by server */
    Bool send_event;      /* true if this came from SendEvent request */
    Display *display;     /* display the event was read from */
    Window event;
    Window window;
    Bool override_redirect;   /* Boolean, is override set */
} XMapEvent;

typedef struct {
    int type;
    unsigned long serial;/* # of last request processed by server */
    Bool send_event;      /* true if this came from SendEvent request */
    Display *display;     /* display the event was read from */
    Window event;
    Window window;
    Bool from_configure;
} XUnmapEvent;
```

Event Structure Members

`event`   The window that selected this event.

`window`   The window that was just mapped or unmapped.

`override_redirect` (XMapEvent only)
        `True` or `False`. The value of the `override_redirect` attribute of the window that was just mapped.

from_configure (XUnmapEvent only)

> True if the event was generated as a result of a resizing of the window's parent when the window itself had a win_gravity of UnmapGravity. See the description of the win_gravity attribute in Section 4.3.4. False otherwise.

MappingNotify

When Generated

`MappingNotify` events occur when any of the following are changed by another client: the mapping between physical keyboard keys (keycodes) and keysyms; the mapping between modifier keys and logical modifiers; or the mapping between physical and logical pointer buttons. These events are triggered by a call to `XSetModifierMapping` or `XSetPointer-Mapping` if the return status is `MappingSuccess`, or by any call to `ChangeKeyboard-Mapping`.

This event type should not be confused with the event that occurs when a window is mapped; that is a `MapNotify` event. Nor should it be confused with the `KeymapNotify` event, which reports the state of the keyboard as a mask instead of as a keycode.

Select With

The X server sends `MappingNotify` events to all clients. It is never selected, and cannot be masked with the window attributes.

XEvent Structure Name

```
typedef union _XEvent {
    . . .
    XMappingEvent xmapping;
    . . .
} XEvent;
```

Event Structure

```
typedef struct {
    int type;
    unsigned long serial;/* # of last request processed by server */
    Bool send_event;       /* true if this came from SendEvent request */
    Display *display;      /* display the event was read from */
    Window window;         /* unused */
    int request;           /* one of MappingModifier, MappingKeyboard,
                            * MappingPointer */
    int first_keycode;     /* first keycode */
    int count;             /* range of change with first_keycode*/
} XMappingEvent;
```

Event Structure Members

request   The kind of mapping change that occurred: `MappingModifier` for a successful `XSetModifierMapping` (keyboard Shift, Lock, Control, Meta keys), `MappingKeyboard` for a successful `XChangeKeyboardMapping` (other keys), and `MappingPointer` for a successful `XSetPointerMapping` (pointer button numbers).

first_keycode
> If the `request` member is `MappingKeyboard` or `MappingModifier`, then `first_keycode` indicates the first in a range of keycodes with altered mappings. Otherwise it is not set.

count
> If the `request` member is `MappingKeyboard` or `MappingModifier`, then `count` indicates the number of keycodes with altered mappings. Otherwise it is not set.

Notes

If the `request` member is `MappingKeyboard`, clients should call `XRefreshKeyboardMapping`.

The normal response to a `request` member of `MappingPointer` or `MappingModifier` is no action. This is because the clients should use the logical mapping of the buttons and modifiers to allow the user to customize the keyboard if desired. If the application requires a particular mapping regardless of the user's preferences, it should call `XGetModifierMapping` or `XGetPointerMapping` to find out about the new mapping.

MapRequest

When Generated

The X server generates `MapRequest` events when the functions `XMapRaised` and `XMap-Window` are called. If this event type is selected, the window is not mapped. This gives the client that selects this event (usually the window manager) the opportunity to revise the size or position of the window before executing the map request itself, or deny the request.

Select With

To receive this event type, you specify the window ID of the parent of the receiving window and pass `SubstructureRedirectMask` as the `event_mask` argument to `XSelect-Input`. In addition, the `override_redirect` member of the `XSetWindow-Attributes` structure for the specified window must be `False`.

XEvent Structure Name

```
typedef union _XEvent {
    . . .
    XMapRequestEvent xmaprequest;
    . . .
} XEvent;
```

Event Structure

```
typedef struct {
    int type;
    unsigned long serial;/* # of last request processed by server */
    Bool send_event;     /* true if this came from SendEvent request */
    Display *display;    /* display the event was read from */
    Window parent;
    Window window;
} XMapRequestEvent;
```

Event Structure Members

parent   The ID of the parent of the window being mapped.

window   The ID of the window being mapped.

532   Xlib Programming Manual

MotionNotify

When Generated

The X server generates `MotionNotify` events when the user moves the pointer, or when a program warps the pointer to a new position within a single window.

Select With

This event type is selected with `PointerMotionMask`, `PointerMotionHintMask`, `ButtonMotionMask`, `Button1MotionMask`, `Button2MotionMask`, `Button3-MotionMask`, `Button4MotionMask`, and `Button5MotionMask`. These masks determine the specific conditions under which the event is generated. See Section 8.3.3.3 for a description of selecting button events.

XEvent Structure Name

```
typedef union _XEvent {
    ...
    XMotionEvent xmotion;
    ...
} XEvent;
```

Event Structure

```
typedef struct {
    int type;               /* of event */
    unsigned long serial;   /* # of last request processed by server */
    Bool send_event;        /* true if this came from SendEvent request */
    Display *display;       /* display the event was read from */
    Window window;          /* event window it is reported relative to */
    Window root;            /* root window that the event occurred on */
    Window subwindow;       /* child window */
    Time time;              /* milliseconds */
    int x, y;               /* pointer coords relative to receiving window */
    int x_root, y_root;     /* coordinates relative to root */
    unsigned int state;     /* button and modifier key mask */
    char is_hint;           /* is this a motion hint */
    Bool same_screen;       /* same screen flag */
} XMotionEvent;
typedef XMotionEvent XPointerMovedEvent;
```

Event Structure Members

`subwindow` If the source window is the child of the receiving window, then the `subwin-dow` member is set to the ID of that child.

`time` The server time when the button event occurred, in milliseconds. `Time` is declared as `unsigned long`, so it wraps around when it reaches the maximum value of a 32 bit number (every 49.7 days).

`x, y` If the receiving window is on the same screen as the root window specified by `root`, then `x` and `y` are the pointer coordinates relative to the receiving window's origin. Otherwise, `x` and `y` are zero.

When active button grabs and pointer grabs are in effect (see Section 9.4), the coordinates relative to the receiving window may not be within the window (they may be negative or greater than window height or width).

x_root, y_root

The pointer coordinates relative to the root window which is an ancestor of the event window. If the pointer was on a different screen, these are zero.

state   The state of all the buttons and modifier keys just before the event, represented by a mask of the button and modifier key symbols: Button1Mask, Button2Mask, Button3Mask, Button4Mask, Button5Mask, Shift-Mask, ControlMask, LockMask, Mod1Mask, Mod2Mask, Mod3Mask, Mod4Mask, and Mod5Mask.

is_hint   Either the constant NotifyNormal or NotifyHint. NotifyHint indicates that the PointerMotionHintMask was selected. In this case, just one event is sent when the mouse moves, and the current position can be found by calling XQueryPointer, or by examining the motion history buffer with XGetMotionEvents, if a motion history buffer is available on the server. NotifyNormal indicates that the event is real, but it may not be up to date since there may be many more later motion events on the queue.

same_screen

Indicates whether the pointer is currently on the same screen as this window. This is always True unless the pointer was actively grabbed before the automatic grab could take place.

Notes

If the processing you have to do for every motion event is fast, you can probably handle all of them without requiring motion hints. However, if you have extensive processing to do for each one, you might be better off using the hints and calling XQueryPointer or using the history buffer if it exists. XQueryPointer is a round-trip request, so it can be slow.

EnterNotify and LeaveNotify events are generated instead of MotionEvents if the pointer starts and stops in different windows.

PropertyNotify

When Generated

`PropertyNotify` events indicate that a property of a window has changed, or at least that a zero-length append has been done in order to get the X server time.

Select With

They can be selected with `PropertyChangeMask`.

XEvent Structure Name

```
typedef union _XEvent {
    ...
    XPropertyEvent xproperty;
    ...
} XEvent;
```

Event Structure

```
typedef struct {
    int type;
    unsigned long serial;/* # of last request processed by server */
    Bool send_event;       /* true if this came from SendEvent request */
    Display *display;      /* display the event was read from */
    Window window;
    Atom atom;
    Time time;
    int state;             /* NewValue, Deleted */
} XPropertyEvent;
```

Event Structure Members

window   The window whose property was changed, not the window that selected the event.

atom   The property that was changed.

state   Either `PropertyNewValue` or `PropertyDelete`. Whether the property was changed to a new value or deleted.

time   The `time` member specifies the server time when the property was changed.

When Generated

`ReparentNotify` events report information about the changing of a window's parent.

Select With

To receive this event type, specify the window ID of the old or the new parent window and pass `SubstructureNotifyMask` as the `event_mask` argument to `XSelectInput`, or specify the window ID and pass `StructureNotifyMask`.

The X server generates this event type when it reparents the specified window.

XEvent Structure Name

```
typedef union _XEvent {
    . . .
    XReparentEvent xreparent;
    . . .
} XEvent;
```

Event Structure

```
typedef struct {
    int type;
    unsigned long serial; /* # of last request processed by server */
    Bool send_event;       /* true if this came from SendEvent request */
    Display *display;      /* display the event was read from */
    Window event;
    Window window;
    Window parent;
    int x, y;
    Bool override_redirect;
} XReparentEvent;
```

Event Structure Members

`window` the window whose parent window was changed.

`parent` The new parent of the window.

`x, y` the coordinates of the upper-left pixel of the window's border relative to the new parent window's origin.

`override_redirect`
The `override_redirect` attribute of the reparented window. If `True`, it indicates that the client wants this window to be immune to meddling by the window manager. Window managers normally should not have reparented this window to begin with.

ResizeRequest

When Generated

`ResizeRequest` events report another client's attempt to change the size of a window. The X server generates this event type when another client calls `XConfigureWindow`, `XResizeWindow`, or `XMoveResizeWindow`. If this event type is selected, the window is not resized. This gives the client that selects this event (usually the window manager) the opportunity to revise the new size of the window before executing the resize request itself, or to deny the request.

Select With

To receive this event type, specify a window ID and pass `ResizeRedirectMask` as part of the `event_mask` argument to `XSelectInput`. Only one client can select this event on a particular window. When selected, this event is triggered instead of resizing the window.

XEvent Structure Name

```
typedef union _XEvent {
    . . .
    XResizeRequestEvent xresizerequest;
    . . .
} XEvent;
```

Event Structure

```
typedef struct {
    int type;
    unsigned long serial;/* # of last request processed by server */
    Bool send_event;     /* true if this came from SendEvent request */
    Display *display;     /* display the event was read from */
    Window window;
    int width, height;
} XResizeRequestEvent;
```

Event Structure Members

window   The window whose size another client attempted to change.

width, height   The requested size of the window, not including its border.

SelectionClear

When Generated

The X server reports SelectionClear events to the current owner of a selection when a new owner is being defined.

Select With

This event is not selected. It is sent to the previous selection owner when another client calls XSetSelectionOwner for the same selection.

XEvent Structure Name

```
typedef union _XEvent {
    . . .
    XSelectionClearEvent xselectionclear;
    . . .
} XEvent;
```

Event Structure

```
typedef struct {
    int type;
    unsigned long serial;/* # of last request processed by server */
    Bool send_event;      /* true if this came from SendEvent request */
    Display *display;     /* display the event was read from */
    Window window;
    Atom selection;
    Time time;
} XSelectionClearEvent;
```

Event Structure Members

window
    The window that is receiving the event and losing the selection.

selection
    The selection atom specifying the selection that is changing ownership.

time
    The last-change time recorded for the selection.

538   Xlib Programming Manual

When Generated

`SelectionNotify` events are sent only by clients, not by the server. They are sent by calling `XSendEvent`. The owner of a selection sends this event to a requester (a client that calls `XConvertSelection` for a given property) when a selection has been converted and stored as a property, or when a selection conversion could not be performed (indicated with property `None`).

Select With

There is no event mask for `SelectionNotify` events and they are not selected with `XSelectInput`. Instead, `XSendEvent` directs them to a specific window, which is given as a window ID: the `PointerWindow` or the `InputFocus`.

XEvent Structure Name

```
typedef union _XEvent {
    ...
    XSelectionEvent xselection;
    ...
} XEvent;
```

Event Structure

```
typedef struct {
    int type;
    unsigned long serial;/* # of last request processed by server */
    Bool send_event;     /* true if this came from SendEvent request */
    Display *display;     /* display the event was read from */
    Window requester;     /* must be next after type */
    Atom selection;
    Atom target;
    Atom property;        /* Atom or None */
    Time time;
} XSelectionEvent;
```

Event Structure Members

The members of this structure have the values specified in the `XConvertSelection` call that triggers the selection owner to send this event, except that the `property` member will return either the atom specifying a property on the requestor window with the data type specified in `target`, or it will be `None`, which indicates that the data could not be converted into the `target` type.

SelectionRequest

When Generated

SelectionRequest events are sent to the owner of a selection when another client requests the selection by calling XConvertSelection.

Select With

There is no event mask for SelectionRequest events and they are not selected with XSelectInput.

XEvent Structure Name

```
typedef union _XEvent {
    ...
    XSelectionRequestEvent xselectionrequest;
    ...
} XEvent;
```

Event Structure

```
typedef struct {
    int type;
    unsigned long serial;/* # of last request processed by server */
    Bool send_event;        /* true if this came from SendEvent request */
    Display *display;       /* display the event was read from */
    Window owner;           /* must be next after type */
    Window requester;
    Atom selection;
    Atom target;
    Atom property;
    Time time;
} XSelectionRequestEvent;
```

Event Structure Members

The members of this structure have the values specified in the XConvertSelection call that triggers this event.

The owner should convert the selection based on the specified target type, if possible. If a property is specified, the owner should store the result as that property on the requester window, and then send a SelectionNotify event to the requester by calling XSendEvent. If the selection cannot be converted as requested, the owner should send a Selection-Notify event with property set to the constant None.

VisibilityNotify

When Generated

VisibilityNotify events report any change in the visibility of the specified window. This event type is never generated on windows whose class is InputOnly. All of the window's subwindows are ignored when calculating the visibility of the window.

Select With

This event is selected with VisibilityChangeMask.

XEvent Structure Name

```
typedef union _XEvent {
    ...
    XVisibilityEvent xvisibility;
    ...
} XEvent;
```

Event Structure

```
typedef struct {
    int type;
    unsigned long serial;/* # of last request processed by server */
    Bool send_event;      /* true if this came from SendEvent request */
    Display *display;     /* display the event was read from */
    Window window;
    int state;            /* Visibility Unobscured,*/
                          /* Visibility Partially Obscured, or */
                          /* Visibility Obscured */
} XVisibilityEvent;
```

Event Structure Members

state   A symbol indicating the final visibility status of the window: Visibility-Unobscured, VisibilityPartiallyObscured, or Visibility-Obscured.

Notes

Table E-5 lists the transitions that generate VisibilityNotify events and the corresponding state member of the XVisibilityEvent structure.

Table E-5. The State Element of the XVisibilityEvent Structure

Visibility Status Before	Visibility Status After	State Member
Partially obscured, fully obscured, or not viewable	Viewable and completely unobscured	`Visibility-` `    Unobscured`
Viewable and completely unobscured, or not viewable	Viewable and partially obscured	`VisibilityPartially-` `    Obscured`
Viewable and completely unobscured, or viewable and partially obscured, or not viewable	Viewable and partially obscured	`VisibilityPartially-` `    Obscured`

F
Proposed Interclient Communication Conventions

This appendix includes the text of David Rosenthal's preliminary Interclient Communications Conventions Manual, which was released with Release 2 of X. The document is incomplete and provisional; but it was thought better to have people following even these preliminary guidelines than working completely independently. A more complete set of conventions is currently under discussion by the X Consortium, and will be part of Release 3. This document is written in terms of the X protocol rather than Xlib, so that it is also useful for the Lisp interface to X. Protocol request names are in some instances different than Xlib routines. In general, the most powerful Xlib routines have direct analogues in the protocol requests, while several convenience routines map to a single protocol request. For example, statements concerning the XConfigureWindow protocol request apply to XConfigureWindow and all the convenience routines like XMoveWindow, XResizeWindow, etc.

In This Chapter:

In This Chapter (continued):

Proposed Interclient
Communication Conventions[*]

Introduction

It was an explicit design goal of X11 to specify mechanism, not policy. As a result, a client that converses with the server using the protocol defined by the *X Window System Protocol, Version 11* may operate *correctly* in isolation, but may not coexist properly with others sharing the same server.

Being a good citizen in the X11 world involves adhering to conventions governing interclient communications in a number of areas:

- The selection mechanism.

- The cut buffers.

- The window manager.

- The session manager.

- The resource database.

- The manipulation of shared resources.

In the following sections we propose suitable conventions for each area, in so far as it is possible to do so *without* enforcing a particular user interface.

---

* This appendix is a very lightly edited reprint of the draft of David Rosenthal's *Inter-Client Communication Conventions Manual* that was included in the X distribution of Release 2. It describes a proposal for the conventions, and is not final. A version of these conventions is currently being reviewed by the X Consortium. The chief architect of the conventions says that the official conventions will be compatible with the R2 conventions except where it is later found to affect their logical integrity.

Status of the Selection Conventions

Apart from the obvious gaps in the specification of the target and type atom lists, the selection conventions described above have caused little controversy. This may reflect the fact that the selection mechanism is, as yet, little used.

It will obviously take some time for these conventions to obtain formal endorsement, and for the toolkits and clients to be changed to conform.

Peer-to-Peer Communication via Selections

The primary mechanism X11 defines for clients that want to exchange information, for example by cutting and pasting between windows, are *selections*. There can be an arbitrary number of selections, each named by an atom, and they are global to the server. The choice of an atom to be used is discussed later. Each selection is owned by a client, and is attached to a window.

Selections communicate between an *owner* and a *requestor*. The owner has the data representing the value of its selection, and the requestor receives it. A requestor wishing to obtain the value of a selection provides:

• The name of the selection.

• The name of a property.

• A window.

• An atom representing the data type required.

If the selection is currently owned, the owner receives an event, and is expected to:

• Convert the contents of the selection to the requested datatype.

• Place this data in the named property on the named window.

• Send the requestor an event to let it know the property is available.

Clients are strongly encouraged to use this mechanism. In particular, displaying text in a permanent window without providing the ability to select it and convert it into a string is definitely anti-social.

Note that, in the X11 environment, *all* data transferred between an owner and a requestor must normally go via the server. An X11 client cannot assume that another client can open the same files, or even communicate directly. The other client may be talking to the server via a completely different networking mechanism (for example, one client might be DECnet, and the other TCP/IP). Thus, passing indirect references to data such as file names, hostnames and port numbers, and so on is permitted only if both clients specifically agree.

Acquiring Selection Ownership

A client wishing to acquire ownership of a particular selection should call Set-SelectionOwner:

```
SetSelectionOwner
     selection:      Atom
     owner:          Window or None
     time:           Time or CurrentTime
```

The client should set *selection* to the Atom representing the selection, set *owner* to some Window, that it created and set *time* to some time between the current last-change time of the selection concerned, and the current server time. This time value will normally be obtained from the timestamp of the event triggering the acquisition of the selection. Clients should *not* set the time value to CurrentTime, since if they do so they have no way of finding when they gained ownership of the selection. Clients must use a window they created, since SendEvent will be used with an empty mask to reply.

> Convention: *Clients attempting to acquire a selection must set the time value of the* SetSelectionOwner *request to the timestamp of the event triggering the acquisition attempt, not to* CurrentTime. *A zero-length append to a property is a way to obtain a timestamp for this purpose; the timestamp is in the corresponding* PropertyNotify *event.*

Note that if the time in the SetSelectionOwner request is in the future relative to the server's current time, or if it is in the past relative to the last time the selection concerned changed hands, the SetSelectionOwner request appears to the client to succeed, but ownership is *not* actually transferred.

> Convention: *Clients are normally expected to provide some visible confirmation of selection ownership. To make this feedback reliable, a client must perform the sequence:*

```
XSetSelectionOwner(dpy, seln, own, time);
if (XGetSelectionOwner(dpy, seln) != own) {
    /* We didn't get the selection */
```

If the SetSelectionOwner request succeeds (not merely appears to suceed), the client issuing it is recorded by the server as being the owner of the selection for the time period starting at *time*. Since clients cannot name other clients directly, they use the *owner* window to refer to the owning client in the replies to GetSelectionOwner, and in SelectionRequest and SelectionClear events, and possibly as a place to put properties describing the selection in question.

To discover the owner of a particular selection, a client should invoke:

```
GetSelectionOwner
     selection:      Atom
=>
     owner:          Window or None
```

There is no way for anyone to find out the last-change time of a selection. At the next protocol revision, GetSelectionOwner should be changed to return the last-change time as well as the owner.

Responsibilities of the Selection Owner

When a requestor wants the value of a selection, the owner receives a Selection-Request event:

```
SelectionRequest
    owner:        Window
    selection:    Atom
    target:       Atom
    property:     Atom or None
    requestor:    Window
    time:         Time or CurrentTime
```

The *owner* and *selection* fields will be the values specified in the SetSelection-Owner request. The owner should compare the timestamp with the period it has owned the selection and, if the time is outside, refuse the SelectionRequest by sending the requestor window a SelectionNotify event with the *property* set to None, using SendEvent with an empty event mask.

More advanced selection owners are free to maintain a history of the value of the selection, and to respond to requests for the value of the selection during periods they owned it before the current one.

Otherwise, the owner should use the *target* field to decide the form to convert the selection into, and if the selection cannot be converted into that form, refuse the Selection-Request similarly.

If the *property* field is not None, the owner should place the data resulting from converting the selection into the specified property on the requestor window, setting the property's type to some appropriate value (which need not be the same as *target*). If the *property* field is None, the owner should choose a suitable property name and place the data as that property on the requestor window, setting the type as before.

> Convention: *All properties used to reply to* SelectionRequest *events must be placed on the requestor window.*

In either case, if the data comprising the selection cannot be stored on the requestor window (for example, because the server cannot provide sufficient memory), the owner must refuse the SelectionRequest as above. See the section *Large Data Transfers* below.

If the property is successfully stored, the owner should acknowledge the successful conversion by sending the requestor window a SelectionNotify event, using SendEvent with an empty mask:

```
SelectionNotify
    requestor:    Window
    selection:    Atom
    target:       Atom
```

```
    property:        Atom or None
    time:            Time or CurrentTime
```

The *selection, target* and *property* fields should be set to the values received in the SelectionRequest event (Setting the *property* field to None indicates that the conversion requested could not be made).

> Convention: *The selection, target, time and property fields should be set to the values received in the* SelectionRequest *event.*

The data stored in the property must eventually be deleted. A convention is needed to assign the responsibility for doing so.

> Convention: *Selection requestors are responsible for deleting properties whose names they receive in* SelectionNotify *events. Owners are responsible for deleting all other properties involved in communicating selections.*

A selection owner will often need confirmation that the data comprising the selection has actually been transferred (for example, if the operation has side-effects on the owner's internal data-structures these should not take place until the data has been successfully received). They should express interest in PropertyNotify events for the *requestor* window and wait until the property in the SelectionNotify event has been deleted before assuming that the selection data has been transferred.

When some other client acquires a selection, the previous owner receives a Selection-Clear event:

```
SelectionClear
    owner:           Window
    selection:       Atom
    time:            Time
```

The *time* field is the time at which the ownership changed hands, and the *owner* field is the window the new owner specified in its SetSelectionOwner request.

If an owner loses ownership while it has a transfer in progress, that is to say before it receives notification that the requestor has received all the data, it must continue to service the on-going transfer until it is complete.

Giving Up Selection Ownership

Voluntarily

To relinquish ownership of a selection voluntarily, a client should execute a Set-SelectionOwner request for that selection atom, with owner specified as None, and time specified as CurrentTime.

Alternatively, the client may destroy the window used as the *owner* value of the Set-SelectionOwner request, or it may terminate. In both cases the ownership of the selection involved will revert to None.

Forcibly

If a client gives up ownership of a selection, or if some other client executes a Set-
SelectionOwner for it, the client will receive a SelectionClear event:

```
SelectionClear
    owner:      Window
    selection:  Atom
    time:       Time
```

The *time* field is the time the selection changed hands. The *owner* argument is the window that was specified by the current owner in its SetSelectionOwner request.

Requesting a Selection

A client wishing to obtain the value of a selection in a particular form issues a Convert-
Selection request:

```
ConvertSelection
    selection:  Atom
    target:     Atom
    property:   Atom or None
    requestor:  Window
    time:       Time or CurrentTime
```

The *selection* field specifies the particular selection involved, and the *target* specifies
the form the information is required in. The choice of suitable atoms to use is discussed
below. The *requestor* field should be set to a window the requestor created; the owner
will use it to place the reply property on. The *time* field should be set to the timestamp on
the event triggering the request for the selection value; clients should *not* use Current-
Time for this field.

> Convention: *Clients should not use* CurrentTime *for the* time *field of*
> ConvertSelection *requests. They should use the timestamp of the event
> that caused the request to be made.*

The *property* field should be set to the name of a property that the owner can use to
report the value of the selection, or to None (in which case the owner will chose a property
name). Note that the requestor of a selection needs to know neither the owner of the selection, nor the window it is attached to.

> Convention: *Requestors should, wherever practicable, use* None *for the pro-
> perty field of* ConvertSelection *requests. By allowing the owner to
> choose the name of the reply property in this way, the need to coin new atoms
> can be reduced.*

The result of the ConvertSelection request is that a SelectionNotify event will
be received:

```
SelectionNotify
    requestor:  Window
    selection:  Atom
```

```
target:        Atom
property:      Atom or None
time:          Time or CurrentTime
```

The *requestor*, *selection*, *time* and *target* fields will be the same as those on the
ConvertSelection request.

If the *property* field is None, the conversion has been refused. This can mean that there
is no owner for the selection, that the owner does not support the conversion implied by
target, or that the server did not have sufficient space to accomodate the data.

If the *property* field is not None, then that property will exist on the *requestor* window. The value of the selection can be retrieved from this property by using the Get-
Property request:

```
GetProperty
      window:       Window
      property:     Atom
      type:         Atom or AnyPropertyType
      long_offset:  CARD32
      long_length:  CARD32
      delete:       BOOL
=>
      type:         Atom or None
      format:       {0, 8, 16, 32}
      bytes-after:  CARD32
      value:        LISTofINT8 or LISTofINT16 or LISTofINT32
```

When using GetProperty to retrieve the value of a selection, the *property* field should
be set to the corresponding value in the SelectionNotify event. The *type* field
should be set to AnyPropertyType, because the requestor has no way of knowing
beforehand what type the selection owner will use. Several GetProperty requests may
be needed to retrieve all the data in the selection; each should set the *long_offset* field
to the amount of data received so far, and the *size* field to some reasonable buffer size (see
the next section, *Large Data Transfers*). If the returned value of *bytes_after* is zero the
whole property has been transferred.

Once all the data in the selection has been retrieved, which may require getting the values of
several properties (see the section *Selection Properties*), the property in the Selection-
Notify should be deleted by invoking GetProperty with the *delete* field set True.
As discussed above, the owner has no way of knowing when the data has been transferred to
the requestor unless the property is removed.

> Convention: *The requestor must delete the property named in the*
> SelectionNotify *once all the data has been retrieved. They should invoke*
> *either* DeleteProperty, *or* GetWindowProperty(delete==True)
> *after they have successfully retrieved all data comprising the selection. See the*
> *section* Large Data Transfers *below.*

Large Data Transfers

Selections can get large, and this poses two problems:

- Transferring large amounts of data to the server is expensive, and it would be beneficial to be able to reuse the data once it has been sent to answer further `Convert-Selection` requests.

- All servers will have limits on the amount of data that can be stored in properties. Exceeding this limit will result in a `BadAlloc` error on the `ChangeProperty` request that the selection owner uses to store the data.

To deal with the first problem, we define the following structure:

```
typedef struct {
    Window window;
    Atom property;
    unsigned long start;
    unsigned long length;
} XPropertyPart;
```

and establish the following conventions:

> Convention: *Selection owners should store the data describing a large selection (where large is defined flexibly, but is definitely less than the maximum-request-length in the connection handshake) in a property on the owner window, not on the requestor window. They should reply to the* `Selection-Request` *with a property of type INDIRECT on the requestor window whose content is an array of* `XPropertyPart` *structures describing the parts of some other properties containing the selection. Normally, there will be a single entry in the array. The properties so named is the owner's responsibility, requestors should not delete it.*

Since the actual selection data remains in properties on the selection owner window, it can be used to reply to futher `SelectionRequest` events. However, owners must be careful not to modify the data in these properties between replying to the `SelectionRequest` and receiving the corresponding `PropertyNotify` indicating that the requestor has the data.

The problem of limited server resources is addressed by the following conventions:

> Convention: *Selection owners should transfer the data describing an immense selection (where immense is defined flexibly, but is larger than large) using the INCREMENTAL property mechanism (see below).*

> Convention: *Any client using* `SetSelectionOwner` *to acquire selection ownership should arrange to process* `BadAlloc` *errors. For clients using Xlib, this involves using* `XSetErrorHandler` *to override the default handler.*

> Convention: *A selection owner must confirm that no* `BadAlloc` *error ocurred while storing the properties for a selection before replying with a confirming* `SelectionNotify` *event.*

Convention: *When storing large amounts (relative to the maximum request size) of data, clients should use a sequence of* ChangeProperty *(*mode==Append*) requests for reasonable quantities of data. This is to avoid locking up servers, and to limit the waste of data transfer caused by a* Bad-Alloc *error.*

Convention: *If a* BadAlloc *error occurs during storing the selection data, all properties stored for this selection should be deleted, and the* Convert-Selection *request refused by replying with a* SelectionNotify *event with* property *set to* None.

Convention: *In order to avoid locking up servers for inordinate lengths of time, requestors retrieving large quantities of data from a property should perform a series of* GetProperty *requests, each asking for a reasonable amount of data.*

Single-threaded servers should be changed to avoid locking up during large data transfers.

Usage of Selection Atoms

It is important to observe that defining a new atom consumes resources in the server, and they are not released until the server reinitializes. Thus, it must be a goal to reduce the need for newly minted atoms.

Selection Atoms

There can be an arbitrary number of selections, each named by an atom. To conform with the interclient conventions, however, clients need deal with only these three selections:

- PRIMARY
- SECONDARY
- CLIPBOARD

Other selections may be used freely for private communciation among related groups of clients.

Problem: *How does a client find out which selection atoms are valid?*

The PRIMARY Selection

The selection named by the atom PRIMARY is used for all commands which take only a single argument. It is the principal means of communication between clients which use the selection mechanism.

The SECONDARY Selection

The selection named by the atom SECONDARY is used:

- As the second argument to commands taking two arguments, for example "exchange primary and secondary selections."

- As a means of obtaining data when there is a primary selection, and the user does not wish to disturb it.

The CLIPBOARD Selection

The selection named by the atom CLIPBOARD is used to hold deleted data. Clients deleting data should:

- Assert ownership of the CLIPBOARD.

- Be prepared to respond to a request for the contents of the CLIPBOARD in the normal way, returning the deleted data. The request will be generated by the clipboard client described below.

Clients wishing to restore deleted data should request the contents of the CLIPBOARD selection in the usual way.

Except while a client is actually deleting data, the owner of the CLIPBOARD selection will be a single, special client implemented for the purpose. It should:

- Assert ownership of the CLIPBOARD selection.

- If it loses the selection (which will be because someone has some newly deleted data):

  — Obtain the contents of the selection from the new owner.

  — Reassert ownership of the CLIPBOARD selection.

  — Respond to requests for the CLIPBOARD contents in the normal way.

Target Atoms

The atom that a requestor supplies as the `target` of a `ConvertSelection` request determines the form of the data supplied. The set of such atoms is extensible, but a generally accepted base set of target atoms is needed. As a starting point for this, Table F-1 contains those that have been suggested so far.

Table F-1. Target Atoms and Their Meanings

Atom	Description
TARGETS	list of valid target atoms
INDIRECT	look in the `ConvertSelection` property
STRING	Uninterpreted ISO Latin 1 text
PIXMAP	Pixmap ID
ODIF	ISO Office Document Interchange Format

Atom	Description
POSTSCRIPT	PostScript[*] program
INTERPRESS	InterPress[†] program
OWNER_OS	operating system of owner
FILE_NAME	full path name of a file
HOST_NAME	see XA_WM_CLIENT_MACHINE
DECNET_ADDRESS	DECnet address for owning host
CHARACTER_POSITION	start and end of selection in bytes
LINE_NUMBER	start and end line numbers
COLUMN_NUMBER	start and end column numbers
LENGTH	number of bytes in selection
USER	name of user running owner
PROCEDURE	name of selected procedure
MODULE	name of selected module
PROCESS	process ID of owner
TASK	task ID of owner
CLASS	class of owner—see XA_WM_CLASS
NAME	name of owner—see XA_WM_NAME

Selection owners are required to support the following targets:

- TARGETS. They should return a list of the targets they are prepared to convert their selection into.

- INDIRECT. The INDIRECT target atom is valid only when a property is specified on the ConvertSelection request. If the *property* field in the Selection-Request event is None and the target is INDIRECT, it should be refused.

- When a selection owner receives a SelectionRequest(*target*==INDIRECT) request, the contents of the property named in the request will be a list of atom pairs, the first atom naming a target, and the second naming a property (or None). The effect should be as if the owner had received a sequence of SelectionRequest events, one for each atom pair, except that:

    — the owner should reply with a SelectionNotify only when all the requested conversions have been performed.

    — the owner should replace any property atoms it received as None with the properties used to store the converted data.

    — the owner should replace any property atoms for targets it failed to convert with None.

---

* PostScript is a registered trademark of Adobe Systems Inc.

† InterPress is a trademark of Xerox.

All other targets are optional.

Usage of Selection Properties

The names of the properties used in selection data transfer are chosen by:

- The requestor, if the *property* field is not None.

- The selection owner, if the *property* field is None, and also in the case of all indirect properties.

The type of the properties involved is always chosen by the selection owner, and they can involve some types with special semantics assigned by convention. These special types are reviewed in the following sections.

Clients receiving properties of these types should ensure that they have retrieved all data they need from the other objects so named *before* they delete the property named in the reply.

STRING Properties

Clients receiving properties of type STRING can assume that for the purposes of displaying them the encoding is ISO Latin 1.

Character strings requiring other encodings are transmitted as properties with other types.

INDIRECT Properties

Clients may receive properties of type INDIRECT. The contents of these properties will be arrays of window/atom pairs. The data in the selection consists of the data in each of the properties so named in turn, starting from the start of the array.

All selection requestors must be prepared to receive properties of type INDIRECT.

It is an error if the types of the second and subsequent properties in the list differ from the type of the first.

The properties named in the INDIRECT property are the owner's responsibility; requestors should not delete them.

INCREMENTAL Properties

Clients may receive properties of type INCREMENTAL. The contents of the property will be a window/atom pair, which the client and the selection owner will use to communicate using the following method.

The selection owner:

- appends the data in suitable-size chunks to the property. The size should be less than the maximum-request-size in the connection handshake. Between each append, the owner should wait for a `PropertyNotify(state==Deleted)` event showing that the requestor has read the data. The reason for doing this is to limit the consumption of space in the server.

- when the entire data has been transferred to the server, waits for a `PropertyNotify` (`state==Deleted`) event showing that the data has been read by the requestor, and then writes zero-length data to the property.

The selection requestor:

- waits for the `SelectionNotify` event.

- loops:

  — retrieving data using `GetProperty` with *delete*==True

  — waiting for a `PropertyNotify` with *state*==NewValue

- deletes the type INCREMENTAL property.

Client to Window Manager Communication

To permit window managers to perform their role of mediating the competing demands for resources such as screen space, the clients being managed must adhere to certain conventions, and must expect the window managers to do likewise.

In general, these conventions are somewhat complex, and will undoubtedly change through time as new window management paradigms are developed. There is thus a strong bias towards defining only those conventions that are essential, and which apply generally to all window management paradigms. Clients designed to run with a particular window manager can easily define private protocols to add to these conventions, but must be aware that their users may decide to run some other window manager no matter how much the designers of the private protocol are convinced that they have seen the *one true light* of user interfaces.

It is a principle of these conventions that a general client should neither know nor care which window manager is running, or indeed if one is running at all. Each window manager will implement a particular window management policy; the choice of an appropriate window management policy for the user's circumstances is not one for an individual client to make but will be made by the user or the user's system administrator. This does not exclude the possibility of writing clients that use a private protocol to restrict themselves to operating only under a specific window manager, it merely ensures that no claim of general utility is made for such programs.

For example, the claim is often made "the client I'm writing is important, and it needs to be on top." Well, maybe it is important when it is being run for real, and it should then be run under the control of a window manager that recognizes *important* windows through some private protocol and ensures that they are on top. However, imagine that the *important* client is being debugged. Then, ensuring that it is always on top is no longer the appropriate window management policy, and it should be run under a window manager that allows other windows (e.g., the debugger) to appear on top.

For clients which need to scan the resource database for information about the window manager's resources, the `res_class` of the window manager is Wm, and the `res_name` is the name of the window manager (e.g. *uwm*). Note that this differs from the normal convention, for two reasons:

- Clients should be able to discover the resources the window manager is using without being forced to know which window manager it is.

- At most one (top-level) window manager should be running, even if the server is driving several screens. The code for *wm* shows how a window manager can deal with multiple screens.

Client's Actions

In general, the object of the X11 design is that clients should as far as possible do exactly what they would do in the absence of a window manager, except for:

- Hinting to the window manager about the resources they would like to obtain.

- Cooperating with the window manager by accepting the resources they are allocated, even if they are not those requested.

- Being prepared for resource allocations to change at any time.

Creating a Top-Level Window

A client would normally expect to create its top-level windows as children of one or more of the root windows, using some boilerplate like:

```
win = XCreateSimpleWindow(dpy, DefaultRootWindow(dpy),
        xsh.x, xsh.y, xsh.width, xsh.height, bw, bd, bg);
```

or, if a particular one of the roots was required, like:

```
win = XCreateSimpleWindow(dpy, RootWindow(dpy, screen),
        xsh.x, xsh.y, xsh.width, xsh.height, bw, bd, bg);
```

Ideally, it should be possible to override the choice of a root window and allow clients (including window managers) to treat a non-root window as a pseudo-root. This would allow, for example, testing of window managers and the use of application specific window managers to control the sub-windows owned by the members of a related suite of clients.

To support this, we define the following extension to the semantics of XOpenDisplay on UNIX systems (similar extensions are required for other operating systems).

On UNIX systems, the display name or DISPLAY environment variable is a string that has the format:

> *hostname*:*number*.*screen*.*prop*

If the *prop* component is present, it should be interpreted as the name of a property on the root window of each screen as returned in the connection handshake. If that property exists, and has the type SCREEN, its contents will be a PseudoScreen structure containing information that, from the client's point of view, should replace the information in the connection handshake describing this screen.

```
typedef struct {
    Window root;                /* root window ID */
    long width, height;         /* width and height of screen */
    long mwidth, mheight;       /* width and height of in millimeters */
    VisualID root_visual;       /* root visual */
    Colormap cmap;              /* default color map */
    unsigned long white_pixel;
    unsigned long black_pixel;/* White and Black pixel values */
    long max_maps, min_maps;    /* max and min color maps */
    long backing_store;         /* Never, WhenMapped, Always */
    Bool save_unders;
    long root_input_mask;       /* initial root input mask */
    Atom depths;                /* list of allowable depths on screen */
} PseudoScreen;
```

The *depths* field is either None, in which case the handshake depths and visuals are valid, or the name of a property of type DEPTHS on the same window, which contains an array of PseudoDepth structures. The number of elements in this array controls the *ndepths* field of the Display structure.

```
typedef struct {
    long depth;                 /* this depth (Z) of the depth */
    long nvisuals;              /* number of Visual types at this depth */
    Atom visuals;               /* list of visuals possible at this depth */
} PseudoDepth;
```

The depth of the Visual whose ID is root_visual controls the *root_depth* field of the Display structure. The *visuals* field is either None, in which case the handshake Visuals for this depth are valid, or the name of a property of type VISUALS on the same window, which contains an array of PseudoVisual structures:

```
typedef struct {
    VisualID visualid;    /* visual id of this visual */
    long class;           /* class of screen (monochrome, etc.) */
    unsigned long red_mask, green_mask, blue_mask;  /* mask values */
    long bits_per_rgb;    /* log base 2 of distinct color values */
    long map_entries;     /* color map entries */
} PseudoVisual;
```

Client Properties

Once the client has one or more top-level windows, it must place properties on that window to inform the window manager of its desired behaviour. Some of these properties are mandatory, and some are optional. Properties written by the client will not be changed by the window manager.

XA_WM_NAME

The XA_WM_NAME property is an un-interpreted string that the client wishes displayed in association with the window (for example, in a window headline bar).

The encoding used for this string (and all other uninterpreted string properties) is implied by the type of the property. Type STRING implies ISO Latin 1 encoding; for other types see the section *Usage of Selection Properties*.

Window managers are expected to make an effort to display this information; simply ignoring XA_WM_NAME is not acceptable behaviour. Clients can assume that at least the first part of this string is visible to the user, and that if the information is not visible to the user it is because the user has taken an explicit decision to make it invisible.

On the other hand, there is no guarantee that the user can see the XA_WM_NAME string even if the window manager supports window headlines. The user may have placed the headline off-screen, or have covered it by other windows. XA_WM_NAME should not be used for application-critical information, nor to announce asynchronous changes of application state that require timely user response. The expected uses are:

- To permit the user to identify one of a number of instances of the same client.

- To provide the user with non-critical state information.

Note that even window managers that support headline bars will place some limit on the length of string that can be visible; brevity here will pay dividends.

XA_WM_ICON_NAME

The XA_WM_ICON_NAME property is an un-interpreted string that the client wishes displayed in association with the window when it is iconified (for example, in an icon label). In other respects, it is similar to XA_WM_NAME. Fewer characters will normally be visible in XA_WM_ICON_NAME than XA_WM_NAME, for obvious geometric reasons.

XA_WM_NORMAL_HINTS

The XA_WM_NORMAL_HINTS property is a XSizeHints structure describing the desired window geometry.

```
typedef struct {
    long flags;
    int x, y;
    int width, height;
    int min_width, min_height;
    int max_width, max_height;
    int width_inc, height_inc;
    struct {
        int x; /* numerator */
        int y; /* denominator */
    } min_aspect, max_aspect;
    int base_width, base_height;
} XSizeHints;
```

Problem: *In this and other property structure definitions, it is assumed that sizeof (int) and sizeof (long) are 4.*

The definitions for the `flags` field are:

```
#define USPosition   (1L << 0)   /* user specified x, y */
#define USSize       (1L << 1)   /* user specified width, height */
#define PPosition    (1L << 2)   /* program specified position */
#define PSize        (1L << 3)   /* program specified size */
#define PMinSize     (1L << 4)   /* program specified minimum size */
#define PMaxSize     (1L << 5)   /* program specified maximum size */
#define PResizeInc   (1L << 6)   /* program specified resize increments */
#define PAspect      (1L << 7)   /* program specified min and max aspect
                                   * ratios */
#define PBaseSize    (1L << 8)   /* program specified base size */
```

The x, y, width, and height elements describe a desired position and size for the window. The coordinate system for x and y is the (pseudo-) root window, irrespective of any reparenting that may have occurred. To indicate that this information was specified by the user, set the USPosition and USSize flags. To indicate that it was specified by the client without any user involvement, set PPosition and PSize. This allows a window manager to know that the user specifically asked where the window should be placed or how the window should be sized and that the window manager does not have to rely the program's opinion.

The `min_width` and `min_height` elements specify the minimum size that the window can be for the client to be useful. The `max_width` and `max_height` elements specify the maximum size. The `base_width` and `base_height` elements in conjunction with `width_inc` and `height_inc` define an arithmetic progression of preferred window widths and heights:

```
width = base_width + ( i * width_inc )
height = base_height + ( j * height_inc )
```

for non-negative integers i and j. Window managers are encouraged to use i and j instead of width and height in reporting window sizes to users. If a base size is not provided, the minimum size is to be used in its place, and vice versa.

The `min_aspect` and `max_aspect` elements are expressed as ratios of x and y, and they allow a client to specify the range of aspect ratios it prefers.

XA_WM_HINTS

```
typedef struct {
    long flags;
    Bool input;
    int initial_state;
    Pixmap icon_pixmap;
    Window icon_window;
    int icon_x, icon_y;
    Pixmap icon_mask;
    XID window_group;
    unsigned int messages;
} XWMHints;
```

The definitions for the *flags* field are:

```
#define InputHint            (1L << 0)
#define StateHint            (1L << 1)
#define IconPixmapHint       (1L << 2)
#define IconWindowHint       (1L << 3)
#define IconPositionHint     (1L << 4)
#define IconMaskHint         (1L << 5)
#define WindowGroupHint      (1L << 6)
#define MessageHint          (1L << 7)
```

The input field is used to communicate to the window manager the keyboard focus model used by the client There are four such models:

• No Input. The client never expects keyboard input.

• An example would be xload, or another output-only client.

• Passive Input. The client expects keyboard input but never explicitly sets the keyboard focus.

• An example would be a simple client with a no subwindows, which will accept input in `PointerRoot` mode, or when the window manager sets the keyboard focus to its top-level window (in click-to-type mode).

• Locally Active Input. The client expects keyboard input, and explicitly sets the keyboard focus, but only does so when one of its windows already has the focus.

• An example would be a client with sub-windows defining various data entry fields, that uses Next and Prev keys to move the keyboard focus between the fields, once its top-level window has acquired the focus in `PointerRoot` mode, or when the window manager sets the keyboard focus to its top-level window (in click-to-type mode).

• Globally Active Input. The client expects keyboard input, and explicitly sets the keyboard focus even when it is in windows the client does not own.

• An example would be a client with a scroll bar, that wants to allow users to scroll the window without disturbing the keyboard focus even if it is in some other window. It wants to acquire the keyboard focus when the user clicks in the scrolled region, but not when the user clicks in the scroll bar itself. Thus, it wants to prevent the window manager setting the keyboard focus to any of its windows.

Clients with the Globally Active and No Input models should set the `input` flag to `False`. Clients with the Passive and Locally Active should set the `input` flag to `True`. For more details, see the `FocusMessage` bit below.

The definitions for the `initial_state` flag are:

```
#define DontCareState     0
#define NormalState       1
#define ClientIconState   2
#define IconicState       3
#define InactiveState     4
#define IgnoreState       5
```

The value of the initial_state flag determines the state the client wishes to be in at the time the top-level window is mapped. In addition, clients may ask the window manager to switch between states by setting the `initial_state` flag (its name has become somewhat misleading). The states are:

- `DontCareState`. The client doesn't care what state it is in.

- `NormalState`. The client wants its top-level window to be visible.

- `ClientIconState`. The client wants its `icon_window` to be visible. If `icon_windows` are not available, it wants its top-level window visible.

- `IconicState`. The client wants to be iconic, whatever that means for this window manager. It can assume that at least one of its `icon_window` (if any), its `icon_pixmap` (if any), or its `XA_WM_ICON_NAME` will be visible.

- `InactiveState`. The client wants to be inactive, whatever that means for this window manager. Inactive windows will normally be available from a pop-up menu, or some other means that doesn't involve permanently allocating screen real-estate.

- `IgnoreState`. The client wants the window manager to ignore this window, and in return agrees that attempts to map it (or its `icon_window`) will be ignored.

The *icon_pixmap* field may specify a pixmap to be used as an icon. This pixmap should be:

- One of the sizes specified in the `XA_WM_ICON_SIZES` property on the (pseudo-) root.

- 1-bit deep. The window manager will select, through the defaults database, suitable background (for the 0 bits) and foreground (for the 1 bits) colors. These defaults can, of course, specify different colors for the icons of different clients.

The icon_mask specifies which pixels of the icon_pixmap should be used as the icon, allowing for non-rectangular icons.

The *icon_window* field is the ID of a window the client wants used as its icon. Not all window managers will support icon windows, but those that do will expect that:

- The icon window is a child of the (pseudo-) root.

- The icon window is one of the sizes specified in the `XA_WM_ICON_SIZES` property on the (pseudo-) root.

- The icon window uses the root visual & default colormap for the screen in question.

- The client will neither map nor unmap the icon window. If the client does map the icon window, it will be treated as if it had set the *initial_state* flag to `ClientIconState`. This treatment is not guaranteed to result in the icon window actually being mapped.

Clients needing more capabilities from the icons than a simple two-color bitmap should use icon windows.

The *window_group* lets the client specify that this window belongs to a group of windows. An example is a single client manipulating multiple children of the root window. Window managers may provide facilities for manipulating the group as a whole.

Convention: *The* `window_group` *field should be set to the ID of the group leader. The window group leader may be a window which exists only for that purpose, and may never be mapped. Its* `window_group` *field should contain its own ID.*

Convention: *The properties of the window group leader are those for the group as a whole (for example, the icon to be shown when the entire group is iconified).*

The definitions for the `messages` flags are:

```
#define ConfigureDenied(1L << 0) /* XA_WM_CONFIGURE_DENIED */
#define WindowMoved    (1L << 1) /* XA_WM_WINDOW_MOVED */
#define BangMessage    (1L << 2) /* XA_BANG! */
#define FocusMessage   (1l << 3) /* XA_WM_TAKE_FOCUS */
```

The meanings of the bits are:

- The `ConfigureDenied` bit enables notification that the window manager has decided not to change the size or position of the top-level window in response to a `Configure-Window` request.

- The `WindowMoved` bit enables notification that the window manager has moved a top-level window without resizing it.

- The `BangMessage` bit enables notification that the session manager feels that termination is likely.

- The `FocusMessage` bit announces that the client sets the input focus to its windows explicitly, and wants notification of when the window manager thinks it should do so.

If the *messages* field is not defined, it defaults to zero.

The four input models and the corresponding values of the `input` and `FocusMessage` bits are shown in Table F-2.

Table F-2. Input Models

Input Model	input field	FocusMessage
No Input	False	False
Passive	True	False
Locally Active	True	True
Globally Active	False	True

WM_CLASS

The `XA_WM_CLASS` property is a string containing two null-separated elements, `res_class` and `res_name`, that are meant to be used by clients both as a means of permanent identification, and as the handles by which which both the client and the window manager obtain resources related to the window. `res_class` is meant to identify the client (e.g. "emacs"), while `res_name` is meant to more specifically identify the particular instance. Resources should be obtained using `res_name`, or if not found under `res_name`, then using `res_class`. The fields should be set using the following rules (non-UNIX systems will differ):

- Set `WM_CLASS.res_class` to the name of the client (for example, "emacs").

- Set `WM_CLASS.res_name` from the first of the following that applies:

  — an optional command line argument (e.g., *-rn name*)

  — a specific environment variable (e.g., RESOURCE_NAME)

  — the trailing component of argv[0]

The `XA_WM_CLASS` property is write-once and must be present when the window is mapped; window managers will ignore changes to it while the window is mapped. If the window is unmapped, and then remapped, window managers will normally reread `XA_WM_CLASS`. However, there should be no need for a client to change its class.

WM_TRANSIENT_FOR

The `XA_WM_TRANSIENT_FOR` property is the ID of another top-level window. The implication is that this window is a pop-up on behalf of the named window, and window managers may decide not to decorate transient windows, or treat them differently in other ways. Dialogue boxes, for example, are an example of windows that should have `XA_WM_TRANSIENT_FOR` set.

It is important not to confuse `XA_WM_TRANSIENT_FOR` with override-redirect. `XA_WM_TRANSIENT_FOR` should be used in those cases where the pointer is not grabbed while the window is grabbed; in other words if other windows are allowed to be active while the transient is up. If other windows must be frozen, use override-redirect and grab the pointer while the window is mapped.

Window Manager Properties

The properties described above are those which the client is responsible for maintaining on its top-level windows. This section describes the properties that the window manager places on clients top-level windows.

XA_WM_STATE

The XA_WM_STATE property is composed of two fields:

```
struct {
    int state;
    Window icon;
};
```

The *state* field can take on some of the same values as the *initial_state* field of the XA_WM_HINTS property. In particular, it can be:

```
#define NormalState        1
#define ClientIconState    2
#define IconicState        3
#define InactiveState      4
```

The *icon* field should contain the window ID of the window which the window manager uses as the icon window for the window on which this property is set, if any; otherwise, it should contain None. Note that this window may not be the same as the icon window which the client may specify.

Clients should be prepared for this property not being set for the standard reasons (no window manager, badly behaved window manager, broken window manager). The *state* field describes the window manager's idea of the state the window is in, which may not match the client's idea as expressed in the *initial_state* field of the XA_WM_HINTS property (for example, if the user has asked the window manager to iconify the window). If it is NormalState, the window manager believes the client should be animating its window; if it is IconicState that it should animate its icon window. Note that in either state clients should be prepared to handle exposure events from either window.

Mapping and Unmapping the Window

Once the top-level window has been provided with suitable properties, the client is free to map it and unmap it as required. Mapping the window should be interpreted as a request to place this window under the control of the window manager, and unmapping it as a request to remove it from the control of the window manager. Typically, the window manager will intercept these calls and *do the right thing*.

Note that mapping or unmapping the window is a heavyweight operation, and that it is *not* the way to change state from open to iconic, and vice versa. An unmapped window is not under the control of the window manager, and its icon will also be unmapped.

A client receiving UnmapNotify on its (top-level or icon) window should regard that as notification from the window manager that animating the window is no longer necessary. They should cease computing new states of the window, and stop sending output to it.

A client can also select for VisibilityChange on their (top-level or icon) windows. They will the receive a VisibilityNotify(*state*=FullyObscured) event when the window concerned becomes completely obscured even though mapped (and thus perhaps a waste of time to update), and a `VisibilityNotify(`*state*`!=FullyObscured)` when it becomes even partly viewable.

Clients should neither map nor unmap their icon windows.

Configuring the Window

There are two possible ways in which a client could resize or reposition its top-level windows:

- Use `XConfigureWindow`.

- Use `XSetNormalHints` to change the size and/or position fields in the `XA_WM_NORMAL_HINTS` property.

Clients wishing to resize or reposition their top-level windows should do *both* of them, as follows:

- Do an `XConfigureWindow` with the desired size and location.

- Do an `XSetNormalHints` with the *same* size and location.

The order is important. The coordinate system in which the location is expressed is that of the (pseudo-) root, irrespective of any reparenting that may have occurred (in this way clients need not be aware that they have been reparented).

Clients must be aware that there is no guarantee that the window manager will allocate them the requested size or location, and must be prepared to deal with *any* size and location. If the window manager decides to respond to a `ConfigureRequest` by:

- Not changing the size or location of the window at all, a client which has requested notification by setting the `ConfigureDenied` bit in `XA_WM_HINTS` will receive a `ClientMessage` whose type field is the atom `XA_WM_CONFIGURE_DENIED`, and which carries no other data.

- Moving the window without resizing it, a client which has requested notification by setting the `WindowMoved` bit in `XA_WM_HINTS` will receive a `ClientMessage` whose type field is the atom `XA_WM_WINDOW_MOVED`, and whose data field contains the new (pseudo-) root x and y. They will not normally receive a `ConfigureNotify` event describing this change, since the window manager will have reparented their window.

- Moving and resizing the window, a client which has selected for `StructureNotify` will receive a `ConfigureNotify` event. Note that the coordinates in this event are relative to the parent, which may not be the root in the window has been reparented.

Keyboard Focus

Clients can, as described above, deal with the keyboard focus in four ways:

- No Input
- Passive
- Locally Active
- Globally Active

Passive and Locally Active clients set the `input` field of XA_WM_HINTS True to indicate that they require window manager assistance in acquiring the keyboard focus. No Input and Globally Active clients set the `input` field False to prevent the window manager setting the keyboard focus to its top-level window.

Clients using SetInputFocus must set the `time` field to the timestamp of the event that caused them to make the attempt. Note that this cannot be a FocusIn event, since they do not have timestamps, and that clients may acquire the focus without a corresponding EnterNotify. Clients must not use CurrentTime in the `time` field.

Clients using the Globally Active model can only use SetInputFocus to acquire the keyboard focus when they do not already have it on receipt of one of the following events:

- ButtonPress
- ButtonRelease
- Passively-grabbed KeyPress
- Passively-grabbed KeyRelease

In general, clients should avoid using passively-grabbed key events for this purpose except when they are unavoidable (as for example a selection tool that establishes a passive grab on the keys that cut, copy, or paste).

The method by which the user commands the window manager to set the focus to a window is up to the window manager. For example, clients cannot determine whether they will see the click that transfers the focus.

Clients which set the FocusMessage bit in XA_WM_HINTS may receive a Client-Message from the window manager whose `type` field is the atom XA_WM_TAKE_FOCUS and whose data field is a timestamp. If they expect input, they should respond with a Set-InputFocus request with its `window` field set to the window of theirs that last had the input focus, or to their *default input window*, and the `time` field set to the timestamp.

Clients will normally receive XA_WM_TAKE_FOCUS when opening from an icon, or when the user has clicked outside their window in an area that indicates to the window manager that it should assign the focus (for example, clicking in the headline bar can be used to asign the focus).

Clients that set the keyboard focus need to decide a value for the `revert_to` field of the SetInputFocus request. This determines the behavior of the keyboard focus if the window the focus has been set to becomes not viewable. It can be any of:

- `Parent`. In general, clients should use this value when assigning focus to one of their subwindows. Unmapping the subwindow will cause focus to revert to the parent, which is probably what you want.

- `PointerRoot`. Using this value with a click-to-type-style window manager leads to race conditions, since the window becoming unviewable may coincide with the window manager deciding to move the focus elsewhere.

- `None`. Using this value causes problems if the window manager reparents the window (most window managers will) and then crashes. The keyboard focus will be `None`, and there will probably be no way to change it.

There isn't a lot of experience to base a convention on, but the tentative convention is:

> Convention: *Clients invoking* `SetInputFocus` *should set* revert_to *to Parent.*

A convention is also required for clients that want to give up the keyboard focus.

> Convention: *When a client with the focus wants to give it up, it should set it to* None, *rather than to* `PointerRoot`.

Colormaps

Clients that use one colormap for each top-level window and its sub-windows should set its ID in the colormap field of the window's attributes, and depend on the window manager to install it at suitable times. They should not set a XA_WM_COLORMAPS property on the top-level window.

If they want to change the colormap, they should change the window attribute, and the window manager will install the colormap for them. Window managers are responsible for ensuring that top-level windows colormaps are installed at appropriate times.

Clients that have sub-windows with different colormap requirements from their top-level windows should install these (sub-window) colormaps themselves. The window manager remains responsible for installing the top-level colormap. They should set the XA_WM_COLORMAPS property on the top-level window concerned to a list of the IDs of the colormaps they will be installing; this informs the window manager that they will do their own sub-window colormap installation, and allows the window manager to uninstall other maps at suitable times.

Clients, especially those installing their own colormaps, should be aware of the min_maps and max_maps fields of the connection startup information, and the effect that the minimum value has on the *required list*:

> At any time, there is a subset of the installed maps, viewed as an ordered list, called the required list. The length of the required list is at most M, where M is the min_maps specified for the screen in the connection setup. The required list is maintained as follows. When a colormap is an explicit argument to `InstallColormap`, it is added to the head of the list, and the list is truncated at the tail if necessary to keep the length of the list to at most M. When a colormap is an explicit argument to `UninstallColormap` and it is in the required

list, it is removed from the list. A colormap is not added to the required list when it is installed implicitly by the server, and the server cannot implicitly uninstall a colormap that is in the required list.

In less precise words, the min_maps most recently installed maps are guaranteed to be installed. This number will often be one; clients needing multiple colormaps should beware.

The XA_WM_COLORMAPS property is merely a hint to the window manager, allowing it to uninstall suitable maps when preparing to install a top-level window's map. If it is inconvenient for a client to collect the complete set of colormaps it will install, the property can be incomplete (or even empty). The only result of an incomplete list is that window manager's attempts to manage the set of installed maps will in some cases be less than optimal.

Icons

A client can hint to the window manager about the desired appearance of its icon in several ways:

- Set a string in XA_WM_ICON_NAME. All clients should do this, as it provides a fallback for window managers whose ideas about icons differ widely from those of the client.

- Set a pixmap into the *icon_pixmap* field of the XA_WM_HINTS property, and possibly another into the *icon_mask* field. The window manager is expected to display the pixmap masked by the mask. The pixmap should be one of the sizes found in the XA_WM_ICON_SIZE property on the root (or pseudo-root). If this property is not found, the window manager is unlikely to display icon pixmaps. Window managers will normally clip or tile pixmaps which do not match XA_WM_ICON_SIZE.

- Set a window into the *icon_window* field of the XA_WM_HINTS property. The window manager is expected to map that window whenever the client is in IconState or ClientIconState. If the icon window is not the window itself, the window manager will treat the window's XA_WM_NORMAL_SIZE property as a hint of a suitable icon size. In general, the size of the icon window should be one of those specified in XA_WM_ICON_SIZE on the (pseudo-) root, if it exists. Window managers are free to resize icon windows.

  Convention: *Clients may ask the window manager to change their state from normal to iconic and vice versa by setting the* initial_state *flag in the* XA_WM_HINTS *property.*

Clients must not depend on being able to receive input events via their icon windows. Window managers will differ as to whether they support this.

Popup Windows

Clients wishing to pop-up a window can do one of three things:

- They can create and map another normal top-level window, which will get decorated and managed as normal by the window manager. See the discussion of window groups below.

- If the window will be visible for a relatively short time, and deserves a somewhat lighter treatment, they can set the XA_WM_TRANSIENT_FOR property. They can expect less decoration, but can set all the normal window manager properties on the window. An example would be a dialog box.

- If the window will be visible for a very short time, and should not be decorated at all, the client can set override-redirect on the window. In general, this should be done only if the pointer is grabbed while the window is mapped. The window manager will never interfere with these windows, which should be used with caution. An example of an appropriate use is a pop-up menu.

Window Groups

A client with multiple persistent top-level windows constitutes a window group, and its top-level windows should be linked together using the *window_group* field of the XA_WM_HINTS structure.

One of the windows (the one the others point to) will be the group leader and will carry the group as opposed to the individual properties. Window managers may treat the group leader differently from other windows in the group. For example, group leaders may have the full set of decorations, and other group members a restricted set.

It is not necessary for the group leader ever to be mapped.

Client Responses to Window Manager Actions

The window manager performs a number of operations on client resources, primarily on their top-level windows. Clients must not try to fight this, but may elect to receive notification of the window manager's operations.

Move

If the window manager moves a top-level window without changing its size, the client can elect to receive notification by setting the WindowMoved bit in the XA_WM_HINTS structure. Notification is via a ClientMessage event whose type field is XA_WM_WINDOW_MOVED and whose data field contains the new (pseudo-) root X and Y.

Clients must not respond to being moved by attempting to move themselves to a better location.

Resize

The client can elect to receive notification of being resized by selecting for `Structure-Notify` on its top-level windows. A `ConfigureNotify` event on a top-level window implies that the window's position on the root may have changed, even though its position in its parent is unchanged, because the window may have been reparented. And note that the coordinates in the event will not, in this case, be meaningful.

The response of the client to being resized should be to accept the size it has been given, and to do its best with it. Clients must not respond to being resized by attempting to resize themselves to a better size. If the size is impossible to work with, clients are free to change the *initial_state* field in their `XA_WM_HINTS` structure and ask to be iconified.

(De)Iconify

Clients can know their open/closed status by examining the `XA_WM_STATE` property on their top-level window. The window manager will set this, using the same bit definitions as the *initial_state* field in `XA_WM_HINTS`, to indicate the state it believes the window is currently in.

Clients needing to take action on changing state (other than painting the window on the opening `Expose` event) can select for `PropertyNotify` and wait for notification of changes to the `XA_WM_STATE` property.

If the only reason for wanting to know whether the window is in open or iconic state is to stop updating it when it is iconic, the client should select for `StructureNotify` on it, and stop updating the display when it receives `UnmapNotify`. `UnmapNotify` does not imply that the window is in any particular state, rather it implies that the window manager believes it is no longer necessary for the client to update the window. For example, consider a window that is open on a pseudo-root that is unmapped.

Colormap Change

Clients that wish to be notified of their colormaps being installed or uninstalled should select for `ColormapNotify` on their top-level windows. They will receive `ColormapNotify` events with the *new* field `False` when the colormap for that window is installed or uninstalled. Window managers will only ever install the colormaps for top-level windows, but a side-effect of them doing so (or of other clients installing sub-window colormaps) may be that other maps are uninstalled.

Clients that need to explicitly install colormaps for sub-windows should do so only when their top-level window has its colormap installed.

> Problem: *There is a race condition here; the* `InstallColormap` *request doesn't take a timestamp, and it may be executed after the top-level colormap has been uninstalled. The next protocol revision should provide the timestamp.*

> Convention: *Clients that need to install their own colormaps, and which expect input, should install them only when they have the keyboard focus and their*

top-level colormap is installed. Clients that need to install their own colormaps, and which never expect input, should install them only when their top-level window has its colormap installed.

Keyboard Focus

Clients can request notification that they have the keyboard focus by selecting for `Focus-Change` on their top-level windows; they will receive `FocusIn` and `FocusOut` events. Clients that need to set the keyboard focus to one of their sub-windows should not do so unless they actually have the focus in (one of) their top-level windows. Clients should not warp the pointer in an attempt to transfer the focus, they should set the focus and leave the pointer alone.

Once a client has the focus in one of its windows, it may transfer it to another of its windows using:

```
SetInputFocus
    focus:        Window or PointerRoot or None
    revert_to:    {Parent, PointerRoot, None}
    time:         Time or CurrentTime
```

> Convention: *Clients using* `SetInputFocus` *must set the* `time` *field to the timestamp of the event that caused them to make the attempt. Note that this cannot be a* `FocusIn` *event, since they do not have timestamps, and that clients may acquire the focus without a corresponding* `EnterNotify`. *Clients must not use* `CurrentTime` *in the* `time` *field.*

ClientMessages

Clients may receive the following messages from their window manager. All will be events of type `ClientMessage`, distinguished by their `type` fields being the following atoms:

- `XA_WM_CONFIGURE_DENIED`. These messages carry no data. They are enabled by setting the `ConfigureDenied` bit of the `messages` field of the `XA_WM_HINTS` structure.

- `XA_WM_WINDOW_MOVED`. These messages carry the new x and y values in root window coordinates. They are enabled by setting the `WindowMoved` bit of the `messages` field of the `XA_WM_HINTS` structure.

- `XA_WM_TAKE_FOCUS`. These messages carry a timestamp. They are enabled by setting the `FocusMessage` bit of the `XA_WM_HINTS` structure.

Status of the Window Manager Conventions

A number of areas in these conventions are still causing considerable controversy. Examples are:

- Keyboard focus handling
- `XA_WM_WINDOW_MOVED`
- The `XOpenDisplay` extension
- `XA_WM_ICON_SIZES`
- `XA_WM_STATE`

It will obviously take some time for these conventions to obtain formal endorsement, and for the toolkits and clients to be changed to conform.

Client to Session Manager Communication

The role of the session manager is to manage a collection of clients. It should be capable of:

- Starting a collection of clients as a group.
- Remembering the state of a collection of clients so that they can be restarted in the same state.
- Stopping a collection of clients in a controlled way.

It may also provide a user interface to starting, stopping and restarting groups of clients.

Client Actions

Clients need to cooperate with the session manager by providing it with information it can use to restart them if it should become necessary, but need not take any other action to assist it.

Properties

The client communicates with the session manager using two properties on its top-level window. If the client has a group of top-level windows, these properties should be placed on the group leader window.

WM_COMMAND

The `XA_WM_COMMAND` property is a string representing the command used to restart the client. In UNIX systems, it will initially be set from *argv*. Clients should ensure, by resetting this property, that it always reflects a command that will restart them in their current state.

WM_CLIENT_MACHINE

The `XA_WM_CLIENT_MACHINE` property should be set to a string forming the name of the machine running the client, as seen from the machine running the server.

Termination

Since they communicate via unreliable network connections, X11 clients must be prepared for their connection to the server to be terminated at any time without warning. They cannot depend on getting notification that termination is imminent, nor on being able to use the server to negotiate with the user (for example, using dialog boxes for confirmation) about their fate.

Equally, clients may terminate at any time without notice to the session manager.

Client Responses to Session Manager Actions

In general, the only action that a client need take in response to the actions of a session manager is to prepare for termination.

Termination

Clients that wish to be warned of impending termination should set the BangMessage bit in the `XA_WM_HINTS` structure. They will receive a `ClientMessage` whose type field is `BANG!` whenever the session manager believes that termination is likely.

Clients that do not set the `BangMessage` bit may be terminated by the session manager at any time without warning.

Clients receiving `BANG!` should place themselves in a state from which they can be restarted, and should update `XA_WM_COMMAND` to be a command that will restart them in this state. The session manager will be waiting for a `PropertyNotify` on `XA_WM_COMMAND` as a confirmation that the client has saved its state, so that `XA_WM_COMMAND` should be updated (perhaps with a zero-length append) even if its contents are correct.

Once it has received this confirmation, the session manager will feel free to terminate the client if that is what the user asked for. Otherwise, if the user merely asked for the session to be put to sleep, the session manager will ensure that the client does not receive any mouse or keyboard events.

Clients should regard BANG! not as a command to terminate, but rather as a warning from the session manager that it believes termination is likely; as a warning shot rather than one to the heart. There is no need to panic and commit suicide when the shot arrives, but clients should be aware that the session manager has more deadly weapons at its disposal, and should ensure their last will and testament is up-to-date, take out life insurance, and prepare for resurrection.

Nevertheless, a client is always free to terminate without giving either the session or window managers notice (and in particular is free to terminate when it receives the BANG! message). When a client terminates itself, rather than being terminated by the session manager, it is viewed as having resigned from the session in question, and it will not be revived if the session is revived.

After receiving a BANG! and saving its state, the client should not change its state until it receives a mouse or keyboard event. Once it does so, it can assume that the danger is over.

Status of the Session Manager Conventions

The question of client termination is still somewhat controversial. It will obviously take some time for these conventions to obtain formal endorsement, and for the toolkits and clients to be changed to conform.

Manipulation of Shared Resources

X11 permits clients to manipulate a number of shared resources, among them the keyboard focus, the pointer, and colormaps. Conventions are required so that clients do so in an orderly fashion.

The Keyboard Focus

Convention: *Clients should set the keyboard focus to one of their windows only when it is already in one of their windows, or when they receive a* XA_WM_TAKE_FOCUS *message. They should set the* input *field of the* XA_WM_HINTS *structure* True.

Convention: *Clients should use the timestamp of the event that caused them to attempt to set the keyboard focus as the* time *field on the* SetInputFocus *request, not* CurrentTime.

The Pointer

In general, clients should not warp the pointer. Window managers may do so, for example to maintain the invariant that the pointer is always in the window with the keyboard focus. Other window managers may wish to preserve the illusion that the user is in sole control of the pointer.

Convention: *Clients should not warp the pointer.*

Convention: *Clients which insist on warping the pointer should do so only with the* src_window *field of the* WarpPointer *request set to one of their windows.*

Colormaps

Convention: *Clients should install their own colormaps only if they have subwindows with colormaps that differ from their top-level window.*

Convention: *Clients should warn the window manager that they will be installing their own colormaps by placing a list of the colormaps they will use in the* XA_WM_COLORMAPS *property of the top-level window concerned.*

Convention: *Clients that need to install their own colormaps, and which expect input, should install them only when they have the keyboard focus and their top-level colormap is installed. Clients that need to install their own colormaps, and which never expect input, should install them only when their top-level window has its colormap installed.*

Acknowledgements

The author's role in preparing this document was limited to asking questions and writing down the answers; the ideas are all due to others. Sources for the questions were the Protocol and Xlib documents, and the answers came from:

* For the Selection section, Jerry Farrell, Phil Karlton, and Bob Scheifler.

* For the Window and Session Manager sections, Todd Brunhoff, Ellis Cohen, Hania Gajewska, Mark Manasse, Bob Scheifler, Ralph Swick, and the participants in the Window Manager discussions at the January 1988 X Conference at MIT.

G
Release Notes

This appendix describes the changes between Release 1 and Release 2 of X Version 11.

D

Release Notes

This appendix describes the changes between Release 1 and Release 2 of X Version 11.

G
Release Notes

This appendix describes differneces between Release 1 and Release 2 of the X Window System. There were only a few changes in the Xlib interface. No changes were made in the underlying X protocol.

The major change was a completely revised resource manager. The resource manager is now merged into the X library; it was a separate library in Release 1. The routines are now entirely different from the ones in Release 1, although they still serve roughly the same purpose. One added feature is the server resource database set up by the *xrdb* program. This allows the user to specify a single defaults file to be set as a property in the server, so that all applications using the defaults mechanism can use those defaults. This was not done in Release 1, and therefore, the user had to maintain a separate defaults file on each machine on which clients were to run. See Chapter 11, *Managing User Preferences*, for a description of the Release 2 resource manager.

Along with the change in the resource manager routines, the *Xdefaults* file has been superseded by a more general resource database file that can have any name. The user runs *xrdb* with this filename as an argument, and *xrdb* sets a property on the root window containing the database. When applications call XGetDefault, this property is the first place where XGetDefault searches for the matching value. This change was made so that an *.Xdefaults* file would not have to be maintained on every system on which client routines run while displaying on a single server.

The XUnionRectWithRegion routine is also new to Release 2. It is provided mainly to simplify the process of coalescing the rectangles returned from a contiguous series of Expose events into a single region before setting the clip mask with XSetRegion. This is done to optimize the redrawing of windows, as described in Section 3.2.13.1.

The XEventsQueued routine was added to Release 2 to tell how many events are on the queue, but in a more flexible way than does XPending. It allows you to choose whether to return immediately if no events are found on Xlib's queue, or to flush the connection with the server first. See Section 8.2.6 for a more complete desciption.

XInsertModifiermapEntry and XDeleteModifiermapEntry were added in Release 2. They make it easier to add or delete a single key to the set of keys mapped to a particular modifier functionality. These routines merely prepare a structure for calling XSetModifierMapping.

Several structures were modified in Release 2. All the event structures had two members added. One is called `serial` that provides the serial number of the last request successfully processed by the server. This member aids in processing errors, and in locating which Xlib call generated the error. The other is called `send_event` and indicates whether the event was sent from the server or from another client using `XSendEvent`. In Release 1, the highest bit in the `type` member was set when the event was sent from another client, but this meant that comparing `type` against the event type symbols such as `Expose` would not work for sent events. In Release 2, all events look the same unless the `send_event` flag is explicitly checked.

Other changes took place in opaque structures (such as `Display`), but programs should only access these through macros and the other interfaces provided in Xlib so that the changes won't affect properly written programs.

H
Sources of
Additional Information

In This Chapter:

Information
Sources

H
Sources of Additional Information

This appendix lists a few of the official and unofficial sources for information about the X Window System and associated software.

Getting the X Software

Release 3 of the X Window System became available on October 27th, 1988. This book documents Release 1 and 2, though the changes in Release 3 are slight. We will be offering a small document that specifies the changes between Release 2 and Release 3 sometime in November. Most people currently have Release 2 and most initial commercial offerings of X from system vendors will be based on Release 2. However, if you want to get the software from one of the sources listed below, you will want to get the latest version. We list here how to get both releases.

You can get the X software directly from MIT on two (for R2) or 3 (for R3) 9-track 1600 BPI mag tapes written in UNIX *tar* format, along with printed copies of MIT's manuals, by sending a check in U.S. currency for U.S. $400 to:

> MIT Software Distribution Center
> Technology Licensing Office
> MIT E32-300
> 77 Massachusetts Avenue
> Cambridge, MA 02139

Their telephone number is (617) 253 - 6966, and the "X Ordering Hotline" is (617) 258-8330. If you want the tapes and manuals shipped overseas, the price is $500. The manual set alone is $125 including U.S. shipping or $175 including overseas shipping.

Other distribution media or formats are not available from the MIT Software Distribution Center. The Release 2 tape comes with source code for sample servers for Sun, HP, IBM, Apollo, and DEC workstations, source code for clients written by MIT, sources for the toolkits Xt, Interviews, and Andrew, contributed software written outside MIT, and sources and postscript files for all MIT's documentation. Note that the servers supplied are sample servers only; they will doubtless differ from commercially released servers for the same machines.

Sites that have access to the Internet can retrieve the distribution from the following machines using anonymous *ftp*. Here are the current sites:

Location	Hostname	Address	Directory
West	gatekeeper.dec.com	128.45.9.52	pub/X.V11R2
			pub/X.V11R3
Midwest	mordred.cs.purdue.edu	192.5.48.2	pub/X11/Release3
East	UUNET.uu.net	192.12.141.129	X/X.V11R2
			X/X.V11R3
Northeast	expo.lcs.mit.edu	18.30.0.212	pub/X.V11R2
			pub/R3

If mordred.cs.purdue.edu does respond on 192.5.48.2, try 128.10.2.2. DO NOT do anonymous *ftp* during normal business hours, and please use the machine nearest you.

The distribution is also available by UUCP from UUNET, for sites without Internet access. The files are split up to be small enough for UUCP distribution.

Bug Fixes

Critical bug fixes as well as a limited number of important new features are available from the archive server *xstuff@expo.lcs.mit.edu*. Electronic mail sent to this address is forwarded to a program which responds with the requested information. Here is the help file that it sends to people:

The *xstuff* server is a mail-response program. That means that you mail it a request, and it mails back the response.

The *xstuff* server is a very dumb program. It does not have much error checking. If you don't send it the commands that it understands, it will just answer "I don't understand you."

The *xstuff* server has four commands. Each command must be the first word on a line. The *xstuff* server reads your entire message before it does anything, so you can have several different commands in a single message. It treats the "Subject:" header line just like any other line of the message. You can use any combination of upper and lower case letters in the commands.

The archives are organized into a series of directories and subdirectories. Each directory has an index, and each subdirectory has an index. The top-level index gives you an overview of what is in the subdirectories, and the index for each subdirectory tells you what is in it.

If you are bored with reading documentation and just want to try something, then send the server a message containing the line

```
send index fixes
```

When you get the index back, it will contain the numbers of all of the fixes and batches of fixes in the archive; send the server another message asking it to send you the fixes that you want:

```
send fixes 1 5 9 11-20
```

If you are using a mailer that understands "@" notation, send to *xstuff@expo.lcs.mit.edu*. If your mailer deals in "!" notation, try sending to *{someplace}!eddie!expo.lcs.mit.edu!xstuff*. For other mailers, you're on your own.

Here is some more documentation. The server has four commands:

help   The command *help* or *send help* causes the server to send you the help file. You already know this, of course, because you are reading the help file. No other commands are honored in a message that asks for help (the server figures that you had better read the help message before you do anything else).

index   If your message contains a line whose first word is *index*, then the server will send you the top-level index of the contents of the archive. If there are other words on that line that match the name of subdirectories, then the indexes for those subdirectories are sent instead of the top-level index. For example, you can say

```
index
```

or

```
index fixes
```

You can then send back another message to the *xstuff* server, using a *send* command (see below) to ask it to send you the files whose name you learned from that list.

index fixes and *send index fixes* mean the same thing: you can use *send* instead of *index* if you want, for getting an index.

If your message has an *index* or a *send index* command, then all other *send* commands will be ignored. This means that you cannot get an index and data in the same request. This is so that index requests can be given high priority.)

send   if your message contains a line whose first word is *send*, then the *xstuff* server will send you the item(s) named on the rest of the line. To name an item, you give its directory and its name. For example

```
send fixes 1-10
```

Once you have named a category, you can put as many names as you like on the rest of the line; they will all be taken from that category. For example:

```
send fixes 1-10 11-20 21-30
```

Each *send* command can reference only one directory. If you would like to get one fix and one of something else, you must use two *send* commands.

You may put as many *send* commands as you like into one message to the server, but the more you ask for, the longer it will take to receive. See "Fairness", below, for an explanation. Actually, it's not strictly true that you can put as many *send* commands as you want into one message. If the server must use UUCP mail to send your files, then it cannot send more than 100K bytes in one message. If you ask for more than it can send, then it will send as much as it can and ignore the rest.

path   The *path* command exists to help in case you do not get responses from the server when you mail to it.

Sometimes the server is unable to return mail over the incoming path. There are dozens of reasons why this might happen, and if you are a true wizard, you already know what those reasons are. If you are an apprentice wizard, you might not know all the reasons but you might know a way to circumvent them.

If you put in a *path* command, then everything that the server mails to you will be mailed to that address, rather than to the return address on your mail. The server host expo.lcs.mit.edu does not have a direct UUCP connection to anywhere; you must go through eddie or somewhere else.

Notes

The *xstuff* server acknowledges every request by return mail. If you don't get a message back in a day or two you should assume that something is going wrong, and perhaps try a *path* command.

The *xstuff* server does not respond to requests from users named root, *system*, *daemon*, or *mailer*. This is to prevent mail loops. If your name is "Bruce Root" or "Joe Daemon", and you can document this, I will happily rewrite the server to remove this restriction. Yes, I know about Norman Mailer and Waverley Root. Norman doesn't use netmail and Waverley is dead.

Fairness

The *xstuff* server contains many safeguards to ensure that it is not monopolized by people asking for large amounts of data. The mailer is set up so that it will send no more than a fixed amount of data each day. If the work queue contains more requests than the day's quota, then the unsent files will not be processed until the next day. Whenever the mailer is run to send its day's quota, it sends the requests out shortest-first.

If you have a request waiting in the work queue and you send in another request, the new request is added to the old one (thereby increasing its size) rather than being filed anew. This prevents you from being able to send in a large number of small requests as a way of beating the system.

The reason for all of these quotas and limitations is that the delivery resources are finite, and there are many people who would like to make use of the archive.

Netnews

The Usenet network news is also a valuable source of information about X. The current list of public news groups that discuss X is as follows:

x11-3D	people interested in X and 3-D graphics
x-ada	X and ada
xfont	people interested in fonts
ximage	people interested in image processing and X
xnonfb	server implementors for non-frame buffers
xpc	people interested in implementing X on PCs
xpert	general discussion of X
xserial	serial line X servers
xtensions	technical discussion of changes to X
xvideo	discussion of video extensions for X

The developers of X post notices of fixes to the software to *comp.window.x*, and this is where users and developers around the world ask and answer questions.

Other Xlib Books

As far as other books on the subject, there are two that should be available in the near future:

Xlib-C Language X Interface, Protocol Version 11

This is the documentation distributed with the X software from MIT. It is to be published by DEC Press, perhaps under a different title. Written by the authors of X (Jim Gettys, Ron Newman, and Robert Scheifler), it has been by necessity the major source of information about Xlib. It has served its purpose. It provides an adequate reference for people already quite familiar with X, with a minimum of effort on the part of the developers whose time was more valuable in improving the software.

We have made every effort to make sure our books contain all the information in MIT's document as it was sent to DEC for addition of figures (this was a later revision than the one that appeared with Release 2 from MIT). Our Volume One and Volume Two are intended as a replacement for the MIT documentation.

I can't claim to be a disinterested observer, but now that I've mentioned MIT's manual I feel obliged to note the weaknesses that I have found after using it extensively myself. It describes only what the routines do, not how to use them. It gives no clue about why the routines were designed the way they are. There are no useful examples. It assumes the reader already has a substantial knowledge of computer graphics and X concepts. As a reference, it is difficult to find individual routines because the organization is in loose groups based on function. The index is useful only for finding the routine descriptions.

Information Sources

Basic X11 Programming, by Oliver Jones

This book, which will be published by Prentice-Hall in the fall of 1988, is likely to be an excellent introduction to X programming. Ollie has taught the Xlib tutorials at the X conferences held at MIT for the past two years, and knows Xlib as well as anyone. The book does not attempt to replace the MIT documentation, but provides many useful programming tips.

The Toolkits

The only information currently available concerning the X toolkit being developed at MIT is contained in the documents supplied on the X release tape. The toolkit is still under development, and therefore most outside efforts to document it or write serious software with it are currently on hold.

The other toolkits on the release tape also come with documentation.

Training

Integrated Computer Solutions (with branches in Cambridge, MA and on Long Island) teaches courses in Xlib programming, and provides consulting services. Contact them at (617) 547-0510 or (718) 361-2811 for more information. ICS also manages an X user's group. Contact them for more information.

X tutorials are now a regular feature of UNIX conventions such as the UNIX EXPO, Usenix, and Uniforum, and at the annual X conference at MIT.

Phone Support

X programming is a very new field, and since everyone who knows enough to help you is overworked, you are likely to hear ''you're on your own'' if you try to call for help. There are currently no support lines, because X was developed by a university, not a system manufacturer or software house. When X becomes widely supported as a commercial product, the situation will change as vendors offer support.

The X Consortium

The X consortium can be reached at:

MIT X Consortium
545 Technology Square Rm. 217
Cambridge, MA 02139

The members of the X consortium at this writing are shown in Table H-1.

Table H-1. The X Consortium

Full Members	Associate Members
Apollo Computer	Adobe Systems
Apple	Ardent
AT&T	Carnegie-Mellon University
Bull	Evans & Sutherland
Calcomp	INESC (Portugal)
Control Data Corp.	Integrated Solutions
Digital Equipment Corp.	Interactive Systems Corp.
Fujitsu	Locus Computing Corp.
Hewlett-Packard	Integrated Computer Solutions
IBM	O'Reilly and Associates
NCR	PCS Computer Systeme
Sequent	Stellar Computer
Sony	Software Productivity Consortium
Sun Microsystems	University of Kent at Canterbury
Tektronix	
Wang	
Xerox	

Most of these companies are preparing products based on X. It should not be long before many different products are available that support X.

Finding Out for Yourself

X is unusual in that the source code is in the public domain. It should be possible for most X programmers to get a copy of the X source code from the sources listed above. Once you understand how the code is organized, you can look up certain details about how X works as long as you have a good knowledge of C and a little persistence.

As described in Chapter 2, *X Concepts*, Xlib and the server are two distinct chunks of code. Each contains code for sending and receiving information to and from the other over the network using protocol requests, replies, events, and errors. The source tree as supplied on the X distribution tape places the Xlib source in the directory *base/lib/X*, where *base* is the top of the entire source tree. There server source is placed in *base/server*.

The procedure for finding out something about an Xlib routine is normally to search for the routine in the Xlib code, and then figure out what it does. Sometimes the answer can be found there. Many of the routines, however, simply place their arguments in a protocol request and send it to the server. Then you will have to look in the server code for the answer. To find the correct place in the server code, you will need the symbol for the protocol request, which is the first argument in the `GetReq` call.

The server code is much more involved than Xlib itself. The device-dependent portions are in *base/server/ddx* and the device-independent portions are in *base/server/dix*. The device-independent code should be your first stop, because it is here that protocol requests from Xlib arrive and are dispatched to the appropriate code. Search for the protocol request symbol you found in Xlib. It will appear in several source files. Start with the occurrence in *dispatch.c*, and try to figure out what the code does. This will require following leads to other routines.

If you don't find a routine in *base/server/dix*, then it must be in the device-dependent code. *base/server/ddx* has one directory in it for each brand of hardware to which a sample server has been ported. It also contains the directories */mi*, */cfb*, */mfb*, and */snf*, which contain routines used in writing the sample server device-dependent code. Note that servers may include code ostensibly for other machines. For example, the Sun sample server appears to use code in several of the directories for other servers such as *dec* and *hp*.

Index

Index

XSizeHints 52, 62, 293, 294
XStandardColormap 200, 201
XTextItem 156
XVisualInfo 33, 109
XWindowAttributes 32, 85 - 88, 102
XWMHints 296
style of line drawing 119
styles of command line option 342
substructure redirect override attribute 32
substructure redirection 99
  definition 18
SubstructureNotifyMask 389
SubstructureRedirectMask 243
subwindow, definition 23
subwindow_mode member of GC 135
switching between GCs 112
symbols
  for window attributes 86
  using 42
synchronizing errors 46

T

tables, association 433
TCP/IP 3
temporary windows 300
  avoiding redirection 18
testing an application 44
text, placing 154
thin line, definition 121
tight bindings 327
tiled window manager 5
tiles 128 - 130
  creating 145
  definition 30
  glossary definition 428
time, glossary definition 428
toolkits
  discussion of 7
  documentation 590
  list of 8
top-level window
  glossary definition 428
  rules for creating 289
tracking the pointer 266
training in Xlib 590
transferring data 311
transformation of coordinates 367
transient windows 300

tree hierarchy 22
true color, glossary definition 428
TrueColor, visual class 33, 178
two-byte fonts 149
type
  determining font 150
  of events 35
  XrmQuark 330

U

union, XEvent 52, 217
UNIX variable DISPLAY 53, 558
unloading fonts 75
UnlockDisplay macro 452
UnmapGravity win_gravity 96
UnmapNotify event 96, 240, 242, 389
  example using 383
unmapped
  configuration while 27
  drawing while 27
  window attributes while 27
usage messages 348
user defaults 40, 315
  getting 339 - 348
user interface
  designing 39
  lack of policy 14
user preferences 40, 315
user vs program size hints 63
uwm window manager 5

V

V10 Function 433
valuemask 86
versions of X 1
vertical placement of text 154
viewable, glossary definition 428
virtual colormaps 181
  definition 196
virtual crossing 510
virtual vs. hardware colormaps 196
visibility 24
  before event handling 216
  conditions for 26, 65
  monitoring 103
VisibilityChangeMask 240 - 241

VisibilityNotify event 240
visible, glossary definition 428
visual 33
  choosing 210
  classes of 33, 178
  default 180
  definition 21, 177, 178, 428
  on monochrome systems 180
  selecting 28
visual class 33, 177
  glossary definition 429
  vs. window class 178
Visual structure 177
  opaqueness of 177

Index

Index

Index

Index

About the Author

Adrian Nye is a senior technical writer at O'Reilly and Associates. In addition to the X Window System programming manuals, he has written user's manuals for data acquisition products, and customized UNIX documentation for Sun Microsystems and Prime. Adrian has also worked as a programmer writing educational software in C, and as a mechanical engineer designing offshore oil-spill cleanup equipment. He has long-term interests in using his technical writing skills to promote recycling and other environmentally-sound technologies. He graduated from the Massachusetts Institute of Technology in 1984 with a B.S. in Mechanical Engineering.

O'REILLY & ASSOCIATES, INC.

SPECIALISTS IN TECHNICAL COMMUNICATION

O'Reilly & Associates, Inc. is a consulting company that specializes in preparing technical documentation and training materials that help people get more out of computers. We also provide troff and PostScript typesetting services.

Our Nutshell Handbooks are concise, down-to-earth books on a variety of UNIX topics. Current Nutshell Series titles:

- ☐ Learning the UNIX Operating System (75 pp.)
- ☐ Learning the Vi Editor (131 pp.)
- ☐ Termcap and Terminfo (248 pp.)
- ☐ Programming with Curses (71 pp.)
- ☐ Managing UUCP and Usenet (242 pp.)
- ☐ Using UUCP and Usenet (185 pp.)
- ☐ Managing Projects with Make (77 pp.)
- ☐ DOS Meets UNIX (134 pp.)
- ☐ UNIX in a Nutshell, System V Ed. (270 pp.)
- ☐ UNIX in a Nutshell, Berkeley Ed. (284 pp.)

- ☐ UNIX Text Processing (665 pp.)
- ☐ Xlib Programming Manual (2 volume set)
- ☐ X Window System User's Guide (344 pp.)

To order, call 1-800-338-NUTS
in MA 617-527-1392 • e-mail to uunet!ora!nuts

Please send us your comments and questions, and any recommendations for future titles. Indicate your particular areas of interest by checking the appropriate boxes and we'll send you a detailed brochure on our current handbooks.

Which of the following areas would you like to see new titles for?

- ☐ SCCS/RCS
- ☐ Sed and Awk
- ☐ Troff and PostScript
- ☐ Shell Programming
- ☐ Xenix in a Nutshell
- ☐ Other _____

- ☐ Mailers and Mail front ends
- ☐ System V IPC
- ☐ Lex and Yacc
- ☐ Basic System Administration
- ☐ System Performance Tuning

☐ Send information on your technical writing services.
☐ Send information on your typesetting services.

Name/Title: _____

Company: _____

Address: _____

City/State/Zip: _____

Daytime Telephone #: _____

From: _____
_____
_____

POSTAGE
NECESSARY

CREATORS OF
NUTSHELL

HANDBOOKS

O'Reilly & Associates, Inc.
981 Chestnut Street
Newton, Massachusetts, 02164

From: _____
_____
_____

POSTAGE
NECESSARY

CREATORS OF
NUTSHELL

HANDBOOKS

O'Reilly & Associates, Inc.
981 Chestnut Street
Newton, Massachusetts, 02164